Language H   Language Change
              and Language Relationship

About the authors:

Hans Henrich Hock is Professor of Linguistics and Sanskrit and of the Classics at the University of Illinois at Urbana-Champaign. He received his Ph.D. in Linguistics from Yale University in 1971 and has been teaching at the University of Illinois since 1967. His major research and teaching interests are historical linguistics and Sanskrit. He has authored and (co-)edited three books, including an advanced book on historical linguistics, and some eighty other publications in general historical linguistics, Indo-European linguistics, the structure and history of Sanskrit from Vedic times to the present, Germanic linguistics, and general phonology, morphology, and syntax.

Brian D. Joseph is Professor and Chair of Linguistics at The Ohio State University. He received his Ph.D. in Linguistics from Harvard University in 1978 and has been teaching at The Ohio State University since 1979. His major research and teaching interests are historical linguistics, the languages of the Balkans, and Greek, covering the ancient up through the modern forms of the language. He has authored or co-authored four books and has written over a hundred articles on topics in general historical linguistics, the history of Greek, Indo-European linguistics, Balkan linguistics, and morphological and syntactic theory.

Language History,
Language Change,
and Language Relationship

An Introduction to
Historical and Comparative Linguistics

by
Hans Henrich Hock
Brian D. Joseph

Mouton de Gruyter
Berlin · New York 1996

Mouton de Gruyter (formerly Mouton, The Hague)
is a Division of Walter de Gruyter & Co., Berlin.

♾ Printed on acid-free paper which falls within the guidelines
of the ANSI to ensure permanence and durability.

Library of Congress Cataloging-in-Publication-Data

Hock, Hans Henrich, 1938−
    Language history, language change, and language rela-
tionship : an introduction to historical and comparative linguistics / by Hans Henrich Hock, Brian D. Joseph.
        p.   cm. − (Trends in linguistics. Studies and
monographs ; 93).
    Includes bibliographical references and index.
    ISBN 3-11-014785-8 (cloth : alk. paper). −
ISBN 3-11-014784-X (pbk. : alk. paper)
    1. Historical linguistics.   2. Comparative linguistics.
I. Joseph, Brian D.   II. Title.   III. Series.
P140.H588   1996
417−dc20   96-32515
                                         CIP

Die Deutsche Bibliothek − Cataloging-in-Publication-Data

Hock, Hans Henrich:
Language history, language change and language relationship :
an introduction to historical and comparative linguistics / by
Hans Henrich Hock ; Brian D. Joseph. − Berlin ; New York :
Mouton de Gruyter, 1996
    ISBN 3-11-014784-X
NE: Joseph, Brian D.:

Diskconversion: Lewis & Leins GmbH, Berlin.
Printing: Gerike GmbH, Berlin.
Binding: Lüderitz & Bauer, Berlin.
Cover design: ramminger Kommunikation · Werbung · Design GmbH, Berlin.
Printed in Germany.

Preface

Why does language change? Why can we speak to and understand our grandparents but may have trouble reading Shakespeare? Why is Chaucer's English of the fourteenth century so different from Modern English of the late twentieth century that the two are essentially different languages? Why are the Americans and the English "one people divided by a common language"? And how can the language of Chaucer and Modern English – or Modern British and American English – still be called the "same language"?

The present book provides answers to questions like these in a straightforward way, aimed at the non-specialist, with ample illustrations from both familiar and more exotic languages. Specific topics covered include:

– The discovery of Indo-European, the far-flung family of related languages that embraces not only English, German, French, Russian, and most of the other modern European languages but also the two classical languages of Europe (Latin and Greek), and a number of languages outside Europe, including Sanskrit, the sacred language of India.

– The history of writing with emphasis on the development of our alphabet. The antecedents of our writing systems in the ancient Egyptian hieroglyphs and the "cuneiform" writing of ancient Mesopotamia. The decipherments that made it possible to read long-forgotten ancient scripts.

– Change in grammatical structure. How do languages change in their pronunciation and grammar? What kinds of changes can be observed? And what are the effects of these changes?

– Change in vocabulary. How do meanings change and how do we create new words? How do we "borrow" words from other languages, such as *rouge* from French or *pundit* from Sanskrit? And what do these developments tell us about change in culture and society or about general tendencies of human nature?

– Change in sign languages. Do they undergo changes that parallel those found in oral languages?

– The relation between "language" and "dialect". Is it really true, as someone claimed, that a language is merely a "dialect with an army and a navy"? What are the effects of the dynamic interaction between language and dialect on language change?

– Multilingualism and its consequences. What happens when languages come in contact, especially if contact is intense and long-lasting? The results range from a simple "foreign accent" to the extreme case of "pidgins", which have a highly simplified structure and a greatly reduced vocabulary, as mirrored in the famous expression *Me Tarzan – You Jane*. What are the social and attitudinal factors that give rise to these and other outcomes of contact?

– The question of language relationship. How can we establish that the members of the Indo-European language family, or any other language family, are really related to each other? Is it possible to establish a common ancestor for all human languages? And how did human language arise in the first place in the distant past?

– Recovering history from language. How do we "reconstruct" the ancestral languages from which the related languages are descended like daughters from a common mother? What does reconstruction tell us about the culture of prehistoric societies? And how can we apply some of the insights of historical linguistics to real-world issues?

In writing this book, we, the authors, have been fortunate to receive support and encouragement from many different sources. Dr. Marie-Louise Liebe-Harkort, then Editor-in-Chief of Mouton de Gruyter, set things in motion by requesting that Hans Henrich Hock produce an elementary introduction to historical and comparative linguistics at a less advanced level than his *Principles of Historical Linguistics* (1986/1991). After Hock had produced a working draft of some eighty-five percent of the present book, Brian D. Joseph was invited to join the project, to provide a fully American perspective, to help with the remaining parts of the book, and to offer comments and additions to earlier parts. Since taking over as Editor-in-Chief of Mouton de Gruyter in 1994 Dr. Anke Beck has provided continued and enthusiastic support for the project. A referee for Mouton de Gruyter provided a first professional reaction with many helpful hints for improvement. Dr. Werner Winter, editor of "Trends in Linguistics", has given encouragement and helpful suggestions on a near-final version of the book. We are very grateful to Mouton de Gruyter for having placed our work in the hands of all such highly capable and helpful colleagues.

We are also grateful for feedback from a class at The Ohio State University, a group of students from many different institutions who attended the 1993 Linguistic Institute at The Ohio State University, and from several generations of students at the University of Illinois who put up with earlier drafts, some of which were highly preliminary indeed. Robert L. Good, a student at the University of Illinois, made extensive comments on an earlier version. Heinrich Sharad Hock provided very helpful comments on the first two chapters of a near-final version, from the perspective of a second-year undergraduate student. To all of these we owe deep gratitude.

Our deepest gratitude must go to Zarina M. Hock, who worked through the entire final draft, making invaluable suggestions on almost every page, both as an experienced editor and as an educated "general" reader. Her insights and suggestions have made the text friendlier and more accessible for those who are not specialists in linguistics.

We hope that the final product accomplishes what we set out to do – to reach a general, non-specialist readership, and to convey to our readers at least some of the excitement that can be derived from understanding language change and the relationship between languages. We encourage our readers to send us suggestions that might help us reach this goal even more effectively in a second edition, and to this end we add our e-mail addresses.

Champaign, Illinois, and Columbus, Ohio
Fall 1995

Hans Henrich Hock (hhhock@uiuc.edu)
and Brian D. Joseph (joseph.1@osu.edu)

Contents

Change in structure

Introductory

Chapter 1
Introduction

> glam·our, glam·or (glam'ər) n. [Scot. var. of *grammar* (with sense of GRAMARYE), popularized by Sir Walter Scott; orig. esp. in *cast the glamour*, to cast an enchantment] **1.** orig., a magic spell or charm **2.** seemingly mysterious and elusive fascination or allure, as of some person, object, scene, etc.; bewitching charm: the current sense
> (*Webster's New World Dictionary of the American Language*, Second College Edition, 1970)

> verve (vûrv) n. **1.** Energy and enthusiasm in the expression of ideas and especially in artistic endeavor: *The play lacks verve.* **2.** Vitality; liveliness; vigor. **3.** *Rare.* Aptitude; talent. [French, from Old French, fancy, fanciful expression, from Latin *verba*, plural of *verbum*, word ...
> (*The American Heritage Dictionary of the English Language*, 1969)

1. Language keeps changing

Hey, it's far out, man.
I don't know if you can, I don't know uh like how many of you can dig how many people there are, man.
Like I was rappin' to the fuzz, hunh, right, can you dig it?
Man, there's supposed to be a million and a half people here by tonight. Can you dig that?
New York State Thruway is closed, man, hunhhunh.
Yeah, lotta freaks, hunhunh.

These are the words that Arlo Guthrie used at the end of his song "Coming into Los Angeles", bantering with the masses of young people – mostly in their late teens and early twenties – who were gathered at Woodstock in August 1969 for the most famous rock festival of the time. What he said is recognizably English, but it is the language of the "youth" and "hip" culture of the late 1960s and early 1970s. It is clearly not the English used today in America at similar gatherings, where words like *rappin'* have very different connotations. Within the time span of only two or three decades, English in America has changed significantly in certain respects.

Of course, these changes have taken place in an area of usage notorious for its fickleness, an area often loosely referred to as slang. The very nature of slang requires constant change, for nothing is worse than out-of-date slang. Where Arlo Guthrie's *far out* was completely in tune with the slang of his time, today he might say *awesome* or *cool*. And even as this book goes to press, *awesome* and *cool* may have become dated, replaced by other, more "awesome" words.

Language change, however, is not limited to slang. It affects all areas of language use, even the staid scholarly world, as the following extended example illustrates.

At a recent meeting of the American Oriental Society the proposal was made to rename the organization: It was argued that although the Society is dedicated to the languages, literatures, and cultures of ALL of Asia, from Israel and Palestine to China and Japan, its name suggests an interest only in the Far East. The proposal was greeted with disbelief, even outrage, and was quickly voted down.

As we shall presently see, this minor incident, in a scholarly society most people have not even heard of, puts into stark relief the fact that language keeps changing inexorably and that even scholars dedicated to the study of language, literature, and culture can be caught unawares by language change.

Evidently, unbeknownst to both sides of the argument, the meaning of the word *oriental* has changed for some speakers of modern American English. When the Society was founded in the nineteenth century, the word was used in the sense it had in Europe, as referring to the area just east of Europe in which the sun rises – the ancient Near East of Israel, Babylonia, and adjacent areas. And scholars grounded in Latin knew that the word *oriental* is derived from Latin *oriens* 'rising (sun)'. (In this regard note that name of the German counterpart of the Society uses the term *morgenländisch* 'connected with the "morning land", the east'.) It was only by extension that the word was used to refer to areas even farther east, eventually to all of Asia.

Since the founding of the Society, several things happened. First, to become a competent scholar of oriental studies it is no longer necessary to know Latin and thus to be able to know the "literal" meaning of *oriental*. Second, America has become much more independent in its thinking from Europe. As a consequence, the term *oriental* cannot be interpreted literally anymore: from the perspective of America, the sun rises in the Atlantic Ocean or, possibly, in Europe, not the Near East. A third, and perhaps most important, element is this: Even though we can look up the established meaning of words in a dictionary, we learn most meanings from the way words are used around us, without any formal instruction as to what is the "real" meaning of a word. As a consequence, we have to figure out most meanings for ourselves. In the process we may not always get things right (from the perspective of the older generation). This is especially true for meaning, since words normally have a fairly broad range of meanings. Consider the word *reader*. We all know what the word basically means, or at least we believe so and act accordingly. But put the word into different contexts and you find that its exact connotations can differ considerably. For instance, the expression *Johnny is a good reader* conveys very different messages, depending on whether Johnny is in first grade or in a poetry-reading class in college. We deal with such issues by assuming that there is a prototypical or core meaning and that other meanings, such as the use of *reader* in the context of a poetry-reading class, are transferred or more peripheral. But, again, for most words we have to figure out the core meaning ourselves, and in the process we may go wrong.

Something along these lines seems to have happened to the word *oriental*, such that a sizable number of speakers of American English have determined for themselves that the prototypical or core meaning of the word refers to East Asia – the area of Asia and its inhabitants which differs most prototypically from Europe and its inhabitants, and from the European-descended majority population of North America. This change in interpretation, however, is a fairly recent development. For a large number of American scholars, the word continues to mean just about the same as *Asian*, at least in scholarly contexts.

But things are even more complex: It is quite doubtful that most scholars are so highly ensconced in their ivory towers that they do not know that *oriental* means 'East Asian' in every-day usage. Rather, it seems that they consider this usage secondary or peripheral, "colloquial" rather than "scholarly", if not downright "slangy". And instead of simply failing to understand why some of their colleagues wanted to change the name of their Society, they probably were outraged at the intrusion of the non-scholarly connotation that *oriental* had acquired.

What is interesting about this reaction is the use of the term "slangy" in reference to a usage considered less correct, i.e., less prestigious. This is a common reaction to linguistic change, especially among those who believe that language must remain pure and unchanged, and that change will somehow reduce not only the purity of language but also our ability to speak and even think clearly. Whole books are written – and indeed have been written for centuries – warning of impending doom, prophesying that our language will go to the dogs if certain usages disapproved by the authors run rampant.

Interestingly, these critics often do not agree with each other on which usages should be disapproved. Many American critics still inveigh against the use of *hopefully* in expressions like *Hopefully, it will rain* and advise the use of something like *I hope it will rain* instead. Their British colleagues generally are amused by this bit of linguistic conservatism and find the use of *hopefully* quite compact and handy. The targets of disapproval may also change over time. Up to about the 1960s the use of *data* as a singular mass noun, rather than a (historically correct) plural form of *datum*, was subject to continued criticism; but nobody objected to the singular use of *agenda*, originally plural of *agendum*. Today, as the singular use of *data* has been accepted by most educated speakers of English, its singular use generally is no longer an issue. Instead, the debate centers around words like *media* and *criteria*, historically plurals of *medium* and *criterion*, respectively, which are undergoing similar changes from plural to singular use.

Most judgmental statements of this sort come from non-linguists. But linguists have not always been free of such prejudices, either. Up to about the 1870s, most historical linguists subscribed to the idea that language change is tantamount to decay. Their initiation to linguistics included a thorough study of the classical European languages, Latin and Greek, and they had been persuaded that these glorious tongues of classical antiquity were the most perfect on earth, and that the modern languages were but poor shadows of them. This view was consonant with traditional Christian and pre-Christian beliefs according to which an original, perfect, and idyllic garden of Eden or "Golden Age" gave way to an ever worsening fall from grace, to ever-increasing decay and depravity.

Anyone who has studied Greek and Latin knows that the word structure (or "morphology") of these languages is "richer" than that of most modern European languages. Thus, Latin nouns had six different "cases", forms of nouns whose choice depended on the syntactic context. There was a nominative for the subject of the sentence (*caesar* 'Caesar'), a genitive to indicate possession (*caesaris* 'of Caesar'), a dative which among other things indicated the recipient of a gift (*caesari* 'to, for Caesar'), an accusative for the object of the sentence (*caesarem* 'Caesar'), an ablative to indicate the source of an action, including the agent of the passive (*caesare* 'from, by Caesar'), and a vocative for addressing a person or, more rarely, a thing (*caesar* 'O Caesar'). In contrast, Modern French nouns have one invariant form (*César*). The situation is similar in English and many other modern languages. (As a consequence, speakers of these languages find it quite difficult to even understand what is meant by "case".) This reduction in morphological richness was considered simply another manifestation of general human sloth and depravity.

Other linguists have claimed that the morphological reduction really is an improvement: Not having to memorize four, five, six, or even more cases for each noun simplifies the language and thereby makes it more efficient and easier to learn.

On the surface, the second view is more appealing, especially in an age that worships the notion of progress. However, "progress" is as much a subjective notion as is "decay". More than that, we have no objective way of telling whether a language with a richer case system is more difficult than one with a "poorer" one. True, learning the six different nominal cases of Latin, or the four cases of German may appear difficult to speakers of English who are used to just two such forms (base form [*wolf*] vs. genitive [*wolf's*]), but when they go to Germany they find, often much to their surprise, that "even the children speak German" and get their cases right most of the time.

Linguists are not surprised: One of the few generally accepted beliefs in linguistics is that all children manage to learn their own native language with equal ease and efficiency and that, by extension, all languages are equally "simple" or "complex".

This does not mean that as individual users of language, linguists are completely free of personal preferences or even prejudices, especially as regards ongoing changes in grammar and usage; and they may do their best to stem particular changes which they consider undesirable. Objectively, however, they are fully aware that over the long haul, these attempts at stemming the tide of change are ineffectual: Language changes inexorably. But interestingly, in the process it does not go to the dogs. We are probably as capable, if we try hard enough, to express our ideas clearly and effectively as our linguistic ancestors were – when they tried hard enough. At any rate, we have not started barking as yet.

The extent to which language changes can be seen more clearly by extending our horizon beyond the two or three decades that separate Arlo Guthrie's language from the present. Compare for instance the Lord's Prayer as it was translated into Old English about a thousand years ago with a more modern version.

Old English (ca. 950 A.D. The original text has been slightly simplified.)

Fader urer ðu arð in heofnum, sie gehalgad noma ðin, to-cymeð ric ðin, sie willo ðin suæ is in heofne ond in eorðo, hlaf userne oferwistlic sel us todæg ond forgef us scylda usra suæ uœ forgefon scyldum usum, ond nc inlæd usih in costunge, ah gefrig usich from yfle.

Modern English (ca. 1985)

Our father who is in heaven, may your name be sacred. Lct your kingdom come. May your will be fulfilled just as much on earth as it is in heaven. Give us today our daily bread. And forgive us our transgressions, as we forgive those who transgress against us. And do not lead us into temptation, but deliver us from sin.

Both in Old English and Modern English, of course, other translations are possible and have in fact been produced. But the difference between the two versions cited here goes much beyond individual word choices; it concerns the entire language. So much so, in fact, that Old English is at least as "foreign" to a speaker of Modern English as, say, Modern German. Nevertheless, Old and Modern English are in some sense the "same" language, with Modern English resulting from centuries of linguistic change taking place in structure and vocabulary. Linguistic change evidently affected not just meaning and usage (as in our earlier examples), but pronunciation, grammar, and everything else.

2. Types of linguistic change

Sound change. What perhaps most saliently distinguishes Old English (OE) from Modern English (Mod. Engl.) is that the two are pronounced very differently, as reflected in part by differences in spelling. In some words, the differences are minor, as in the word for 'father' where the major difference is Old English *d* : Mod. Engl. *th*. In others, the difference is much greater, as in OE *hlaf* 'bread' (with a vowel similar to the *a* in Mod. Engl. *father*) vs. the corresponding Mod. Engl. *loaf*, which lacks the initial *h* and has a different vowel. In addition, of course, *loaf* has changed in meaning, no longer referring to 'bread' in general, but to a certain quantity of bread. (This is the reason that the word cannot be used in the modern version of the Lord's Prayer.)

Linguists use the term SOUND CHANGE to refer to such changes in pronunciation; and like many other technical terms, it is defined more narrowly than in ordinary usage, to refer only to certain types of change in the pronunciation of words. Sound change understood in this sense has been claimed to be completely regular, in the sense that all words that can undergo a given change do so. Recent research shows this claim to be an overstatement; still, sound change does turn out to be overwhelmingly regular.

It is this overwhelming regularity of sound change that makes it possible for us to trace words through history, or across different, but related languages, and to be confident that we are really comparing different versions of the same word, rather than words which just happen to sound similar. Understanding how sound change operates often helps us explain otherwise strange facts about language. For instance, English has a number of words pronounced with initial *n* but preceded in spelling by a "silent" *k*, such as *knee, knight,* and *knave.* The *k* of these words was pronounced in early English (as in OE *cneo, cniht, cnafa*) and is still pronounced in the related German (e.g. *Knie* 'knee'). It was lost in English by a regular sound change that operated in word-initial position before *n*. The modern spelling with *k* preserves an earlier stage when the *k* was still pronounced.

Analogy. Sound change is not the only change that may affect pronunciation. Words often change their pronunciation under the influence of, or by ANALOGY with, other words. For instance, the early Modern English plural of *cow* was *kine,* a form still found in nineteenth-century poetry. The present-day plural *cows* came about in the seventeenth century under the analogy of the most common, productive mode of plural formation, as we find it in *pig : pig-s, horse : horse-s.* Unlike sound change, analogy is not normally regular; and Modern English has retained many irregular plural forms such as *men, women, children, feet.*

Analogy comes in many different forms, some of which may be consciously exploited for creating new words. One of these is a process called blending which produces something like a compromise form between two competing words. An example of an ordinary, unconscious blending is *feets,* a form frequently used by children as a compromise between the "correct" plural *feet* (insisted on by grown-ups) and a more regularized analogical *foots,* comparable to our earlier *cows.* More conscious applications of the same process are found in words like **bru**nch, something like a compromise between **breakfast** and **lunch,** *transceiver,* something which is simultaneously a **trans**mitter and a **receiver,** or *modem,* a **mode**lator-**dem**odulator. A similar explanation may hold true for *irregardless,* a form used in a variety of English that is commonly considered "non-standard", "vernacular", or even "ungrammatical". The word may owe its existencc to a blending of ***irrespective*** and ***regardless.***

Analogy, combined with sound change, may have profound effects on word structure (also known as MORPHOLOGY). Thus, Old English was similar to Latin in having a fairly "rich" nominal case system. For instance, the word for 'stone' had the following inflection, with three different case endings, each distinct for singular and plural:

	singular	plural
nominative/accusative:	*stān*	*stānas*
dative:	*stāne*	*stānum*
genitive:	*stānes*	*stāna*

Modern English has just two cases:

base form	*stone*	*stones*
genitive	*stone's*	*stones'*

The primary factor underlying the change from Old English to Modern English is sound change, which eliminated all of the vowels in the case suffixes, as well as the *m* of the dative plural. But if only sound change had applied we would have a system that differs from the one actually found:

nominative/accusative:	*stone*	*stones*
dative:	*stone*	*stone*
genitive:	*stones*	*stone*

As can be readily seen, this hypothetical system does a very poor job of keeping the different case forms apart. The same form is used for the nominative/accusative and dative singular and also for the dative and genitive plural; and another form is employed for the nominative/accusative plural and genitive singular.

At this point, analogy stepped in and put some greater order into the system, by extending the *-s* of the nominative/accusative plural to all other forms of the plural. As a consequence, neither singular nor plural distinguished between nominative/accusative and dative, making this distinction superfluous in English grammar. If the development had been carried to its logical conclusion, the genitive forms would have been affected, too, and Modern English would no longer distinguish the genitive from the base form. But as we just noted, analogy does not apply with the same regularity as sound change; and the English genitive singular merrily retained its *-s*. (The different *s*-forms were then differentiated in writing, but not in pronunciation, by a judicious use of apostrophes.)

Semantic change. As we have seen in §1 above, in addition to their pronunciation, words may change in their meaning. This type of change, referred to as SEMANTIC CHANGE, is notoriously unpredictable and "fuzzy", probably because of the way in which we readily stretch and extend the meaning of words to cover new situations. (Recall the different uses of the word *reader* mentioned in section 1.) One of the consequences of the fuzziness of semantic change is that semantic flip-flops may occur. As noted earlier, OE *hlaf* 'bread' corresponds to Mod. Engl. *loaf* through sound change, but the modern word designates a narrower semantic range, namely a certain quantity of bread. Exactly the opposite happened in the case of the modern word *bread*. This word can be traced back to OE *bread* (probably different in pronunciation); but the meaning of the Old English word was more narrow: '(bread) crumb, morsel'. One of the most remarkable flip-flops of this kind is the relatively recent change in African American Vernacular English of *bad* to mean its exact opposite, 'excellent, cool, etc.'.

Semantic change can lead to many other, quite radical and unexpected results. Perfect examples for such changes are the words **glamour** and **verve**.

Consider first the word *glamour*. The ultimate source of the word is Greek *gráphein* 'to scratch'. By a fairly mundane change the verb came to mean 'write' after the advent of writing. (This semantic shift has parallels in many other languages, such as Latin *scribere*, English *write*, Sanskrit *likh-*, all of which originally meant 'scratch'.) Once *gráphein* had changed its meaning, nouns derived from it, such as *grámma* and *grammatikē* came to refer to the products of writing: a letter of the alphabet, a letter of communication, or *letters* 'learning in general' as in *Arts and Letters, Doctor of Letters*, etc. From Greek the word entered Latin as *grammatica*, with roughly the same range of meanings.

In Old French, a new derivative was created, *grammaire*, whose meaning underwent a certain amount of expansion, referring not only to '(Latin) grammar' and 'philological learning', but to all traditional learning, including the occult sciences of alchemy and astrology. The latter meaning was especially prevalent among the "unlettered", for whom the notion literacy conjured up images of wizards poring over books on alchemy, magic, and the supernatural. After all, being able to read and write was itself an esoteric phenomenon in a society where literacy was limited to just a small portion of the population. (In French, this popular understanding of 'grammar' survives in the word *grimoire* 'a book on magic'. Another meaning, 'scribbles', reflects a different, less awestruck attitude.)

The word was borrowed as *gramer* into Middle English, with the same range of meanings as in Old French and, again, with magical connotations mainly among the "unlettered". Along the way, the two meanings of the word, the educated one of '(Latin) grammar and learning in general' and the popular magical interpretation, came to be differentiated in writing, giving rise to Mod. Engl. *grammar* vs. *gramary(e)*.

The form *glamour* is in origin a Scots English variant of *gramary(e)* and was introduced into modern standard English by Sir Walter Scott with the meaning 'magic; magic charm'. The later semantic development to 'charm' and related meanings reflects a common metaphorical extension from 'magic charm', similar to the more transparent metaphorical use of words like *bewitching*. In fact, the word *charm*, as well as *enchanting*, exhibit the same development; the more original meanings are preserved in expressions like *cast a charm on someone* and the somewhat archaic *enchantress* 'female sorcerer'. (Both of these words originally referred to acts of *chanting*; but that is a different story.)

Along the way, the word *grammar* lost a lot of its earlier glamour, as it were, and increasingly was used to refer to instruction in linguistic structure, often with emphasis on "correctness". Its earlier, more general meaning remains in fixed expressions like *grammar school*, a school which was intended to inculcate not just grammar in the modern sense, but learning in general.

The word *verve*, too, can be plausibly derived from a word dear to linguists, namely from Latin *verba*, plural of *verbum* 'word'. (Along a different path this word furnished Mod. Engl. *verb*, likewise an important element in the vocabulary of linguists.) The Latin word could by extension also refer to general sayings or proverbs and to something like 'mere, empty words'.

The early French outcome of *verba* was *verve*, whose meanings, ranging from 'proverb' to 'verbosity', can easily be explained as specializations of the Latin meanings. In later medieval French, *verve* came to be used in the meaning 'caprice, fantasy', possibly an extension from 'verbosity' via something like 'verbal exuberance'.

From the later medieval connotations it is only a short step to the modern French meaning 'enthusiasm, vitality, etc.'; and it is with this meaning that the word was borrowed from French into English. (An earlier borrowing from French, found in earlier English, shows yet another semantic development, to 'talent', perhaps from 'verbosity' via 'verbal skill'.)

Syntactic change. In addition to their pronunciation, morphology, and meaning, words can also change in their SYNTAX – the way they are put together into sentences, and how these sentences, in turn, are related to each other. Take for instance the order of subject, verb, and object in sentences like *The dog* (subject) *bit* (verb) *the man* (object). In Modern English the normal order places the verb in a "medial" position between the subject and the object, not only in sentences like *The dog bit the man* but also in more unusual sentences like *The man bit the dog*. By contrast, "verb-initial structures" like *Bit the man the dog* or "verb-final" ones like *The man the dog bit* do not qualify as well-formed complete English sentences (although they may be part of well-formed sentences, as in *The man the dog bit is getting rabies shots*).

Old English had a much greater freedom of word order and the Old English counterpart of *Bit the man the dog* was perfectly acceptable. The most unmarked sentence structure, however, would have been closest to the verb-final type *The man the dog bit*. (Students of Latin will find this aspect of Old English syntax quite familiar.)

The change from the Old English verb-final syntax to the modern verb-medial pattern was partly shared by German, a closely related language. However, in German the development stopped in midstream, as it were: Only those verb forms which have personal endings (such as Engl. third person *has* vs. non-third person *have*) appear in medial position. If the verb consists of more than one word (as in Engl. *has gone* : *have gone*), the elements without personal endings stay at the end of the sentence. To make matters even more complicated, German verb-medial syntax is limited to main clauses; dependent clauses are verb-final. This accounts for the curious mismatch in word order between English and similar languages (such as French) with more or less solidly medial verbs on one hand, and German on the other:

English	German
HE **loves** *his wife*	ER **liebt** *seine Frau*
SHE **has** LOVED *her husband*	SIE **hat** *ihren Mann* GELIEBT
that THE CHILDREN **love** *their parents*	*dass* DIE KINDER *ihre Eltern* **lieben**

It is this mismatch which is in large measure responsible for the notorious difficulties experienced by speakers of languages like English when confronted with German (or with Modern Dutch and Frisian, which in their word order are very similar to German.)

Change resulting from language contact. The developments illustrated so far are the major linguistic changes that affect languages under all circumstances. A number of other changes take place only when different languages (or dialects) are in CONTACT with each other.

The most common development in contact situations is a process called
BORROWING, the adoption or adaptation of words from one language to another. Modern English is full of such borrowings; note for example such
culinary expressions as *curry* (from India), *frankfurter* (German), *bagel* (Yiddish), *paté* (French), *enchilada* (Spanish), *spaghetti* (Italian), *pita* (Greek),
kimchee (Korean). Many other languages are much more reluctant to adopt
foreign words to this large extent. In fact, languages like Chinese have severe
limitations in this regard.

Extended bilingual or multilingual contact between languages (or more
accurately, their speakers) can lead to an increase in STRUCTURAL similarities
as well. Many areas of the world are notorious for developments of this sort,
for instance the Balkans, South Asia, Southeast Asia, and the Indigenous
American languages of the northwestern United States and adjacent areas of
Canada. The idea that structural elements should diffuse from one language
to another often meets with incredulity. People are prepared to accept the
existence of lexical borrowings, since these presumably go hand in hand with
the borrowing of the objects, ideas, or concepts expressed by the words; but
why would languages borrow, say, a "passive" construction – if, presumably,
earlier they were perfectly happy without it?

Actually, structural elements usually do not diffuse through borrowing,
but are the cumulative results of a different, very common phenomenon.
This is the transfer of pronunciation and other aspects of linguistic structure
that leads to the "accent" with which people speak a foreign language, even
after long years of residence in the country where the language is natively
spoken. What is especially significant is that the development does not seem
to be entirely unilateral. True, we tend only to notice the accent with which
the foreigner speaks our language; but when that foreigner returns home after
many years abroad, those who remained behind will notice a certain accent in
his or her speech as well. This is often considered an affectation, and to some
extent it may be. But to a certain degree the "foreign" accent in one's native
language is as natural and normal as the accent in one's second, non-native
language.

Under certain extreme conditions, language contact can lead to yet other
results. One of the most striking is the development of PIDGINS, languages
with minimal linguistic structure and, perhaps even more important, with
minimal vocabulary. The lexicon of such languages has been estimated to
contain no more than 1,000 to 2,000 words. Many ideas which find compact
single-word expressions in "normal" languages therefore have to be rendered
by circumlocutions. It is said that the word *piano* is rendered in one of the
pidgins as something like *big fellow box you fight him he cry*. A large number

of pidgins arose in the wake of European imperialist-colonialist expansion around the world, when speakers of European languages came in contact with speakers of languages that were totally unfamiliar to them.

Even such extreme developments can be explained (at least in part) by principles commonly observable elsewhere. Sentences with extreme structural and lexical simplifications are frequently used in one of two contexts: (a) with babies who are not yet able to speak the full form of the language, (b) with speakers whose language we do not understand, and who do not understand ours. Examples are expressions like *Baby want (to) seep? = Does the baby/do you want to sleep?* and the famous *Me Tarzan – You Jane = I am Tarzan, you are Jane.* Though there are considerable differences in details, especially in friendliness or rudeness of intonation, both types of discourse share one thing beyond structural and lexical simplification: They are used in situations where we believe that we cannot successfully communicate in ordinary language and that, therefore, we must simplify our language, on the assumption that we will somehow get through – if we simplify enough and, in the case of foreigners, speak slowly and loudly enough.

3. Language relationship

Language change, thus, is not only pervasive but also takes many different forms. More than that, even within a single type of linguistic change, such as sound change, there are many different possible subtypes. In the preceding section, for instance, we have seen that English lost initial *k* before *n* (as in *knee*), while German did not. Similarly, we have observed that English developed a solidly "verb-medial" syntactic pattern, while German stopped in midstream, as it were. Such differences in development are very common, especially when lines of communication are attenuated or even broken.

We can observe many examples of this phenomenon in the different varieties of English, especially between American and British English. The differences affect pronunciation, vocabulary, word formation, and even syntax. Thus, British English generally "drops" the *r* in words like *cart* and *car*, American English generally does not; American English "drops" the *h* of *herb*, British English does not. Where British English has *lorry, bonnet, boot*, American English offers *truck, hood, trunk.* Differences between British and American English can sometimes lead to genuine misunderstandings. It is said that at a joint-staff meeting of the Allied Command during the Second World War, a British officer proposed that an important matter be *tabled*, whereupon his American counterpart became angry. He interpreted the word the American way, as a near-synonym of *shelve* (i.e. 'delay'), whereas the intended meaning was the British one of *placing the matter on the table for immediate discussion*. One of the most commonly encountered differences in word formation concerns the past participle of the verb *get*. While American English makes a distinction between *I have gotten a letter from home* 'I have received a letter ...' and *I've got a letter from home* 'I have a letter ...', British English uses *got* in both contexts. In the area of syntax, questions like *Did you give Mary the hat?* can perfectly acceptably be answered in British English by saying *I gave her it yesterday*, whereas such a structure would be considered unacceptable in (standard) American English.

Divergent changes of this type, if continuing over a long enough period, can be pervasive enough to change what originally were different varieties of the same language into effectively different languages, much as a millennium of linguistic changes has effectively turned Old and Modern English into different languages.

In fact, it is through such divergent developments that Latin, the language of the Roman empire, came to be differentiated into the Romance languages (Portuguese, Spanish, French, Italian, Romanian, etc.). Similar developments can be observed in northern India, whose modern languages are the differentiated outcomes of Sanskrit. Linguistic relationships of this type have been known for a long time. Many other relationships had long been suspected, but it was not before the end of the eighteenth century that linguists began to establish some of these relationships beyond a reasonable doubt. Some modern linguists even believe that they can establish that all human languages are related to each other; and their claims have received a fair amount of attention in the popular press. The claims, if correct, would add another important element to the continuing discussion of the question of human origins. At this point, most historical linguists still consider the issue controversial, but the ensuing debate has introduced an element of excitement – as well as acrimony – into an otherwise rather staid profession.

What distinguishes some of the relationships that were established later from the Romance "LANGUAGE FAMILY" is this: Latin, the ANCESTOR from which the Romance languages have "descended", is historically attested. There could therefore be no doubt about the fact that the Romance languages are "daughter" languages sprung from the same "mother" (or better, perhaps, "offspring" languages sprung from the same "parent").

The Germanic languages (English, German, Dutch, Frisian, Norwegian, Danish, Swedish, Icelandic, etc.) exhibit a degree of similarity with each other that is not substantially different from the one between the Romance languages. Note especially the striking similarities in such an idiosyncratic pattern as Engl. *good : better : best*, Germ. *gut : besser : best*, Icel. *góður : betri : bezt-*. However, no mother language is historically attested from which the Germanic languages might have developed as daughters. Claiming that the Germanic languages are nevertheless related, therefore, requires the assumption of a linguistic ancestor which happened to be spoken before the arrival of literacy.

In the case of Germanic, this was actually not a major problem, since in the Middle Ages the languages were still quite similar to each other. It was much more difficult to accept that languages as disparate as Latin, Sanskrit, and the Germanic languages might be related to each other. In this case there was both an absence of a known linguistic ancestor and a much greater degree of differentiation.

The linguistic relationship of Latin, Sanskrit, and Germanic now is firmly established, too; and so are similar relationships between many other languages of the world. A method called COMPARATIVE RECONSTRUCTION has made it possible to develop at least some ideas on the structure and vocabulary even of unattested linguistic ancestor languages. Linguists and prehistorians even have drawn on reconstructed vocabulary to draw inferences about the culture and society of the speakers of reconstructed languages.

The results of reconstruction clearly are only theories or hypotheses, and as such they are subject to revision as new evidence is considered or as old evidence is reconsidered. Nevertheless, an attempt to test the method on the Romance languages (where we can compare the reconstructed ancestor language with the attested Latin) suggests that the method can yield amazingly accurate results.

4. A word of caution, or "Long live the speaker"

The work of historical and comparative linguists has yielded interesting and illuminating results and can explain many things that are otherwise "strange", such as the "silent" *k* in Engl. *knee*, the differences in word order between English and German, or the amazing similarity in the idiosyncratic pattern of Engl. *good : better : best*, Germ. *gut : besser : best*, Icel. *góður : betri : bezt-*. But most language users are neither historians nor linguists. In many cases, their behavior goes counter to historical and comparative evidence.

For instance, as noted earlier, linguists believe that the attempts of self-appointed critics to stem the tide of linguistic change must ultimately be futile – linguistic change takes place inexorably, whether we like it or not. And yet, the actions of critics can have an effect.

A most remarkable example is found in Icelandic, a language which like Chinese today greatly restricts the number of foreign words that it adopts. At an earlier period, a lot of foreign words were employed quite freely, such as *dedicera* from Latin *dedicare* 'dedicate', or *borgmeistari* from Germ. *Bürgermeister* 'mayor'. Linguistic critics deplored such borrowings, arguing that they alienated Icelanders from their own language and tradition. And, apparently because they struck a sympathetic chord among most Icelanders, the critics won out: Words such as *dedicera* and *borgmeistari* were eliminated from the language, and severe restrictions were placed on the adoption of new words. As a less "global" example, consider a process known as popular etymology or folk etymology, which gives words a new, historically inaccurate etymology. For instance, French *andier* 'metal support for a fireplace grid' was borrowed into English first as *andire* (with various spelling variations). With substitution of English for French pronunciation, this word can hardly be argued to be an unacceptable word in English (acceptable words such as *endeavo(u)r, Andrew, Andover* are very similar in structure). Nevertheless, for some reason *andire* must have been felt to be "strange", and various attempts were made to make it more like a "recognizable" English word. The first attempt was the replacement of the final *-ire* by *-iron*, no doubt because the object designated by the word is made of metal. Further developments along the same lines have led to the less established variants *endiron* (presumably because it is located at the two ends of the fireplace grid) and *handiron* (probably simply because of the similarity of sound). As a consequence of these processes, the word now has a shape that suggests a derivation very different from the historically correct one.

Spelling pronunciations, such as the British "sounding out" of the initial *h* of *herb* are similarly historically inaccurate. The word belongs to a set of borrowings from French which includes *hono(u)r* and *hour* and whose written initial *h* originally was not pronounced, because French itself did not pronounce it. (The situation is similar to that of the *k* in *knee*: The spelling with *h* is an "echo" of the fact that an *h* was once pronounced – in Latin.) But because the word is spelled with an *h*, and because an *h* in initial position usually is sounded out (as in *he, him, hymn*), some speakers pronounced the *h* of *herb* as well, and in British English their pronunciation eventually prevailed.

In this case the spelling pronunciation is not completely inaccurate from a historical perspective, since Latin, the ancestor of French, actually pro-

nounced an *h* here. In other cases, spelling pronunciation may lead to historically incorrect results. For instance, during the Renaissance people in western
Europe became aware that many words borrowed from Latin with the letter
t were ultimately from Greek where they were written with the letter θ, transcribed as *th* and, in English, pronounced the same as the *th* of words like
thing. This discovery led to the reintroduction of *th* in many words, such as
Dorothy and *Thomas*. In some of these, spelling pronunciation then led to the
introduction of the *th* sound *(Dorothy)*, while in others, the old *t* pronunciation remained *(Thomas)*. In at least one word, *Anthony*, British and American
English went different ways: British English has retained the pronunciation *t*,
while American English has opted for the spelling pronunciation *th*.

So far so good, especially since by the time that these spelling changes
occurred, the Greeks had come to pronounce θ as *th*, just as in English. However, in the process some innocent bystanders were re-spelled and, eventually,
re-pronounced as well – words which were of genuine Latin, not of Greek
origin, and which never had a θ in them. This is how the word *author* (Middle English *autour,* from Lat. *auctor* via Fr. *auteur*) got its *th* spelling and
pronunciation.

Historical linguists cannot – and should not – ignore such "ahistoric" behavior. Speakers' attitudes, whatever their historical or linguistic justification,
play a significant role in language change. (In fact, in language contact situations, even non-native speakers' attitudes and behavior play a significant
role.) Even if speakers of British English are made aware of the fact that the
initial *h* of *herb* is historically as incorrect as – heaven forfend – sounding out
the initial *h* of words like *honour* or *hour*, they will adopt an *h*-less pronunciation for *herb* only at the risk of being considered Cockney by their peers,
and Americans would run into a similar problem if they pronounced *Anthony*
with *t*. Similarly, insisting on saying *andire*, instead of *andiron, endiron,* or
handiron, will hardly be appreciated as a more correct pronunciation; it is
most likely to be met with confusion, if not utter lack of comprehension.

5. A note on transcription and terminology

In this introductory chapter, words have been cited in the form they are usually written (or transliterated), and phonetic interpretations have been given
approximately, using English spelling conventions. However, English spelling
is notoriously "non-phonetic": Especially as far as vowels are concerned,

there is little consistency in the relation between spelling and pronunciation. English speakers themselves are keenly aware of this and can cite expressions such as

Though the rough cough ploughed him through and through

as examples of the inconsistency of English spelling: Here, the sequence *ough* designates five different pronunciations. Yet further phonetic variants of *ough* spellings are found in *hiccough* and *lough*.

Consider further the case of the past tenses of the verbs *read* and *lead*: For *read*, we have *read*, presumably to distinguish it from the color *red* but as a consequence spelled the same way as the present-tense form. On the other hand, for *lead* we have *led*, which is nicely differentiated from the present-tense form, as well as from the name of the mineral, *lead*; but the latter is not distinguished from the present-tense *lead*, even though sounding different.

George Bernard Shaw, an ardent supporter of spelling reform, is said to have proposed the spelling *ghoti* for *fish* to demonstrate the vagaries of English spelling, with *gh* as in *rough* or *cough*, *o* as in *women*, *ti* as in *nation*. This, of course, is an exaggeration, since *gh* never has the value *f* in initial position, and *ti* does not designate the sound of *sh* except before vowels; English spelling is not quite that "crazy". Still, as long as we are having fun, we can expand on Shaw's *ghoti* by proposing *ghubtoti* as the spelling for *fetish*, where the additional *u* has the value as in *bury*, and *bt* as in *debt, doubt,* and *subtle*.

Even if we ignore such exaggerations, the fact remains that English spelling is not an ideal way of transcribing speech sounds, especially of languages very different from English. In the remainder of this book, a standardized method of transcription will be followed, using symbols widely used among linguists (especially historical linguists). Readers not familiar with these symbols should consult the Appendix to this Introduction, which also lists a few additional, non-phonetic symbols used in this book.

While a familiarity with phonetics is essential for the study of most forms of language, there is one class of languages for which it is not. These are SIGN LANGUAGES (also referred to as signed languages), found all over the world as a means of communication between the deaf (see Chapter 16, § 8), and also used by speakers of "oral" languages in communicating with deaf people. There are many misconceptions about sign languages; and the study of the history of sign languages is still rudimentary. But increasingly intensive research shows no significant differences in structure, in complexity, or in expressivity between sign languages and oral languages; and some aspects of linguistic change in sign languages are beginning to be known. Where appropriate, we therefore add brief remarks on sign languages to the discussion of linguistic change.

Most of the examples in this book come from members of the Indo-European language family, including its ancestor, "Proto-Indo-European". Of all the known language families, this one has been most thoroughly researched and, in addition, is most familiar to the authors of this book. Chapter 2, following the Appendix on Phonetics, provides an account of the discovery of Indo-European, information on the reconstructed Proto-Indo-European language and the symbols and terminology used to describe it and its early descendants, a brief overview of the members of the Indo-European family, and a list of abbreviations for the names of Indo-European languages. (A survey of other language families can be found in Chapter 16, § 8.) Chapter 3 surveys the origin and history of writing and the decipherment of ancient scripts which give us access to early texts that otherwise would have been lost to us. Our discussion of language change begins with Chapter 4, on Sound Change.

Appendix to Chapter 1
Phonetics, phonetic symbols, and other symbols

> Scientific phonetics [is] the indispensable foundation of all study
> of language ... above all, of historical grammar.
>
> (Henry Sweet, *Collected Papers*)

Henry Sweet was a nineteenth and early-twentieth century scholar of Old English and speech science who founded the modern discipline of PHONETICS, the scientific study of speech sounds. He reportedly was the model for Henry Higgins, the male lead character in George Bernard Shaw's play *Pygmalion*, upon which the musical *My Fair Lady* was based. Just as Henry Higgins needed to know about speech in order to "improve" the speech of his Cockney-speaking subject, Eliza Doolittle, so we must, as Sweet suggests, understand the phonetic basis of language, before we can get seriously into the examination of language change.

SPEECH SOUNDS are wave-like variations in air pressure produced by vocal organs, especially the tongue, interfering with the flow of air from the lungs through the vocal tract. In this regard they are not substantially different from the sound made by slapping your hand on a table or breaking a stick, which also sets air in motion and creates sound waves. However, while we perceive the slapping or breaking noise as a single, undifferentiated event, we perceive speech sounds as differentiated into discrete units. Thus, we hear a word such as *peer* as consisting of three speech sounds, a *p*, an *ee*, and an *r*; similarly, we hear *wreath* as consisting of a *r*, an *ee*, and a *th*-sound (as if it were spelled *reeth*).

But what do we mean by such symbols as *p*, *ee*, or *th*? Does *p* designate the initial sound of *peer, pieced, pill*, etc., does it have the same value as in *philosophy*, and what about the "silent letter" in *pterodactyl* or *pneumonia*? Does *ee* stand for the vowel sound in Engl. *peer, geese, feet* etc., or for the vowel in German *leer* (which sounds close to Engl. *lair*)? Which *th*-sound do we mean, the one in *thing*, the one in *this*, or the one in *Thomas* or *Thames*? And how do we distinguish the two similar, and yet different, sounds in *thing* and *this*?

These examples confirm what we saw at the end of the preceding chapter: English spelling is not an ideal way of transcribing speech sounds. But even if other languages may have more consistent spelling systems, these systems are accurate only for the language for which they were designed. No ordinary spelling system can be expected to be usable for all languages.

In linguistics, by contrast, we need a system that can in principle be used for any language. This is especially true for historical linguistics, which by its very nature deals with the relationship between different languages or different stages of the same language, each of which has its own phonetic and orthographic peculiarities.

In addition, we need a firm grasp of the nature of speech sounds, such as the question of the distinction between the two *th*-sounds in *thing* and *this*. Without such an understanding we cannot understand sound change. Without understanding sound change we cannot establish that, say, OE *hlāf* and Mod. E *loaf* are really different versions of the same word, not just words that happen to sound similar. And without establishing such identifications across time and space, the whole enterprise of historical and comparative linguistics comes to a grinding halt.

In what follows, therefore, we will develop a vocabulary for talking about the nature of speech sounds, and introduce an inventory of symbols that we can use to represent them. You will recognize many of the symbols from the English alphabet, though some of the specific values we assign might be unfamiliar. Other symbols will be adaptations of familiar ones, often with "diacritical" marks above or below the symbol.

If at this point you find the large number of phonetic terms and symbols quite bewildering, you are in good company. Just about everybody who has studied linguistics has had the same initial reaction. As you see the terms used throughout this book, you will become more and more familiar with them, and at the end of the book you should find, much to your surprise, that they have become second nature.

Along the way, you may treat what follows as a source of reference which you can return to whenever needed. Summaries of the terms and symbols are given in Tables 1–4, which are placed at the end of this appendix for easy reference.

Analyzing speech sounds. As noted earlier, speech sounds are produced by various speech organs obstructing the air that is being forced out of the lungs and through the vocal tract. Differences between speech sounds result from differences in the type of obstruction (the MANNER OF ARTICULATION), in the organ of speech that makes the obstruction (the ARTICULATOR), and the place in the vocal tract where the obstruction is made (the PLACE OF ARTICULA-TION). Most important among these three parameters of speech articulation

are manner of articulation and place of articulation. Speech sounds can generally be described in terms of these parameters, although some sounds can
be produced in more than one way. Figure 1 provides a view of the vocal
tract, the major articulators and places of articulation, and the names used to
designate them.

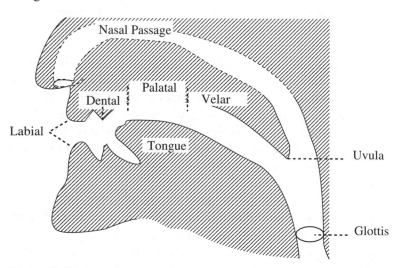

Figure 1. Major articulators and places of articulation

Stops and places of articulation. The most radical articulation, which is
also easiest to observe, consists of completely blocking the airflow at one of
the places of articulation. Sounds produced in this manner are called STOPS.
Depending on their place of articulation, English stops are classified as LABIAL
(*p, b*), DENTAL (*t, d*), PALATAL (*č* and *ǰ*, similar to the initial and final sounds of
Engl. *church* and *judge*, although the English sounds really are affricates; see
below), and VELAR (*k* and *g* as in *get*). A GLOTTAL stop occurs marginally in
emphatic speech (before initial vowel, as in *ʔoff with his head*) or in dialectal
British English for written *t(t)* in words such as *little, got*. In Semitic and
many other languages, the glottal stop is a regular speech sound, and so is the
UVULAR stop *q*. Yet other types of stops are found in other languages. One
of these will make an occasional appearance in the chapter on writing; this
is the Semitic "pharyngeal" stop, articulated somewhere between the uvula
and the glottis. Together with the glottal and uvular stop, the pharyngeal stop
forms a class of sounds that in Semitic linguistics is referred to as "gutturals".
(A complete listing of the major sounds and symbols relevant for this book
appears in Tables 1–4.)

Nasals. Although NASALS like *n* and *m* sound very different from stops, they are articulatorily closely related – as anyone who has had a cold or hay fever can readily understand. Nasals essentially are oral stops of the type *b, d, g,* except that the opening to the nasal passage is left open. This permits air to escape through the nasal passage, producing a nasal resonance that turns the oral stop into a nasal. If a cold or hay fever interferes with the passage of air through the nose, the difference between oral *b, d* etc. and nasal *m, n* etc. disappears, and nasals seem to turn into "dasals".

In addition to labial *m* and dental *n*, English has a velar nasal ŋ, often written *ng*, which occurs in *sing* and *sink*.

Fricatives, sibilants, and voicing. A less radical obstruction than for stops and nasals narrows the air passage sufficiently to produce a friction noise at the place of articulation. Not surprisingly, the resulting sounds are called FRICATIVES. The English labial fricatives (*f, v*) are actually LABIODENTAL, articulated with the upper teeth against the lower lip; fricatives involving both lips ("BILABIAL") occur in some languages, but the general tendency is for labial fricatives to be labiodental. Dental fricatives are found in Engl. *thing* and *this*. The initial sound of *this* is transcribed as ð; for the initial sound of *thing* two transcriptions are employed: θ and þ. The transcription þ is traditional in talking about early Germanic languages; θ is used elsewhere. A glottal fricative is the *h* of Engl. *horse*. Closely allied to the fricatives are the SIBILANTS (*s, z,* and the sounds in *share* and *measure*, transcribed š and ž). Sibilants differ from ordinary fricatives by being articulated with some additional friction noise. The exact location and manner in which that hissing noise is produced may vary from speaker to speaker; even the primary place of articulation may vary – as long as the acoustic effect comes close to the expectations of other speakers of the language.

The sibilants *s* and *z* are ideal for beginners to understand something that we have glossed over so far; that is the difference between such pairs as *s* and *z, p* and *b* – or the initial θ and ð of Engl. *thing* and *this* which we talked about earlier. The difference is one of "VOICING", which is present in sounds like *z, b,* and ð, and absent in their counterparts *s, p,* and θ. Voicing is a kazoo-like effect produced by the vocal folds (more commonly known as vocal cords), two membranes in the glottis, deep down in the vocal tract and therefore difficult to observe. Fortunately, the sibilants *s* and *z* provide an easy means to get around this difficulty: Hold your fingers over your ears while you first articulate a *z* and then an *s*; you should feel a strong buzzing vibration during the *z* which should be absent in *s*. The source for the buzz in the VOICED sound *z* is the kazoo-like vibration of the vocal folds. VOICELESS sounds like *s* are articulated without this vibration, with the vocal folds at rest, in an open position.

Affricates and aspirates. Many languages have a set of complex sounds which are called AFFRICATES. These begin as stops; but in contrast to ordinary stops, the stoppage of the airflow is released into a fricative or sibilant that is produced at the same place of articulation. In English, the palatal stops *č* and *ǰ* are affricates, rather than simple stops, and could therefore be transcribed as *čš* and *ǰž* if we wanted to make fine phonetic distinctions; a certain degree of affricate articulation is normal for palatal stops in all languages. (In most cases we can ignore the difference between palatal stops and affricates.) Some languages have other types of affricates.

Articulatorily, ASPIRATED consonants can be considered a special type of affricate, with the stop released into something like the glottal fricative *h*. In English, voiceless stops tend to be aspirated, especially in initial position, before an accented vowel; but aspiration does not serve to distinguish stops from each other in the same way as voicing does. In many early Indo-European languages aspiration plays a much more important role. For instance, Sanskrit makes a distinction between *phala-* 'fruit', *pala-* (a unit of weight), *bhala* (an interjection), and *bala-* 'strength'. Even if we may not be able to make such distinctions ourselves, it will be important to remember that they can be made when we get to the discussion of linguistic change.

Liquids. If the obstruction of the airflow is reduced even farther than for fricatives and sibilants, the result will be various *r*- and *l*-sounds. Especially the *r*-sounds exhibit a great amount of variation, both within and across languages. While Scots English, Spanish, and many other languages have a trilled *r*, the *r* of American English is rather similar to *w* (with which it is often confused by children), and many varieties of French, German, and other languages have a uvular or velar *R*. But differences in *r*-sounds usually do not distinguish different words. In most cases it will be sufficient to use a single symbol, *r*. There is less variation in *l*-sounds, but some languages (including conservative Spanish) distinguish between a dental and a palatal. Since *l*-sounds are articulated with "lateral" (i.e., side) contact of the tongue, they are commonly called LATERALS.

It is difficult to find a common articulatory or acoustic feature that would define *r*-sounds and laterals as a group. But children often have great difficulties distinguishing them in the early stages of learning their first language; and many languages have only one or the other of the two classes of sounds.

To express this affiliation between *r*-sounds and laterals, it is convenient to use the term LIQUIDS.

Semivowels, palatalized consonants, and labiovelars. The consonants with the least amount of obstruction to the airflow are so close to the vowels that they are often referred to as SEMIVOWELS. English examples of semivowels are the initial consonants of *yes* and *woman*.

Just as fricatives and sibilants can combine with stops to produce affricates and aspirates, so semivowels can combine with stops and other consonants into special types of speech sounds. A *y*-like element frequently combines with consonants to produce PALATALIZED consonants. The term "palatalized" is confusing, because it sounds very similar to "palatal". But in linguistic change, palatalized consonants are closely related to palatals (see Chapter § 5.1.1); and the term "palatalized" is too deeply ingrained in linguistic terminology to be abandoned anyway. A rarer combination is that of a *w*-like element with a velar consonant to form a LABIOVELAR. This, too, is a confusing term, since it might suggest that the lips touch the velum, a physical impossibility even for the most acrobatically inclined. The "labio" element merely refers to the fact that the lips are rounded while the back of the tongue articulates against the velum. As we will see in Chapter 2, labiovelar stops are a feature of Proto-Indo-European.

A summary of the major consonant symbols that will be needed for this book is given in Table 1 with examples mainly drawn from English. Parentheses indicate symbols that are used only rarely. The table does not include aspirates, palatalized consonants, and labiovelars; these consonants are designated by diacritics that modify the symbols in Table 1. See Table 3 for the most important of these diacritics.

Vowels. The speech sounds examined up to this point are jointly referred to as CONSONANTS. They differ in significant ways from the VOWELS (such as *a, i, u*):

– Vowels normally are the center, the "syllabic peak", of the syllable (as in *consonant*); consonants usually are not.
– Vowels are formed with the least amount of obstruction of the airflow; in fact, the articulator does not even touch the place of articulation.
– Vowels further differ from consonants in that they are all produced in a very limited space, the velar area; and in that small area, a large number of different vowels can be articulated.

Vowels therefore have to be characterized by terms that are different from those used for the consonants. The most basic classification is in terms of relative tongue position, on a front-to-back scale (FRONT, CENTRAL, and BACK), and a high-to-low scale (HIGH, MID, and LOW). See Table 2 for illustrations of these distinctions.

In addition, many languages make a distinction in terms of "rounding": ROUND vowels are articulated with lip rounding, UNROUND vowels are not. The general tendency is for front vowels to be unround (e.g. the vowel in Engl. *sit*) and for back vowels to be rounded (as in Engl. *soot*); but languages like German and French are well known for their front rounded vowels, often called "umlaut vowels", and difficulties these sounds cause for speakers of languages like English (which do not have them) are notorious.

The symbols used for the basic vowels are given in Table 2 with examples mainly from English. Symbols in parentheses may occasionally be used for finer distinctions; for most purposes the unparenthesized symbols are sufficient.

The low back vowels in the lower right corner of Table 2 may cause some difficulties, for this is the area of the vowel spectrum where different varieties of English show the greatest amount of variation. Many varieties of American English, for instance, pronounce *caught* and *law* with the same vowel as *father*. In the midwest this tends to be the low central vowel [a]; but in other areas it may be closer to [ɔ]. Such differences in pronunciation, however, do not affect the use of our phonetic terms and symbols; on the contrary, it is through these terms and symbols that we can characterize the differences.

Two of the vowels and the symbols used for them have special names; these are the central vowels ə, called *schwa* (a term from Hebrew grammar which came into English via German) and i, called "barred *i*" (because the symbol *i* has a "bar" across it). The vowel ə occurs in most varieties of English corresponding to the final "a" of *sofa*; i is found in many varieties of American English in the pronunciation of the adverb *just* (as in *I just can't wait till I get to find out more about how languages change*).

Diphthongs. Vowels can combine with each other or with semivowels to form more complex "syllabic peaks", as in Engl. *my*, pronounced [may]. The name for such complex structures is DIPHTHONG (literally, 'double sound').

Vowel length and nasalization. For vowels, we need to use diacritics much more frequently than for consonants. In addition to relative tongue position and rounding, vowels often are distinguished in terms of LENGTH, as in

Engl. *sit* vs. *seat*, with short vs. long vowel. English long vowels tend to be slightly diphthongal (e.g., *seat* may be transcribed as [siyt]); but in many other languages, length is the major or only relevant distinction.

Vowels also may be NASALIZED by opening the passage to the nasal cavity, just as for nasals like *m* and *n*. Nasalized vowels are a well-known feature of French; but they are found in many other languages, including Portuguese and Hindi. Length and nasalization are indicated by diacritic symbols modifying the basic vowel symbols. These diacritics are given in Table 3.

Other diacritics and their phonetic values. In the course of examining consonants and vowels we have introduced several diacritics (for aspiration, palatalization, labiovelars; and for vowel length and nasalization). A few other diacritics will be used in this book.

Retroflex and alveolar consonants. Where English and most other European languages have just one class of consonants articulated at or near the front teeth, most languages of South Asia distinguish between two classes. One of these, the dental class, is articulated at the same place as Engl. *θ* and *ð*, the other much farther back than Engl. *t* and *d*, close to the area where Am. Engl. *r* is pronounced. This second group is distinguished from the dentals by the name "RETROFLEX" (because the tongue is flexed backward in their articulation). Retroflex consonants are marked by a subscript dot, as in *ṭ* and *ḍ*. Some South Asian languages add a third class of consonants, right in between the dentals and retroflexes. These are referred to as "ALVEOLARS" and are marked by a subscript line, as in *ṯ* and *ḏ*. (English "dentals" actually are alveolars, too, being usually articulated just behind the dental area; but since we do not need to distinguish them from other consonants in the same general area, no special symbols or terms are needed.)

Consonants marked by superscript diacritics. In transcriptions of Sanskrit you may occasionally find the symbol *ṁ* (an *m* with superscript dot) which designates a complex nasal "glide" or transition sound between a vowel and a following consonant. Sanskrit examples also may contain the symbol *ś* (an *s* with superscript accent mark); this is the conventional symbol to transcribe the palatal voiceless sibilant of Sanskrit. Superscript accent marks are even more commonly used for Proto-Indo-European reconstructions, where they indicate a class of "palatal-prevelar" consonants (see Chapter 2, § 2).

Syllabic nasals and liquids. At the beginning of the vowel section we observed that consonants differ from vowels by usually not forming the "syllabic peak". Occasionally, however consonants may do so anyway, especially the nasals and liquids. In fact, English has such SYLLABIC NASALS and LIQUIDS in words like *bottle, button, bottom*, but they are hidden by the spelling and, complicating things even more, they may in super-careful speech be pronounced with a ə-vowel + non-syllabic liquid, as in [bɔtəl] or [batəl]. Syllabic liquids are indicated by a subscript circle, as in [bətn̥] = *button*; they are a prominent feature of Proto-Indo-European (see Chapter 2, § 2).

Accent or stress: In many languages, words of more than one syllable contain one syllable that is more prominent than the rest, in terms of loudness, pitch, or some other feature. This syllable is conventionally referred to as bearing ACCENT or STRESS. Where necessary in this book, the accented syllable is designated by a superscript acute accent mark, as in *áccent* or, in phonetic transcription, [ǽksent]. Stress can be the sole phonetic characteristic distinguishing between two words, as in Engl. *áccent* (noun) vs. *accént* beside *áccent* (verb).

Conclusion. We now have the tools to describe and transcribe the various sounds of different languages that you will encounter in the rest of the book. In many cases we will simply cite words in the form they are usually written (or transliterated). This is especially the case if the actual pronunciation of a word or phrase is not at issue; but many writing and transliteration systems are close enough to our transcription that a phonetic interpretation is not necessary even when talking about sound change. Where phonetic interpretations are crucial, though, familiarity with our phonetic terminology and phonetic alphabet will be indispensable, as Sweet would put it.

Before we can begin to apply our terminology and phonetic alphabet in examining language change, however, we need to become familiar with a few additional special symbols that are employed in this book. These are given in Table 4.

Table 1. Consonants

		Labial	Dental	Palatal	Velar	Uvular	Glottal
Stops	vl[1]	*p* **pet**	*t* **Tom**	*č* **church**	*k* **kid**	*(q[3])*	*ʔ* *bottle*[4]
	vd[2]	*b* **bet**	*d* **dumb**	*ǰ* **judge**	*g* **go**		
Fricatives	vl.	*f (Φ[5])* *ʃat*	*θ/þ*[6] **thorn**	*(ç)* Germ. *ich*	*x* Scots. *loch*	*(χ[3])*	*h* **hand**
	vd.	*v (β[5])* *vat* (Span. *debe*)	*ð* **that**	*(ɉ)*	*γ* Span. *lago*		*(ɦ)* *behold*
Sibilants	vl.		*s* *see*	*š* *she*			
	vd.		*z* *zeal*	*ž* *measure*			
Affricates[7]	vl.	*pf* Germ. **Pferd**	*ts* Germ. *Katze*	*(čš)*	*(kx)*		
	vd.			*(ǰž̆)*			
Liquids			*r, l* **red, lead**	*(λ)* (conservative	*Span. ella)*	*(R)* (Germ. *rechts*)	
Nasals		*m* **mow**	*n* **no**	*ñ* Span. *señor*	*ŋ* *sing*		
Semivowels		*w* **woo**		*y* **you**			

[Notes: [1]voiceless; [2]voiced; [3]used in many non-Indo-European languages; [4]in Scots English and many British urban dialects; [5]bilabial fricatives; [6]þ is traditionally used in Germanic, θ elsewhere; [7]in languages with a contrast between affricates and stop + fricative, the fricative element may be raised to avoid confusion.

General note: In addition to velar, uvular, and glottal stops and fricatives, other back consonants are possible; the Semitic languages, for instance, have a set of stops and fricatives (called GUTTURALS) articulated between the uvula and the glottis, including ʕ (stop) and ħ or ḥ (fricative); in addition, note ḫ = [x].]

Table 2. Vowels

	Front		Central	Back	
	unround	round[1]		round	unround[2]
High	*i* (i^3)	*ü*	*ɨ*	*u* (U^3)	(ɪ)
	seat, sit	Fr.*rue*	(*just* [adverb])	*boot, foot*	
Mid	*e* (ε^3)	*ö*	*ə*	*o*	
	bate, bet	Fr. *feu*	*sofa*	*boat*	
Low	*æ*		*a*	*ɔ*	
	bat		*father*	(*caught, law*)	

[Notes: [1]same position as *i, e*, but lips rounded; [2]same position as *u*, but lips unrounded; [3]these symbols are used occasionally to indicate slightly lower vowels, as in [sɪt] = *sit* vs. [sīt] = *seat.*]

Table 3. Diacritics

Aspiration:	*ph*, *bh*, etc. (In languages with contrast between aspirates and stop + *h*, the *h*-element of aspirates may be raised to avoid confusion.]
Palatalization and labiovelars:	*t*ʸ, *d*ʸ, etc. and *k*ʷ, *g*ʷ, etc.
"Dottings" and other diacritics:	The languages of South Asia have a contrast between pure dental consonants (articulated at the same location as Engl. [θ]) and "retroflex" consonants (for which the tongue tip points back, roughly as in Am. Engl. [r]). The latter consonants are distinguished from the former by subscript dots, as in *ṭ*, *ḍ*, *ṇ*. (In the Semitic languages, subscript dots indicate "emphatic consonants".) The Dravidian languages of Southern India distinguish yet another, intermediate series, called alveolar, which is transcribed by means of subscript hyphens, as in *ṯ*, *ḏ*, *ṉ*. For Sanskrit, an *ṁ* with superscript dot is used to indicate a special nasal glide. Accent marks over consonants indicate palatal or "palatal/prevelar" pronunciation, as in Sanskrit *ś*, or Proto-Indo-European *k̂*, *ĝ*, etc.
Nasalized vowels:	*ã*, *õ*, etc. (Fr. *en* [ã] 'in' etc.)
Long vs. short vowels:	*ī* vs. *ĭ*, *ā* vs. *ă*, *ū* vs. *ŭ*, etc. (roughly as in *seat* vs. *sit*, etc.). (Vowel shortness is indicated only when necessary; ordinarily, short vowels are left unmarked.)
"Syllabic" nasals/liquids:	*ḷ*, *ṛ*, *ṇ*, *ṃ* (*bottle, button, bottom*) (As the examples show, syllabic liquids and nasals behave like vowels in constituting the most prominent part of a syllable. In English, these sounds may in very slow, careful pronunciation be pronounced with a ə-vowel + nonsyllabic liquid, as in [bɔtəl]. See also Chapter 2, § 2.)
Accent or stress:	indicated by an acute accent mark over the vowel in the stressed syllable, e.g. *áccent* or, in phonetic transcription, [ǽksent].

Table 4. Other special symbols

"Arrows": To indicate sound changes, unshafted arrows are used. For instance, a >
b means "a changes to b"; and b < a means "b results from a".

For analogical replacements, shafted arrows are used (→ and ←).

To indicate borrowings, double-shafted arrows are used (⇒ and ⇐).

Asterisks: A preposed asterisk indicates a reconstructed form (one not actually attested but hypothesized to have existed – see Chapter 16); a postposed
asterisk designates any other hypothetical form.

Brackets: Where it is necessary to distinguish phonetic transcriptions from customary
spelling, the transcription is placed in square brackets, [ ]; angle brackets,
< >, may be used to focus on the written form, as distinct from its phonetic
value.

Chapter 2
The discovery of Indo-European

The Sanfcrit language, whatever be its antiquity, is of a wonderful ftructure; more perfect than the Greek, more copious than
the Latin, and more exquifitely refined than either, yet bearing
to both of them a ftronger affinity, both in the roots of verbs and
in the forms of grammar, than could poffibly have been produced
by accident; fo ftrong indeed, that no philologer could examine
them all three, without believing them to have fprung from fome
common fource, which, perhaps, no longer exifts: there is a fim-
ilar reafon, though not quite fo forcible, for fuppofing that both
the Gothick and the Celtick, though blended with a very different idiom, had the fame origin with the Sanfcrit; and the old
Perfian might be added to the fame family, if this were the place
for difcuffing any queftion concerning the antiquities of Perfia.
(*Sir William Jones, Third Anniversary Discourse, on the Hindus,
Royal Asiatic Society, 1786*)

1. Language relationship

The preceding remarks, made by Sir William Jones at the close of the eighteenth century, present a turning point in our understanding of historical
and comparative linguistics in general. Scholars were specially impressed by
Jones's suggestion that the similarities between certain languages of India and
Europe are too great to be attributed to chance and can only be explained by
assuming that the languages are related by descent from a common ancestor.
This suggestion stimulated a veritable explosion of new research. Over the
years, the research resulted in an increasing confidence that not only the disparate and far-flung languages mentioned by Jones, but many others as well
(see § 3 below), are in fact members of a family of closely related languages
and descended from a common, unattested ancestor.

In the early nineteenth century, the family of languages came to be called
Indo-European, because its known members extended from India in the east

to Europe in the west; and the common ancestor is now referred to as Proto-Indo-European. (Since then, another member of the family – Tocharian – has been discovered in Chinese Turkestan, farther east than the northwestern part of India where Sanskrit was first spoken, but the name "Indo-European" has stuck.)

The idea that languages might be related to each other through descent from a common ancestor was not entirely without precedent. The similarities among the Romance languages could be, and were, easily explained as resulting from their descent from a known common ancestor, Latin. (One of the earliest to propose such an account was the famous poet and scholar Dante.) Note for example the similarities in the word correspondences below:

	Latin	Italian	Spanish	French	Romanian
'one'	*ūnus*	*uno*	*un*	*un* [õ]	*un*
'two'	*duo*	*due*	*dos*	*deux* [dö]	*doi*
'three'	*trēs*	*tre*	*tres*	*trois* [tRwa]	*trei*
'fish'	*piscis*	*pesce*	*pez*	*poisson*	*peşte*
'heart'	*cor*	*cuore*	*corazón*	*cœur*	(*inimă*[1])
'winter'	*hiberno-*	*inverno*	*invierno*	*hiver*	*iarnă*

([1]The Romanian word for 'heart' comes from a different source: Lat. *anima* 'soul'. Cases like this, where one or more related languages exhibit a non-cognate word, are not unusual – or unexpected – given the fact that vocabulary, too, is subject to change.)

The situation is similar for the medieval and modern languages of northern India whose structure and vocabulary were routinely derived by indigenous grammarians from their attested common ancestor, Sanskrit. The following correspondences for the numerals 'one' to 'three' may illustrate the ease with which a relationship can be established.

	Sanskrit	Bengali	Hindi	Marathi	Gujarati	Kashmiri
'one'	*ēkaḥ*	*ēk*	*ēk*	*ēk*	*ek*	*akh*
'two'	*dvau*	*dui*	*dō*	*dōn*	*bɛ*	*ziʔ*
'three'	*trayaḥ*	*tin*	*tīn*	*tīn*	*t(r)ən*	*triʔ*
	neut. *trīṇi*					

However, attempts at longer-range comparisons, going beyond easily recognized families like Romance, were less successful. In Europe, it was commonly assumed that all languages ultimately were descended from Hebrew, since that, presumably, was the language spoken by Adam and Eve in the Garden of Eden. Similarly in India, where Sanskrit had exerted a strong influence on the Dravidian languages of the south, especially on their vocabulary, it was assumed that these languages were descended from Sanskrit. We now know that both of these interpretations are erroneous. And that knowledge is founded on the vastly improved understanding of historical and comparative linguistics that was stimulated by Jones's pioneering remarks.

Although Jones also made some very wrong guesses about language relationships, his comments came at an opportune moment in history, when earlier European attitudes, limited by religious, social, and cultural isolation, were giving way to new modes of thinking.

During the medieval period western Europe scholars had become linguistically parochial, limiting their attention almost exclusively to Latin. But, although Latin was the common currency of all scholars in western Europe, the form of the language that was used had become far removed from the Classical Latin of Caesar and Cicero – indirectly mirroring the great distance between medieval and Classical Latin thought and life.

In the late thirteenth century, with the great Renaissance (lit. 'rebirth') of interest in the literary and philosophical traditions of Classical Latin antiquity, scholars attempted to reform Latin usage by making it conform more closely to the language of the great classical authors. But in the process, a profound change in linguistic thinking occurred: Scholars like Dante realized that there were vast differences between the Latin language that was learned in schools and the Italian, Spanish, French etc. vernaculars that children learned in early childhood. They began to account for the differences by determining the linguistic changes that differentiated the vernaculars from the ancestral Latin language. Moreover, they began to advocate an increased use – and cultivation – of the vernaculars. As a consequence, grammars of Italian and Spanish were published in the fifteenth century, to be followed by grammars of French, Polish, and other languages in the sixteenth century.

The Renaissance emphasis of returning *ad fontes* 'to the sources [of western European culture]' had implications far beyond linguistic scholarship. Religious reformers like Luther, Zwingli, and Calvin attempted to return to the early Christian idea that the Gospel should be preached in the language of the people and therefore began to translate the Bible into the vernacular languages. The resulting translations expanded the cultivation of western European vernacular languages; and this cultivation, in turn, encouraged closer examination of the earlier, medieval forms of these languages.

The Renaissance received an unexpected boost from the Ottoman Turks' conquest of the Byzantine empire. Greek scholars began to flee to western Europe; and an early trickle of westward migration turned to a flood with the fall of Constantinople in 1453. The result was a vast increase in awareness of classical Grcck antiquity and its vehicle, Classical Greek. And Greek was added to Latin as a language to be studied in school by anyone who wanted to be considered properly educated.

The Ottoman conquest of Byzantium, however, also had other, more indirect, effects on western linguistic awareness: It seriously interrupted the trade routes with India and China, sources of highly treasured silks and spices. Portugal therefore began to look for alternative routes around the coast of Africa. And in 1492, Columbus set sail for what he believed to be India, to discover what turned out to be an entirely "new world" – the Americas. The voyages by the Portuguese and Spanish explorers, and their later rivals from France, the Netherlands, and the British Isles, set in motion not only an expansion of European power across the world but also the subjugation, even destruction, of non-European societies. (Some of the linguistic effects of these developments are taken up in Chapter 14.) The travels of European explorers and missionaries also led to an increase in familiarity with languages beyond Western Europe's cultural horizon.

One of the results was an ever expanding set of comparative word lists, with at least some attempts at establishing families of related languages on the basis of vocabulary similarities.

Some of these attempts were rather naive from our present perspective. For instance, one scholar classified languages in terms of their words for 'God', grouping Latin and Greek closely together because of their correspondence *deus : théos*, and Slavic with Iranian because of *bogŭ : baga*.

At first glance, these correspondences appear to be excellent, both in form and in meaning. But after more than a century of working out the sound correspondences in inherited words, we know that the similarities in *deus : théos* are accidental. Lat. *deus* is from the root underlying Gk. *Zéus* (genitive *Diós*), and if Greek *théos* had a good Latin cognate, it would have to have an initial *f*. (A possible, but controversial, cognate is Lat. *festus* 'festive'.) The similarity of *bogŭ: baga* results from secondary contact between Slavic and Iranian and does not reflect close genetic relationship. In fact, Iranian is most closely related to Sanskrit, and that language has *dēva*, a fine cognate of Lat. *deus*.

Some attempts at establishing relationship, however, were remarkably mature, especially those by Sajnovics (1770) and Gyármathi (1799) to relate Hungarian to Finnish.

In the remainder of this chapter we will take a closer look at Indo-European, since this is the most thoroughly investigated language family, as well as the source for most of the examples in this book. Brief discussions of other language families are found in Chapter 16.

2. Proto-Indo-European

What makes it possible to rule out correspondences like Lat. *deus* : Greek *théos* is the fact that Jones's famous "discovery" of 1786 brought about a sea change in the way scholars think about language relationship. Jones inspired a dramatic outburst in comparative research on the Indo-European languages; and, most important, that research soon went beyond the stage of superficial comparison of individual words and began to examine recurrent and systematic correspondences in hundreds, even thousands, of words, including words like the following:

	Sanskrit	Greek	Latin	Old English	Old Church Slavic
'one'	*ēkaḥ*	*(heis)*	*ūnus*	*ān*	*edi:nǐ*
'two'	*dvau*	*duō*	*duo*	*twā*	*dǔva*
'three'	*trayaḥ*	*treis*	*trēs*	*þrīe*	*trǐje*
'that'	*tad*	*to*	*(is-) tud*	*þæt*	*to*
'father'	*pitā*	*patēr*	*pater*	*fæder*	*(otǐcǔ)*
'foot'	*pad-*	*pod-*	*ped-*	*fōt*	*(noga)*
'blood, gore'	*krūra-*	*kreas*	*cruor* [**k-**]	*hrēaw*	*krǔvǐ*

(As in the earlier Romance example, some languages display non-cognate words for particular lexical items. These are put in parentheses. The parenthesized *is-* of Lat. *istud* is an added element that originally reinforced the demonstrative force of *tud*.)

One of the most important developments was a discovery by the Danish scholar Rasmus Rask (1818) which was popularized by the German linguist Jacob Grimm (1819) and therefore came to be known as GRIMM'S LAW. As Rask observed, the consonant system of the Germanic languages differed from the systems of most of the other Indo-European languages in a manner that was remarkably systematic. For instance, where other languages have *p*, *t*, *k*, early Germanic offers the fricatives *f*, *þ*, *h*, as in the boldface consonants in the above examples. (These systematic correspondences are discussed in further detail in Chapter 4.)

The regularities summed up by Grimm's Law encouraged scholars to look for similar regularities in other correspondences between various Indo-European languages. As a result of this work historical linguists were able to tackle another task with much greater confidence and vastly improved results, namely the comparative reconstruction of the Proto-Indo-European parent language.

The language thus reconstructed had a very rich system of CONSONANTS, which by the end of the nineteenth century was classified as follows.

	Labial	Dental	Palatal	Velar	Labiovelar
voiceless	*p*	*t*	*$\acute{k}$*	*k*	*k^w*
voiceless aspirated	*ph*	*th*	*$\acute{k}h$*	*kh*	*k^wh*
voiced	*b*	*d*	*$\acute{g}$*	*g*	*g^w*
voiced aspirated	*bh*	*dh*	*$\acute{g}h$*	*gh*	*g^wh*
fricative/sibilant		*s*			
nasals	*m*	*n*			
liquids		*r, l*			

In addition, there were the SEMIVOWELS *y* and *w*.

The VOWEL system, however, is less "exotic". With the exception of ə, all vowels come in long and short varieties:

$$
\begin{array}{ccc}
i & & u \\
e & ə & o \\
& a &
\end{array}
$$

In addition to the vowels, Proto-Indo-European had a set of SYLLABIC nasals and liquids (also called SYLLABIC RESONANTS or SONORANTS), variants of consonantal (nonsyllabic) nasals and liquids which, like the vowels, were the center or syllabic peak of their respective syllables. These are commonly written as follows:

$$
\begin{array}{cc}
\d{m} & \d{n} \\
& \d{r}, \d{l}
\end{array}
$$

The relationship between syllabic and nonsyllabic sonorants (such as $\d{m}$: *m*) closely mirrors the relationship between syllabic *i* and *u* and their nonsyllabic semivowel counterparts *y* and *w*, respectively. For instance, the Sanskrit root *k$\d{r}$-* 'do, make' appears with syllabic sonorant before a consonant (as in *k$\d{r}$-ta-* 'done'), but with nonsyllabic sonorant before a vowel (as in *kr-āna-* 'doing'), just as *prati-*' in return, re-' appears with syllabic *i* before a consonant (*prati-vadati* 'replies'), but with nonsyllabic *y* before a vowel (*praty-avadat* 'replied').

Proto-Indo-European was reconstructed with a fairly rich system of noun and verb inflection. In the nouns, eight cases were distinguished with the following major functions. Examples are given from Sanskrit. (Adjectives and pronouns had essentially the same inflectional system.)

Nominative: Subject case (*dēvas* 'God')
Accusative: Direct object case (*dēvam*)
Instrumental: 'With' or 'by' case, i.e., accompaniment, instrument,
               agent of passive (*dēvēna*)
Dative: Indirect object, beneficiary of an action (*dēvāya*)
Ablative: 'From' case, i.e., source (*dēvāt*)
Genitive: 'Of' case: possession, modification of other nouns
               (*dēvasya*)
Locative: Location in place and time (*deve*)
Vocative: Address case, used to address or call persons (*dēva*)

In addition to case, nouns were inflected for number, distinguishing not only singular and plural, but also a "dual" (for pairs of persons or things, such as *dēvau* 'two Gods'). Nouns also distinguished three "genders": masculine, feminine, and neuter. As in modern German and French, and unlike modern English, there was no straightforward relationship between sex and grammatical gender. True, most nouns for males and females were masculine and feminine respectively, but some exceptions are found. Many nouns for inanimate things could be masculine, feminine, or neuter. While some of these peculiarities of Indo-European noun gender have been explained, many other aspects still remain uncertain or controversial.

Verbs were inflected for person ("first", "second", and "third") and number ("singular", "dual", and "plural"). Verb inflection further distinguished between different "tenses", "moods", and "voices". In the "tense" system, we can distinguish between a present and three formations that tend to have past tense value, the "imperfect", the "aorist", and the "perfect". Corresponding to our future, Proto-Indo-European used the present tense, modal formations such as the subjunctive, or formations indicating a desire to do something. The following mood distinctions were postulated for Proto-Indo-European languages: "indicative" (unmarked), "imperative" (for commands), "optative" ('should, could, might do something'), and "subjunctive" ('shall, can be expected to do something'). In voice, there was a distinction between active and "medio-passive", the latter expressing a range of functions, including "reflexive" ('hurt oneself') and passive ('is hurt').

3. The Indo-European languages

The focus of Jones's famous statement were the three classical languages – Greek, Latin, and Sanskrit. This should not come as a surprise. As we have seen earlier, the rediscovery of Greek in western Europe had led to the inclusion of Greek, beside Latin, as a language to be studied by anyone aspiring to an education. And Jones, a judge in the British administrative system of the East India Company, certainly was an educated man. He added Sanskrit to the other two classical languages in the course of his duties as judge in India. What made him and other Britishers do so was a set of fortuitous events and decisions quite unconnected with language or linguistics.

In the eighteenth century, Britain began to establish its Indian colonial empire by setting up the East India Company for trading purposes in the area around today's Calcutta. From the start, the British took political control of the territory that they dominated by adopting the administrative system of the Mughal empire, which once had held sway over most of India but was now in decline. The Mughals were Muslims, and like all traditional Islamic rulers believed that Islamic law applied only to Muslims, and that non-Muslims had to be governed by their own laws. In India, where most non-Muslims are Hindus, this meant that legal disputes between Hindus had to be settled by their own law. And Hindu law was handed down in Sanskrit. Fortunately for comparative linguistics, when the British took over the Mughal administrative system, they also took over the pattern of separate codes of justice – Islamic law for Muslims, and Hindu, i.e. Sanskrit, law for Hindus. But wanting to be able to administer these laws effectively, they felt it necessary to acquire first-hand knowledge of the languages in which the laws were handed down – Arabic for Muslim law, Sanskrit for Hindu law. In addition, Jones and his fellow administrators had to learn Persian as well, since this was the administrative language of the Mughals.

It is to Jones's great credit that he was not satisfied with learning Sanskrit and Persian merely for administrative reasons, but that he drew on his classical education, compared the structures of the three classical languages that he had mastered (Greek, Latin, and Sanskrit), and came to the conclusion that their similarities point to descent from a common ancestor. More than that, he suggested that even some modern languages might have to be added to this family: Persian, Celtic, and "Gothick" – a term by which he probably meant Germanic, the family that includes English, German, as well as Gothic.

Since then, comparative linguists have established beyond any doubt that Persian, Celtic, and Germanic are in fact relatives of Greek, Latin, and Sanskrit, as are many other languages, some of which were discovered or deciphered much later. The remainder of this section provides a brief outline of the major languages that have been shown to belong to the Indo-European language family, of their history, and – where appropriate – of the manner in which they were discovered.

The map below gives an approximate indication of the geographic location of Indo-European languages at an early period (ca. 1000 B.C.). The map is only approximate and does not account for prehistoric or historic migrations. Thus, the British Isles are shown as Celtic territory, since Celtic is the Indo-European language for which we have the earliest attestations there. The later arrival of the Germanic Anglo-Saxons is not accounted for. Similarly, Indo-Aryan is placed into the northwest portion of South Asia. Its later expansion to the east and south is ignored.

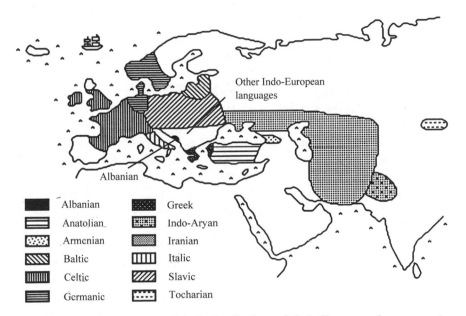

Map 1. Approximate geographical distribution of Indo-European languages (ca. 1000 B.C.)

3.1. Celtic

At an early period, the westernmost group of the Indo-European languages consisted of the CELTIC (or Keltic) languages. While today confined to the western periphery of Europe and the British isles, the Celts once ranged over a vast territory: The names Bohemia and Bavaria, Belgrade, Louvain, and London are all Celtic in origin. In late prehistoric times, Bohemia and all of Southern Germany were Celtic. From this home base, Celtic peoples expanded westward into Gaul (today's France) and Belgium where they had long been settled when Caesar conducted his famous campaign to conquer Gaul. Celts likewise had settled in northern Spain and the British Isles. In all of this vast territory, the Celts appear to have been the vanguard, as it were, of Indo-European westward expansion. But the movement of the Celts was not limited to the west. In the fourth century B.C., Celts crossed the Alps, settled in northern Italy, laid siege to Rome, and exacted tribute from the city of Rome. A century later, they invaded the Balkan peninsula, thrust into Greece, and threatened the sanctuary of the famous oracle at Delphi. Some Celts even settled in Anatolia, where they were known as Galatians, the people addressed in one of Paul's epistles in the New Testament.

By the time of late antiquity, however, the power of the Celts had greatly diminished, partly perhaps because they had overextended themselves, but no doubt also because in much of western Europe they became integrated into the Roman empire and adopted Roman customs and Latin speech. Only a small number of Celtic inscriptions, either in the Roman or the Greek alphabet, are found on the continent, in Gaul and neighboring parts of Spain. These date from about the third century B.C. to the third century A.D.

The richest attestations come from the British Isles: Old Irish in Ireland and spreading into Scotland (from ca. 400 A.D.), Welsh in Wales (ca. 8th c. A.D.), and Cornish (now extinct) in Cornwall (9th c. A.D.). Breton (9th c. A.D.), now spoken in Britanny, on the western coast of France, originally was an insular Celtic dialect as well, whose speakers fled the British Isles to escape the onslaught of the Anglo-Saxons. Old Irish is the ancestor both of modern Irish and Scots Gaelic.

The earliest Old Irish texts consist of short inscriptions on memorial stones, giving the genitive form of the name of the person in whose memory the stone was erected. They tell us a fair amount about early Irish names and the phonetics of Old Irish, and more than we need to know about the case endings of the genitive. Beyond that they are interesting mainly for the special, and quite unusual, script in which they were written, the so-called Ogham characters. Later Insular Celtic texts (including those of Breton) are all in Roman script. The modern Irish script of Ireland is a regional, "Insular" modification of the Roman script which was used also for medieval English. (On the Ogham and Insular scripts, see Chapter 3, § 2.6.)

Although Cornish, as noted, is now extinct, there have been recent attempts to revive it. Modern Irish, Scots Gaelic, Welsh, and Breton have been able to maintain their spoken tradition, but centuries of discrimination in favor of the official or unofficial state language (English or French) have led to a great reduction in the number of speakers. To varying degrees, these languages are all now considered to be endangered.

There is some uncertainty whether Pictish, originally spoken in the area of today's Scotland and replaced early on by Gaelic, is part of the Celtic languages, part of the larger Indo-European language family, or even Indo-European at all. Basque, in the northwest of the Iberian peninsula and the southwest of present-day France, certainly is not an Indo-European language, a living – and tenacious – testimony to the fact that Europe had been settled by human beings long before the arrival of Indo-European speakers.

3.2. Italic (Latin)

To the south and east of the original position of the Celts is the group of ITALIC languages. The most richly attested of these is Latin, whose earliest attestations, brief inscriptions, begin about the sixth century B.C. (Literary texts start to appear in the third century B.C.) Originally the speech of a small area around Rome, Latin became the dominant language of western Europe, first through conquest and domination of the rest of Italy, followed by the far-flung military conquests of the Roman empire, and eventually the spiritual conquest by Roman Christianity of Europe from the Baltic to the Mediterranean, and from Poland and Hungary to Ireland and Iceland. The Roman empire's policy of encouraging conquered peoples to acquire Roman citizenship by adopting Roman customs, including the Latin language, led to the adoption of Latin as the language first of Italy, and then of most of the rest of Southern Europe, as well as parts of the Balkans.

The spoken Latin that spread in this way, slightly different from the written Latin of Caesar and Cicero, became the source of the modern Romance languages, including Portuguese, Spanish, Catalan, French, Italian, Romantsch (the fourth official language of Switzerland, beside Italian, French, and German), as well as Romanian. Romanian originally was connected with the rest of the Romance languages through Dalmatian, spoken in present-day Croatia and Bosnia-Hercegovina; but the language eventually was replaced by varieties of Slavic, as well as by Italian. The last speaker of the language is reported to have been killed in 1898, in a mine explosion.

Three of the Romance languages spread beyond their original territories and became world languages as a result of the "age of discovery" and the subsequent period of western imperialism. Spanish and Portuguese have large numbers of native speakers, especially in Latin America. French has become the official state language of a number of former colonies, particularly in

Africa; it also is one of Canada's two official languages and the dominant language in the province of Quebec.

Although the Romance languages clearly developed out of spoken Latin by undergoing divergent linguistic changes, we cannot trace these developments directly. Latin remained the written medium for many centuries after the Romance languages began to develop. The earliest texts clearly written in Romance come from the ninth century A.D. and are limited to the French area.

Latin, in fact, for a long time was the dominant written language throughout western Europe, not just in Romance territory. More than that, it also was the dominant SPOKEN language of the educated. As a consequence, a scholar, say, from Finland, could attend a university in France and communicate with other scholars entirely in Latin, without having to learn the local language. Especially in the Romance area, the coexistence of spoken Latin with the emerging Romance vernaculars had profound effects on the vernaculars, especially in their vocabulary, where forms inherited from Latin, such as Spanish *dueño* 'lord' (< Latin *dominus*) coexist with borrowings from Latin, such as *dominar* 'to dominate'.

Before Latin spread throughout Italy, it coexisted with several other "Italic" languages. The two best-known among these are Oscan (from about the fourth century B.C.) and Umbrian (3rd c. B.C.). Both of these, attested in relatively short inscriptions, were replaced by Latin in about the first century B.C.

Ancient Italy was home to a number of other languages. Some of these are Indo-European, but not part of Italic, others are of controversial origin. None of these is attested sufficiently well to be of great help for comparative or historical linguistics. Perhaps the most fascinating of these languages is Etruscan. At an early period, the Etruscans held much vaster territory and had a much higher degree of civilization than the Romans. In fact, they are commonly believed to have been the major source for the early transmission of ancient Greek culture – including the art of writing – to the Roman world. They have left behind more than nine thousand inscriptions, in a script which can be perfectly read, in the sense that we understand the phonetic values of its letters. But like the Old Irish Ogham inscriptions, most of the texts are short and simply contain names which do not tell us very much about the structure and vocabulary of the language. The few texts that might be more informative have so far resisted successful interpretation. And no outside relatives or later descendants of Etruscan are known. In short, except for the structure of names (and of a few pronouns), we do not really understand the language of the Etruscans; and its relationship to other languages remains a mystery. (If the

Greek historian Herodotus is to be trusted, the Etruscans hailed from Lydia in Asia Minor – an intriguing suggestion, especially because the genitive singular ending *-l* of Etruscan is similar to a genitival suffix *-l* attested in Hittite and other early Indo-European languages of Anatolia. But similarity in a single ending could well be due to chance.)

3.3. Germanic

As the Celts moved westward, they were closely followed by the GERMANIC peoples, who settled Southern Germany and Austria. At the dawn of history Germanic peoples are found throughout most of present-day Germany and Austria, present-day Belgium and the Netherlands, as well as Scandinavia. But in Scandinavia they remained confined to the more southern and western areas.

During the early historic period, the Germanic peoples rival – perhaps even surpass – the Celts in mobility and in the vast area over which they range. The Goths, the Burgundians, and the Vandals, originating in the Scandinavian area, migrate as far east as the Caspian Sea, temporarily make common cause with the Iranian tribe of the Alans and with the dreaded Huns, then turn west again, to besiege and – temporarily – conquer parts of the Roman Empire. Ostro-Goths ('East Goths') establish a short-lived empire in Italy; Visi-Goths ('West Goths') rule over parts of Spain; the Burgundians eventually settle in a part of France which even today bears their name: Burgundy; and the notorious Vandals, after sacking Rome and wreaking havoc all over the empire, establish a kingdom in North Africa. In the meantime, a southern expansion brings the Alemannic tribes into Switzerland, and the Frankish tribes into present-day France, whose name is derived from that of the Franks. Although they had help from such non-Germanic peoples as the Alans and Huns, the migrating Germanic tribes bear much of the responsibility for the collapse of the Western Roman Empire. Ironically, it was a Germanic ruler over the French – Charlemagne – who, having been crowned emperor by the Pope of Rome, reestablished the Western Roman Empire. And as ruler over much of Germany, he incorporated that country into the empire – something which none of the emperors of the original Roman Empire had been able to accomplish.

The extended invasions of the Germanic peoples left a rich legacy of borrowings in the Romance languages. Not surprisingly, these borrowings include martial terms such as Span. *guerra*, Fr. *guerre* 'war' from **werra-* (compare Engl. *war*) or Fr. *gonfalon* 'battle flag' from **gund-fano*. Many personal names were borrowed, too, presumably because of the prestige or power of Germanic rulers. Examples are Fr. *Henri, Charles*, Span. *Enrique*,

Carlos which correspond to the native Germanic names reflected in Germ. *Heinrich, Karl.* (The English versions of the names, *Henry* and *Charles*, do not continue the original Germanic forms of the names; they are borrowings from French that came to England in 1066 and reflect the power and prestige of the Norman invaders. History, in a way, repeated itself; and the names were "recycled" to a Germanic language.) Curiously, the borrowings from Germanic also included the word for 'soap': Fr. *savon*, Old Span. *xabon*, Mod. Span. *jabón*.

These great migrations – or barbarian invasions, depending on one's perspective – generally did not lead to a geographic expansion of Germanic languages; but many other, slightly later migrations did. One of these was the migration of the Angles, Saxons, and Jutes into England under the leadership of two chieftains whose names have come to us as *Hengest* and *Horsa*. (The names of these two gentlemen can be roughly translated as *Stallion* and *Stud*.) Pushing back the indigenous Celtic population into the marginal areas of Wales and Cornwall, they settled in the southern part of the island up to Northumberland.

In the meantime, the Scandinavians, too, began to migrate. They settled Iceland and, as Vikings and Varangians, roamed far and wide. They probably sailed to the North American continent. They certainly laid siege to and plundered many a Mediterranean harbor and kingdom, including Sicily. They invaded and settled a part of France which came to be named Normandy in their honor, soon adopting a regional variant of French as their language. Pursuing an eastern route, the Swedish Varangians took up trade with the Iranians in Southern Russia and established the first royal dynasty of Russia, the house of Rus. The quintessentially "Russian" names *Oleg* and *Olga* in reality reflect Varangian domination; they are derived from earlier forms of the modern Scandinavian names *Helge* and *Helga*. Finally, known as "Danes", Scandinavians from Denmark, Norway, and Iceland engaged in extended warfare with the Anglo-Saxons, furnished some of the Anglo-Saxons' rulers (e.g. Canute), and settled down in the so-called Danelaw, an extensive strip on the east coast of England, stretching from Yorkshire down to the vicinity of London. After settling and intermarrying with the Anglo-Saxons, the Danes exerted considerable influence on the development of the English language, especially in terms of extensive contributions to the vocabulary, including such words as *give, get, take; skin, skirt, sky, egg;* and even the pronoun forms *they, their, them.*

Soon after the Danish threat had abated, the Vikings that had settled in Normandy and had, as we have seen, become Francophone, conquered England in 1066 and left a lasting mark on the English language. Words such as *beef, pork, mutton; court, royal, justice;* and even the second part of the function word *because* owe their origin to French influence. The immense French influence on English vocabulary may also have set the precedent for a tradition which treasures a huge vocabulary and, consequently, encourages continued borrowing. Compared to most other languages, English seems to be almost voracious in adopting words from all the languages of the world.

Like French, Spanish, and Portuguese, English became an international language as the result of colonialism and imperialism. The 314 million (+) native speakers in North America and the Caribbean, Australia, New Zealand, and South Africa vastly outnumber the 56.5 million speakers in the United Kingdom plus 3.5 million in the Republic of Ireland. But in addition, English is used as a fluent means of communication by about another 300 million speakers in former British and American colonies around the world, including India, Singapore, the Philippines, Kenya, and Nigeria. The impact of this immense spread of English on the languages of the world – as well as on English – is only beginning to be researched and understood. New standard varieties of English are emerging, such as South Asian English which is used by millions of South Asians to communicate with each other – not just with native speakers of English. In the process, English is being indigenized, in vocabulary, structure, and pronunciation. We will take a closer look at some of these developments in Chapter 12.

Developments like these could hardly have been foreseen when the Germanic languages first appeared on the historical scene. The earliest attestations of Germanic come in brief inscriptions beginning about the first century A.D. The inscriptions are written in a special offshoot of the alphabets used in Greece and Rome, the runes. (For the script, see Chapter 3, § 2.6.) The language of these texts is virtually identical to the reconstructed Proto-Germanic ancestor.

The oldest extensive text is a Gothic Bible translation produced by the Gothic bishop Wulfilas ('Little Wolf') in the fourth century, which has come down to us in fragmentary form. Manuscripts have been found in Germany, Italy, and even Egypt; and new finds are still being made. The earliest discovery, made in the Ruhr area of Germany, attracted the attention of sixteenth-century German and Dutch scholars who, in the spirit of the Renaissance, studied the manuscript in their endeavor to unravel the history of their language. Because of its early attestation and the relative richness of the text, the Gothic Bible translation has ever since been a valuable source of information on early Germanic sound and word structure. But because it followed the word order of the Greek original quite slavishly, it is less useful in the area of syntax. Most varieties of Gothic seem to have died out quite early; but in the sixteenth century, the Dutch traveler van Busbecq brought back a few vocabulary specimens of a remnant of Gothic from the Crimea, in southern Ukraine. We do not know if this last remnant of the language survived much longer. No modern descendants of Gothic are known.

The earliest documents of the other Germanic languages appear still later than the older runic inscriptions and Gothic: seventh century A.D. for Old English, thirteenth century for Old Frisian (spoken in the coastal areas of present-day Holland and Germany), tenth century for Old Low Frankish (the ancestor of modern Dutch and Flemish), ninth century for Old Saxon (the ancestor of "Low" German in northern Germany), eighth century for Old High German (in the southern, mountainous area of Germany, hence the term "High" German), twelfth century for Old Norse (mainly Old Icelandic, with embedded verse passages that go back to about the ninth century A.D.).

The major modern Germanic languages are English (see above); German (the official language of Germany, Austria, Liechtenstein, and parts of Switzerland and Belgium); Dutch (in the Netherlands) and the closely related Flemish (in Belgium), as well as a colonial offshoot, Afrikaans, spoken in South Africa; the Scandinavian languages Danish, Norwegian, and Swedish; and Icelandic and Faroese.

3.4. Slavic

The SLAVIC languages, to the east of Germanic, now cover a vast territory, especially if we include Russian, the lingua franca of the former Soviet Union and the major language of the Russian Republic. Prehistorically, the languages occupied a smaller region. Recall that Bohemia originally was Celtic territory. The place names of much of the Russian core area, from St. Petersburg to Moscow, have been claimed to be Baltic in origin. Most of present-day Russia is colonial territory, with a large variety of non-Indo-European indigenous languages, many of which belong to the Uralic and Altaic language families.

From around the fifth century A.D., Slavic speakers begin to push into the Balkan peninsula, engaging in protracted warfare with the Eastern Roman Empire (whose capital was Constantinople). The word *slave*, a phonetic variant of *Slav*, bears testimony to the warfare: In ancient times, prisoners of war, if permitted to live, became slaves. The fact that for a long period in the history of the East Roman Empire, most prisoners of war were Slavs made it possible to reinterpret the word Slav as meaning 'slave' and to use it in this new meaning even when referring to prisoners from other ethnic groups.

The situation in the northwestern Slavic area is especially complicated. Over the centuries, large portions of Poland and eastern Germany alternated in seesaw fashion between Slavic and German. Even today, two Slavic speech islands, Upper and Lower Sorbian, are located in eastern Germany. Many places in Germany (almost as far west as Kiel and Hamburg) bear names that are of Slavic origin, including the cities of *Berlin, Leipzig*, and *Dresden*. On the other hand, the city of *Gdańsk* in present-day Poland was for many centuries, up to 1945, essentially a German city, *Danzig*. The name *Danzig*, in turn, is a Germanization of the Polish name of the city, *Gdańsk*, which clearly is older, suggesting that the city originally was Polish. But the story doesn't end there. A yet earlier form of the name, *Gŭdansk-*, contains *Guda-*, which has been plausibly connected with *Guta-*, the name the Goths used for themselves. We can therefore conclude that this was once Gothic, i.e. Germanic, territory. But, again, this does not preclude the possibility that at an even earlier time, the area had been Slavic or even Baltic.

Some evidence suggests that Slavic had strong prehistoric contacts with Iranian in present-day southern Russia. Note for instance the shared word for 'God': Old Persian *baga* : Old Church Slavic *bogŭ*. It is possible, therefore, that the original homeland of the Slavs was close to southern Russia. But given the mobility of the Slavs in historical and even prehistoric times, we cannot be certain.

The literary attestation of Slavic begins in the ninth century A.D. with a Bible translation commissioned by the ruler of Moravia in what is the present-day Czech Republic and produced by two brothers, Cyril and Methodius, who hailed from Thessalonica, a city in what is now northern Greece. Although the local Slavic then spoken in Thessalonica must already have differed from the Slavic of Moravia, it was apparently close enough for the two brothers to use their own variety of the language. But while in this respect they can be said to have compromised, they did not compromise on another issue: Faced with considerable linguistic differences between Slavic and the original Greek text, they devised a new writing system, based on the Greek alphabet, but with letters added to accurately transcribe the sounds of their native language. (See Chapter 3, § 2.6.)

Ironically, Moravia, for which the Bible translation had been produced, became part of Western Roman Christianity and consequently accepted the Latin Bible translation, as well as the Latin (or Roman) alphabet. Cyril and Methodius's translation and the script they had devised came to be adopted by Eastern Orthodox Slavic Christianity, and the "Old Church Slavic" of their translation became a language of liturgy and learning comparable to Latin in western Christianity. And like Latin in the Romance area, Old Church Slavic was used as the major written language in much of South and East Slavic, masking the developments taking place in the regional forms of Slavic.

Although exhibiting dialectal features belonging to southern Slavic, the Old Church Slavic texts come fairly close to the ancestral, Proto-Slavic language. Like Gothic, they are therefore extremely useful for comparative linguistic research. But, again like Gothic, they closely follow the word order of the Greek original and therefore are not as helpful as far as syntax is concerned.

The Slavic languages are usually divided into three groups: West Slavic (Czech, Slovak, Polish, Sorbian), South Slavic (Slovenian, Serbo-Croatian, Macedonian, Bulgarian), and East Slavic (Russian, Byelo-Russian, Ukrainian). Serbo-Croatian is one of several languages which are "divided against themselves" because of religious and ethnic differences between their speakers. Although the two speech varieties have virtually identical grammars, they are traditionally used by different communities: Serbian by Eastern Orthodox Christians, Croatian by Roman Catholics. The difference in religion is mirrored by a difference in script: Serbians use Cyrillic, Croats the Roman alphabet. Where Serbians tend to be fairly open to borrowings from other languages, Croats prefer to create new words from their own native resources. (On this issue see Chapter 8, § 5.2.) While the government of the former Yugoslavia emphasized the essential unity of Serbo-Croatian and linguists who are not emotionally involved would agree, nationalists on both sides dwell on the differences of Serbian and Croatian and consider the two varieties fundamentally different languages. At present, the nationalists clearly have the upper hand, demonstrating the importance of speakers' attitudes which we talked about in Chapter 1.

3.5. Baltic

The BALTIC languages include Lithuanian (from 16th c. A.D.), Latvian (16th c.), and the now extinct Old Prussian (ca. 14th c.). They were originally spoken over a much larger territory than today. During the historical period, much of Baltic gave way to Slavic, and a relentless campaign of forced Germanization led to the demise of Old Prussian in the seventeenth century. Ironically, the names Prussia and Prussian were taken over by the Germans and through a series of events came to be associated with an important regional and dynastic element in German politics. (Such secondary associations of traditional names are not unusual. Compare for instance the case of Frankish : French and Burgundian : Burgundy. Similarly, Modern Greeks use the term *Roméikos*, literally 'Roman', to refer to themselves, in reminiscence of the fact that Greece once was the center of the Eastern Roman Empire. See also Chapter 9, § 3.1.)

Though attested relatively late, Baltic has been rather conservative in certain aspects of its linguistic structure, especially in the area of noun inflection. Thus, of the original eight cases reconstructed for Proto-Indo-European (see § 2 above), the early classical languages Sanskrit, Latin, and Greek preserved eight, six, and five, respectively. And as we have seen earlier, modern languages like French and English have reduced the number of cases even more. Modern Lithuanian and Latvian preserve seven of the original eight cases. Similarly, among the classical languages, the Proto-Indo-European distinction singular : dual : plural was fully preserved only in Sanskrit; Greek showed the dual only in moribund form; and Latin had lost it as a grammatical category. Modern European languages such as English, German, and French likewise have no trace of the dual. But again, Lithuanian preserves the dual number. In spite of their relatively late attestations, the Baltic languages thus provide valuable information for comparative Indo-European linguistics.

This does not mean that Baltic is archaic in every respect. For instance, the Indo-European triple gender distinction masculine : feminine : neuter has in Lithuanian and Latvian been reduced to one between masculine and feminine; only Old Prussian preserved the neuter gender. Even the case system is not entirely archaic, for Lithuanian and Latvian actually have ADDED three cases to the inherited system. The development of these cases, an "illative" (specifying the direction into something), an "allative" (the direction toward something), and an "adessive" (the location near something) represents a structural convergence with the neighboring Uralic languages (such as Estonian) which have an abundance of such locational and directional cases. Structural convergence of this sort is not unusual under conditions of extensive bilingualism (see Chapter 13). One suspects, therefore, that the Baltic Indo-European and Uralic languages have been in prolonged bilingual contact.

There has been a continuing controversy as to whether Baltic and Slavic form a special, "Balto-Slavic" subgroup of Indo-European which underwent enough common developments in their prehistory to set them off from the rest of the Indo-European languages. To some extent the debate has been fueled by nationalism: Slavic scholars and their sympathizers tend to argue for "Balto-Slavic", with the implicit assumption, perhaps, that Slavic was the senior partner in this relationship. Baltic scholars and their sympathizers, who are fearful of Slavic attempts at domination, tend to emphatically reject the relationship. Such intrusion of personal prejudice into linguistics unfortunately is not as rare as it should be. But if backed up by evidence, prejudice does not necessarily invalidate the force of an argument.

In the case of Baltic and Slavic, strong arguments have been mustered by both sides. It may well be that many of the similarities shared by Baltic and Slavic reflect not just a period of common prehistory, but the fact that they were neighbors from Proto-Indo-European times to the present and thus kept influencing each other for millennia, both in structure and in vocabulary.

3.6. Albanian

To the south of Baltic and Slavic, on the west coast of the Balkan peninsula in present-day Albania and neighboring areas of Serbia and Greece, we find ALBANIAN, attested very late (from the 15th c. A.D.); it had been subject for many centuries to the influences of neighboring languages, including Greek, Latin and its descendants, Gothic, and South Slavic. Some ninety percent of its vocabulary is of foreign origin. Nevertheless, a sufficient core of indigenous vocabulary remains for comparative linguistic work.

Not much is known about the historical antecedents of Albanian or whether it has any close relatives within the Indo-European language family. According to a traditional view, modern Albanian is descended from Illyrian, a language spoken in ancient times in the north of modern Albania. But what little is known about Illyrian argues against close affiliation with Albanian, because it belongs to a very different group of Indo-European languages and therefore cannot be the ancestor of modern Albanian. The basis for this argument lies in the exciting discovery by nineteenth-century Indo-Europeanists that there was a regional distinction in early Indo-European: At a very early time, a central group of Indo-European languages changed the Proto-Indo-European (PIE) palatal stops (for which see § 2 above) into sibilants; compare PIE *$\acute{k}m̥tom$ '100' > Avestan *satəm*. Other languages preserved the stop articulation, as in the Latin outcome *centum* [k-] '100'. (See also Chapter 11, § 3.) Using the Avestan and Latin outcomes of the word for '100', the two groups of languages were then distinguished as "satem" vs. "centum" languages. What is significant for the debate over the affiliation of Albanian is the fact that Albanian is a satem language; Illyrian, on the other hand, is a centum language.

Another language mentioned as a possible ancestor of Albanian is Thracian, the language of ancient Thrace in the southeastern part of the Balkan peninsula. Although linguistic evidence makes this affiliation more likely (Thracian is a satem language), the geographic separation between Thrace and Albania causes difficulties. Most important, however, like many other early Indo-European languages of the Balkans, including Illyrian, Thracian is attested much too sparsely to permit successful comparative linguistic work.

3.7. Greek

The GREEK language, in the extreme south of the Balkan peninsula, was until recently believed to have been first recorded about 800 B.C. Some time prior to that date, alphabetic writing had been developed from Semitic sources in Asia Minor (see Chapter 3, § 2.5). The introduction of the alphabet was a technological innovation which some scholars believe made it possible for the Homeric epics, the *Iliad* and the *Odyssey*, to be given a more permanent written codification, even though they had been successfully handed down for centuries in an oral tradition (see Chapter 3, §2.1 on the oral transmission of texts), and the earliest manuscripts of the epics date from much later times. Still, the introduction of the alphabet was a well-documented historical event, so it was generally believed that no Greek texts older than the ninth century B.C. would ever be found.

All of this changed dramatically in 1952, when it was discovered that the non-alphabetic "Linear B" script of Minoan times was used to write an early form of Greek (see Chapter 3, § 3.3). This discovery pushes back our knowledge of Greek to a time between about 1400 and the twelfth century B.C., a period when some of the linguistic changes that differentiate Greek from the rest of the Indo-European languages had not yet taken place. The decipherment of Linear B has made it possible to confirm certain hypotheses about these changes and to disconfirm others, in addition to raising new issues which still await full resolution.

The exact reasons for the end of Minoan literacy, which necessitated a "reinvention" of literacy in the ninth century, are still under dispute. A fair amount of evidence suggests that Minoan society collapsed under the on-slaught of the so-called Sea People, who also wreaked havoc on Egypt and other areas of the mainland. But the identity of the Sea People is uncer-tain. Another possibility is that the invaders were the Doric or "West Greek" tribes: Both Greek tradition and the geographic distribution of these tribes (see Chapter 11, § 5) suggest that they were late intruders. But instead of destroying the Minoan civilization, they may have simply filled the void left behind by the Sea People. In short, we really do not know what caused the downfall of Minoan civilization.

In historical times, Greek is characterized by a strong differentiation of dialects, each associated with one of the many city states of ancient Greece and jealously guarding its identity. The major early Greek dialects are: At-tic and Ionic (closely related), Arcadian and Cypriot (also closely related), Aeolic (with several subdialects), and the Doric or "West Greek" dialects. Attic (the speech of Athens) and Ionic were the major literary languages of classical Greek society. Doric, with many regional dialects, covered a large area of Greece. Of the many dialects of Doric, those of Corinth and Sparta were politically quite important. Arcadian, Cypriot, and the Aeolic dialects were politically and, to a large degree, geographically more marginal.

From the time of the Persian wars, a variant form of Attic, with some influence from Ionic and other dialects, began to emerge. As the "Koiné" (from Gk. *koinè glôssa* 'the common language') it became the common language of the Greek empire established by Alexander the Great and eventually replaced virtually all the ancient dialects. (See Chapter 12, § 5.) As a consequence, nearly all the modern Greek dialects are descended from the Koiné, though one dialect, Tsakonian, spoken in the interior of the Peloponnesus, preserves some features of Laconian (an ancient Doric dialect).

3.8. Anatolian

Anatolia, to the east of Greece, is the home of a large number of ancient languages, many of which were written in the cuneiform ("wedge-shaped") script of ancient Mesopotamia. In the early part of this century it was shown that one of these languages, Hittite, is Indo-European, even though in its structure and vocabulary it differs considerably from the other early attested Indo-European languages. (See Chapter 3, § 3.1.) Its oldest texts come from the seventeenth century B.C. and are among the earliest texts in any Indo-European language; the latest texts date from about 1200 B.C.

Beside Hittite, several other, fairly closely related languages have been found in Anatolia, including Palaic and Luwian (roughly contemporary with Hittite), Lydian (6th–4th c. B.C.), and Lycian (5th–4th c. B.C.). Because of their geographical location, Hittite and its relatives are referred to as ANA-TOLIAN.

Because they are attested so early, Hittite and the other early Anatolian languages could be expected to yield important information for comparative Indo-European linguistics. To some extent, this expectation has not gone unfulfilled, especially for certain issues in sound and word structure. But many other aspects of Anatolian linguistic structure have created more problems than they have solved. For instance, Hittite has a verb 'to have', as in 'I have no money', whereas the comparative evidence of the other Indo-European languages shows that Proto-Indo-European expressed the notion 'I have no money' by something like 'Of me (there) is no money' or 'For me (there) is no money'. Although in the case of 'have', Anatolian most certainly innovated, in other areas the rest of Indo-European may have been more innovative. The problem is that Indo-Europeanists do not yet agree on the interpretation of many of the differences between Anatolian and the rest of Indo-European.

3.9. Armenian

Yet farther to the east, in the Caucasus region, we find ARMENIAN. Though attested from a rather early period (5th c. A.D.), it is much less archaic in vocabulary and structure than Baltic and Slavic. Partly this is due to strong prehistoric influence from Iranian. In fact, the large amount of Iranian words taken into Armenian, such as *hazar* '1000' : Old Iranian **hazahra*, Mod. Pers. *hazār*, led early researchers to consider Armenian an Iranian dialect. We now know that Armenian is historically quite distinct from Iranian, or any other attested Indo-European language group, for that matter. Another important source for the "changed" character of Armenian may be convergence with non-Indo-European, Caucasic languages, such as Georgian.

Recent hypotheses about the nature of Proto-Indo-European dispute the traditional view that the structure of Armenian underwent profound changes that differentiated it from the rest of the Indo-European languages. Instead, some of the special characteristics of Armenian, such as the existence of a series of "glottalized" consonants (with glottal-stop coarticulation), are considered highly archaic, direct inheritances from Proto-Indo-European. This new, "glottalic" view of Indo-European is still a matter of great controversy (see Chapter 16, § 7). One of the difficulties with the assumption that the glottalized consonants of Armenian are an archaism is that these consonants can also be explained as a regional innovation, a convergence of Armenian with the neighboring non-Indo-European languages. In this regard, note that an Iranian language, Ossetic, displays the same "glottalic" sound system as Armenian and most of the other languages of the Caucasus; but in the case of Ossetic, glottalized consonants clearly are a late, regional development.

Old Armenian texts begin in the fifth century A.D. and are composed in a literary language that combines elements from a number of different dialects. It was written in a special script said to be devised by the Christian priest Mesrop. Some scholars believe the script was developed out of an earlier northern Iranian script with some influence from the Greek alphabet; others think that it is overwhelmingly of Greek origin. As in the case of Gothic and Old Church Slavic, the earliest text was a Bible translation. Like Old Church Slavic, the language of that translation soon became a literary standard, and this "Classical Armenian" remained in use into the nineteenth century.

During the twelfth century, a Middle Armenian language acquired currency at the court of Cilicia. During this period, a major sound change began to differentiate Western and Eastern Armenian, which has given rise to two modern standard languages, West and East Armenian. East Armenian is the language of the Republic of Armenia, while West Armenian is used by Armenians hailing from Turkey who as the result of persecution are now largely dispersed in countries such as Syria, Lebanon, Egypt, and even the United States. Armenian enclaves are also found in Iran. The division between the East and West Armenian literary languages masks a much more profound diversity of local and regional dialects.

3.10. Indo-Iranian

IRANIAN and INDO-ARYAN, at the southeastern periphery of the attested Indo-European languages, though distinct subgroups, are more closely related to each other than any other subgroups of Indo-European. The INDO-IRANIAN subgroup is therefore the most uncontroversial subdivision of the Indo-European family. The close relationship between Iranian and Indo-Aryan is manifested by a large number of common innovations in phonetic structure, as well as in vocabulary. For instance, the fairly rich vowel system of Proto-Indo-European given in § 2 above has been reduced to an early Indo-Iranian system with just three vowel distinctions: $\breve{\imath} : \breve{a} : \breve{u}$. More than that, Iranians and Indo-Aryans even agreed on the name that they used to refer to themselves – *ārya*. (The name *Iran* originally is the genitive plural of this word, designating the country as the land 'of the Aryans'.) In the nineteenth century the term Aryan was extended to designate all Indo-Europeans, under the false assumption that the Irish word *Eire* is cognate with *ārya*, and ill-founded theories about the racial identity of these Aryans were propounded, which ultimately were used to justify the racist excesses of the Nazis. For these reasons, the term Aryan fell into disfavor for a while, and Indo-Aryan was commonly referred to as Indic (German "indisch"), especially among German scholars. The preference of Indian scholars for the name Indo-Aryan eventually led to the readoption of the term.

3.10.1. Iranian

The two major Old Iranian languages are Avestan and Old Persian. Of these, Avestan is attested in much earlier – and much more archaic – texts, dating back to at least the seventh century B.C. These are the sacred writings of Zoroastrianism, hymns composed by the founder of that religion, Zarathushtra, handed down orally for a long time, and put into written form quite late by persons no longer fully competent in the language. (The oldest extant manuscripts come from about the thirteenth century.) Unlike Old Persian, Avestan seems to have come from a more eastern part of Iranian, close to Indo-Aryan. Both because of its early attestation and, perhaps, because of its greater proximity to Indo-Aryan, Avestan is quite close to the oldest form of Indo-Aryan, Vedic Sanskrit (see below). In fact, the two languages are so similar that it is possible to change an entire Avestan hymn into an acceptable Vedic hymn by merely adjusting the pronunciation.

Some general information about Zoroastrianism was available from Greek sources, which also are responsible for the form of the name, Zoroaster, that came to be known to the West. But the texts of the religion were unknown. It was only in the seventeenth and eighteenth centuries that a few manuscripts came into western hands, unfortunately in a script that nobody could decipher. A young Frenchman, Anquetil du Perron, was deeply impressed by these manuscripts and determined to learn to read them. To do so, he joined the French military and sailed to India in 1754. Taking leave, he set out on his own to Bombay, where he contacted Zoroastrian priests who, like other Zoroastrians or "Parsis", had fled Persia at the time of the Muslim conquest. The priests at first regarded him with great suspicion, but after repeated efforts on his part to learn from them, they eventually opened up, teaching him their rituals, as well as the language and script of their sacred texts. Armed with some manuscripts that they had given him, Anquetil du Perron returned to France in 1761 and busied himself with the study of the texts and their language. In 1771 he finally published a three-volume translation of the Avestan texts. Although many of his readings turned out to be flawed, his work opened the way to an understanding of this important ancient Iranian language. Subsequent research, informed by a fuller understanding of related Iranian languages and of Sanskrit, has greatly improved our understanding of Avestan so that, unlike William Jones, we are now able to include Avestan among the most ancient Indo-European languages.

Unlike Avestan, Old Persian can be dated confidently, being attested in rock inscriptions by the great Persian kings (Darius I, Xerxes I, and Artaxerxes II and III) who lived in the sixth to fourth centuries B.C. The inscriptions had been noticed for a long time by travelers, but the cuneiform script of the inscriptions could not be read until its nineteenth-century decipherment (see Chapter 3, § 3.1). Although not as archaic as Avestan, the language of the inscriptions is sufficiently old to establish beyond any doubt what William Jones had only considered a possibility, namely that Persian is related to Sanskrit, Greek, Latin, and the other Indo-European languages.

At an early period, Iranian dialects were spoken over a vast territory, ranging from Iran to the Hindukush, at some times even into what is now China, and into the steppes of Southern Russia. Iranian tribes in Southern Russia, commonly known as Scythians, are probably responsible for the early Iranian borrowings in Slavic mentioned in § 3.4.

Modern Iranian languages include Modern Persian (or Farsi), Kurdish, Pashto (in Afghanistan), and Ossetic (in the Caucasus Mountains). Like Armenian, Ossetic has a structure that bears great similarities to the structures of the non-Indo-European languages of the Caucasus. In the case of Ossetic, it is quite clear that these similarities result from secondary convergence. (See also § 3.9.)

3.10.2. Indo-Aryan (Sanskrit)

Early Indo-Aryan is represented by Sanskrit, whose earliest texts, the Vedas, go back at least to about 1500 B.C. Like the Avestan texts, the Vedas were transmitted orally; but their oral transmission continued just about to the present day. Thanks to an elaborate "back-up" system (including a highly developed formal grammar), the texts have come down to us with only minor changes.

Classical Sanskrit, attested in texts from about the fifth century B.C. to the present, was mainly a language of the educated. From an early period it coexisted with Prakrit, a later form of Indo-Aryan that was the language of the common people. This coexistence is mirrored in a literary convention of Classical Sanskrit drama, where Sanskrit is reserved for the educated protagonists (mainly male), while Prakrit is used by the uneducated (including most women).

At an early time, Indo-Aryan appears to have been limited to the extreme northwest of South Asia. Settlement of the Ganges valley, especially of the more eastern area of Bengal, is believed to have taken place only slowly, over the course of several centuries. In historical times, we can see an even farther expansion of Sanskrit, both in India (where it becomes the sacred language and, for many centuries, also the literary language even of the Dravidian south) and outside. A major vehicle for the spread of Sanskrit outside India was Mahayana Buddhism which expanded, via Central Asia, as far east as China and Japan. An early form of Prakrit, Pali, experienced a more moderate spread to Sri Lanka and parts of Indo-China as the vehicle of Hinayana Buddhism. Unlike Sanskrit, however, it did not survive on the Indian mainland.

As Sanskrit, and Indo-Aryan in general, spread within South Asia, its speakers came into contact with many speakers of non-Indo-European languages. In India, the two most important groups of such languages are Dravidian and Munda. The Dravidian literary languages, Tamil, Malayalam, Kannada, and Telugu, are all spoken in the south of the subcontinent. But "tribal" Dravidian languages are found as far north as the central mountain range of India and even in present-day Pakistan. The Munda languages are part of an Austro-Asiatic family, which includes members like Mon and Khmer in Indo-China. All Munda speakers belong to "tribal" societies and, like Dravidian – and Indo-Aryan – "tribals", live in relatively inaccessible areas in the central mountains.

There is some controversy over when the Indo-Aryans first came into contact with Dravidian and Munda speakers. Some linguists argue for very early contact between Indo-Aryan and Dravidian, attributing features of Indo-Aryan structure to convergence with Dravidian. Others have proposed that Indo-Aryan speakers first came into contact with Munda speakers. One scholar has postulated an unknown northwestern language which supposedly influenced Indo-Aryan. The available evidence may simply be too limited to decide between these hypotheses. (See also Chapter 13.) There is no doubt, however, that eventually Indo-Aryan, Dravidian, and Munda all came to structurally converge with each other through multilingual contact extending over several millennia.

Like Latin in the western world, Sanskrit functioned as a scholarly lingua franca of India long after the emergence of regional languages that had descended from it. And like Latin, Sanskrit has slowly been losing ground. Unlike Latin, however, Sanskrit has remained in spoken form to the present day. (In fact, after hearing two American colleagues gossip in Sanskrit at a scholarly meeting, the lead author of this book went to do research in India on spoken Sanskrit and learned to speak Sanskrit, too.) During the past two decades, however, the spoken use of Sanskrit has decreased so dramatically that it may become extinct within a generation or two.

The most widely spoken modern Indo-Aryan language is Hindi-Urdu. Like Serbo-Croatian, it is a language that is "divided against itself" because of religious and political differences. Hindi is used by Hindus and other non-Muslims; it is also one of the two official link languages of the Republic of India. Urdu today is primarily the language of Muslims, and the official state language of the Islamic nation of Pakistan. Hindi draws on Sanskrit sources for its religious and cultural terminology, as well as to translate English technical terminology. Urdu uses Persian and Arabic sources for the same purposes.

The two forms of language differ most markedly in their highly literary and intellectual varieties. There is virtually no difference in their everyday forms of use. During the Indian independence struggle, leaders like Gandhi advocated the use of a common, non-sectarian "Hindustani" language, based on these everyday varieties. The subsequent political separation of British India into Islamic Pakistan and secular India led to an increased polarization between Urdu and Hindi, putting an end to attempts at promoting Hindustani. (See also Chapter 8, § 5 and Chapter 12, § 1.)

Other modern Indo-Aryan languages are Panjabi, Marathi, Gujarati, Bengali, as well as Sinhala (in Sri Lanka). Yet another modern Indo-Aryan language is Romani, the language of the Gypsies or Dom, an Indo-Aryan tribe that migrated from northern India in the Middle Ages, first to Central Asia, and from there to much of Asia and virtually all of Europe.

3.10.3. Indo-Iranians in the ancient Near East: The Mitanni

Documents from Anatolia and other parts of the ancient Near East (ca. 15th c. B.C.), containing names and other words of Indo-Iranian origin, show that an Indo-Iranian group (called the Mitanni) had migrated to this area of the world. Among these are passages in a treatise which suggest that the Indo-Iranians brought with them an improved method of horse training that may have added to the military prowess of the Hittites. Some of the words contained in these passages are phonetically closer to the earliest attested Indo-Aryan than to Old Iranian. It has therefore been suggested that the people in question really were Indo-Aryans, not Iranians or speakers of an as yet undivided Indo-Iranian. Assuming that they indeed were Indo-Aryans, a number of questions arise: How did these Indo-Aryans get to the Near East? Were they just an isolated tribe that strayed from the India-bound path of the rest of Indo-Aryan? Or did perhaps all of the Indo-Aryans meander through the Ancient Near East before settling in India? Although the last-mentioned scenario is rather unlikely, we have no hard evidence to answer these questions.

3.11. Tocharian

The easternmost branch of Indo-European, if we disregard the later eastward expansion of Indo-Aryan, consists of a group of two closely related languages, TOCHARIAN A and B. Documents in these languages (going back to the sixth to eighth centuries A.D.) were found in Chinese Turkestan in the late nineteenth and early twentieth century, and the languages were recognized as Indo-European in the early part of this century.

Like Armenian, Tocharian appears to have been greatly affected by outside influence. It is probably due to this influence that, again like Armenian, Tocharian is markedly less archaic than Baltic and Slavic, even though both of these languages are attested later. This is especially true for Tocharian sound structure, whose historical derivation from Proto-Indo-European is extremely complex. Some aspects of its verb inflection, however, seem to preserve archaic elements.

3.12. Other Indo-European languages

In addition to the subgroups of Indo-European briefly outlined above, ancient Europe and the Near and Middle East offer evidence for quite a number of other languages that seem to belong to the Indo-European language family, such as Phrygian (Asia Minor, 5th c. B.C.), Thracian (Asia Minor to eastern Balkans, attested mainly in citations in ancient Greek and Roman writers), or Venetic (Northern Italy, 2nd–1st c. B.C.). Many such languages seem to have been used in the central unmarked area of the map above, between Slavic, Albanian, and Greek. However, their attestations are too fragmentary to be useful for historical and comparative linguistic work. (See also the earlier discussion of Albanian.)

4. Abbreviations of Indo-European language names

In the remainder of this book it will be useful to abbreviate the names of languages from which examples are cited. For many languages, different stages are distinguished by prefixes, such as "Modern", "New", or "Old". A key to these abbreviations is given below, first of prefixes, then of the various language names.

Prefixes:

Class. = Classical	N = New
Mod. = Modern	P = Proto- (= reconstructed)
O = Old	pre- = an earlier stage, without indication
M = Middle	of the exact location in time

The most usual designations of the old, middle, and modern stages of a given language are O, M, and N (for 'new'), as in OE = Old English, ME = Middle English, NE = New or Modern English.

Language names:

Alb. = Albanian	Arm. = Armenian
Att. = Attic (Greek)	Av(est). = Avestan
BS = Balto-Slavic	Bulg. = Bulgarian
Celt. = Celtic	E(ngl.) = English
Fr. = French	G(erm.) = German
Gaul. = Gaulish (Celtic)	Gk. = Greek (usually ancient Gk.)
Gmc. = Germanic	Go(th). = Gothic

HG = High German
Icel. = Icelandic
Ir. = Irish
It(al). = Italian
Latv. = Latvian
N = Norse
OCS = Old Church Slavic
Pol. = Polish
Rom. = Romance
Rum. = Rumanian/Romanian
Serb. = Serbian
Slav. = Slavic
Swed. = Swedish
W = Welsh

IAr. = Indo-Aryan
IE = Indo-European
Iran. = Iranian
Lat. = Latin
Li(th). = Lithuanian
Norw. = Norwegian
Pers. = Persian
Port. = Portuguese
Ru(ss). = Russian
SCr. = Serbo-Croatian
Skt. = Sanskrit
Sp(an). = Spanish
Toch. = Tocharian

Chapter 3
Writing: Its history and its decipherment

Alpha es et O
'You are the beginning and end'
(from the old Christmas carol *In dulci jubilo*)

1. Introduction

The great advances of historical and comparative linguistics in the nineteenth
and twentieth centuries would have been impossible without the availability,
interpretation, and (in many cases) decipherment of written documents.

It is, of course, fairly obvious that written texts are important for historical
linguistics, for they are the only source for earlier language stages (such as
the Old English version of the Lord's Prayer cited in Chapter 1). But their
significance goes much farther. For instance, some of the early Indo-European
languages, such as Hittite and Tocharian, are only attested in written form; no
modern descendants have survived. Without written texts of these languages,
our knowledge of Indo-European would be greatly diminished. Moreover,
both the Hittite and the Tocharian texts yielded their information only because
the scripts in which they were written were already known from their use
in other languages: The Hittites had adapted the so-called cuneiform script
of ancient Mesopotamia, and the Tocharians an offshoot of scripts used in
India.

This, however, is not where the importance of understanding written texts
ends. The cuneiform script of ancient Mesopotamia had long died out, together with the civilizations that employed it. It was only the decipherment
of cuneiform script by nineteenth-century scholars that made it possible to
read this script and the documents in which it was used, and to understand
how these texts were pronounced.

In this chapter we take a closer look at the nature of writing, written texts,
their origin, development, interpretation, and decipherment.

2. History of writing

2.1. Oral traditions

In the modern industrialized world, writing has become such an essential component of all of our activities that we find it hard to imagine a world without writing. But even in the western world we do not need to go back far before we come to periods in which writing was limited to a small elite, so much so that literacy itself could be considered something like magic by the common people. (See Chapter 1.) And if we go back far enough we come to a time, somewhere before the fourth millenium B.C., when nobody knew how to read and write.

This does not mean that human beings were condemned to living without the benefits that we can so easily derive from reading: access to the wisdom and also the follies of earlier generations. Preliterate societies have their own ways of handing down such information, within the oral medium. Many readers will be familiar with the system of Griots in West Africa, bards who committed the history of their society to memory and who thus maintained a continuity of tradition. It was this system, and its amazing accuracy, that made it possible for Alex Haley to reestablish the link with his own African ancestors as reported in his book *Roots*.

We tend to disbelieve the accuracy of such orally transmitted texts, because preoccupation with written transmission and prejudice against rote learning has greatly diminished our ability, or willingness, to learn texts accurately by heart. In societies where rote learning – at least of important things – is treasured, we can even today observe feats of memorization that we find hard to believe. During this century an eminent expert in indigenous Indian grammar is said to have set aside a few years to memorize the entire *Rāmāyaṇa*, one of the two great epics of India which is about three times the length of the *Iliad* and *Odyssey* combined. But his internalization of the text went far beyond an ability to recite the text from beginning to end, or any particular section. If asked where a particular word occurred within the text, he was able to recite every single passage in which the word occurred. (In this, of course, he was aided by being a grammarian.) Put differently, he had memorized the text in such a fashion that he could operate on it more or less in the same fashion as one would on a text stored in computer memory.

This feat of memorization should not come as a surprise in India, a country which until very recently preserved all of its early sacred literature entirely in oral form, along with supporting texts on the function, meaning, and even grammar of these texts – over a period of between 2500 to 3500 years. To accomplish this task without serious lapses, an extremely intricate support system was developed. One of the systems was an amazingly sophisticated grammatical tradition. Perhaps most interesting, however, is the early development of an elaborate back-up system through which the texts were memorized in two, three, or even more different versions. One of these operated as follows: Let *a, b, c* ... stand for the words of the original text; the back-up, then, goes *abba, bccb,*... (Using an English translation of an early Sanskrit hymn, we can illustrate this method as follows: The original text is *I invoke Agni* ... ; the back-up text runs *I invoke invoke I invoke Agni Agni invoke* ...) Rules of conversion made it possible to restore the original text from any of the back-up versions.

Modern scholarship has been able to show that at an early period there was some corruption within the Indian oral tradition. However, once the back-up systems had been put in place, the texts were handed down with such amazing accuracy that from one end of the South Asian subcontinent to the other, a particular text would exhibit no significant variations, except for differences attributable to the fact that the pronunciation is to some extent "colored" by the native language of the reciters.

2.2. Forerunners of writing

Oral traditions often employ non-oral "props" to increase their accuracy, or for contexts in which oral communication is not possible. Some, fairly elementary props continue to be used even today; others disappeared with the arrival of literacy.

A very wide-spread phenomenon is the use of MNEMONIC DEVICES, which help in remembering numbers or other information that can be quantified or is in some way related to counting. A very simple device of tallying numerical information is presented in Illustration 1. This device, of course, is still in wide use today. But evidence for its use appears to go back at least 10,000 years.

Illustration 1. Mnemonic counting device

More complex is the system of rosary beads, employed to keep track of sequences of prayers in traditional Christianity, but also in other religions such as Buddhism. Counters of greater size and different material or color may mark the beginning or end of different prayer sequences, while other counters help keep track of individual prayers within the sequence. The cultural importance of rosaries in medieval Europe can be gauged from the fact that the modern English word *bead* is derived from an Old English word *bede* 'prayer': When people keeping track of their prayers on the counters of the rosary were asked what they were doing, they might well have said *I'm counting my beads*, meaning '. . . my prayers'. But seeing counters being manipulated, those asking the question were free to interpret the word *beads* as referring to the counters, not to prayers.

The most elaborate system of mnemonic devices seems to be presented by the quipus of the pre-Spanish Inca empire of Peru and adjacent areas of South America. (See Illustration 2.) Quipus were primarily used for recording

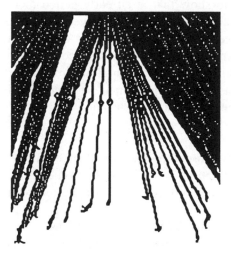

Illustration 2. Section of a quipu bundle

numerical information by means of a combination of different string colors and knots. The often complex statistical information thus stored "triggered" memorized recitations concerning particular transactions, such as the inflow and outflow of goods in the imperial treasury. Secondarily, apparently, the quipus were also used as mnemonic devices for other types of texts, such as historical accounts, that likewise had been committed to memory. However, like the strokes in Illustration 1, the quipus provided an accurate record only of numerical information. They could not be used for accurate, verbatim transcriptions of non-numerical texts.

Especially significant is the appearance during the ninth to sixth millennia B.C. of clay tokens in the ancient Near East, which came in different sizes, shapes, and designs and were used for identifying goods exchanged in

Illustration 3. Clay tokens of the Ancient Near East

trade, and different quantities of such goods. (See Illustration 3.) It has been claimed that these clay tokens played a very important role in the eventual development of full writing in this area, since they bear a strong resemblance to some of the symbols used in the early stages of Near Eastern writing.

Beside mnemonic devices, preliterate societies seem to have employed PICTORIAL representations to convey messages. Many such representations have been found all over the world. However, lacking information on the context for these representations, their purpose, or the language of those who produced them, the interpretation of these representations usually is quite uncertain. A common joke among prehistorians, commenting on earlier practices, is that "When in doubt, give a mystical interpretation." Although such an interpretation may be correct for some representations, a fair amount of evidence suggests that more mundane interpretations are more appropriate. First, in the Ancient Near East, where we can follow the development of writing in greatest detail, writing was initially employed for keeping track of commercial transactions. A perfect parallel is found in the case of the Inca quipus. Secondly, we have direct evidence that at least some pictorial representations had rather mundane purposes. Consider Illustration 4, a note sent in the nineteenth century by an Ojibwa girl to her boyfriend. The message of this note is quite clear and was confirmed by the boy's reaction: He did indeed come to the girl's place as requested. The message conveyed can be roughly paraphrased as follows:

> From the girl of the Bear Totem [see sign on upper left] to the boy of the Mudpuppy Totem [sign on lower left]: Take the path which leads toward the lakes [right]. After it is joined by a path from the right, a path goes off to the left, leading to two tepees with three Christian girls in them [see crosses]. I'm in the left one and want you to come [see waving hand symbol in left teepee].

However, highly successful as it may have been, the representation in Illustration 4 does not convey a specific linguistic message and in this sense is

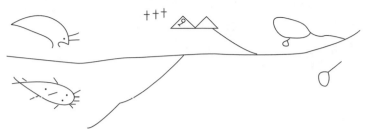

Illustration 4. Letter of an Ojibwa girl to her boyfriend (adapted from G. Mallery (1893): Picture Writing of the American Indians [10th Annual Report of the Bureau of Ethnology])

not much different from the secondary use of the quipus to keep track of non-numerical information. It merely conveys certain ideas, and its interpretation depends heavily on knowing enough about the cultural and other contexts in which it was sent. Without knowing the context, it would be impossible to come up with the correct interpretation simply by looking at Illustration 4; one might just as well assume that it conveyed some deep mystical meaning. More than that, the message of Illustration 4 can be paraphrased in many different ways and, evidently, in many different languages – not just Ojibwa, but also English. In short, unlike writing, it fails to express a specific linguistic message.

A similar, but more elaborate, use of pictorial symbols is found in the Ancient Near East – cylinder seals that were rolled into wet clay to produce an impression identifying a person or clan. These seals continued to be used when writing was introduced (much like modern seals and sealing wax) and, at that time, even could incorporate writing into the pictorial representation. See Illustration 5. Like the clay tokens in Illustration 3, these seals may have been an important precursor of writing in the area.

Impression   Cylinder (side view)

Illustration 5. Ancient Near Eastern cylinder seal and impression (adapted from E. Chiera (1938): *They Wrote on Clay*)

2.3. The development of writing in the Ancient Near East

As noted earlier, the development of writing, from the early, pre-writing stages of mnemonic devices and pictorial descriptions, via early attempts to combine and expand them, to full writing can be best observed in the Ancient Near East of Mesopotamia, especially in the civilization of ancient Sumer. In other areas of the world, such as ancient Egypt, China, or Meso-America, the early history of writing is shrouded in mystery.

Some scholars have proposed that, in fact, writing originated only once in the "Old World" of Eurasia and Northern Africa, in the place where we can see it develop most clearly – Mesopotamia. According to this view, the fact that we lack specific evidence for such a development elsewhere in the "Old World" is no accident: Writing outside Mesopotamia was not an independent invention, but resulted from the spread of writing – or the idea of writing – to the rest of the world. This view appeared to receive further support from the fact that the earliest attestations of writing in Mesopotamia date back to about 3100 B.C. Writing in Egypt (to the west) and in ancient Elam (to the east) was considered to come in somewhat later (about 3000 and 2900 B.C., respectively). Written records appear even later in the Indus Valley (about 2400 B.C.), and yet later in China (commonly dated as beginning about 1300 B.C., but see below). That is, the farther from Mesopotamia, the later the appearance of writing.

This diffusionist view of the origin of writing has in recent years lost much of its earlier persuasiveness. The most important reason for a change in perspective is the increasing realization that the characters used by the Meso-American Mayans in their inscriptions represent genuine writing, recounting not just astronomical information (as had earlier been believed) but also the chronicles of royal families and their kingdoms. (There is some evidence that Mayan writing was taken over from the Olmecs, an earlier important civilization of the area, whose language is considered to be related to the modern Mixe-Zoquean group of languages.)

Scholars now are ready to accept at least three different, independent origins of writing: Mesopotamia, China, and Meso-America. On the other hand, the writing systems of Egypt and Elam are generally considered diffused from Mesopotamia. (The Indus Valley writing still awaits successful decipherment, a fact that makes it difficult to determine whether it is an independent creation or not.)

Whatever the merits of these scholarly debates, one should note that the traditionally posited time difference between the earliest appearance of writing in Mesopotamia, Egypt, and Elam is exceedingly small, given the time depth we are talking about. In fact, recent research suggests that Elamitic writing developed at just about the same time on the Iranian plateau as it did in Mesopotamia, that is, about 3300–2900 B.C. And as work on Chinese proto-history continues, the date for the development of Chinese writing gets pushed back farther and farther, currently to at least the seventeenth century B.C. by conservative estimates (see § 5 below).

Even in their earliest stages, the different writing systems of the Old World exhibit significant differences in detail; see Illustration 6. And the observable similarities (as in the symbol for 'sun') can easily be explained in terms of the properties of the designated objects. The possibility of independent development, therefore, should not be ruled out entirely.

	Sumerian	Egyptian	Chinese
God	✳	◁	✳
Sky	✳	⊓	🕴
Star	✳	✕	▫▫
Sun	(⊙)	◯	▭

Illustration 6. Some pictograms in early Sumerian, Egyptian, and Chinese writing

What may be more important is to look at the conditions under which writing appears, not only in Mesopotamia, but also in Egypt, Meso-America, and elsewhere. As it turns out, in all of these areas writing was introduced at a time when large states had developed, with a centralized system of collecting revenue. The revenue, in turn, had to be distributed to the king's court, the nobles or warriors, and the priests; and some of it had to be kept as a reserve for the general populace in time of need. In Mesopotamia and Egypt, it was clearly for the purpose of keeping track of these transactions that writing was developed. And it is probably no accident that under very similar conditions, the Inca empire developed its elaborate system of quipus.

Meso-America appears to be an exception. Even the earliest attested inscriptions deal with calendrical information and events at the royal court. But perhaps the inscriptions do not tell the whole story: The word used to refer to writing, *tz'ib*, literally means 'paint', which suggests that an earlier phase of writing consisted of "painting" symbols on paper-like material, and that the documents have been lost to us because of the perishability of the material. At present we do not know what kinds of texs were written in the early "painted" form of writing; but it is at least possible that these texts dealt with commercial matters. (Evidence for a continued tradition of "painted writing" is found in several late codices that survived the organized effort of Spanish colonialists to destroy all native documents because of their "heathen" nature.)

At any rate, the commercial origin of writing in Mesopotamia becomes very clear when we look at early transitional phases, between the pre-writing stage and full writing. An example is found in Illustration 7. As can be seen from this example, the intermediate phase tends to combine mnemonic and pictorial devices to produce more specific messages than earlier precursors of writing. Still, the messages are quite limited. This shortcoming was partly compensated for by the addition of cylinder seal impressions (see Illustration 5 above), which identified the persons involved in the transaction. (Compare the similar use of the totem symbols in Illustration 4.) Even then, a message like the one in Illustration 7 does not tell us what exactly happened to the 54 cattle it refers to.

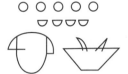   54 "ox/cow" = 54 CATTLE

Illustration 7. Example of "proto-writing" in Ancient Near East

In spite of their shortcomings, these early attempts at increasing the power of graphic symbols must have been successful enough to stimulate the development of even better presentations. This development was accomplished by an increasingly conscious – and also increasingly confident, even daring – expansion of the original code. To illustrate these developments more vividly, most of the following examples are drawn from English, as if English were now in the process of developing writing out of pre-writing.

One of the methods to expand the code was the principle of SEMANTIC TRANSFERENCE, the use of symbols for easily depicted objects so as to designate semantically related concepts that are abstract and thus more difficult to draw. See for instance Illustration 8 in which the easily drawn symbol for 'sun' is used to refer to the semantically related 'day', a notion that is quite difficult to draw. See also the genuine Sumerian examples for 'God', 'sky', and 'star' in Illustration 6 above. In some cases, of course, the use of the same symbol for two different notions might lead to confusion (as in the case of 'sun' and 'day'). To remedy this situation, the symbols sometimes were secondarily differentiated; see again Illustration 8, as well as the genuine Sumerian example in Illustration 9, where 'king' is differentiated from 'man' by a stylized crown.

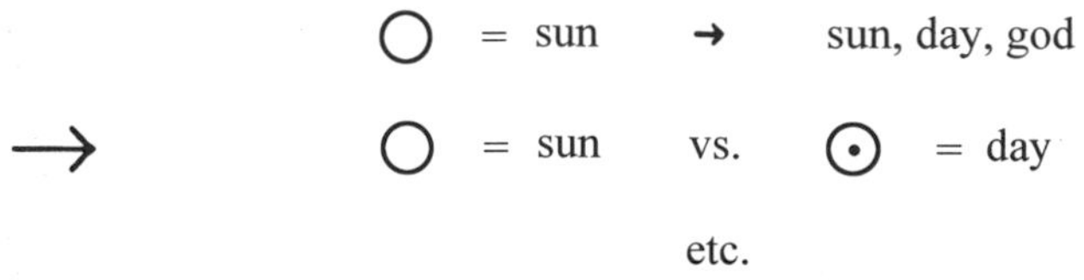

Illustration 8. Semantic transference and secondary symbol differentiation

man   king

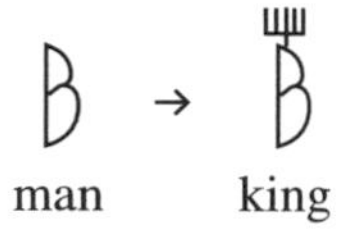

Illustration 9. Symbol differentiation in Sumerian

A similar expansion was achieved through PHONETIC TRANSFERENCE, the use of an easily drawn symbol to designate a phonetically similar or identical word that is difficult to render graphically. Illustration 10 gives a genuine example from Sumerian, an ingenious solution of the otherwise nearly insoluble problem of how to depict the notion 'life'.

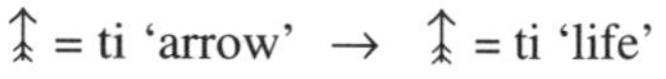

Illustration 10. Phonetic transference

Yet other ways were devised to expand the code. One of these was the use of PHONETIC INDICATORS to help differentiate which of several possible interpretations of a given symbol was intended. Phonetic indicators, thus, are used very much like the statement "sounds like" in the game of charades. For instance, in the Ancient Near East, there was a sexist metaphor equating two women with strife, discord, or quarrel. As a consequence, the notions 'strife', 'discord', 'quarrel' could be designated by a picture of two women facing each other, as in the upper part of Illustration 11. To indicate which of these readings was intended, the picture of a cord might be added to narrow down the choice to 'discord', as in the lower part of Illustration 11. (See Illustration 18 further below for a different phonetic indicator used with the same base symbol, and compare the real examples from Egyptian and Mayan in Illustrations 13 and 19 below.)

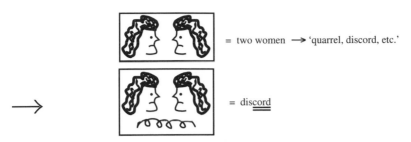

= two women ⟶ 'quarrel, discord, etc.'

⟶

= dis<u>cord</u>

Illustration 11. Phonetic indicators

An alternative solution consisted in the introduction of SEMANTIC INDICA-TORS, in which the meaning of subsidiary symbols narrows down the range of possible interpretations. See Illustration 12, where the addition of an anchor narrows down the choice of possible readings to 'sea'. As the real Ancient Egyptian example in Illustration 13 shows, phonetic and semantic indicators may be employed simultaneously. Here we have phonetic transfer from a conventionalized pictograph for *pr* 'house' to *pr-* 'go out', plus addition of a phonetic indicator *r* **and** a semantic indicator for 'MOTION'.

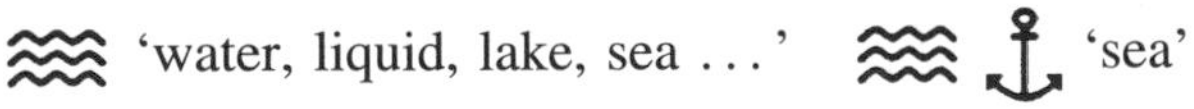

≋ 'water, liquid, lake, sea ...'   ≋ ⚓ 'sea'

Illustration 12. Semantic indicators

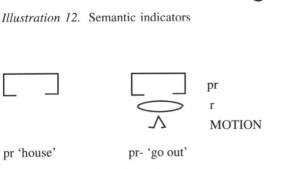

pr

r

MOTION

pr 'house'   pr- 'go out'

Illustration 13. Semantic and phonetic indicators in Ancient Egyptian

An even more powerful means of expanding the code is known as the REBUS PRINCIPLE, after a parlor game in which words or component parts of words are expressed by pictures of objects, or by other symbols that have (nearly) the same sound. (An English example would be a picture of a bee followed by the symbol *4*, spelling out *before*.) Combining existing characters in their phonetic values made it possible to express longer and more complex words, as in Illustration 14. On the left side, a sequence of a

Illustration 14. Expansion of the code through the rebus principle

kneeling person = *kneel* [nīl] plus the by now well-known symbol for 'sun' [sən] spells out the name *Neilson*. On the right side, the combination of the symbols for 'sun' and 'day' is employed to spell out both *Sunday* and the identical-sounding ice cream concoction *sundae*. This method was especially useful in expressing foreign names. While such names tend to be meaningful in their original language, they often are "meaningless" in another language and therefore difficult to represent in terms of meaningful symbols. (Consider for instance the name *Mississippi*, which quite appropriately means 'big river' in the Algonquian language from which it was adopted, but which in English is just an arbitrary combination of sounds.)

The increasing use of the rebus principle brought about an increasing PHONETICIZATION of the writing system, in contrast to the early LOGOGRAPHIC system which mainly focused on the SEMANTICS of words. (Sometimes the term pictographic is used for the early system, because its symbols generally are pictorial representations. But the term logographic is more useful, since writing systems may be logographic without using pictorial representations. A perfect example of such a writing system is that of Chinese; see § 5 below.)

Ultimately the most powerful and, at the same time, most daring method was the principle of ACROPHONY and similar arbitrary phonetic reductions. Nowadays, the related process of acronymy is used mainly as a means of abbreviation, generally by drawing on the initial letters of words, as in US = *United States*. Occasionally, it may use the first syllables or parts of syllables, as in *Benelux* = *Be*lgium, the *Ne*therlands, and *Lux*embourg. In any event, acronymy usually is based on spelling. At the early period in the development of writing that we are concerned with, acrophony operated on the initial syllables of words as they are PRONOUNCED, or on parts of these syllables. Moreover, the purpose of the process was simply to create a more flexible code for spelling out words phonetically, without regard for the original semantics of the symbols employed. And to accomplish this goal, other, non-acrophonic "mutilations" of words might be used to create new phonetic symbols.

Illustration 15 exemplifies various different routes that may be taken in this process. One is to abstract the initial consonant plus the following vowel as the essential phonetic value of the writing symbol. Alternatively, the final consonant plus the preceding vowel might be abstracted in this way. Even

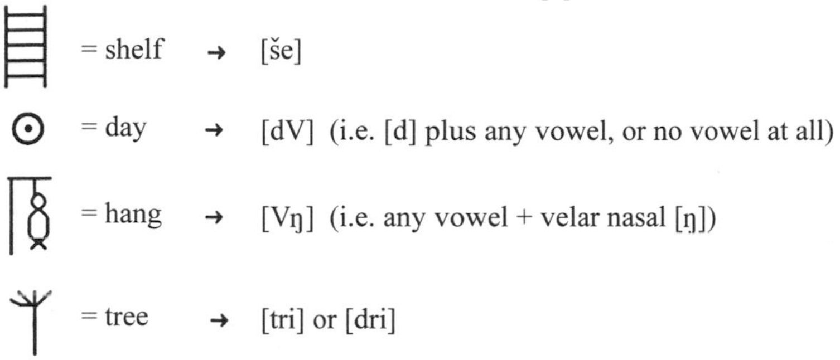

= shelf   →   [še]

= day   →   [dV] (i.e. [d] plus any vowel, or no vowel at all)

= hang   →   [Vŋ] (i.e. any vowel + velar nasal [ŋ])

= tree   →   [tri] or [dri]

Illustration 15. Creation of phonetic symbols by acrophony and related processes

more daringly, the precise quality of the vowel may be ignored, so that a symbol like the one for 'day' may stand for [d] plus any vowel or even no vowel at all. And again, the same may be done for a final consonant plus preceding vowel. Yet another daring step is to ignore the difference in voicing between, say, [t] and [d] and to permit the same symbol to stand for both [tri] and [dri].

If pushed to its logical conclusion, the principle of acrophony can lead to the development of a SYLLABARY, in which, ideally, written symbols consistently designate particular phonetic syllables, no matter which word they might occur in. In many writing systems, symbols actually express PARTS of syllables, so that complete syllables have to be spelled out by combinations of "syllabic" signs. (Compare Illustration 16 for some examples.) Whatever the details, however, at this stage, the writing system has become completely phoneticized.

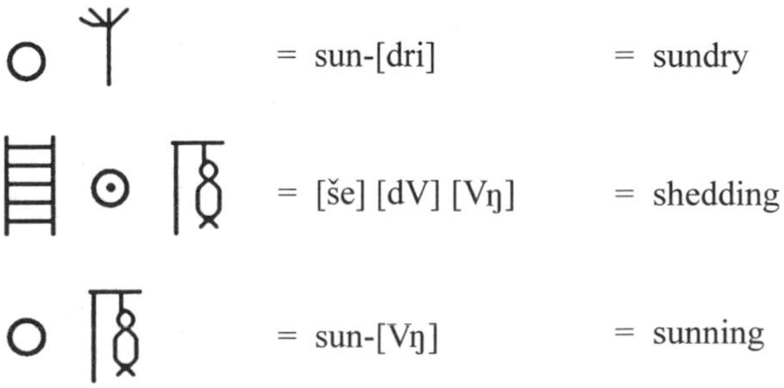

= sun-[dri]   = sundry

= [še] [dV] [Vŋ]   = shedding

= sun-[Vŋ]   = sunning

Illustration 16. Development of syllabary

In the Sumerian tradition, the syllables or parts of syllables designated by syllabic symbols could be of the shape consonant + vowel (CV), vowel

+ consonant (VC), consonant + vowel + consonant (CVC), or just plain vowel (V). See Illustration 16 for some hypothetical examples. In Egyptian, on the other hand, syllabic symbols consistently were of the shape CV (Illustration 17). Moreover, as in the case of the symbol 'day' = [dV] of Illustration 15, the "V" of these syllabic symbols could be any vowel, or even no vowel at all.

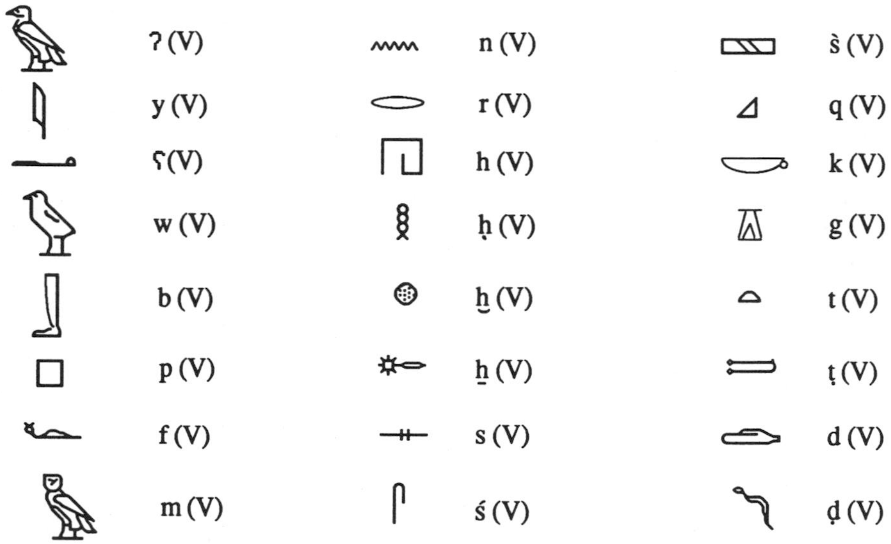

𓅃	ʔ (V)	𓈖	n (V)	𓄑	š (V)
𓏭	y (V)	𓂋	r (V)	𓂤	q (V)
𓂝	ʕ (V)	𓉔	h (V)	𓎡	k (V)
𓅱	w (V)	𓎛	ḥ (V)	𓎼	g (V)
𓃀	b (V)	𓐍	ḫ (V)	𓏏	t (V)
𓊪	p (V)	𓄡	ẖ (V)	𓍿	ṭ (V)
𓆑	f (V)	𓋴	s (V)	𓂧	d (V)
𓅓	m (V)	𓏏	ś (V)	𓆓	ḍ (V)

Illustration 17. Egyptian syllabary (or abjad)

While from one perspective the Egyptian method of phonetic writing is still syllabic, it is easy to see how this writing system might be reinterpreted as a "consonantal alphabet", a system very much like our alphabet, except that it writes only consonants and has no special symbols for vowels. The term ABJAD, the Arabic word based on the initial letters of the Arabic writing system (ʔabǰad), has recently been proposed as a designation for this type of writing system. In fact, there has been some controversy over whether the Egyptian writing system should be considered to be a syllabary or an abjad. Whatever the resolution of this controversy may turn out to be, the Egyptian type of writing was very important for the development of writing. (See § 2.4 below.)

In the traditional cultures of the ancient Near East and Egypt (and also of Meso-America), syllabic writing never completely replaced the earlier logographic systems with or without phonetic or semantic indicators. The two coexisted, just as in the hypothetical examples of Illustration 18 or the real Egyptian example in 13. Note also Illustration 19, which shows a similar coexistence of logographs with or without phonetic indicators and syllabic writing in another traditional writing system, that of the Mayans. (What complicates things in Mayan writing is that phonetic indicators are combined with the logographic base symbol into a complex symbol whose parts are difficult to distinguish for the beginner, and the syllabic symbols are combined in a similar fashion.) Readers familiar with Japanese may find a parallel in that language, too, in that Chinese logographic symbols are used side by side with syllabic writing. Even languages like English exhibit traces of mixed writing, as in the combination of logographic numeral symbols with something like phonetic indicators in expressions such as *1st, 2nd, 3rd, 4th*.

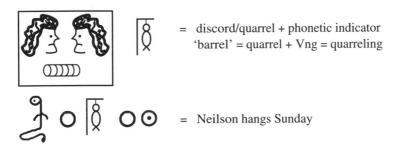

= discord/quarrel + phonetic indicator
'barrel' = quarrel + Vng = quarreling

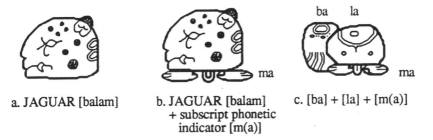

= Neilson hangs Sunday

Illustration 18. Mixed system of logographic and phonetic writing

		ba la
a. JAGUAR [balam]	b. JAGUAR [balam] + subscript phonetic indicator [m(a)]	c. [ba] + [la] + [m(a)]

Illustration 19. Mixed system in Mayan (adapted from M. D. Coe (1992): *Breaking the Maya code.*)

In Mesopotamia, things got even more complicated: At a fairly early period, Semitic peoples such as the Assyrians and Babylonians replaced the Sumerians and took over their writing. As they did so, they retained many symbols with the old Sumerian values, whether syllabic or logographic. This meant that in order to read and write it was necessary to learn Sumerian; and grammars of Sumerian were prepared for this purpose.

At the same time, the Babylonians and Assyrians began using symbols with the phonetic values of their own languages. Symbols thus could have their logographic meaning, the phonetic value of Sumerian, or the phonetic value of Semitic languages like Babylonian. Yet another layer of complications was added when the Indo-European Hittites adopted the writing system. As a consequence, the symbol on the (a)-side of Illustration 20 below could have both its Sumerian value *ē* 'house' and the Assyrian value *bītu* 'house'. In many cases, the range of phonetic values of particular symbols became even more formidable, as in item (b) of Illustration 20.

(a)   (b)

Phonetic values: *ē*   *tar, kud, sil, ḫas*
Logographic value: 'house' (= Sum. *ē*, Assyr. *bītu*)

Illustration 20. Multiple values of symbols in Mesopotamian tradition

With an increasing development away from the early pictographic system toward a logographic or even phonetic one, there was less and less motivation in the tradition of Mesopotamia to draw pleasing or realistic pictures. Symbols became increasingly simplified and standardized. But more than that, in order to make the process of writing easier, the orientation of symbols was changed in many cases (see stage II in Illustration 21). Most noticeable, however, is the fact that slowly, and by no means affecting all symbols at the same time, the shape of the letters began to change radically in response to the material and implements used for writing (see stages III and IV). In the tradition of Mesopotamia, most writing was produced on wet clay tablets which, after they had been covered with writing, were either sun-dried or, for more permanent storage, baked into brick. The "stylus" with which the clay tablets were engraved was wedge-formed (see Illustration 22) and, unless scribes were very careful, would leave a wedge impression at the insertion point, followed by a narrow groove. With the increasing trend away from pictography, there was no longer any need to avoid the wedge; and in keeping with a general tendency to make writing simpler, lines were made straight, and the resulting shapes were rearranged for yet further simplification. The wedge shape characteristic of the resulting system is responsible for the name CUNEIFORM (lit. 'wedge-form').

The developments just discussed may appear extreme, especially if one considers that the ancient Egyptian script in Illustration 17, referred to as

Stage I   Stage II   Stage III   Stage IV

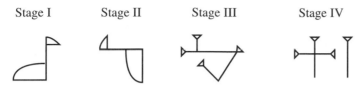

Illustration 21. Development of cuneiform characters

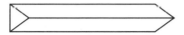

Illustration 22. Stylus used for cuneiform writing

HIEROGLYPHIC, remained essentially pictorial. However, this pictorial script was retained only in monumental inscriptions. Side by side with it there arose another, simplified system which, like the cuneiform script, was greatly influenced by the implements and material used for writing (a narrow ink brush on papyrus). The latter system of writing is referred to as DEMOTIC. A modern analogue to this influence of writing material and instrument is the perhaps short-lived development of relatively grainy characters on dot-matrix printers, where the lines and curves of written characters are decomposed into dots or "pixels". Here, too, the medium of writing, a pixel-oriented graphics system on the computer plus the mechanics of the dot-matrix printer, changed the shape of characters. A further parallel can be seen in the shape of the early Germanic runes; see § 2.6 below.

2.4. The origination of full syllabaries and consonantal alphabets

As noted earlier, in the traditions of Mesopotamia and Egypt, the step toward a fully phonetic, syllabic (or even alphabetic or abjad) system of writing was never completed. The reason, no doubt, was the fact that there was a more or less unbroken cultural tradition; and logographic, beside syllabic, writing was part of that tradition. (Another reason may have been that the complex system that resulted suited the scribes very well, as it was virtually impenetrable to the majority of the population, thus assuring the small class of scribes continued employment and a good income.)

Full phonetic writing, in the form of syllabaries or even abjad forms of alphabets, however, developed on the periphery of Mesopotamia and ancient Egypt, among peoples influenced by these great civilizations, but not beholden to their traditions. (The term "full phonetic writing" is perhaps a little too strong. Just as in modern alphabetic systems, a few logographic symbols remained, similar to, say, the $ or £ of English.)

By a process sometimes referred to as STIMULUS DIFFUSION, these societies adopted the idea of writing, especially that of syllabic or abjad writing, as well as the "look" of the characters employed; but the symbols they created, as well as their phonetic values, were quite independent. (A similar development took place more recently in the case of the CHEROKEE SYLLABARY, whose symbols, such as **A** and **H**, are inspired by the shape of the alphabet used for English, but whose phonetic values differ greatly: **A**, for instance, designates the syllable *go*, and **H**, *mi*. See § 5.3 below.)

Two of these writing systems were especially important historically. The Old Persian one provided the starting point for the decipherment of the cuneiform script and thus, ultimately, for the understanding of the Ancient Near Eastern texts – whether Sumerian, Semitic Assyrian and Babylonian, or Indo-European Old Persian and Hittite. The other system, used by various South and West Semitic peoples, became the source for a large number of modern writing systems. These include the consonantal alphabets or abjads of Hebrew and Arabic, possibly the writing systems of India, and certainly the alphabetic script of ancient Greece which, unlike its Semitic ancestor and relatives, designates both vowels and consonants. From this script, in turn, are derived the Roman alphabet, used in western Europe (and its "Insular" offshoot, used for medieval English and still employed for Gaelic), the runic script of early Germanic, and the Cyrillic alphabet used in large parts of eastern Europe and adjacent parts of Asia.

Let us begin with a brief look at the Old Persian syllabary. As in many syllabaries, the symbols of this script must be read with different values, sometimes with and sometimes without an inherent vowel; and long vowels are written as combinations of two short vowels (see Illustration 23). Ideally, the script would have had a different symbol for each consonant + vowel combination; but as Illustration 24 shows, only the set of consonant characters with an inherent *a*-vowel is complete. These are the "base consonants", which are also used to designate consonants without an inherent vowel. Missing characters for other consonant + vowel combinations are produced by placing the *i*- or *u*-vowel symbol after the base consonants.

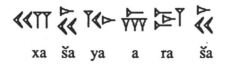

xa ša ya   a   ra ša

= xšayārša

Illustration 23. The name of King Xerxes in the Old Persian syllabary

	a	i	u			a	i	u
Vowels	◆	◆	◆					
b	◆				l	◆		
č	◆				m	◆	◆	◆
ç	◆				n	◆		◆
d	◆	◆	◆		p	◆		
f	◆				r	◆		◆
g	◆		◆		s	◆		
h	◆				š	◆		
x	◆				t	◆		◆
y	◆				θ	◆	◆	
ǰ	◆	◆			w	◆		
k	◆		◆		z	◆		

Illustration 24. Old Persian syllabary

Various explanations have been advanced for the evidently inconsistent character of the script. The most plausible is that at a certain point, the decision was made not to wait any longer for the completion of the script, but to go ahead and use whatever had been developed by that time, not unlike an early release of software before all the "bugs" are worked out. Presumably, the great rulers of the mighty Persian empire were getting impatient with the slow progress of the scholars who were working on the writing system and decided to go ahead and use an incomplete "prototype" version in order to proclaim their great deeds to the world and to posterity.

Even though using characters with very different shape, the Old Persian syllabary shows certain similarities to the Egyptian system, at least as far as the base consonants are concerned: In both cases, symbols stand for a consonant ± vowel. The systems differ in that the Old Persian symbols stand for $C(a)$, while the Egyptian ones indicate a consonant ± **any** vowel.

This more radical development becomes important in the writing systems of South and West Semitic peoples in the area of Syria/Palestine in the early part of the second millennium B.C. At an early period, a large variety of writing systems is found, some with characters similar to cuneiform, others with more pictorial symbols reminiscent of the Egyptian hieroglyphs. These facts suggest that the inhabitants of this centrally located area were influenced by both the Ancient Near Eastern and the Egyptian traditions. (What complicates matters is that at this point, a number of other pictorial or hieroglyphic writing systems have made their appearance in the area, such as that of Hieroglyphic Luwian in Asia Minor or the hieroglyphs of early Crete and neighboring areas.)

In their phonetic character, however, these writing systems were most similar to the Egyptian syllabary which, as noted earlier, was inherently open to reinterpretation as an abjad or consonantal alphabet. Although there may still be some controversy over whether this reinterpretation took place in Egyptian, it is quite certain that it was completed in the new systems of the South and West Semitic peoples.

The development of a writing system which indicates only consonants was possible and made sense because of the word structure of the Semitic languages and of the distantly related Ancient Egyptian. In these languages, the basic building block of words is the "root", a configuration of (generally) three consonants which carry the basic "lexical meaning", such as √*ktb* 'write'. By insertion of different vowel patterns into this "consonantal skeleton" (with or without prefixes or suffixes), different types of words are created, such as *katab* 'he wrote', *kātib* 'writer', *kit(ā)b* 'book', *mi-ktab* 'letter', etc. Given enough context, it is quite predictable which of the various forms of √*ktb* must be intended and what, therefore, the vocalism of that word must be. It is thus possible to write without specifying the vowels. (Even in English this is marginally possible, as in *f y cn rd ths y cn bcm a gd scrtry*, an advertisement for a shorthand system seen on many subways in the US, where only the word *a* causes difficulties, since it contains no consonant.)

In the Semitic languages (and the related Egyptian) the acrophonic principle therefore could and did lead to characters which spell a particular consonant without further specification of the following vowel (if any). Hence:

p (V) = *pa, pi, pu, p* etc. See Illustration 17 above for part of the Egyptian syllabary or abjad and Illustration 25 below for the two first symbols of the early Semitic abjad of Canaan, and the further developments of these symbols in Arabic and Hebrew, the two best-known modern Semitic languages.

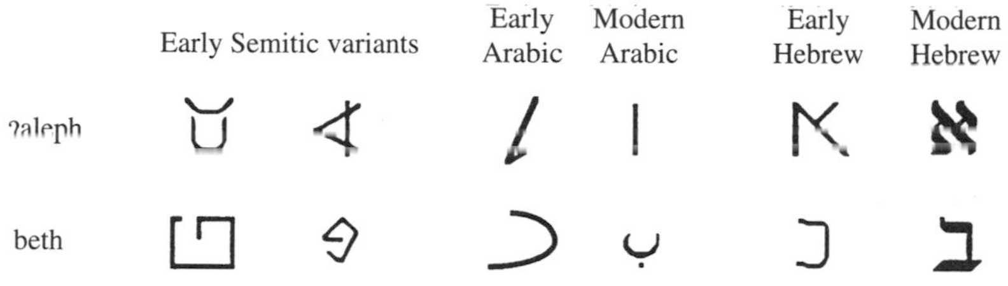

	Early Semitic variants	Early Arabic	Modern Arabic	Early Hebrew	Modern Hebrew
ʔaleph	♉ ◁	⟋	׀	⟨	𐤀
beth	⊓ ⟨	⟩	◡	⟩	⟩

Illustration 25. Developments of Semitic consonantal signs

Illustration 25 further shows a number of other features of Canaanite writing: First, although greatly simplified and conventionalized in their shape, the letters are pictographic in origin. Thus, the letter *ʔaleph* is a stylized picture of an ox; and *beth* represents the ground plan of a house. The selection of these symbols is not just due to chance: *ʔaleph* and *beth* mean 'ox' and 'house', respectively. Moreover, *ʔaleph* and *beth* are the names of the two letters, and the phonetic values of the letters are identical to the initial sounds of the letter names/pictographs, i.e., *ʔ* and *b*. A similar acrophonic relation between letter name and speech sound holds true for the rest of the writing symbols.

The great advantage of this system over the traditional mixed systems is (a) its much smaller number of symbols (20 to 30 vs. 600 to 700 in cuneiform and hieroglyphic script), and (b) the easy manner in which the phonetic value of each symbol can be derived from the corresponding letter name. Memorizing a relatively small number of letter names in a fixed order therefore made it possible to learn how to write in about a week, rather than the months or years required to master the traditional scripts of Egypt and the Ancient Near East.

Note that while a number of letters, in addition to ♉ and ⊓, are clearly pictographic in origin, other letters, such as � = *ḥēth*, are not. Moreover, some letters are quite patently secondary modifications of other characters, created to increase the number of speech sounds that could be distinguished. Compare for instance ⧻ = *hē* beside ⧻ = *ḥēth*, where one is no doubt derived from the other by addition or deletion of strokes, although the direction of derivation is uncertain. Developments of this type reflect the same tendency that we observed earlier in the often daring methods of expanding the code during the early stages of the development of writing: Once people have discovered a good thing, they usually find ways to make it even better.

We find here another parallel to earlier developments: Once writing symbols become conventionalized, their pictorial origin becomes irrelevant and their shapes change to suit the writing materials, the scribes' convenience, or even more artistic, calligraphic concerns. This accounts for the change of early Ʊ to ⊀, ⊔ to ⌀, and many other, similar developments, including those in later Semitic.

2.5. The development of the alphabet

At some time during the early ninth century B.C. (or perhaps even earlier), the consonantal alphabet of the Semitic Phoenicians was adopted by the Greeks through commercial contacts in Asia Minor. Superficially, the writing systems of the two peoples look very similar, as can be seen in Illustration 26. The difference in language, however, combined with the way in which the writing system was memorized and recited, brought about a major change – from an abjad system that clearly distinguished only consonants to a fully alphabetical one which had distinct symbols both for the consonants and for the vowels. Thus, whereas in the Semitic languages, the symbol in column (a) of Illustration 26 had the value of a consonant, transcribed [ʔ], the corresponding Greek symbol (column (a')) represents a **vowel**, [a].

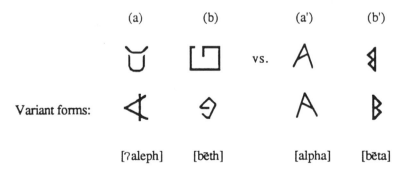

(a)	(b)		(a')	(b')
Ʊ	⊔	vs.	A	∤
⊀	∽		A	Ƀ
[ʔaleph]	[bĕth]		[alpha]	[bĕta]

Variant forms (row two, left labels).

Illustration 26. Semitic abjad vs. Greek alphabet

What made this change possible is the fact that the Greeks took over from the Phoenicians not only the letters of the writing system, but also (a) the order in which the letters were recited, (b) the letter names, and (c) the acrophonic principle according to which the first sound of the letter name designates the speech sound denoted by the letter.

Lacking the consonant [ʔ] in their language, the Greeks omitted that sound in the name of the first letter of the writing system, [ʔaleph], and pronounced the name as [alpha]. And presto, given the acrophonic principle, they acquired a letter which designated a vowel, not a consonant!

Similar developments led to the development of the vowel letters for *e* and *o*. The former developed out of a letter designating an *h*-sound in Semitic, the latter, from a letter transcribing the "pharyngeal" stop [ʕ] and lacking any counterpart in Greek. See the two columns on the left of Illustration 27 below.

	Phoenician	Early Greek	Later Greek	Roman	
ʔ	⊲	A	A	A	a
b	⌐	⅃	ℬ	B	b
g	𝟣	𝟣	Γ	C/G	g → k/g
h	⅃	⅃	⪢	E	e
ḥ	目	日	H (Ion. ēta WGk. hēta)	H	ē / h
ʕ	O	O	O	O	o
			Ω (Ionic)		ō

Illustration 27. The development of selected letters of the alphabet

The remaining vowels of the early Greek alphabet derive from characters which could, under certain circumstances, be used as vowels in Semitic. One of these was the letter *yod* whose basic value, given the acrophonic principle, was *y*; but between consonants it was realized as *i*. Since Greek at this point lacked the sound *y*, but had an *i*, the symbol was naturally appropriated to designate the vowel, and the name of the letter changed to *iota*. The case of Semitic *waw*, with base value *w* but inter-consonant realization as *u*, is even more interesting: In this case, early Greek had both sounds. So the question arose: In what value should *waw* be adopted? The answer was to have it both ways, by splitting the letter in two, one (Y) having the value *u*, the other, ⅂, a doubled version of Y, being used to designate *w*. Interestingly, an almost exactly parallel development occurred when the Roman alphabet was adopted for writing the early Germanic languages: The Roman alphabet used a single symbol (V) for both *u* and *w*. Germanic users of the alphabet seem to have felt the need for a clearer distinction, and V was doubled to VV or W to indicate *w* – hence the modern English name of the letter, *double-u*. (Just as the other letters, the symbol ꟻ soon changed direction, becoming F.)

Within Greek, the development continued: When Ionic, an important dialect of early Greek, lost its initial "aitches", the letter which previously had the value *h* acquired a vowel value, namely the long front vowel *ē* [ɛ̄]; and this value was adopted in many of the other Greek dialects. In West Greek, by contrast, the letter retained its value *h*, and it was this pronunciation that was adopted in Latin.

Once this precedent was set, a new letter was devised for the corresponding long back vowel, *ō*, by opening up the lower part of the old letter O and changing it to Ω. For these developments, see the last three rows of Illustration 27. In both these developments and in the earlier "splitting" of *waw* we can see the same creative processes at work that we have encountered several times already: Once people have recognized a good thing, they like to make it even better.

In addition to these changes, there was a general tendency for the letters to change "direction", presumably to make them easier to write. (Note the Mesopotamian parallel in Illustration 20 above.) For instance, while in early Greek, the letter *B* faced to the left, as it had done in Semitic, later on, it faced to the right. In this case, the change in letter orientation appears to be connected with a change in the direction of writing: While the Semitic languages were written from right to left (and still are), the Greek alphabet soon changed to being written from left to right. (At an intermediate stage, the direction of writing shifted in alternate lines. Starting, say, from the right in the first line and ending on the left, the writer continued at the left side of the next line and went to the right, much as one plows furrows with a team of oxen. The technical term for this writing therefore is BOUSTROPHEDON, lit. 'in the manner of oxen turning'.)

Though the starting point for the development of a full alphabet can be characterized as "sheer dumb luck", the alphabet turned out extremely useful for Greek and other Indo-European languages. The word structure of Indo-European is quite different from Semitic: Vowels are not just modifiers of essentially consonantal roots, but may be primary meaning carriers, as in Engl. *a*, or Gk. *eî*, pronounced [ē], 'you (sing.) are'. A purely consonantal script would find it very difficult to express structures of this type.

2.6. A note on the further fate of the alphabet

From the Greeks, specifically from West Greek dialects, the alphabet spread to Italy. One of the languages for which it came to be used early was Etruscan. In the process, certain changes took place in the value of individual letters, much as what happened in the earlier adoption of the Phoenician writing system by the Greeks, except that the alphabetic character of the system remained unchanged. One of the modifications was the use of the letter *gamma* to designate the voiceless velar stop, [k], presumably because Etruscan made no distinction between voiced [g] and voiceless [k].

As the Romans adopted the alphabet from the Etruscans, they introduced further modifications. Some of these were motivated by considerations of writing ease, others by the structure of their own language, Latin. One change, introduced only after some time, was "splitting" the original letter *gamma* into two – C (phonetically [k]) and G (= [g]) with an added stroke – because, unlike Etruscan, Latin did make a distinction between voiceless [k] and voiced [g]. (See Illustration 27.) Another innovation resulted from the fact that Latin had a sound *f* that was absent in Greek and therefore lacked a corresponding character in the Greek alphabet. At the same time, West Greek dialects had a combination FH = *wh*, designating a sound combination absent in Latin. And just as Engl. *wh* can sound similar to *f* to speakers lacking this sound combination, so the Romans identified FH = *wh* with their own *f* and used it to transcribe that sound. But since F occurred only in combination with H, the latter symbol was soon felt to be redundant, and F was used by itself to designate *f*. In both of these developments we see the same ingenuity at work as in earlier Semitic ⊟ vs. ⊒ or early Greek Y vs. ⅂.

Other (direct or indirect) offshoots of the Greek alphabet include the runic writing system (see Illustration 28), and the Cyrillic alphabet. The runic alphabet, usually named *futhark* after its first six letters, is found in early Germanic inscriptions from the early A.D. period to at least the eighth century. Eventually it gave way to the Roman alphabet, but some of its characters, especially the single letter *þ* for the sound designated in Modern English by *th*, was retained in many of the early Germanic scripts and is still used in Modern Icelandic.

Early Roman reports tell us that the Germanic people used runes inscribed on small wooden chips or tablets for oracular purposes, and great magical powers were commonly ascribed to the runes. (On this matter see the discussion below on the early Irish Ogham script.) But the extant inscriptions are on stone or metal, and, to the extent that they are complete or that we can interpret them, they convey rather mundane messages. For instance, one of the most celebrated inscriptions, found on a golden drinking horn, states (in

f   u   th   a   r   k   g   w

h   n   i   y   E   p   z   s

t   b   e   m   l   ng   o   d

Illustration 28. Older Germanic runes

transcription): *ek hlewagastiz holitijaz* (or *holtingaz*) *horna tawido*, which translates as 'I, Hlewagasti of Holt (or: Holting) made the horn'.

There must, however, be something to the Roman reports about the use of runes on wood. First, this would explain the **shape** of the runes. Observant readers may have noticed that only vertical or diagonal strokes are used in runic writing; there are no horizontal strokes. If we assume that runes commonly were written on wood, we can explain this peculiarity: Vertical or diagonal strokes that cut through the wood grain leave marks that remain legibible, while horizontal strokes, along with the grain of the wood, are quickly filled up again and become invisible. Note further that the Germanic words for 'book', including Engl. *book* and Germ. *Buch*, are related to the word for 'beech tree'; see especially the German word for 'beech tree', *Buche*. To this must be added the German word for 'letter, writing symbol', *Buchstabe*, which literally means 'book staff' (or even 'beech staff'). The fact that no early wooden inscriptions have been preserved can be explained by the fact that wood is more perishable than metal and stone.

The Cyrillic alphabet is said to have been developed by the great Slavic Apostles, Cyril and Methodius, with the specific idea of devising an alphabet that adequately transcribes all the distinctive sounds of Slavic. Actually, there is some question as to whether Cyril and Methodius really invented the Cyrillic alphabet. Scholars now believe that they invented a similar alphabet, called Glagolitic, which was in early use among the Southern Slavs. Whatever the details, however, the creator or creators of the Cyrillic alphabet exhibited the same ingenuity as the Greek and Semitic peoples before them. For instance, the Greek letter B, at this point probably pronounced as a bilabial fricative [β], was split into two letters, Б and В, to designate the two distinctive sounds *b* and *v*, respectively. The writing system betrays its origin

from the major literary tradition of Greek in which the letter *H* was used for
ē, by using a symbol derived from it as a vowel sign – И designating [i].
(The actual shape has changed slightly to differentiate this letter from the
sign H, evidently a later development of earlier N, used to designate [n].)

Just as the Roman alphabet became the common currency of the part of
medieval Europe that embraced Roman Catholicism, so the Cyrillic alphabet
became the property of the more eastern, mainly Slavic, parts of Europe
that adhered to the Eastern Orthodox variety of Christianity. Most important
was its use in Russia, for through Russian domination over a large variety
of non-Slavic peoples it has come to be used for the languages of many of
these peoples, too – as usual, with appropriate modifications in response to
linguistic differences.

There are many other offshoots of the Greek and Roman alphabets. One
of these is the Morse Code which substitutes different sequences of dots
and dashes (or short and long beeps) for the letters of the alphabet, as in
$\cdots - - - \cdots = \text{SOS}$.

A curious parallel is found in the Ogham script of very early Irish texts.
Here lines of different lengths and numbers are drawn in one direction or another at the edge of a stone memorial (or across the edge); see Illustration 29.
Scholars of writing are agreed that in principle, the symbols are a code version of the Roman alphabet, very much in the same way as the Morse Code.
What is less clear is the principle for the fact that the Ogham characters
are arranged in a different order from the traditional Roman alphabet. One
intriguing explanation starts with the observation that the traditional names
of the letters originally are tree names. In the early Irish law texts, trees are
divided into four classes which can be glossed as 'ordinary trees', 'chieftain
trees', 'shrub trees', and 'bramble trees'. Interestingly, the letter names in the
four groups of the Ogham alphabet follow the same system of classification,
the first group having names of the ordinary tree family, the second of the
chieftain tree family, and so on.

It is tempting to speculate that the use of tree names for letter names is a
cultural parallel to the early Germanic use of wood for runic writing and of
terms derived from the notion 'beech tree' to refer to books and even letters.
In fact, the parallel can be extended further.

In the later, specifically Scandinavian period of runic writing, there existed
an alternative system of "feather runes" as in Illustration 30 below. In this
case we can discern a clear motivation for the code: Like the Ogham alphabet,
the runic alphabet is divided into groups. In early Germanic, these are the
three rows of characters in Illustration 28 above. (In the later, Scandinavian
system, the number of characters in each row has changed; but the principle

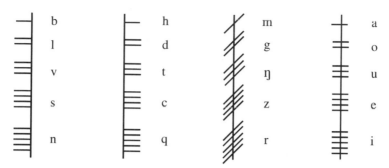

Illustration 29. The Ogham alphabet

'Row 1, letter 3':   Þ = þ   'Row 2, letter 1':   Ͱ = h

Illustration 30. Scandinavian "feather runes"

of letter groups remains.) Now, the number of left branches of feather runes indicates the letter group in the runic alphabet, the number of right branches, the position of the letter within that group.

The similarities between feather runes and Ogham symbols are remarkable enough to suggest that one of the systems may have been influenced by the other. And the fact that the feather runes can be clearly motivated as a code based on an ordered alphabet makes it likely that the Irish Ogham symbols arose in a similar fashion, except that in this case the underlying alphabet is not independently attested.

There is much independent evidence to indicate cultural exchange between early Celtic and Germanic, with Celtic generally the donor and Germanic the receiver (see Chapter 8, §2 for an example). One might suspect that the parallel between Ogham symbols and feather runes owes it origin to the same early Celtic influence on Germanic. However, chronological and geographical considerations make it difficult to substantiate this view. Perhaps the problem lies in the fact that we are dealing with a later, more regionally limited phenomenon, not with an instance of the above-mentioned early interaction between all of Celtic and all of Germanic. In this regard, note the use of the term *rūn-* both in early Irish and in Germanic – and only in these languages – to refer to secret wisdom that can be conveyed by Ogham or runic characters.

In Germanic the meaning of the term is further extended to refer to the characters themselves.

Note, incidentally, that here we do have evidence in traditional lore that the runes were associated with magic. But that magic may well be nothing more remarkable than the *glamour* of this book's introductory chapter – the power attributed to literacy in a society where writing was limited to a chosen few.

So far, we only have traced the history of the Greek and Roman CAPITAL letters. LOWER-CASE letters are a later development and seem to have first arisen in cursive writing. The original form of many of the letters required several strokes of the pen (or whatever other writing instrument was used). Thus, three strokes were needed for the letter A. Cursive writing in general favors fewer strokes. Illustration 31 shows how replacing the three strokes needed for the letter A by one gave rise to the shape of the letter which we now classify as lower case. Similarly, replacing the two strokes needed to write the letter T led to the (lower-case) "Insular" form of *t*, found in medieval English and still used in Gaelic.

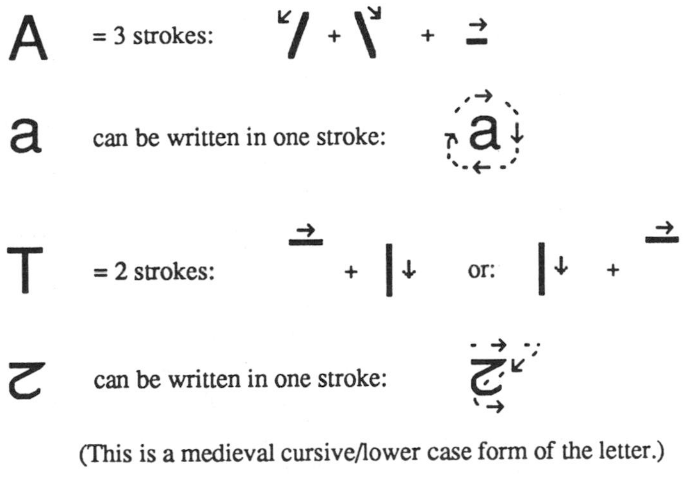

(This is a medieval cursive/lower case form of the letter.)

Illustration 31. Development of lower-case, cursive letters

Designating these early cursive letters as lower case actually required a further step. It seems that the continued use of the original letter forms in more important public inscriptions led to the reinterpretation of these letters as "more important", too. Consequently, the cursive letters were reinterpreted as less important. By mixing the two types of letters, it was then possible to indicate the importance of some words or even whole passages by writing

them with the "more important" letters or, to make things easier, by just let-
ting them begin with one of these letters. And once the distinction between
capital and lower-case letters was introduced, it was possible to put the distinction to new uses, such as the English use of capitals to indicate proper
names. (Note incidentally that the distinction between capital and lower-case
letters is by no means universal; many writing systems, such as the indigenous
systems of South Asia, do not make it.)

3. The decipherment of ancient scripts

While the literary traditions of Arabic, Hebrew, Greek, and Latin have to
some extent survived to the present day, together with their writing systems,
the scripts of ancient Mesopotamia, Persia, and Egypt, as well as many others
around the world, died out together with the cultures that employed them.
Our knowledge of these scripts results from the work of many scholars who
succeeded in deciphering them. (As indicated earlier, the Indus Valley script
has not yet been successfully deciphered, and the situation is similar for many
others.)

Deciphering a script draws on techniques very similar to code breaking.
And like code breaking, it requires some idea of what is being expressed. It
also helps to know something about the language expressed by the writing
system. But even without this information, it is possible to make certain
guesses on the nature of the writing system, and these may help in the ultimate
decipherment.

Given even relatively small amounts of texts, it is relatively easy to determine whether a script is logographic, a syllabary, or alphabetic. Alphabetic
scripts usually do not have more than fifty different symbols; syllabaries may
range from about thirty to about 150; logographic systems tend to have thousands of characters. However, more specific clues are needed to identify the
precise values of the individual characters.

3.1. The decipherment of the cuneiform scripts
The first of the ancient scripts to be deciphered was that of Old Persian.
For a long time, travelers had returned with reports about inscriptions found
in the ruins of the ancient Persian empire and about great inscriptions on
isolated rocks from the same era. The temptation was great to attribute them
to the rulers of that empire, whose names were familiar from Greek sources:

Darius, Xerxes, Cyrus, and Artaxerxes. However, the cuneiform script of the inscriptions was uninterpretable.

The first steps in the direction of decipherment were made in 1788 by the German scholar Carsten Niebuhr and, building on his findings, in 1802 by the Danish scholar Frederik Münter. Their work suggested that the great inscriptions contained three parallel texts, in three different writing systems: While all of them were in cuneiform, the number of discrete symbols in the first text was small enough to suggest an alphabetic system; that in the second was compatible with a syllabary; while the third text had to be logographic. Münter also plausibly argued that the first text had to be in the language of the Persian empire, (Old) Persian, and must therefore be relatively close to Avestan, the only ancient Iranian language known at that time. Finally, he suggested that certain recurring symbol sequences mean 'king' and 'king of kings'. Most of these suggestions turned out to be accurate, except for the suggestion that the first text was alphabetic. We now know that it is written in the Old Persian syllabary given in Illustration 24.

The first actual decipherment of the Old Persian script was accomplished in the same year as Münter's work, 1802, by Georg Friedrich Grotefend, a German high school teacher with virtually no knowledge of Avestan or other relevant languages, but with a lot of experience in breaking secret scripts. His initial assumptions about the nature of the text were very similar to those of Niebuhr and Münter. Beyond that, he suggested specific readings for the first text, not only of titles like 'king' and 'king of kings', but also of the names of the kings. Many details of his readings had to be revised. For instance, like Münter, Grotefend assumed that the Old Persian text was written in an alphabet; he therefore analyzed the sequence of symbols referring to Xerxes as *xšharša*, instead of the correct syllabic *xa-ša-ya-a-ra-ša-a* (see Illustration 23 above). Nevertheless, his work opened the door for the successful interpretation of the Old Persian inscriptions, which was undertaken by an international succession of scholars, including Rasmus Rask (of Denmark), Christian Lassen (of Germany), Henry Rawlinson (of Britain), and Jules Oppert (of France).

Excavations in Assyria, undertaken in the early forties of the nineteenth century, yielded a large number of inscriptions whose writing could be identified as identical to the third text of the great inscriptions of ancient Persia. Since the message of these inscriptions had by now been sufficiently identified in the Old Persian portions of the royal Persian inscriptions, the task of deciphering the script was made easier. Still, it took nearly a decade before the British scholar Rawlinson determined that the symbols of the script could have a broad range of values (see Illustration 20 above) and that the texts could be interpreted under the assumption that they were in a Semitic language.

Scholars like Rawlinson further discovered that in addition to the ancient Semitic language(s) expressed in these inscriptions, there was a layer of vocabulary that belonged to a very different language. This language came to be identified as Sumerian. And it became possible to learn more about this language from a somewhat unexpected source: As noted earlier, reading and writing in ancient Mesopotamia meant being literate in Sumerian, as well as in Assyrian or Babylonian. In order to facilitate the learning of Sumerian, lists of grammatical paradigms, dictionaries, and bilingual Sumerian-Babylonian texts had been composed. As fragments of these documents became available, the knowledge of Sumerian increased; and several grammars of Sumerian are now available.

In the early part of this century, excavations near Ankara (Turkey) led to the discovery of the Hittite state archives which yielded a large number of written records. The script used in these documents was the same as that employed for Assyrian, Babylonian, and Sumerian. But large portions of the text clearly presented a different language – Hittite. The credit for having successfully identified this language as Indo-European goes to the Czech scholar Bedřich Hrozný, who in 1915, during the First World War, published a paper on the "Solution of the Hittite problem" in the journal of the German Oriental Society. The passage that was instrumental in this finding is said to have been the following:

> *nu* NINDA-*an e-iz-za-at-te-ni wa-a-tar-ma e-ku-ut-te-ni*

Drawing on his experience with the often clumsy nature of cuneiform syllabary writing, Hrozný was able to interpret the text as spelling out the message

> *nu* NINDA*n ezzatteni watar-ma ekutteni*

Only one word in this passage actually was known, the logogram NINDA 'bread'. However, it stood to reason that 'bread' is 'eaten' and that therefore there might be a word meaning 'eat' in this passage, occurring near the word for 'bread'. Of the two words flanking NINDA, *ezzatteni* contained an element *ezz-* [ets-] which looked amazingly similar to the Indo-European root for 'eat', **ed-* found in Lat. *edō* 'I eat', as well as in Engl. *eat*. Once this identification had been made, it became possible to interpret nearly all the other elements of the sentence as Indo-European as well. Thus, the initial *nu* could be identified with **nu*, the word for 'now' found widely in the Indo-European languages, including Engl. *now*. Similarly, *watar* could be identified with Engl. *water* and its cognates in the other Indo-European languages. Even the *eku-* of the last word can be identified as the element found in the Latin word *ēbrius* 'drunk', the source of the modern English borrowing *inebriated*. Given these identifications, then, it was possible to give a perfectly sensible interpretation to the hitherto nearly incomprehensible passage as meaning

'Now you eat bread, and you will drink water'

As in the case of Grotefend's decipherment of Old Persian, many of Hrozny's interpretations have since been revised. But his identification of Hittite as Indo-European has proved to be correct.

3.2. The decipherment of ancient Egyptian

In 1799, during Napoleon's expedition into Egypt, workmen digging fortifications near Rosetta came across a stone bearing inscriptions in three different scripts. The lowest one of these was in a language well-known to scholars: Greek. The topmost was in hieroglyphic characters, a writing system which from ancient times had been known as the script of ancient Egypt and which prominently figured on virtually all of the archaeological remains. (The script in the middle turned out to be a cursive variant of the hieroglyphs; its decipherment played a less important role than that of the hieroglyphs and the script is therefore ignored in the following discussion.)

Early attempts at interpreting the hieroglyphic texts operated under the assumption that their script was ideographic, expressing in pictures complex philosophical ideas; and fantastic interpretations were proposed which, in hindsight, were nothing short of outrageous. At this point it became clear that the inscription found by Napoleon's workmen, called the Rosetta Stone, provided the key to deciphering the hieroglyphs, much as the Old Persian inscriptions were the key for the decipherment of the cuneiform script of Mesopotamia.

The Greek text of the Rosetta Stone contained a number of well-known names, including *Ptolemaios* (= Ptolemy) and *Alexandros* (= Alexander). Some of these could be identified in the hieroglyphic part of the inscription. However, not much else could be done, especially since the hieroglyphic portion had been heavily damaged. Along the way, however, scholars identified Coptic, a language now surviving as a liturgical language among Egyptian Christians, as a late descendant of Egyptian. Drawing on such earlier work, a young Frenchman, François Champollion, who at the age of eleven had decided to become the decipherer of the hieroglyphs, succeeded in doing so in a series of publications beginning in 1813. By demonstrating that certain suffixal elements (e.g. *-f* 'he', *-s* 'she') in the hieroglyphic text recurred in

contexts where the Greek text had personal pronouns, he was able to identify the meanings of these elements. This made it possible to identify these
elements with Coptic suffixes of similar meaning and thus to determine an
approximate pronunciation. As a consequence, the number of symbols with
identifiable values increased, and substituting the same values in other passages made it possible to read additional words. Along this route, then, he was
able in 1822 and 1824 to propose a decipherment of the hieroglyphs which,
in spite of later revisions in detail, made it possible to read the hieroglyphs
of ancient Egypt and to understand the nature of the writing system.

3.3. Other decipherments

A number of other writing systems of the ancient Near East and neighboring
areas, as well as the script of the Mayan kingdoms of Meso-America have
been deciphered by employing similar methods. In the ancient world, these
include Elamite, the language of the non-Indo-European predecessors of the
ancient Persian rulers, as well Hieroglyphic Luwian and a number of other
languages more or less closely related to Hittite.

The perhaps most amazing decipherment, in 1952, led to the discovery
that centuries before the appearance of alphabetic writing in ancient Greece,
Greek had been written in a very different, syllabic script called "Linear B".
In 1900, the British archaeologist Arthur Evans had discovered in Knossos,
on the island of Crete, the remains of the archives of the Minoan civilization.
In the documents found there, Evans was able to distinguish three phases:
(i) An early stage (about 2000–1600 B.C.) using a pictorial writing system;
(ii) a later stage partly overlapping with the preceding one (about 1700–1550
B.C.) in which the characters were simplified to their barest outlines, whence
the name Linear A; and (iii) a third variety, Linear B, also starting around
1700 B.C., whose characters, though similar to Linear A, differed in many
important details. Linear B died out around the twelfth century B.C., together
with the Minoan civilization, apparently under the onslaught of newcomers.
Although possibly Greeks too, the new arrivals did not take over the script
they encountered. As a consequence, the Greeks returned to illiteracy for
about 500 years, until contact with the Phoenicians reintroduced writing (see
§ 2.5 above).

The decipherment of Linear B and the identification of its language as an
early, regional form of Greek came as a great surprise even to the decipherers.
The common opinion had favored just about any language other than Greek,
including Etruscan or even some ancient relative of Basque. There was little
motivation for looking to Greek as a possible key to breaking the code.
Things were made even more difficult by the fact that not even a trace of

a bilingual text could be found. Only one thing was certain: The number of distinct characters was too large for the script to be alphabetic, and too small to be logographic; it had to be a syllabary. Attempts were made to use the computers then available to help in breaking the code: Exhaustive lists of symbols were established, as well as of the various combinations into which they entered. It was possible to show that certain symbol groups recurred, suggesting possible lexical units. Moreover, some symbol groups recurred only partially, with different symbols following them under what seemed to be syntactically different conditions. This suggested that the language of Linear B had a system of roots followed by something like inflectional endings. In addition, attempts were made to randomly assign different phonetic values to different symbols and to examine whether the resulting structures bore any resemblances to forms of known languages.

The breakthrough came in 1952 when a British architect and amateur linguist, Michael Ventris, was able to demonstrate that certain phonetic substitutions yielded results which could be read as place names in ancient Crete, such as *ko-no-so* which would be a rather standard way of spelling the name *Knossos* (ancient Greek *Knōsós*) in a syllabary. Substituting the same phonetic values in other contexts made it possible to read other words, and slowly it became clear that these words – and their structure – did not just sound similar to place names and other words of ancient Greek, they **were** ancient Greek. For instance, beside *ko-no-so*, a putative adjective form of the same word *ko-no-si-jo* 'of Knossos' could be identified, and this corresponded magnificently to the Greek adjective *Knōsío-*.

As in all the other decipherments, further work suggested modifications of Ventris's original interpretations. But again, as in the other successful decipherments, the basic breakthrough had been made.

As a postscript it might be mentioned that attempts to decipher Linear A by means of the same methods so far have not yielded any satisfactory results. One scholar, Cyrus Gordon, claims that Linear A was used to write a Semitic language; but his claim does not seem to have been accepted so far in the scholarly community. Perhaps the language written in that script has left no known descendants. The situation is similar for many other scripts, ancient and relatively modern, including the script of the ancient Indus Valley civilization, which like Linear A has so far resisted satisfactory decipherment, in spite of repeated claims by different scholars that they have been able to break the code. (The problem with such claims is that they are usually subscribed to only by those who propose them.)

The most recent breakthrough, the decipherment of the Mayan script, is important for a number of reasons. First, it took place in the face of preconceived notions that, except for numerical information, largely of calendrical and astronomical nature, the Mayan hieroglyphs did not present real writing, but were ideographic, expressing complex ideas in picture form, much like the pictorial representation in Illustration 4 above. These preconceptions, similar to pre-decipherment views on the Egyptian hieroglyphs, had the backing of the most authorative scholars in the field, who ostracized and ridiculed occasional attempts (generally by amateurs or linguists) at interpreting the Mayan hieroglyphs as representing genuine writing. Underlying this attitude were two factors: One was the theory by the then greatest authority on writing, the American scholar I. J. Gelb, that true writing only originated once, in the Ancient Near East, and that all other forms of writing spread from this original source through diffusion. (As Mayan scholars realized, there was no credible evidence for cultural diffusion from Eurasia to Meso-America.) The second factor, closely allied to the first, was a Eurocentric, or more correctly "Old-World-centric" view which linked the development of writing to "civilization", which believed "primitive" people only to be able to imitate the writing of "civilized" people, and which – of course – considered the indigenous peoples of the Americas to be "primitive" compared to the "civilized" people of the "Old World" of Eurasia and Northern Africa.

The credit for having laid a solid foundation for the eventual decipherment of the Mayan script goes to a 1952 article by the Russian scholar Yu. V. Knorosov who showed that like the traditional scripts of the Ancient Near East and Egypt, Mayan writing represented a mixed code with logographic characters with or without phonetic indicators as well as syllabic signs; see Illustration 19 above. Although many details still need to be worked out, a loosely organized international team of linguists, archaeologists, and specialists in writing systems has since then succeeded in unraveling many of the mysteries of Mayan writing and, in the process, has shown that the Mayan hieroglyphs are indeed true writing, not just a quaint, "primitive" ideographic code. Moreover, although much of the information conveyed by Mayan writing is indeed of calendrical and astronomical nature, there are also reports of historical events and personalities. Finally, recent research suggests that Mayan writing continues an older tradition of the Olmecs, an earlier Meso-American civilization probably speaking a different language.

The significance of the Mayan decipherment is obvious: First, it casts serious doubts on such preconceived notions as "Old World" = "civilized" vs. "New World" = "primitive". Clearly, the development of advanced civilizations which find it useful to develop writing is possible among ALL human beings, in ALL areas of the world. (At the same time, it does seem to be true that a certain advancement in civilization is necessary for writing to develop. As a consequence, the Mayans and Olmecs had writing; other indigenous peoples of the Americas did not.) Secondly, the fact that the Olmecs and Mayans evidently developed true writing independently from the "Old World" has brought about serious rethinking about the development of writing in the "Old World": Whereas Gelb had argued for a single origination of writing, in ancient Sumer, and for diffusion of writing from Sumer to the rest of Eurasia and North Africa, we now have to admit the possibility that writing originated independently, in a number of different societies, as these societies developed economic, social, and cultural structures that were conducive to the development of writing as a more effective means of record keeping and communication.

4. The phonetic interpretation of written records

One of the questions that arises in dealing with ancient scripts is "How do we know how the symbols of this system were pronounced?" In fact, given the vagaries of English spelling (see Chapter 1, § 5), we might have great doubts as to whether it would ever be possible to assign consistent – or even inconsistent – phonetic values to written symbols. Fortunately, many of the "inconsistent" English spellings are reflexes of earlier linguistic stages. (Compare the initial *k* of words like *knight*, or the *gh* of the same word, both of which reflect sounds – [k] and [x] – that were actually pronounced in earlier English.) In the earliest stages of writing in a particular language, there is no earlier history which might motivate such historical spellings. In this regard, at least, early writing systems tend to be free of the inconsistencies of languages like English.

Even for modern English, however, it would be possible to come up with pretty good phonetic interpretations – if, say, as the result of some major disaster, English had died out and a scholar of the twenty-third century were trying to decipher documents written in English, dug up from the ruins of our society. In fact, putting ourselves into the position of that scholar may serve to demonstrate how people go about interpreting the phonetic values of ancient scripts.

4.1. Determining the nature of the script
Investigators would very quickly be able to determine that there are two different sets of written characters in English, which rarely combine with

each other. On one hand there are characters like *b, r, e*, on the other, *1, 2, 3*, as well as *$, £*, etc. The fact that members of the set *1, 2, 3* appear consecutively at the top or bottom of pages would make it easy to recognize these as logographs designating numerals. And the fact that symbols like *$* and *£* combine mainly with these numerals suggests that these symbols are logographs, too, referring to some kind of "operators" or "classifiers" related to the numerals.

These and other considerations would suggest that only the members of the set *b, r, e*, etc. qualify as writing symbols. Moreover, the limited number of characters would suggest that the writing is alphabetic.

Within the set of writing symbols, it would be possible to isolate a subset *e, a, i, u, o* and another subset *s, d, r, t*, etc., which differ from each other in terms of their combinability: Members of the second set can enter into more complex combinations (such as *str, sts, rts*), while *e, a, i, u, o* are more limited in their combinations (we find *ei, ie, ai, ia, oi, io*, etc., but combinations like *eia* or *oae* would be difficult, if not impossible to locate). A scholar familiar with general tendencies in linguistic structure would be able to conclude from this and other, similar information that the set *e, a, i, u, o* designates vowels, while the set *s, d, r, t*, etc. characterizes consonants. Moreover, an observant investigator would note that one letter, *y*, sometimes behaves like a vowel (as in *my*), and sometimes as a consonant (as in *your*).

4.2. Beginning to crack the code

The major task, now, would be to assign specific values to the vowels and consonants of the script. And this is where things get to be much more difficult. The fact that across the different human languages, dentals tend to be the most frequent consonants may suggest that the most frequent English consonants, *s, d, r*, and *t*, are dentals. Perhaps it would be possible to make a few similar guesses concerning other sets of symbols. But this still leaves open the question of which consonant symbol designates which consonant, not to speak of the values of the vowel symbols. The fact that the same sounds may be spelled in many different ways in English would only add to the problems faced by the investigator.

A way to deal with the latter problem is to look for evidence that might establish that certain spellings, though using different symbols, refer to the same sounds. One area of evidence helpful in this regard consists of misspellings or variant spellings, such as *nite* (for *night*), *insure* beside *ensure*, *plough* beside *plow*.

Another area which an experienced investigator might look to is poetic language, which frequently draws on phonetic similarities or identities as the foundation for creating poetic lines. In English, poetic texts are relatively easily isolated, since each line is treated as if it were a paragraph. Moreover, even cursory examination would show that in many poetic texts, the words at the end of neighboring lines (or of alternate lines) tend to end in the same spelling. This would suggest that English uses the principle of end rhyme. If in poetic texts we find not only end rhymes like *ring : king*, but also *rite : night* etc., this evidence would provide further support, in addition to variant spellings like *night : nite*, for the phonetic equivalence of the spellings *ite* and *ight*, at least in some words. And given enough patience or a good enough computer, it would be possible to establish a large set of such "equivalent" spellings.

Of course, English poetry offers occasional examples of "eye rhymes", words that are permitted to rhyme because they are spelled the same, even though sounding different; e.g. *bomb : womb : comb*. But the special nature of these rhymes can be established by noting that, say, *womb* elsewhere rhymes with *groom, doom, bloom*, etc., while *comb* rhymes with *home, gnome*, etc.; but *groom* etc. cannot rhyme with *home* etc.

In this manner it is possible to establish sets of letter combinations likely to express the same pronunciation and to contrast them with other sets with different pronunciation. However, this still leaves open the exact pronunciations expressed by these spellings.

4.3. Establishing phonetic values

To more firmly establish the phonetic identity of given spellings it is necessary to draw on evidence beyond the writing system and its nature. Such evidence may come from at least two types of sources.

We may find in our texts statements by indigenous grammarians about the nature of their sound system and the relationship between sound and spelling. Statements of this sort may be highly accurate, but they may also be quite vague and unhelpful. In English, for instance, depending on the texts we might find, the difference between the vowels in *bit* and *bite* might be described phonetically accurately as [ɪ] vs. [ay] or in a phonetically misleading manner as "short *i*" vs. "long *i*". The situation is similar in the pre-modern world. On one hand are the Sanskrit phoneticians who made very detailed and accurate phonetic observations and thus were able to distinguish consonants such as *b, bh* as voiced from voiceless consonants such as *p, ph*. On the other hand there is the traditional western approach, where for instance in German, *b, d, g* are called "soft" vs. "hard" *p, t, k*, without any phonetically verifiable definition of these terms.

The investigator may be lucky enough to come across modern English texts that provide an accurate description, not just of the sound system, but also of the many different ways in which the sounds of that system are spelled. But what if such texts have not survived or if the quality of the texts that have survived is not very high?

In many cases, another approach is available by examining borrowings: For instance Engl. *strike* has been borrowed as *Streik* in German and as στραϊκ (= *straik*) in Greek. Now, in both languages, the borrowed words are spelled with an orthographic diphthong, *ei* in German and *ai* in Greek (where it is specifically characterized as a diphthong by the double dot over the *i*). Evidence of this sort suggests that Engl. *strike* is pronounced with a diphthong. Given enough patience it would further be possible to determine that in one or more of the borrowing languages the "fit" between spelling and pronunciation is much closer than in English. If in addition one or more of the languages offers texts by indigenous grammarians that provide reliable information on their sound system and its relation to spelling, the investigator can begin to assign specific phonetic values to particular English spellings. For instance, if it can be determined that German *ei* regularly spells a diphthong [ay], then the spelling *Streik* suggests that Engl *strike* is pronounced with a similar diphthong, [ay].

In this way, a good amount of knowledge about the pronunciation of written records may be gained. However, some details can be known only in those rare cases where indigenous grammarians' description are very meticulous and reliable. Elsewhere we may well miss out on such fine details as whether a *t* is really dental (as in French or Spanish), or post-dental (as in English).

More than that, a fair number of cases remain where even the experts cannot agree on the phonetic interpretation of certain letters or letter combinations. This is the case, for instance, for the Old English "digraphs", *eo, ea,* etc., which by some are claimed to have been diphthongs, by others to have been monophthongs with a phonetic value intermediate between the sounds normally designated in Old English by the individual vowel letters. Fortunately, such cases of uncertainty are rather rare in most of the early Indo-European languages, which form the basis for the most extensive – and intensive – study of linguistic change. Moreover, the occasional cases of uncertainty cause no major difficulties – as long as we do not draw on them to build grandiose theories about the nature of language change.

5. Writing in the rest of the world

Up to this point, we have been focusing mainly on writing systems in the Middle East and Europe, though there have been references to writing elsewhere, especially to the Mayan hieroglyphs and the significance of their decipherment for theorics on the origin of writing. Writing, however, has a much wider distribution, both in time and in space; examining the development of writing elsewhere in the world therefore can provide a valuable balance.

In particular, writing has a long history in East Asia, where there are three major writing traditions: Chinese, Japanese, and Korean. The logographic Chinese system and the phonetically-based Korean system present characteristics that allow them to be called unique; they are therefore discussed in some detail. The Japanese system, on the other hand, is not examined here, since in effect it combines the two different approaches of Chinese and Korean. The East Asian systems we examine confirm some of the principles of the development of writing systems that we have seen before, but they also provide new insights.

In addition, a brief look at some indigenous writing systems in America and Africa can shed important light on how such systems can emerge.

5.1. The Chinese system

Chinese writing is the oldest known system in East Asia, appearing in the fourteenth century B.C., during the late Shang dynasty, with a few small texts coming from slightly earlier periods. The system used at the time of first attestation is already considerably elaborated, suggesting an extended period of earlier development which, depending on one's estimate, may have lasted for 400 to 700 years.

The earliest Chinese writing is found in so-called oracle texts, responses by oracular interpreters to questions posed about future events (similar to our horoscopes). Most of the texts were written on animal bones and tortoise shells.

The writing system at that stage bears strong similarities to the early systems of the Near East. Pictorial symbols are used as logographs, with the possible addition of phonetic and semantic indicators. And as in ancient Mesopotamia, the shape of the symbols, traditionally called "characters", changed over time, in response to the materials that were used for writing. Illustration 32 gives an example of an early stage of these changes. The change in letter shape was greatly accelerated once brush and ink came to be used. It has been estimated that one cannot guess the meaning of a single

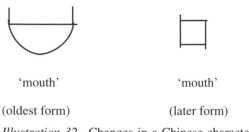

'mouth'   'mouth'

(oldest form)   (later form)

Illustration 32. Changes in a Chinese character

modern character from its form, in contrast to the transparent relation between meaning and form in Ancient Chinese. In this respect, too, the development of Chinese writing is similar to that in the Ancient Near East and its later abjad and alphabetic successors.

But as anyone familiar with Chinese can readily tell, in one important respect Chinese writing followed a very different course from the writing systems farther west. Even to the present day, Chinese writing has remained essentially logographic (with the possible addition of phonetic and semantic indicators). The main reason for this different development also is quite obvious to anyone who has any familiarity with Chinese. As the common wisdom goes, Chinese is a "monosyllabic language", that is, most Chinese words and other meaningful elements consist of just one syllable. With few exceptions, then, words are syllables – and syllables are words. In contrast to other languages, therefore, it makes no sense in Chinese to distinguish between word symbols (logographs) and syllabic symbols; there is no difference to begin with. Since the overall structure of Chinese has remained pretty much the same as it was in ancient times, it is not surprising that the writing system has retained its essentially logographic nature to the present day. In fact, Chinese writing is the only major logographic system now in use, with a set of between 1,850 and 4,000 distinct characters.

Using a logographic system with so many different symbols has definite disadvantages in the modern world. For instance, for telegraphic transmissions, a special numerical code had to be devised for the representation of each graph, and Chinese typewriters were enormously complex, and therefore slow and clumsy to use. The twentieth century therefore has seen several attempts to radically reform Chinese writing by adopting, and adapting, the Roman alphabet of the west.

The efforts at introducing an alphabetic system, however, have not succeeded. One reason is that logography is felt to be an integral part of Chinese culture and identity. But there are other, more practical reasons as well.

The most important practical reason is that the logographic system has the advantage of bridging gaps of communication within Chinese: Although it is customary to speak of "the" Chinese language, in fact there are numerous Chinese languages (often, but erroneously, called dialects) which in their spoken form are mutually unintelligible. Use of a common logographic system makes it possible for these speakers to communicate in writing, no matter how differently they may pronounce the characters. As a parallel in societies with alphabetic writing, compare the use of numerical symbols, such as 2, which can be read by anyone, no matter whether the symbol is pronounced [tū] (English), [dü] (Albanian), [kaksi] (Finnish), [wili] (Swahili), or [iki] (Turkish).

In fact, the use of Chinese writing to communicate across different languages is not limited to Chinese; speakers of many other East Asian languages employ Chinese characters for the same purposes, including the Japanese and the (South) Koreans. This is because Chinese writing spread far beyond its original boundaries, along with many other aspects of Chinese culture and civilization, as well as Chinese words. Even where different writing systems developed, they did so under the influence of Chinese writing and generally came to coexist with Chinese characters which continued to be used for a massive number of words borrowed from Chinese.

5.2. Writing in Korea

The most striking case in point is Korean. From about 600 A.D., the people of Korea began to use an adaptation of the Chinese writing system to write their own language. Korean, however, is a language very different from Chinese. Whereas Chinese is "monosyllabic", Korean words tend to be quite complex, with roots followed by strings of suffixes. Chinese logography was thus not particularly well suited for writing Korean, although South Koreans still use it to write Chinese words borrowed into Korean. To write native Korean words, Chinese writing has generally given way to a system designed specifically for Korean by an enlightened monarch, King Sejong, who ruled in Korea from 1418 until 1450. (In present-day North Korea, the Korean writing system is even used for words of Chinese origin.)

The system that King Sejong invented (or perhaps, had a committee of scholars invent under his direction) was completed in 1444 and has come to be called Han'gǔl (meaning 'great script'). In principle it is an alphabet, with 28 letters, but it differs from ordinary alphabets in its organization. There are no separate symbols for all of the distinctive sounds of the language. Rather, there is a set of consonantal and vocalic "base symbols", and a set of phonetically based diacritics that differentiate, or "derive", the symbols for other sounds from these base symbols. For example, Korean has a set of "lax" stops (produced with relatively reduced muscle-tension), which can be somewhat imperfectly transcribed as [t], [č], etc., and a corresponding set of aspirated "tense" stops (produced with relatively greater muscle tension), such as [tʰ] or [čʰ]. Han'gŭl base symbols are used to represent the lax stops, while the tense stops are written by modifying the corresponding base symbols by means of a superscript horizontal line (which in the case of [tʰ] is connected to the base symbol by a vertical); see Illustration 33.

ㄷ　　ㅌ　　　ㅈ　　ㅊ

t　　tʰ　　　č　　čʰ

Illustration 33. Some Han'gŭl symbols

The Han'gŭl system is a remarkable achievement showing considerable originality and linguistic insight. While there have been some changes in spelling conventions since its invention, Han'gŭl's place in the history and typology of writing systems in the world is secure – as is its place in Korean life. Until recently, for instance, the ninth of October was a national Korean holiday, celebrating the invention of Han'gŭl!

5.3. Writing elsewhere

While the development of Mayan writing of Meso-America shows that writing can develop independently in different parts of the world, and yet with remarkably similar results (if we disregard differences in the shape of the letters), Korean demonstrates that writing can also spread by "stimulus diffusion", and that the results of the spread can differ remarkably from the original.

There are several examples in nineteenth-century North America and Africa of the similar creation of writing systems under stimulus diffusion. Particularly well-known in North America is the syllabary that Sequoyah (1770?–1843) developed for writing his native Cherokee (an Iroquoian language). He had learned of writing from contact with Europeans, especially English speakers, although he could not read or write English; and he set out to develop a writing system for Cherokee. After experimenting with a logographic system, he hit on the idea of a syllable-based graphic representation, and as the basis for his syllabary took some of his symbols from English books that he had seen. Since he did not read English, he was not bound by the alphabetic values of the letters in English, but could use them in completely novel syllabic values; for instance, **H** stood for [mi], **h** for

[ni], and **M** for [lu]. Other symbols were simply invented. The result was an initial syllabary of some 200 signs which Sequoyah later simplified to 85. The syllabary was used for publishing books and newspapers in Cherokee, and it is still in use today.

Syllabaries were developed to write other Native American languages also, some by missionaries in the nineteenth century and some possibly native adaptations (via stimulus diffusion). One that has achieved rather wide use was invented by the English missionary J. Evans, around 1840, to write Cree, an Algonquian language spoken across much of Canada but mainly in the western provinces. This syllabic script utilizes geometric symbols such as small circles, angles, triangles, some oriented in a variety of positions, some together with various diacritical marks, to spell all the consonant-vowel syllables of Cree; the symbol >, for instance, stands for [po], and a superscript dot marks all syllables with an *a*-vowel. Cree syllabics are still used, and in fact their use spread in Canada; Evans's syllabic script was adapted, for example, for the writing of Slave, an Athabaskan language spoken in Canada's Northwest Territories, and the Eastern Arctic Eskimo spoken on Baffin Island, also in the far north of Canada (a Latin-based alphabet is used for other Eskimo dialects, including Greenlandic Eskimo).

Nineteenth-century Africa also witnessed the creation of several similar indigenous writing systems, especially in West Africa. One assumes that these systems, too, arose under stimulus diffusion, but the role of contact with Europeans is not always clear. Noteworthy is the Vai system, developed prior to 1848 by Bukele, a speaker of Vai. As with Cherokee, the Vai system was at first logographic but soon developed a syllabic basis, with some syllabic signs being taken from logograms for monosyllabic words. Other syllabic systems in West Africa that emerged in roughly the same period, such as the Mende syllabary invented by Kisimi Kamala or the Toma syllabary used in part of Liberia, seem to have been stimulated by the Vai system.

An interesting parallel to King Sejong's invention of Han'gŭl is found in the Bamum syllabary of Cameroon, which was invented by a local ruler named Njoya (with some help apparently from a European missionary). Bamum is especially interesting since it developed some alphabetic principles, thus showing the independent development of an alphabet out of a syllabary, parallel to the development of alphabetic writing in Semitic.

In spite of all their differences, these writing systems show patterns of development that are remarkably similar to developments in the Near East and Korea and thus bear testimony to the fact that, given similar circumstances, human beings tend to respond in very similar ways.

Change in structure

Chapter 4
Sound change

> Etymology is a science in which consonants count for little, and
> vowels, for nothing at all.
>> (*Statement attributed to Voltaire, probably apocryphal.*)

> Sound change, in so far as it takes place mechanically, takes
> place according to laws that admit no exceptions.
>> (*Osthoff and Brugmann, 1878*)

1. Introduction

The early days of comparative Indo-European linguistics concentrated heavily on studying the similarities and differences in word structure in the Indo-European languages. This line of investigation in fact was a continuation of earlier scholarship which predated comparative Indo-European linguistics. Special attention was given to attempts to derive all noun and verb endings from earlier independent words which were said to have fused with the preceding noun and verb stems. For instance, the *-s-* appearing in forms like Gk. *lú-s-ō* 'I will loosen', a marker of future tense, was claimed to be related to the *s* of the root *es-* 'be'. Similarly, the *-dēdun* of the Gothic past tense (as in *nasidēdun* 'they saved') was considered derived from the root underlying modern Engl. *do*. Some of the proposed ideas may have some merit, such as the derivation of the Gothic ending *-dēdun*; but even this is still a matter of controversy. Many other ideas turned out to be premature and, by hindsight, rather naive.

They were naive especially because they were proposed without a proper understanding of linguistic change, particularly of the way in which sound change operates.

2. Grimm's Law

A major breakthrough in comparative Indo-European linguistics came when
the Danish scholar Rasmus Rask and, following him, the German linguist
Jacob Grimm began to take a closer look at the relationship between the
Germanic languages and the rest of Indo-European. Recall that William Jones,
in his famous pronouncement of 1786, had hedged his bets as to whether
Germanic (designated by the term Gothick) was related to Sanskrit or not:

> ... there is a similar reason, though not quite so forcible, for supposing that
> ... the Gothick ..., though blended with a very different idiom, had the same
> origin with the Sanscrit ...

Jones's reason was that Germanic looked very different from the classical languages, Greek, Latin, and Sanskrit, especially in the way it was
pronounced. For instance, where the classical languages had voiced stops, as
in Gk. *édomai*, Lat. *edō*, Skt. *admi* 'eat', the Germanic languages had voiceless ones, as in Engl. *eat*, Goth. *itan*, or even sibilants, as in Germ. *essen*. At
the same time, some Germanic words seemed to preserve the voiced stops
of the other Indo-European languages, such as Engl. *day*, corresponding to
Lat. *dies* 'day'; but again, German differed by offering a voiceless stop in its
cognate, *Tag* 'day'. It was perhaps this inconsistency in the way Germanic
corresponded to the classical Indo-European languages that led Jones to talk
about Germanic being "blended with a very different idiom".

The purpose of Rask's and Grimm's work was to elucidate more clearly
the relationship between Germanic and the classical Indo-European languages
and, in the process, to show that Germanic was in fact part of the Indo-
European language family. To this end, Rask and Grimm conducted thorough
investigations into the nature of precisely those aspects which appeared to
make Germanic quite "alien", namely the differences in pronunciation.

The result of the work, published in 1818 and 1819, was twofold: First, the
work succeeded in establishing once and for all that the Germanic languages
are indeed part of Indo-European. Secondly, it did so by providing a brilliant
account for the differences between Germanic and the classical languages in
terms of a set of amazingly systematic SOUND CHANGES, and a similar set of
sound changes differentiating German from the rest of Germanic.

To simplify matters, let us concentrate on the sound changes differentiating
all of Germanic from the rest of Indo-European. The discovery of this set of
systematic changes has been so influential in the development of historical

linguistics that the name soon attached to it, GRIMM'S LAW, has become a stock expression for everyone interested in language change and linguistic relationship. The name actually is a misnomer: The credit for discovering the systematic correspondences between Germanic and the classical languages must go to Rask. However, Grimm was so successful in formulating the changes – and in marketing them – that he received the recognition of having the "law" named after him, at least outside the German-speaking countries. (Note expressions like *Grimm's Law*, Fr. *le loi de Grimm*.) In German, the law is more commonly known as the (First) Germanic Sound Shift to distinguish it from a similar wholesale remaking of the Germanic stop system in Old High German, often referred to as the Second or High German Sound Shift; see Chapter 11, § 2.3.

Having talked so much about Grimm's Law, let us see how it operates. Let us begin with a brief look at the differences between Germanic, represented here by Gothic and Old English, and the classical Indo-European languages, concentrating on the initial consonants; see example (1). (In some cases, the initial consonant is preceded by a prefixed element. Such elements are put in parentheses.)

(1) Classical Indo-European languages Germanic languages

	Greek	Latin	Sanskrit	Gothic	Old English	
a.	*patér*	*pater*	*pitá*	*fadar*	*fæder*	'father'
	treîs	*trēs*	*trayas*	*þreis*	*þrī*	'three'
	(he-)katón	*centum* [k-]	*śatám*	*hund*	*hund*	'hundred'
b.	*déka*	*decem*	*dáśa*	*taihun*	*tēon*	'ten'
	geúomai	*gustus*	*jōṣ-*	*kiusan*	*cēosan*	'taste, test, choose'
c.	*phérō*	*ferō*	*bharāmi*	*baira*	*beoru*	'I carry'
	(é-)thē-ka	*fē-c-ī*	*(a-)dhā-m*	*(ga-)dē-þ-s*	*dæd*	'put/do; deed'
	kheúō	*fu-n-d-ō*	*ho-tar-*	*giutan*	*gēotan*	'pour'

As these examples show, change is not limited to Germanic. Especially in the last three items (set (c)) we notice some major differences between the initial consonants of Greek, Latin, and Sanskrit. Still, the greatest differences separate Germanic from the rest of Indo-European.

Starting with a reconstruction of Proto-Indo-European (PIE) that postulated voiceless stops for set (a), voiced ones for set (b), and voiced aspirated ones for set (c), Rask and Grimm accounted for the different look of Germanic by postulating three sweeping and highly systematic sound changes, affecting whole classes of sounds at the same time:

(2) Grimm's Law:
  i. PIE voiceless stops become voiceless fricatives;
  ii. PIE voiced stops become voiceless stops;
  iii. PIE voiced aspirates become voiced stops or fricatives (depending on the context in which they occur).

Change (i) accounts for the differences in set (a) of (1) above, e.g. Gk *treîs*, Lat. *trēs*, Skt. *trayas* corresponding to Goth. *þreis*, OE *þrī* 'three'. Change (ii) explains correspondences like Gk. *déka*, Lat. *decem*, Skt. *dáśa* : Goth *taihun*, OE *tēon* 'ten'. And change (iii) derives Goth. *(ga-)dē-þ-s*, OE *dǣd* 'deed' from the PIE root **dhē* 'put, make' underlying Gk. *(é-)thē-ka*, Lat. *fē-c-ī*, Skt. *(a-)dhā-m*.

What is especially remarkable is that these changes apply not just to a few words. Their effects recur in hundreds of other words. Grimm's Law, thus, is not only phonetically highly systematic, by affecting all classes of stop consonants, but it also is lexically systematic, by applying to so many words.

This dual systematicity greatly impressed other Indo-Europeanists and inspired a massive outburst of research on sound change, compensating for its neglect in earlier Indo-Europeanist studies.

Since Rask's and Grimm's times, many similar systematic sound changes have been found in many other areas of the world. For instance, among the early Indo-European languages, Armenian had a similar sweeping sound shift; see the initial consonants in the examples in (3) below. (Some of the Armenian consonants underwent further changes, such as original **p > h*.)

(3)   Armenian sound shift

	Greek	Latin	Sanskrit	Armenian	
a.	*patér*	*pater*	*pitá*	*hayr*	'father'
	tó	*(is-)tud*	*tad*	*thē*	'that'
	téttares	*qu*attuor	*čatvāri*	*čhorkh*	'four'
b.	*déka*	*decem*	*dáśa*	*tasn*	'ten'
	gunḗ		*ǰani/gnā-*	*kin*	'woman'
c.	*phérō*	*ferō*	*bharāmi*	*berem*	'I carry'
	(é-)thē-ka	*fē-c-ī*	*(a-)dhā-m*	*dir*	'put, place; make, do'
	thermós	*fornax*	*gharma-*	*ǰerm*	'hot, heat; oven'

A similar change, but restricted to the voiceless stops, differentiated Southern Bantu languages from the other Bantu languages; see example (4). In this case, different languages exhibit different outcomes, but they share the fact that they systematically change all voiceless stops of the ancestral Proto-Bantu language. Moreover, the fricative outcomes of *p and *k in Sotho can easily be related to the aspirates of Xhosa; see § 5.4 below. (The development of *t to Sotho *r* is more difficult to explain and therefore is not discussed here.)

(4)   Southern Bantu sound shift
        Proto-Bantu Xhosa Sotho
        kama   *khama* *xama*   'wring'
        tatu   *thathu* *raru*   'three'
        pa   *pha*   *Φa*   'give'

Another parallel to Grimm's Law, affecting voiceless stops, has been observed in the "Chipewyan consonant shift" of Athabaskan. That such changes need not be limited to ancient and/or "exotic" languages is shown by the British English dialect of Liverpool, in which voiceless stops are shifting toward fricatives, as in *lock* which, via [lɔkh] with heavily aspirated velar stop, is changing to [lɔx] with velar fricative. (The change is actually more widespread in British English. For instance, during a stop-over at Gatwick airport (near London), the lead author of this book heard the announcement *Transit passengers please proceed to gate thir*[**ts**]*een*, with shift [t] > [ts].)

Though clearly interesting and impressive, changes such as those in (3) and (4) were discovered much later, too late to create the same excitement as Grimm's Law. But the very fact that they were discovered is ultimately the result of the interest in sound change generated by Rask's and Grimm's discoveries.

In recent times, doubts have been voiced about both Grimm's Law and the Armenian consonant shift. Some scholars have claimed that the Armenian and Proto-Germanic consonant systems are archaic, close to the one of Proto-Indo-European, and that the systems of the other Indo-European languages are the result of innovating changes. This is the so-called "glottalic" view of Proto-Indo-European mentioned in the discussion of Armenian and Iranian (Ossetic) in Chapter 2. As noted in that discussion, the glottalic view is highly controversial. Many linguists are not convinced by the cogency of the arguments and evidence marshalled in its support, while others are just as certain that the theory is correct. Even if the theory should eventually become generally accepted, this does not diminish the importance of the work of Rask, Grimm, and their successors and its significance for the development of historical linguistic thinking and methodology. For case of exposition, the subsequent discussion ignores the glottalic theory and proceeds under the assumption that the traditional, Grimm's Law, view is correct. (The issue is taken up again in Chapter 16.)

3. From Grimm's Law to Verner's Law

While Rask and Grimm, as well as their contemporaries, were highly impressed by the systematicity of the sound changes they had discovered, they did not expect the changes to be absolutely regular. They were too much influenced by the idealism of the Romantic movement to believe that human beings were capable of behaving with complete, exceptionless regularity, as if they were automata or machines.

In fact, correspondences such as Lat. *dies* 'day' : Engl. *day* suggested that Grimm's Law did not apply in all words. Even more examples could be found in which Grimm's Law and other changes separating Germanic from the rest of Indo-European applied inconsistently, affecting most sounds, but leaving one or two sounds unaffected. Some examples of such apparent exceptions to Grimm's Law are given in (5), where Latin represents the classical Indo-European languages, and Old English, Germanic. (Note that Lat. *c* designates the sound [k].) The first two examples are especially interesting, since here [k] and [p] have undergone Grimm's Law in the early part of the words, changing to the voiceless fricatives *h* [x] and [f]; but voiceless stops occurring toward the end of the word, marked in boldface, do not exhibit the change. One might toy with the idea that, having applied Grimm's Law once or twice within a given word, the speakers of early Germanic got tired and therefore did not change voiceless stops occurring later in the word. But the other two examples show that even voiceless stops not preceded by other Indo-European voiceless stops in the same word may fail to undergo the change. That is, the exceptions seem to be completely random.

(5)   Latin   Old English
    captus   *hæft*   'captured, prisoner'
    piscis   *fisc*   'fish'
    spuō   *spīwan*   'spew, spit'
    stō   *standan*   'stand'

In addition to such words in which Grimm's Law failed to apply (or applied only partially), there were a number of other words in which there was a change, but the outcome of the change was different from the one predicted by Grimm's Law: Instead of being reflected by the expected voiceless fricatives, Indo-European voiceless stops came out as voiced. Compare the examples in (6). Here again, it seemed impossible to come up with any generalization about the words in which such exceptional outcomes are found. True, the examples in (6.a) all refer to close family relatives; but so does (6.b). More than that, within one and the same PARADIGM (= the set of inflected forms of a given word) we find some forms exhibiting outcomes conforming to Grimm's Law, whereas others have exceptional voiced outcomes. Compare examples (7.a) vs. (7.b), where the classical Indo-European languages and Germanic are respectively represented by Sanskrit and English. Such alternations within the same paradigm are now commonly called MORPHOPHONEMIC ALTERNATIONS.

(6)

	Latin	Sanskrit	Gothic	Old English	
a.	*pater*	*pitá*	*fadar*	*fæder*	'father'
	māter	*mātá*		*mōdor*	'mother'
b.	*frāter*	*bhrátā*	*brōþar*	*brōþor*	'brother'

(7)

	Sanskrit	OEngl.	
a.	*vártate*	*weorþan*	'turn, become' (pres.)
	vavárta	*wearþ*	(past sing.)
b.	*vavr̥túr*	*wurdon*	(past plur.)
	vr̥taná-	*(ge)worden*	(past participle)

As time progressed, scholars discovered that some forms originally considered exceptional were simply irrelevant. For instance, closer examination of the evidence and of the regular sound correspondences between the Indo-European languages showed that the similarities between Engl. *day* and Lat. *dies* are accidental. The two forms are not really cognate. A genuine English cognate of the root in Lat. *dies* is, believe it or not, the first element in the word *Tuesday*: The root underlying both of these is PIE **dy(e)u-*, originally meaning 'sky, light, day'. The Latin word represents a fairly straightforward outcome. The Germanic word presents no difficulties from the perspective of sound change either, since its initial *t* is precisely what we would expect by Grimm's Law. The meaning of the word represents a more special development, but that development has parallels elsewhere in Indo-European: In the meaning 'sky', **dy(e)u-* became the name of the God of the sky, often with the addition of the word 'father'; compare Skt. *dyaús pitá*, Gk. *Zeús patér*,

Lat. *Juppiter*. It is this name of the Sky God that underlies the *Tues* of Engl. *Tuesday*. (See also Chapter 18, § 4.3.)

In addition, scholars realized that some apparent exceptions to Grimm's Law are in reality borrowings. Thus, Latin has a word *pondus* 'weight', which in pronunciation and meaning is close to Engl. *pound*, OE *pund*. If the two words were inherited from Proto-Indo-European, the English word would be a double exception to Grimm's Law: Neither the voiceless stop nor the voiced one would have changed. In fact, however, OE *pund* is an early borrowing from Latin, made at a time when Grimm's Law had taken its course and therefore did not affect any new words. Other borrowings from that early period include *street*, OE *strǣt*, from Lat. *(via) strāta* 'a prepared road', and *cheap*, OE *cēap* 'bargain, purchase', from Latin *caupō* 'merchant'. These are part of a large amount of vocabulary exchanged between Latin and Germanic during the time of the Roman expansion into Germanic territory and the slightly later "return visits" of the Germanic tribes. Among the words going from Germanic to Latin and its descendants is the word for 'soap': PGmc. **saipōn-*, hence Engl. *soap*, Germ. *Seife* : Fr. *savon*, Span. *jabón*, etc. (See Chapter 2.)

A better understanding of etymological relationships and of borrowings thus managed to clear away some of the apparent exceptions to Grimm's Law. But by its very nature, this approach produced only piecemeal solutions. A much more sweeping solution, which has not received the recognition it deserves, is C. Lottner's discovery in 1862 that exceptions of the type (5) above, far from being totally random, exhibit an amazing degree of regularity: The unshifted voiceless stops all occur after a voiceless fricative, whether that fricative is the original PIE sibilant *s* or the result of Grimm's Law (such as the *f* of OE *hæft*).

Lottner's insight suggests that part one of Grimm's Law as originally stated needs to be revised, so as to systematically exempt voiceless stops after Germanic voiceless fricatives (or after their equally voiceless PIE sources).

This still left the exceptions in (6) and (7), and these were much more difficult to explain. It was only in 1877 that the Danish linguist Karl Verner found a solution which showed that these, too, were not really irregular but exhibited a regularity of their own. The reason for the long wait was that the regularity of these forms could not be accounted for by modifying Grimm's Law; they required a law of their own. Moreover, the conditions under which the law applied were far from obvious if one restricted one's horizon to Germanic, the group of languages in which the "exceptional" voiced outcomes occurred. Rather, it was necessary to look to other languages, mainly Greek and Sanskrit, for an explanation. And if that were not enough, one had to attribute the change at least in part to a conditioning factor considered quite unlikely to bring about voicing, namely the location of the Indo-European stress or accent. Once all of these elements were brought together, however, the solution was so clear, so obvious, and so "neat" that no doubt many scholars asked themselves, "Why couldn't I have thought of that?" But they didn't, and the change responsible for the voiced outcomes came to be called VERNER'S LAW.

To see how Verner's Law works, consider again the forms in (6) and (7) and note that the voiced outcomes are found only in those forms in which the PIE voiceless stops occur between vowels or between *r* and vowel, and where the syllable preceding the stop is not accented in Sanskrit (which preserves the PIE accent placement). Elsewhere, the voiceless stop occurs.

Now, as example (8) shows, this distinction between voiced and voiceless outcomes is not restricted to PIE voiceless stops; it is also found in the reflexes of PIE **s*. (The *r* found in Old English goes back to an earlier **z*.) Verner's Law, thus, can be said to affect all Germanic fricatives, whether they reflect original **s* or result from PIE voiceless stops by Grimm's Law.

(8)   Sanskrit   Old English
        jóṣate   *cēosan*   'taste, choose' (pres.)
        jujóṣa   *cēas*   (past sg.)
        jujuṣúr   *curon*   (past pl.)
        juṣaná-   *(ge)coren*   (past participle)

Keeping in mind these various factors, as well as some others which it would take too long to exemplify, Verner's Law can be formulated as follows:

(9)   Verner's Law:
        Proto-Germanic fricatives (including sibilant *s*) become voiced if the following three conditions are met: They are not initial, what precedes and follows them is voiced, and the PIE accent is not on the immediately preceding syllable.

Before we can proceed to show how Verner's Law operated in relation to Grimm's Law, we need to mention one other change. After Verner's Law ceased to operate, another sweeping change occurred: The accent shifted to the root syllable of the word which, in most cases, coincides with the initial syllable. It was this change that obscured the accentual condition of Verner's Law and, consequently, made it so difficult to recognize.

If we let GL stand for Grimm's Law, VL for Verner's Law, and AS for the early accent shift to the initial or root syllable, we can illustrate the way these three processes interacted. As example (10) shows, only the order GL before VL before AS will yield the right results. Other sequences fail to do so. See for instance the unsuccessful derivations in (10′) and (10″), where the incorrect forms are marked by a following asterisk.

(10)	PIE	*pətér*	*bhrátēr*
	GL	*faþér*	*bróþer*
	VL	*faðér*	INAPPLICABLE
	AS	*fáðer*	*bróþer*
	Old English outcomes	*fæder*	*brōþor*

(10′)	PIE	*pətér*	*bhrátēr*
	VL	INAPPLICABLE	INAPPLICABLE
	GL	*faþér*	*bróþer*
	AS	*fáþer*	*bróþer*
	Old English outcomes	*fæþer**	*brōþor*

(10″)	PIE	*pətér*	*bhrátēr*
	AS	*pə́tēr*	*(bhrátēr)*
	GL	*fáþer*	*bróþer*
	VL	INAPPLICABLE	INAPPLICABLE
	Old English outcomes	*fæþer**	*brōþor*

Situations like these, where only one sequence of changes will yield the correct results, establish what linguists call a RELATIVE CHRONOLOGY: Even when we cannot be sure about the "absolute" chronology (i.e. when the changes took place in historical time), we are at least able to demonstrate their relative ordering. When looking at demonstrations of the type (10)–(10″), non-linguists often get the feeling that linguists are just playing a shell game, imposing their own view on history. In fact, however, it is the history of the language that imposes the solution on linguists: If history had been different, the outcomes would be different, and a different relative chronology would suggest itself.

The influence of Verner's Law on historical linguistics was profound. The fact that the law was conditioned by phonetic factors previously not considered even remotely relevant stimulated the linguistic community to pay much greater attention to fine phonetic details that had not been examined in earlier studies. And this closer look at the factors that condition sound change has greatly enriched our understanding of language history. This is not to say that all the after-effects of Verner's Law were beneficial. There was, as in many other cases, a certain bandwagon effect that resulted in a large variety of attempts at explaining historical developments in terms of accentual differences – even in cases where there simply was no evidence for such differences. But these misuses of accentual explanations do not diminish the significance – and correctness – of Verner's Law.

4. The regularity hypothesis and the neogrammarians

In addition to stimulating greater attention to the phonetic conditions of sound change, Verner's Law provided the final stepping stone toward solving the apparent exceptions to Grimm's Law. If allowances were made for the operation of certain additional changes, such as analogy (see Chapter 5), it appeared that the nearly sixty years of scholarly endeavor since Rask and Grimm published their findings had succeeded in establishing that Grimm's Law was not just amazingly sweeping and systematic. It seemed to have, in fact, operated with COMPLETE regularity, affecting every single word it could affect at the time that it took place.

Developments like these suggested a very different meaning for the slogan "Sound change is regular", which had been voiced by a number of earlier scholars. Now a group of young linguists working at the University of Leipzig (Germany) felt justified in raising this slogan to an axiom of historical linguistics, with the assumption that "regular" meant not just "overwhelmingly regular" or the like, but ABSOLUTELY REGULAR. (See the second motto at the beginning of this chapter.) Another way of putting it was to say that sound change "operates blindly". Because this new view on the nature of sound change had been proposed by a group of young linguists at Leipzig, the group and its later followers came to be known as the NEOGRAMMARIANS ("Junggrammatiker" in German). Their claim, in turn, has been labeled the REGULARITY HYPOTHESIS.

To understand what is meant by the claim that sound change is absolutely regular, however, it is necessary to understand what is meant by the term sound change. A number of other factors also need to be taken into consideration in order to interpret the claim. Without these modifications, the claim is meaningless.

Sound change, in the sense that the term is used here, refers to change in sounds conditioned only by phonetic factors or, even more accurately, but less elegantly, change in sounds not conditioned by non-phonetic factors. Clearly there were all kinds of changes that could affect the pronunciation of words, but were not conditioned just by phonetic facts. For instance, as mentioned in Chapter 1, the early Modern English plural of *cow*, *kine,* changed to *cows* on the analogy of other, more regular plurals, such as *pig : pig-s, horse : horse-s*. Changes of this type were known to be quite irregular. For instance, *swine* did not change to *swows**, or *wine* to *wows**.

Similarly, we find that tabooed words often are deliberately distorted in polite company, making it possible to use the tabooed word without "actually saying it". Examples in English are expressions like *gosh, darn, doggone ...; blasted, blessed, bleeding ...; shoot; friggin'* instead of well-known taboo words which are better left unprinted. Here again, it is quite clear that the changes in question affect the pronunciation of the words, but that they are by no means regular. Thus, *rod* is not replaced by *rosh*, *ham* by *harn*, *muddy* by *masted*, *hit* by *hoot*, or *tucking* by *triggin'*. (On taboo distortion see also Chapter 7.)

It was believed that processes like analogy and taboo distortion do not take place with the regularity of, say, Grimm's Law because they heavily depend on the mental association of forms with each other or on meaning, whereas sound change, properly understood, operates without any regard to such mental associations or meanings – or even the effect that it might have on our ability to communicate such mental associations or meanings.

There is a lot of empirical evidence that sound change does, in fact, take place "blindly", without consideration of the havoc it may create on our ability to communicate. Thus, in Southern U.S. English, *pen* and *pin* have come to be pronounced identically, by a process that regularly changed [e] to [i] before nasal. As a consequence it is now necessary in these dialects to resort to circumlocutions like *writing* [pin] vs. *needle* or *stick* [pin] in order to properly distinguish the two words. Similarly, in many varieties of American English, *can* and *can't* are not distinguished, except in very slow, deliberate speech, necessitating speakers to ask things like *Do you mean you are able to or not?* In New York English, the vowel of words like *can* and *man* has changed to such an extent that the common woman's name *Ann* sounds like the relatively rare man's name *Ian*. It is reported that children, being more familiar with the name *Ann*, asked their parents why they gave their baby brother, *Ian*, a girl's name. Similarly, in some varieties of the English in and around Chicago, *John* has acquired a pronunciation that outsiders hear as *Jan*, again resulting in all kinds of confusion. (More on the New York and Chicago changes in § 5.4 below.)

Changes of this sort are not restricted to modern English; they have taken place at all stages of the language. Compare for instance *cleave* 'stick to' and *cleave* 'chop, split'. The second of these two words goes back to OE *cleofan*, is related to regional Germ. *klieben* 'chop, split', and derives from a PIE root **glewbh-*, while the first reflects OE *cleofian*, is related to Germ. *kleben* 'stick', and goes back to PIE **gleybh-*. (Speakers of Modern English may consider the difference between *cleofan* and *cleofian* to be trifling; but the distinction in the suffixes, *-an* vs. *-ian*, made a great deal of difference in Old English.) Since 'stick to' and 'chop, split' convey meanings that are just about diametrically opposed, the use of the two words must have led to a lot of confusion. In modern English, this confusion is to a large extent resolved by avoiding the use of *cleave* in the meaning 'stick to'. But this change took place only after sound change made it impossible to distinguish the two words. As in all the other examples above, there is no evidence that speakers tried to block the changes in mid-stream, in order to avoid possible confusion. (On matters like these see also Chapter 7.)

In addition to understanding properly what is meant by the term sound change, it is further necessary to be aware of a lot of "fine print". For instance, in the natural sciences the expression "absolutely regular" would be taken to mean that a particular change takes place under the same conditions, anywhere, and at any time that it has a chance to do so. In the regularity hypothesis, this can hardly be the intended meaning. For even a moment's reflection will tell us that Grimm's Law took place at some point between Proto-Indo-European and Germanic, and that it took place only at that point, and only in Germanic (although some other languages, such as Armenian, may have had similar changes). If Grimm's Law were not restricted this way, we should expect all the other Indo-European languages – in fact, all the languages of the world – to have had the same change. The change also should have applied again and again, so that a *d* going back to earlier **dh* by part (iii) of Grimm's Law, would next undergo part (ii) of the same law and become *t*, only to undergo part (i) and turn into *þ*. As a consequence, PIE **dhē-* should not have stopped at the stage represented by Mod. Engl. *deed*, but should have changed further to *teet**, and then to *theeth**. The regularity hypothesis, therefore, is a statement about particular sound changes as historical events, limited by place, time, as well as language (or even dialect).

One final restriction on the regularity hypothesis must be mentioned: The neogrammarians were keenly aware that certain types of change which do not easily qualify as analogy or the like, nevertheless are notoriously irregular. These prominently include the following two processes: (i) "metathesis", the transposition of sounds, as in OE *bryde* > Mod. Engl. *bird*; and (ii) "dissimilation", as in Engl. *col(o)nel* > [kərnəl], where the first of two [l] sounds has changed to [r] so as to become "dissimilar" to the second. The neogrammarians made several attempts to account for the irregularity of these changes. Perhaps the best among these is the claim that dissimilation and metathesis are similar to speech errors, a lapse in some special control faculty, perhaps the same faculty that we put to the test in tongue twisters. (See also § 5.5 below.)

From the time that it was formulated, the neogrammarian regularity hypothesis ran into strong opposition. Even so, the hypothesis was widely accepted by most historical linguists. Recent research has raised questions about many of the neogrammarians' assumptions and has shown that sound change is not always regular. But even this research confirms that much of sound change is so close to regular that the neogrammarian hypothesis can still be accepted as a general guideline.

Even if we may have to give up the notion that sound change is absolutely regular, in favor of the more modest proposition that it is overwhelmingly regular, the regularity hypothesis has proved enormously fruitful in historical linguistics. It challenges linguists to look more carefully at linguistic change in order to explain apparent irregularities. And any closer investigation is bound to yield new and interesting results – in any field of inquiry. In the field of historical linguistics, the regularity hypothesis certainly has done just that.

5. Some types of sound change

Except for the restriction discovered by Lottner, Grimm's Law is a set of changes that take place across the board, and no special phonetic conditions are discernible that might motivate them. Verner's Law, by contrast, depends on a lot of conditions. Why the most celebrated of these, the accentual one, should have induced voicing of original voiceless fricatives is still open to question. However, the fact that the voicing takes place in a medial voiced environment seems to make intuitive sense: The fricative "assimilates" to the voicing of its surroundings. Here, then, we have a perfect case of the context in which the change takes place in some way triggering the change. Processes of this sort can be called CONDITIONED changes.

5.1. Assimilation, weakening, loss
Over the 200-odd years that modern historical linguistics has been practiced, a large number of conditioned types of changes have been observed. By far

the most common of these are changes which in some ways ease the process of pronunciation. This, however, should not be taken to suggest that all sound change leads to phonetic simplification. Some changes consist of the addition of new sounds, a phenomenon that could hardly be considered simplification; see § 5.2 below. Others appear to be neutral as regards simplicity; see § 5.3. Moreover, there clearly must be limits on the extent to which simplification can progress: If phonetic simplicity were permitted to run its full course, it would change all words to something like [ə], a simple central vowel without any complex distinctions of vowel position (high, mid, low; front, central, back; etc.), to say nothing of the effort of producing a large variety of different consonants. But how would we convey with this one, maximally simple utterance the plethora of different meanings that we are able to express through our more "complicated" words? Human language requires a certain degree of complexity to successfully communicate meaning, variation, and creativeness. (See also § 6 below.)

Nevertheless, it is true that changes which seem to ease pronunciation make up the bulk of regular sound change. That these changes have not, over the long history of human language, led to the ultimate stage of simplification, [ə], suggests that language has enough resilience, as it were, to counteract the ravages of simplificatory change and to keep reintroducing enough "complications", whether by sound change or other changes, to retain its functionality.

5.1.1. Assimilation

One type of simplificatory change, briefly mentioned in the preceding section, is ASSIMILATION. As the name suggests, the process consists of making the pronunciation of a given sound more similar to that of another sound and thus simplifies the articulatory gestures required to pronounce the word. The sound triggering the change may precede or follow, but usually it is an immediate neighbor of the sound that is changing.

The word *assimilation* itself provides a perfect illustration of the process it designates. It is derived from the Latin elements *ad-* 'to' and *similis* 'similar', which combined to form the basis of Lat. *assimilare* 'to make similar to', in which the *d* of *ad* so successfully assimilated to the following *s* that it acquired the same articulation. A less radical example of assimilation is found in the formation of English plurals. Although we write the plural ending as -*s*, no matter where it occurs, in pronunciation it assimilates to preceding voiced sounds by becoming voiced; compare *bed-s* [bedz] vs. *bets* [bets].

Several subtypes of assimilation occur frequently enough, with interesting results, to have been given special names. One of these is UMLAUT, a process common in early Germanic; see example (11). Umlaut typically involves the assimilation of a root vowel to a vowel occurring in a suffix; see Stage II in example (11). Moreover, typically some of the suffix vowels triggering the change are subsequently lost, so that the conditions for the vowel change are no longer fully recoverable; see Stage III. The example in (11) further illustrates a common outcome of umlaut: If the entire suffix is lost, the vowel change produced by umlaut may take over the function of the original suffix, in this case, the function of indicating plurality. Many of the "irregular" plurals of Modern English owe their origin to umlaut; compare *foot : feet, tooth : teeth, mouse : mice, louse : lice, man : men, woman : women.*

(11)   Stage I   Stage II   Stage III
             (= pre-Old Engl. I) (= pre-Old Engl. II) (= Old English)
             kū-z   *kū-z*   *cū* [kū]   'cow'
             kū-iz   *kǖ-iz*   *cȳ* [kǖ]   'cows'

A process in some ways similar to umlaut is PALATALIZATION. Like umlaut, the change typically proceeds in three stages: A stage without assimilation is followed by a stage in which a class of consonants, mainly the dentals or velars, assimilates to following front vowels producing a palatalized consonant (indicated by a following superscript *y*), and a final stage at which some of the triggers for the change are lost. At that point, the palatalized consonant tends to become a palatal which, in turn, has a strong tendency to change into a sibilant or fricative. Compare the example in (12). Traces of the palatalization in (12) are found in many English borrowings from French. And because French palatalization was a conditioned process, which took place only before front vowel, many of the words borrowed from French alternate between the original velar and the sibilant reflex of palatalization, depending on the originally following vowel. Compare alternations of the type *electric* [-k] : *electricity* [-s-]. As noted in § 3 above, such systematic changes in the pronunciation of words, depending on the context in which they occur, are commonly referred to as morphophonemic alternations.

(12)   Stage I   Stage II   Stage III   Further changes
        (= Latin)   (= Proto-   (= Proto-
                         Romance I)   Romance II)
        faciat [fakiat] *fakʸya*   *fakʸa > fačə >* Mod. Fr. *fasse* [fas(ə)]
        'would make'

Many words borrowed with *s* resulting from French palatalization underwent another process of English palatalization, if the *s* was followed by a suffix-initial front vowel, as in *electrician*. (The vowel triggering this second round of palatalization has since ceased to be pronounced.)

Before turning our attention to other simplificatory processes, let us briefly mention a type of change which often is considered assimilatory, namely FINAL DEVOICING. As the name suggests, this process involves the devoicing of final consonants. The starting point for the change seems to lie in utterance-final position where even languages like standard English, not otherwise known to have final devoicing, exhibit a slight degree of devoicing. In many other languages, such as German and Russian, the change goes much farther and leads to a complete "merger" of voiced stops and fricatives with their voiceless counterparts. Moreover, the change is not confined to utterance-final position but applies word-finally, as well. Compare the example in (13).

(13)   OHG Mod. Germ (NHG)
          tag   *Tag* [tāk]   'day'
   vs.   *taga*   *Tage* [tāgə]   'days'
          stab   *Stab* [štāp]   'staff, stick'
   vs.   *staba* *Stäbe* [štebə]   'staffs, sticks'
          etc.

Assimilatory changes can also be observed in sign languages. A type of assimilation that is very common in American Sign Language has come to be known as SYMMETRY. For instance, the sign for 'angry' once consisted of one hand moving away from the waist; now it is articulated instead with both hands moving in symmetry. A slightly different example of the change is found in the development of the sign for 'final'. This sign used to involve the index finger of one hand striking the little finger of the other; now, however, little finger strikes against little finger.

5.1.2. Weakening

A process that even more clearly simplifies pronunciation is WEAKENING (also referred to as LENITION), a relaxation, reduction, or even total omission of the articulatory gestures required to make particular speech sounds. Weakening occurs most commonly in a medial voiced environment (just like Verner's Law), but may be found in other contexts as well. In modern English it is especially the voiceless dental stop [t] that is liable to be weakened. In American English, for instance, we find *better* pronounced as [beɾər] (with an *r*-like flap), [bedər] (with voicing), or in some areas apparently even [beØər] (with loss of the *t* indicated by the symbol Ø). Many varieties of British English have the pronunciation [beʔə(r)] (with glottal stop). What is common to all of these pronunciations is a relaxation in the gestures required to make a voiceless [t] in intervocalic voiced environment: In the case of [ɾ], contact is made less firmly, resulting in a flap; in [d], the switch from voicing to voicelessness and back to voicing has been eliminated; [ʔ] omits the oral closure required to make a [t], but leaves something like an "echo" of that closure in the shape of the glottal stop; and the most radical solution is represented by Ø – a complete omission of all gestures required to articulate [t].

Alert readers may have noticed that the voicing in [bedər] could also be interpreted as a simple case of assimilation of voiceless [t] to its voiced surroundings. Intervocalic voicing is an area in which the two processes, assimilation and weakening, overlap. But perhaps there is more to it: One could argue that assimilation in general is simply a special case of weakening, in that the articulatory gestures required to pronounce sounds differently are relaxed, leading to more similar pronunciations.

In some languages, weakening can be quite sweeping, affecting all intervocalic stops. This is the case in the western Romance languages. See for instance the Spanish examples in (14), where intervocalic Latin [p, t, k] become voiced fricatives and where [d, g] are lost altogether.

(14)   Latin   Spanish
        lupus   *lobo* [β]   'wolf'
        status   *estado* [ð]   'state'
        locus   *luego* [ɣ]   'place'
        habere   *haber* [β]   'have'
        videre   *ve(e)r* [Ø]   'see'
        legere   *leer* [Ø]   'read'

5.1.3. Loss

The LOSS of speech sounds is not limited to the contexts that typically exhibit weakening, but occurs frequently in other environments as well. As we already have seen in Chapter 1, English lost initial [k] before nasal, as in OE *cnyht* > Mod. Engl. *knight* [Øn-]. A context especially liable to undergo loss is the end of words; compare (15). The reason for this presumably is the fact that our voice often "trails off" at the end of utterances, both in intonation (which goes down to a fairly low pitch) and in the precise articulation of speech sounds. Like final devoicing, the results may subsequently be generalized to all word-final positions.

(15)   Old English   Mod. English
      singan   *singØØ*
      stānas   *stones* [-nØz]

A repeated process of loss in final syllables is responsible for the fact that English has lost most of the inflectional endings of Old English: Old English had endings to differentiate four different noun cases (nominative, genitive, dative, and accusative) and to distinguish these cases in two different numbers (e.g. dative sg. *stān-e* 'to the stone' : dative pl. *stān-um* 'to the stones'). Of these different endings, only two have remained in Modern English, both sounding identical: the plural marker *-s* and the genitive marker *-s*. Here, then, loss may be said to have simplified not only pronunciation but the whole inflectional system of English. (Note, however, that analogy played a role, too, in this development. See Chapter 5, § 4, as well as the brief discussion in Chapter 1.)

Sometimes, loss of a sound is compensated for by lengthening of the preceding vowel, where lengthening maintains the timing of the structure from which the sound is lost. For example, Engl. *tooth* derives from PIE **dont-* (as in Gk. *o-dónt-*), via PGmc. **tanþ-* which changed into OE *tōþ* with loss of the nasal *n* and with COMPENSATORY LENGTHENING of the preceding vowel, hence OE *ō*. There is an interesting parallel in sign languages: When an original compound symbol of American Sign Language is reduced through loss of one of the component signs, the remaining sign is lengthened through repetition. For instance, 'orange', originally a compound of 'slice' and 'yellow', now is formed without the element 'yellow' and with repetition of the sign for 'slice'.

5.2. Epenthesis, the gain or insertion of speech sounds

Although loss is a very wide-spread phenomenon and, as we have just seen, can have far-reaching effects on the structure of languages, some sound changes have the opposite phonetic effect – they introduce speech sounds. This type of change is generally referred to as EPENTHESIS.

A common subtype of epenthesis consists of the insertion of vowels before word-initial consonant groups or into such groups elsewhere. A well-known example is the process of PROTHESIS in early Spanish and French, which inserted an [e] in front of *s* + stop clusters. Compare Lat. *spata* 'sword' : Span. *espada*, Fr. *épée*. As these two words show, epenthesis in one context of a given word does not prevent weakening or even loss in others. Note especially the French word in which the *s* which had triggered the prothesis of *e* was lost by a later weakening change.

Not only vowels may be inserted, but consonants as well. This is an especially common phenomenon between nasals and following liquids, as in OE
þunØrian 'to thunder' > *þundrian*, whence Mod. Engl. *thunder*. The motivation for this change seems to be as follows: Nasals are pronounced with the
same articulation as voiced stops, except that the passage to the nose is left
open, permitting nasal resonance to be audible. (As noted in the Appendix
to Chapter 1, this articulatory fact is strikingly confirmed if you have a cold:
The blockage of your nose leads to a reduction in nasal resonance; and the
result is that your *nasals* sound like *"dasals"*.) Switching from the nasal to
the following non-nasal liquid requires a delicate timing in the adjustment
of articulatory gestures. Ideally, the change from stop to liquid should take
place at the same time as the change from nasal to non-nasal. Epenthetic
developments as in *þunrian* > *þundrian* result if the two gestures are not
properly timed, i.e., if speakers switch too early from nasal to non-nasal,
producing a stretch of oral stop articulation. Compare the schematic presentation in Illustration 1. Here a solid horizontal line indicates the presence of a
particular articulation, a broken line, its absence. If in the original sequence *n*
+ *r* the stop articulation is held out longer than the nasal articulation (see the
circled part of on the right hand of Illustration 1), the result is an interval of
a non-nasal – i.e., oral – stop *d*. (The vertical lines in Illustration 1 indicate
the boundaries between the sounds.)

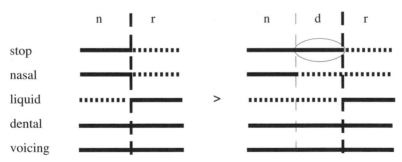

Illustration 1. Consonant epenthesis as the result of wrong timing

The very common phenomenon of aspiration, as in the change from Proto-
Bantu *tatu* 'three' to Xhosa ***thathu*** (example (4) above), can likewise be
considered an example of wrong timing; see Illustration 2. If the switch
from voiceless (stop) to voiced (vowel) is not timed correctly, an interval of
voiceless articulation results, without the stop to "support" it; and the [h]-
like hissing noise of that interval is what we call aspiration. (Aspiration, once
present, can be extended to contexts without following vowel; and the hissing

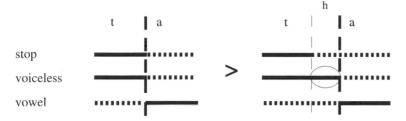

Illustration 2. Aspiration as the result of wrong timing

noise of aspiration may become stronger and more turbulent. But these are secondary developments.)

5.3. Acoustically or auditorily conditioned changes

The types of sound change we have looked at so far are best explained as being triggered by articulatory factors. However, when we learn our first language, no one tells us how to articulate. No one says, "Now, in order to make a [t] you press your tongue tip firmly against the back of the teeth, make sure not to let your glottis vibrate, and then release the closure." We have to find out for ourselves how to articulate the sounds we hear. And in the process we may make mistakes. Glaring mistakes are usually corrected over time. But less obvious deviations may persist. Moreover, misunderstanding the phonetic output of others is not limited to children. Adults, too, may mishear and consequently mispronounce words they are not familiar with. Many speakers of American English, for instance, pronounce the abbreviation *etc.* as [ekseterə], instead of the correct form [etseterə]; another common example is *aestetic* for *aesthetic*.

It is therefore not surprising that we can find occasional examples of sound changes which appear to result from such misunderstandings. An example is the substitution of uvular [ʀ] for trilled (post-)dental [r] . The substitution has been reported to be frequent among Spanish children; but in most Spanish dialects, children are corrected and told to use [r]. In rural dialects of Puerto-Rican Spanish, [ʀ] has caught on; and the second part of the name Puerto Rico is now pronounced [ʀiko]. In French, a similar substitution has become effectively the norm, except in theatrical stage pronunciation, where [r] is still preferred. Note however that [ʀ] has a strong tendency to weaken toward a voiced or voiceless velar (or uvular) fricative or "scrape". The usual Modern French pronunciation of a word like *rouge* has an initial voiced velar fricative [ɣ]. And the rural pronunciation of Puerto Rico commonly is [puelto xiko], with voiceless velar fricative.

The pronunciation of orthographic *gh* as [f] in certain English words likewise results from an acoustically or auditorily based misidentification. The original value of *gh* was [x], as it still is in Scots English. While in some English dialects, the [x] was lost across the board, in others [x] was dropped only after an original front vowel (as in words like *night*). Where [x] remained it was later misidentified as a labial fricative [f], because labials and velars share certain acoustic properties. This accounts for the pronunciation of words like *laugh, rough,* and *cough.* (Words of the type *though, plough,* and *through* came into the English standard language from dialects with across-the-board loss of [x].)

Since acoustically or auditorily based misidentification can cut both ways, it should not come as a surprise that other languages misidentified [f] as [x]. This has happened in Dutch, where earlier *luft* 'air', *graft* 'ditch, waterway', etc. have changed to *lucht, gracht,* etc., with *ch* = [x].

5.4. Structurally conditioned changes, "chain shifts"

Although the neogrammarians firmly believed that sound change is conditioned only by purely phonetic factors, research in the latter part of this century, especially by the French scholar André Martinet, has shown that changes may to some extent be triggered by more abstract considerations, such as the STRUCTURE of phonetic SYSTEMS. The most famous examples of this type are represented by so-called CHAIN SHIFTS in vowel systems. To illustrate the structural motivation of such chain shifts, let us look at two concrete examples of change in present-day American English. (Similar changes are found in many other languages and dialects.)

Certain lower middle-class dialects in New York, Chicago, and many other large urban areas of the northeastern part of the United States, exhibit the diphthongization of [æ] to something like [æə] under certain conditions (which need not detain us here). The diphthong tends to be strongly nasalized, and its initial element, [æ], tends to rise to mid-vowel or even high-vowel position, yielding something like [eə] or [iə]. As a consequence, words like *Ann* tend to be pronounced [æən], [eən], or even [iən]. (The latter pronunciation is, of course, identical to that of the name *Ian.* See § 4 above.)

Now, as long as nothing else happens, the changes in question may not appear particularly remarkable. But something else did happen, both in New York and in Chicago, even if that "something else" was different in the two cities. In both cities, there was a system-based reaction to the fact that old [æ] was vacating its position as a low front vowel and thus introducing a certain imbalance in the vowel system. In Chicago, the old central vowel [a] began to shift to the position vacated by [æ], thus rebalancing the system. Hence the pronunciation of words like *John* [ǰan] becomes sufficiently similar to that of words like *Jan* [ǰæn] in other dialects to confuse people not familiar with this dialect. In New York, on the other hand, the imbalance is redressed by the fact that the vowel [a] begins to follow the example of old [æ], diphthongizing and moving up toward the position of [u], as in the change of *coffee* [kafi] to [koəfi] or even [kuəfi]. Both of these chain shifts are outlined in Illustration 3, where the arrows marked with the numeral 1 indicate the initial change, the raising of old [æ] toward the position of [i] in [iə]; and the arrows marked by 2 represent the follow-up changes, of old [a] toward [æ] in Chicago and toward the position of [u] in [uə] in New York.

Chicago shift		New York shift	
i	u	i	u
1 ↑		1 ↑	
	2		2↑
æ	← a	æ	a

Illustration 3. Chicago and New York chain shifts

Chain shifts can lead to major rearrangements of phonetic systems. For instance, the change in New York, if carried to its logical conclusion, would eliminate the low vowels [æ] and [a] from the system. The capacity of chain shifts to bring about such major rearrangements has led scholars to suspect that similar sweeping rearrangements of phonetic systems in earlier or even prehistoric times, such as Grimm's Law, may likewise have resulted from chain shifts, even if the details of these shifts may escape us. For Grimm's Law, for instance, it is possible to cook up three or four different scenarios, all of them chain shifts. (Some of them may be more likely than others, but which of them actually took place remains anybody's guess.)

The most traditional interpretation, going back in spirit to the time of Grimm and Rask, assumes that the voiceless stops changed first by becoming aspirates (see the Xhosa example in (4) above and also Illustration 4 below). Under this view, the aspirates further changed into fricatives by the following steps: In aspirates with turbulent aspiration, the [h]-like hissing noise of aspiration may assimilate to the position of the preceding stop, so that [th] > [ts], [ph] > [pΦ], etc. The resulting combinations of stop + fricative offglide are commonly referred to as AFFRICATES. Thus in certain British English dialects words like *nineteen* may come out as [nayntsīn] instead of [naynthīn]. Similarly, in many varieties of modern Indo-Aryan, words like *phūl* 'flower' are pronounced [pΦūl]. Affricates, in turn, may be simplified by losing their stop element. This is found in other varieties of the same Indo-

Aryan languages, where [pΦūl] 'flower' is realized as [Φūl]. At this point, then, the fricative stage attested in Proto-Germanic (as well as in Sotho) has been reached. Changes of voiceless stops to voiceless fricatives are also observed in Northern Dravidian languages (in Central India and present-day Pakistan), and in Hungarian and other members of the Uralic language family (in Eastern Europe and adjacent parts of Asia). The whole series of developments, from (aspirated) voiceless stop through affricate to fricative, has been observed in a change that is still unfolding in the British English dialect of Liverpool, with words like *lock* changing to [lɔkh] with heavy aspiration > [lɔkx] > [lɔx]; see § 2 above. (Note, incidentally, that some linguists reject aspiration and affrication as intermediate steps between voiceless stops and voiceless fricatives and assume that voiceless stops can change directly into voiceless fricatives by a kind of weakening process.)

Once this complex set of developments has been set in motion, the position of plain voiceless stops has been vacated. And just as old [a] started to fill the position vacated by the diphthongization and raising of old [æ] in Chicago, so – it is claimed – the voiced stops begin to move into the position of the old voiceless stops in early Germanic. But this change leaves the position of the old voiced stops empty, and so the old aspirates move to fill that position. Compare Illustration 4, which ignores the further development of the voiceless aspirates *ph, th, kh* toward *f, þ, x*. This kind of shift, where sounds are "dragged" into a vacated position is commonly referred to as a DRAG CHAIN.

	ph	th	kh
		₁ ↑	
voiceless:	p	t	k
		₂ ↑	
voiced:	(b)	d	g
		₃ ↑	
voiced aspirate:	bh	dh	gh

Illustration 4. Grimm's Law as a chain shift

One of the other proposed chain-shift explanations is very similar, except that it reverses the order of events: The voiced aspirates are considered to shift first, toward the position of the voiced stops. To avoid merging with the voiced aspirates, the voiced stops move toward the voiceless stops. And these change their articulation to voiceless aspirate to escape merger with the old voiced stops. For obvious reasons, this type of shift is called a PUSH CHAIN. (A third approach focusses on the fact that the voiced labial stop *b* is rare in Proto-Indo-European and makes this the basis for a slightly more complex scenario.)

In the absence of relevant historical evidence, these scenarios must remain speculative, and a choice between them is not possible on purely empirical grounds. At the same time, some kind of chain-shift no doubt is responsible for Grimm's Law. It is hardly conceivable that some speakers of Proto-Indo-European woke up one fine morning to discover that their entire stop system had mysteriously changed over night, making their speech radically different from that of their fellow Indo-Europeans and branding them as Germanic "oddballs".

As something of a postscript to this section, it can be mentioned that the GREAT ENGLISH VOWEL SHIFT, too, resulted from some kind of chain shift. This change radically transformed the English vowel system and is largely responsible for the multiple phonetic values attached to English vowel letters. As a consequence *i* can denote both [i] and [ay], depending on whether it originally designated a short or long vowel, and the vowel letters *a, e,* and *i* are pronounced [ey], [ī], and [ay], in contrast to most other European languages which have [a], [e], and [i] (long or short, depending on the language). Examples are given in Illustration 5.

Old Engl.	Mid. Engl.	Mod. Engl.		Old Engl.	Mid. Engl.	Mod.Engl.
bītan	*bīten*	*bite* [ay]	vs.	*biten*	*biten*	*bitten* [i]
hūs	*hūs*	*house* [aw]		*sungen*	*sungen*	*sung* [ə]
hē	*hē*	*he* [ī]		*better*	*better*	*better* [e]
dōm	*dōm*	*doom* [ū]		etc.		
dǣd	*dǣd*	*deed* [ī]				
stān	*stȭn*	*stone* [ow]				
nama	*nāme*	*name* [ey]				

Illustration 5. The Great English Vowel Shift

As in the case of Grimm's Law, opinions differ as to how the change unfolded. The most widely accepted hypothesis assumes a drag chain, with the high long vowels *ī* and *ū* changing first, becoming diphthongs – most likely [əy] and [əw] respectively. The high-vowel positions vacated in this way then were filled by the long mid vowels, whose emptied positions, in turn, attracted the long low vowels, and so on. Compare the simplified presentation in Illustration 5a, which distinguishes two phases, one prior to Shakespeare, the second post-Shakespearean and affecting the outputs *ē* and *ǣ* of the pre-Shakespearean phase.

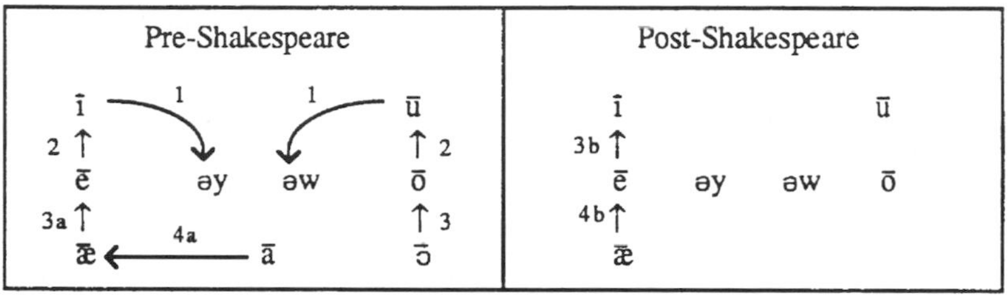

Pre-Shakespeare	Post-Shakespeare

Illustration 5a. The Great English Vowel Shift as a chain shift

Instead of a drag chain, some linguists postulate a push chain, where the change was initiated by a general raising of the vowels putting pressure on the highest vowels. Since these could not be raised any further, they diphthongized instead.

In this case, empirical evidence makes it possible to decide in favor of the drag chain: Spelling variation and testimony by contemporary observers show that only the shifts on the left side of Illustration 5a had been completed by the time of Shakespeare. Old *ǣ* and *ā*, which by now had become *ē* and *æ* respectively, lagged behind and reached their modern positions only in the post-Shakespeare period; compare the right side of Illustration 5a. The fact that these two low vowels lagged behind is precisely what we would expect in a drag chain. If the shift had been a push chain, one would expect them to have been in the vanguard of the change.

5.5. Fast, furious, and faulty speech: Typically sporadic changes

While the types of sound change examined in the preceding sections by and large exhibit the regularity postulated by the neogrammarians, a few changes are notoriously irregular or SPORADIC.

Consider for instance words like Engl. *ma'am* or *bye*. The first of these is patently derived from *madam*; but just as patently, the change involved is not a regular change. For instance, we do not say *A'am* for *Adam*. Moreover, *madam* still coexists with *ma'am*. Regular sound change supposedly does not leave such unchanged residue. The expression *bye* is derivable from *good bye*, which itself is derived from *God be with ye* (with *good* substituted for *God* for taboo reasons). And again, the changes that link *God* or *good be with ye* to *good bye* and *bye* are isolated, limited to just this expression.

Irregular shortening developments of this type are rather frequent in forms of address and formulas of greeting and leave-taking, i.e., in expressions of verbal POLITENESS. Compare further It. *mona* (as in *Mona Lisa*) < *Madon(n)a* 'my lady'; the polite second-person address forms Skt. *bhavat* < *bhagavat* '(your) lordship' and Span. *usted* < *vuestra merced* 'your grace'; and the German greeting *Mo(ə)ŋ* < *Morgen* < *Guten Morgen* 'good morning'. While developments like *Morgen* < *Guten Morgen* may be considered something like ellipsis (see Chapter 5), reductions like *Mo(ə)ŋ* < *Morgen* cannot be explained in this manner. Like *ma'am* they seem to be clear examples of sporadic sound change, and thus an acute embarrassment to the regularity hypothesis.

Note however that reduced pronunciations of the type *Mo(ə)ŋ* are not limited to politeness expressions. They are a common phenomenon in FAST or ALLEGRO SPEECH and other forms of less than carefully monitored speech. In fast speech, German speakers are just as likely to say *mo(ə)ŋ* for the adverb *morgen* 'tomorrow' as for the expression *(Guten) Morgen*. In fact, fast speech is notorious for its extensive and pervasive reduction of phonological structure. Even sound sequences that would not be permissible in careful or LENTO speech occur quite freely in fast speech, as in English [ŋaygow], with initial velar nasal, for careful *Can I go?*

In general, we filter out such highly reduced forms and pretend that only the lento forms exist. And because we, as speakers, filter out allegro forms, linguistic change generally operates on these, and not on allegro forms. The fact that politeness expressions are frequent exceptions can be explained as follows: While society expects us to be polite, we may not necessarily want to lose too much time over it. Even sticklers for etiquette may find excessively lengthy politeness expressions in bad taste. As a consequence we tend to use the shorter forms furnished by fast speech (as well as ellipsis).

Similar extensive, even excessive, reductions are commonly found in expressions like *you know* when we use them – much to the dismay of self-anointed critics – as speech fillers or in order to reassure ourselves that the addressee is still listening. Reductions of *you know* may range from the fairly innocuous [y(ə)now] to things like [nyə] or even [yow]. Here it is the relatively subordinate semantic or communicative value of the expression that is responsible for the phonological reduction.

One suspects that similar factors are responsible for the very common phonological reduction of CLITICS. These are a special class of words with the following characteristics: They are typically function words and thus, like the type *you know*, of reduced communicative significance. Probably as a consequence, they do not bear an accent of their own. As a result, they differ from "well-behaved", "normal" words which do bear accent. Furthermore, unlike normal words they cannot occur by themselves, and must therefore "lean on" another word, called the HOST. (The name clitic is derived from the Greek root *kli-* 'to lean on'.)

Elements of this type take something of an intermediate position between full words and affixes. Examples of English clitics are the *n't* of forms like *can't, hasn't, isn't* and the *'s* of forms like *John's got the flu, Mary's at work*. As can be readily seen, these elements cannot be pronounced by themselves (except by linguists who have learned to pronounce all kinds of things that ordinary speakers don't). They have to lean on a preceding host. In fact, if there is a slight break in the utterance, separating the host from the element in question, the clitic cannot occur and the full form must be used instead. Compare unacceptable *Mary – 's at work** with acceptable *Mary – is at work*.

What is relevant in the present context is that all of these English clitics have undergone a large variety of weakenings or reductions. Compare the reduced forms *n't* and *'s* with their corresponding full, non-clitic forms *not, has,* and *is*. Phonological reductions of this type are very common in clitics.

If we try to generalize, we may say that the different forms of irregular reduction and weakening processes we have examined above originate in speech that is "down-graded", either because it is less than carefully monitored, or because it is communicatively of minor importance.

In addition to down-grading, we may also "up-grade" our speech. For instance, although glottal stops do not occur in the lento speech of most varieties of English, they are not uncommon in speech that expresses anger or other forms of strong psychological affect. While in examples like *shut [ʔ]up already*, such glottal stops are a rather transitory phenomenon, in some expressions they have become institutionalized. In the U.S. military, for instance, the command *attention* usually is pronounced with a glottal stop instead of the final *n*. In the absence of a conventional spelling for glottal stops, this variant pronunciation is commonly spelled *(at)ten(s)hut*. The spelling *nope* may hide a similar glottal-stop pronunciation [noʔ]. (Spelling and/or the absence of [ʔ] from the inventory of "normal" English speech sounds may be responsible for the fact that some speakers may actually pronounce *attenshut* and *nope* with a final dental or labial stop.)

Upgrading is not limited to angry speech. In English, expressions like [**mm**a(r)vələs] or [**bi**yūtiful] for normal *marvel(l)ous* [ma(r)vələs] or *beautiful* [byūtiful] serve to express the fact that the speaker feels that something is especially 'marvelous' or 'beautiful'.

In Modern English, the expressive consonant doubling, or GEMINATION, in expressions like [**mm**a(r)veləs] is a fairly transitory phenomenon, presumably because the normal language does not have phonetic geminates. (Written double consonants, as in *lass*, are pronounced the same as single consonants, as in *gas*.) Modern Italian, however, has geminates and, interestingly, expressive gemination appears in *mammà*, a word for 'mother' which like its cousins in other European languages (Fr. *maman*, Germ. *Mama*, or Engl. *mama*) belongs to the affective vocabulary of nursery talk, the form of language used by adults with very young children and modeled on the babbling of early childhood. Expressive gemination may also account for the shape of Mod. Engl. *lick*, OE *liccian* vs. Goth. *(bi)-laigon* 'lick', or German *Zicke* 'goat', *Zicklein* 'kid' beside *Ziege* 'goat'. In both cases, the single voiced *g* is what we would expect from regular sound change. (For instance, the PIE root for 'lick' was **l(e)iǵh-*. And as we know by now, Grimm's Law would change voiced aspirate **gh* to voiced *g*.) The words with modern [k], from early Germanic [kk] (as in OE *liccian*), reflect expressive gemination, plus a further "strengthening" of the geminates by making them voiceless. In *lick*, the gemination seems to reflect the fact that licking frequently is a repeated and thereby intensive act. In *Zicke, Zicklein* one suspects that gemination originated in affective usage, referring to the proverbial liveliness of goats or the cuteness of their kids.

Like the reductions of "down-graded" speech, expressive gemination or glottal-stop insertion affects only individual words and leaves most words unaffected. Thus, while there is an English *nope*, there is no *gope** for *go*. Moreover, changed *nope* coexists with unchanged *no*, just as *ma'am* coexists with *madam*. Affective changes, thus, are just as irregular or sporadic as the effects of downgrading. Moreover, both types of sporadic change play a very marginal role in language change.

A much more significant role is played by a group of sporadic changes that were recognized by the neogrammarians as systematic exceptions to their regularity hypothesis. The two most prominent of these changes are known by the names dissimilation and metathesis. Before trying to explain their irregularity, it is useful to take a closer look at the changes.

DISSIMILATION is the logical opposite of assimilation. Where assimilation makes different sounds more similar to each other, dissimilation makes similar sounds more different. An English example, cited earlier in this chapter, is *colonel* pronounced as if it were written *cornel*, where the first of the two [l]-sounds dissimilates to [r]. An even more radical dissimilatory step is found in the common non-standard pronunciation of *library* as if it were written *libary*. Here the first of two [r]-sounds dissimilates by simply disappearing. Examples like *contrary*, with both [r]-sounds retained, show that the change is in fact sporadic, not regular.

Note however that some instances of dissimilation have all the appearance of having once been completely regular. For instance, in the early history of Sanskrit, all but the last of several aspirated stops in a given word lost their aspiration by dissimilation; see example (16). Like Grimm's and Verner's

Laws, this change has received a great amount of attention in historical linguistics (and even in other branches of linguistic research); and like these changes it was named after its discoverer – GRASSMANN'S LAW.

(16)   Proto-Indo-European Sanskrit
  bhudh-ye-toy   **budh**-ya-tē 'is awake'
  bhe-bhowdh-e   **bu-bōdh**-a   'was awake'
  dhi-dhē-ti   **da-dhā**-ti   'puts, places'

METATHESIS consists of the transposition of sounds within a given word. An example in modern non-standard English is the pronunciation of *ask* as [æks] or [aks]. This pronunciation, actually, has hoary antecedents. Already in Old English we find the ancestor of this word spelled both as *ascian* and as *acsian*. Metathesis has been quite frequent in English vowel + liquid or liquid + vowel combinations. But the examples in (17) show that the process was far from regular: Many words that might have qualified did not undergo the change.

(17)   a. OE *bryde* NE *bird*
               frist   *first*
               þridde   *third*
         vs.   *þrysce*   *thrush*
        b.   *beorht*   *bright*
         vs.   *word*   *word*

Metathesis frequently goes beyond individual words and affects whole utterances. In such cases it has received a special name, SPOONERISM, after an English cleric who was famous for his often amusing transpositions, such as *Let me sew you to your sheets* instead of the intended *Let me show you to your seats*. (However, many Spoonerisms cited in the literature cannot be attributed to the Rev. Spooner with any degree of certainty.)

Spoonerisms suggest that dissimilation and metathesis have a great affinity to SPEECH ERRORS, in the sense of "faulty" phonetic production. This impression is reinforced by incidents such as the following. In the early seventies, the lead author of this book heard an announcer on a local radio station attempt to say ... *in rural areas*. What actually came out was something like ... *in* [rūəl], *uh*, [rūləl], *uh*, [rūrəl] *areas – I always have problems with that word*. Evidently, the sequence of three liquids, [r ... r ... l], caused the announcer considerable difficulties and resulted in two different dissimilations. Difficult sequences of this type, of course, are the foundation for tongue twisters, such as the infamous *Peter Piper picked a peck of pickled peppers*. Dissimilations and metatheses are especially frequent when people are tired or drunk (or both), i.e., when their ability for monitoring their speech production is diminished. (In addition, of course, tired and drunk speech also is full of reductions comparable to those of fast speech.)

It may very well be that the only thing distinguishing speech errors like these from historically attested dissimilations and metatheses is that they remain temporary mistakes, while changes as in *bryde* > *bird*, for some reason, caught on and became a permanent feature of the language.

In addition to dissimilations and metatheses, "faulty speech" abounds in distant assimilations, such as *heroic pouplets* for *heroic couplets*. In fact, tongue twisters like *Peter Piper picked a peck of pickled peppers* normally are cleverly constructed such that our choice of dissimilating the repeated [p]s in sequences like **Peter Piper** is biased by the assimilative influence of the [k]s of words like *peck* and *pickle*.

Like dissimilation and metathesis, distant assimilation frequently catches on in the historical development of languages. For instance, Old French had the verb *cercher* [serčer] 'search, look for', from which Engl. *search* was borrowed. The expected Modern French outcome is [serše]. Instead we find *chercher* [šeršč] with distant assimilation of the initial [s] to the later [š], as in the famous expression *cherchez la femme*. But again, like dissimilation and metathesis, distant assimilation normally is a sporadic phenomenon.

6. Why sound change?

6.1. Early views

Ordinary human beings, not influenced by what linguists think on this matter, generally view all linguistic change, including sound change, as a matter of decay. This view, in fact, was shared by many of the pioneers of historical linguistics, as well. Only occasionally do we find a dissenting voice, such as that of Grimm, who attributed his famous sound shift, not to decay, but to the Germanic people's "drive for freedom".

Since early Indo-Europeanists came to historical linguistics from a background in – and great love for – classical languages, it is understandable why they reacted the way they did. As already noted in Chapter 1, the great classical languages had five noun cases (Greek), six cases (Latin), or even eight (Sanskrit), whereas the number of different case endings is vastly reduced in the modern languages. The majority of Romance languages have no case distinctions whatsoever in their nouns, English only marks genitives by separate endings, and even a language like German, which nominally preserves four cases, does not distinguish the different cases as clearly as the classical languages. If you have grown up loving rich case systems, the modern languages do indeed look as if they had undergone massive decay. Of course, the premise here is that you love cases. Some linguists have claimed that those many different case endings of the classical languages are a useless burden on people's memory and that languages like English have improved by getting rid of this unnecessary baggage. This view, again, rests on an a priori assumption, namely that case endings somehow are bad for you. Linguists nowadays find it difficult to be comfortable with either view, considering that the speakers of languages such as English are quite happy without all those case endings, while speakers of modern "case-rich" languages such as Finnish or Turkish are just as happy with them. This insight, incidentally, goes back to the neogrammarians and is one of their many great contributions to linguistics.

Decay and progress are not the only motivations proposed for linguistic change. As noted above, Grimm attributed his famous changes to the Germanic people's "drive for freedom" which supposedly led to a more energetic pronunciation. As a consequence, the voiceless stops became heavily aspirated stops which, by later changes, turned into fricatives. (See § 5.4 above.) Other scholars operated with the same idea of more energetic pronunciation, but attributed it to factors such as a move to higher elevations which made it necessary to breathe more vigorously, or a change in diet which required more energetic chewing. These explanations and many others like them, however, failed just as much as the notions decay and progress. First of all, we have no evidence suggesting that the Germanic people lived in a relatively mountainous area at the time of Grimm's Law, or that they changed to a different diet. Secondly, given our much broader knowledge of linguistic change, we can say for certain that there is no correlation whatsover between climate or diet and linguistic change. Finally, it is not even certain that the Grimm's-Law change of voiceless stops to voiceless fricatives proceeded via such "more energetic" heavily aspirated stops. As noted in § 5.4 above, some linguists have claimed that the change proceeded directly from voiceless stops to voiceless fricatives and therefore constituted a weakening of articulation.

6.2. Neogrammarian explanations

Although many individual neogrammarians continued to cling to such older ideas about the reasons for linguistic change, their major theorists attempted to give different explanations. In these they were strongly influenced by the work of contemporary phoneticians. Relying on vastly improved instruments, the phoneticians had come to the realization that all human speech is full of low-level deviations from an idealized norm. No two utterances are ever completely alike; there is no such thing as an exact repetition (except by mechanical means). The feeling that there is a norm results only from the fact that variation follows the classical bell-shaped curve pattern (see the top part of Illustration 6), with most of the deviations staying fairly close to the norm, so close in fact that only a trained phonetician can observe them. Building on this empirically well-established foundation, the neogrammarians proposed that sound change results from a SHIFT OF THE IDEALIZED "TARGET" within the area of variation; see the lower part of Illustration 6.

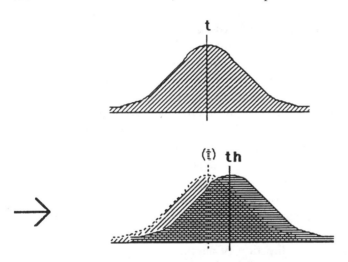

Illustration 6. Sound change as deviation from an idealized norm

While at first quite appealing, this explanation runs into serious difficulties once we examine it more closely. The very idea expressed by a bell-shaped curve is that the deviations from the norm cancel each other out and thereby confirm the idea of the norm. Why, then, are we to assume that all of a sudden the rules of the game no longer apply and there is a cumulative deviation in the direction of a new target?

One might suppose that a certain direction is built into linguistic change in so far as it leads to SIMPLIFICATION. Assimilation, weakening, and loss, the three most common types of change certainly can be argued to reduce the amount of effort required to speak. And the fact that speakers of English find it very difficult to pronounce the word-initial [kn-] in foreign words like *knish* or names like *Knut* might be considered to corroborate the view that the change of earlier initial [kn-] to [n-] was a genuine simplification.

Similarly, speakers of English, German, and many other languages find initial [sr-] difficult to pronounce, as in *Srinagar*, the name of the capital of Kashmir (in northern India). And lo and behold, PIE *sr- was eliminated in Germanic by changing to *str-, as in Engl. *stream*, Germ. *strömen* 'to stream' vs. Skt. *sravati* 'flows', all containing the PIE root *sr(e)u- 'to stream, to flow'. So again, sound change simplified matters, didn't it? It even has been claimed that the replacement of trilled [r] by [ʀ] (see § 5.3 above) was a simplification, not just an acoustically-based misidentification. And from the perspective of those who have it, [ʀ] is in fact simpler than [r].

But, those who have trilled [r] find [ʀ] difficult. And those who have neither find both sounds difficult. Similarly, speakers of languages that tolerate initial *sr-* (Kashmiris, for instance) have no difficulties with this combination and might consider *str-* more "complex". In fact, for cases like [r] vs. [ʀ], *sr-* vs. *str-* it is difficult to come up with any objective evidence that supports the view that the new pronunciation is any easier than the old one – except the circular argument that otherwise the change would not have taken place. For [kn-] vs. [n-] it is much easier to consider [n-] a simpler structure. Nevertheless, speakers of languages that tolerate initial *kn-*, such as German, have no difficulties at all. Here as elsewhere, the maxim holds that "even the children speak the language" which has the supposedly more difficult sounds or combinations of sounds. (See also Chapter 1, § 1.)

Even if we dismiss the notion of simplification, it might be claimed that processes like assimilation have a built-in directionality and thus would motivate a cumulative deviation from the norm, as in Illustration 6. After all, one sound assimilates in the direction of another.

But many other linguistic changes are possible, beside assimilation. What motivates the choice of assimilation, rather than one of these other changes? Even if the choice were to be in favor of assimilation, this does not in itself provide a directionality for deviation. Assimilation comes in many different degrees and varieties. For instance, if we are given a sequence *tm* and told to assimilate, we can a priori go into at least the following different directions: *pm, bm, mm* with various degrees of assimilation of the first sound to the second; *tn, dn, nn* with a similar variety in assimilation of the second to the first; or even *tp, db, tt, dd, pp, bb* with both sounds assimilating to each other. Even closely related languages may choose different paths. For instance, some of the early descendants of Sanskrit changed *tm* to *tp*, others to *tt*, and yet others to *pp*, as in. Skt. *ātman-* 'self' : *atpan-, attan-, appan-*.

Realizing the difficulties with this approach, the neogrammarians came up with a second explanation: CHILDREN learn the basics of their first language without any instruction, simply by imitating the speech of their elders. In the process, they may misperceive the norms of their elders and come up with different norms of their own.

This explanation, too, seems very plausible at first. In fact, even today it can claim many adherents. But the same problem arises as in the case of the first explanation: Why should the deviations be cumulative, in one direction? In fact, when we examine early stages of child language we find a great degree of variation, both for individual children and across different children. Recent research shows that although early child language deviations and linguistic change show certain similarities, there are also considerable differences. We only need to look at what commonly happens to the children of immigrants to convince ourselves that the effect of parents' input and of deviations in early language learning are minimal at best: No matter what the original language of the parents, or the children's early attempts to learn it, once children are socialized into peer groups, they quickly adopt the speech of their peer group. As a consequence, British parents who proudly maintain their accent for the rest of their lives in America, find – much to their horror – that their children speak with a "broad midwestern accent", a "Southern twang", or what not, depending on the speech of their peers.

Sensing that this explanation does not provide satisfactory answers either, some of the neogrammarians proposed that sound change originates as deviations in the IDIOLECT, or individual speech variety, of a prestigious person. Here, of course, we must again ask why the deviations of such a speaker should be consistent. Now, in some cases, they might result from a speech defect. For instance, it has been claimed that the French change of trilled [r] to uvular [ʀ] originated with Louis XIV, who could not articulate [r]. His great prestige supposedly was responsible for the adoption of the change by other speakers. This claim receives some support in the fact that the change apparently spread to many urban speakers of German, along with many patterns of behavior that emanated from the court of Louis XIV. However, the change [r] > [ʀ] has been observed in many other areas of the world, including isolated rural areas of northern Germany which hardly were influenced by the court of Louis XIV. In fact, in Germany, the uvular pronunciation has been observed as early as about 1600, well before Louis XIV. Most important, however, the idea that change might originate with some prestigious person is just a thought experiment. There is no empirical evidence whatsoever that behind every one of the thousands and thousands of sound changes that have occurred in human language there has been a famous person.

6.3. Labov and the social motivation of change

The fundamental difficulty with all three of the explanations proposed by the neogrammarians is that they are based on thought experiments, not on the observation of changes as they actually take place. The reason is that the neogrammarians firmly believed that sound change is unobservable. They came to this conclusion by the following line of argument: Sound change takes place "blindly", without regard for its effects on the structure of words or our ability to communicate; the fact that speakers make no attempts to remedy these effects until the change has run its course indicates that sound change is actually unobservable to them.

So far, so good. But then the neogrammarians made a grave mistake: They assumed that sound change is unobservable not only to speakers, but to linguists as well. For some reason the neogrammarians failed to realize that the phoneticians had no difficulties in observing the low-level variation in human speech which ordinary speakers were not even aware of. As a consequence, the neogrammarians made no attempts to observe sound change in progress.

Meanwhile, a number of linguists had serious reservations about many of the neogrammarians' views, including the belief that sound change and analogy differ fundamentally from each other, one being "mechanical" and regular, the other, based on mental associations and irregular. They argued that instead, the two types of change were fundamentally the same and differed from each other only in degree. In the hope of finding empirical evidence for this view, they began to investigate sound changes in progress. By hindsight, some of their results were quite revealing and would at least have required some serious rethinking about the nature of change. Unfortunately, however, the number of scholars pursuing this "unorthodox" line of inquiry was small, much smaller than the orthodox followers of the neogrammarians.

It was not before the mid-1960s that a major change took place, in response to a series of detailed empirical investigations by the American scholar William Labov which were presented clearly and forcefully enough to catch the attention of most historical linguists.

Like his "unorthodox" predecessors, Labov found that the neogrammarians' views on sound change were in serious need of revision: Sound change is observable, at least by trained linguists. As sound change takes place, it may be conditioned not just by phonetic factors, but also by such factors as word structure and meaning. Even more significant, during its propagation, sound change exhibits a lot of irregularity. It is only in its final outcome that sound change is overwhelmingly regular.

Interesting as these findings may be, Labov came up with an even more radical proposal: Sound change and, in fact, all linguistic change is ultimately motivated not by purely linguistic factors, but by SOCIAL considerations.

This claim is most strikingly supported by Labov's study of a recent sound change on Martha's Vineyard, an island off the coast of Massachusetts. If we simply consider the "input" and "output" of the change, there is nothing much remarkable about it: The vowel [a] was centralized to the position of the mid-central vowel [ə] in the diphthongs [ay] and [aw], as in *right* [rayt] > [rəyt] or *rout* [rawt] > [rəwt]. However, the manner in which the change unfolded is quite remarkable.

Labov found that at the earliest stage, only a few words exhibited a variation between [a] and a slightly more centralized variant, only in the diphthong [aw] if followed by voiceless sounds, and only in the speech of a few individuals.

Somewhere along the way, the variant with centralization was perceived by speakers as a symbol of identity, differentiating "islanders" from the "mainlanders". (Note that there has been a long tradition of animosity by Martha's Vineyarders toward the mainland of Massachusetts. Occasionally, this animosity results in attempts to secede from the Commonwealth of Massachusetts, even though – so far – these attempts have failed.)

When it had come to be perceived as socially relevant, the centralized variant began to get generalized along a number of different parameters, including the following:

– the number of speakers using the variable in their speech
– the number of words exhibiting the variant
– the phonetic contexts in which it occurred, including an extension of the variable to the diphthong [ay]
– the degree of centralization (from a slightly centralized [a] toward a fully mid-central [ə])

All of these generalizations followed the pattern of a classical S-curve: An initial phase with fairly little change, followed by a period of rapid change, and eventually a point near saturation where the change slowly peters out. (See the simplified presentation in Illustration 7.)

Moreover, Labov found an interesting correlation between attitude toward the mainland and the degree to which the centralized variant was adopted: Those with the most polarized attitude toward the mainland tended to have the highest degree of centralization, in the largest number of words, and in the broadest range of phonetic contexts. On the other hand, those with a

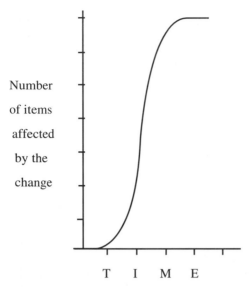

Number

of items

affected

by the

change

T   I   M   E

Illustration 7. A classical S-shaped curve

positive attitude toward the mainland exhibited the change to a much lesser degree, if at all.

Based on this study and others that he conducted at roughly the same time Labov proposed that sound change (and all other change, as well) proceeds in the following manner:

(i) The starting point for sound change is the inherent variability of human speech. (Labov did not differ on this count from the neogrammarians and the nineteenth-century phoneticians.)

(ii) For reasons that perhaps must remain a mystery forever, a particular variable is interpreted by a certain group as socially significant. At this point, the variable ceases to be a "mere performance" variant and takes on not only social, but also linguistic significance.

(iii) Under the pressure of its social significance or "marking", the variable gets generalized to new contexts, in terms of both social and linguistic parameters. (On the role that male : female differences can play in social marking and in the extent to which a change may be generalized, see Chapter 11, § 1.) What makes it possible for the generalization to continue is the fact that the new pronunciation does not immediately replace the old one, but that old and new pronunciations coexist with each other for some time. The variation between old and new pronunciations, then, can be extended to new forms, much along the lines of analogical change: If, say, we have a variation [aw] : [əw] in the word *house*, then this variation can be extended to, say, *mouse* or *louse*.

(iv) If, as usually happens, the process of generalization continues long enough and without anything to disturb it, the eventual outcome may be a regular sound change, which affects all instances of the sound, and all speakers in the speech community.

This view of sound change as socially conditioned has since then been confirmed by a number of other studies. It also explains a number of things about language change which otherwise would be difficult to account for.

One of these is the fact, noted earlier, that even if a language "decides" to have a specific type of change such as assimilation, the direction of assimilation cannot be predicted on purely linguistic grounds. This is to be expected under Labov's view of linguistic change: The low-level variation of human speech includes a large variety of small-scale assimilations, going in many different directions. Which of these is chosen as socially significant is, from the linguistic perspective, quite arbitrary.

Another aspect of linguistic change explained by Labov's view is the fact that there appear to be changes which are moving extremely slowly, so much so that there can be some legitimate doubt as to whether they will ever reach completion. One of these, noted already in the early part of this century, is the English change of long [ū] (as in *boot*) to short [u] (as in *foot*) found in many varieties of English (and difficult to localize geographically). Let us refer to this change as *oo*-shortening. Unlike the centralizing change on Martha's Vineyard (which was completed in about three generations), this change seems to have been going on for several centuries but still shows no sign of coming to completion. And whereas in the steep part of its S-shaped-curve development, the Martha's Vineyard change affected many lexical items at the same time, *oo*-shortening even now is affecting only a few lexical items: Variability is limited to just a few words (such as *roof, room, root*), while many others only have the long-vowel pronunciation (such as *food, mood, groom, groove*).

Interestingly, the difference in social connotations between, say, [rūt] and [rut] (for written *root*) is minimal. At best we can say that [rūt] may strike some people as perhaps a little too formal, while others consider [rut] a little too informal. This is a far cry from the strong social connotations associated with centralization on Martha's Vineyard. If social marking is indeed the driving force behind linguistic change, then the differences between *oo*-shortening and the centralization of Martha's Vineyard make eminent sense: The fact that centralization took place quite rapidly reflects the strong social motivation of the change, while the slow-moving nature of *oo*-shortening is explained by its weak social motivation.

As a final illustration of the explanatory power of Labov's view of linguistic change, let us take up the issue of typically regular vs. typically sporadic sound change. As noted earlier, sporadic changes are very similar to speech errors and, as such, would be highly noticeable. Regular changes, by contrast, may start as rather minor deviations from an idealized norm, so much so that if somebody said to us, "Hey, you didn't make your [a] in *house* low enough", we would not even understand what the person is saying – except, of course, if we are linguists. (But, as noted in Chapter 1, most speakers are not linguists!)

If these arguments are on the right track, then we can explain the difference between regular and sporadic sound change: The fact that most sporadic changes are noticeable as speech errors makes it very difficult for them to be seized upon as marker of social identity. After all, who would want to be identified with a speech error?

Labov's new view of linguistic change has proved its usefulness in many other areas. But perhaps its greatest importance lies in the fact that it provides a satisfactory answer to the question, "Why sound change?"

Chapter 5
Analogy and change in word structure

> "I never heard of 'Uglification'," Alice ventured to say. "What is it?" The Gryphon lifted up both its paws in surprise. "Never heard of uglifying!" it exclaimed. "You know what to beautify is, I suppose?" "Yes," said Alice doubtfully: "it means – to – make – anything – prettier." "Well, then," the Gryphon went on, "if you don't know what to uglify is, you *are* a simpleton."
>
> (Lewis Carroll, *Alice's Adventures in Wonderland*.)

1. Introduction

As noted in the preceding chapter, early historical linguists believed that linguistic change is tantamount to decay, a falling away from a pristine stage at which language was perfect and wonderful. (This, in fact, is still the prevailing view among non-linguists.)

While phonetic deviations were considered the result of slovenly speech, the major reason for decay in linguistic structure was thought to be "false analogy". Ancient Greek and Latin grammar and linguistic philosophy had introduced and popularized the notion of analogy as a designation for structural pattern or regularity. "False" analogy, then, lay in permitting a word to deviate from the "true" or "proper" pattern. For instance, in Early Modern English, the "true" pattern of making a plural of the word *cow* consisted of a vowel change (reflecting the sound change of umlaut) and the addition of an ending [-n]; hence *cow*, plural *kine*. When the plural form was replaced by the form we use today, *cow-s*, the word was permitted to follow the – "incorrect" or "false" – analogy or pattern of words like *pig : pig-s, horse : horse-s*. False analogy was considered characteristic of late, decaying languages.

One of the great achievements of the neogrammarians, generally overshadowed by the fame of their regularity hypothesis, was the insistence that such notions as decay and false analogy are inappropriate in historical linguistics. Reconstructed languages and their early offshoots should not be considered any more perfect than later, or even modern, descendants. There is no indication whatsoever that speakers of ancient Greek (or, we might add, Old English) were able to communicate any more effectively than speakers of Byzantine or Modern Greek (or of Modern English). Similarly, the neogrammarians argued, all linguistic phenomena encountered in observable history must be accepted as possible in reconstructed Proto-Indo-European as well, or in its early descendants. This view, which liberated historical linguistics from earlier, prescientific ideas, has since become known as the UNIFORMI-TARIAN HYPOTHESIS, a term borrowed from geology (where the notion of uniformitarianism brought about a similar revolution in thinking).

Consequently, changes of the type *cow : kine* → *cow-s* could no longer be claimed as limited to late, "decaying" languages, but had to be accepted as a possibility at all stages of linguistic development. This change in perspective led to a rejection of the term false analogy and its replacement by the simple term ANALOGY.

Note, however, that as a consequence of this relabeling, the term analogy underwent a considerable change in meaning, from "pattern" or "regularity" to something like "change in phonetic structure conditioned by non-phonetic factors in other lexical items, such as word structure, syntactic function, and semantics". Analogical change, as defined now, tends to introduce greater phonetic similarity between semantically, formally, or functionally similar linguistic forms.

2. Relatively systematic analogy

The neogrammarians considered all analogy to be essentially irregular or sporadic. Still, they recognized that two analogical processes are considerably more systematic than others: FOUR-PART ANALOGY and LEVELING. Four-part analogy is the process that gave rise to Mod. Engl. *cow-s*. Leveling is responsible for the disappearance in English of many of the MORPHOPHONEMIC ALTERNATIONS created by Verner's Law (see Chapter 4, § 3). Recall that one of the results of Verner's Law was an alternation between *s* and *r*, as on the left side of (1) below. This alternation has been eliminated in Modern English, where *s* (now pronounced [z]) has been generalized throughout; see the right side of (1). Both of these processes are sensitive to very general aspects of word structure, or MORPHOLOGY. At the same time, both processes, especially four-part analogy, can have profound effects on morphology. These effects are taken up in § 4 below.)

(1)   OE *cēosan*   (present)   : Mod.Engl. *choose*
             cēas   (past sing.)   :   *chose*
             curon   (past plur.)   :   *chose*
             (ge)coren (past participle) :   *chosen*

2.1. Leveling

Leveling can be defined as the complete or partial elimination of morpho-phonemic alternations that do not seem to signal important differences in meaning or function. This elimination takes place within a PARADIGM, i.e., in the set of inflected forms of a given word (or in a subset of such forms), such as the verbal paradigm in (1). The motivation for leveling has been plausibly expressed in the slogan ONE MEANING – ONE FORM.

The development in (1) is a perfect example of leveling. As noted earlier, the Old English morphophonemic alternation was the result of Verner's Law (Chapter 4, § 3), which like all other regular sound change operated without regard for the complications that it might introduce in word structure (see Chapter 4, § 4). As long as the alternation was still in place, the word for 'choose' had (at least) two different variants, one with *s*, the other with *r*. The distinction between *s* and *r*, however, did not correlate with any significant difference in meaning or function, since *s* is found both in the present and in the singular of the past, while the other forms of the past have *r*. Eliminating the alternation, thus, did not entail sacrificing any important distinctions. Moreover, it served beautifully to bring the various forms of the verb 'choose' closer to the ideal of "one meaning – one form".

The situation is a little different as far as the root vowels are concerned. In Old English, these vowels differed for all of the four different forms: *ēo* (whatever its precise pronunciation) in the present, *ēa* in the past singular, *u* in the past plural, and *o* in the past participle. Modern English clearly shows some effects of leveling, in that the three past forms have the same root vowel [ō]. But the present tense has escaped this leveling and uses a different root vowel, [ū]. How are we to explain this incomplete or partial leveling?

The answer becomes clear if we ask ourselves, What would have happened if the leveling had affected the entire paradigm? Clearly, in that case, there would be no formal distinction between present and past. Leveling, then, must have been blocked so that the important distinction between present and past tense was not lost. On the other hand, the vowel alternations in the three past tense forms did not signal any important distinctions, since all of the forms had the same tense value.

Leveling is a fairly systematic process. For instance, most of the *s : r* alternations created by Verner's Law were eliminated in English. Words which once exhibited the alternation include Mod. Engl. *lose, freeze, rise.* (The same holds true for the other alternations produced by Verner's Law.) However, the systematicity of leveling is a far cry from the regularity of sound change. For instance, the verb *rise* had undergone leveling in the prehistory of English, while *lose, freeze,* and *choose* were changed after the Old English period. Even today, one verb, the notoriously "irregular" verb 'be' has escaped leveling in the past tense, retaining the *s : r* alternation in *was : were.* Other, less obvious RELICS are *for-lorn,* whose second element is the old past participle of *lose,* and *rear,* originally a derived form of *rise* meaning 'make rise, make grow up'. (Mod. Engl. *raise,* which seems more closely related to *rise,* is a borrowing from Scandinavian.)

English is not the only language that has leveled out most of the effects of Verner's Law. German did likewise. But, interestingly, the direction of leveling was different. While in the dialects underlying Standard English the sibilant was generalized, in German it was *r.* Compare example (2), the German counterpart of the English example (1). The difference between English and German suggests that even if languages start out with essentially the same alternation, they may differ about the direction of leveling. At the same time, it is remarkable that English consistently extended the sibilant alternant, while German equally consistently generalized the *r.*

(2)   OHG *kiosan*   (present)   : NHG (archaic) *küren*
              kōs   (past sg.)   :   *kor*
              kurun   (past pl.)   :   *koren*
              (gi)koran (past partic.) :   *gekoren*

Things are even more complex. Some dialects of English appear to have done the same thing as German. For instance in the Newfoundland dialect of English, some people say *frore* instead of Stand. Engl. *froze.*

It appears, then, that the direction of leveling is unpredictable, at least across different languages and dialects.

In fact, there are further complications. In many cases it may be perfectly clear whether a given alternation is significant or not; however, there are cases where different speakers evidently had different ideas about this matter. For instance, the effects of umlaut have in English largely been eliminated. Only a small set of "irregular" forms preserves them, such as *tooth : teeth, goose : geese, foot : feet.* In German, by contrast, umlaut is still very much alive, as in the present-tense verb paradigm in (3). More than that, in the nouns it has actually been extended (by four-part analogy, see the next section). Compare example (4) and note that this extension of umlaut has affected many other nouns. It has been plausibly argued that this extension serves to make the plural forms more clearly distinct from the singular. We must therefore conclude that the effects of umlaut were considered significant in German, in contradistinction to English where they were considered insignificant.

(3)   OHG   NHG

		OHG	NHG	
sg.	1	*faru*	*fahre*	'go' (compare Engl. *fare*)
	2	*ferist*	*fährst*	
	3	*ferit*	*fährt*	
pl.	1	*faram(es)*	*fahren*	
	2	*faret*	*fahrt*	
	3	*farant*	*fahren*	

(4)

OHG		NHG		
sg.	pl.	sg.	pl.	
gast	*gest-i*	*Gast*	*Gäst-e*	'guest'
boum	*boum-a*	*Baum*	*Baum*-e* → *Bäum-e*	'tree'

In general, leveling affects what we might call the phonetic representation of words and affixes. And in so doing it tends to undo the effects of sound change. Leveling thus confirms the somewhat paradoxical maxim:

> Sound change, though inherently regular, creates irregularities in the morphology. Analogy, though inherently irregular, attempts to undo the effects of sound change and thus to make morphology more regular.

(Many linguists believe this to be true about all of analogy. The statement, however, is most saliently true about leveling. Other analogical processes may be triggered by factors that have no relation to sound change.)

In some cases, the effects of leveling can go beyond the phonetic representation of words and affixes. This is especially so when, as the result of other linguistic change, a given morphological category exhibits an alternation between a "Ø-affix" (i.e., the absence of an affix) and an affix with phonetic content. Consider, for instance, the example of English plurals. In Old English, the nominative plural forms of the most productive masculine and neuter nouns were as in the left column of (5), with *-as* in the masculines and -Ø in the neuters. As gender distinctions became irrelevant in English noun inflection, the two endings came to be interpreted as variants of a single plural affix, realized as *-(e)s* in some nouns, -Ø in others. In Modern

English, the phonetically full ending *-(e)s* generally was leveled out, at the expense of the Ø-ending; compare the right column of (5). This development is not surprising, given that the singular : plural distinction can be considered important. Significantly, however, its effect goes much beyond ordinary leveling: In examples like (1) and (2), individual lexical items are affected, whereas in (5), the effect is on the overall MORPHOLOGY.

(5)

	OE		Mod.Engl.	
	sg.	pl.	sg.	pl.
masc	*stān*	*stān-as*	*stone*	*stone-s*
neut.	*word*	*word-Ø*	*word*	*word** → *word-s*

Note however that, just like the German extension of the umlaut pattern in certain noun plurals in (4), the development in (5) can also be explained in terms of the concept of four-part analogy (see the next section). This seems to be true for all cases in which leveling affects the overall morphology of a given language. Leveling and four-part analogy thus are not always clearly distinguishable from each other. In some cases they may "cooperate"; and it is this cooperation, it seems, which makes it possible for leveling to have a general effect on morphology.

As a kind of postscript, it might be mentioned that the earlier English plural alternation between *-(e)s* and *-Ø* was not always leveled out in favor of *-(e)s*. A few sets of English nouns referring to animals have kept the Ø-plural and, in fact, extended it to words which originally had an *s*-plural. Two major sets of nouns can be distinguished, a set of words referring to animals that are or may be hunted (especially *deer*) – the "hunt" type – and another set consisting mainly of words for (different types of) fish (such as the word *fish* itself, as well as many other words such as *haddock*) – the "fish" type. What complicates matters and at the same time makes things more interesting is that there is a fair amount of vacillation between the two sets. Finally, there are a few words such as *sheep* and *swine* which are not easily classified.

For the "hunt" type it may be significant that *deer*, the word for the quintessential object of the hunt, had a Ø-plural even in Old English. But most other words had original *s*-plurals (or other forms marked by a plural suffix). In fact, even in present-day usage, many of the hunt words may have alternative *s*-plurals when they are not used in the context of hunting; thus beside expressions such as *they were hunting (wild) fowl* or *boar* we may get references to *barnyard fowls* or *five boars*. (The Old English plurals of *fowl* and *boar* were *fugl-as* and *bār-as*, from which the modern *fowl-s* and *boar-s* can be derived by regular changes.) The reason for the somewhat surprising extension of the Ø-ending for hunt words may have been a social one: One suspects that the starting point for the Ø-plural was the word for 'deer', in which the Ø-plural was inherited, and that this form of the plural was generalized among the medieval and early modern British gentry as a grammatical marker associated with the hunt, one of the favorite activities of that class and one from which the commoners tended to be excluded. It is the same social setting that sported such hunt-related expressions as *An exultation of larks, A pride of lions, A pack of wolves*. Further support for this account of our Ø-plurals comes from the fact that the words *deer* and *fowl* have been semantically specialized to refer to animals or birds that are hunted, while OE *deor* and *fugal* simply meant 'animal' and 'bird', just as their modern German cognates, *Tier* and *Vogel* [f-]. (For another meaning of *fowl*, see below.) A similar semantic development can be seen in the word *hound*, now generally a hunting dog, but in Old English meaning 'dog' in general. (Again, German has preserved the original meaning in the cognate *Hund* 'dog'.)

For the "fish" type, it may be relevant that a fundamental distinction was made in traditional Roman Catholic society between *meat*, which could be eaten on most days of the week, and *fish*, which had to be eaten on Fridays instead of meat. (Recall that up to the sixteenth century, Roman Catholicism was the dominant religion in all of England.) This distinction is reflected in fixed, idiomatic expressions such as *neither fish nor flesh* (where *flesh* is used in the older meaning 'meat') or *neither fish nor fowl*, which contrast *fish* with other types of meat that can be consumed on days other than Fridays. Now, when talking about things such as meat and fish as prepared food, as in *Are we having meat or fish tonight?*, we regularly use the singular form in a collective sense, even for words that normally have *s*-plurals and even for words that may belong to the hunt type. Thus we would normally say *We are having chicken* or *(game) fowl for dinner*; an expression like *We are having chickens for dinner* would suggest rather that we would have to consume uncooked individual chickens or that we would have to do the cooking ourselves. One suspects that because of its special significance in traditional Roman Catholic society, the word *fish* and other words referring to different types of fish extended the collective singular form *fish* to contexts where a plural form might have been appropriate, such as *They caught six fish*. This extension evidently was a slow process, for the old *s*-plural (reflecting OE *fisc-as*) persisted into the seventeenth century.

Vacillation between the two sets, then, may be explained as resulting from the fact that words such as *fowl* can be used both to refer to an animal of the hunt and to a particular type of meat. Those who use the term *fowl* only (or mainly) as a word for food will treat the word as belonging to the fish category, while those who are familiar with the word in broader contexts, including the hunt, may treat it as belonging to the hunt category.

Finally, the Ø-plurals *sheep* and *swine* correspond to Old English Ø-plurals and may therefore simply be archaic retentions. The retention of the Ø-plural could perhaps be motivated by the fact that sheep and swine are thought of, not so much as individuals, but as collection of animals; however, related words such as *lamb* and *pig* have *s*-plurals, even though they could just as easily be thought of as collections of animals.

2.2. Four-part analogy

The process designated four-part analogy involves the remaking of a morphologically "derived" formation on the model of another, generally more productive derivational pattern by means of an analogy which can be expressed by a proportion involving four parts:

$$a \quad : \quad a'$$
$$b \quad : \quad X \ (= b')$$

(or "*a* is to *a'* as *b* is to X = *b'* "). The process may also be characterized as a PROPORTIONAL ANALOGY; but that term is used in a broader meaning (to include processes such as backformation and hypercorrection; see later in this section as well as § 6 below).

FOUR-PART ANALOGY is the process that gave rise to the regular *s*-plural of Mod. Engl. *cow*; see (6). The proportion in (6) reflects the fact that most English plurals are morphologically derived from the corresponding singular by the addition of the plural marker -*s*. Proportions like the one in (6) have characteristics very similar to mathematical equations. The new form, *cow-s* therefore can be obtained by solving for X, on the derived – plural – side of the equation.

(6)   Engl.   *stone* : *stones*
                    arm   : *arms*
                    . . .   : . . .
                    cow   : X = *cows* (replacing earlier *kine*)

Now, not all imaginable proportions lead to analogical replacements. Some fail to do so simply out of "inertia". For instance, words like Mod. Engl. *tooth : teeth, goose : geese, foot : feet* have not changed their plurals to *tooths*, gooses*, foots**. Given the fact that analogy normally is not regular, the failure of certain forms to undergo a possible analogical replacement should not come as a surprise. Still, if somebody were to say *tooths* or the like, we would be able to understand what she or he is saying – even if we might consider the form to be wrong. (Actually, for expressions like *silly goose*, the plural commonly is of the form *silly gooses*.)

Our reaction would be very different if we heard someone say something like *thang* as the past tense of *thing*. True, we can set up a neat proportion of the type *ring : rang = thing : X*. But there is no morphological relation between *ring*, a verb, and *thing*, a noun. This lack of relationship makes the proportion meaningless: The derivational pattern giving rise to *rang* as the past tense of *ring* simply cannot be extended to *thing*. This shows that to be meaningful, four-part analogy has to operate on forms that are morphologically related. (The vernacular pronunciation [θæŋ] of *thing* reflects sound change, not analogy; [θæŋ] does not mean something like 'a thing of the past'.)

Morphological relationship, however, is not enough. If someone were to say to us that a skunk *roke* or *rought to high heaven*, our reaction would be the same as for *thang* – a complete lack of comprehension. Now, *roke* and *rought* can easily be motivated by proportions of the type *speak : spoke = reek : X* or *seek : sought = reek : X*. More than that, if we reversed the proportions, as in *reek : reeked = speak : X* and solved for X = *speaked*, the situation would be quite different. True, as in the case of *foots*, people might take exception to our "bad grammar", but they would have no difficulty understanding us. The reason for this difference in reaction is that patterns of the type *speak : spoke*, *seek : sought* are not productive in English, while the type *reek : reeked* is. Four-part analogy, thus, has a greater chance for success if it extends a PRODUCTIVE pattern of morphological derivation.

This is not to say that patterns that are less productive cannot be generalized. For instance, the verb *dive* made its past tense with the productive suffix *-(e)d* as early as Old English. Even so, Modern English permits *dove* as an alternative form of *dived*. The model for this development must have been *drive : drove*. But this pattern of forming past tenses is not productive in English.

Some developments of this type, which run counter to expectation, are difficult to explain. For others, however, it is possible to think of an explanation.

Consider for instance the case of Engl. *bring : brought : brought*. In many vernacular forms of English, this pattern is replaced by *bring : brang : brung* or *bring : brung : brung*, on the model of verbs like *sing : sang : sung* or *fling : flung : flung*. Both of these model patterns are "irregular" and non-productive. (For instance, the relatively recently derived verb *to king*, referring to the process of making a checker piece into a "king", has the past tense *kinged*; a form such as *kang* or *kung* would be unthinkable, except perhaps as a joke.) However, the patterns *sing : sang : sung, fling : flung : flung* are found with a fair number of other verbs and thus are less irregular than the pattern *bring : brought : brought*, which is limited to just one word. Replacing *brought* by *brang* or *brung*, thus, makes the inflection of *bring* more regular. True, it is not as regular as a potential *bring : bringed : bringed*; but that might be considered going too far, considering that this is an irregular verb and that even words like *sing* and *fling* have resisted complete regularization.

Even cases where a productive pattern is replaced by a non-productive one can sometimes be motivated. For instance, the original Modern English plural of *dwarf* is the completely regular form *dwarf-s*, but in many varieties of American English, the plural has changed to *dwarv-es*, whose formation follows a much more irregular plattern.

The most likely model for this change is the semantically closely related word *elf*, whose plural *elves* has been irregular for many centuries. And the reason for the extension of this irregular pattern to *dwarf* may be that both words belong to the vocabulary of fairy tales and similar types of stories, in which elves make a frequent appearance and in which at least one other word ending in *f* and making an irregular plural is commonly used, namely *wolf*. The irregular plurals in *-ves*, thus, may have been felt to be characteristic of fairy-tale or fantasy characters, much as the Ø-plural of words like *deer* appears to have been interpreted as characteristic of hunt-related terms (see the preceding section).

Though productivity plays a major role in four-part analogy, it is by no means clear what makes a particular type of formation productive and others non-productive. In this regard, note that the English *s*-plural has not always been the single most productive form of making plurals. In Middle English it competed with another plural formation, using the suffix *-(e)n*; and in some Middle English words, this suffix actually replaced the *s*-ending. Thus, while the Old English plural of the word *shoe* had an *s*-plural, Middle English shows both *s(c)hoes* and *s(c)hoon* or *s(c)hoen*. In Modern English, by contrast, the *n*-plural remains only in a few relics: *oxen, children, brethren*, and early Mod. Engl. *kine*.

Some scholars have attributed the eventual victory of the *s*-plural to outside influence. After 1066, French exerted a great influence on English, especially in the area of the lexicon. And the normal, productive plural marker of French is *-s*, which in medieval times was still pronounced as [s]. (As those who have learned French know, in the modern language the plural marker *-s* normally is "silent".) However, the idea that the *s*-plural of French lent a helping hand in the eventual victory of the English *s*-plural runs into difficulties – the victory took place much later, at a time when the importance and potential influence of French had greatly diminished. During the time of greatest French influence, the *s*-plural had serious competition from the *n*-plural (see above). More than that, even if the *s*-plural did become productive due to French influence, the Middle English productivity of the *n*-plural cannot be attributed to outside influence. The issue of how productivity arises, therefore, still remains an open question.

The notions productivity and morphological relatedness, important as they may be, are not sufficient to make four-part analogy successful. Consider the reaction you might have if somebody talked to you about a *Chinee* who will be coming to visit. Your reaction would probably be very much the same as in the case of *thang* (as the past tense of the noun *thing*) or *the skunk roke to high heaven*.

As a matter of fact, though currently not acceptable as an English word, *Chinee* is found in eighteenth-century travel descriptions. And it is perfectly possible to explain *Chinee* on the basis of a productive plural : singular proportion, as in (7). In contrast to *thang*, this proportion cannot be simply ruled out on the grounds that there is no morphological relatedness, for the word *Chinese* clearly can be used in the sense of a plural, as in *The Chinese are a people in East Asia*.

(7)   *employee-s* [-īz] : *employee* [-ī]
       Chinese [-īz]   : *X*.

The fact that the word *Chinee* nevertheless causes great difficulties can be explained by observing that we have solved the equation on the "wrong" side – not on the morphologically derived side, but on the basic side. To be fully successful, four-part analogy evidently needs to be solved on the derived side of the proportion.

This does not mean that developments of the type (7) are impossible. Even though significantly rarer than "well-behaved" developments, they are sufficiently common to have received a name of their own, BACKFORMATION.

Examples of fully successful backformations are Mod. Engl. *pea, sherry,* and *orate*. The ancestor of Mod. Engl. *pea* is early Mod. Engl. *pease*, a mass noun like *rice*. The word survives in the nursery rhyme *Pease porridge hot* ... Now, a mass of *pease* consists of individual pieces. Moreover, *pease* happens to end in [-z], the variant of the plural marker -*s* that would be appropriate after vowel. It was therefore possible to reinterpret the word as a plural, referring to a plurality of individual pieces. Given this reinterpretation, the pattern *beans : bean* (etc.) = *peas(e) : X* made it possible to create a new singular, *pea*.

The word *sherry* came about in very much the same way. Originally it was a borrowing from earlier Spanish *Xerez (de la Frontera)*, now *Jerez de la Frontera*. The word entered English as referring to the fortified wine coming from the city of *Xerez*, whose *X-* was pronounced [š], and was nativized as *sherries*. (This form is found for instance in Shakespeare's *Henry IV, Part 2*.) The rest is history, as it were.

Orate and many (but not all) other verbs ending in *-ate* are backformations from "agent nouns" like *orator*, created on the model *speak-er* [-ə(r)] : *speak* = *orat-or* [-ə(r)] : *X*. Verbs of this sort are motivated by the fact that nouns like *orator* clearly designate someone who engages in a particular activity, but as the result of historical accident there was no morphologically related verb to express the activity of an *orator*. Backformation solved the problem by furnishing a handy verb from which the agent noun can be considered to be derived. (Other backformations, such as *orientate*, are probably derived from "action nouns" of the type *orientation*.)

If some speakers of Modern English use forms like *to drug-deal*, these result from essentially the same process, although the details differ. The starting point clearly is *drug-dealer*, i.e. a 'dealer in drugs'. Ordinarily, the word would correspond to a verbal expression *to deal in drugs*, from which it can be said to be derived – just as *car-dealer* is derived from *deal in cars*. For some speakers, this derivational relationship seems to have become unclear, perhaps because the noun *drug-dealer* is used much more frequently than the corresponding verbal expression. The verb *drug-deal*, then, could be created for the same purpose as *orate* and the like – to furnish a handy verbal counterpart to the agent noun.

Unlike leveling, four-part analogy has a clear and very strong impact on morphology. As we have seen, it can lead to the integration of particular words into more productive morphological patterns, sometimes even less productive ones. And, as noted in § 2.1, in combination with leveling it can bring about an extension of particular affixes (as in example (5)), or even the elimination of affixes (as in the case of *deer, fish, fowl*).

Combined with the effects of sound change, especially the very common phenomenon of loss in final syllables, four-part analogy (with or without the help of leveling) can have far-reaching repercussions for morphology. These are discussed in fuller detail in § 4 below.

3. Sporadic or non-systematic analogy

As we have seen in the preceding section, leveling and four-part analogy (if operating in the right direction or in favor of productive forms) can be highly systematic, even if not regular in the manner of sound change. The reason for this systematicity no doubt lies in the fact that both types of change operate within well-defined and fairly general parameters. Leveling works within paradigms, and most paradigms accommodate more than one or two words. In fact, productive paradigms may work for hundreds of words. Four-part analogy operates with derivational patterns, especially productive ones which, again, may accommodate hundreds of words.

Most other types of analogical influence on linguistic form are not conditioned by such well-defined and general parameters. Instead, by their very nature they tend to affect only one or two words at a time. This does not mean that they are rare. As a matter of fact, they are quite common. But their effect usually is much more "helter-skelter" than that of four-part analogy and leveling.

3.1. Blending, contamination, and similar processes

Consider for instance the phenomenon of BLENDING, also referred to as portmanteau. Example (8), a citation from Lewis Carroll's *Through the Looking-Glass*, provides an excellent definition of the process.

(8)   Humpty Dumpty to Alice:
       Well, *slithy* means "lithe and slimy". "Lithe" is the same as "active".
       You see it's like a portmanteau – there are two meanings packed into
       one word.

As in the *slithy* of example (8), blending often is a deliberate process, employed to coin new words, often with a wisp of humor (at least when they are first coined). Compare the examples in (9). In many cases, the results of blending express something like a compromise between "competing" words, as in the examples in (9a). For instance, the word *brunch* designates a meal that combines properties of both *breakfast* and *lunch*; the latter two terms therefore are in something like a competition as names of that meal. But blendings may also "telescope" the components of a compound expression into a single, more neatly packaged unit. Thus, *telethon* in (9b) is a *telephone marathon*, an American fundraising event calling for telephone pledges, and long and exhausting like a marathon race. Such "packaging" makes blends especially useful for advertising purposes, as in (9c).

(9)   BLENDING   SOURCES
    a. *chortle*   *chuckle : snort*   (Lewis Carroll)
        brunch   *breakfast : lunch*
        broccoflower   *broccoli : cauliflower*
        motel   *motor : hotel*
        boatel   *a boat converted into a hotel*
    b. *Dixiecrat*   *a Dixie Democrat* (i.e., from the US South or
                           Dixieland)
        exercycle   *exercise (bi)cycle*
        telecast   *television newscast*
        bik(e)athon   *bike marathon*
        telethon   *telephone marathon*
    c. *Toyotathon*   *a Toyota marathon sale*
        Croisan'wich   *a croissant sandwich*

Blending may also occur unconsciously, as a kind of compromise between actually competing forms. For instance, the first form in (10), frequently heard among children, is a compromise between the correct form *feet* of adult language and the regularized (four-part analogical) form *foots*. Similarly, the early Modern English plural form *kine* appears to be a compromise between the phonetically regular outcome of OE *cy* [kü], *kye* (preserved in British English dialects), and an *n*-plural of the type *oxen*, **cow-(e)n*; see the second example in (10). Other similar non-deliberate blendings are given in the remainder of (10).

(10)   *feets*   *feet : foot-s*
        kine   *kye : *cow-(e)n*
        children   *child-er* (OE *cildru*) : **child-en*
        irregardless   *irrespective : regardless*
        near miss   *near hit : miss* (in aviation)

The last two of these blendings are commonly considered substandard or incorrect, and a fair amount of ink has been spilled on *near miss* as being a logically flawed recent development. Whatever its logical shortcomings, however, *near miss* has been around for quite some time: It was used, for instance, in an Allied news report on the bombing of the French city of Caen at the end of World War II.

Blends even may affect whole utterances, at least in one-time speech errors. For instance, the lead author of this book overheard the following sentence on National Public Radio (7 February 1991): *Thomas's death will be missed.* Evidently, the person who scripted this line conflated the following two sentences into one: *Thomas will be missed* and *Thomas's death will be regretted/mourned.*

A process very similar to blending, and sometimes difficult to distinguish from it, is CONTAMINATION. Before trying to define what is meant by the term, let us take a brief look at an example.

Latin had two adjectives whose meanings were polar opposites, *gravis* 'heavy' and *levis* 'light'. (Such words are called ANTONYMS.) In the form of Latin which, as "Proto-Romance", underlies the modern Romance languages, *gravis* changed to *grevis*, hence OFr. *grief*, OSpan. *grieve*, Ital. *greve* 'heavy'. (Original Latin *gravis* would have yielded OFr. *gref*, OSpan. *grave*, Ital. *grave*. Mod. Fr. *grave* 'heavy' clearly is a later borrowing from Latin, and the *grave* of Modern Italian and Spanish is no doubt likewise.) What has happened here is that *gravis* has been "contaminated" by *levis* by adopting the pronunciation *grevis*, whose *e* is closer to the *e* of *levis*.

Changes of this sort are very common in antonyms, as well as in numerals. Both antonyms and numerals are often uttered in close succession (with perhaps a short conjunction intervening), as in *Is it **heavy** or **light**?* or ***One two three.*** One possible interpretation, therefore, is that contamination starts out as a distant assimilation, a speech error similar to spoonerisms (see Chapter 4, § 5.5). The fact that the assimilation catches on would be due to the close semantic relationship between the words in question. A different interpretation, not necessarily incompatible with the preceding, is that antonyms and numerals form psychologically closely related sets and that their adjacency in mental storage might favor some kind of formal assimilation, irrespective of whether they occur next to each other in actual speech.

Some additional examples of contamination may be found in (11). As these examples show, contamination differs from blending in that the two words or their meanings are not telescoped into one but remain as distinct words, albeit phonetically more similar ones. For instance, Engl. *eleven*, whose *n* results from the influence of *ten*, does not designate something like '10½', but just plain '11'.

(11) | Engl. | *male : female* | ⇐ Fr. *male : femelle* |
|---|---|---|
| Engl. | *ten : eleven* | PGmc. **tehun : *ainlif* |
| | | (compare Germ. *zehn : elf*) |
| Dial.Gk. | *hepta : hoktō* | Standard Gk. ***hepta** : oktō* '7' : '8' |

A nearly opposite development is observed in cases like U.S. Armed Forces Engl. *niner* for *nine*, used to distinguish this numeral from *five* under poor communication conditions. Similar circumstances have given rise to Germ. *eins, **zwo**, drei* for *eins, zwei, drei*, and ***Juno, Julei*** for *Juni, Juli*.

In some cases, such differentiations involve selection of a dialectal or archaic variant (Germ. *zwo*); Germ. *Julei* with -[ay] may have been modeled
on Engl. *July*, and *Juno* is the name of a Roman Goddess, boldly substituted for the similar sounding *Juni* to avoid confusion. In cases like U.S.
Armed Forces Engl. *niner*, the differentiation seems to result from deliberate
distortion. As examples like *niner* vs. *five* show, in contrast to contamination, distortions or substitutions of this type are not limited to neighboring
numerals.

The examples of blending and contamination so far examined would certainly entitle us to believe that neither process has much chance of being
systematic: In each case, the analogical process involves just two lexical
items – in stark contrast to leveling and four-part analogy which potentially
affect hundreds of words.

Nevertheless, some blendings have broader effects. For instance, once
forms like *bik(e)athon* and *telethon* in (9b) have arisen, it is possible to
reanalyse them as containing a suffix *-(a)thon*. Four-part analogy, then, can
extend this suffix to new forms, such as *rentathon* or *saleathon*. (Expressions
like this are special favorites of the advertising industry, as in (9c) above.
A recent TV commercial by one car maker pokes fun at the competitor's
saleathon by staging a fake *thonathon*.)

Other processes, very similar to blending and contamination, can lead to
patterns that are quite productive. Consider for instance the English onomatopoetic set *bang, bash, batter; clang, clap, clash, clatter; crack, crash;
smack, smash, smatter;*... There are at least thirty-two words of this sort
in current use; and several others sprang up during the history of English,
only to die again. If the written tradition of English can be trusted, the set
started out from very humble beginnings. Only one word, *clatter*, is attested
as early as the eleventh century, and the thirteenth century adds *dash*. It is in
the fourteenth century that the pattern begins to take off, with the appearance
of *batter, clap, crack, patter, rap, ram, rap, rattle, slash, smatter*. And some
words, such as *whang* and *wham*, have made their appearance as late as the
nineteenth and twentieth centuries.

The exact process by which this set propagated itself is not entirely certain.
It is tempting to set up proportions of the type *bang : batter = clang : X*. But
the problem is that words of this type do not seem to have any morphological
structure to speak of. What, for instance, would be the meaning or function
of *b-* or of *-ang* or *-atter*? Proportions of this type would not be any better
than *sing : sang = thing : X*. Rather, what seems to be going on is some kind
of more vague influence of forms on each other, similar to what we find in
blending and contamination.

Some scholars have referred to very similar phenomena as RHYMING FOR-MATION: Words that agree in part of their phonetic representation and are similar in meaning often get to be more similar by coming to rhyme with each other or, alternatively, to alliterate, i.e., to acquire identical initial consonants. (While rhyme is a very common principle of poetry, alliteration can serve a similar poetic function, as for instance in early Germanic.)

Sometimes, this rhyming principle operates simply by combining compatible pre-existing words that happen to rhyme or alliterate, such as Engl. *wining and dining*, or *rest and relaxation, bed and board, rock and roll*. In most cases, such expressions are quite transparent. But note occasional examples like *kit and caboodle*. What's a *caboodle*?

A more interesting type is represented by such things as *helter-skelter, hoity-toity, hocus-pocus, hodgepodge, hurdy-gurdy, hurly-burly, nitwit, pell-mell*. In some words of this type, it is possible to account for the origin of one or, even more rarely, both of the rhyming components. For instance, in *pêle-mêle*, the French source of *pell-mell*, it is possible to etymologize the second element as *mêle* 'mix'. But the source of the other part of the word is wrapped in mystery. In many other words of this type, the entire etymology is uncertain.

In English, expressions of this type are fairly common if they involve rhyme. Pure alliterating examples are much more difficult to find. Perhaps words like *know-nothing, go-getter, two-timer, tattle-tale* belong here. Much more common is the type *flim-flam, riff-raff, zig-zag, mish-mash, pitter-patter; drip-drop, flip-flop, sing-song; hee-haw, gew-gaw*. Here we find not only repetition of the initial consonants, but also the final ones (if there are any). In addition, most of these words exhibit one of a very limited set of vowel alternations, which recur in such sets as *sing : sang* or *sing : song*. Linguists refer to these alternations as ABLAUT or apophony.

There is thus a strong general tendency toward rhyming formation. Moreover, words of the type *drip-drop, pitter-patter* are remarkably similar to the words in sets like *bang : bash : batter*. Not only are they onomatopoetic, some of the words agree in the phonetic shape of their rhyme as well. Compare for instance *pitter-patter* and *batter, shatter*, etc. Finally there are rhyming pairs in other onomatopoetic words, such as *thump : bump, drip : blip*.

Given these facts we are perhaps entitled to explain sets like *bang : bash : batter* etc. as resulting from rhyming formation.

In some languages, rhyming patterns of this type may become generalized, to such an extent that we can talk about a morphologically productive pattern and invoke four-part analogy (or some kind of rule) to account for thc propagation of the pattern. Some varieties of English have acquired just such a pattern from Yiddish. Compare such expressions as *school-shmool, linguistics-shminguistics,* or *nice-shmice.* Here the second part of the rhyming word has a completely arbitrary and standardized initial consonant combination, and the connotations of the combination are completely predictable. For instance, *school-shmool* means something like 'school – who cares?' or 'school – who needs it?' Moreover, given the right circumstances, the pattern can be extended to just about any noun or adjective.

Sign languages, too, offer sporadic instances where one sign affects the form of another because of a close relationship in meaning. For example, in American Sign Language the sign for 'patient' (adject.) used to be formed with the head nodding down and an index finger drawn against the lips. Now it is formed by a downward movement of the hand over the lips – the hand movement telescopes the original separate gestures of the head and of the hand into a single sign. In addition, however, another development has taken place: The sign for 'patient' is no longer formed with the index finger, but with the hand in the shape of a fist and the back of the thumb touching the lips. This change has been attributed to contamination by the semantically related sign for 'suffer' which employs the fist shape.

3.2. Other sporadic processes

While blending and contamination involve at least two words at a time, other analogical developments tend to affect single words and thus would normally be highly sporadic.

One of these is REANALYSIS or REINTERPRETATION of morphological structure. If for instance a child responds to the admonishment *Behave!* by saying *But I'm being have,* he or she evidently has misunderstood the morphology of *behave.* Instead of interpreting the expression as a simple lexical item, the child has (re-)interpreted it as being morphologically composite, parallel to the many other commands that grown-ups tend to direct at children, such as *Be quiet!* or *Be nice!* Given this interpretation, the response *But I'm being have* is no different from responses like *But I'm being quiet.*

One wonders how many reinterpretations of this sort take place in the early stages of first-language learning. That this is a common phenomenon is suggested by recurrent anecdotes. One that has been so widely told and retold as to have entered English folklore is the following: When asked why she kept calling her bear *Gladly,* a child answered *Oh you silly, don't you know? It's Gladly, my cross-eyed bear.* Evidently the child had misunderstood the beginning words of the well-known church hymn, *Gladly, my cross I'd bear.*

Other children are reported to have said things like *Lead us not into Penn Station* for the passage *Lead us not into temptation* in the Lord's Prayer.

Most such reinterpretations of early childhood do not make it into adult speech or become part of the language in general. This is, of course, not surprising, given Labov's observation that linguistic change takes place in the post-childhood social setting of peer groups. (See Chapter 4, § 6.3.)

Nevertheless, some reinterpretations have caught on. This seems to be especially common in the area of "linking" or LIAISON phenomena: In English, for instance, the indefinite article has two forms, *an* which is used before vowel, and *a* which occurs elsewhere. Now, the *n* of *an* generally is phonetically linked to the following vowel, so that things like *an apple* are pronounced as if they were written *a napple*. This fact is often drawn on for the purpose of punning, as in *He's a nice man : He's an ice man*.

What is important for present purposes is that liaison can create ambiguities, especially in rarer, less well-known words: Should the sequence *a-n*-vowel be morphologically resolved as *a* plus a word beginning in *n* + vowel, or as *an* plus a word beginning in a vowel? Evidently, such uncertainties have in some cases led to reanalyses. For instance, the two English words *napkin* and *apron* ultimately both derive from a French word stem *nape* '(table) cloth'. While *napkin* has faithfully preserved the original initial *n*, the combination *a-n-apron* must have been reinterpreted as *an* + *apron*. Even common words may be affected by reanalysis. Witness the common English expression *A whole nother one*, instead of "correct" *A whole other one*, with *nother* reanalyzed in the combination *another*.

Just like blending and contamination, reanalysis can sometimes lead to new morphological patterns. In fact, we already have seen one example of such reanalysis, the *-(a)thon* of forms like *bik(e)athon, telethon*, etc. While the starting point for this particular reanalysis lies in blendings, reinterpretation may affect much more mundane morphological structures. For instance, the *-ician* of Engl. *beautician* and *mortician* arose by a reanalysis of forms like *electrician, mathematician, logician* as containing a suffix *-ician* indicating a skilled professional. As a matter of historical fact, of course, words like *electrician* are to be analysed as *electric* plus a suffix *-ian* which, among other things, indicates a skilled professional. Words like *beautician* and *mortician* therefore were attacked as "incorrect" when they first were used, because there is no *beautic** or *mortic** from which they could be derived. The fact that they have become part of the general English vocabulary confirms the observation in Chapter 1 that attempts by purists to stem the tide of linguistic change by and large are ineffectual, and that the ultimate authority lies with the speaker.

The role of linguistically unsophisticated speakers is even more noticeable in two closely related analogical processes, "recomposition" and "folk
etymology", especially in the latter. To understand the nature of these processes it is useful to observe that sound change often obscures the structure
of compounds. For instance, Mod. Engl. *lord* derives from OE *hlāf-weard* by
a series of regular sound changes, and *lady* goes back to *hlāf-dige*. The Old
English words literally meant 'bread-warden' and 'bread-kneader'. Given the
importance of bread as a staple of medieval diet, those who controlled the
production and distribution of bread in an extended household wielded considerable power. This accounts for the fact that the meanings of these words
quickly acquired much more powerful and "noble" connotations.

Similarly, *daisy* derives from MEngl. *daies-ei(e)* 'day's eye' = '(little)
sun', and *boatswain* (a petty officer on a boat), pronounced [bōsn̥], comes
from MEngl. *bot(e)swayn(e)* 'young man on the boat'.

Many "faded" compounds of this type have remained unchanged, effectively becoming morphologically non-composite lexical items. Others, however, have been renewed, made more transparent, by RECOMPOSITION. Compare for instance the examples in (12). In the word *hussy* of (12a), sound
change obscured the outcome of OE *hūswīf* 'house-wife' beyond recognition;
and the meaning of the word changed drastically, too (on this see Chapter 7).
The sound changes involved were of a sort that affect longer words which
contain internal consonant combinations of the type [sw], [tsw], etc. These
changes would naturally fail to apply to OE *hūs* 'house' and *wīf* 'woman,
wife' when they occurred by themselves, and these words simply developed
into Mod. Engl. *house* and *wife*. Modern English, then, in effect undid the
results of the sound changes that led to *hussy*, by recombining the independent words *house* and *wife*. The examples in (12b) may perhaps be explained
along the same lines. Here, too, the result of sound change as it applies in
longer words appears to have been undone by recombining the component
parts in the shape that they received as independent words. However, the
examples in (12b) can alternatively be explained as spelling pronunciations:
The component parts are spelled the same as when they are used as independent words. The pronunciation associated with the spelling of the independent
words then may have been introduced into the compounds.

(12)   Early form of the Outcome by sound Recomposition
          compound   change
     a. OE *hūswīf*   *hussy*[1]   *housewife*
     b. OE *tōweard*   *toward* [tɔrd]   *toward* [tuwɔrd]
          OE *forhēafod*   *forehead* [fɔrɪd]   *forehead* [fɔrhɛd]

([1]In British English, this word was until recently pronounced as if written *huzzif* or *huzzive*.)

Examples of the type (12) represent cases where the results of recomposition are historically correct. For instance, the elements in Mod. Engl. *housewife* are historically the same as those in OE *hūswīf*. As noted in Chapter 1, however, most speakers are not linguists. They are therefore not aware of what the historically correct etymology of a given word may be. All they are concerned about is that a particular form "looks like it ought to be a compound", but is not easily recognizable as such.

There are quite a few such words in English. Note for instance *cranberry* or *raspberry*, which are clearly compounds containing the word *berry* as their second element and in this respect resemble fully transparent compounds like *blackberry* and *blueberry*. But what is *cran-* or *rasp-*(pronounced [raz/ræz])? (The element *cran-* is often connected with *crane*, but from the English perspective that is a folk etymology, since the word is a borrowing of Germ. *Kronsbeere*. Interestingly, however, from the German perspective, the etymology is sound, since the German word contains a dialectal form of the word *Kran/Kranich* 'crane'. This, then, is a case of a folk etymology which is correct in spite of itself.)

Many words of this type go on their merry way without being remade. Others, however, are subjected to attempts to make them more transparent. For instance, Old English had a compound *brȳd-guma* 'man of the bride', consisting of *brȳd* 'bride' and *guma* 'man'. By regular sound change, this compound would have come out as something like *bridegum* or *bridgum*. If OE *guma* 'man' had survived into Modern English, this outcome would have caused no great difficulties, except perhaps for a need for recomposition. However, the word *guma* has been lost from the English vocabulary. Still, the word *brid(e)gum* looks like a compound, containing the word *bride* as its first element. But what about the second part? What does it mean? Faced with this quandary, English speakers at a certain point replaced the expected *gum* by a word that sounds similar and has a recognizable meaning, namely *groom*. The outcome, *bridegroom*, has the advantage of being a transparent compound. And if the original meaning of *groom*, 'attendant, servant', isn't as appropriate as 'man' (the original meaning of *guma*), well, that's too bad. At least the word has an "etymology".

Historical linguists refer to such historically incorrect etymologies as FOLK ETYMOLOGY or POPULAR ETYMOLOGY.

Folk etymology, because it does not depend on knowledge of the history of words, is not necessarily limited to words that originally were compounds. It is sufficient that in some way they "look" like compounds and therefore should also "behave" like compounds. For instance, the word *asparagus*, a borrowing from Greek via Latin, can be considered a compound in that it is a bit "too long" to be an ordinary, uncompounded word. In some varieties of English, the word consequently has received a popular etymology, being remade into *sparrow-grass*. (In the process, the initial *a-* evidently was reinterpreted as the indefinite article *a*.) Those who do not speak this variety of English will find this particular popular etymology amusing or even utterly ridiculous. But this is a common reaction to folk etymology when it first arises. Those who do use the word *sparrow-grass* are perfectly convinced of its semantic appropriateness and will justify their belief by saying things like *You see, it has long stalks like grass, and sparrows and other birds hop around in it*. (As a matter of historical fact, *sparrow grass* has been attested since the seventeenth century.)

In fact, many words that we use in Modern English without feeling that they are "amusing" or even "utterly ridiculous" attempts at folk etymology, do in fact owe their present shape to this process. Some additional examples are given in (13).

(13)   Modern English word   Source
        andiron (also *handiron, endiron*)   Fr. *andier* 'firedog'
        breaker 'water cask on lifeboat'   Sp. *bareca* 'barrel'
        buckaroo   Sp. *vaquero* 'cowboy', with
                                                     some help from
                                                     Engl. *buck* (?)
        buckwheat   Dutch *boekweite* 'beech wheat'
        carry-all   Fr. *carriole* 'small carriage'
        chaise lounge   Fr. *chaise longue* 'long chair;
                                                     couch'

In some cases, popular etymology has given rise to further developments. A case in point is *gridiron* – like *andiron* above, an incomplete or partial popular etymology, with substitution of the recognizable English word *iron* for the final element of a French borrowing, which in this case was *gredyre*. (The latter word might be related to Engl. *griddle*, by way of dissimilation.)

Once *gridiron* had come into use, the question must have arisen as to what the first element, *grid*, might mean. Evidently, somebody made the inference that this part is what distinguishes 'gridirons' from other 'irons' and thus carries the basic meaning in the word *gridiron*. Something like backformation, then, made it possible to extract *grid* from *gridiron* and to use it as an independent word.

The development of *grid* from *gridiron* can alternatively be explained by another process, ELLIPSIS, the elimination or deletion of what is considered redundant verbiage. The fact that *gridirons* are prototypically made of iron may have made the element *iron* appear to be redundant. As a consequence, it could be deleted. (In traditional rhetorical theory, ellipsis was grouped together with clearly semantic processes, e.g. hyperbole and litotes (see Chapter 7). It is therefore sometimes included in discussions of semantic change. Unlike these other processes, however, ellipsis is sensitive both to meaning and to form, and in this way more similar to analogy.)

Ordinarily, ellipsis is quite limited in its application, as can be illustrated with the following additional example. With the advent of the women's liberation movement, males opposed to equality for women often were referred to as *male chauvinists*. This expression contained a metaphorical extension of the word *chauvinist* which earlier had been employed to refer to an overly ardent nationalist, a jingoist. In the context *male chauvinist*, however, the word began to be reinterpreted as meaning a 'male supremacist'. As a consequence of this reinterpretation, *male chauvinist* could be considered redundant, being equivalent to saying *male male supremacist*. At this point, ellipsis eliminated the redundancy by deleting the redundant element *male* – and in the process establishing a new meaning for *chauvinist*.

Under special circumstances, ellipsis can go much farther. For instance, the original Old English word of negation was *ne*, as in *ic ne wāt* 'I don't know'. This ordinary mode of negation could be reinforced by the hyperbolic use of either *wiht* 'something, anything' or *nāwiht* 'nothing, not anything'; see example (14), Stage I. (Evidently, at this stage the phenomenon often called negative spread, as in non-standard Mod. Engl. *I don't know nothing*, was not yet considered unacceptable in the standard language.) As time progressed, the hyperbolic force of *(nā)wiht* began to fade. First the word became an all-purpose emphasizer with negation, as in Stage II. Over time, even the emphatic force began to fade, and the form *nāwiht* came to be interpreted as part of a two-part, "discontinuous" marker of negation *ne ... nāwiht*; see Stage III. But once ordinary negation was expressed by two words, *ne* and *nāwiht*, the stage was set for ellipsis to come in and to eliminate the seeming redundancy. The result was that *ne*, the word that originally had bccn the marker of negation, was deleted, and *not*, the reflex of originally hyperbolic *nāwiht* became the only marker of negation. See Stage IV. The result of this development, however, was not limited to effectively replacing the lexical item *ne* by *nāwiht* > *not*. It affected the entire syntax of negation, not only in the sample sentences of (14), but in all sentences: Whereas in Old English, the particle of negation preceded the verb, in the English of Shakespeare it follows. (Modern English has introduced further changes through the introduction of the "helping verb" *do*.)

(14)   Stage I   *ic ne wāt* 'I don't know'   :   *ic ne wāt (nā)wiht* 'I don't
                                                        know (no)thing'
         Stage II   *ic ne wāt* 'I don't know'   :   *ic ne wāt (nā)wiht* 'I don't
                                                        know at all'
         Stage III   *ic ne wāt nāwiht* 'I don't know'
         Stage IV   *I wot(e) not* 'I don't know' (Shakespeare)
         → present-day *I don't know* (by further changes, including obsoles-
         cence of *wot(e)*)

While sweeping developments of this type may not be particularly common, the specific changes exemplified in (14) have parallels in a number of other modern European languages, including German, the Scandinavian languages, and many non-standard varieties of French. Standard French, however, has not yet reached Stage IV; instead, we find a complex coexistence between Stage I/II forms with the original negation *ne*, the discontinuous negation of Stage III, *ne ... pas*, and the Stage-IV elliptical *pas*. (The original meaning of Fr. *pas* is 'step', as in OFr. *je ne vais pas* 'I don't go a step'.)

4. Morphological change

Examples like the ellipsis in (14) show that analogy can have profound effects on the structure of languages. This particular development had a multiplicity of effects. First, like a number of other analogical processes (especially blending), it resulted in LEXICAL CHANGE. (This phenomenon will be discussed in greater detail in Chapter 9.) It also brought about, as its most far-reaching effect, a CHANGE IN SYNTAX. (For this type of change see the following chapter).

But along the way it also affected the morphology, by creating a discontinuous marker of negation, *ne ... nāwiht*. This effect on the MORPHOLOGY is in fact the more usual characteristic of analogical change; and some linguists have referred to analogy as morphological change. However, as we will see in this section, morphological change – understood as change in morphological SYSTEMS – results from a complex interplay between analogical change and sound change, at times involving even syntax.

Many historical linguists would consider the interplay between sound change and four-part analogy to be the prototypical vehicle for morphological change. An example we have looked at before (Chapter 1, § 2, and Chapter 4, § 5.1) involves the English case system.

To recapitulate: Old English had four different cases, with each case potentially differentiated between singular and plural. Moreover, it had, depending on one's count, between six and fourteen different inflectional classes, in which the same cases were distinguished, but by means of different suffixes. Compare for instance the two paradigms on the left side of example (15). Modern English has only two cases: nominative and genitive; the suffix used to distinguish the genitive from the nominative is phonetically identical to the plural marker -*s*; and nothing has remained of the different inflectional classes. Compare the right side of (15).

(15)

		Old English		Modern English	
		sing.	pl.	sing.	pl.
	Nom.	*stān*	*stānas*		
	Acc.	*stān*	*stānas*	*stone*	*stones* [-z]
	Dat.	*stāne*	*stānum*		
	Gen.	*stānes*	*stāna(na)*	*stone's* [-z]	*stones'* [-z]
	Nom.	*caru*	*cara*		
	Acc.	*care*	*cara*	*care*	*cares* [-z]
	Dat.	*care*	*carum*		
	Gen.	*care*	*cara/carena*	*care's* [-z]	*cares'* [-z]

In Chapter 1 we noted that the primary factor underlying the change from the Old English to the Modern English case system is sound change: Both vowels and nasals were regularly lost in final syllables. For the top paradigm in (15), these changes would have yielded the following outcomes:

(15′)   Expected Modern English
                  sing.   plur.
          Nom.   *stone*   *stones*
          Acc.   *stone*   *stones*
          Dat.   *stone*   *stone*
          Gen.   *stone(')s* *stone*

The usual view is that at this point four-part analogy stepped in. The identity of the nominative, accusative, and dative forms of the singular was extended to the plural, yielding a nominative/accusative/dative plural form *stones*. At the same time, the genitive plural was analogically remade to have the same final -*s* as both the genitive singular and the new nominative/accusative/dative plural. (The different "*s*-forms" were then differentiated in writing, but not in pronunciation, by a judicious use of apostrophes.) The modern inflection of *care* can then be explained as having adopted the pattern of *stone : stones* etc. by four-part analogy.

One can easily imagine that if this interplay between sound change and four-part analogy continues unabated, English may eventually lose all remaining traces of affixal morphology. Languages of this type, without any morphology to speak of, are called ISOLATING languages. English evidently is still far removed from being isolating. (See below.) But Classical Chinese is a near-perfect example of an isolating language. Interestingly, it has been suggested that the ancestor of that language, Proto-Chinese, had inflectional affixes that distinguished a nominative/genitive form from an accusative/dative; see example (16). Although somewhat controversial, this proposal seems to be supported by outside evidence from the distantly related Burmese. As example (17) shows, that language makes a similar case distinction between nominative and "oblique". True, the distinction is made in terms of tones (designated by superscript 1 and 2); but we know from other evidence that loss of word-final sounds may lead to tonal differences. A development along these lines is in fact demonstrated in another instance of loss of an earlier affix in Chinese: Proto-Chinese had a derivational suffix *-*s* which differentiated the two reconstructed items in the left column of (18). In Modern Mandarin Chinese, final consonants are lost, and the two forms differ mainly in terms of tone (indicated by different accent marks), although there is also some difference in the vowels. Evidence of the type (16)/(18), then, suggests that Chinese became isolating secondarily, presumably through a combination of sound change and analogy.

(16)   Proto-Chinese pronominal case inflection (Karlgren 1920 and 1949)
               First Person Second Person
       Nom./Gen. *ng-o *$ñy$-o
       Acc./Dat.   *ng-$â$ *$ñy$-$â$

(17)   Burmese pronominal case inflection
               First Person Second Person
       Nom. $ŋa^1$ $nĩ^1$
       Oblique $ŋa^2$ $nĩ^2$

(18)   Proto-Chinese derivational *-s
       *kit 'to tie'   : Mod. Chin. *jié*
       *kit-s 'hair-knot' :   *jì*

Sound change is not the only process that can trigger morphological innovations. As we have seen in the preceding section, the analogical processes
of blending, reinterpretation, and ellipsis can introduce new morphological
structures which then can be generalized by four-part analogy. Compare the
cases of *tele-thon*, *beaut-ician*, and *ne ... (nā)wiht*. And, as these examples
patently show, the result may increase morphological complexity, rather than
decrease it.

Borrowing, too, can enrich the morphology of a language. In fact, one
of the major factors that prevented Modern English from becoming an isolating language, or coming very close to being one, is the rich morphology
introduced by massive borrowings from Latin and Greek, often via French.
Consider the case of *-able*. This affix came into English through words like
debatable and *capable* and originally was limited to being used with borrowed root elements, such as *debate* and *cap-*. But patterns such as *debate :
debatable = do : X* (= *doable*) led to the extension of the affix to native
words, such that, given the proper occasion, nearly every transitive verb can
now be extended by *-able* to indicate that it is possible to engage in the action
indicated by the verb. (Incidentally, the suffixes of both the type *tele-thon*
and the type *beaut-ician* also originated in borrowed vocabulary.)

New English affixes were even introduced from purely native sources;
and these, too, counteracted the general tendency of English toward becoming an isolating language. For instance, in Old English compounds of the type
frēond-līc, literally 'having the body [= manner] of a friend', the second element *-līc* slowly lost its original force and came to be interpreted as an affix
for deriving adjectives from nouns. Once reinterpreted in this manner it was
extended by four-part analogy to many other nouns and acquired a certain productivity, reflected in Modern English adjectives like *friendly* and *heavenly*.

Along a similar route, the adverbial Old English form of this reinterpreted adjective suffix, *-līc(e)*, became even more productive: It is the source of the adverbial ending *-ly* (as in *merrily, quickly, gently*) which, through four-part analogy, can be extended to virtually any adjective of Modern English.

Even syntax, mainly in the form of the syntax of clitics, has contributed to Modern English morphology. A common traditional view of the genitive *'s* (or *s'*) of Modern English is the one summarized above: The suffix originated in the genitive singular of certain noun classes and was extended from there to the genitive plural, as well as to the genitive singular and plural of other noun classes. This account works well if we limit ourselves to single nouns, but it fails to account for the placement of genitive *'s* in structures like (19), where it follows not the noun to which it belongs – the head noun, but an "appendage" to that noun: an *of*-genitive in (19a) and a relative clause in (19b).

(19)   a. *The present Queen of England's castle ...*
        b. *The man I saw yesterday's dog ...*

In earlier English, the *s* would have had to be attached to the head noun, as an upstanding, "God-fearing" inflectional suffix should; but structures of that sort are patently unacceptable in Modern English; see (19').

(19')   a. *The present Queen's of England castle ...*
         b. *The man's I saw yesterday dog ...*

The placement of Modern English *'s* could presumably be explained as an analogical extension from the head noun to the total "noun phrase" composed of the head noun + appendage. But historical evidence shows that the development was more complex. In early Modern English we find structures of the type (19") with a full word, *his*, following the noun phrase. (The example in (19"b) is a citation from Shakespeare's *Twelfth Night*.) This *his* no doubt is the genitive of the third person singular pronoun, except that at this stage it could be used both for the masculine and for the neuter. The existence of such structures suggests that Modern English *'s* results from something like a blending of the original genitive ending *-s* with *'s*, a CLITIC form of *his* with clitic reduction (see Chapter 4, § 5.5). In the process of blending, the syntactic character of *'s* as an element following entire noun phrases was generalized. And subsequently, the use of *'s* was extended from masculines and neuters to feminines, which earlier had used the appropriate feminine form *her* or *hir*; see (19"c) from Lyly's *Euphues*. The effective transformation of a clitic to an affix observed in Engl. *'s*, in fact, is a rather common phenomenon. (See below.)

(19″)   a. *The man I saw yesterday **his** dog* ...
        b. *... a sea-fight 'gainst the Count **his** gallies*
        c. *Lucilla **hir** company*

It can easily be imagined that developments of this type, as well as of the type *quick-ly* or *do-able*, could lead to a considerable INCREASE in morphological complexity – if they continued unabated. In English, such developments generally have had a very selective effect.

To illustrate the effect, it is useful to distinguish between INFLECTIONAL and DERIVATIONAL morphology. Derivational morphology can be illustrated by the word *derivational* which is derived from another word of the English language, *derivation*, and this word, in turn, comes from *derive*. Both of the latter two words can be inflected, to indicate such abstract grammatical notions as plural and third person singular, as in *derivation-s* and *derive-s*.

With the exception of inflectional *'s*, the new morphology that English has required through the developments we have just examined is overwhelmingly derivational.

In other languages, developments like these can affect inflection as well. Consider for instance the case of Burmese. Although the old inflectional morphology, going back to the ancestral language of Chinese and Burmese, persists only in tonal relics of the type (17) above, Modern Burmese exhibits complex morphological structures of the type (20), of which a literal English gloss would run as follows: 'Ganges-river-interior-in-also-indeed'. The suffixes of these structures are originally independent words that became quasi-suffixal via an intermediate clitic stage. At least one of the suffixes, *-hma¹*, has clearly inflectional function, corresponding to the locative case endings of Proto-Indo-European and a number of early Indo-European languages. (As in (17), superscript numerals indicate different tones.)

(20) $k\tilde{h}i^3kh a^1$ *-myi⁴* *-the²* *-hma¹*   *-le²* *-phe²*
       Ganges   river interior in (Locative) also emphasizer
       ' ... also (emphasis) in the interior of the river Ganges ... '

The result of such an introduction of inflectional affixes may either be an AGGLUTINATING or an INFLECTIONAL language. These differ from each other in terms of the transparency of affixation: In agglutinating languages, the affixes retain their phonetic identity to such an extent that it is easy to tell where one affix begins and the next one ends. If sound change obscures the boundaries between affixes and brings about their amalgamation, the result is an inflectional language.

In the case of Burmese, we clearly have agglutination. Other typical agglutinating languages are Finnish, Hungarian, and especially Turkish. (Compare for instance Turk. *sön-dür-ül-e-me-mek* 'not to be able to be extinguished', where the root *sön-* means 'extinguish (intransitive)', *-dür-* makes the verb transitive, *-ül-* turns the transitive verb into a passive, *-e-* indicates possibility, *-me-* marks negation, and *-mek* is the infinitive affix.)

Proto-Indo-European was more of the inflectional type. In some of its forms it is easy to isolate different suffixes, as in the third singular **bher-e-t-i* 'carries' = root **bher-*, an extension or "theme vowel" *-e-* which makes the stem appropriate for the present tense, *-t-* the third singular marker, and *-i* a marker of present tense. In others, however, it is impossible to do so. For instance, the first singular corresponding to **bher-e-t-i* is **bher-ō* whose *-ō* simultaneously serves as theme vowel, person marker, and present tense indicator.

The distinction between agglutinating and inflectional languages is not always clear-cut. Many agglutinating languages exhibit fused suffixes. Inflectional languages of the Indo-European and Afro-Asiatic (including Semitic) type have complex vowel alternations, as in Mod. Engl. *sing : sang : sung,* or the Semitic type √*KTB* 'write', *KaTaB* 'he wrote', *KāTiB* 'writer', *KiT(ā)B* 'book', *mi-KTaB* 'letter' (see Chapter 3, § 2.4). The origin of some of these alternations is uncertain or controversial. However, the discussion of umlaut in § 5.1.1 of Chapter 4 illustrates one of the ways in which such vowel alternations can arise.

A number of Indigenous American languages, as well as Eskimo, now commonly referred to as Inuit, have even more complex, INCORPORATING (or "polysynthetic") morphological structures, in which single words correspond to complete sentences in languages like English or Chinese. Compare the Inuit example in (21). It is likely that the noun, verb, and other forms "incorporated" into the basic verbal expression started out as clitics which were fused with their hosts much in the same way as Engl. *'s* or the complex Burmese structure of (20). (Example (21) illustrates another phenomenon often found in inflectional and incorporating languages, the use of an infix, *-niaʀ-* which is inserted into the middle of the root *sipu*. Although infixes are not at all uncommon, their historical origin in most cases is quite uncertain.)

(21)   *āwlisa -ut   -issʔaʀ si -niaʀ-   pu -ŋa*
        fish   -ing usable   try   sg. 1
                              sipu = 'find'
        'I try to find (something) usable for fishing.'

As noted earlier, while English developments like the introduction and generalization of the adverbial suffix *-ly* constitute steps toward a more complex, agglutinating system of derivational morphology, in its inflectional morphology English has rather tended toward the isolating type. In fact, even in its derivational morphology, English has strong isolating tendencies. Consider "Ø-derivations" of the type *crown* (noun) → *crown* (verb), where no affix serves to signal the derivation. Some new Ø-derivations of this type, such as *impact* (noun) → *impact* (verb), are the object of the ire of self-appointed critics. But the same critics have no problems about using old ones like *crown* (noun) → *crown* (verb).

A similar mix of isolating and agglutinating tendencies can be observed in most other Indo-European languages. Thus, over the course of some three thousand years, the rich morphology of Sanskrit, with eight different cases, has been reduced to just two in the early stages of its modern descendants, such as Hindi. Somewhere along the line, however, the course has been reversed. Original postposed prepositions have become clitics in Hindi (similar to what happened in Burmese) and are now fusing with the preceding noun stems. The result is a shift toward an agglutinative system.

The fate of morphology from Sanskrit to its modern descendants gives credence to the common belief that languages tend to develop in cycles: from isolating to agglutinating, from agglutinating to inflectional (through amalgamation of different affixes into one), from inflectional to isolating (through sound change and analogy), and so on.

However, in many languages and language families we cannot observe the complete cycle. Languages like Turkish appear to have been agglutinating as far back as we can trace them in history. More than that, as already noted, English simultaneously exhibits both agglutinating and isolating tendencies, even though the latter seem to be stronger, especially in inflectional morphology. Moreover, what remains unexplained is why, say, the overall tendency of English is toward isolation, while the overall tendency of a language like present-day Hindi is toward agglutination. Why don't the isolating and agglutinating tendencies simply cancel each other out, creating some kind of equilibrium? Completely satisfactory answers to these questions do not seem possible at this time.

Nevertheless, there are some indications that in spite of the great morphological differences between classical isolating languages (such as Chinese) and classical agglutinating languages (such as Turkish), language as a whole maintains some kind of equilibrium. For instance, as the case systems of the various Indo-European languages underwent attrition, the use of prepositions increased. As a consequence, where Old English could express the difference between direct and indirect object in terms of case (accusative vs. dative), Modern English does so by marking the indirect object with the preposition *to* and leaving the direct object unmarked (as in *They gave the book to Mary*). Alternatively, Modern English indicates the difference through word order, by placing the unmarked indirect object obligatorily before the direct object (as in *They gave Mary the book*). In this regard, too, Modern English differs from Old English where the relative order of direct and indirect object was not fixed, presumably because case marking made it possible to distinguish the two kinds of objects, no matter where they occurred.

In this manner, then, reductions in one component of the grammar (morphology) can be compensated for by expansions (and other changes) in a different component (the syntax).

5. Analogy and phonology: Rule-governed, regular analogy

All of the analogical processes that we have looked at so far conform to the neogrammarian view that analogy is inherently irregular, in contradistinction to regular sound change. Under certain special conditions, however, clearly analogical developments can unfold with the same regularity (and speed) as sound change. Some of these developments were known to the neogrammarians, but they did not realize – or appreciate – the regularity of the changes.

Many examples of regular analogy are quite complex in their analysis and presentation. One example, however, from the history of English, can be presented without going into difficult technical details. This is a change that has taken place in certain varieties of British English, involving original word-final *r*.

The common wisdom is that British English has lost final *r*, so that words like *matter* are pronounced [mætə]. And in certain varieties of British English this may be true. In others, however, word-final *r* was linked to the following word, if that word began in a vowel and followed without any break. (See § 3.2 above for the similar linking of the *n* of *an*.) Being linked to the beginning of the next word, however, the *r* was no longer phonetically final and thus did not qualify for the final *r*-loss.

The result was a word-final variation between *r* and Ø; see (22). And since this variation did not depend on the nature of the words involved, but entirely on phonetic facts, there would have been no motivation to laboriously learn for each originally *r*-final word that it has two variants, one with *r*, the other, without. Speakers would be better off learning a general rule to account for the alternation.

(22)   *the butter* [-ə] *was*   :   *the butter* [-ər] *is*
        the matter [-ə] *was*   :   *the matter* [-ər] *is*
             . . .   :   . . .

From the historical perspective, the correct rule would have to be an "*r*-deletion", which can be informally expressed as follows:

r-deletion: Phonetically word-final [r] → Ø

In this formulation, then, the forms with [r] are considered basic, and the forms without [r], derived.

However, here again we need to remember that most speakers are not linguists and therefore have no great motivation to be "historically correct". There is nothing to prevent them from taking the forms without [r] as being more basic, and the ones with [r], as derived. In fact, this might be considered a much better analysis: Forms with [r] occur only before words with initial vowel. By contrast, forms without [r] occur much more frequently, in all other contexts, including if nothing follows. They can therefore be considered to be more basic.

Of course, if we go in for this analysis, then the rule formulation above won't do. Instead, we have to reformulate the rule as an "*r*-insertion":

r-insertion: Insert [r] between word-final vowel and
                 word-initial vowel

This formulation might be felt to be additionally motivated by a general tendency in languages to break up groups of neighboring vowels by the insertion of some kind of consonant. Both rules will perfectly well account for the [r] : Ø alternation in (22) and, in that sense, their effects could not be distinguished from each other. However, the way *r*-insertion is formulated makes much broader claims. Not only should words like *butter* and *matter* exhibit an alternation between [r] before vowel and Ø elsewhere; all other words in final vowel should do likewise. Otherwise, *r*-insertion wouldn't be much of a rule. Faced with this situation, speakers have a choice: Either forget about *r*-insertion and try *r*-deletion instead, or fix things up so that *r*-insertion works. The varieties of British English under discussion evidently opted for the second alternative. As a consequence, all words in final vowel, whether originally *r*-less or *r*-ful, insert an [r] if they precede a vowel-initial word. Compare the examples in (23).

(23)   *the idea* [-ɔ] *was*   : *the idea* [-ər] *is*
                            Australia [-ə] *was*   : *Australia* [-ər] *is*
                                . . .   :   . . .
            just like: *the butter* [-ə] *was*   : *the butter* [-ər] *is*
                        the matter [-ə] *was*   : *the matter* [-ər] *is*
                                . . .   :   . . .

Significantly, in these varieties of English, the change brought about by this reformulation of the rule has taken place with the same degree of REGU-LARITY and speed as regular sound change. One suspects that this is because, like sound change, the change operates without any regard to morphology, semantics, or syntax (except that speakers have to know where words begin and end). An added factor is that it is a RULE that is being reinterpreted and generalized: In a manner of speaking, the regularity of the rule begets the regularity of the change. Whatever the explanation for the regularity of the development, however, developments like this suggest that the neogram-marian distinction between regular sound change and irregular analogy may have been too strict. As a postscript it might be mentioned that the rule of *r*-insertion at present is being extended to word-internal contexts, as a vari-able process very much in keeping with Labov's view on the nature of sound change (see Chapter 4, § 6.3). As a consequence, forms like *drawing* may now be heard either as [drɔiŋ] or as [drɔriŋ]. (The change does not seem to affect words like *going* or *seeing*, presumably because they are pronounced with an intervocalic semivowel, as in [gowiŋ] or [siyiŋ].)

6. Hypercorrection: An interdialectal form of analogy

Certain American English dialects present phenomena that are superficially similar to the British rule of *r*-insertion: Speakers of originally *r*-less dialects such as those of New England, New York, and the old South, often pronounce an [r] in words like *paw, saw,* or *sofa*. This "intrusive *r*", however, seems to owe its origin to a very different process, namely HYPERCORRECTION. Unlike the other analogical processes that we have examined so far, hypercorrection crucially is motivated by the relationship between different dialects or lan-guages – or rather by the relationship between these as perceived by their speakers.

In many cases, speakers focus on differences in prestige. Speakers of less prestigious dialects try to imitate a more prestigious one by adaptations in their pronunciation. This is no doubt the case with the intrusive *r* of American English. It is found with speakers who are switching from their old *r*-less pronunciation to the *r*-ful pronunciation that is more prestigious in the United States. If speakers of these dialects want to use the pronunciation which is more standard in American English, they will quite naturally stick [r]s into words like *pore* [pɔ̄], *sore* [sɔ̄], and *better* [beɪə]. So far, so good. Evidently, however, speakers do not always know where to draw the line. In many cases they go overboard and stick [r]s even into words like *paw, saw,* and *sofa,* or even word-internally in words like *wash* [wɔrš] or *popcorn popper* = [pɔrpkɔrn pɔrpər]. Presumably because of its different origin, the intrusive *r* of American English differs from British English *r*-insertion by being a fairly sporadic phenomenon, with a lot of variation between different speakers and even for individual speakers.

A similar, and somewhat related, phenomenon is observed in some of the less prestigious dialects of New York, where words like *pearl* or *earn* are pronounced with [oy], instead of the more standard American [ər]. When speakers of these dialects try to use the more standard pronunciation, they often substitute [ər] for [oy] not only in words like *pearl* and *earl*, but even in words that are pronounced with [oy] in the standard dialect. Example (24) illustrates one of the results of this development. Moreover, it serves to show that hypercorrection is very similar to four-part analogy by operating with a proportional schema. It differs from four-part analogy by operating across dialects.

(24)   NY dial. *pearl* [poyl] : *pearl* [pərl]
           earn [oyn] : *earn* [ərn]
           oil [oyl] : x = [ərl] (just like *earl*)

Another case of hypercorrection is found in many vernacular varieties of English. As the result of a variety of sound changes and analogical developments, English at a certain stage had two competing forms of the so-called gerund, a form in *-ing* (as in *going*) and a form in *-en* (as in *goen*). At a later stage, Standard English leveled out the form in *-ing* at the expense of *-en*. Many non-standard dialects generalized *-en*, instead. This difference has since become one of the major features distinguishing standard from non-standard English, and the use of the form in *-en* is often referred to as "dropping one's *g*s". As speakers who "drop their *g*s" try to speak the prestige dialect, they replace their *-en* by *-ing*. And again, in many cases they go too far and extend this substitution to words like *taken* (as in *I have taking it*).

In these and many other cases, hypercorrection is indeed motivated by prestige differences. However, hypercorrection can occur even when prestige differences are irrelevant. For instance, in the dialect of Norwich (England) words like *daze* and *days* originally had different pronunciations: [dēz] vs. [dæiz]. Among younger speakers, the distinction has been lost in favor of [dæiz]. When younger speakers try to imitate the older dialect, without nec-essarily wanting to switch to it, they tend to pronounce both *daze* and *days* as [dēz] – on the model *daze* [dæiz] : [dēz] = *days* [dæiz] : X. The phenomenon has been labeled HYPERDIALECTISM by Peter Trudgill, the British scholar who first observed the Norwich situation.

Chapter 6
Syntactic change

Why did the chicken cross the road?
(Popular riddle)

1. Introduction

The preceding two chapters have illustrated two major areas of change that affect GENERAL LINGUISTIC STRUCTURE – sound change, which for obvious reasons affects the sound structure or PHONOLOGY, and analogy, which typically affects the MORPHOLOGY. But as we have seen in the preceding chapter, analogical change can interact with SYNTAX, too.

For instance, ellipsis in earlier English structures of the type *Ic ne wāt nāwiht* 'I do not know (anything)' yielded the Shakespearean type *I wot(e) not* with the negation following, rather than preceding, the verb. See Chapter 5, § 3.2. And section 4 of the same chapter showed that syntactic constituents which become clitics can wind up as morphological affixes.

In fact, syntax can even interact with phonology. Recall that clitics, besides being syntactic constituents, have special phonological properties (see Chapter 4, § 5.5). One of these phonological properties, namely that they cannot occur by themselves, has clear syntactic consequences, in that they need a "host" to lean on and are therefore dependent in their syntactic behavior on the behavior of their host. (See § 3 below.)

Because of these multiple interactions it is not always easy to determine where syntax begins and where morphology or phonology ends. Even linguists are not always in agreement on this matter. (See § 3 below.)

To further complicate matters, much uncertainty exists among non-linguists who – as noted in Chapter 1 – constitute the majority of language users. For them, syntax is often synonymous with style. For instance, English-speaking children frequently say things like (1a); and just as frequently, adults correct them by responding with something like (1b).

(1)   a. *Me and Charlie went to the movies.*
         b. *Don't say "Me and Charlie", say "Charlie and I".*

In making such comments, adults are not properly distinguishing syntax from style. According to prescriptive standard grammar, it is syntactically incorrect to use the form *me* for the subject of the sentence, even if it is conjoined with another subject (*Charlie*, in this case). The correct form is *I*. At the same time, it is not considered polite to talk about yourself first; and for this – purely stylistic, not grammatical – reason the first person pronoun should follow, not precede, *Charlie*. Put differently, in the standard form of English, both (1′) and (1″) are syntactically correct, by having the right case on the pronoun; but stylistically, (1″) would be preferred. When adults say things like (1b) they confuse these issues and, as it turns out, wind up confusing the children as well. But more on that in § 5 below. (Interestingly, a recent popular book on the English language by a well-known linguist labels sentences such as (1′) ungrammatical. It may be true that structures like these do sound a little odd, but that is perhaps only because they are used so rarely.)

(1′)   *I and Charlie went to the movies.*
(1″)   *Charlie and I went to the movies.*

2. Questionable "syntactic" changes

Confusion between syntax and style, combined with an insufficient under- standing of syntax, lies at the foundation of many of the dire warnings by self-appointed critics about usages such as *Hopefully, it will rain*, or the use of *data* as a singular noun. (Recall the discussion of these structures in Chapter 1.)

Let us begin with *data*. Like many other English nouns in *-a*, this is an original neuter plural of Greek and/or Latin origin. Specifically, *data* is the plural of Lat. *datum* 'something given (that can be used as the basis for discussion)'. Even Shakespeare confessed to knowing only "a little Latin, and less Greek"; and since Shakespeare's time, the study of Latin has become even more limited. It is therefore not surprising that the average English speaker would not know, without being expressly told, that *data* is a plural form in Latin. Moreover, *data* normally come collectively as a set; the need to talk about an individual *datum* arises rarely, indeed. Speakers may therefore be forgiven if they reanalyze *data* as a singular mass noun, and consequently use it with a singular verb (as in (2a)), not with the plural verb in (2b) which is required under a plural interpretation of *data*.

(2)   a. *The data presented here shows that Professor Boondoggle's analysis is wrong.*
        b. *The data presented here showØ that Professor Boondoggle's analysis is wrong.*

Critics commonly refer to structures like (2a) as syntactically incorrect. But that assessment is highly questionable. The syntax of (2a) is impeccable, once *data* is reinterpreted as a singular mass noun. If there is a mistake, it does not lie in the syntax, but in the morphological analysis of *data*. Moreover, it is a mistake only in comparison with the traditional analysis of *data* as plural. But, then, *cows* once was a "mistake" for *kine* which, in turn, was a "mistake" for even earlier *kye* < OE *cȳ.* (See Chapter 4, § 5.11, and Chapter 5, §§ 2.2 and 3.1.) More than that, the same critics who object to *data* as singular have no difficulties with a number of other original plural expressions that are now routinely used as singulars. Consider such terms as *linguistics* or *politics*, which are clearly marked as a plural by their final *-s*, or the expression *United States*, also clearly marked as plural and even in its original meaning a plurality of *States*.

As noted in Chapter 1, *data* is now used so widely that critics generally have lost interest. This does not mean, however, that the battle is over. Even historical linguists who are naturally open-minded about linguistic change may personally prefer to treat *data* as plural. In the meantime, the critics are directing their attention to new *a*-plurals that are undergoing a similar reanalysis, such as *media* (originally plural of *medium*, as in *information medium*) and *criteria* (originally plural of *criterion*). On the other hand, similar reinterpretations seem to be escaping the critics' attention, a fact which reinforces the impression that the critics are inconsistent, and their dire warnings, ultimately, quite ineffectual.

Two examples of such reinterpretations that seem to have slipped by the critics are *stigmata*, originally plural of *stigma*, used by educated English speakers as a singular in reference to the crucifixion wounds on Christ's hands or a psychologically based medical condition with similar markings; and *schemata*, originally plural of *schema*, now similarly used among certain linguistic theorists as a technical term construed as singular. Even some words derived from Latin plurals in simple *-a* are routinely used as singular, such as *agenda*, originally the plural of Lat. *agendum* '(something) to be done'.

3. Clitic *n't* in English

The discussion in § 3.2 of Chapter 5 shows how ellipsis and other developments brought about a change in English, not only in the morphology of negation, but also in its syntactic placement. The syntactic part of the development was portrayed as an effective shift of negation from preverbal to postverbal position.

If we limit ourselves to simple declarative sentences, that portrayal is not bad, except that in modern English a form of the helping verb *do* came to be inserted before the negation if the verb is SIMPLE, as in (3a). (The developments that gave rise to this requirement are quite complex and need not concern us here.) A systematic exception is the verb 'to be' when, as in (3b), it is used as a COPULA, i.e. as a mere "linker" between subject (*you*) and predicate (*happy*). With COMPLEX verbs, as in (3c–d), the negation is placed after the AUXILIARY (the *has* and *was* of (3c/d)). (Auxiliaries are "helping verbs" which "help" in making temporal distinctions as in (3c) or in forming the passive (3d). English has a similar class of "modal" verbs, such as *can, may, must*, but these can be ignored in the present discussion.)

(3)   a. *I do **not** go*
       b. *You are **not** happy*
       c. *He has **not** gone*
       d. *She was **not** seen*

The result is that negation always occurs after the first verb within the verb complex. Let us refer to this first verb as the FINITE VERB. (More discussion on finite verbs is found in § 6 below.)

This statement, however, holds true only for declarative sentences. In questions, the finite verb is placed into the position in front of the subject, and the negation is left "stranded" before the rest of the verb complex (if there is any). Compare (4).

(4)   a. *Do I **not** go?*
       b. *Are you **not** here?*
       c. *Has he **not** gone?*
       d. *Was she **not** seen?*

So far, so good. But as we observed in Chapter 4, § 5.5, beside the full form *not*, English has acquired a clitic form *n't*. And like all good clitics, this variant of negation has to lean on a host. Now, while some clitics go to all kinds of lengths to find a proper host to attach to (see § 6 below), *n't* was content to choose the immediately preceding word as its host, as in (3′). And again, so far nothing very remarkable has happened.

(3′) a. *I don't go*
     b. *You aren't here*
     c. *He hasn't gone*
     d. *She wasn't seen*

But notice what happens when we form questions with clitic *n't*. As (4′) shows, the negation cannot remain stranded in its usual position (as it did in (4)) but has to move along with the finite verb. Contrast the grammatical structures on the left with the ungrammatical ones on the right (marked by a postposed asterisk.)

(4′) a. *Don't I go?*   *Do I **n't** go?* *
     b. *Aren't you here?*   *Are you **n't** here?* *
     c. *Hasn't he gone?*   *Has he **n't** gone?* *
     d. *Wasn't she seen?*   *Was she **n't** seen?* *

This phenomenon, of clitic *n't* moving along with the finite verb, can be called "pied piping", after the Pied Piper of Hamlin and the mice (or children) that moved along with him out of town.

The pattern of "fronting" the finite verb in questions goes back to at least Old English. But as we have seen, post-finite-verb negation is a much more recent phenomenon. And cliticization is even more recent. This means that the pied piping in the grammatical structures of (4′) must be yet more recent, which raises the question of how pied piping came about.

One answer might be that the rule of placing negation after the finite verb (as in (3) above) was reapplied after that verb was fronted. But in that case we have to ask ourselves why this reapplication was limited to clitics. Why, for instance, don't we also get *Am not I going?*

A more likely answer is the following: Originally, all that mattered is that clitic *n't* needed a host, and the preceding finite verb happened to be available for that purpose. Subsequently, the finite verb was reinterpreted as the only possible host for clitic *n't*. And once that reinterpretation had taken place, *n't* had to follow the finite verb wherever it moved.

However, an alternative, non-syntactic explanation is also possible: As we saw in § 4 of Chapter 5, clitics may become affixes. Some linguists claim that this is what happened to our *n't*. If we accept this analysis, it stands to reason that *n't* will move along with the finite verb, just like the third singular affix *-s* in structures like *Wa-s she seen?* or even *Wa-s-n't she seen?* If this analysis is correct, then just as the singular use of *data*, pied piping of clitic *n't* is not the result of a syntactic change.

4. Syntax, analogy, or both?

The case of *hopefully* looks more promising as a genuine case of syntactic change, at least at first sight. This is because those who decry the use of *hopefully* in structures such as (5a) resort to the following syntactic argument. The word *hopefully* behaves syntactically similar to words like *fortunately, unfortunately, regrettably*, and *luckily* (see example (6a)) and like these words expresses a speaker's attitude to what is being reported in the rest of the sentence. These correct (read: traditionally established) attitudinal adverbs all correspond to structures of the type (6b) which contain the corresponding adjective. For *hopefully*, however, parallel structures like (5b) are unacceptable, as indicated by the postposed asterisk.

(5)   a. **Hopefully**, *it will rain tomorrow.*
        b. **It is hopeful** *that it will rain tomorrow.**
        c. **We are hopeful** *that it will rain tomorrow.*

(6)   a. **Fortunately**, *it will rain tomorrow.*
        b. **It is fortunate** *that it will rain tomorrow.*
        c. **We are fortunate** *that it will rain tomorrow.*

Under closer examination, this syntactic argument against *hopefully* quickly evaporates. First, underlying the argument is the hidden assumption that the b-versions in (5) and (6) are more basic, and that the a-versions can be justified only if they can be derived from the b-versions. But this assumption is quite arbitrary. It would be just as easy to choose the c-structures of (5) and (6) as the basis for derivation. And as the examples show, such a derivation would permit (5a).

Secondly, at least one attitudinal adverb established in traditional English usage, *happily*, cannot be explained by derivation from a b-version, but only from a c-version; see (7). This might suggest that syntactically there is nothing wrong with (5a).

(7)   a. ***Happily**, it will rain tomorrow.*
       b. ***It is happy** that it will rain tomorrow.**
       c. ***We are happy** that it will rain tomorrow.*

Things get even more complex if we consider additional examples, such as *presumably* and *actually*. See examples (8)–(9). Here one, or the other, or both, of the putative base structures is either strange (indicated by a question mark) or unacceptable (characterized by an asterisk). Still, the adverbs are well established in traditional usage, presumably even among the critics who inveigh against *hopefully*. For (8) it is possible to come up with another, alternative "base structure", as in d., which "works", but is quite different from b. and c. For (9), yet a different base structure could be postulated, see (9d). But the need for such ever-new, ever-different base structures casts serious doubts on the whole syntactic approach.

(8)   a. ***Presumably**, it will rain tomorrow.*
       b. ***It is presumable** that it will rain tomorrow. ?*
       c. ***We are presumable** that it will rain tomorrow. **
       d. ***It can be presumed** that it will rain tomorrow.*

(9)   a. ***Actually**, it will rain tomorrow.*
       b. ***It is actual** that it will rain tomorrow. **
       c. ***We are actual** that it will rain tomorrow. **
       d. ***It is an actual fact** that it will rain tomorrow.*

Nevertheless, the use of *hopefully* in (5a) clearly is an innovation and must be motivated by something. If a "hard-core" syntax approach fails to provide a satisfactory explanation, what does?

An answer is possible, but unfortunately also quite complex: The adverb *hopefully* has been around for a long time in such structures as (10). In this context its use was parallel to that of other attitudinal adverbs, such as *happily*; see (11a). Now, *happily* also occurred in structures like (11b). The coexistence of structures like (11a) and (11b), and the existence of structures like (10) then could give rise to the pattern in (5a) above by simple four-part analogy, see (12).

(10)   *"Tomorrow it will rain," Mary said **hopefully**.*
(11)   a. *"Tomorrow it will rain," John said **happily**.*
       b. ***Happily**, it will rain tomorrow.*

(12)   *"Tomorrow it will rain," John said* **happily**   :   **Happily**, *it will*
                                                                  rain tomorrow.
          "Tomorrow it will rain," Mary said **hopefully**. :   X

Note, however, that unlike ordinary four-part analogy, this one operates
on syntactic structures, not just words. In this sense, then, the development
that probably gave rise to *hopefully* is syntactic, after all.

Attitudinal adverbs like *fortunately* and *sadly* presumably arose in a similar
manner. For some of these, the analogy may have been motivated by the
pattern (6b) : (6a). Others no doubt require different patterns. Given the
relatively non-systematic nature of analogical change, it is not surprising
that the developments – and their outcomes – likewise are relatively non-
systematic and therefore defy a straightforward syntactic account.

The use of *hopefully* in (5a) can thus be explained as the result of a rather
ordinary type of linguistic change. This should put to rest the critics' claim
that it is syntactically anomalous. But one suspects that the real reason for
the critics' objections to *hopefully* is that they consider it newfangled and
therefore undesirable. It is too early to tell whether the usage will prevail
against these feelings. But many other innovations have caught on, in spite
of the critics. And, as noted in Chapter 1, the usage is now generally accepted
in British English. These facts suggest that the new use of *hopefully* is here
to stay.

5. *Me* revisited, or the critics' revenge

For a number of the developments discussed in the preceding sections it is
questionable whether they really constitute syntactic change. Moreover, cases
like *data* and *hopefully* involve just one or two words at a time. Generally,
however, syntactic change is highly systematic, affecting whole classes of
words and their syntactic behavior. This is true, at least, for its eventual
outcome. However, just like sound change (see § 6.3 of Chapter 4), syntactic
change may exhibit a lot of irregularity during its propagation. And, again
as in the case of sound change, some developments may be propagated quite
rapidly, others very slowly, depending on their social value.

The issue of social evaluation once again raises the specter of the critics,
or more specifically, of prescriptive grammarians who in the seventeenth and

eighteenth centuries tried to establish the ground rules for a standard variety of English.

Through the time of Shakespeare, English had been relatively free of prescriptive regulation. One reason for the new prescriptivism must have been the increasing emphasis of the Renaissance on using and cultivating the vernaculars instead of Latin (Chapter 2, § 1) and the feeling that for the vernaculars to compete with Latin, they had to be provided with a prescriptive grammar that could rival that of Latin. Another factor is that French had been giving way to English as the language of Parliament, the King's court, and the courts of justice; but English was not ideally suited to this new task, since it exhibited very high variability, both geographically and socially, which made communication between different groups quite difficult. Under the circumstances, the development of a common, standard language was highly desirable. (Most European languages underwent similar standardizing developments at roughly the same time, and for roughly the same reasons. See for instance Chapter 10.)

The grammarians who busied themselves with laying down rules for a standard English language were faced with the near-total absence of an English grammatical tradition and an overwhelming presence of a Latin grammatical tradition. As a consequence, they tended to formulate rules that were better founded in Latin grammar than in the realities of English usage.

For instance, in the area of morphology they set up English nominal paradigms with six cases, for no other reason than that Latin distinguished six cases; compare the singular paradigm in (13). But while in Latin the case forms were distinguished by different endings, English had just two overtly distinguished case forms: *boy* and *boy's*. The rest of the paradigm had to be eked out by combinations of preposition + noun. But note that English has many other such combinations, e.g. *with the boy*, which were not incorporated into the paradigm because they lacked Latin counterparts. Paradigms such as the one on the left of (13), thus, were quite arbitrary and uninformative as far as the structure of English goes. Nevertheless, paradigms of this type became an integral part of English school grammar, much to the dismay of generations of school children who, after laboriously learning them by heart, could only say *O boy!* The tradition came to an end only in the middle of the twentieth century, when linguists finally were able to persuade school teachers that paradigms of this sort, while appropriate for Latin, are meaningless for English.

(13)   English   Latin
            Nominative   *the boy*   *puer*
            Genitive   *the boy's*   *pueri*
            Dative   *to the boy*   *puero*
            Accusative   *the boy*   *puerum*
            Ablative   *from the boy*   *puero*
            Vocative   *O boy!*   *puer!*

The effect of Latin grammar, however, was not limited to the teaching of morphology. Syntax, too, was affected. And while in morphology, Latin influence mainly resulted in the minor annoyance of unnecessarily complicating grammatical description, in syntax the influence had far-reaching effects.

For instance, Latin had a rule according to which doubled negative particles within the same sentence cancel each other out and, in fact, may create a strong positive, as in (14). From the Old English period, English had inherited a very different rule, namely that doubled negatives reinforce each other, as in (15).

(14)   ***Nullus non*** venit
        no-one not   came
        'Someone (certainly) came.'

(15)   a. *þe on land Dena*   *laðra **nænig** ...   *sceððan*
           whom in the land of the Danes none of the enemies injure
           ***ne**-meahte* (Beowulf)
           not might
           '... whom none of the enemies might injure in the land of the Danes.'
        b. *I cannot go **no** further* (Shakespeare, *As You Like It* 2.4.9)

Influenced by the Latin model, the grammarians of the new English standard inveighed against the traditional use of double negation and promoted the Latin rule that double negatives cancel each other out.

In this particular case, the grammarians slowly won out. Structures like (15b) are ungrammatical in Modern Standard English in the meaning intended by Shakespeare, even though they appear quite often in non-standard varieties; in the Modern Standard, (15b) is possible only in the meaning 'I can (certainly) go further'.

The success of the grammarians may have been aided by two factors: One was an appeal to logic: If negation is equated with $-X$, and a positive statement with $+X$, then simple mathematics will tell you that $-(-X) =$

+X. Secondly, and perhaps even more significant, adopting the Latin rule of double negation provided an easy, and very effective, way of distinguishing standard from vernacular and of linguistically marginalizing speakers of the vernacular. In Modern English, sentences like *I don't want to give nothing to nobody, nohow, no time* are clearly vernacular and "uneducated". Educated, upper-class speech instead uses structures like *I don't want to give anything to anybody, under any conditions, ever*. (More on such distinctions between vernacular and standard in Chapter 10.)

In other areas, the Latin-influenced efforts of the prescriptive grammarians were much less successful. For instance, English had inherited from its earliest attested stages a rule that permitted relative pronouns and particles to be fronted to clause-initial position without pied-piping their prepositions. As a result, the prepositions could remain stranded later in the clause. An Early Modern English example is given in (16).

(16)   ... *that* *the old carlot once was master* *of*
        (Shakespeare, *As You Like It* 3.5.108)

Latin did not permit structures of this type. So the schoolmaster-grammarians began to inveigh against this inherited English usage too and declared that prepositions should not be permitted to end a sentence. But in this case their success was much more limited than in the case of double negation. Even Winston Churchill, a man hardly known as a knee-jerk liberal, is said to have poked fun at the rule. "This," he said, "is something up with which I will not put."

Let's now return to the *Me and Charlie went to the movies* of example (1) above. Here, too, the grammarians tried their hand at legislation – and still do. But the result has been very mixed, and still is. In fact, to some extent the attempts at prescriptive legislation appear to have backfired.

The issue at hand concerns the case marking of pronouns: Just as in many other languages, English case marking has survived longer in the pronouns than in the nouns. Thus, English pronouns distinguish between a nominative case (*I*) and an objective case (*me*); nouns do not. In that sense, pronouns are somewhat anomalous and therefore vulnerable to developments that might tidy up the situation.

In the second-person pronoun, *you*, these developments have been carried to their logical conclusion, and the distinction between nominative and objective has been lost. In the other pronouns, the developments have been less radical.

To understand these developments it is necessary to look at the system of case marking that early Modern English inherited. Simplifying things a little, this system can be characterized by the following rules:

(a) Subject pronouns are in the nominative case;
(b) Pronouns that are the predicates of equational sentences of the type *X is Y* containing the verb 'be' also are marked nominative;
(c) Pronouns that are the objects of verbs (other than the verb 'be') or of prepositions are in the objective case.

Traces of this earlier system are clearly present in the early Modern English of Shakespeare, as in (17). But side by side with it we find signs of an innovated system with different case marking conventions; compare (17').

(17)   a. *Why, so **I** do ...*
            (*Twelfth Night* 1.1.18)
        b. *A sister! You are **she***
            (*Twelfth Night* 5.1.326)
        c. *I saw **him** hold acquaintance with the waves*
            (*Twelfth Night* 1.2.16)
            *Say I do speak with **her**, my lord, what then?*
            (*Twelfth Night* 1.4.23)

(17')   a. *Mistress, dispatch you with your safest haste*
            And get you from our court.
                            ***Me**, uncle?*
            (*As You Like It* 1.3.41–42)
        b. *That's **me**, I warrant you*
            (*Twelfth Night* 2.5.79)
        c. *You know my father hath no child but **I***
            (*As You Like It* 1.2.18)
            *Let fortune go to hell for it, not **I***
            (*Merchant of Venice* 3.2.21)
            *... all debts are cleared between you and **I***
            (*Merchant of Venice* 3.2.319)

In examples like (17'c) the nominative case of the pronoun does not occur directly after the verb or preposition. This suggests that rule (c) above is getting relaxed, requiring objective marking only on pronouns that are directly preceded by the verb or preposition. Let us refer to these pronouns as ADJACENT to the verb or preposition.

Examples like (17′a) and (17′b) are more difficult to interpret. One possibility is that, as in French, the objective case of the pronoun is beginning to be used as an emphatic form. This interpretation would account for both (17′a) and (17′b). But the type (17′b) is also amenable to another analysis: The objective case here is the result of an extension of rule (c) so that it applies after all verbs, including the verb 'be' (at least if the pronoun is adjacent to the verb). If carried to its logical conclusion, this development would eliminate the need for rule (b) and, in that sense, simplify the grammar of English.

The development of case marking in vernacular or untutored Modern English, uninfluenced by the rules of the prescriptivists, suggests that two of these accounts are especially appropriate: the notion that adjacency plays a role in case marking and the explanation of (17′b) as reflecting an extension of rule (c) and incipient loss of rule (b). Interestingly, however, the results are somewhat different. Consider the examples in (17″).

(17″)   a.   *I went to the movies*
             (subject pronoun adjacent to the verb)
             Me and Charlie went to the movies
             (subject pronoun not adjacent to the verb)
        b.   *It's me*
        c.   *They saw me*
             They saw me and Charlie
             They gave it to me
             They gave it to me and Charlie

Whereas in early Modern English, adjacency affected the case marking of object pronouns, in untutored Modern English it applies to subject pronouns. Contrast the two examples under (17″a). And while in early Modern English the "default" case marking of pronouns not adjacent to the verb was the nominative, as in (17′c), in Modern English it seems to be the objective case, as in the second example of (17″a).

Now, the rules for Latin case marking are very similar to rules (a)–(c) above. Given what we have seen so far, it is not surprising that the grammarians insisted that Standard English should follow these rules, and not the new rule systems underlying (17′) and (17″).

In the case of structures like (17″b), the critics' success has been quite mixed. Many speakers of Standard English feel that *It's I* is overly formal, even stilted, and prefer to say *It's me*, at least in informal, more friendly or intimate, contexts.

As for structures like (17″a), we have seen in the beginning of this Chapter that present-day critics tend to correct expressions like *Me and Charlie went to the movies*, by insisting on *Charlie and I* ... , confusing syntax and style. Moreover, in doing so, they provide no reliable grammatical guidelines for correctness. As a consequence, there is nothing to prevent the poor target of such corrections to interpret them as generally prohibiting sequences like *me and Charlie* and requiring instead the general use of structures like *Charlie and I*.

The result is that speakers come up with hypercorrect sentences such as *They saw Charlie and I* and *They gave it to Charlie and I*. These structures seem to comply with the demand to say *Charlie and I*, not *Me and Charlie*, yet they obviously violate rule (c) above which requires object pronouns to be in the objective case in Standard English. Critics shudder at such sentences, and so do many other, more liberal speakers of Standard English. But most of the critics don't realize their own role in bringing about such structures – by not providing proper guidelines as to when one should say *Charlie and I* and when *Charlie and me*. To do so, however, requires making a proper distinction between syntax and usage. The usage issue is very simple: It is considered impolite to talk about yourself first, so you should mention *Charlie* first and then yourself. The syntactic issue is a bit more complex, but can be explained in fairly simple terms, too: When you say *Me and Charlie went to the movies* you are basically saying that you went and Charlie went. But, except for Cookie Monster on Sesame Street, Tarzan, and speakers of pidgins (see Chapter 14), no English speaker would say *Me went to the movies*, everybody would say *I went to the movies*. That's why you should say *Charlie and I went to the movies*. On the other hand, nobody would say *He saw I* or *They gave it to I*, people use *me* instead. So, why don't you also say *He saw Charlie and me* and *They gave it to Charlie and me*?

While structures such as *He saw Charlie and I* are superficially similar to Shakespeare's *Let fortune go to hell for it, not I* and *all debts are cleared between you and I* in (17′c), it is more likely that they are hypercorrections than direct descendants of the Shakespearean constructions, for children are constantly subjected to admonishments of the type *Don't say "me and Charlie"; say "Charlie and I"*, without any guidelines as to when *Charlie and I* is appropriate. Nevertheless, just like morphological hypercorrections, these hypercorrect uses of the nominative pronoun have the potential of becoming accepted as normal. There are some indications that this has happened in some varieties of English.

6. A successful major shift: Word order in English and related languages

Attentive readers may by now have realized that syntactic change differs markedly from most forms of sound change and analogical/morphological change: It does not affect just individual words or classes of words, not even individual sentences, but the patterning of a large number of sentences. For instance, the developments in pronoun case marking were not limited to the sentences cited above, but instead affected all sentences containing subject and object pronouns. In order to trace syntactic change it is therefore necessary to examine the fate of abstract patterns for sentences, patterns whose structural make-up may vary considerably. Moreover, by their very nature, such sentence patterns are quite complex; and to discuss how they are put together requires using fairly extensive and specialized terminology. This is especially true if we examine more complex syntactic changes than the ones we looked at in earlier sections.

For these reasons let us look at only one example of a complex syntactic shift. This is a sequence of changes which significantly altered major word order from early Germanic to Modern English. The example has been chosen because, among the various more complex syntactic changes that can be observed, word order changes are most easily illustrated.

Assume you wanted to say that a chicken crossed the road in Modern English. And assume you are interested only in stating the facts – no questions asked, no commands, and no passive. You wouldn't have much of a choice, would you? The most natural way of stating the message would be as in (18a), with the subject (in small caps) preceding the verb (in boldface) which, in turn, precedes the object (in italics). For some speakers (18b) would be acceptable, too, but clearly more "marked", with particular emphasis on the road. Many other speakers would prefer to express such an emphasis by saying something like *It's the road that the chicken crossed*, or they would use a passive *The road was crossed by the chicken*. (See § 7 below.) Other permutations of (18a) would be entirely unacceptable, such as (18c)–(18f).

(18)   a. THE CHICKEN **crossed** *the road*
            [Basic, "unmarked" order]
         b. *the road* THE CHICKEN **crossed**
            ["Marked" order; *the road* is "in relief"
            ≠ *The road the chicken crossed (was wide)*]
         c. THE CHICKEN *the road* **crossed** *

    d. *the road* **crossed** THE CHICKEN *
    [But note constructions like: *Out of the cave came* A TIGER.]
    e. **crossed** *the road* THE CHICKEN *
    f. **crossed** THE CHICKEN *the road* *

In this respect, Modern English differs markedly from the majority of the early Indo-European languages, as well as from Old English, especially the very archaic stage of Old English found in the famous epic *Beowulf*. In these languages, any of the six different orders in (18) would be acceptable; see (19). (To save space, the Old English nouns are given without preceding demonstrative pronouns, the forerunners of the modern definite article.)

(19)   Old English (Beow.)   Sanskrit

	Old English (Beow.)	Sanskrit	
a.	HENN **oferēode** *rāde*	KUKKUṬAḤ **atarat** *mārgam*	[Marked]
b.	*rāde* HENN **oferēode**	*mārgam* KUKKUṬAḤ **atarat**	[Marked]
c.	HENN *rāde* **oferēode**	KUKKUṬAḤ *mārgam* **atarat**	[Basic]
d.	*rāde* **oferēode** HENN	*mārgam* **atarat** KUKKUṬAḤ	[Marked]
e.	**oferēode** *rāde* HENN	**atarat** *mārgam* KUKKUṬAḤ	[Marked]
f.	**oferēode** HENN *rāde*	**atarat** KUKKUṬAḤ *mārgam*	[Marked]

Latin

a.	PULLUS **transiit** *viam*	[Marked]
b.	*viam* PULLUS **transiit**	[Marked]
c.	PULLUS *viam* **transiit**	[Basic]
d.	*viam* **transiit** PULLUS	[Marked]
e.	**transiit** *viam* PULLUS	[Marked]
f.	**transiit** PULLUS *viam*	[Marked]

Moreover, the basic, "unmarked" order is not (19a), but (19c), with the subject (S) before the object (O), which in turn precedes the verb (V). Other orders convey special connotations. For instance, in (19b), (19e), and (19f) the first word is in relief. It may simply be emphasized, it may be treated as the topic of the rest of sentence, or it may be in some other way under special focus. Placing constituents in a position on the extreme left of clauses to convey such connotations is such a widespread phenomenon in languages other than English that the position has received a special name, namely TOPIC. Patterns of the type (19a) and (19d), with a constituent following the verb are rarer than the others. They, too, convey special connotations. For instance, (19d) might be used to place special emphasis or focus both on the road and on the chicken.

Ignoring Old English, Sanskrit, and Latin patterns of the type (19a) and (19d) in which a constituent follows the verb, we can diagram the differences in sentence patterns between Modern English and the earlier Indo-European languages as follows.

	Basic structure	Structure with TOPIC
Modern English	SVO	(TOPIC SV ...) [in marginal use]
Early Indo-European	SOV	TOPIC S ... V [productive pattern]

Figure 1. Word order differences between Modern English and early Indo-European

How, then, did English change from the early basic SOV pattern in (19c) to its modern SVO pattern in (19a)?

To understand this development, it is necessary to consider sentences with complex verbs, such as Engl. *had crossed*, consisting of an AUXILIARY (*had*) and a MAIN VERB that carries the main lexical meaning (*crossed*). In Modern English, the basic order of these two is as given in (20a), with the auxiliary preceding the main verb. This contrasts with the basic order of Sanskrit and Latin, in which the main verb precedes the auxiliary; see (20b) and (20c). (The Sanskrit and Latin structures corresponding to (20a) are construed as passives; but this does not affect the argument.)

(20)   a. THE CHICKEN **HAD crossed** *the road*
        b. KUKKUṬENA *mārgaḥ* **tīrṇaḥ** ĀSĪT
        c. (A) PULLO *via* **transita** ERAT

Given the parallelism between Beowulfian Old English and Sanskrit/Latin in (19), we might expect a similar parallelism as regards the order of auxiliary and main verb. In fact, we do find structures of the type (21a), with the main verb followed by the auxiliary, both placed at the end of their clause. But in structures with complex verbs, *Beowulf* tends to prefer a different order, given in (21b), with the auxiliary in second position, but the main verb stranded at the end of the clause. (Note that the verb 'go', contained in the Old English word for 'cross', is an irregular verb which makes its past tense and past participle from different roots.)

(21)   a. HENN *rāde* **ofergangen** HÆFDE
        b. HENN **HÆFDE** *rāde* **ofergangen**

This placement of the auxiliary in second position clearly is an innovation. The innovation may have been motivated by the fact that the early Germanic auxiliaries had properties characteristic of clitics (see Chapter 4, § 5.5). For

instance, one of the two auxiliaries of early Germanic, the verb 'be', underwent clitic-reduction developments similar to what we find in the Modern
English auxiliaries. Just as in Modern English, *has* and *is* often occur in the
reduced form *'s* (compare *He's come; She's here*), so PGmc. *ist* had been
reduced to *is* in Old English. (Contrast OE *wāst* 'you (sg.) know', with its
final *-t* retained in the same phonological context (after *s*) in which the *t* of
*ist was lost.)

There is a general tendency in the languages of the world for clitic auxiliaries to go to the second position of the clause. Perhaps this is because in
languages like Old English, the first position of the clause tends to be the
topic, which can be expected to be accented and thus to serve as the host
for the clitic auxiliary, in a sense like a magnet. Whatever the explanation,
however, we must accept that at the time of *Beowulf*, auxiliaries had begun to
move into second position. We can diagram this development as in Figure 2.

Figure 2. First stage of word order shift

Syntactic changes, however, do not happen all of a sudden. We don't wake
up one fine morning and discover, much to our surprise, that our syntax has
changed! Rather, change in syntax has many of the properties of sound change
as observed by Labov (Chapter 4, § 6.3). There is a lot of variation between
the old and the new pattern, but slowly the innovated pattern gains ground,
and eventually the old pattern may disappear entirely.

In the case of our syntactic change, patterns of the type (21a) persisted
throughout the history of Old English. They did so especially in DEPENDENT
CLAUSES. This may be because dependent clauses did not make as much use
of the clause-initial topic position that served as the host for clitic auxiliaries.
Whatever the explanation, however, dependent clauses lagged behind in the
development – throughout the history of Old English, not just as regards the
movement of auxiliaries to second position, but in the later changes as well.

In a complex verb like OE *ofergangen hæfde* or *hæfde … ofergangen*,
only one element usually is inflected for person, number, and the like, namely
the auxiliary. Thus if we wanted to say that several chickens had crossed the
road, the verb would have to take the form *ofergangen hæfdon* or *hæfdon …
ofergangen*. A verb which thus inflects for person, number, etc. is referred
to as a FINITE VERB.

Now, the original motivation for the auxiliary to move into second position was that it was a clitic. However, as we have just seen, auxiliaries also are finite verbs. This made it possible to reinterpret the movement to second position as conditioned, not by the clitic status of the auxiliaries, but by their finite status. Compare Figure 3:

TOPIC ———— S   O   Main Verb Auxiliary
                            non-finite   finite

Figure 3. The second stage in the development – Reinterpretation

Such a reinterpretation would be very similar to the British English reinterpretation of *r*-deletion as *r*-insertion discussed in Chapter 5, § 5. And just as in the latter case, both the old and the new interpretation would perfectly well account for the situation for which they were originally intended. But recall that the reinterpreted rule of *r*-insertion made much broader predictions than the old *r*-deletion, for it could apply not only to originally *r*-ful words like *matter*, but also to originally *r*-less ones, such as *idea*. And once it was applied to the latter, the rule radically changed British English phonology.

The situation is similar for the reformulation in Figure 3. Whereas in structures of the type (20a/b), the auxiliary is the finite verb and the main verb is non-finite, in the Old English structures of the type (19), the main verb, *oferēode*, is finite. (For instance, if several chickens had crossed the road, we would have had to say *oferēodon*.)

If the formulation in Figure 3 is to remain valid, finite main verbs like *oferēode* likewise must move into second position. And this is what happened in post-*Beowulf* Old English, which would have increasingly expressed the idea 'The chicken crossed the road' as (22b), not (22a). (Again, however, the change did not take place overnight, and the two types of structure coexisted for a long time.)

(22) a. HENN *rāde* **oferēode**
      b. HENN **oferēode** *rāde*

Toward the end of the Old English period a further development set in: The "stranded" main verb of structures like (21b) = (23a) began to line up immediately after the second-position auxiliary; see (23b). The reason for this development seems to be that auxiliary and main verb functionally belong together, as component parts of a morphologically complex, but functionally simple verb.

(23)   a. HENN HÆFDE *rāde* **ofergangen**
        b. HENN HÆFDE **ofergangen** *rāde*
        c. THE CHICKEN **HAD crossed** *the road*

The resulting structure (23b) looks remarkably similar to its Modern English counterpart, given in (23c). One might be tempted to believe that the late Old English stage represented in (23b) is completely identical to Modern English and that, therefore, the change from SOV to SVO had been completed by this time. Things are a little more complex, however. In late Old English, both (23a) and (23b) were still grammatical, whereas the counterpart of (23a), *The chicken had the road crossed* is not acceptable in Modern English, at least not in the meaning 'the chicken had crossed the road'. More than that, not only did (23a) and (23b) both continue to be grammatical in late Old English, (22a) continued to coexist with (22b), and (21a) with (21b). That is, the change toward SVO had by no means been concluded.

In addition, Modern English differs from Old English not just in having SVO, but also by increasingly disfavoring structures with initial topic. (Recall that structures such as *It's the road the chicken crossed* provide a handy alternative.) Moreover, to the extent that it still tolerates structures with topic, Modern English usually does not place the verb directly after the topic. For instance, it is impossible in Modern English to say *The road crossed the chicken* in the sense of 'The chicken crossed the road', with emphasis or some other kind of prominence on *the road*. If we can place *the road* in initial position at all, we have to place the subject immediately after it, and the verb has to follow the subject, as in *The road the chicken crossed*. That is, Modern English generally requires that the subject precede its verb in simple declarative statements. Only traces of the older pattern, with verb before subject, remain, such as *Out of the cave came a tiger* and especially *There is a chicken on the road*. (Non-standard English tends to treat even structures of the latter type as having the order of subject preceding the verb, making the verb "agree" with the singular (i.e., non-plural) form *there*, even if the (original) subject is in the plural. Compare *There is many chickens on the road*, or even more common: *There's many chickens on the road*.)

Finally, recall that in Old English, dependent clauses tended to lag behind in the development from SOV toward SVO. Whereas main clauses increasingly favored the (b) versions of examples (21), (22), and (23), dependent clauses tended to favor the older (a) patterns. In this respect, too, syntax has changed on the way toward Modern English, for now there is no longer any major difference in word order between main clauses and dependent clauses; both types of clauses have SVO.

The developments outlined so far took place not only in English, but with certain variations, in the majority of the other European languages. German, Dutch, and Frisian, however, participated only in the first two stages of the development. As a consequence, they place all main-clause finite verbs into the second position (whether they are auxiliaries or main verbs), but leave non-finite main verbs stranded in final position. Compare the German examples in (24a) and (24b). However, the fact that dependent clauses lagged behind was reinterpreted in these languages as being syntactically significant: Dependent clauses generalized the older, verb-final patterns at the expense of the innovated second-position structures and, as a consequence, came to systematically differ from main clauses. This accounts for the ordering of elements in (24c) and (24d). (To simplify matters, the remainder of this discussion will concentrate on German.)

(24)   a. DAS HUHN **überquerte** *die Strasse*
           'the chicken crossed the road'
        b. DAS HUHN **HATTE** *die Strasse* **überquert**
           'the chicken had crossed the road'
        c. dass DAS HUHN *die Strasse* **überquerte**
           'that the chicken crossed the road'
        d. dass DAS HUHN *die Strasse* **überquert** HATTE
           'that the chicken had crossed the road'

These divergent developments are responsible for the differences between English and German word order noted in § 2 of Chapter 1.

German differs from English in another important respect: In contrast to English, structures with initial topic are still productive, at least in main clauses. And in main-clause structures, the finite verb still directly follows the topic, while the subject is placed after the finite verb; see (25). This retention of topic structures, however, is not limited to German. Many other European languages likewise have retained topic structures, although the degree to which such structures are used may differ considerably.

(25)   a. *Die Strasse* **überquerte** DAS HUHN
        b. *Die Strasse* **HATTE** DAS HUHN **überquert**

Even in German, structures like (24) are subject to certain restrictions. For instance, the fact that expressions like *die Strasse* and *das Huhn* do not distinguish nominative from accusative case may make structures like (25) ambiguous. Instead of interpreting them as meaning that 'the chicken crossed the road' or 'the chicken had crossed the road', it would be possible to understand them to mean 'the road crossed the chicken' or 'the road had crossed the chicken'. In the present case, such an interpretation is rather unlikely, simply because roads don't normally cross chickens. But in sentences like *Die Mutter* **liebt** DAS KIND, there could be genuine confusion as to whether we should translate this as THE CHILD **loves** *the mother* or THE MOTHER **loves** *the child*. In sentences of this type, therefore, the topic construction is generally avoided – if there is no context that might help to disambiguate. (This is especially true in written texts, which lack most of the intonational clues of spoken language and where readers cannot ask for clarification.) If enough disambiguating context is present, however, sentences of this type can be – and are – used. (This is especially true in informal conversations where listeners can watch out for intonational clues or, if necessary, ask for clarification.)

7. Conclusion

Although many of the changes discussed in this chapter, if they are syntactic at all, have relatively minor consequences, the extended example in § 6 shows that syntactic change can be at least as sweeping and general as Grimm's Law or the Great English Vowel Shift, and that its effects on the structure of the language can be at least as great as the morphological changes which ideally can turn a language from isolating to agglutinating to inflecting, and back again to isolating.

In fact, in English there seems to be a certain connection between the morphological development toward a more isolating type of language and the loss of free word order. While in German, ambiguities of the type *Die Mutter* **liebt** DAS KIND can be considered somewhat minor annoyances, the total loss of nominative/accusative case distinctions in English nouns would have led to systematic ambiguities in all structures of this type – unless English eliminated free order and adopted the convention that the subject must necessarily precede the verb directly in unmarked declarative sentences. This is probably a major reason for why Modern English can topicalize only by moving the direct object in front of the subject, but leaving the order of subject and verb untouched, as in *The child, the mother loves*.

As noted earlier, even this relic of topicalization is beginning to fade, and many speakers of English, especially in the American Midwest, are quite uncomfortable with such structures. But since there are great communicative advantages to placing a topic element in sentence-initial position, they use alternative devices for accomplishing this task. One of these is the passive construction, as in *The child is loved by the mother*. Another one employs periphrases, such as *As for the child, the mother loves her*, or *It is the child the mother loves*.

In the development of these alternatives, the same principle seems to be at work as in the case of morphological change from inflectional or agglutinating to isolating: Loss or attrition in one component of the grammar tends to be compensated for in another component. In this manner, the communicative capability of language is maintained, and something like a "steady-state dynamic equilibrium" prevails (to borrow a term from the natural sciences).

Change in the lexicon

Chapter 7
Semantic change

"When *I* use a word," Humpty Dumpty said, in a rather scornful tone, "it means just what I choose it to mean – neither more nor less."

(Lewis Carroll, *Through the Looking-Glass.*)

1. Introduction

The preceding three chapters have been devoted to changes in linguistic STRUCTURE – the topic which probably interests linguists most. The majority of speakers, however, are not linguists, and linguistic structure is something they hardly ever think about. There is a good reason for this: In order to use linguistic structure effectively we have to place its knowledge safely below the level of consciousness. We can see this when we first learn a new language and are still consciously trying to get the grammar right. Uttering even a single, simple sentence can be agony. Or consider a totally different activity – driving a car. In the beginning, when we are too conscious of all the discrete actions we have to coordinate, we find driving very exhausting, and technically speaking we are pretty poor drivers. Only when we internalize the mechanical rules of driving do we get to be technically good drivers – although, of course, we may still be poor drivers in other ways, such as speeding or taking other kinds of risks; but such risks are taken at a more conscious level.

Stretching the metaphor a little, the manner in which we use – safely internalized – linguistic structure in order to convey meaning is similarly a more risky, as well as conscious, activity. Although the syntactic structures of the following two expressions are the same, it makes a great deal of difference whether we say *Let me show you to your seats* or *Let me sew you to your sheets*. And when a spoonerism changes one into the other (see Chapter 4, § 5.5), we will try to quickly correct ourselves – or some-one else will. The main purpose of language, after all, is to convey meaning.

As a consequence, non-linguists are much more aware of – and fascinated by – the SEMANTIC purpose of language. This is especially true for the meaning of individual words, i.e. lexical semantics. Linguists, by contrast, find lexical semantics extremely elusive and therefore difficult to deal with, because meaning is inherently fuzzy and non-systematic (see § 2 below). They greatly prefer to deal with the much more "orderly" structure of language.

While this difference between linguists and non-linguists is understand-able, we need to keep in mind that to be able to use language successfully, we need both structure and meaning. Structure without meaning would be quite useless, except as an intellectual exercise. And similarly, meaning needs structure to be expressed. At a minimum, it needs phonological structure, such that we can express ideas such as 'dog', 'bite', and 'kid' in articulatable words. But putting the words together helter-skelter, as in *dog bite kid* or *kid dog bite*, is not sufficient either; we need to put the words together according to syntactic rules, together with the proper morphological machinery (where appropriate), as in *The dog was biting the kid* vs. *A kid bit a dog*, and so on.

The number of new, or even old, ideas that we may want to convey through language is virtually without limit. But even if the number of lexical items that we use to convey these meanings may be huge, it has to be finite. If every idea had to be expressed by a different sound, we would soon run out, because the number of discrete speech sounds that we can make is limited. Languages generally operate with about twelve to eighty-two different speech sounds. And the hitherto observed upper limit of eighty-two comes close to the maximum range that human beings are able to produce or recognize.

To some extent we make up for this limitation by conveying meaning not through individual speech sounds, but through combinations of sounds. Thus, the sounds [s], [a], [w], [n], and [d] by themselves have no meaning, but put these meaningless sounds together in that order and you have the word [sawnd] = *sound*. Even then, there are limitations on how we can combine speech sounds. For instance, if we take the same five sounds and reverse their order, we come up with a sequence [dnwas] which is unacceptable in English and many other languages. There is some question as to whether it is possible to establish any absolute limits across the different languages. Even so, any given language seems to impose some limitations on the combinations of sounds. (Although these might ultimately be motivated by such considerations as learnability or distinctiveness, historical accident plays a certain role as well.) The result of this indirect encoding of meaning through combinations of meaningless speech sounds is that there is no direct relationship between meaning and the sounds which spell out the words that convey meaning. In other words, the relationship between meaning and form is ARBITRARY. (See § 4 below.)

Even if we were capable of producing a virtually infinite number of different speech sounds, how would we ensure that our listeners understand us? A simple thought experiment illustrates the difficulty. Assume we want to unambiguously convey the linguistic idea of sound change, so that there can be no confusion about the fact that this differs considerably from the ideas non-linguists would associate with the term. We could do this by saying something like [sownč]. But this word would be utterly meaningless to our listeners, unless we went through a long explanation of what we intend to designate by the word. It would have been just as easy to stick to the expression *sound change* and to explain to our listener that it has a special, technical meaning in linguistics. But imagine our doing this for every different new idea. We would have to have a lexicon of virtually infinite proportions. Who would be able to memorize all those different words and the meanings associated with them?

To gauge the difficulty of this undertaking, just ask yourself how many of the million or so words of English you are actually familiar with. What, for instance, is the meaning of *thermion*, or *thigmotaxis*, or *thill*, or *thimerosal*? You would have to be an expert in physics, biology, the art of driving animal-drawn wagons, as well as pharmacy in order to know all of these. (*Thermion* = 'an ion emitted by conducting material at very high temperatures', *thigmotaxis* = 'movement of an organism in response to outside tactile stimulation', *thill* = 'either of a pair of shafts or poles between which an animal is hitched to pull a wagon', *thimerosal* = '$C_9H_9HgNaO_2S$ in powdered form used as an antiseptic'.) And even if you happened to be an expert in all of these areas, would you know terms like *thaumaturge* (a performer of miracles), *theta-marking* (a convention in a certain framework of syntactic theory), or *threnody* (a song of lamentation)? One suspects that even lexicographers, who are in the business of compiling the dictionaries in which we find such words, do not know the meaning and use of all these words. The idea of a virtually infinite lexicon therefore would be nothing but preposterous.

2. The inherent fuzziness of meaning: Polysemy, semantic overlap, metaphor

To avoid the difficulties just outlined, natural language permits a great amount of flexibility in meaning. Note for example the expression in (1) which, depending on the context or reference, may have a variety of different interpretations. If John is in kindergarten, his just barely being able to sound out written words may merit the response in (1). But if John is in his teens or older, with normal abilities, this would not be a probable interpretation. He would have to be able to do something more spectacular, such as excel in a speed reading class, in a poetry reading contest, or the like. The expression in (1), however, is able to convey all of these interpretations, by being sufficiently vague or "fuzzy". This vagueness or fuzziness of meaning is referred to as POLYSEMY.

(1)   *John reads very well*

In many cases we are not even aware of such polysemy. But if we think about it, we tend to say that there is a true or CORE meaning and that other meanings are transferred or EXTENDED. For instance, the core meaning of *read* might be something like 'comprehend the meaning of written symbols'. Meanings such as 'comprehend the meaning conveyed by written symbols' might be a first extension of the core meaning. A further extension might be 'sound out written symbols'. Yet another extension would be 'sound out a poem for an audience'. This is very much what we find in dictionaries, as in the following excerpt from the entry for *read* in the *American Heritage Dictionary of the English Language* (first edition). But note that even the most comprehensive dictionary can only list a small subset of the total range of meanings that can be related to each other in this way.

> **read** ... **1.** To comprehend or take in the meaning of (something written or printed). **2.** To utter or render aloud (something written or printed). **3.** To

have the knowledge of (a language) necessary to understand printed or written material . . .

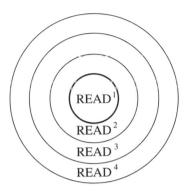

Figure 1. Core and extended meanings as concentric circles

This relationship between the different meanings in a word like *read* can be modeled as in Figure 1, with a core meaning surrounded by a set of extended meanings arranged in concentric circles. However, this diagram greatly simplifies matters. For instance, a derivation of the type READ[1] 'comprehend the meaning of written symbols' → READ[2] 'comprehend the meaning conveyed by written symbols' → READ[3] 'sound out written symbols' is highly unlikely. Rather, READ[2] and READ[3] are both extensions of READ[1], but they go in different directions. And READ[4] 'sound out a poem for an audience' would be an extension of READ[3]. A more realistic, but also more unwieldy, model therefore would look more like Figure 2 (p. 220), with a core meaning surrounded by concentric amoeba-like extensions.

Examples like READ readily show that the range of meanings of a given word can vary considerably. Depending on the circumstances that range may be BROADER or NARROWER.

Moreover, because the meanings of words ordinarily are polysemous and extend over a larger area of references, the meanings of different words may OVERLAP, as in Figure 3 (p. 220). Thus, for at least one of the interpretations of (1) we can also say something like (2). (Although more realistic, models of the type illustrated in Figure 2 are rather unwieldy, as noted above. This is especially true for relationships between the meanings of different words. Figure 3 therefore uses the simpler, concentric-circle model.)

(2)   *John recites very well*

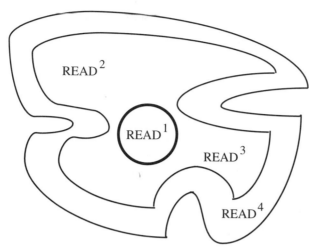

Figure 2. More realistic model of core and extended meanings

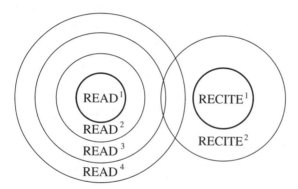

Figure 3. Semantic overlap

The fuzziness in meaning resulting from semantic extension and semantic overlap can be much more extensive than the example of *read* and *recite* suggests. Consider the following, much more complex cases.

What is the meaning of *animal*, either taken by itself or contrasted with *plant* or other words? Are bacteria animals or plants? What about corals? Insects? Birds? Human beings? Speakers may disagree greatly with each other. But even more significant, they may disagree with themselves. For instance, the following sentences might be uttered by the same person, at different times, without any feeling of contradiction. In some of these, *animal* is used in a fairly restricted sense as a near-synonym of *mammal*, in others it has a more general, scientific, meaning, conforming to dictionary definitions such as 'Any organism of the kingdom Animalia, distinguished from plants by ... locomotion, fixed structure ... and non-photosynthetic metabolism' (*American Heritage Dictionary of the English Language*, first edition). But other factors play a role, too, for the way many people use the word, such as land-based vs. air- or water-based, human vs. non-human. And expressions like (7) and (8) illustrate a similar vacillation for *fish* and its relation to *animal*.

(3)   *This powder kills noxious insects, but is harmless to humans and animals.*

(4)   *It's incorrect to call bacteria "bugs", because bacteria are plant-like, but bugs or insects are animals.*

(5)   *Birds and human beings are two-legged animals.*

(6)   *Noah gathered pairs of all the birds and animals on his ark.*

(7)   *Whales aren't really fish, they're animals.*

(8)   *Jonah was swallowed by a great fish, probably a whale.*

What about the word *star*? Again, speakers can accept a wide range of different, often contradictory meanings conveyed by this word, as in (9)–(12). And here, again, one of the contributing elements is a difference between scientific and ordinary use.

(9)   *Venus is the brightest star in the early night sky.*

(10)   *Venus is a planet, not a star.*

(11)   *Stars shine at night.*

(12)   *The sun is a star.*

It is tempting to model the relationship between these two different interpretations of *star* as an ellipse, with two core meanings as its foci, see Figure 4 (p. 222). However, even those who insist on considering the sun a (fixed) star would find it very strange if in broad sunlight somebody said to them *Look at that beautiful starlight*. (See the cartoon at the beginning of this chapter.)

Moreover, an elliptic model would do nothing for the apparently multifocal semantic range of *animal*. A much more appropriate model probably would be one which considers the broad semantic RANGE of the scientific or dictionary definition to be the true or basic meaning of *animal*. Within that range, the meaning 'mammal' would hold a special status, similar but not identical to a

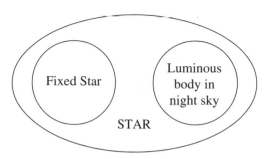

Figure 4. A semantic ellipse with two foci

core meaning, since we tend to think of mammals as the most PROTOTYPICAL animals. For obvious reasons, the notion 'human being' would at least partly overlap that of 'mammal'. The meanings 'fish' and 'bird' are clearly less close to the prototypical 'mammal', 'reptile' even less; and 'insect' would be quite peripheral. An attempt to model these relationships is found in Figure 5 (p. 223).

This model of semantic relationship differs considerably from the models that we looked at earlier. The models in Figures 1–3 operate with the assumption of an increasing semantic broadening or expansion of a core meaning. In the case of *animal*, by contrast, a broad range of meanings undergoes a variety of semantic narrowings; and among these narrower meanings one can be considered prototypical. Such tendencies toward semantic narrowing plus development of a prototypical quasi-core meaning are quite typical of inherently broad cover terms such as *animal, France, Asia*, or *Orient*. (See § 5.6 below for further illustration.)

The major vehicle for expanding the range of meanings of a given word is METAPHOR. The term metaphor is most commonly used in reference to the often quite daring or arcane expansion of meanings in poetic language, such as, say, *arrows* for the sun's rays or *mother of the waters* for the ocean. But it is a much more widespread phenomenon which we constantly draw on to creatively expand the power of words.

The effects may be relatively subtle, as in the ever-increasing semantic range of *read*. But they may approach the boldness of poetic metaphor. For instance, the word *clear* originally referred to visible objects such as liquids or air, but then, by metaphorical extension, came to be used also about invisible objects, such as statements and arguments. It is true, metaphorical extensions such as that of *clear* may not strike us as particularly daring; that is because the metaphoric link, like linguistic structure, has been pushed below the level of consciousness. But it is not difficult to bring it back to consciousness. This

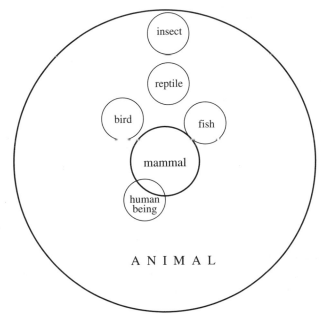

Figure 5. A semantic range with prototypical center plus other more peripheral meanings

for instance happens if somebody answers the question *Is everything clear?* with something like *Clear as mud.*

Metaphor comes in many different guises, some based on perceived similarity, others on contiguity or physical association. Examples of the former are the just-mentioned *arrows* and *clear*. Consider further the metaphorical extension of *animal* in expressions like *John's a real animal*. Examples of extension by contiguity are the different meanings of *read*, or the use of *hands* to refer to *laborers*. (Further illustrations are found in later sections.)

3. Synonymy and homonymy

The need to use a finite number of words to express a virtual infinity of meanings has further consequences. One of these is that absolute SYNONYMY, i.e., identity in meaning between phonetically different expressions, tends to be avoided and is consequently rare. Having more than one linguistic form to express exactly the same range of meanings would simply not be economical. True, thesauruses are full of supposed synonyms, intended to help us avoid excessive repetition. But uncritical use of a thesaurus can have very strange, even ridiculous, consequences because the listed alternatives are only partial, not absolute, synonyms, exhibiting semantic overlap, not identity.

Thus, although the meanings of *subconscious* and *unconscious* overlap to a considerable degree, even a cursory look at examples like (13) shows that they cannot be used completely interchangeably. Their synonymy, thus, is only a partial one.

(13)   *She knocked him* _____

There is yet another consequence: In order to make it possible for words to clearly and unambiguously signal different meanings, there is a tendency to avoid HOMONYMY, i.e., the use of phonetically identical words with divergent references. This is true at least when the two words can occur in the same context and can create undesirable confusion. Thus, there is no difficulty about Engl. *read* [red] (past tense of *read*) and *red* (the color). But in varieties of American English in which *can* and *can't* are pronounced identically (as something like [kæən], see Chapter 4, § 4), problems do arise, and people will ask questions such as *Is she able or not?*

Although in principle homonymy is fundamentally different from polysemy, the two phenomena are not always easy to distinguish. For instance, are the two expressions *ear* of corn (etc.) and *ear* of animals just homonymous, or are they a single, polysemous word? What about *reader*, the noun corresponding to the *read* of (1) above, compared to the British English university rank of *Reader* = roughly 'Associate Professor'? And what about the two highlighted words in (14)?

(14)   *The Air **Marshal** of the People's Republic declared **martial** law today.*

For literate speakers of English, the spellings of *marshal* and *martial* would just about guarantee that the words are considered mere homonyms, in spite of their identical pronunciation as [maršəl]. But what about speakers that are not literate? As for *Reader*, many speakers might consider the word a specialized use of the normal word *reader*, because *Readers* read out their lectures. Historically, this is no doubt how *Reader* acquired its meaning. But do all *Readers* read out their lectures? Don't some of them lecture without a written text? And what about the British university rank of *Lecturer* = roughly 'Assistant Professor'? Does a *Reader* lecture any less than a *Lecturer* and a *Lecturer* read any less than a *Reader*? As for *ear* and *ear*, American speakers might see a relationship, since *ears of corn* for them refer to 'cobs of the maize plant'. And such cobs stick out from the plant in such a manner that with some imagination they could be compared to the ears of human beings or animals. In British English, such an interpretation would be quite preposterous: The word *corn* commonly designates a plant such as 'wheat', whose *ears* are of a very different shape and therefore could hardly be considered even remotely similar to human or animal ears.

It is possible to argue that the tendency to avoid both absolute synonymy and excessive homonymy springs from a common principle. That principle, in fact, is identical to the one invoked earlier as the motivation for the analogical process of leveling, which in Chapter 5, § 2.1 was characterized by the slogan ONE MEANING − ONE FORM. In the present case, this means that if there are two different forms, then we expect there to be two different meanings; and if there is no formal distinction, then we expect no semantic distinction, either. But just as in the case of leveling, our response to violations of the principle will be selective, based on an evaluation of the significance of the violation.

4. The relationship between sound and meaning

As noted earlier, the indirect encoding of meaning through combinations of meaningless speech sounds in effect entails that the relationship between meaning and form is ARBITRARY. This can be seen from the fact that different languages use phonetically very different expressions to express (roughly) the same meanings. See for instance the words for 'dog' in (15a). The converse is true, too − different languages may assign very different meanings to forms that are phonetically identical or quite similar, as shown by (15b).

(15)   a. Engl. *dog*, Germ. *Hund* [hunt], Fr. *chien* [šyẽ], Span. *perro* [peřo], It. *cane* [kane], Lith. *šuo*, Finnish *koira*, Hindi *kuttā*, Tamil *kūraṇ*, Arabic *kalb*, Amharic *wuššā*

b. Arabic *kalb* 'dog'   : Germ. *Kalb* 'calf'
    Turkish *beter* 'worse'   : Engl. *better*
    Turkish *alt* 'bottom'   : Germ. *alt* 'old'
    Turkish *kar* 'snow'   : French *car* 'because', Engl. *car*
    Sanskrit *yunaǰmi* 'I join'   : Engl. *you nudge me*
    Gk. *hén* 'one'   : Engl. *hen*
    Mod. Gk. *míti* 'nose'   : Engl. *meaty*
    Cree *tanse* 'how?'   : Germ. *tanze* 'I dance'
    Albanian *nis* 'begin'   : Ukrainian *nis* 'nose'

Note especially cases such as Arabic *kalb* : Germ. *Kalb*, where both words refer to a type of animal to be sure, but to very different animals ('dog' vs. 'calf') and pairs like Turkish *beter* : Engl. *better*, where the meanings literally are opposite, 'worse' vs. 'better'.

Further evidence for the arbitrariness of the meaning-sound relationship can be seen in the fact that sound change and/or other changes may alter the shape of words beyond recognition, without affecting their meaning. For instance, believe it or not, Germ. *Hund*, Fr. *chien*, It. *cane*, and Lith. *šuo* all are reflexes of the same word, PIE *ḱuon-*.

In spite of these facts, however, ordinary speakers, without training in linguistics, tend to believe that the relation between word and meaning is in and of itself meaningful, not arbitrary. Note for example the statement in (16) or the story, possibly apocryphal, of the German-speaking traveler from Tyrol (Austria) who, upon coming to Italy, was struck by how senseless it was of the Italians to say *cavallo* for the animal (the horse) that everyone knows is called a *Pferd*! Linguists may consider such statements and stories naive and irrelevant for the discipline of linguistics. But here as elsewhere we should keep in mind that the majority of speakers are not linguists and, as will be seen below, their opinions do matter, by providing the motivation for linguistic changes – whether linguists like it or not.

(16)   *It's very clear why pigs are called pigs – they're very dirty animals.*

The feeling that the sound-meaning relationship is not arbitrary is especially prevalent and appropriate as regards ONOMATOPOEIA, i.e., words intended to capture sounds of nature through similar speech sounds. Compare for instance the English animal sounds in (17).

(17)   rooster: *cockadoodledoo*
        young bird: *peep, cheep, chirp*
        dog: *arf, bow-wow*
        cow: *moo*

The special relationship between meaning and sound in onomatopoeia becomes especially obvious if we consider possible alternatives. Forms like *peep, cheep,* and *chirp* simply won't do as imitations of the rooster's call; nor will *moo* for the dog's bark, or *bow-wow* for the sound of cows. Even less radical changes would in many cases be inappropriate. For instance, it would be strange to refer to the sounds of young birds as *choop*, or to the sound of cows as *mee*.

Examples like *cheep* vs. *moo* illustrate a very general tendency of onomatopoeia to use high front vowels to refer to the sounds of young or small animals and human beings, and back vowels (or at least, vowels that are not high and front) to depict the sounds of adult or large creatures. This tendency is grounded in the fact that the sounds emitted by small creatures tend to be higher pitched and as a consequence acoustically closer to high front vowels.

The relation between high front vowels and 'small' may be exploited in areas that do not involve onomatopoeia, such as *teeny* vs. *tiny*, *leetle* vs. *little*, where the forms with *ee* [ī] have front vowels higher than the other forms and designate something even smaller. Such non-onomatopoetic relationships between sound and meaning are referred to as SOUND SYMBOLISM.

Another area in which non-linguists commonly find an especially salient non-arbitrary relationship between meaning and form is TABOO, i.e., words which are considered forbidden or at least impolite under certain social circumstances. Here it is not so much the meaning that is found unacceptable, but the linguistic expression of that meaning. In English, for instance, expressions like (18a) are acceptable in most circles, even if they may appear excessively severe. But the nearly synonymous (18b) is not, either in this form or without an object, used as a general expletive. The fact that the offensiveness of (18b) lies in its linguistic form becomes especially clear when we contrast it with the expressions in (18c), where a simple alteration in phonetic form renders the expression much less offensive. Evidently, the different distortions in (18c) permit speakers to have their cake and eat it too: They can utter the tabooed expression, but forestall reprimand by being able to claim that they did not really use it. (See also Chapter 4, § 4.)

(18)   a. *(May) God punish them by sending them to hell*
       b. *(May) God damn them*
       c. *dang, darn, gosh darn, doggone, dad burn(ed)* ...

While ordinary speakers (i.e. non-linguists) may be convinced that there is a clear connection between sound and meaning, at least in onomatopoeia, sound symbolism, and taboo, linguists are just as firmly convinced that even here the relation is to some degree arbitrary. To support this view they can point out that other languages often employ different onomatopoetic means to express the same animal sound. Compare for instance (17'). Similarly, languages – or their speakers – may disagree over what is taboo. While there is a great tendency for words for excrement, sexual activities, or the name of the divinity to be taboo, in some societies it is the name of one's elder sister, the names of deceased persons and everything which sounds like these names, or yet other words. Even so, the belief of linguistically naive speakers that the sound-meaning relationship in such words is not arbitrary is sufficiently powerful to bring about linguistic change.

(17')   German   French   Hindi
    rooster: *kikeriki*   *cocorico*   *kuk(a)rūkū*
    dog: *wauwau*   *tou-tou*   *bhõ-bhõ*

5. Factors responsible for semantic change

In large measure, semantic change results from the same factors that are responsible for the fuzziness of meaning, namely the semantic relation between words, and the relationship that we perceive between meaning and form. The effects of these, as well as other factors, are discussed in the following sections.

5.1. Metaphor
The major vehicle through which words acquire new or broader meanings is metaphor.

Metaphoric language comes in many different shapes, which in traditional rhetorical theory have been classified in various subtypes. One of these is SYNECDOCHE, the designation of a thing or person by means of its most salient part, as in (19). The extended meaning in (19a) results from the fact that in a traditional setting, employers would consider the hands to be the most important part of laborers for their work. (Their minds, obviously, are of little concern.) Similarly, the meaning in (19b) reflects the fact that the most important part of a table is the board on top. (Legs are there merely to support the top board.)

(19)   a.   Engl. *hands* = 'laborers'
      compare Span. *braceros* 'laborers' : *brazo* 'arm'
      b.   Engl. *board* = 'table'
      c.   Engl. *wheels* = 'car'

A very similar broadening of meaning can be accomplished through METONYMY, the designation of a group of things or persons by means of a word referring to something with which that group is habitually associated. Compare (20). The developments in (20c,d), presupposing the synecdoche in (19b), show that metaphorical extensions can build on other, previous metaphorical extensions. In principle there is no limit on how far such chains of metaphorical extensions can go.

(20)   a. *The pulpit* = 'the clergy'
      b. *The bar* = 'the legal profession (which pleads its case at the bar separating the jury etc. from the rest of the court)'
      c. *The board (of directors)* = 'those who sit around a table in order to make decisions'
      d. *(Bed and) board* = 'the food served at a table'

A large number of metaphoric uses are motivated by what can be called social factors, employing a fairly broad definition of the term social. For instance, we may choose to give our claims greater impact by exaggeration or to mitigate their force through understatement. In one case we tend to produce HYPERBOLE, in the other, LITOTES. Compare (21) and (22), where the examples under (a) illustrate current extended metaphorical uses, while the (b) examples illustrate original metaphors which have lost their metaphorical flavor.

(21)   a. Engl. *I'm **terribly, awfully, frightfully** sorry*
                 I'm ***sorely*** disappointed
                 *This is the **most unique** experience I've ever had*
      b. Germ. *sehr* 'very', cognate of Engl. *sore.*
           Engl. *very* < ME *verai* 'true, truly' (⇐ OFr. *verai* 'true')

(22)   a. Engl. *I feel **a little, a bit** under the weather*
                 *The danger is **not inconsiderable***
      b.   *Give me a **couple** of oranges* (= a few, several oranges)

Other socially motivated metaphors include EUPHEMISM and PARONOMASIA or punning. Euphemisms may be used to avoid words that are under taboo (see below), but also to avoid a large range of other unpleasant connotations. The examples in (23) may serve to illustrate the range of possible developments. Politicians are notoriously adept at employing euphemisms in order to "pretty up" their actions and ideas. The use of euphemism in totalitarian states has been caricatured in the Newspeak of George Orwell's *1984*, with expressions such as *joycamp* (a forced-labor camp) and *Ministry of Love* (a prison in which dissenters are tortured). Some euphemisms, such as *pre-owned automobile* and *pacified village*, may never succeed in becoming part of the regular vocabulary. But words such as *mortician* and *beautician* have. (See Chapter 5, § 3.2 on the morphology of these two words.) Paronomasia, on the other hand, does not normally seem to make lasting contributions to the lexicon. In present-day American English, it is a favorite device for creating names of business establishments, see (24). Note however that something very much like paronomasia played a great role in the early development of writing. (Recall for instance the Sumerian use of the symbol for *ti* 'arrow' to refer to *ti* 'life'; Chapter 3, § 2.3.)

(23)   *deceased, loved one* = 'dead body, corpse'
         mortician = 'undertaker'
         beautician = 'hair dresser'
         pre-owned automobile = 'used car'
         pacified village = 'village which has been forced to side with "us"'
         liberation = 'killing or putting into "reeducation camps" people who sided with "them"'
         ethnic cleansing = 'killing or expelling "unwanted" ethnic groups'
         final solution = '"elimination" of Jews, Gypsies, and other "undesirables"'

(24)   *The Mane Event, Head Hunters, Cost Cutters, From Hair to Eternity, Shear Delight* (all names for hair cutting salons)
         Cuttin' Corners, The Mower's Edge, The Lawn Ranger (names of lawn mower servicing and lawn mowing businesses)
         Chin's Wok'n Roll Cafe, The Great Impasta, Lox Stock & Bagel, Wiener Lose, Snaks Park Avenue (names for restaurants, delis)
         The Daily Grind, Common Grounds (names of coffee houses)
         The Laser's Edge (name for an establishment that produces laser-printed resumés)

The use of metaphor is especially widespread in certain types of language use. Beside the language of politicians, with its heavy reliance on euphemisms, the most notorious areas of such language use are AR-GOTS, JARGONS, and SLANG. These are discussed more fully in Chapters 9 and 10.

As noted in § 2 above, in many cases the metaphoric link is pushed below the level of consciousness. In cases like *clear*, the link can easily be brought back to the surface. But in other cases the relationship has become much more tenuous. Compare for instance the relationship between *reader* and the British university rank of *Reader* (§ 3 above).

This common tendency for the metaphoric link to become attenuated is referred to as semantic FADING. If fading goes far enough, the link between original and derived meaning becomes severed, and synonymy results in homonymy, as in the case of Mod. Fr. *pas* 'not' and *pas* 'step' (Chapter 5, § 3.2). Similarly, there is no obvious semantic connection between *very* and *verity* or *veritable*, in spite of their historical relationship (all of them ultimately go back to forms derived from Lat. *vērus* 'true').

5.2. Taboo

Taboo likewise tends to lead to frequent vocabulary renewal. This can be gauged by the large number of lexical replacements for tabooed words, especially for the ones considered most objectionable. In addition to the examples in (18) above, see for instance the set in (25a) which serves to avoid *bloody*, a word which is considered taboo in British English. (25b) illustrates the fact that words for 'toilet' are subject to similar constant lexical renewal. The Victorian era is said to have been especially notorious for the degree to which at least some speakers placed all kinds of words under taboo because of their – often marginal – sexual connotations. Some of the taboo-induced replacements of that era have been retained, and those in (25c) are often cited as examples. But modern speakers usually are no longer aware that these result from taboo. In the case of *white meat* and *dark meat*, the retention may be due to the fact that the linguistic distinction made by the terms corresponds to a widespread distinction in taste preference.

(25)   a. Brit. Engl. *blasted, bleeding, blighted, blooming, blessed*, etc.
       b. *bathroom, powder room, ladies'/men's room, lavatory, WC, loo*, etc.

c. *chest*   'breast'
    limb   'leg'
    white meat   '(chicken) breast'
    dark meat   '(chicken) legs and thighs'
    drumstick   '(chicken) leg'

The examples in (18) and (25) show that there may be different lexical reactions to taboo. While (25b) and (25c) simply replace the tabooed words without any consideration for the way they are pronounced, the replacements in (18) and (25a) sound similar to the words under taboo. In many cases, the result is a pre-existing word which simply gets to be used in a new meaning. In others, such as *gosh*, the result is a totally new word. Words of the latter type make it useful to distinguish between TABOO-INDUCED REPLACEMENT and TABOO-INDUCED DEFORMATION.

In spite of the social restrictions against them, tabooed words may be remarkably persistent. Some of the "Anglo-Saxon four-letter" words considered most offensive can be traced back to Old English and beyond. While it is not appropriate to use these tabooed words in polite company, there are many other areas of language use in which they may be quite appropriate (such as among adolescents or in the military). And sometimes, breaking the taboo may be considered appropriate, as a sign of deep anger. Even persons who would never permit themselves to utter such words certainly know them. Thus, a famous lexicographer is said to have been approached by an elderly lady who congratulated him on his new dictionary, but added, "You naughty man; there are a lot of naughty words in your dictionary." Whereupon the lexicographer replied, "You naughty lady; you knew precisely where to look."

Lexical replacement is not necessarily limited to the tabooed words. "Innocent bystanders", words that happen to be mere homonyms, may be affected as well – or instead. For instance, American English has generally replaced *ass* by *donkey* and *cock* by *rooster* because of their homonymy with words under strong taboo. In the case of the perhaps most heavily tabooed word of English, the process of replacement seems to have gone even farther, eliminating all independent words with short vowel in the context between [f] and [k]; see the data in (26), where dates in parentheses indicate the last attestation cited in the *Oxford English Dictionary*. Significantly perhaps, most of these last dates come from the Victorian era.

(26)   *fuk* (a sail) (1529)
         fac 'factotum' (1841)
         feck 'effect, efficiency' (1887) (now only in *feckless*)
         fack/feck (one of the stomachs of a ruminant) (1887)
         feck(s)/fack(s) '(in) faith, (in) fact' (1891)

The effects of taboo-induced replacement and deformation can be quite far-reaching. Many Polynesian and Micronesian societies, for instance, have the tradition that upon the death of a person, his or her name becomes subject to taboo. Moreover, since names tend to be compounds of ordinary words (of the type 'noble warrior', 'slim-waisted', or 'dances with wolves'), their component parts likewise may be subject to taboo. Even derivational and inflectional affixes may be affected. The result has been such a large turnover in the lexicon that it is quite difficult to establish the degree of relationship between different languages on the basis of vocabulary correspondences.

Deformation due to taboo likewise can create difficulties in comparative linguistics. Note for instance the word for 'tongue' in Indo-European. Being the organ of speech, the tongue was in earlier, more "primitive" times considered to be mystically identical with speech and therefore, like speech, a supernatural force: Giving a name to somebody or something would give one power over that person or thing. We see echoes of this identification of 'tongue' and 'speech' in such expressions as *the English tongue* or *speaking in tongues*, as well as in our word *language* which, via French, derives from Lat. *lingua* 'tongue, language'; note also Arab. *lisan* 'tongue, language'.

Below are given the words for 'tongue' from most of the (ancient) Indo-European languages, together with the forms from which they could be derived by regular sound change, if they had developed only according to sound change. As can be seen, although there clearly was a word for 'tongue' in Proto-Indo-European, which probably contained the sounds [n̥ǵhwā/ū-], taboo-induced deformation has taken its toll to such an extent that the phonetic nature of the reconstructed word cannot be determined with greater precision. For instance, the question whether there was an initial consonant and what the nature of that consonant was cannot be resolved on the basis of the extant evidence. (Similar difficulties can be encountered in the words for other important body parts, especially the words for 'liver' and 'spleen'. Interestingly, the word for 'heart' has remained much more constant, suggesting either that the early Indo-Europeans were not yet aware of the physiological importance of the heart or that they had a different attitude toward it.)

(27)   Indo-European 'tongue':

Lat.	*lingua*, OLat. *dingua*	: *$dn̥ǵ(h)wā$- (with some help from *lingō* 'lick'?)
Oscan	*fangva*	: *$dhn̥ǵ(h)wā$-
OIr.	*tengae*	: *$tn̥ǵ(h)wā$-t-
Engl.	*tongue*	: *$dn̥ǵhwā$-
OCS	*językŭ*	: *$Øn̥ǵ(h)ū$-
Lith.	*liežuvis*	: *$Øn̥ǵ(h)ū$- (?) (with help from *liež*- 'lick')
Avest.	*hizvā*	: *$siǵ(h)wā$
Skt.	*jihvā*	: *$ǵ(h)iǵhwā$

5.3. Onomatopoeia

Even if there is a certain arbitrariness to onomatopoeia (see § 4 above), its purpose is to mirror sounds of the real world. If sound change makes a given onomatopoetic expression too different from the real-world sound it is to depict, one of two things can happen. Either the word ceases to be onomatopoetic, or its pronunciation is remade so as to restore the fit between speech sounds and the real-world acoustic effect.

For instance, Middle English had a verb *pīpen* 'to chirp, make the sound of little birds' whose [ī] very nicely approximated the acoustic impression created by the sounds of little birds. As a result of the Great Vowel Shift (see Chapter 4, § 5.4), *pīpen* turned into Mod. Engl. *pipe*, pronounced [payp]. The verb is still listed in the dictionaries; but it is rarely used, except perhaps in the expressions *to pipe up* and *to pipe down*. In ordinary language it has been replaced by words like *peep, cheep, chirp* whose sounds more closely mirror the chirping of little birds. Similarly, Classical Greek had a word *bē* [bɛ̄] to depict the sound made by sheep. Regular sound change would have turned the word into Mod. Gk. [vi], a far cry, we might well say, from the sound of sheep. The word has been productively replaced by [bɛ] which, given the vagaries of Modern Greek spelling, is written μπε = *mpe*.

Onomatopoeia also may be responsible for the creation of new linguistic expressions. For instance, among the words for 'dog' in example (15), the Hindi one is onomatopoetic in origin.

Interestingly, the Hindi word is not the only onomatopoetic replacement of an earlier word for 'dog' in the history of Hindi. The Proto-Indo-European form *$ḱu$-*on*- underlying the Germ. *Hund*, Fr. *chien*, and Ital. *cane* of (15) above came out as *śvan-* in Sanskrit. A Modern Hindi descendant of this word is *sōnhā*, whose meaning however has become specialized to 'wild dog'. Within the history of Sanskrit, a new, onomatopoetic word was created, namely *kurkura-*, literally no doubt 'the one that snarls, growls, or barks, i.e. makes the sound [kurkur]'. (Compare in this regard the German word for 'growl, snarl', *knurren*.) The Modern Hindi reflex of this form is *kūkar*, whose meaning tends to be specialized as 'puppy'. The normal Hindi word, *kuttā*, cannot be traced to any Sanskrit antecedents and thus must reflect an even later instance of onomatopoeia. Similarly, Mod. Engl. *cur* is derived from MEngl. *curre*, a shortened form of *cur-dogge* 'growling, snarling dog', whose *cur* may be from Scand. *kurra* 'growl, snarl'. One suspects that its Modern German semantic equivalent *Köter* has a similar origin. In both cases the negative associations of snarling are reflected in the negative connotations of the words. Similar developments are found outside Indo-European, as in Tamil *kurai* 'to bark' : *kūraṇ* 'dog'. (On Engl. *hound* see § 6.1 below.)

For another effect of onomatopoetic considerations, see the discussion of Engl. *bang, clang; bash, clash, crash, smash; batter, clatter, smatter, shatter* in Chapter 5, § 3.1.

5.4. Avoidance of excessive homonymy

Although there is a great amount of homonymy in language, mere homonymy does not cause any great difficulties. Engl. *read* (pres.) and *reed* sound the same, and so do *read* (past) and *red*. However, *reed* and *read* hardly ever have a chance of occurring in the same context and of being mistaken, one for the other. And even if, with some imagination, we can think up a context that might be ambiguous, such as *This is a good* [rīd], structures of this sort are hardly ever uttered out of context. Thus, if the sentence is uttered by someone pointing at a book (or in a context where someone has just mentioned a book), we can be sure that the word *read* is meant. If the reference is to something like the mouthpiece of a saxophone or plants on a lake shore, then *reed* must be intended.

Some instances of homonymy, however, can create genuine confusion with potentially quite undesirable results. For instance, Old English had two verbs, *lǣtan* 'let, permit' and *lettan* 'hinder, prevent', both of which became Mod. Engl. *let* through regular sound change. Now, assume someone had robbed us and were running down the street. If we called out, *Let that man*, nobody would be sure whether we meant 'stop that man' or 'let/permit that man (to run through)'. Similarly, Lat. *cattus* 'cat' and *gallus* 'rooster' both came out as *gat* in Southwestern French. The resulting ambiguity could be disastrous in a rural society, for it makes quite a difference whether the *gat* reported to have entered the hen house is a rooster or a cat.

In cases of such "excessive homonymy", one of the two homonymous words soon gets replaced. For instance, English no longer uses *let* in the meaning 'hinder' or 'prevent', except in a few opaque relics, such as *without let or hindrance* or *let ball* (in tennis). (But note that *let ball* frequently is made more transparent by folk-etymological change to *net ball*.) Similarly, Southwestern French *gat* 'rooster' was replaced by a variety of other words, such as the dialectal word for 'vicar'. (See also § 5.6 below, as well as Chapter 4, § 4 for *cleave* 'stick to' vs. *cleave* 'chop, split' and Southern U.S. Engl. *pen* [pin] and *pin* [pin].)

5.5. Avoidance of synonymy, semantic differentiation

As we have seen, language is designed so as to convey the maximum amount of meanings through a minimum amount of lexical items. One would expect, then, that complete synonymy – where two phonetically distinct words would express exactly the same range of meanings – is highly disfavored.

This expectation has been met, for where other types of linguistic change could give rise to complete synonymy, we see that languages – or more accurately, their speakers – time and again seek ways to remedy the situation by differentiating the two words semantically. For instance, it is well known that analogical processes do not always lead to the complete replacement of the old form by the new. In many cases, the two forms continue to coexist. In all cases, however, their meanings get differentiated, so that the new form almost invariably will take on the more productive, basic meaning, while the old form persists in more specialized, marginal functions. Examples are given in (28).

(28)   New form   Old form
       brothers   *brethren*
       older   *elder*
       orientate   *orient* (verb)
       housewife   *hussy*

Borrowing can lead to similar doublets, and again we see that they tend to be semantically differentiated. The only difference from analogical examples such as (28) is that the direction of differentiation cannot be predicted. In some cases the native word remains more basic, in others, the borrowing wins out, and in yet others it is difficult to tell which is more basic. Compare for instance the examples in (29).

(29)   Native word Borrowed word
      kingly   *royal* (from French)
      cow   *beef* (from French)
      shirt   *skirt* (from Scand.)

Even other semantically induced changes, such as onomatopoeia, can lead to semantic differentiation. This is no doubt the reason for the semantic differentiation of Hindi *sōnhā* 'wild dog' vs. *kūkar* 'puppy' vs. *kuttā* 'dog' (see § 5.3 above).

5.6. Reinterpretation

Another major reason for shifts in meaning is REINTERPRETATION. A fairly simple case of reinterpretation is found in the development of earlier Engl. *bead* 'prayer' to 'counter on a rosary, bead'; see Chapter 3, § 2.2.

Another, more complex, case is the one of *oriental*, discussed in Chapter 1. Originally the term referred to the areas just to the east of the Graeco-Roman world, also known as Anatolia or the Levant, in ancient times also as Asia. In fact, just like *Anatolia* and *Levant*, the term *orient* originally referred to the rising (sun) and then, by metaphorical extension, to the east where the sun rises. (See § 6.2 below.) Unlike *Anatolia* and *Levant*, but like *Asia*, the term slowly came to be used in a broader range of meanings, so that ultimately it could refer to the entire continent of Asia. As we have seen in § 2, however, words with such a broad semantic range tend to acquire a quasi-core meaning, based on the prototypical understanding of the term. This is no doubt what happened with *oriental*: East Asians, being most clearly different from Europeans, have come to be considered prototypical *orientals*, not only by Europeans and European Americans, but also by East Asians or their descendants in countries like the United States. The final step in the development lies in the reinterpretation of this prototypical meaning as the core meaning of the word.

Interestingly, a similar development is affecting the word *Asian*. However, in this case the change is running into active opposition from citizens of other Asian countries such as India or Sri Lanka (or their descendants in countries like the United States) who do not look kindly at the prospect of being left without a name for the continent they share with the East Asians.

Reinterpretation is not always easily distinguishable from some of the minor, more sporadic analogical changes, especially popular etymology. For instance, through sound change the Old English words *wēod* 'plant' and *wǣd(e)* 'garment' both became Mod. Engl. *weed*. The resulting homonymy apparently was too great. In the meaning 'garment' the word generally was replaced by other lexical items (such as *garment*); *weed*, by and large, survived only in the meaning 'undesirable plant'. However, relics of 'garment' remained in the rare term *weed* 'a token of mourning, such as a black armband' and the somewhat more common compound *widow's weeds* 'a widow's mourning clothes'. Most speakers of Modern English familiar with these terms no doubt have reinterpreted *weed* in these expressions as a specialized use of the "victorious" word *weed* 'undesirable plant', with the rationalization that mourning clothes or cloths are less colorful and fashionable, and more weedy than others. This rationalization can be explained as the result of reinterpretation. But for those speakers who only know the term *widow's weeds*, the development can equally well be attributed to folk etymology, motivated by the fact that the word *weed* has not survived in the meaning 'garment' outside the compound. (Compare the similar case of Engl. *bride-gum** → *bridegroom* in Chapter 5, § 3.2.)

Reinterpretations often reflect changes in culture and society. For instance, Old French had a word *marechal*, a borrowed form of the word *māre-skalk* found in the Frankish speech of their Germanic overlords. The original meaning of the word was 'a stable hand (*skalk*) in charge of horses (*māre*)'. Now, horses were very important war equipment in medieval times. Hence, the word *marechal* was reinterpreted as 'somebody in charge of important war equipment'. Further extensions and reinterpretations along similar lines led to increasingly loftier connotations: 'somebody in charge of horses and horsemen' → 'somebody in charge of the cavalry' → 'a (high) military officer', and so on.

Similarly, Gk. *presbúteros* originally designated an 'older (person)'. In a society governed by older and presumably wiser persons, the meaning of the word came to be extended to 'older person who is a community leader', whence it could be reinterpreted as simply meaning 'community leader'. As a consequence, now even younger persons can become 'presbyters'. (A further development is found in the early Christian use of *presbúteros* for church elders, whence much later the term *Presbyterian*.) Compare also NE *elder*, an earlier form of the comparative of *old*, but now commonly used to refer to 'community leaders', especially of religious communities, without regard to age.

Reinterpretation can proceed in many different, often contradictory directions. Thus, Old English had the words *cnafa* 'boy' and *cniht* 'servant'. While the connotations of the former were relatively neutral or even positive, those of *cniht* were relatively lowly. In the Modern English reflexes, *knave* 'villain' and *knight* 'nobleman', the connotations are just about reversed. (For a similar semantic flip-flop see the discussion of *bread* and *loaf* in Chapter 1.

Note further that the improvement in the connotations of *glamour* and *verve* observed in Chapter 1 contrasts with the semantic deterioration in another word referring to language and linguistics: The chiefly British English word *gloze* 'flattery, deceit' is derived from the same source that gives us the word *gloss*.)

The shifts in meaning of *cnafa* and *cniht* can be explained in terms of well-precedented extensions and reinterpretations. In medieval society, *cnafas* > *knaves* 'boys' tended to be apprentices, and apprentices were treated like servants or even serfs. And since servants and serfs do not necessarily like the treatment meted out to them by their masters, they may act in a way that their masters perceive as "uppity, insolent, not-to-be-trusted"; hence the modern meaning of *knave*. The word *cniht* acquired its lofty meanings in a slightly different, but contemporary context: In medieval warfare, noblemen often took some of their servants with them into battle. In this context, the word *cniht* could be reinterpreted as referring to a lower-rank warrior and subsequently, because war was considered a noble enterprise, even to a lower-rank nobleman. (See also § 6.1 below.)

The role of cultural factors in reinterpretation can be seen in the development of the Modern English word *write*. As noted in Chapter 3, § 2.6, in early Germanic runic writing, letters were mainly produced by means of scratching or engraving into wood. (Other favorite writing media were stone and metal.) As a consequence, the verb **wrītan-* 'scratch' could be used very appropriately to refer to the act of writing. The arrival of Christianity introduced not only a new alphabet (the Roman one), but also new writing materials such as parchment, and letters were no longer scratched into the material but applied to it in ink, by means of a quill. In some of early Germanic, these differences were apparently considered too great for the old verb still to be appropriate, and the Latin verb, *scrībō*, was borrowed; compare Mod. Germ. *schreiben* 'write'. In English and Icelandic, on the other hand, the similarities outweighed the differences: Both the runes and the Roman letters served to put words into written form. As a consequence, the word *wrītan* was reinterpreted as referring to this shared process. This led to a certain complication, in that now there was a question as to whether *wrītan* 'write' was the same word as *wrītan* 'scratch'. In English, the difficulty resolved itself as *wrītan* 'scratch' became obsolete. Icelandic preserves *ríta* 'scratch' beside *ríta* 'write'; but because of their semantic remoteness, the two words probably have become simple homonyms. (Note that Gk. *gráphō*, Lat. *scrībō*, and their borrowed descendants in modern English likewise derive from words that originally meant 'dig, make incisions, etc.')

Interestingly, semantic reinterpretations such as the one of Germanic
wrītan owe their existence not so much to active processes like metaphoric
extension, but rather to INERTIA: The old term simply continues to be used
even though the activity or phenomenon designated by it has undergone significant change.

5.7 Other linguistic changes

As we have seen in § 5.5, semantic differentiation can be triggered by analogy,
borrowing, and even semantically induced changes. Non-semantic linguistic
changes have led to many other types of semantic change.

For instance, the fact that American English speakers can at least entertain
the idea that *ear* (of corn) and *ear* (of a human being or animal) might be
the same word (§ 3 above) was made possible by sound change. Originally,
the two words were quite different: *ear* (listening organ) goes back to PGmc.
*auzō, while the *ear* of corn reflects **ahuz-*. Similarly, as noted in Chapter 5
(§ 3.2), Mod. Engl. *daisy* derives from MEngl. *daies-ei(e)* 'day's eye', a
metaphor for 'sun', much as *sunflower* in present-day English. As sound
change obscured the compound character of *daisy*, the sense of metaphor
was irretrievably lost (to all, of course, but historical linguists).

Borrowing often is accompanied by semantic change. For instance, Lat.
comprehendere, meaning 'grasp, include' could, like Mod. Engl. *grasp*, be
used metaphorically to mean 'understand'. The English borrowing *comprehend* is generally used only in the originally metaphorical meaning. But in
the absence of the originally basic meaning, the word no longer feels like a
metaphor. (The original meaning, however, is preserved in *comprehensive*.)
Similarly, the German word *Angst* has been adopted in English as a technical term of Freudian psychology. In German, the Freudian use is merely an
extension of the basic meaning of *Angst*, namely 'fear, anxiety, anguish'.

Sometimes, the special connotations associated with borrowings give rise
to linguistic change. For instance, Japanese has borrowed many English words
for non-traditional, "western-value" concepts, such as *gārufurendo* ⇐ *girl
friend*. The somewhat morally loose connotations of such words then led to
the coinage of new terms with similar connotations, made up from borrowed
words, such as *rabu hoteru* 'love hotel' = a place where people have illicit
sexual relations. Something similar happened in American English advertising, where the fashionable connotations associated with French borrowings
spawned a whole set of "quasi-French" expressions like ***le*** *car* and ***le*** *bag*.
(See Chapter 8, § 4 for similar "quasi-foreign" forms in English.)

6. The effects of semantic change

If we look at the semantic changes so far examined, we can observe a wide variety of effects. The sound structure of words may be affected by taboo-induced deformation and onomatopoetic considerations. Taboo and the avoidance of excessive homonymy can lead to vocabulary loss. Such loss can, of course, likewise result from changes in society and culture which render par ticular words unnecessary. For instance, the word *thill* 'either of a pair of shafts or poles between which an animal is hitched to pull a wagon' has effectively ceased to be used, except perhaps by the few remaining individuals that still drive animal-drawn wagons. In fact, many other similar words became obsolete with the introduction of the internal combustion engine. (Other words, however, such as *car* or *wheel* have survived through inertia, albeit with rather different meanings.)

Of course, what most saliently gets affected by semantic change is the meaning of words, including their connotations. Original homonyms may sometimes become, or threaten to become, polysemous variants of the same word, such as *ear* and *ear*. Just about the exact opposite may occur, too, as in the case of PGmc. *wrītan 'scratch/write' : Mod. Icel. *ríta* 'scratch' and *ríta* 'write'. And so forth.

In some cases, whole fields of words undergo similar semantic changes, such as those words referring to animal-drawn wagons and chariots that were retained by inertia after the introduction of the internal combustion engine. Similarly, when Britain changed from an absolute form of monarchy to a parliamentary one, words like *king, queen, prince, princess, court* all acquired connotations appropriate to the new political context.

6.1. Social attitudes and change in connotations

Especially noteworthy are the semantic developments of words like OFr. *marechal*, OE *cniht*, Gk. *presbúteros* on one hand, and OE *cnafa* on the other (see § 5.6 above). While the words of the first set have acquired connotations that are considerably more favorable, the connotations of *cnafa* have become much less favorable. Developments of the former type are referred to as MELIORATION, those of the latter, as PEJORATION.

Both types of development are quite common and tell us a lot about social attitudes. Pejoration, for instance, has time and again affected words referring to young, innocent, or defenseless people. Just consider the sources for the English words *silly* and *daft*, as well as the semantically similar Germ. *albern* 'silly', Fr. *niais* 'stupid'.

The word *silly* ultimately derives from OE *sælig* which had the meaning 'happy, blessed, blissful', a meaning preserved in Middle English (as in *þurh seli martirdom* 'through blessed martyrdom'; 13th c.). Middle English also offers extended meanings that come closer to the modern semantics of *silly*, such as *Vp an seli asse he rod* 'he rode on a humble (or simple) donkey' (13th c.). Humility and simplicity, however, unfortunately are often equated with feebleness; and expressions like *seely Idiotes* (16th c.) illustrate another unfortunate, but common development – the extension of words meaning 'weak' or 'feeble' to mean 'feeble-minded' or 'stupid'. Brit. Engl. *daft* 'crazy' developed along very similar lines from ME *dafte* 'gentle, mild', OE *(ge)dæfte* 'mild, meek'. Similarly, Germ. *albern* 'silly' is derived from MHG *alware* 'simple', which itself comes from OHG *alawāri* 'kind, gentle'. French *niais* can be derived from Lat. **nīdax* 'nestling', via 'helpless', 'simple', 'foolish'. Some of the connotations of Engl. *simple* point in the same direction; and *simpleton* only has the pejorative meaning.

Interestingly, the association of 'simple' or 'foolish' with 'young', 'helpless', or 'delicate' sometimes can lead to reverse developments of melioration. An example is found in Engl. *nice*, a borrowing from Old French *ni(s)ce* 'stupid, foolish' which, in turn, reflects Lat. *nēscius* 'unknowing, ignorant'. In earlier English, the word still preserves the meaning 'ignorant, foolish'. The modern meaning seems to have developed via the meanings 'shy, bashful' and hence 'delicate, dainty'.

A different development, also common in words referring to the powerless, is seen in examples like OE *cnafa* : NE *knave*. For parallels see the following examples.

The word *boy* may be used by, say, a stereotypical Southern U.S. sheriff, in addressing a black man even if that man is in his eighties. Similarly, Gk. *paîs* and Lat. *puer*, whose literal meaning is 'boy, child', were also used to designate 'servants' and 'slaves'. Developments of this type are not necessarily limited to western or Indo-European languages. In Kharia (a Munda language in India), for instance, *kɔn-ghɛr* 'young man' likewise has come to be used to mean 'servant, slave'.

Note also *common, mean*, originally 'common; normal, average'; *villain*, originally 'belonging to the villa (= the landlord's mansion) or the village (= a peasant)'; *varlet*, a relative of *valet*, both from French and originally meaning 'young servant' (ultimately derived from Celt. **wasso- < *upo-sto-* 'standing by, waiting on'). Interestingly, the word *vassal*, derived from the same source as *varlet*, acquired more positive connotations when it was used to refer to feudatories of a king or prince.

Similarly *churl* is from OE *ceorl* '(free) man' → 'commoner' → 'person lowest in the social order' → 'peasant' → 'rude person'; and dial. Engl. *carl*, a borrowing from ON *karl* 'man', changed to 'peasant, serf' → 'rude person'. Here, too, we find that a related word, the Frankish variant *Karl*, gave rise to the much more lofty French name *Charles* (whence the English name) = Lat. *Carolus*, Germ. *Karl*. And because of its association with the emperor *Charlemagne, Carolus Magnus, Karl der Große*, this word was borrowed with the meaning 'king' into various Slavic languages; compare Serbo-Croatian *kral* 'king'. (An earlier parallel is found in the Latin name *(Julius) Caesar*, from which are derived Germ. *Kaiser* 'emperor' and its Russian counterpart, *car'* (pronounced [tsar^y]) 'czar'.)

Sexist attitudes are reflected in the fate of many words referring to women: Shakespeare's *quean* 'loose woman' reflects OE *cwene* 'woman'; NE *hussy* is earlier *hūswīf* 'housewife'; *whore*, Germ. *Hure* are related to Goth. *hōrs*, Lat. *cārus* 'dear (one)'. Other examples are: *wench*, originally 'girl, young woman'; *mistress* 'a kept woman', originally a femininized form of *mister* which itself reflects earlier *master*; *madam* 'proprietress of a brothel', originally the same as the respectful term of address *madam(e)*, variant *ma'am*, from Fr. *madame* 'my lady'. Other words for 'loose woman', many of them of uncertain origin, are *harlot, slattern, strumpet, trollop*. Note also Fr. *putain*, Sp. *puta* 'prostitute' from PRom. **pūtta* 'girl'; NHG *Dirne* 'prostitute' from OHG *thiorna* 'maid(en)'; Avestan *ǰahi(kā)-* 'woman' → 'prostitute'; Hindi *raṇḍī* 'widow' → 'prostitute'; Telugu *tottu* 'female servant, slave' → 'prostitute'; Arab. *xalīlā* 'dear (fem).' → 'prostitute'.

Significantly, there are few counterparts for men. (But note words like *lecher*, often abbreviated as *le(t)ch*.) In fact, the notion 'loose man' strikes many people as anomalous, if not ridiculous, and words like *stud*, which come close to denoting something of this sort, tend to be used even with some degree of admiration. A rare example of a male-reference word with negative connotations is *pimp*, but even this word is used generally about men who are connected with females of sexually "questionable character" (and who have power over such females). The word *pimp* is generally considered to be of uncertain origin. However, the *Oxford English Dictionary* (*OED*) gives a phonetically very similar form *pimping* (adj.), meaning 'small, trifling, insignificant, ... petty, mean, sickly'. The *OED* compares this word to Dutch *pimpel* 'weak little man', Germ. *pimpelig* 'effeminate, sickly, puling', which, it adds, "implies a stem *pimp*". In addition, there is a German form *Pimpf* 'young male' which looks remarkably similar (although the difference between initial [p] and medial [pf] causes difficulties). Perhaps these similarities are simply accidental; but if they are not, then it is possible that Engl.

pimp originally meant 'young boy', and that its current meaning came about through pejoration, via an intermediate meaning 'weak, effeminate man'.

Similar examples of pejoration in terms referring to young, innocent persons, young males, and females of all ages are found in language after language and, apparently, at all stages of human language.

Developments of this type show a rather unpleasant side of the human character, which glorifies strength and power and holds in contempt the weak, the gentle, and the female. Occasionally, however, we get a glimpse of the underdog's getting even, such as Engl. *surly*, originally *sirly* 'lordly, masterful', hence 'imperious, domineering', and then 'rude, uncivil'.

At the same time, words designating warriors and rulers, such as OFr. *marechal* : Engl. *marshal*, Engl. *knight*, Gk. *presbúteros*, Engl. *elder*, tend to acquire positive connotations, as we have seen before. Note also Fr. *Charles,* Lat. *Carolus*, Germ. *Karl*, Serb.-Croat. *kral*; Lat. *Caesar*, Germ. *Kaiser*, Ru. *car'*. This was especially the case in medieval and early modern society, when the lords of the manor considered themselves greatly superior to the common people and reserved for themselves the right to hunt and to indulge in elegant living. It is this context that may have given rise to Ø-plurals for animals that are hunted, such as *deer* and *fowl*, and to cultivating such witty expressions as *an exaltation of larks, a pride of lions, a pack of wolves.* (Chapter 5, § 2.1.) Here, too, French borrowings such as *beef, veal, mutton, venison*, as well as *dine* acquired their more elegant, lofty connotations compared with the corresponding Anglo-Saxon terms *cow, calf, sheep, deer*, and *eat*. (See Chapter 8.) And this is the context as well for the special development of Engl. *hound*, the cognate of Germ. *Hund*, Fr. *chien*, Ital. *cane* (§§ 4 and 5.3 above), to designate not just any dog, but a dog used for hunting.

Sometimes we can see both pejoration and melioration in succession, as social factors cause words to change from one sphere to the other. For instance, Old French had a word *ber/barun* 'man' which, like *churl* above, could be used to refer to 'common men' or even 'servants'. As these became 'servants' and 'vassals' of the king, their status became elevated to *king's barons*, and eventually they could be *The Great Barons* who were members of the Great Council, the House of Lords.

6.2. Sporadic vs. systematic effects

Because of its inherently fuzzy nature, meaning can be expected to change in a fuzzy, non-systematic manner. Most of the changes examined so far clearly are sporadic, as expected. For instance, while some tabooed words undergo deformation, others are replaced by euphemisms. Yet others remain unaffected themselves, but induce replacements of innocent homonyms.

Metaphor, including metonymy, synecdoche, hyperbole, litotes, generally affects individual words. Sound symbolism operates to change Engl. *tiny* to *teeny*, *little* to *leetle*, but fails to affect *small*, whose rounded back vowel does not conform to the correlation "high vowel : small". Note the similar difficulty with Engl. *big*, whose high front vowel is in conflict with the expected correlation "non-front vowel : big, large". Moreover, the direction of semantic change may differ in contemporary varieties of the same language, as in the case of *table* 'put on the table for immediate discussion' (Brit. Engl.) vs. 'shelve' (Am. Engl.); see Chapter 1.

More systematic, sweeping developments are observable in the medieval and early modern developments of terms associated with war, nobility, and the activities of the nobility. Here, whole semantically definable FIELDS of words underwent similar meliorative developments. But as we have seen, at roughly the same time that terms such as *knight* show the effects of melioration, *knave* develops negative connotations. And the ancestor of Mod. Engl. *baron* successively underwent both pejoration and melioration. Although more sweeping than other semantic changes, changes in semantic fields, thus, are far from fully systematic.

This does not mean that there are no systematic semantic changes at all. But such changes tend to be restricted to fairly narrowly confined and more or less self-contained subparts of the lexicon or to lexical items whose use is intimately tied up with linguistic structure.

6.2.1. Cardinal-point systems

An example of a self-contained subpart of the lexicon is presented by the words for the cardinal points or directions in early Indo-European: East (E), west (W), north (N), and south (S). Two major tendencies for naming the cardinal points can be observed. One refers to the rising sun or to dawn to designate E, the midday sun for S, and the setting sun or evening for W; see (30) below. In this system, terms for N are derived from various sources, such as Gk. *boréas* named after a northerly wind, or Lat. *septentrio* from the constellation also referred to as *ursa minor* 'the Little Dipper', which contains *Polaris*, the northern beacon in the night sky.

(30)   a. East: Source
        Gk.   *anatolḗ* (hence *Anatolia*) *anatéllō* 'rise'
        Lat.   *oriens* (hence *Orient*)   *orīri* 'to rise'
        Ital. *levante* (hence *Levant*)   *levare* 'to rise'
        OCS   *vŭstokŭ*   *vŭstekǫ* 'rise'
                   (hence *Vladivostok* 'ruler of the east')

Gk.	*héōs*	
Gmc.	*aust-* (hence Engl. *east*)	PIE **(a)wes-*‘dawn’
Avest.	*ušastara-*	

b. South:

Gk.	*mesēmbría*	*meso-* ‘mid’ + *(h)ēméra* ‘day’
Lat.	*meridies*	*medio-* ‘mid’ + *dies* ‘day’
Gmc.	*sunþa-* (Engl. *south*)	*sunnō* ‘sun’ (‘towards the sun’)

c. West:

Lat.	*occidens*	*occido* ‘fall down, sink’
Ital.	*ponente*	*porre* ‘put, set down’
Gmc.	*west-*	PIE **wes-* ‘stay, spend the night’ (?)
OCS	*zapadŭ*	*za-padǫ* ‘fall down, sink’
Gk.	*hespéra*	= ‘evening’
Lith.	*vakarai*	plural of *vakaras* ‘evening’
Avest.	*daoštara-*	*daoš-* ‘evening, dark’

Beside this relatively loose system of designations, another, more systematic one is found. The system is fully operative in Sanskrit and Old Irish, but traces are also found in Germanic and Welsh words for N and/or S. In this system, orientation is strictly to the east, the *orient* (i.e. the rising sun). E, therefore, is called ‘forward’ or ‘in front’, and the names for the other cardinal points are ‘left’ = N, ‘right’ = S, and ‘back, behind’ = W. Compare (31). Note incidentally that the Sanskrit word for ‘left’, *uttara-*, is a euphemism which in some ways tries to compensate for the widespread prejudice against left-handers. Its original meaning is ‘upper’, hence ‘better’. Such euphemisms are not unusual for the notion ‘left’; compare Gk. *aristerós* (lit. ‘better’) and *euṓnumos* (lit. ‘well-named’), Lat. *sinister* (lit. ‘older’, hence ‘better’), or OEngl. *winstre* (lit. ‘friendlier’). (A remarkably similar euphemism is found in the sexist expression *my better half* for ‘my wife’.)

(31) a. Sanskrit:

E:	*prāñč-*; *pūrva-*	lit. ‘directed forward; first’
N:	*uttara-*	lit. ‘left’
S:	*dakṣiṇa-*	lit. ‘right’
W:	*pratīča-/paśčima-*	lit. ‘(directed to) behind’

b. Old Irish:
   E: *airther*   lit. 'directed forward'
   N: *tuascert*   lit. 'left direction'
   S: *descert*   lit. 'right direction'
   W: *iarthar*   lit. 'directed to behind'

c. Other languages:
   N: Gmc. *norþ-*   Compare Osc.-Umbr. *nertro-* 'left'
       Welsh *gogledd* Compare *cledd* 'left'
   S: Welsh *deheu*   lit. 'right (hand)'

What is significant for present purposes is that one early Indo-European language, Avestan, systematically shifted the system in (31) clockwise by one point, so that 'forward' became S, 'behind' N, and 'right' W; see (32). The remaining term, the one for E, should be 'left', but no unambiguous examples are attested, perhaps by accident. (There is, to be sure, a *vātō uparō* 'east wind', whose *uparō* literally means 'upper' and thus could be compared to Skt. *uttara-* 'upper' → 'better' → 'left' (see above); but a more literal interpretation as 'wind from the up-country' has also been proposed.)

(32)   Avestan:
             S: *pauruua-* lit. 'directed forward; first'
             N: *apāxtara-* lit. 'directed to behind'
             W: *dašina-*   lit. 'right'

The reasons for this shift in orientation may perhaps lie in the fact that the Zoroastrian religion of the Avestan texts presents a deliberate break with the earlier Indo-Iranian tradition (as represented by Sanskrit). But this is mere speculation, for it is not at all clear why the general break in religious tradition should have brought about the specific break in terminology for the cardinal points.

A similar systematic shift in orientation is suggested by comparison of various Afro-Asiatic languages; see the roots and forms in (33). In this case, perhaps, the southern orientation of Egyptian can be attributed to the overwhelming significance of the river Nile and the fact that it runs from south to north. Compare for instance the root √*ḫdy* 'go downstream, go north'; and note that √*ḫntw* 'in front; south' can also means 'upstream'. But again, that is sheer speculation. Moreover, in Hausa, which like Semitic, Berber, and Ancient Egyptian is a member of the Afro-Asiatic family, the root corresponding to Sem./Egypt. √*ymn* means 'west', just as in Egyptian.

(33)   Semitic   Berber   Ancient Egyptian
                                          S: √ḫntw   lit. 'in front'
        N: √šml (Arab.)   E: √yʔb   lit. or alternative
                                                            meaning 'left'
        S: √ymn   W: √ymn   lit. 'right'
                                          W: ḍəffər   Compare Sem.
                                                            √dbr 'be behind'

Interestingly, the religious significance of Mecca in Islam may have been
responsible for a similar shift: The root √qbl 'facing, in front' acquired the
meaning 'the direction faced when praying'. A further reinterpretation as
'south' must have taken place in areas where Mecca lies to the south.

Altaic furnishes further evidence for a pattern of naming the cardinal points
in terms of a southern orientation: Mongol *bara-gun* 'right', Kalmük *ömnö*
'in front', and Mongol *aru* 'back' also mean 'west', 'south', and 'north',
respectively. The evidence of Altaic may be significant, since here we do not
have an alternative eastern orientation. This fact may suggest that southern-
orientation systems need not always be considered secondary realignments
of original eastern-orientation systems. In Indo-European, however, eastern
orientation is pervasive and southern orientation limited to Avestan. Under the
circumstances it is more likely that in this language family, eastern orientation
is original, and southern orientation just an areally restricted innovation.

The northern orientation of modern times reflects a later perspective, in
which reference to the magnetic north pole became the basis for navigation.
This northern orientation has given rise to completely new uses of 'left' and
'right' as referring to 'west' and 'east', respectively. Moreover, they have
introduced the terms 'up' and 'down' as referring to 'north' and 'south'.

6.2.2. Syntax and systematic semantic shifts

In the discussion of ellipsis (Chapter 5, § 3.2) we have already seen one
example of how semantic change, interacting with other changes, can have a
systematic effect on linguistic structure, both on morphology and on syntax.
That is the case of Engl. *ne ... nāwiht → not*, involving the hyperbolic
use of *nāwiht* 'nothing' as reinforcement of the negation *ne*, fading of the
hyperbolic connotations of *nāwiht > not*, and ellipsis of the original negation
ne. Note further the similar development in French, through which *pas* '(a)
step' is coming to be a particle of negation. In both cases, the systematicity
of the change is due to the fact that negation is not just a semantic, or even
morphological, phenomenon, but directly interacts with syntax, which by its
very nature is highly systematic.

Even more remarkably systematic effects can be found when a semantically well-defined subsystem of the lexicon interacts with morphology and syntax. This frequently is the case in the development of pronouns, especially when the semantic trigger is POLITENESS.

In ordinary usage, politeness is more or less the same as being considerate to your fellow human beings, by not hurting their feelings, saying nice things to them, and so on. In linguistics the term is often used in a more restricted sense, which might be defined as showing appropriate deference or intimacy through highly conventionalized means. In present-day English, politeness in this sense is just about limited to the choice of address forms, such as *sir* or *ma'am*, the use or non-use of titles, and the use of first or last names.

Earlier English, from about the thirteenth century till about 1700, had an additional means at its disposal for expressing politeness, namely a choice between singular and plural forms of the second person pronoun in reference to singular addressees. The use of plural forms usually indicated a higher degree of politeness or deference, while singular forms were used either with subordinates or as signs of great intimacy. Compare the examples in (34) from Chaucer's *Book of the Duchess*. In (34a) Juno, Queen of the Gods, addresses her messenger, a clear subordinate, and uses the singular form of the pronoun, *thou*; in (34b) Morpheus, God of Sleep, uses a form of the plural pronoun *you* to address his wife, Alcione, a Goddess herself. For speakers of Modern English who are not familiar with such pronoun usage, it should perhaps be added that second plural forms sometimes are used with subordinates and second singular forms with persons who should normally be addressed in the plural. Such violations of the norm convey special connotations of irony, opprobrium, or insult, very similar to, say, a sudden switch from first name to last name (or vice versa) in Modern English.

(34)   a. *"Go bet," quod Juno, "to Morpheus*
            ***Thou** knowest hym wel . . . "*
            ' "Go quickly," said Juno, "to Morpheus – you know him well." '
        b. ***Ye** shul me never on lyve yse*
            'You shall never see me alive (again).'

Although this earlier English pronoun usage may have arisen under French influence, it ultimately reflects a semantic tendency found in many other languages, namely to associate plurality with greater importance or "weight". Modern English preserves a trace of this in the so-called royal or editorial *we*.

If this were all, earlier English would differ from the modern language merely by having an additional lexical category for indicating politeness. However, when used as subjects, the singular and plural second person pronouns controlled different agreement markers on the verb. Compare (34′), where the singular of (34a) is replaced by the plural, and the plural of (34b) by the singular. In (34′a), the verb agreeing with plural *ye* appears without the second singular ending *-st*, in (34′b) the singular form *thou* requires the verb to have the second singular ending *-t*. This shows that the semantically determined choice of singular vs. plural has direct repercussions in the syntax.

(34′)   a. ***Ye** know-Ø hym wel ...*
        b. ***Thou** shul-**t** me never on lyve yse*

As time progressed, the members of the upper crust of English society increasingly used only the plural pronoun, together with plural verb agreement – not so much as a sign of deference or politeness in the usual sense, but as an indication of their own refinement, as a sign of politeness to themselves and to their class, as it were. Use of the old singular structures, by contrast, came to be reinterpreted as a sign of lack of refinement, even boorishness. The behavior – and prejudices – of the upper crust soon came to be imitated by the burgeoning bourgeoisie. And in order not to be considered boors, the burghers did the same thing as the barons: They increasingly gave up the use of *thou* in favor of *you*. Eventually, the use of *you* instead of *thou* was adopted by the lower classes as well. The Quakers were the only major source of resistance to these developments, and into the twentieth century they insisted on retaining the use of the old singular pronoun, in the form *thee*. (They did, however, accept one innovation: the use of the third singular ending *-s* instead of the old second singular agreement markers.) Elsewhere, forms of the pronoun *thou* disappeared from the standard spoken language, surviving only in fossilized form in religious contexts.

Interestingly, and perhaps ironically, because of its restriction to religious use, *thou* has undergone a significant reversal in connotations. Originally the second singular pronoun was used, as in most other languages with similar politeness conventions, to signal the same kind of intimacy between God and worshiper as the use of the word *father* in the Lord's Prayer. Its modern restriction to the religious sphere invites a very different evaluation of *thou*, as a symbol of the very special and deep reverence that human beings owe to the Lord. This re-evaluation is no doubt one of the reasons that many forms of English-speaking Christianity have begun changing from *thou* to the more familiar and intimate *you* in their Bible translations and liturgical texts.

The semantically driven developments outlined above had their own lexical, morphological, and syntactic effects: First, the second person singular disappeared from the lexicon of ordinary Standard English. Or rather, the distinction between second singular and plural pronouns disappeared. Secondly, the second singular verb endings disappeared as well. Finally, as a consequence, the syntax of English no longer requires a syntactic agreement distinction between second singular and plural. In fact, English now has just one verbal agreement marker, the third person singular ending -*s* (as in *he know*-*s*) which, moreover, is limited to the present tense.

Some linguists have argued that the loss of the singular : plural distinction in the second person was a great gain, not only because it simplified morphology and syntax, but also because it made English speakers more democratic than the speakers of most European languages who still use pronoun differences to pay – or withhold – respect. But English speakers are able to do the same thing by using different address forms: Not calling an officer *sir* or *ma'am* in the military can have as disastrous consequences as using the "familiar" form of address, the second singular, in earlier English or in most European languages. And conversely, calling your buddy *sir* or *ma'am* may be as inappropriate, ironic, or even insulting, as the use of the "polite" second plural (or some other polite pronoun form) in earlier English and many other languages. Moreover, the loss of the singular : plural distinction in the second person has clearly been felt to be a drawback by many English speakers. Otherwise, there wouldn't be so many different attempts at restoring the distinction by creating special pluralized forms such as *y'all* [yɔl], *you'uns* [yɨnz] (< *you ones*), or *yous(e)* [yūz], not to mention the very widespread colloquial *you guys* or *you chaps*.

Even so, English is not alone in having lost the singular : plural distinction in the second person. Many varieties of Latin American Spanish have similarly generalized the old plural pronoun *vos* at the expense of the old singular *tu*, through strikingly similar developments.

On the other hand, some languages expand the pronominal system to express an even greater range of politeness distinctions. Thus, in Modern Hindi the old second singular pronoun *tū* indicates either great intimacy or great rudeness, depending on the social context; the old plural *tum* is the ordinary, unmarked form of second-person address; and a new pronoun *āp* is used to indicate deference or social distance. And as in Middle and early Modern English, each of the different pronouns controls a different kind of verb agreement.

7. Conclusion

Examples like the ones discussed in the preceding sections show that, given the right circumstances, semantic change can have very sweeping and systematic effects, even on linguistic structure. This should not, however, distract from the fact that in the majority of cases semantic change is as fuzzy, self-contradictory, and difficult to predict as lexical semantics itself. This is the reason that after initial claims that they will at long last successfully deal with semantics, just about all linguistic theories quickly return to business as usual and concentrate on the structural aspects of language, which are more systematic and therefore easier to deal with.

At the same time, even linguists must admit that semantic change can have profound effects on the lexicon and is, in fact, so intimately tied to the lexicon that some historical linguists subsume it under the heading of lexical change. In the following two chapters we take a closer look at other processes that bring about lexical change.

Chapter 8
Lexical borrowing

> And I must borrow every changing shape
> To find expression
> (T. S. Eliot, Portrait of a Lady)

> Neither a borrower, nor a lender be
> . . .
> This above all: To thine own self be true
> (Shakespeare, Hamlet)

1. Introduction

Languages and dialects normally do not exist in a vacuum. They – or more accurately, their speakers – always have some contact with other languages or dialects. The degree of contact may vary considerably. It may involve the whole range of language use, from informal, spoken to highly formal, written; or it may remain confined to just one level of use, such as written discourse. A very common result of linguistic contact is lexical BORROWING, the adoption of individual words or even of large sets of vocabulary items from another language or dialect. Examples of such borrowings, or LOANS abound in English, such as *rouge* (from French), *macho* (from Spanish), *yen* 'craving' (from Chinese), or *schwa* (from Hebrew via German).

Generally, such "borrowed" items are not returned, nor is there any intent to return them at the time of borrowing. In this regard, then, the terms theft or embezzlement would be more appropriate, but they sound less genteel. Besides, the DONOR language does not actually lose the borrowed word.

Such semantic quibbles aside, what is important is that like all other linguistic terminology, terms such as borrowing, loan, and donor are used in historical linguistics with special, technical connotations. The connotations of such terms are bound to differ from those found in the real world, no matter what terms we use.

Although in the act of borrowing there is no intention to return the borrowed word, occasionally, essentially by sheer coincidence, words do get returned, or are stolen back. Consider for instance the English words *redingote* (a long, open, lightweight coat without lining) and *contredanse* (a type of musical composition), or the French *sport* 'sport'. The first two words were taken from French which, in turn, had borrowed them from English earlier; see (1a,b). Conversely, *sport* came into French (and many other languages) from English which, in turn, had taken the ancestor of the word from French; see (1c). We even may encounter something like mistaken returns, not to the original donor, but to a language closely related to it. Compare the words in (2) which had been taken from Old Frankish, the language of the Germanic overlords of Romance Gaul (see Chapter 2, § 3.3), and were then passed on to English, another Germanic language, when England came to be ruled by the French-speaking Normans. Interestingly, these words coexist in English with native words which are still quite similar to the words that French had borrowed; compare *wise* (as in *in no wise*) and *ward*.

(1)   a. Engl. *riding* coat ⇒ Fr. *redingote* ⇒ Engl. *redingote*
      b. Engl. *country dance* ⇒ Fr. *contredanse* (with popular etymology: *contre* 'counter, opposite' + *danse* 'dance') ⇒ Engl. *contredanse*
      c. OFr. *de(s)porter* 'divert; amuse' → MEngl. *disporten* 'divert, amuse (oneself)' → 'play, frolic' → NEngl. *sport* ⇒ Fr. *sport*
(2)   a. OFrank. **wīsa* ⇒ OFr. *guise* ⇒ Engl. *guise*
      b. OFrank. **wardōn* ⇒ OFr. *guarder* ⇒ Engl. *guard*

In some cases, words spread over vast territories through a chain of borrowings. In German, such words are referred to as "Wanderwörter" ('migrating words'). Words for cultural items or concepts are especially apt to become widely dispersed. Compare for instance the examples in (3).

(3)   a. Skt. *śarkara-* 'sand, grit; sugar in granulated form' ⇒ Pers. *shakar* ⇒ Arab. *sukkar* ⇒ (O)Ital. *zucchero*, OSpan. *azúcar* ⇒ OFr. *sucre* ⇒ Engl. *sugar*; compare Germ. *Zucker* ⇐ Ital. *zucchero*, as well as Medieval Greek *sákkharon* 'sugar', the source for Engl. *saccharin*.
      b. Skt. *khaṇḍa-* 'broken piece; sugar in large pieces, rock sugar' ⇒ Pers. *qand* ⇒ Arab. *qandi* ⇒ OIt. *zucchero candi* ⇒ OFr. *sucre candi* ⇒ Engl. *sugar candy* (hence by further developments, *candy*); compare Germ. *Kandis(zucker)*.
      c. Lat. *centēnārius* 'a hundredweight' ⇒ Gk. *kentēnárion* ⇒ Aramaic *qintinārā* > *qintārā* ⇒ Arab. *qintar* ⇒ Medieval Lat.

quintāle (a "returnee" word) ⇒ OFr. *quintal* ⇒ Engl. *quintal*; compare also Germ. *Zentner*, which is more directly from the original Latin.

2. The substance of borrowing

The first thing that comes to mind when we think of borrowing is the adoption of individual lexical items, such as *rouge, macho, realpolitik*, or one of our favorite linguistic terms, *umlaut*. However, through vocabulary borrowing other linguistic elements may be acquired.

For instance, extensive vocabulary borrowing can introduce new MOR- PHOLOGY (see Chapter 5, § 4). Heavy borrowing from French, as well as Latin and Greek (often via French), has introduced into English words like the ones in (4). Many of these coexist with other borrowed words from which they can be considered derived, see (5). They can therefore be analyzed as con- taining these basic words plus the suffixes *-able/ible, -ation/tion, -ance/ence*. As a result, English has acquired a considerable amount of originally foreign derivational morphology – in addition to the words that it borrowed. Some of the new elements may combine only with other borrowed elements, such as the *-duct, -ceive* of (6), words coined in English from borrowed elements. Others can freely combine with non-borrowed, native elements, such as the *-able* of (7). One of the most commonly used derivational suffixes of English, the agentive suffix *-er* of words like *singer, baker*, or *transceiver*, ultimately is a loan from (late) Latin *-ārius* ⇒ OE *-ere* (as in OE *leornere* 'learner; disciple').

(4)   *equatable, legible, potable*
        derivation, deliberation, equation
        deliverance, occurrence
(5)   *equate*
        derive
        deliver
(6)   *trans-duct, trans-ceiv-er*
(7)   *readable, laughable, drinkable*

Vocabulary borrowing also can introduce new SOUNDS, or new contexts for old sounds. The latter, perhaps more common development is observed in words like *rouge, prestige, garage* with [ž] in word-final position. In more established English words, [ž] is limited to medial position, as in *measure, leisure.* And the relative foreignness of final [ž] is responsible for the common substitution of [ǰ], especially in less prestigious words like *garage.* (In British English, the pronunciation [gǽriǰ] has become more or less standard.)

The introduction of a new sound is found for instance in the pronunciation of the composer's name *Bach* as [bax] by English-speaking aficionados of Baroque music. The same sound has been introduced in the New York English expression *yecch* [yex] which seems to be of Yiddish origin. Speakers familiar with Scots English, which has preserved the [-x] of earlier English, may also affect the sound in the word *loch* (as in *Loch Ness*).

In addition to individual lexical items, languages may adopt combinations or COLLOCATIONS of words, such as Engl. *court martial,* an expression which comes from French. Such collocations, in turn, may influence the grammar of the borrowing language. For instance, expressions like *court martial* have introduced into English a new manner of plural formation. In native English collocations, the plural suffix *-s* normally attaches to the last word, as in (8a). In French expressions of the type (8b), plural *-s* is attached to the "head noun" of the construction, *court,* not the following adjective, *martial.* From the perspective of prescriptive grammar, this is the correct pattern in English, too, even though many speakers may no longer understand that *martial* is an adjective, and that *court martial* really means 'martial (i.e., military) court'. For these speakers, then, the structure in (8b) is anomalous, and they tend to replace it with the regularized pattern in (8c), with the plural *-s* following the last word of the constituent just as in (8a). For speakers who use the pattern (8b), on the other hand, the borrowing has introduced a new syntactic pattern of noun + adjective which is not generally found otherwise in English.

(8)   a. *parade marshal-s*
       b. *court-s martial*
       c. *court martial-s*

In other cases the influence may be much greater. For instance, the French mode of forming comparatives by means of *plus* 'more' plus the simple adjective (9a) has given rise in English to the pattern (9b), with Engl. *more* substituting for Fr. *plus.* And this pattern came to coexist with the native pattern (9c). The competition between these two different modes of comparative formation eventually was resolved such that monosyllabic adjectives (generally) take the inherited comparative in *-er,* as do disyllabic ones in *-y.* Many speakers also have this pattern in disyllabic adjectives in *-er*; but for some this is only optional. Adjectives which do not qualify for taking *-er* make their comparatives by means of *more*. Compare example (10).

(9)	a.	*beau*	: *plus*	*beau*
	b.	*beautiful*	: *more*	*beautiful*
	c.	*long*	: *long-er*	
(10)	Monosyllabic:	*long*	: *long-er*	
	Disyllabic:	*pretty*	: *pretti-er*	
		clever	: *clever-er/more clever*	
		handsome	: *more handsome*[1]	
	Polysyllabic:	*beautiful*	: *more beautiful*	

([1] Some English speakers can say *handsomer*. There are further variations, especially in non-standard varieties of English; but note also Lewis Carroll's *curiouser and curiouser*. On the other hand, some monosyllabic adjectives that are rarely used in the comparative may prefer the pattern with *more*, such as *more vague*.)

Examples like these may suggest that anything can be borrowed: lexical items, roots and affixes, sounds, collocations, and grammatical processes. To some extent this impression is well justified. Still, there are some differences.

From a purely linguistic perspective, the most important fact is that different spheres of the vocabulary are borrowed more easily, others significantly less easily. For instance, the most successful resistance to borrowing is offered by BASIC VOCABULARY, words referring to the most essential human activities, needs, etc., such as *eat, sleep; moon, rain; do, have, be,* or function words essential in syntax, such as the demonstrative pronouns *this* and *that*, the definite article *the*, or conjunctions like *and, or, if,* and *when*. In English, this is evident from the fact that in spite of its pervasive and domineering influence, French contributed virtually nothing to the most basic vocabulary. The only exception is the *-cause* of *because*. But note that the initial *be-* of the word is solidly Anglo-Saxon, derived from earlier *bi* 'by'. The word *because*, thus, clearly is not a borrowing, but was put together in English, by combining the native prefix *be-* with the borrowed word *cause* 'reason, etc.' Words of this type sometimes are referred to as HYBRIDS.

Although verbs are borrowed more easily than basic vocabulary, they nevertheless are not as readily borrowed as nouns. And if the need for borrowing a verb does arise, many languages instead borrow a nominal form of the verb and employ a native all-purpose verb such as *do* or *make* as a means of turning that form into the equivalent of a verb. See for instance the examples in (11). The reason for this particular resistance probably lies in the fact that it is easier to ask questions like "What do you call this (thing)?" than something like "What is the verb you use to designate that somebody is doing this/acting in this way?" Eventually, English expressions of the type (11) came to be used without the verb 'to do', on the model of correspondences like (12).

(11)   Latin   Early Modern English borrowing
        Verb   Verbal Adject.
        imitāre   *imitātum*   *do imitate*
        speculāre *speculātum*   *do speculate*
        corrigere *correctum*   *do correct*

(12)   *they do go*   : *they go*
        they do imitate : X

The relative resistance of verbs and especially of basic vocabulary does not mean that they are totally impervious to borrowing. Under the right social circumstances (see § 5 below) both types of lexical items can be borrowed. For instance, English borrowed the basic-vocabulary pronouns *they, their, them* from the language of the so-called Danes. (On the identity of the Danes and their relationship to the Anglo-Saxons see Chapter 2, § 3.3.) The same "Danish" language also was the source for the fairly basic English verbs *give* and *take*. Moreover, English borrowed a considerable number of not so basic verbs from French, such as *perceive, receive,* and *derive*.

The most easily borrowed words belong to more specialized forms of discourse, often referring to technology or other phenomena that require a good deal of mental and linguistic abstraction. Compare words like *nation, inflation, machine, engine, atom, finance,* all of which are borrowings.

Other words, too, are commonly borrowed, especially the names for new artifacts and other cultural items which are subject to frequent change. Here belong words such as *telephone* (made up of the borrowed components *tele-* 'far' and *phone* 'speech', both from Greek) and *lac/lacquer* (ultimately from Hindi *lākh* or its cognate in some other Modern Indo-Aryan language).

Borrowing of technological vocabulary is not just a modern phenomenon. For instance, the ancient Gauls of what is now France had a highly developed technology in metallurgy; and the Germanic words for 'iron', such as OE *isern* (Mod. Engl *iron*), OHG *isarn*, were borrowed from Gaul. *isarno*, a native Celtic word found also in Irish *iarn*.

3. Nativization, or how do you deal with a word once you have borrowed it?

The major difficulty with borrowing from a foreign language is that languages may diverge considerably in their phonology. Thus, *r* is generally pronounced as a velar fricative [γ] in Modern Standard French. Not having this sound in their own language, English speakers find it very difficult to articulate the sound in words like *rouge*. Even those who have learned French and in the process have acquired the pronunciation when speaking French usually have difficulties in maintaining the pronunciation when speaking English. The problem basically is this: In order to speak English, we have to "configure" our articulatory organs – and the neurological processes that control articulation – for English, unless we want to speak with a foreign accent. If, then, a word like *rouge* comes up in an English context, such as *She put on rouge*, we can affect the French pronunciation only by reconfiguring for French. That, however, is not only difficult and inconvenient, normally it also brings about a noticeable and undesirable break in the utterance. Perhaps even more important, our listeners may feel that we are putting on airs. To avoid all these difficulties, we have to do what most English speakers do, we have to pronounce the *r* as an English [r].

There are many other adjustments, beside changes in pronunciation, that tend to accompany borrowing. What is common to all of them is that they NATIVIZE the borrowing by integrating it more firmly into the linguistic structure of the borrowing language.

The most important nativization processes clearly involve PHONOLOGY. Even if we do nothing else, we have to see to it that the borrowed word becomes pronounceable in our language.

When faced with a foreign sound that does not exist in our own language, we think that the most natural thing to do is to substitute the MOST SIMILAR NATIVE SOUND. In principle, this usually is what happens. However in many cases it is quite difficult to determine which sound should be regarded as most similar.

The problem is that similarity or lack thereof comes in many different shades. For instance, a voiced French sibilant (as in *zéro*) is very similar to a voiced English sibilant (as in *zero*), even though the French sound may be more fully voiced than its English counterpart. Under the circumstances, substituting anything but a voiced sibilant would be perverse.

A slightly more complicated example is the English substitution of [k] for foreign [x], as in the usual English pronunciation of *Bach* as [bak]. Here the phonetic difference between donor language and borrowing language is considerably greater, and English (outside of Scots English) simply has no sound that would closely match the foreign sound. Still, the substitution of [k] for [x] makes sense, since both sounds share the fact that they are velar and voiceless. A substitution of voiced velar [g] would make much less sense; and substitutions such as [p] and [b] would be preposterous.

The situation often is much more complex. English is one of only a few European languages that have the voiceless dental fricative [θ]. When words with English [θ] are borrowed, such as the word *thriller*, there is a great amount of variation in the nativization of [θ]. It comes out as [s] in standard French and German, but as [t] in many other European languages, including many non-standard varieties of French and German. These different choices cannot be fully explained by the notion most similar sound. It is difficult to see how in standard German or French [s] is more similar to [θ] than [t], while in other forms of speech, [t] is more similar. Rather, it appears that [θ] is in some ways equally similar – and dissimilar – to both [t] and [s]: Sibilants like [s] are super-fricatives which differ from ordinary fricatives by having extra, "sibilant", friction. The simple fricative [θ] therefore can be considered to take an intermediate position between non-fricative [t] and super-fricative [s]. Under the circumstances, the choice between [t] and [s] is arbitrary; and the fact that different languages opt for one or the other substitution seems to result from something like conventionalization. In fact, some German speakers use neither [s] nor [t], but [f] to nativize [θ], presumably because it is acoustically closer to [θ] than either [s] or [t]. (Russian similarly substituted [f] for Byzantine Greek [θ] in words like *Fyodor* < Gk. *Theódōros* [θ-].)

At times it is not just one sound which is substituted, but rather a combination of sounds which together can be said to be most similar to the foreign sound. Thus, Fr. *salon* is borrowed as Engl. [səlɔn]. What motivates this development is the following: The French word contains [ɔ̃](written *on*), a single nasal vowel that is absent in English. The nativization as corresponding oral vowel [ɔ] plus *n* manages to "factor out" the vowel and nasal features of the French sound in terms of permissible English sounds. Here again, there is some element of arbitrariness, in the selection of [n] to encode French nasality. Non-standard German uses the velar nasal [ŋ] for the same purposes, as in [zalɔŋ]. (Standard German has adopted the nasal vowel from French, as in [zalɔ̃].)

Another example of such a process of factoring out the features of a non-native single sound is the Middle English substitution of [iu] for Fr. [ü]; see example (13a). Here, the frontness of Fr. [ü] is rendered by the front vowel [i], and its rounding by the round vowel [u]. This substitution had important consequences for English. In many varieties of English [iu] became [yū]; and the [y] of this new pronunciation triggered a subsequent process of palatalization. It is this development which accounts for phonetic correspondences like Fr. *mesure* with [zü] : Engl. *measure* with [žə] from earlier [zyū]. Similar examples can be found elsewhere, see (13b).

(13)   a. Fr. *pur* [pür] ⇒ ME [piur] 'pure'
          b. Turk. *göl* ⇒ Bulgar. *gyol* 'lake'

In modern literate languages, nativization frequently takes place through SPELLING. For instance, the common English pronunciation [rɔθ(s)čayld] for the name *Rothschild* [rōtšild/t] is based on the fact that *th* and *ch* usually are pronounced as Engl. [θ] and [č], respectively. Similarly the common English pronunciation of words like *Sanskrit* [sənskrit] as [sænskrit], with [æ] rather than [ə], results from the fact that the word is transcribed with the letter *a*, which in this context usually is pronounced as English [æ]. To forestall such pronunciations, some Indian words with [ə] are spelled with *u*, as in [pənǰāb] : *Punjab*. But interestingly, spellings of this type may give rise to the pronunciation [punǰab], a hypercorrection based on the fact that the letter *u* is commonly pronounced [u] in foreign words. (A similar phenomenon is observed in the pronunciation [rāžā] for the South Asian word *raja(h)* [rāǰā]. This hypercorrection arises from the belief that a foreign word must have a "foreign" sound, so [ž] is substituted for [ǰ] to make the word sound like other foreign words, such as *prestige*. More in § 4 below.)

Even more "exotic" nativization processes can be observed. One of these can be termed ETYMOLOGICAL nativization. For instance, literate speakers of Russian normally nativize foreign [h] as [g], as in *gospital'* 'hospital'. None of the nativization processes so far discussed would account for this substitution. But once we note that languages like Ukrainian, closely related to Russian and in intensive contact with it, have changed Proto-Slavic *g* to *h*, an explanation is possible: The relationship between native Russian words and their Ukrainian cognates provides a quasi-analogical pattern which suggests that foreign *h* corresponds to native *g*; see (14).

(14)   Ukrainian *hospod'* : Ru. *gospod'*   'God, Lord'
                  etc.

        Germ.   *Hospital* : X = Ru. *gospital'* 'hospital'
                  etc.

Phonological nativization may also be sensitive to phonological STRUC-
TURE. Many languages nativize foreign borrowings to make them conform to
native restrictions on word or syllable structure. For instance, in the northern
varieties of Standard German, all final stops have become voiceless by final
devoicing (see Chapter 4, § 5.1.1). Foreign words that do not conform to this
pattern of final voicelessness, such as Engl. *trend* with final voiced [d], are
made to conform, through substitution of the nearest voiceless sounds, as in
Trend [trent].

Similarly, foreign borrowings in Japanese are consistently reshaped in
order to conform to the syllable structure of Japanese which tolerates only
syllables of the type CV, with just one initial consonant (if any), plus a vowel
(or syllabic nasal), and with no syllable-final consonants. This is commonly
achieved through vowel insertion, as in (15a). But it may be accomplished
by other means, such as the reduction of the initial consonant group and the
dropping of the final consonant in (15b), or by turning semivocalic [w] into
the corresponding vowel [u], as in (15c). (The final vowel in *kuizu* (15c),
of course, reflects the same insertion as in (15a). Example (15a) additionally offers an instance of a nearest sound substitution, with [r] replacing
English [l].)

(15)   a. Engl. *baseball*   ⇒ Jap. *bēsubōru*
                   crawl   ⇒   *kurōru* (a swimming style)
        b.   *sweater*   ⇒   *sētā*
        c.   *quiz* [kwiz] ⇒   *kuizu*

Phonological nativization, thus, can be accomplished by a large variety
of developments, some fairly simple, others quite complex. In some cases,
however, none of these (or yet other) nativization processes are employed.
Nativization, if it can be called that, is accomplished by the simple ADOPTION
of a foreign sound or by adoption of a sound in a context where it does not
occur natively. The latter development, for instance, accounts for the final [ž]
of Engl. *prestige, rouge*, etc. The former is found in the English pronunciation
of *Bach* with [x], rather than native English [k].

In many cases, nativization also takes place at the LEXICAL level. And
here again we encounter the possibility of adoption, in this case without
morphological modification. Examples are Engl. *rouge, conceive, compas-*

sion, sympathy which, respectively, are from Modern French, Old French, Latin (via French), and Greek (via Latin and French). Such instances of lexical adoption, however, are usually accompanied by phonetic or phonological nativization. The need to make a foreign word pronounceable is much more basic than the need for lexical nativization.

Interestingly, in some cases of complete adoption, folk etymology secondarily leads to greater nativization, in that it makes better sense of the often opaque structure of borrowed words. (See Chapter 5, § 3.) English examples are the Algonquian animal name *otček* which by popular etymology has been made more transparent by being changed to *woodchuck*, and Fr. *chaiselongue* 'sofa; lit. long chair' which in many varieties of English has been recast to *chaise lounge* or *lounge chair*. In like manner, German has folk-etymologized a borrowing from Lat. *arcuballista* 'crossbow; lit. bow-thrower' as *Armbrust* lit. 'arm-chest/breast'. In fact, borrowings are perhaps the most favored target of popular etymology, because their structure frequently is opaque to the speakers of the borrowing language.

The polar opposite of lexical adoption is represented by LOAN SHIFTS. These involve changing the meaning of an existing native word so as to accommodate the meaning of a foreign word. Put differently, a foreign concept is borrowed only at the semantic level, without its linguistic form (which is supplied from native sources) and consequently, no new lexical item is introduced into the borrowing language.

Examples of this much more subtle and often undetectable process are found in the semantic shifts which many older Germanic religious terms underwent in response to the introduction of Christianity through the vehicle of Latin. For instance, the words *heofon* 'sky', *hel* 'underworld', and *god* (non-Christian deity) acquired new Christian meanings beside, or instead of, their earlier native connotations. The semantic shifts were possible because the corresponding Latin terms had a range of meanings that included both Christian and pre-Christian connotations. The partial semantic agreement between Latin and Old English, then, made it possible to extend the Old English meanings into new, Christian usages covered by the Latin terms. As the formulation in (16) shows, developments of this sort operate on something like a proportional model, similar to the one in the analogical processes of four-part analogy, backformation, and hypercorrection (see Chapter 5).

(16)   Latin   Old English

caelum	'sky'	:	*heofon*	'sky'
	'abode of the gods'	:		'abode of the gods and of warriors fallen in battle'
	'Christian heaven'	:		**X**

| *inferna* | 'abode of the dead (be-low the earth)' | : | *hel* | 'abode of the dead who have not fallen in bat-tle (below the earth)' |
| | 'Christian hell' | : | | **Y** |

| *deus* | 'deity' | : | *god* | 'deity' |
| | 'God' | : | | **Z** |

A process that is in a sense intermediate between adoption and loan shift is that of producing loan translations or CALQUES. The process consists of translating morphologically complex foreign expressions by means of novel combinations of native elements that match the meanings and the structure of the foreign expressions and their component parts. Compare for instance the examples in (17). Like loan shifts, these words do not introduce foreign elements into the language; but they do introduce new forms. Thus in (17b), the English term *world view* owes its existence to Germ. *Weltanschauung* 'view/outlook on the world', of which it is a loan translation. But unlike its occasional rival *weltanschauung*, it is composed entirely of native elements. Calquing was especially common as an alternative to loan shifts when Christianity was introduced to the early Germanic peoples; compare (17c).

(17)   a.   Engl.   *chain smoker*   :   Germ.   *Kettenraucher*
                         skyscraper   :   *Wolkenkratzer*
                                                  Fr.   *gratte-ciel*
          b.   Germ. *Weltanschauung* :   Engl.   *world view*
          c.   Gk. ⇒ Lat. *ev-angelium* :   OEngl.   *gōd-spell* (both lit. 'good message')
                                            >   Mod.Engl.   *gospel*

The examples in (17a) further show that the elements used to translate the component parts of a foreign word are usually put together according to native morphological patterns and processes. For instance, Engl. *chain* corresponds to Germ. *Kette* and *smoker* to *Raucher*. But the German compound is *Kette-**n**-raucher*, not *Ketteraucher**, in accordance with a productive German process of compound formation. Similarly, French translates Engl. *skyscraper* as *gratte-ciel*, lit. 'scrape-sky', because that is the productive mode of making compounds corresponding to the English pattern *skyscraper* (compare *ouvre-porte* 'door opener', lit. 'open-door').

Germ. *Wolkenkratzer*, lit. 'cloud scraper' or 'cloud scratcher', further shows that calques may occasionally be less than exact translations. In the present case, the motivation for the inexact translation may be something like taboo. German does not make a distinction between *heaven* and *sky*, but like Old English, uses a single word, *Himmel*. A calque *Himmelskratzer** thus might have been interpreted as 'heaven scraper', invoking unfortunate associations with the Tower of Babel.

It might be added that calquing presupposes a certain familiarity with the donor language and its grammatical structure. Otherwise, it would not be possible to recognize that a given item in the donor language is morphologically complex, or to furnish a translation of the component parts. (This issue will become important in § 5.)

Calques are not necessarily limited to structures like (17), in which the component parts of morphologically complex expressions are independent lexical items in their own right. They can involve affixes. Consider for instance (18), where Latin substitutes its native suffix *-us* for the *-os* of Greek, but leaves unchanged the preceding root, *Petr-*.

(18)   Gk. *Pétr-os* : Lat. *Petr-us* (name of the apostle Peter)

The suffix substitution in (18) probably has a special, MORPHOLOGICAL, motivation: The suffix *-os* is well established in Greek morphology, where it goes along with a genitive singular *-ou* and other case forms. In Latin, however, the suffix does not fit into the native inflectional system. At the same time, like Greek, Latin requires nouns to be inflected for number and case. The substitution of native *-us* introduces a suffix which can be inflected (e.g. genitive singular *Petr-i*) and thus makes it possible to use the borrowed word in a grammatically correct manner.

Such structural nativization is possible only if the donor and borrowing languages have similar grammatical systems. Where the systems diverge, different strategies need to be resorted to, at least in the case of languages which have fairly complex morphological systems.

To illustrate the problem and how it is resolved, let us look at the gender assignment of borrowings in languages which obligatorily have to mark every noun for gender.

Gender assignment for borrowings seems to operate in terms of the following parameters: (i) formal criteria; (ii) general semantic criteria; (iii) considerations of the gender of semantically related native words; (iv) a default class to which words are assigned if none of the other criteria provides a solution.

Consider for instance the case of German. German has three genders – masculine, feminine, and neuter. In this regard it looks similar to English. What complicates matters is that gender assignment is "grammatical", i.e., to a large extent semantically arbitrary. Thus, 'tables' may be masculine, 'doors' feminine, and 'books' neuter, as in the examples of (19). At the same time, gender assignment is obligatory and has important syntactic consequences, since pronouns and adjectives have to agree in gender with the nouns they refer to; see again the examples in (19). To make things even worse, there is no consistent formal distinction between the three genders of German. The best that can be said is that masculines and neuters tend to inflect alike and in their nominative form tend to end in a consonant, while feminines tend to end in a vowel, most commonly in -*e* [-ə].

(19)   Masculine: *Das ist ein alter Tisch; **er** kostet viel Geld.*
                   'That is an old table. It costs a lot of money.'
        Feminine: *Das ist eine starke Tür; **sie** kostet viel Geld.*
                   'That is a strong door. It costs a lot of money.'
        Neuter: *Das ist ein gutes Buch; **es** kostet viel Geld.*
                   'That is a good book. It costs a lot of money.'

Let us now look at how German assigns gender to words borrowed from other languages. Most examples are drawn from English which has "natural", or sex-based gender, but only for human or animate beings. One example comes from French which has two genders, masculine and feminine.

The French system is more similar to the German one in that gender is semantically largely arbitrary. However, in terms of its morphology, the grammatical gender system of French is no more similar to that of German than the natural gender system of English. German speakers, therefore, tend not to look to the donor language for guidance in assigning gender but to rely on the criteria outlined above. And remarkably, in spite of the fact that the principles are quite vague and heterogeneous in nature, German speakers show an amazing degree of agreement in how they apply them. Consider for instance the examples in (20).

(20)   a. Early NFr. *garage* [garažə] (m.) 'garage'
        b. Engl.   *computer*
        babysitter
        trend
        rush hour
        panel

The French word in (20a) is masculine and should not cause any difficulties if German gender assignment were based on the system of the donor
language; it should come out as a masculine. However, formal criteria are potent enough to tilt gender assignment in a different direction. French *garage*
and all other French words in *-age* come out as feminine in German, as in
die Garage. The reason must be sought in the tendency for German nouns
in *-e* to be feminine.

The fact that German has many borrowings from French ending in *-age* and
has consistently nativized them as feminines has an interesting consequence:
When Germans learn French, they naturally assume that French words in
-age are feminine. But when they use them as feminines they soon find
out – much to their annoyance – that the French "perversely" use them as
masculines, not realizing that if there has been perversion it has taken place
on the German side. Such mismatches between apparently cognate native and
foreign words are actually quite common, not only as far as formal issues such
as gender are concerned, but also in meaning. (For instance, the *convenance*
of French *mariage de convenance* means 'agreement', not 'convenience', in
spite of the English calque *marriage of convenience* which is based on a
misunderstanding of *convenance*.) In language teaching, mismatches of this
sort are often referred to as "false friends".

The problem of gender assignment is of course greatest in borrowings from
languages like English which have natural, not grammatical, gender. Here,
too, German may draw on formal criteria. For instance, the word *computer*
fits the native German class of instrument nouns in *-er*, such as *Kratz-er*
'scraper' (as in the *Wolkenkratzer* of (17a) above). And since nouns of this
type are masculine in German, *computer* is assigned masculine gender.

By a similar reasoning we should expect *babysitter* to be nativized with
masculine gender, since German agent nouns in *-er* are masculine, such as
Bäck-er 'baker'. However, while masculine gender causes no difficulties if
this word is used in a generic sense, it becomes inappropriate if used in reference to a prototypical babysitter who, as in English, is female. In that case,
German morphology requires that the form be marked by the feminine suffix
-in, as in *Bäcker-in*, the female counterpart of *Bäcker*. But many Germans

would balk at using *Babysitter-in*, presumably because the word *Babysitter* has not been sufficiently nativized to accept native derivational suffixes. Germans therefore are in something of a quandary as to how to use *Babysitter* and tend to use the word only in the generic sense, as in *Sie arbeitet für uns als Babysitter* 'she works for us as babysitter', while avoiding expressions corresponding to Engl. *The babysitter just called to say she is late.*

Gender assignment for *Trend* is more complex, since semantic criteria generally work only in words for humans or animates. Moreover, formal considerations provide only negative guidance. The word ends in a consonant, which suggests masculine or neuter gender, rather than feminine; but the choice between masculine and neuter is left undetermined. In this case, principle (iii) takes over, namely consideration of the gender of semantically related native words. Native near-synonyms which like *Trend* are monosyllabic and end in consonant are *Zug* and *Hang*; and these are masculine. As a consequence, the word is nativized with masculine gender.

An example like *rush hour*, which comes out as feminine (*die Rush-hour*), suggests that when formal and semantic criteria disagree, the latter may win out. Formally, the word ends in consonant and should therefore get either masculine or neuter gender. But semantically, Engl. *hour* corresponds to the German feminine *die Stunde* 'the hour' and it is this gender that gets assigned to *Rush-hour*. (In addition, the etymological German equivalent of *hour* is *Uhr* 'watch, clock', also a feminine. Speakers familiar with the relationship between *hour* and *Uhr* may draw on the relationship as another factor in favor of assigning feminine gender to *Rush-hour*.)

Finally, in cases like *Panel*, none of the criteria examined so far will unambiguously assign a specific gender. Here the default provision takes over and turns the word into a neuter, as in *das Panel*.

Similar considerations play a role in other languages. For instance, like other Bantu languages, Swahili has a system of "noun classes", with different "class prefixes", as in M-*toto* 'child', pl. WA-toto, or KI-*swahili* 'Swahili language'. As in German, adjectives and other words have to agree in class with the nouns they refer to (for illustrations see Chapter 12, examples (12) and (13)). Words borrowed from non-Bantu languages therefore have to be integrated into the noun class system. In some cases, nativization takes place, as in German, on the basis of formal criteria (sometimes with structural reinterpretation). Thus the Arabic word *kitāb* 'book' is assigned to the "*ki*-class" as *ki-tabu* because of its initial *ki-*, even though that *ki-* is not a prefix in Arabic. And accordingly, it makes its plural as *vi-tabu*. What helped in this reassignment is the fact that *ki-* is the prefix for languages and other "linguistic things" and thus is perfect for a word meaning 'book'. Similarly, a traffic pattern enjoined by signs with the verbal message *keep left* is now referred to by the nativized expression *ki-plefti* whose plural, not surprisingly by now, is *vi-plefti*.

General semantic considerations decide the assignment of words like Engl. *settler* to the *m-* (pl. *wa-*) class of human beings: *m-setla*, pl. *wa-setla*.

And again, a default class accommodates words that are not assignable by other criteria. In Swahili this is the Ø-prefix class (with Ø-prefix also in the plural), a class to which are assigned borrowings like Port. *mesa* [-z-] 'table', hence Swah. *Ø-mēza*, pl. *Ø-mēza*.

The issue of nativization also arises in sign languages. For instance, American Sign Language (ASL) borrows many words from (oral) American English. The mechanism for borrowing has been the use of finger-spelling, in which words that do not have their own ASL sign can be spelled out in their English form, using the manual alphabet where different hand-shapes correspond to letters of the English alphabet. Borrowings from the oral language may be either short words (usually two or three letters, and generally no more than five) or abbreviations, such as *if* and *OK* (whatever its origin in English – see Chapter 9, § 1). Similar borrowings are *KO* for 'knockout' (a boxing term) and *NG*, as an acronym for 'No Good', which, though not common today, had some currency in American English usage in the 1950s and beyond.

Finger-spelled loan words often undergo nativization, just like loan words in oral languages. For example, the finger spelling for *OK* has undergone assimilatory changes (see Chapter 4, § 5.1.1). Instead of the thumb contact and arcing of the fingers characteristic of an independent finger-spelled *O*, we find that in one version of the sign, the *O* has assimilated to *K*, so that the thumb is in contact only with the first two fingers, the fingers used in the formation of the *K*. In many instances, the changes to these loan words are so drastic that they lose all trace of their origin as finger spellings. ASL users, for instance, are said to identify the sign *NG* with the similarly formed sign for 'eliminate', the idea being that something no good is to be thrown away. This identification constitutes a form of folk etymology (see Chapter 5, § 3.2).

4. "Hyper-foreignization": A further effect of borrowing

As shown by the example of *raja(h)* in the previous section, the belief that foreign words must have "foreign" sounds may lead to the introduction of hypercorrect, or "hyper-foreign" substitutions, such as [ž] for the original [ǰ] of *raja(h)* – in spite of the fact that the correct [ǰ] is a perfectly normal speech sound of English.

HYPER-FOREIGNIZATION is a relatively common phenomenon in English. One that has been observed since at least the 1930s is found in pronunciations such as [kū də gra] for *coup de grâce* 'final blow' (lit., 'blow of mercy [to relieve an animal of incurable pain]'), whose French pronunciation is [ku də gʀas]. The motivation for this pronunciation is the belief that "French drops its final consonants". Now, it is perfectly correct that French commonly drops its final consonants, as in *gras* 'grease' [gʀa]; but this holds true only if the consonants are final in the spelling. Words with final orthographic -*e* follow a different rule which drops the -*e*; *grâce* therefore is pronounced [gʀas] in French. English speakers who pronounce *coup de grâce* as [kū də gra] evidently are not familiar enough with the intricacies of French spelling and extend the drop rule to consonants that are final in pronunciation, not in spelling. The resulting [kū də gra] may be amusing to those more familiar with French (including of course the French), because it corresponds to a spelling *coup de gras* – which means a 'blow of grease'; but the joke is lost on those whose familiarity with French is more limited.

Hyperforeignisms are not restricted to pronunciation but can also be based on misperceptions of what constitutes foreign morphology. Thus the phrase *No problemo*, which has had some currency in recent American usage and is uttered, for instance, by Arnold Schwarzenegger's character in the film *Terminator 2*, is a morphological hyper-Spanish form. The actual Spanish form for 'problem' is *problema*, with a final -*a*, but based on English borrowings from Spanish such as *taco, burrito, nacho,* or *macho*, the perception has emerged that final -*o* is a typically Spanish word-ending – whence *problem-o*. (Note also quasi-foreign forms such as *le car*; see Chapter 7, § 5.7.)

At work in these cases is a phenomenon we have seen before and will see again – most speakers are not linguists. What matters are ordinary speakers' perceptions of what makes a word or sound seem foreign, not what the actual facts of the foreign language are. These facts are for linguists to worry about; speakers are too busy using their own language to be concerned with such fine details.

5. Why borrow? Motivations for borrowing strategies

The motivation for borrowing which most readily comes to mind is NEED. If the speakers of a given language take over new cultural items, new technical, religious concepts, or references to foreign locations, fauna, flora, there obviously is a need for vocabulary to express these concepts or references. The easiest thing, then, is to take over the foreign word together with the foreign article or idea. Many of the examples which we have looked at so far are of this nature. Compare especially (1a,b) and (3) above.

But need will not account for all borrowings. What need, for instance, would English have had for borrowing words from French like the ones on the left side in (21) below? As the inherited, Anglo-Saxon lexical items on the right show, there were perfectly workable indigenous words for these animals. The reason for the borrowing must be sought in a different area, namely PRESTIGE: The words on the left side refer to the animals as they were served at table, i.e., in a social sphere where French culture and prestige dominated after the conquest of England in 1066. The terms on the right side, by contrast, belong to the social spheres of raising and herding the animals which after 1066 were relegated to the non-French-speaking community. And even though we may no longer think of *beef* or *veal* as more prestigious, the semantic differences between the terms on the left and those on the right are still an echo of the original prestige difference. (Before the French words were borrowed, of course, the Anglo-Saxon words were the general designations for the animals, whether served at table or raised in the barnyard.)

(21)   *beef* : *cow, bull, ox*
             veal : *calf*
             pork : *pig/hog/swine*

Prestige, rather than need, also accounts for borrowings like Germ. *Trend* (see § 3) or the loan shift by which Germ. *Papier* '(sheet of) paper' came to include in its range of meanings the notion 'journal article, presentation at a professional meeting'; see (22).

(22)   English   German
       paper 'piece, sheet etc. of paper' : *Papier* 'piece, sheet etc. of paper'
                'article etc.'   :   **X**

Just as English had perfectly serviceable indigenous words for the items in (21) prior to the Norman conquest, so German has perfectly adequate native words for *Trend* and the new meaning of *Papier* – *Zug, Hang, Anlage, Tendenz*, etc. for the first word, *Aufsatz, Vortrag*, etc. for the second.

If we look at the context in which these words entered the German language, we can see the motivation for their getting borrowed. They were first used in post-1945 Western German sociology and related social sciences, in conscious imitation of the corresponding English terms. The initial purpose was to indicate to the world – or at least to one's colleagues – familiarity with the most up-to-date and prestigious literature in the field; and that literature happened to be written in English. Even now, the terms *Trend,* and *Papier* in the meaning 'article', tend to be limited to the somewhat trendy professional jargon of sociologists, pollsters, and journalists.

It is of course possible to argue that the difference between need and prestige is not really that great – if something is PRESTIGIOUS, we may feel a NEED to imitate or borrow it. Nevertheless, the notion of prestige plays a significant role in determining the extent of borrowing, as well as what kinds of words are likely to be borrowed. Moreover, other, related social concepts affect the extent to which foreign words are nativized, especially when that nativization is non-phonological.

5.1. Prestige relations and their effects
The varying effects of prestige on borrowing can be illustrated by a brief look at the relationships of English with the different languages it has come in contact with during the course of history.

Let us start with the Anglo-Saxons' contact with the speakers of Celtic languages that they encountered upon their arrival in England. In this particular situation, the Anglo-Saxons clearly had the upper hand, militarily and politically. As a consequence, they must have considered the Celts inferior. The LOW PRESTIGE of the Celts, in turn, must be the reason that very few words of Celtic origin were borrowed. The words that were borrowed were quite restricted in their denotations and connotations. They were limited, in effect, to a few names for animals, articles of clothing, and topology, such as *brock* 'badger' ⇐ Celt. *brokko-*, OE *bratt* 'cloak' ⇐ Gaelic (compare OIr. *bratt*), and *crag* 'steep rock' ⇐ Celtic (compare W *craig*, Ir. *carraig*, Scots Gael. *creag*). In addition there are a fair number of place names, including *London*, whose *-don* recurs in other place names of Celtic origin, both in the British Isles and on the continent. Many of the place names appear to have come to the Anglo-Saxons in Latinized form, reflecting the earlier Roman domination of much of present-day England and the relatively greater prestige of Roman culture. (Old English *bratt* is said to be the ancestor of

Modern Engl. *brat*, as in *spoiled brat*; the semantic changes leading to the modern meaning are fairly complex.)

The second important historical contact was with the Old Norse of the so-called Danes who, after the typical raping and pillaging of medieval warfare, eventually settled in the so-called Danelaw, intermarrying and otherwise acting as EQUALS with the indigenous English population. (See Chapter 2, § 3.3.) From this relationship between equals resulted a very large number of borrowings, by some estimates more than 1,700. These borrowings affected everyday vocabulary, and included words such as *egg, guest, hit, husband, raise, skill, skin, skirt, sky*. Even basic vocabulary was borrowed, such as *get, give, like, take*, and the pronouns *they, their, them*. Names, too, were affected, including the numerous English place names ending in -*by* (ON *bý* 'abode') and the widespread pattern of family names ending in -*son*, reflecting an Old Norse "patronymic" naming pattern preserved in Modern Icelandic (as in *Stefán Einarsson* = Stefán, son of Einar). Interestingly, this naming pattern affected at least some Gaelic names as well, such as *Fergus(s)on* = 'son of Fergus'.

In addition to the large amount of borrowing and the fact that even basic vocabulary was affected, there are no special connotations (either positive or negative) attached to these loans. For instance, Scandinavian borrowings like *skirt* or *to raise* do not differ significantly in social connotations from their Anglo-Saxon counterparts, such as *shirt* or *to rear*.

The next important contact of English was with the French of the Norman conquerors who in 1066 became overlords over the native English (and Anglo-Scandinavian) population. This contact resulted in the largest number of borrowings. Moreover, to the extent that special connotations are attached to the loans, they almost invariably reflect the HIGHER PRESTIGE enjoyed by the speakers of French. Compare the examples in (21) above. At the same time, as in the case of the earlier contact with Celtic but in contrast to the Danish contact, the most basic vocabulary remained unaffected.

The last contact to be examined closes the circle in more than one sense. This is the contact between English and the indigenous languages of North America. From the perspective of the conquering Europeans, this was a contact of unequal relationship very similar to the much earlier one between Anglo-Saxons and Celts. The difference in prestige, again, is reflected in the types of borrowings that were made from the Indigenous American languages. The most general sphere of borrowings is that of place names – of the forty-eight contiguous states of the United States, more than half bear names derived from indigenous languages. Note for instance *Illinois,*

Michigan, Ohio, Wisconsin. But even here we find a strong tendency to use European-derived names, such as *New York, Washington, Virginia.*

Beyond place names, borrowings most commonly are found in names for fauna and flora, such as *woodchuck* and *moose* from Algonqu. *otček* and *mōs.* (Other borrowings of this sort include *opossum, skunk, wapiti, hominy (grits), tupelo (tree), persimmon,* and *succotash.*) However, here too the tendency is to adapt European words to the new surroundings. Compare for instance the word *robin* which in America refers to a bird quite different in size and taxonomic classification from the European bird of the same name.

Other borrowings are even more limited and tend to refer exclusively to Indigenous American life (compare *moccasin, pow-wow, squaw, teepee, toboggan, totem, wampum*), very often with derogatory connotations, as in *squaw,* or with specifically American Indian connotations (such as *teepee* and *wampum*).

The contact situations just outlined and the nature of the borrowings associated with them are fairly typical of linguistic contact in general. The different types of relative social status of the participants in such contact situations can be characterized by the terms ADSTRATUM, SUPERSTRATUM, and SUBSTRATUM. Languages of roughly equal prestige, such as English and Norse in early England, are referred to as adstrata. Where prestige is unequal, as between Normans and Anglo-Saxons, between Anglo-Saxons and Celts, or between English-speaking Europeans and Indigenous Americans, the terms superstratum and substratum are used, the former referring to the language with higher prestige, the latter to the one with lower prestige.

Adstratal relationships, then, are most conducive for borrowings of everyday-life vocabulary, even basic vocabulary. In contrast, there are much greater limitations in contacts between languages of unequal prestige. Moreover, in such contacts, the borrowings tend to reflect the social status of the donor language. If that language is a superstratum, loans tend to come from the more prestigious sections of the lexicon and their connotations likewise tend to be prestigious, at least at the beginning. If the donor language is a substratum, loans tend to be limited to need borrowings (such as new place names) and/or to have derogatory connotations.

5.2. Linguistic nationalism or the effect of social attitudes on nativization

In § 3 we have noted a large variety of routines through which foreign words are integrated into the borrowing language. In most of these, foreign words are nativized in phonological or morphological structure. But occasionally, they may be adopted in unmodified form, without any significant degree of nativization. Though such unmodified adoption is rare in the phonological structure of words, it is quite common in morphology. In fact, all of the borrowings discussed in § 4.1 are of this type. But as we have seen, processes like calquing and the development of loan shifts offer an alternative to morphological adoption – the creation of words made up entirely from native sources. Let us contrast these two different approaches to morphological integration as ADOPTION VS. ADAPTATION.

As we have seen in the preceding section, the notion of prestige plays a powerful role in determining the kinds of words that are borrowed and the quantity of borrowings. The question of what determines the choice between adoption and adaptation likewise finds a satisfactory answer only when social factors are considered.

At first sight, one might suspect to the contrary, that the choice between adoption and adaptation is entirely determined by linguistic factors. Adoption would be preferred where the structures of donor and borrowing language are sufficiently similar to permit the process to apply. Elsewhere, adaptation would be preferred. In support of this view one might point to the difference between Chinese and English. Chinese heavily favors adaptation. For instance the adaptation *dian hua*, lit. 'lightning speech', is much more readily accepted as the rendition of Engl. *telephone* than the rival adoption *de lü feng*, even though the latter sounds more similar to the English original. English on the other hand quite readily adopts foreign words, e.g. *macho, rouge, umlaut*.

This difference might be attributed to the fact that in its structure, Chinese differs radically from the European languages, by having essentially monosyllabic words (although compounding is possible), with severe restrictions on the occurrence of consonants, plus a rich system of tonal contrasts (not marked in the above examples). Moreover, as noted in Chapter 3, § 5.1, Chinese has a virtual one-to-one relationship between word and syllable – words are syllables, and syllables are words. When Chinese speakers try to adapt by substituting similar-sounding syllables for the syllables of a foreign word, they face the difficulty of having to match up the meanings of these syllables with the meaning of the foreign word. For instance, a nativization of Engl. *telephone* as *de lü feng* is quite good from the phonological perspective, but semantically it causes difficulties, for *de lü feng* literally means 'power-law-wind', which only vaguely fits the meaning of *telephone*. Chinese speakers therefore prefer to adapt foreign words, by creating compounds of native words whose meanings are more compatible with those of the foreign originals, such as *dian hua*, lit. 'lightning speech', for *telephone*. (Even worse is the case of *mai ke feng* as a phonetic approximation of Engl. *microphone*:

Its literal meaning, 'wheat-gram [unit of weight]-wind', cannot be considered even remotely related to the meaning of the English word. But interestingly, in spite of these difficulties *mai ke feng* has been accepted as the normal word for microphone.)

Structure, however, cannot be solely responsible for preferring adaptation to adoption. This is shown by the case of Modern Icelandic. Although the structure of Icelandic is much less different from that of English and other European languages, it behaves like Chinese, generally preferring adaptation and limiting adoption to foreign place names and terms for foreign fauna and flora. Contrast the adoptions in (23a) with the adaptations in (23b). (English here is used as a representative for the majority of European languages, which have a more tolerant, or at least mixed, attitude toward adoption.) In many cases, the adaptations are more or less literal calques, as in (23b.i). Others are loan shifts; compare (23b.ii), which actually involves the resurrection of an Old Icelandic word whose meaning roughly was 'wire', as a translational equivalent of the English term *wire* 'telegram'. In many other cases, the words are recreated from Icelandic elements, without even attempting to provide a more or less precise translational equivalent of the foreign words; see (23b.iii). On the other hand, adoptions like *jeppi* 'jeep' and *berkill* 'tubercle' are exceedingly rare. In fact, as examples like *samríkismaður* 'member of the U.S. Republican party' show, even foreign terms often are adapted, rather than adopted.

(23)   a.   *Arabi*   *Arab*
                Evrópa   *Europe*
                melóna   *melon*

        b. i. *ljóshvolf* *photosphere*   'light concavity'
                                                    = 'photo' + 'sphere'
                fjarverða *absence*   'far-being'
                                                    ≈ 'ab-' + 'sence'
                samtal   *conversation*   'together-speak'
                                                    ≈ 'con-' + 'versation'
                úrval   *selection*   'out-choice'
                                                    ≈ 'se-' + 'lection'[1]
           ii. *síma*   *telegram, telephone,*
                             telecommunication   'wire'
                talsíma   *telephone*   'speech wire'
                ritsíma   *telegram*   'write wire'

iii. *samríkismaður* *(U.S.) Republican* 'together-state-man'
      hershöfðingi   *general*   'army-chieftain'
      bókmentir   *literature*   'book-arts'

(^{1} This word may actually be a calque on Dan. *ud-valg*, Germ. *Aus-wahl*, which themselves are calques of *se-lection*. A number of other calques may be similarly derived via German and Danish intermediaries; but these calques are motivated by very similar attitudes.)

We know that this avoidance of adoption has not always been dominant in Icelandic. In texts of the sixteenth through early nineteenth centuries, innumerable adoptions of foreign words can be found; compare (24). These came to Icelandic through the Scandinavian languages, especially Danish. The Scandinavian languages themselves had undergone extensive influence from the Low German trade language of the Hanse, a commercial league of Northern German and Dutch cities. As a consequence, many of the adopted words ultimately derive from Low German. In addition, of course, there was the ever-present influence of Latin, mediated through Danish and often also through Low German.

(24)   *borger* 'citizen, burgher' (ultimately from Low German)
        borgmeistari 'mayor'   (ultimately from Low German)
        dedicera 'to dedicate'   (ultimately from Latin)
        disputatía 'dispute'   (ultimately from Latin)

The reason for this large-scale adoption of foreign words must be sought in two factors: political domination by Denmark, and the introduction of Lutheran Christianity. Danish domination made Danish the prestige language. And the change from Roman Catholicism to Lutheranism brought with it a large amount of new Danish (ultimately German) terminology which was intimately linked with the new form of religion and which, through this association, carried considerable prestige as well.

Even at the height of their use in Icelandic, these adopted borrowings occurred more frequently in informal writings than in more formal texts, suggesting that they were trendy prestige borrowings, rather than need-based. Significantly, the very writers of these informal texts inveighed against the use of foreign words. They feared that the excessive use of such words would alienate Icelanders from their own rich medieval literature, a literature still highly revered by the Icelandic people. This attitude no doubt is responsible for the fact that the Icelanders of that time used adopted foreign words much more sparingly in their formal writings, when they were on their best linguistic behavior. As nationalist feelings increased markedly during the nineteenth century, virtually all the foreign words adopted since the sixteenth century were eliminated or replaced by adaptations, and with the exceptions noted above, new borrowings were accepted only in adapted form.

The socially based motivating force behind these developments is now commonly referred to as LINGUISTIC NATIONALISM or linguistic purism, the use of language to assert the identity and prestige of one's own people – in contrast to the prestige that might be attached to foreign languages and their speakers.

Ironically, to the extent that it resorts to calquing, linguistic nationalism requires a much fuller understanding of foreign linguistic structure than plain adoption. When adopting a foreign word like *photosphere*, it is not strictly necessary to understand that it is composed of the elements *photo* 'light' and *sphere* 'sphere, concavity'. But such an understanding is essential for calquing *photosphere* as *ljóshvolf*. As a consequence, adaptations usually are introduced by persons with a good understanding of the donor language's morphology.

In spite of its present-day aversion to adopting foreign words, Chinese, too, has not always been resistant to adoption. When Buddhism came to China during the Middle Chinese period, the speakers of Chinese struggled valiantly to adopt the Sanskrit terminology of Buddhism, in spite of the fact that, if anything, the structural differences between Chinese and Sanskrit are even greater than those between Chinese and English. One of the words that were borrowed in this contact was later adopted in Japanese and is now known to us in its Japanese form. This is the word *zen* whose ultimate source is Skt. *dhyāna-* 'meditation'. The linguistic nationalism of Modern Chinese, then, must be a more recent development – or a rekindling of an earlier attitude after the influence of Buddhism had abated.

Linguistic nationalism is by no means limited to Icelandic and Chinese. It is found in many other languages, although most of them show its effects only in a very inconsistent, even erratic fashion.

Consider for instance German. The erratic nature of linguistic nationalism is reflected in two ways. First, in many cases, foreign words appear both in adapted and in adopted form; see (25). Secondly, there is no consistency in the connotations associated with adaptations vs. adoptions. As (25) shows, in some cases it is the adopted borrowing, in others, the adapted word that is the more natural or popular. The other word, then, often is used mainly in "officialese" or in specialized jargons. Thus, people might enter a phone booth which is marked *Öffentlicher Fernsprecher* 'Public Far-Speaker' = 'Public Telephone' (an officialese expression), but in the booth they use the *Telephon* (which is the normal word). And there is at least one case (*Auto : Wagen*) where both words are commonly used, with different speakers preferring one or the other term, but with no consensus as to which one is more natural or popular. The degree of inconsistency becomes especially clear if we contrast the words for 'telephone' and 'television': In the case of 'telephone', normal use prefers the adoption, while the adaptation is officialese. For 'television', the situation is just about the opposite.

(25)   ADOPTION   ADAPTATION
         Auto (general use)   *Wagen* (general use)
                                       Kraftwagen (officialese)
         Radio (general use)   *Rundfunk* (officialese)
         Telephon (general use)   *Fernsprecher* (officialese)
         Television   *Fernsehen* 'TV institution'
         (TV industry jargon)   (general and officialese)
                                       Fernseher 'TV set' (general)
                                       Fernsehgerät 'TV set' (officialese)
         Kopie 'xerographic copy'   *Ablichtung* (small-town, officialese)
         (large city, academia)

The situation is very similar in most other languages of Europe (excepting Iceland). Even in France, where linguistic nationalism has the powerful support of the prestigious and centralized Académie Française and of the political and educational establishment, attempts at purging the language of foreign adoptions have met with only limited success. Words like *redingote* 'riding coat' (see (1a) above) and *club* (borrowed from nineteenth-century British English) are fully integrated into the French lexicon. And everybody knows that the Académie's attempts to proscribe "Franglais" have been rather ineffectual, at least in more trendy circles. Expressions like *le hot dog, le hamburger*, mainly of American English origin, have found wide acceptance.

Even in Israeli Hebrew, linguistic nationalism has had less than spectacular success. This is so in spite of the fact that the founders of the Hebrew revival in the early part of the twentieth century made a deliberate, nationalistically inspired attempt to revive the language in a truly Semitic guise, with total elimination of the various European influences that had crept into the language over the centuries. The founders of the movement expected the total elimination of European influence to free Hebrew and its speakers from the yoke of 1,700 years of diaspora, second-class citizenship, and recurrent persecution. However, not even the killing of six million Jews in the Nazi holocaust – an event that precipitated the founding of the state of Israel – has been able to block the entrance of adopted words like *viza* 'visa', *student,* or *gymnazia* (a type of secondary school).

Native speakers of English often find it very difficult to understand why linguistic nationalism should manifest itself in a preference for adaptations over adoptions. Not that linguistic nationalism is alien to modern English. It is very clearly present in the area of pronunciation, which favors phonological adaptation over the adoption of foreign sounds. Thus, most speakers would consider the pronunciation of the composer's name *Bach* with final [x] to be an affectation. (Contrast this with the fact that educated German has adopted nasal vowels from French, as in [zalɔ̃] 'salon', and [ǰ] from English, as in [meneǰər] 'manager'.) At the lexical level, however, adaptation is rare in Modern English and adoption just about the norm.

Even the preference for lexical adoption, however, is a fairly recent phenomenon. The introduction of Christianity in the Old English period, for instance, was accompanied by a large number of loan shifts and calques; see (16) and (17c) above. In this case, adaptation may have sprung not so much from linguistic nationalism as from a conscious attempt by the missionaries to make the Christian religion less unfamiliar and therefore easier to accept by using terms that the intended converts were familiar with. (This, in fact, is standard procedure in Christian missionary efforts.)

Linguistic nationalism did, however, play a strong role in English during the sixteenth and seventeenth centuries. As in many other parts of Europe, the Renaissance had brought with it a rekindled interest and reverence for the languages of (western) European classical culture and civilization, and this interest and reverence led many English writers to draw heavily on the classical languages as sources for new vocabulary; compare (26). Many of the resulting borrowings, such as the ones in (26a), have become an integral part of the English vocabulary. Many others, however, have not; see the examples in (26b).

(26)   a. *affirmation*
           negation
           maturity
           modesty
           persist
        b. *adiuvate* 'help'
           dominical 'lordly'
           ingent 'enormous'
           obtestate 'beseech'

Words of the type (26b) failed to become generally accepted for several reasons. Some of the words may have been considered excessively trendy by most contemporaries and thus would have passed out of usage anyway.

But what may have been even more important is that the large influx of unassimilated or poorly assimilated foreign words met with a reaction very similar to the Icelandic response to the influx of Danish words. English writers and scholars began to inveigh against the excessive use of foreign words, often ridiculing them as "inkhornisms". The words in (26b) are all found in an 'ynke-horne letter' published by Thomas Wilson as an illustration of usage that he condemned.

Attacks against inkhornisms came especially from two sides, the "Anglo-Saxonists" and the Puritans. Like the Icelandic critics of excessive Danish borrowings, the Anglo-Saxonists wanted to maintain the linguistic link with medieval literature and tradition and regarded the flood of foreign words as a serious obstacle. The Puritans equated "plain speech" with truth and saw the excessive use of borrowings as overly ornate and, therefore, as a deviation from truth. One of the strongest advocates of plain speech, John Cheke, used terms such as *yeasay* and *naysay* instead of the words *affirmation* and *negation* (26a). Many other, similar adaptations were proposed, such as *unboundedness* for *infinity* and *gainrising* for *resurrection*.

English differs from Icelandic in that most of these proposed adaptations have met a similar fate as the inkhorn terms in (26b). Only a few, such as *unboundedness*, have retained some degree of currency. This difference no doubt results from the fact that the use of adopted borrowings from Greek and Latin found strong, even vociferous, support among many other English writers and scholars, who viewed the use of such terms highly appropriate "for the necessary augmentation of our language" (Thomas Elyot). Moreover, while medieval Icelandic was fairly free of foreign influence, the medieval language of poets like Chaucer was too clearly influenced by the French of the Norman conquerors to be describable as pure Anglo-Saxon. Finally, "plain speech" may have come to be too closely associated with the sectarian activities of the Puritans. Whatever the reasons, linguistic nationalism failed to become the same powerful force as in Iceland.

This does not mean that linguistic nationalism faded away entirely. Occasionally it was rekindled, especially when fueled by political nationalism. For instance, antipathy to Germany during the First World War led to attempts to replace adopted German borrowings such as *weltanschauung* by adaptations like *world view* (see (17b) above), or even more daring replacements such as *victory cabbage* for *sauerkraut* (⇐ Germ. *Sauerkraut* 'sour cabbage'). But many of these replacements, such as *victory cabbage*, did not succeed in the long run.

In general, the argument that adoptions enrich the English language has carried the day. (See also the next section.) Linguistic nationalism survives mainly as an anti-intellectual undercurrent, especially among vernacular speakers who abhor the "high-falutin" sesquipedalianisms of the educated.

The unqualified success of linguistic nationalism in Modern Icelandic as well as in Modern Chinese, then, is quite unusual and must be attributed to very special circumstances. In both cases, the immediate reason for this success is the fact that the attitude of linguistic nationalism is shared by virtually all layers of society.

In Icelandic, linguistic nationalism seems to have been supported by the movement to achieve independence, as well as by a genuine fondness and reverence in all layers of society for medieval literature whose written form remained remarkably intelligible to the speakers of Modern Icelandic.

In the case of Chinese, linguistic nationalism is supported by a highly traditional, ethnocentric attitude. It has been claimed that an added factor lies in the nature of Chinese writing which, as we have seen in Chapter 3, § 5.1., is essentially logographic. The problem therefore is not simply that phonetic adoption creates difficulties because all syllables are meaningful; after all, there would be nothing to prevent Chinese from using for nativization phonetic syllables that are not associated with any specific meaning. Much more important is the fact that the writing system does not offer any symbols for such meaningless syllables – all writing symbols are meaningful. Put differently, Chinese has a triple identity between word, syllable, and logographic symbol, and this identity places enormous obstacles in the way of the phonetic adoption of foreign borrowings.

There is probably some truth to this argument; but as observed earlier, Modern Chinese does offer instances of phonetic adoption, such as *mai ke feng* for Engl. *microphone*, even though the literal meaning of the logographic symbols employed, 'wheat-gram [unit of weight]-wind', clashes with the semantics of the English word. Even more significant, Middle Chinese nativized a massive amount of Sanskrit words through phonetic adoption. As in the case of Icelandic, therefore, the real reason for preferring adoption over adaptation is more likely to lie in the social attitude of linguistic nationalism.

In most other societies, the general populace seems to have a more ambivalent attitude toward linguistic nationalism. However, even if its effects may be mixed, there can be no doubt that in most societies, linguistic nationalism provides an important counterbalance to the prestige of foreign culture and vocabulary.

The two socially based notions of prestige and linguistic nationalism, thus, are the most important factors that determine the manner in which foreign words are integrated into the lexicon of the borrowing language. In English, to be sure, foreign prestige or domestic linguistic nationalism play a subordinate role, as compared to the notion that adoptions enrich the language. But like prestige and linguistic nationalism, the notion of enrichment is based on social attitude, not on linguistic structure.

Before concluding this section, it may be appropriate to mention that linguistic nationalism can take rather unexpected forms. For instance, during Japan's highly nationalistic phase, prior to its defeat in 1945, the speakers of Japanese strongly resisted the adoption of foreign words. Instead, they preferred adaptations. But these generally were made not in terms of native Japanese vocabulary, but by means of words of Chinese origin. In fact, many of the Modern Chinese adaptations of foreign words, such as *dian hua*, were created in Japan and spread from there to China.

The Chinese words had been adopted in the first millennium A.D., partly because the Japanese adopted Buddhism from China. Chinese, thus, had acquired in Japan a very similar role to that of the classical European languages, Latin and Greek, in much of Europe. As a consequence, its vocabulary could be regarded as indigenous and East Asian and thus much more congenial to the Japanese language than adoptions from western languages.

We find a similar situation in Modern Indonesian, which draws heavily on Sanskrit lexical resources to adapt foreign words and concepts. Here Sanskrit had been the source for a large number of earlier borrowings and thereby acquired the role of an indigenous, Asian prestige language whose vocabulary can be drawn on to indigenize foreign western words and concepts.

Understandably, Sanskrit, as the language of traditional Indian culture and civilizations, plays a very similar role in most of the modern languages of the Republic of India, both Indo-Aryan and Dravidian. Compare for instance the Sanskrit-based Hindi adaptations from English in (27). As in Icelandic, some of the adaptations are straightforward calques (27a). Others are recreated from Sanskrit elements, only partly influenced by the structure of the English model. Thus in (27b), the first element of *viśvavidyālay(a)* echoes the *univers-* of Engl. *university*, but the rest combines Sanskrit elements into a compound 'knowledge-abode' = 'school'. Similarly, in (27c), the *pro-* of Engl. *professor* is calqued by its cognate *pra-*, to which then is added one of the Sanskrit words for 'teacher', *adhyāpaka*.

(27)	Hindi	English model	Sanskrit elements
a.	*prag(a)ti*	*progress*	*pra-* 'forward' + *gati-* 'going' (= Engl. *-gress* from Lat. *gradior* 'step, walk')
	prasār(a)	*promotion*	*pra-* 'forward' + *sār(a)* 'causing to move'

lalit(a)kalā	*fine arts*	*lalita-* 'lovely, charming' = 'fine' + *kalā* 'art'
b. *viśvavidyālay(a)*	*university*	*viśva-* 'all, universal' + *vidyā-* 'knowledge' + *ālaya-* 'abode, place'
bhāṣāvijñān(a)	*linguistics*	*bhāṣā-* 'language' + *vijñāna-* 'knowledge, science'
c. *prādhyāpak(a)*	*professor*	*pra-* 'forward, in front' + *adhyāpaka* 'teacher'

Although such adaptations are Sanskrit in form, semantically they are eminently English. For instance, Hindi uses the terms *ārambh(a)-* or *samāroh(a)-* in the meaning 'festive occasion'. In terms of the Sanskrit elements of which these words are composed, one would expect meanings such as 'beginning'; and these are in fact attested for these words in traditional Sanskrit. The meaning 'festive occasion' could only have arisen via the English semantics of *commencement* which can mean both 'beginning' and 'festive occasion (especially at a university)'. The pervasive influence of English semantics can be noticed even in extended uses of Sanskrit-based adaptations. For instance, the term *pragati* in (27a) is beginning to be used not only to designate the idea and ideology of 'progress' in an abstract sense, but also the use of *progress* in expressions like *work in progress*, which is calqued as *kām pragati mẽ* – much to the chagrin of purists who consider such usage to be excessively influenced by English.

Two Indian languages resist adaptations by means of Sanskrit elements – Urdu and Tamil. As an Islamic counterpart of Hindi (see Chapter 2, § 3.10.2), intent on maintaining its distinctiveness vis-à-vis Hindi, Urdu draws on Arabic and Persian sources to create counterparts for English terminology, such as *lisaniyat* 'linguistics' (from Arab. *lisan* 'tongue, language' + a derivative suffix *-iyat*) and *funūn ē latīfā* 'liberal arts' or 'fine arts' (where *funūn* = plural of Arab. *fan* 'activity', *ē* = a Persian linking element, and *latīf(ā)* = 'good, fine').

Although Tamil has borrowed heavily from Sanskrit in the past (e.g. words like *āsiriyaṉ* 'teacher' ⇐ Skt. *ācarya*), it now prefers to draw on its own resources for adapting foreign terminology, including the Sanskrit-derived terminology of other Indian languages. Thus, for *viśvavidyālay(a)* 'university' Tamil uses the word *palkalaikkaṛakam*, composed of *pal* 'various' ≈ *viśva* 'all, universal', *kalai* 'art' ≈ *vidyā* 'knowledge, science', and *kaṛakam* 'assembly' ≈ *ālay(a)* 'abode'. And as a counterpart to *prādhyāpak(a)* 'professor' it offers *pērāsiriyaṉ* = *pēr* 'great' + *āsiriyaṉ* 'teacher' = *adhyāpak(a)*.

These "Tamilizations" of Sanskrit-based terminology are motivated by a more regionally defined form of linguistic nationalism – the widespread feeling that Indo-Aryan political and cultural domination, whether by Modern Hindi or by Sanskrit – has been excessive and has threatened the separate, Dravidian identity of the Tamil people. (Ironically, some of the Tamilizations contain early borrowings from Sanskrit, such as the *āsiriyan* of the word for 'professor'. Evidently, linguistic change has made these words sufficiently different from their Sanskrit sources to escape detection.)

6. The effects of borrowing

As we have seen in the preceding section, English has a strong tendency to adopt foreign vocabulary, usually restricting adaptation to phonology. In fact, since the time of the Renaissance, English writers and scholars generally have claimed that lexical adoptions lead to an enrichment of English vocabulary.

The extent of this enrichment may be gauged from the fact that between sixty-five and seventy-five percent of present-day English vocabulary is of foreign origin. Much of that vocabulary comes from Romance. In most cases of Romance borrowings, the source is French; see (28a). Less commonly, other Romance languages, especially Spanish and Italian, are the donor languages, as in (28b). In addition, of course, there is an abundance of borrowings from Graeco-Latin sources. But the phonetic shape of these borrowings usually is closer to French than to either Greek or Latin; see (28c). In some cases, this is because the word was borrowed via French. This may be the case for *nation*. In others, the reason is that the English word has been assembled from elements received via French, as in *intercontinental*. (See § 1 on this matter.) In yet others, the word may have been similarly assembled in French, such as in the case of *hydrogen*. Note further that in some cases, English words may owe their phonological shape to etymological nativization (see § 3) based on the phonetic correspondence between earlier borrowings from French and their English equivalents, such as Fr. *nation* [nasyɔ̃] : Engl. *nation* [neyšn̩]; this is no doubt the case for *negation*.

(28)   a. *place, receive, rouge, veal*
          b. *plaza* (from Spanish)
               piazza (from Italian)

    c. *nation* (Lat. *natiō, -ōnis*, Fr. *nation*)
      intercontinental (Fr. *inter-* 'between', *continental* 'continental';
      compare Lat. *inter-* and *continentālis*)
      hydrogen (Fr. *hydrogène*; compare Gk. *hudro-* 'water' + *genēs*
      'engendering')
      carbon (Lat. *carbō, -ōnis*, Fr. *carbone*)
      negation (Lat. *negatiō, -ōnis*)

The effect of these borrowings is especially striking in technical prose, where English and French (and other Romance languages) show a great degree of terminological similarity, whereas German, with its adapted *Wasserstoff* 'hydrogen' (lit. 'water matter'), *Kohlenstoff* 'carbon' (lit. 'coal matter'), etc., appears to be quite different and "Teutonic". Many popular writers on English therefore claim that English now really is a Romance, not a Germanic language.

    Historical linguists have difficulties with such claims. First, although more than sixty percent of the total vocabulary may be of foreign, largely Romance origin (especially if Latin is included under the definition Romance), much of that borrowed vocabulary is restricted to certain, highly technical or specialized, spheres of usage. Compare the examples in (29).

(29)   *quadrant*
        quadrivium
        questionnaire
        quincunx
        quodlibet

On the other hand, in basic vocabulary, cognates are much easier to find between English and German than between, say, English and French; see (30a). The similarities between English and German become especially striking if we look at the morphology of basic vocabulary, such as the principal parts of irregular verbs, as in (30b). Clearly, then, in this most basic, most indispensable, and most frequently used part of its vocabulary, English looks very much like a "Teutonic" language, not like Romance. Even where English and German do not agree (as in *sky* : *Himmel*), English does not show any closer agreement with French (*ciel*).

(30) a. English French   German

English	French	German
I	*je*	*ich*
you	*tu/vous*	*du/ihr/Sie*
he	*il*	*er*
she	*elle*	*sie*
it	*il*	*es*
do	*faire*	*tun*
be	*être*	*sein*
eat	*manger*	*essen*
drink	*boire*	*trinken*
earth	*terre*	*Erde*
sky	*ciel*	*Himmel*
and	*et*	*und*
to	*à*	*zu*
of	*de*	*von*

   b. English *drink* (pres.), *drank* (past), *drunk* (past pple.)
       German *trinken* (pres.), *trank* (past), *getrunken* (past pple.)
  vs. French *boire* (pres.), *buvais* (imperf.), *bus* (passé défini),
       boirai (fut.), *bu* (past pple.)

More than that, the so-called Romance component of English comes from
different, distinct Romance languages. For instance, the *place* of (29a) above,
and the *plaza* and *piazza* of (29b) all go back to Latin *platēa* 'wide street',
which itself was borrowed from Greek *plateîa (hodós)* 'wide street'. But
place shows developments peculiar to French, *plaza* to Spanish, and *piazza*
to Italian. There are many similar sets of multiple borrowings, made at very
different periods and from different sources, but coexisting in modern English; see (31).

(31) a. Modern English forms derived from Latin *discus* 'quoit, disk'
          (⇐ Gk. *dískos*)

	SOURCE
dais	< ME *deis* ⇐ Fr. *deis* < Lat. *discus*
desk	⇐ Mediev. Lat. *desca* ⇐ Ital. *desco* < Lat. *discus*
dish	< OE *disc* < West Germanic **diskaz* ⇐ Lat. *discus*
disk/disc	⇐ Fr. *disque* ⇐ Lat. *discus*
discus	⇐ Lat. *discus*

b. Modern English forms derived from the word for 'brother' in various languages

SOURCE

fraternal, fraternity ⇐ Lat. *fråter* 'brother' (and derivatives)

Fra ⇐ Ital. *fra* 'brother; designation of a friar' < Lat. *fråter*

friar ⇐ OFr. *frere* 'brother' < Lat. *fråter*

phratry ⇐ Gk. *phratría/phrátra* 'a clan group' (consisting of 'brothers' or 'brethren' in the extended sense)

pal ⇐ Romani *p(h)al, phral* 'brother; buddy' < Skt. *bhråtar-*)

Examples like (28a,b) or (31a) show that the "Romance" component of English is a more or less accidental amalgam from different Romance languages.

Moreover, while the majority of Romance borrowings are French or Latin in character, they have entered English at various times, with very different subsequent developments within English. In addition to the examples in (30a), compare Engl. *petty* vs. *petite*, both borrowings from Fr. *petit* (m.), *petite* (f.) 'small', but adopted at different times. While the more recently borrowed *petite* is phonetically quite close to its French counterpart, *petty*, borrowed in the medieval period, has an accentuation which is more fully nativized. Consider also correspondences like Engl. *chant* with [č-] vs. Fr. *chant* with [š-]. Here English preserves the initial [č-] of Old French, while Modern French [š-] is the result of a later French sound change. That is, English cannot be identified with any single chronological layer of Romance.

Finally, with a few exceptions (such as *rouge*), the borrowings from Romance (and other languages) have been completely nativized in their phonology and thus have ceased to be French, Italian, or Spanish, but have become English. As a consequence of having become nativized, they have undergone subsequent changes that are peculiar to English and may alter the pronunciation of the words considerably, sometimes beyond recognition. Compare the borrowings from French in (32).

(32)   Modern English   Modern French
measure [mɛžə(r)]   *mesure* [məzüʀ]
beef [bīf]   *bœuf* [bɔ̈f]
curfew [kərfyū]   *couvre-feu* [kuvʀ(ə)fö]

The case is very similar for Swedish (with some sixty-five to seventy-five percent of its vocabulary of foreign, much of it Low German, origin) and even for Albanian, with about ninety percent of its lexicon of foreign provenience, coming from Greek, Latin, Slavic, and many other sources. In both cases the basic structure and vocabulary are distinctly native. And as in English, the overall structure of the language, including its lexicon, cannot be identified with any of the source languages for the borrowings, or with any particular chronological stage of these languages.

In summary, then, it appears that lexical borrowing, even on a massive scale, is highly unlikely to lead to a change in the genetic affiliation of a given language. (For certain complications see Chapter 12, § 3.) On the other hand, the adoption of borrowings may be conceived of as enriching the lexicon of a given language. As we have seen, this belief is most widespread in English and probably accounts for the fact that unlike most other languages, English almost voraciously adopts foreign words.

Even in this respect, however, it is advisable to exercise caution. Languages that adapt foreign words by means of calquing (as in Germ. *Wasserstoff* lit. 'water matter' ≈ Fr. *hydrogène* 'water engendering/matter') expand their vocabulary just as much as languages that adopt (such as Engl. *hydrogen*).

There is, however, one form of adaptation that does not enrich the lexicon, namely adaptation through loan shift. By definition, loan shifts simply redefine the meanings of existing lexical items, without adding new words. Moreover, the result of loan shifting is an increase in polysemy, which potentially can lead to ambiguities. Consider the case of Germ. *Papier* discussed in § 4 above. The increase in the semantic range of this word from '(sheet of) paper' to '(sheet of) paper; journal article, presentation at a professional meeting' increases the possibility of misunderstanding such sentences as *Ich kann mein Papier nicht finden* 'I can't find my paper' (is it a sheet of paper or a journal article?), which can be avoided by the old-fashioned distinction between *Papier* '(sheet of) paper' and *Aufsatz* 'article'. The situation is even worse for the plural use, *Ich kann meine Papiere nicht finden*, since *Papiere* (plur.) has the additional, specialized meaning 'documents'.

As an alternative to loan shifts, therefore, borrowing by adoption can be justifiably argued to enrich the language, by conveying the new meaning without any ambiguity. In English, for instance, the German borrowing *angst* manages to more clearly indicate the intended psychoanalytical connotations than *anxiety* or *fear*.

Even in other respects, adoption may enrich a language. For one thing, many loans are not need-based, but prestige borrowings that introduce novel

linguistic forms for already existing linguistic concepts and their corresponding native forms. Thus when English borrowed from French the adjective
royal, it already had its own indigenous adjectival formation corresponding
to *king*; namely NE *kingly*. The new term *royal* then came to compete with
the inherited form. And as noted in § 5.5 of Chapter 7, such a competition
usually is resolved through semantic specialization. In the present case, therefore, *royal* became the normal adjective corresponding to *king*, while *kingly*
survived in more specialized functions.

A less obvious enriching effect of adopted borrowings is that in many
cases they bring with themselves their own, novel morphological inventory
and rules for the combination of morphological elements. This is of obvious
benefit in the area of word COINAGE, the creation of new linguistic terms to express novel concepts. One obvious benefit, noted already in § 1, is that the borrowed morphology provides an increase in the morphological elements and
rules which form the basis for coining new words. This can be especially important for a language like English, in which the ability of native derivational
morphology to create complex new structures is fairly limited. For instance,
native English morphology rarely goes beyond structures like *like-li-hood*
or *own-er-ship*. The morphology abstracted from Latin and Greek sources,
on the other hand, permits the creation of complex derivations such as *dis-*
establish → *dis-establish-ment* → *dis-establish-ment-ary* → *dis-establish-*
ment-ari-an → *dis-establish-ment-ari-an-ism* or *dis-establish-ment-ari-an-ist*
→ *dis-establish-ment-ari-an-ist-ic* → *dis-establish-ment-ari-an-ist-ic-al* →
dis-establish-ment-ari-an-ist-ic-al-ly.

Additionally, the borrowed morphology frequently signals that the new
word is a technical term, not just an ordinary, everyday word. This is clearly
the case for such sesquipedalianisms as *dis-establish-ment-ari-an-ist-ic-al-*
ly, or the word *sesquipedalianism* for that matter. But it affects many other
spheres of the vocabulary as well. Consider for instance the case of *auto-*
mobile. The word was created from the elements *auto-* 'self' and *mobile*
'moving', extracted from borrowings from Greek and Latin, respectively.
The novel combination of these elements into *automobile*, then, signaled the
technical nature of the resulting word much more clearly than would have
Engl. *self-moving* or Fr. *mouvant par soi*. Nevertheless, some technical terms
in English do not use borrowed morphology, but are quite mundane Anglo-
Saxon collocations; compare for instance *black hole* in astrophysics. (The
issue of coinage is discussed in fuller detail in the next chapter.)

In fact, perhaps the most important and overriding effect of large-scale
adoptive borrowing on English is the creation of a clearly marked formal distinction between an educated/technological variety and other, more everyday

varieties of the language. As can be seen from epithets like "sesquipedalian" or "high-falutin" for the technological vocabulary, this distinction is very clear to native speakers, no matter whether they are educated or not.

However, the special connotations just observed are limited to the vocabulary that is more clearly of Latin and Greek origin. Contrast the difference in connotations between expressions like *automotive, capability, antidisestablishmentarianism* on one hand and *target practice, royal pain, enterprise* on the other. Technically, both sets of words are borrowings; but only the first set has special technological or educated, if not pedantic, connotations.

There is reason to believe that the special connotations are directly attributable to the fact that the words are borrowed from Greek and Latin, scholarly prestige languages in which many of the words had already been used with special scholarly or technical connotations. The connotations of Graeco-Latin borrowings therefore are exactly what one would expect.

In addition, recall that in languages like German it is adaptations like *Fernsprecher* and *Rundfunk* which often have special technical or officialese connotations, while adoptions like *Telephon* and *Radio* belong to the ordinary, non-technical layer of the language. Facts like these suggest that in many cases it is more the sphere of usage than the origin of a particular lexical item which determines its special connotations. Note in this regard that even in English, Anglo-Saxon collocations like *black hole* have very special connotations if used in astrophysics, and so do terms like *borrowing*, when employed in historical linguistics.

Finally, recall that many of the Graeco-Latin technical borrowings in English are restricted to very specialized uses. Compare words like *thermion*, *thigmotaxis*, and *thimerosal* in Chapter 7, § 1.

The common belief of English speakers that the adoption of vocabulary is desirable, in that it "enriches the language", thus, is difficult to justify on purely linguistic grounds. But ultimately that may not be relevant. As in many other cases we must remember that most speakers are not linguists. They are consequently free to ignore what makes sense to linguists and instead to act according to their own beliefs, however naive these may appear to linguists. If, then, most English speakers are persuaded that enlarging their vocabulary is a good thing, they can be expected to behave accordingly and to adopt foreign words at a rate that far exceeds that of other languages. Moreover, although the outward manifestations are quite different, the English thirst for borrowings ultimately is remarkably similar to the linguistic nationalism of other languages. Linguistic nationalism, after all, is just as much based on irrational beliefs, not on purely linguistic or structural facts.

Chapter 9
Lexical change and etymology: The study of words

Good words are worth very much, and cost little.
(George Herbert, *Jacula prudentum.*)

What do you read, my lord?
Words, words, words.
(William Shakespeare, *Hamlet* II. 191–2)

1. Introduction

The preceding chapters have emphasized the processes of change, detailing the various forces that can bring about change in different domains of a language. We have presented the types of change in terms of the different components of grammar (phonology, morphology, syntax, semantics). Yet there is at least one factor that goes beyond these different grammatical components and thereby unifies these changes: All can have a profound effect on all the numerous and varied elements that together make up a language's lexicon.

A very basic, almost trivial, type of lexical change comes about through regular sound change. When sound change affects a sound or class of sounds, clearly the pronunciation of lexical items containing those sounds will undergo a change. For instance, when the Latin word for 'father', *pater* [pater], became French *père* [pɛr] as the result of regular vowel changes and the regular loss of intervocalic *t*, the lexical item for 'father' changed.

Analogical change can likewise bring about lexical change. For instance, the leveling of the sibilant : [r] alternation in OE *cēosan* [čēozan] : *cēas* [čēas] : *curon* : *(ge)-coren* in favor of *-s-* [z], ultimately yielding Mod. Engl. *choose : chose : chosen* (Chapter 5, § 2.1), may be said to have produced a change in this lexical item, in that its morphophonemic behavior was altered.

More interesting are developments involving rhyming formation and related processes discussed in Chapter 5, § 3.1, for these may introduce new words to the language. Consider for instance the English words in (1). All of these end in *-ag*, and all have something to do with 'slow, tired, or tedious action'. But as noted in Chapter 5, the morphological composition of such forms is difficult to determine. If, for instance, we were to say that the meaning 'slow, tired, or tedious action' is associated with *-ag*, what then would be the meaning of *dr-, f-, fl-, l-,* or *s-*?

(1)   a. *drag* 'lag behind' < ME *draggen* < OE *dragan* or ON *draga* 'drag, pull'

         b. *fag* 'exhaust, weary, grow weary', presumably < ME *fagge* 'droop'

         c. *flag* 'hang limply; droop', probably of Scandinavian origin, from a word akin to Old Norse *flögra* 'flap about'

         d. *lag* 'fail to keep up; straggle' < earlier English *lag* 'last person', ME *lag-* 'last', possibly from Scandinavian

         e. *sag* 'sink; droop' < sixteenth century Engl. *sacke*, ultimately probably of Scandinavian origin, compare Swed. *sacka* '(to) sink'.

The words in (1a–d) do in fact go back to earlier forms which already contained *-ag*; so for these we might claim that the phonetic similarity does not result from change, but is simply accidental. However, the matter is not so simple if we look at the semantics. Only two items had earlier meanings compatible with 'slow, tired, or tedious action', namely (1b) and (1d). Semantically, then, all the listed words have undergone a change which has brought them closer together. And this fact suggests that the relationship is not entirely accidental. The smoking gun (if we can use that term for words meaning 'slow, tired, or tedious action'), which virtually proves that the similarity is not due to chance, is seen in (1e), a word whose final consonant has actually changed from [k] to [g]. Other words ending in [k], such as *sack* 'bag', *lack, crack* have not undergone the change; the development in (1e) therefore cannot be the result of regular sound change. The only explanation of the final voiced *-g* of *sag*, then, is that it came to be associated with the *drag/fag/flag/lag* "gang of four" because of its meaning.

Thus an irregular, analogical change (sometimes referred to by the fancy term "phonesthematic attraction"), led to a change in a lexical item, and to the strengthening in semantic coherence of a whole cluster of related lexical items.

These examples of lexical effects of various changes have started with well-understood items whose history is easily documented. But there are vast numbers of other words whose history we are uncertain of. What is the source of *t-shirt*, for instance? Is it so named because it is shaped like the letter *t*, or like a golf tee, or is it an abbreviation for *t(ennis)-shirt*? What about the incredibly common English lexical item *OK* (also spelled *O.K.* and *okay*), which has spread practically all around the world? Scholars have long been divided on the source of *OK*. Some consider it an acronymic abbreviation for *Old Kinderhook* (a nickname of 1840 U.S. presidential candidate Martin Van Buren); others see it as shortened from a jocular spelling "*oll korrect*", supposedly popular in the 1840 election; and still others treat it as an Africanism that entered American English through contact with the usage of African slaves in the South (see § 4.4 below for words that can be more clearly derived in this manner).

The study of the origin of words is known as ETYMOLOGY. The first part of this word comes from Greek *étymon* 'true sense of a word', so that etymology is the study of the true, i.e. original, forms of words. In a larger sense, etymology is concerned with the history of words, how they arise, the factors that have affected their ultimate shape and meaning, the semantic paths they have taken in their development though time, and so on. Moreover, once one starts exploring word origins, the question arises, too, as to where various phrases and expressions – idiomatic groups of words – come from. Why, for instance, do we say *madder than a wet hen, rarer than hen's teeth, raining cats and dogs*, or *on a wild goose chase*, to take just a few animal-related expressions?

Etymology is fascinating in its own right, and clearly has great popular appeal, as the large number of books on word and phrase origins indicates. And many etymologies – or facts showing the absence of an etymological connection among words – do make for interesting trivia. For instance, although this may be hard to believe, the term *canary* ultimately derives from Lat. *canis* 'dog'. The birds known as *canaries* bear their names because they originally came from the *Canary Islands*. These islands, in turn, were named in Latin after the large *canes* (pl.) 'dogs' found there. On the other hand, there is no etymological relationship between *canary* and the French word *canard* 'duck', even though one might at first glance be led to think of such a connection; once you have *canary* and *canard, can-* in bird names seems like a logical morphological division to start with ("birds of a feather ..."). Actually, though, the *can-* of *canard* apparently is a syllable that onomatopoetically reflects the duck's quack, and thus is unrelated to *canary* – even though it is conceivable that for speakers of French, in which the word for *canary* is *canari*, a folk etymological connection (see Chapter 5, § 3.2) between *canari* and *canard* might seem right. (In English, *canard* was borrowed only in the extended, metaphorical meaning 'hoax' → 'malicious story', or as a specialized term in aeronautical jargon, referring to a particular type of plane or its distinctive control and stabilizing surfaces.)

Far from being just a matter for trivial pursuits, etymology is in a real sense the basis of historical linguistics, for establishing the origin of a word is crucial to understanding the changes it has undergone and the factors that have influenced its development. Without a well-worked-out account of how *bead* could shift in meaning from an abstract meaning 'prayer' to a very concrete meaning 'small roundish glass or ceramic object' (through the use of rosary beads for counting prayers, see Chapter 3, § 2.2), we could not really establish its etymology, nor could we be sure about the effects of sound changes such as Grimm's Law in Germanic without first positing etymologies for various lexical items that connect them with cognate words in other languages (e.g. *father* as being from the same source as Latin *pater*, or *ten* from the same source as Greek *déka*). Thus, once a good many well-established cases are examined, working out the general principles that govern language change can be undertaken. And it all starts with etymology.

Most of the changes discussed so far in a sense do nothing to alter the basic inventory of lexical items. Whether 'father' is pronounced [pater] or [pɛr], whether the past participle of 'choose' has an -*r*- or a -*z*-, or whether we say *sag* or *sack* to convey the meaning 'sink, droop', there is still a single form linked to a given meaning, and thus no net gain in the number of lexical entries.

Other types of change, as we have seen in the chapters on semantic change and borrowing, can significantly affect the lexical inventory of languages. In this sense, then, etymology is also the study of the sources of words, of the word-formative resources that languages have, and of how speakers use these resources. And the study of etymology necessarily involves us in a study of lexical change, how words rise and fall through time.

For instance, borrowing almost invariably adds to the vocabulary, even in cases of calquing. The only exception is represented by loan shifts, which broaden the meaning of existing words but ordinarily do not introduce new ones. Occasionally, even loan shifts can enrich the lexicon. Consider the case of Modern Icelandic *síma* 'telecommunication', used to translate Engl. *wire, cable = telegram*. In this case, the loan shift was accomplished, not by expanding the meaning of a word already in Modern Icelandic use, but through resurrecting an obsolete Old Icelandic word of somewhat obscure signification which, however, from context could be guessed at as meaning something like 'cable' or 'rope'.

Conversely, cultural and social changes may lead to obsolescence, the loss of words, sometimes on an equally impressive scale. When Horatio tells

Hamlet (Act I.230) that he did not see the face of Hamlet's father's ghost because *he wore his beaver up*, we need a textual note or a dictionary to tell us that a *beaver* is a term for the visor on a helmet. If more of us wore suits of armor, this meaning would be more commonly known. Consider also what happened to terminology such as *snaffle* and *thill* (see Chapter 7) when the horse and buggy were replaced by automobiles.

The social, cultural, and technological factors that lead to the obsolescence of words at the same time may also necessitate the development or COINAGE of a great deal of new vocabulary, not necessarily through borrowing. This phenomenon is evident in the lexical explosion occasioned by the introduction of the internal combustion engine or, more recently, the advent of the computer.

In the sections that follow, we will examine a number of processes by which the lexical store of a language can be enriched, by considering the etymology of new lexical items and expressions.

2. Coinage

In the preceding chapter we have seen many examples of borrowing of technical terms, whether by adoption or by adaptation (calquing). Compare sets like the one in (2) – perfect examples of the fact that speakers tend to borrow the words which go along with the new artifacts or ideas that they adopt.

(2)	English	French	Spanish	Mod. Greek
	telephone	*téléphone*	*teléfono*	*tiléfono*

German	Icelandic	Hindi
Telephon	*tal-síma*	*(ṭēli)fōn*
Fernsprecher		*dūr-bhāš*

What we have not examined is the question of how the language in which the artifact or idea first originated acquired the new term to designate it. Clearly, that language cannot resort to borrowing, but must create the term from its own resources. In the case of *telephone*, this was accomplished by combining the elements *tele-* 'far' and *phone* 'speech, voice; speak' which had entered English through earlier borrowings from Greek (via Latin). In principle, this is not different from the process that gives rise to the German alternative word, *Fernsprecher* = *fern* 'far' + *sprecher* 'speaker', or the similar Hindi *dūr-bhāš* = *dūr* 'far' + *bhāš* 'speech, voice'. But while the German and Hindi words are re-creations, modeled on the English form, the English word was an original creation, a new COINAGE.

In the case of *telephone*, the new word came about by combining the elements *tele* and *phone* in a productive morphological pattern through something like four-part analogy; compare similar formations such as *tele-scope*, *tele-graph*, or *micro-phone*. The same process is responsible for many other NEOLOGISMS. The word *neologism* itself is a neologistic coinage from the Greek elements *neo-* 'new' and *log-* 'word' that had previously entered English, and thus literally means something like 'new word'.

Other neologisms include *hard disk, dark matter,* and *black hole.* Compared to words like *telephone*, these expressions are much more mundane, in that they do not significantly draw on the Graeco-Latin morphological elements that might be considered typical of technical terminology (see Chapter 8, § 5). But that does not diminish their being new coinages, on a par with more technical-sounding ones like *disk operation system* or *magnetic resonance imaging.*

In addition to four-part analogy, two other analogical processes frequently are used for creating neologisms: blending (as in *brunch* or *Amerindian*) and backformation (as in *orientate* or *drug-deal*). Compare the discussion in Chapter 5 and see also below. (Folk etymology and recomposition, too, may introduce new lexical items. But these two processes are not commonly employed for consciously coining new words.)

Coinage may be accomplished by a large variety of other changes. In some cases, something akin to loan shifting is involved, namely a simple semantic extension. This has been the case for instance when horse-and-buggy terms like *wheel* and *tire* came to be used in reference to automobile parts. Many slang terms involve extension (see § 4 below), often utilizing the "part-for-the-whole" strategy of synecdoche (see Chapter 7, § 5.1), as with *wheels* as a term for *car, skirt* for *woman,* and *suit* for *businessman, lawyer,* or *administrator* (i.e., someone forced to wear a suit to work). And just as in some cases loan shifts may be accomplished by resurrecting obsolete words of somewhat obscure meaning (see Icel. *síma* above), so neologisms sometimes are created by adopting a word of obscure significance.

This has been the case for the word *quark*, used in physics to designate a set of elementary particles. The word has been adopted from an enigmatic passage in James Joyce's *Finnegan's Wake: Three quarks for Muster Mark!* (The whimsicality that led to selecting this word is carried further with the attributes by which different kinds of *quarks* are distinguished – *top, bottom, strange, charmed, up,* and *down.*)

The processes of coinage are seen quite vividly in the names given to new products. *Kleenex* is clearly built on *clean, Jell-O* on the verb *jell* or the noun *jelly*, and *Xerox* on the Greek *xero-* for 'dry'. But the source of the final parts (*-ex, -O,-ox*) is not entirely clear. Perhaps they represent extensions from similar pieces in other words (such as the *-o* suffix in a word like *kiddo*). Many of these well-known product names have spread into general usage, as a generic term for the type of product they refer to, e.g. *kleenex* for any type of facial tissue, *jello* for any type of flavored gelatin dessert, *xerox* for any type of xerographic reproduction. Despite strenuous objections of the manufacturers, who have paid huge sums of money to some advertising team to think up the name for their product, such developments are difficult to prevent; they are paralleled by many other, similar extensions in sphere of usage. (See many of the examples in the discussion below.)

Coinage can also involve raw creation, sometimes for the sound or even visual effect alone. For instance, the product name *Kodak* is said to have been created because the letter < k > is somewhat rare in the spelling of English words, and thus a word with an initial and a final < k > would make a striking – and thus presumably lasting – visual impression. Similarly *Kleenex* with an initial < K- > and a medial < ee > has its own distinctive look visually, and the initial and final < x > in *Xerox* is eye-catching too. Thus the final parts of these product names may simply represent visually motivated creative word invention.

More usually, perhaps, a striking sound impression is involved in such raw creations. The word *googol* for 'the number 10 raised to the power 100' was created out of the blue by Milton Sirotta, the nine-year-old nephew of the American mathematician Edward Kasner in the mid-twentieth century, apparently because it sounded good! Note also that once *googol* was part of the language, it was easy to create the word *googolplex*, for 'the number 10 raised to the power googol', as a BLEND of *googol* and the *-plex* of words like *duplex*.

Many so-called NURSERY WORDS in virtually all languages involve creations that are commonly believed to have an "appropriate" sound structure, e.g. Engl. *Momma, Papa, Daddy, Nanny*, even nicknames like *Bubba* or *Sis(sie)*; Goth. *Atta* 'father' (from which the name *Attila* was derived), *aiþei* 'mother'; It. *papà, mamma, bambino* 'child'; Turkish *baba* 'father', *ana/anne* 'mother'; Hindi *bāp, mã̄, baččā* 'child'; Georgian *deda* 'mommy', *mama* 'father'; and so on. The structure, sounds, and often also the connotations of these words suggest that they come from "baby talk", i.e., the words and meanings which adults assign to the early babbling of infants (see Chapter 14, § 1). Like other items that occur in this kind of language, the words tend to have reduplicated syllables (as in *pa-pa*). And the predominance of the vowel *a* and of the relatively unmarked consonants *p/b, t/d, m,* and *n* in these words is a common feature of early babbling. In a sense, then, these words represent a type of borrowing. Note further that despite modern American and European sensibilities as to what is "appropriate" sound structure in these words, there is nothing universal about the attachment of particular meanings to particular combinations of sounds. Most of us might believe that words of the type *mama* must refer to 'mother', and *tata, dada* to 'father'; and in fact, one famous linguist has claimed universal validity for this generalization. But Georgian *deda* 'mommy', *mama* 'father' show that the generalization is not universally true.

Many other processes can be drawn on to coin new words. Consider for instance the word *car* in the meaning 'automobile'. At first glance we might be tempted to assume that it originated by the same semantic transfer as other automotive terms, such as *wheel* and *tire* above. But the common use of the term *motor car* in the early period of the automobile suggests that *car* instead results from ellipsis: Once *motor cars* had become the normal means of transportation, the element *motor* could be considered redundant and therefore was deleted.

Many modern words have originated in this fashion. Consider the examples in (3). Because of their derivations from place names and personal names, examples of the type (3a) and (3b) are often singled out for special treatment, as TOPONYMS (3a) and EPONYMS (3b), respectively. In some cases, such developments can take strange turns, as the earlier discussion of *canary* indicates. Moreover, as (3c) illustrates, words that have arisen via ellipsis, such as the *jeans* and *canary* of (3a), may enter new compounds which may be subjected to another round of ellipsis (recall how *googol*, once coined, could spawn *googolplex*).

(3)   Modern English Source
    a. *damask*   *Damask cloth* (= cloth from Damascus)
       (blue) jeans   *Gene* (= Genoa) *cloth*
       denim   Fr. *serge de Nîmes* = cloth from Nimes
       canary   a bird from the Canary Islands
    b. *bowler*   *Bowler hat* (after a famous hat maker)
       hansom   *Hansom car* (after a famous carriage maker)
    c. *jeans*   *blue jeans*
       canary   *canary yellow* (after the coloring of canaries)
       gum   *chewing gum*

However, the terms toponym and eponym cover much wider territory, referring not only to the results of ellipsis, but also to other secondary uses of place or personal names, mainly by way of metaphoric extension, as in (4). Thus, a *maverick* is somebody who is like the rancher Maverick in not going along with prevailing behavior. An even bolder extension of personal names can be seen in the nomenclature for measurements prevalent in physics, such as *ohm, newton,* and *volt,* all named after famous physicists of the past. (The relationship between *volt* and the physicist's name *Volta* seems to involve some kind of phonological abbreviation, similar to *lab* for *laboratory,* for which see below.) A very different secondary use of names is found in the selected use of personal names, generally ones that are or once were quite common, in various colloquial or even slang expressions, in principle as a generic word for 'human being', 'man, male', 'woman, female', but often with humorous or nasty overtones; see the examples in (4b) and (4c). The use of *john* as a colloquial expression for 'toilet' probably owes its origin to such a development.

(4)   a. *maverick* name of a nineteenth-century Texas rancher who un-
                  like other ranchers did not brand his cattle

            dunce   John Duns Scotus, a philosopher whose followers
                  were opposed to the humanism of the Renaissance
                  and thus failed to grasp the significance of the new
                  movement

            maudlin   Mary Magdalene, who was iconographically portrayed
                  as weeping over the death of Jesus

       b. *jack-of-all-trades*
          jack-o'-lantern
          Billy Goat
          John Doe
          Jane Doe

       c. *Joe Blow*
          Johnny-come-lately
          jack-ass
          jenny(-ass)
          Plain Jane
          john (a customer of a prostitute)
          Dick, Peter (American English colloquial/slang/vulgar terms for
          the male organ; note also Brit. Engl. *Willy*)

Moreover, while examples of the type (3) can be accounted for as reflecting ellipsis, there are many other cases of lexical shortening for which such an explanation is much more difficult, or even out of the question. For instance, examples like (5a) can with some stretch of the imagination be considered elliptical, eliminating the "redundant" elements *show* or *filling*. But what about examples like (5b): Is the element *ham* here really redundant? If so, what is its meaning? Surely it is not 'ham'! Now, it is possible to argue that *cheese burger* is a blending of *cheese* and *hamburger*. But that explanation does not account for the similarities between (5a) and (5b). In both cases, a somewhat lengthy compound is made shorter, more manageable, through some kind of reduction. It is this reduction that seems to count most; and the method by which the reduction is accomplished is of much lesser significance. Reanalysis of words like *cheeseburger*, or backformation, in turn has given rise to the word *burger*. (Note that *hamburger* in origin is a toponym, going back to the German expression *Hamburger Rundstück* 'round piece of Hamburg', a round piece of meat prepared à la Hamburg, i.e., as it would be prepared in the city of Hamburg.)

(5)   a. *TV host*   *TV show host*
            gas station   *gas filling station*
         b. *cheeseburger* *cheese hamburger*
            tacoburger   *taco hamburger*

Some such shortenings can be quite extreme, and it is often difficult to figure out how their parts end up going together to make the new whole. For example, the *Columbus Dispatch* in the early 1980s reported on a dog owner who was repeatedly in violation of the law for some minor offense concerning the dog (e.g. not cleaning up after him) but routinely ignored the tickets that were issued, and thus acted like a scofflaw. The newspaper article referred to the dog as a *scoffdog*, apparently an extreme shortening for something like *scofflaw-owned dog*. Obviously, the dog was not the scoffer! Similarly, some grocery stores in Columbus have an aisle sign for *Baked Needs*, where the intent is 'items needed for (making) baked goods', and thus we see a shortening for (the somewhat clumsy) *Baked Goods Needs*, even though in the resulting shortening, it would seem that the *needs* are *baked*! Perhaps all that is needed is a vague associative reference to the words underlying the shortened form.

The view that the basic motivation for words like *gas station* and *cheeseburger* lies in a tendency toward ABBREVIATION is supported by a wide variety of other abbreviatory developments. Consider for instance the examples in (6). Cases of the type (6a) still bear a certain similarity to those in (5), in that the abbreviated version (such as *phone*) is a meaningful component of the longer version (*tele-phone*). But the shortened forms in (6b) cannot possibly be explained by some kind of morphological reduction. Reduction here operates entirely on PHONOLOGICAL principles, commonly by eliminating all but the accented syllable of the word, as in *fridge*, though accented syllables can also be eliminated, as in the slang forms in (6c) and the ordinary English word in (6d). The outcomes of this reduction of phonological material are commonly referred to as CLIPPINGS.

(6)   a. *phone   telephone*
             auto   automobile
        b. *mike   microphone*
             lab   laboratory
             fridge refrigerator
             frank   frankfurter (⇐ Germ. *Frankfurter Würstchen* 'little sausage à la Frankfurt')
        c. *'rents   parents*
             'za   pizza
        d. *bus   omnibus* (⇐ Lat. *omnibus* 'for all', where *-bus* is the dative plural ending)

In some cases, one and the same form may be subjected to clipping in more than one direction. For instance, *taxicab* (itself a shortening for *taximeter cabriolet*) has yielded both *taxi* and *cab* as clipped forms with the meaning 'taxicab'.

Even more daring reductions can be seen in the common use of ACRONYMS, such as *US = United States* or *MRI = Magnetic Resonance Imaging*. A special subtype of such acronyms arranges the basic words in such a way that the combination of their initial letters or sounds is a pronounceable word, as in *laser = Light Amplification by Stimulated Emission of Radiation* or *scuba = Self Contained Underwater Breathing Apparatus*. Noteworthy, too, are acronyms based on successive syllables of a single word, such as *TV = TeleVision* or *PJs = PaJamas*. Interestingly, abbreviations of the latter type are not significantly shorter in terms of their pronunciation; they are shorter only in spelling. (Some scholars reserve the name acronym for structures like *laser*, which are pronounced more like ordinary words, and use the term initialism to distinguish abbreviations of the type *US*, which are merely sequences of conventional letter names.)

In modern literate societies, acronyms generally operate in terms of the written medium. Moreover, in fully alphabetic writing systems, they usually select single initial letters. Examples of the type Germ. *Flak = FLugzeug-Abwehr-Kanone* 'aircraft-defense-cannon', operating with the initial consonant group of the first element of the compound, are much less common. In pre- or non-literate societies, acronyms seem to be more naturally based on initial (or final) syllables. Thus, in the oral tradition of indigenous Sanskrit grammar, going back to about the sixth century B.C., finite verbs can be referred to as *tiŋ*, based on the initial (*tip*) and final (*mahiŋ*) elements in an oral listing of finite-verb endings. And as the discussion in Chapter 3 has shown, syllabic acrophony of this type played a major role in the development of syllabaries.

3. Proper names: A case study in lexical origins

Proper names play a role in lexical change in providing a source for new ordinary (or "common") nouns, as in the cases of *maverick* or *john* discussed above. Yet where do proper names come from in the first place? Many, it turns out, come from a specialized use of common nouns, though there are other sources as well. As an extended case study in the processes by which words arise, we examine here the origins of various types of proper names and the occasional improper (so to speak) uses to which proper names are put.

3.1. Names of peoples and places

A good place to start is with names of groups – what are often termed "peoples", and by extension the names of the countries these peoples are located in.

All human peoples have names for themselves, as well as names for others, and often consciously distinguish themselves from other groups in terms of their names. Quite frequently, the group name is simply the word for 'people' or 'human being', in the language of the group – making an implicit contrast between "us", the group members = human beings, and "others", the nonmembers = nonhumans or nonpeople. This ideology underlies names of peoples all over the world, including Indigenous American names such as the *Illinois*, the *Lakota*, and the *Kiowa*; Uralic names, such as *Mari* (the Cheremis name for themselves), *Nenets* (the Yurak self-designation), *Komi* (the name of the Ziryenes for themselves), *Hanti* (the Ostyak self-label); the Munda ethnic name *Kurku*; and the Santal self-designation *Hoṛ*. The German self-label *Deutsch* looks like it belongs here, too, since its original meaning is 'of the people'. But in this case it is more likely that the term originated in the medieval period when Latin was the dominant language of education and when *diutisk > diutsk > deutsch* referred to the language of the people, in the sense of "vernacular language" (as distinguished from the Latin prestige language). A similar use is found for the Old English cognate of *diutisk, þeodisc.*

Related to the common self-definition as 'the (real) people' is a traditional tendency to draw a distinction between one's own group as speaking a real language and others as incapable of doing so. A well-known example is the Ancient Greek use of *bárbaros* (the source of Engl. *barbarian*) to refer to non-Greeks. To Greek ears, other languages sounded like an inarticulate stammering, *bar bar*. (The Latin adjective *balbus*, (roughly) cognate with Greek *bárbaros*, means 'stammering'.) A term *barbara-* with the same meaning is also found in Sanskrit, alongside a word *mlēččha-* which no doubt, too, is intended to characterize foreigners as only capable of producing ugly sounds. Interestingly, when the Romans conquered Greece they took over, along with Greek culture, the term *bárbaros* ⇒ *barbarus*, but because of their great respect for just about everything Greek, they could not use the word to refer to the Greeks. So from then on, the Romans considered everyone a barbarian, except themselves and the Greeks.

Very commonly, names given to familiar groups by others bear negative connotations similar to *bárbaros*. For instance, *Eskimo* has been traced (via Spanish and French) to Micmac *eskameege* 'raw fish eaters'. *Nemets*, the name for Germans among Slavic speakers, literally means 'mute, unable to speak a real human language', i.e. the language of the Slavs. (The name *Slav*, by contrast, may either be derived from *slovo* 'glory; word' or result from a folk-etymological connection with *slovo* after a dissimilatory change had altered original **svobēn-* 'one's own; our own [people, language]' to **slobēn-*.) Similarly, the word *Apache* derives from the Zuñi word for 'enemy', and *Comanche*, from the Ute word *kima* 'stranger'.

In some instances, the name of rulers has come to be used for the ruled people. Such was the case with the names for French and France, named after the Germanic Frankish peoples who conquered Gaul in the sixth century A.D. and built a powerful empire there for some 400 years.

In many of the above examples, the group's self-designation differs markedly from our conventional name for the same group. (Consider for instance *Nenets* vs. *Yurak*, or *Deutsch* vs. *Nemets*.) This conflict between self-designation and name assigned by others is a very widespread phenomenon. For instance, the Greeks nowadays refer to themselves as [élines], reflecting (via regular sound changes) an Ancient Greek name, *Héllēnes*, that was used originally (e.g. in the *Iliad*) for a group from Thessaly (in central Greece) and later extended (e.g. by the Ancient Greek historian Herodotos) to designate Greeks in general. Occasionally modern Greeks may also use the term [rómii], lit. 'Romans', reflecting the Byzantine heritage of Greece and the fact that Byzantium once was the Eastern Roman Empire. Nonetheless, speakers of English and most languages of Western Europe, refer to them as *Greeks* (or the equivalent thereof, e.g. French *grec*, Spanish *griego*), reflecting the term *Graeci* used by the Romans for all Greeks, though the Ancient Greek source, *Graikoí*, was originally applied properly just to one group, in the northwest part of Ancient Greece.

Similarly, Germans are referred to as *aleman*, lit. 'Alemannic', in French and Spanish, and as *Saxon* in the Carpathian area of Romania. In addition, of course, they are referred to as *German* in the English-speaking world and in countries originally dominated by England, such as India, where we find Hindi *ǰarman*. The original English word for 'German' was *Dutch*, based on Germ. *deutsch*, and was used in reference to the Germanic-speaking inhabitants of Germany at a time when that country included the Netherlands. But the *Dutch* that the English had the greatest contact with came from the Netherlands. After the Netherlands became independent in 1648 the English naturally used *Dutch* to refer to the inhabitants of that country – which left them without a name for the inhabitants of the remainder of Germany. In this situation they resorted to a word used by the Romans to refer to their northern, Germanic neighbors. But while this choice fixed the immediate problem, it turned out to cause difficulties for future students of historical linguistics who may find the terms *German* and *Germanic* to sound confusingly similar. (The Germans have no such problems, distinguishing *deutsch* from *germanisch*. The case is similar for all other nationalities that do not use the term *German*.) A further complication results from the fact that the English term *Dutch* has survived here and there as a designation of some groups of German, not Dutch, origin – most notably in reference to the *Pennsylvania Dutch*.

Another case with similar complications is that of *India* and *Indian*. The Indo-Aryans who centuries ago occupied what is now India referred to themselves as *ārya-*, from the Indo-Iranian self-designation meaning 'noble' (see Chapter 2, § 3.10). The outside world has come to use a different name, of the type represented by English *India* (the country) and *Indian* (the inhabitants). This terminology derives from Greek *Indós*, an adaptation of the Old Persian name *hindu* for a river that in Sanskrit is called *sindhu*. The Indus River frequently formed the boundary between Iranian and Indo-Aryan peoples, so that the Iranians could use *hindu* to elliptically refer to the country and the people living 'beyond the Indus'. (The correspondence Skt. *sindhu-* : OPers. *hindu-* reflects regular sound changes. The absence of initial *h-* in Greek reflects the fact that the Greeks living closest to the Iranians, the Ionians, had lost their aitches, just like Cockneys.)

The Iranian term *hindu* has become widely known with a different connotation, referring to the most widespread indigenous religion of India. This connotation developed when Persian-speaking Muslims conquered much of South Asia and began to use the term *hindu* to refer to the majority population's religion. At the same time, they retained the more original meaning of *hindu* in the name for the country, *Hindustan*, a term nowadays commonly used by Indians and other South Asians to refer to India. (The more official name of the country is *Bhārat(a)*, 'the land of the descendants of *Bharat(a)*', the mythological ancestor of an important early royal dynasty.)

The use of the word *Indian* as a term for the indigenous peoples of the Americas is an interesting misnomer resulting from Christopher Columbus's belief that he had reached India after crossing the Atlantic Ocean. In English, the "politically correct" term for these peoples now is *Native* or *Indigenous Americans*; and given the possible confusion between *Indian*$_1$ 'citizen of India' or, at an earlier time, 'inhabitant of South Asia', and *Indian*$_2$ 'Indigenous American', this choice of terminology has a lot to recommend it. (German ingeniously differentiates between the two types of "Indians" by referring to the first group as *Inder*, and the second as *Indianer*.) At the same time, the term *Native American* causes difficulties, since members of virtually all human races may be born in the United States and in that sense be native Americans (where *America* = *U.S.*). Moreover, U.S.-born whites like to distinguish themselves as *native Americans* in contrast to the recent large influx of non-white immigrants – an ironic twist of events, since at an earlier time, whites used the term *natives* to refer to indigenous non-white peoples around the world. Yet a further wrinkle in this complex, even convoluted, situation derives from the fact that many Indigenous Americans prefer to be called *Indians*.

As in the use of *Indian* as a term for the indigenous peoples of the Americas, group names can be misapplied or perceived as misapplied, sometimes with serious political consequences. A case in point is found in the terms *Macedonia* and *Macedonian*. In ancient times, the *Macedonians* (whose name possibly derives from Gk. *makednós* 'tall') spoke a language that may have been a sister-language of the Hellenic (Greek) branch of Indo-European – or even a separate branch with close affinities to Hellenic. Under Philip of Macedon and especially his illustrious son Alexander the Great, Hellenistic culture and Greek language were introduced, and Macedonia became part of Greece. Incursions of the Byzantine period brought speakers of Southern Slavic who settled especially in the north of the area and who have referred to themselves and their language as *Macedonian* for over a hundred years now. Politically, part of Ancient Macedonia now is a province of Greece, with Greek as its official language. Another part was a state in the former Republic of Yugoslavia, has recently become independent, and refers to its Slavic majority population and its language as *Macedonian*.

There is thus no straight-line connection between the ancient Macedonians and the modern country or province of Macedonia or their speakers – other than the name. Yet the terms *Macedonia* and *Macedonian* have become potent symbols in a bitter political struggle between Greece and the newly formed (Slavic) Republic of Macedonia, with Greece claiming that it alone is entitled to use the name *Macedonia*. "What's in a name?" one might ask. The answer is "Plenty!", especially if it is invested with the right sort of emotional and political appeal.

Just as the proper name *Maverick* was the basis for a common noun *maverick*, and names like *John* or *Peter*, as noted above, have taken on other meanings as common nouns, so too the names of various groups may be used "improperly", often with negative connotations. For instance, the word *slave* is ultimately (through a Greek rendering of the name) related to *Slav* (see Chapter 2, § 3). The word *gyp* derives from *Gypsy*, a misnomer related to *Egyptian*, based on the mistaken belief that the Gypsies, who originated in India and call themselves *Roma(ny)* (< Prakrit *ḍoma*), came instead from Egypt. The word *cannibal* comes from Christopher Columbus's rendering *Caníbalis* of the Arawak ethnic name *caniba* for the *Carib* peoples of Cuba and Haiti, who, it was alleged, ate other human beings – an allegation not substantiated by evidence. (Widespread ethnocentric prejudice against foreigners is common to many cultures and expresses itself through various stereotypes. The "others" are often said to eat human beings; they may be characterized as *eskameege* 'raw-meat-eaters', or as only able to stammer *bar bar*, or as being *nemets* 'mute'. Reports of cannibalism therefore must be taken with a fair amount of skepticism.) Note also such usages as *to welsh* (or *welch*) *on a bet* or *to jew someone*. And so the list goes on.

In western society today, with an increasing awareness of cultural differences and a resurgence of ethnic pride, many of these negative terms are disappearing, such as the verb *to jew*. For others terms, alternative words are being proposed, such as *Inuit*, originally the name of a subgroup, for all *Eskimos*. As in other cases of taboo, the success of these attempts can be expected to be mixed. And some names, such as Slavic *Nemets* for 'German', are so deeply ingrained and their literal, etymological meaning so much lost in history that change is unlikely to take place.

Moreover, those who find the misuse of ethnic names regrettable can take some solace in the existence of relatively innocuous terms or phrases derived from ethnonyms, such as *Dutch treat*, or *It's Greek to me*. Interestingly, the Modern Greek equivalent is *mu íne kinézika*, literally 'It is Chinese to me'; and German has *Das kommt mir spanisch vor* 'That strikes me as Spanish'.

3.2. Names of persons

What is true for group names also holds for personal names. Names of individuals show a variety of sources, in terms of both the type of source and the language.

Most names were once meaningful words that presumably came to be applied to some individual in recognition of some defining quality, and thus resemble nicknames. For instance, the widespread name *Paul* (Span. *Pablo*, Ital. *Paolo*, Russ. *Pavel*, Mod. Gk. *Pávlos*, etc.) is ultimately from Latin *paulus* 'small', the name given to Saul of Tarsus when he converted to Christianity, and thus surely a characterizing epithet at first. Similarly, *Philip* is ultimately from Greek *phíl-ippos* 'lover of horses', again no doubt an epithet that originally characterized the designee or the hopes that his parents had for him when he was born.

Biblical names commonly are of Hebrew origin: The name *Adam* is from the Hebrew for 'red' (perhaps originally designating a characteristic skin color), *David* is from a nursery word for 'darling' (later 'friend'), *Joseph* originally means 'may Jehovah add' (with an understood object 'children'), and *Mary* is possibly from an expression meaning 'desired, longed-for [child]'.

From Germanic come names such as *Edward* (Old English *Ead-weard* 'rich guardian') and *Robert* (Old English *Hreod-beorht*, Old High German *Hrode-bert*, literally 'bright of fame'). But as noted in Chapter 2, § 3, many names of Germanic origin have come to English via French after the Norman conquest of 1066.

The Romans used ordinal numbers as the basis for some proper names, e.g. *Sextus* (literally 'the sixth [child or son]') or *Octavius* ('the eighth'); compare English names like *Six*, a character on the TV show *Blossom*. In rural England and the Southern United States, names such as *Easy* or *Early* are attested, characterizing the nature of their bearers' birth. Christian virtues became names such as *Faith, Hope, Charity*, in America at least, among settlers in Puritan New England. The month-names *April, May*, and *June* are the basis for some women's names, originally perhaps motivated by the joyous, spring-like connotations associated with these months.

In more recent years, people have found even more daring or, some would say, outrageous, names for their children or for themselves. For instance, girls have been named *Georgia* after the U.S. state of the same name; many English girls are called *Chelsea* (originally after London's artists' quarter); and the British actress Catherine Oxenberg called her daughter *India*. Note also the American author **Tennessee Williams**, the fictional character **Indiana Jones**, and a New York author named *Gary Indiana* (after the town *Gary, Indiana*). Some of these names may be motivated by emotional attachment to the state or country, others simply by a desire to be different.

A special case is the use, in the rural U.S. South of the 1930s, of such names as *Syphilis* or *Gonorrhea*. Here the words have presumably no referential meaningfulness, and the phonic value alone prevails. A similar, more widespread phenomenon is the use of alternate, supposedly more refined or melodious spellings. For instance, the former U.S. president *Lyndon B. Johnson* owed his first name to a respelling of *Linden* because the use of *y* and *o* was considered more euphonic. A caricature of this convention is found in the jocular spelling of a very refined dog *Fido* as *Phideaux*.

Just like common nouns, names can be borrowed, for their sound, their meaning, or their symbolic value. Many, perhaps most, English names are borrowed. This includes Germanic names like *Henry* or *Robert*, which came to English via French; Celtic names such as *Brian* (from **bre* 'hill'); French names of Latin and Greek origin, such as *Renée, Pierre*, and *Philip*; and Biblical names such as *Adam, David,* and *Joseph*. Names of foreign origin that have not been nativized in English may be used as an indication of ethnicity. For instance, families from Germany and Scandinavia may call their sons *Hans* and their daughters *Helga*, African and Arabic names such as *Abdul, Biko, Jamaal,* and *Kareem* are especially popular among African Americans; and *Hillel* as a given name is typically Jewish.

But with all names there is tendency toward bleaching of the original meaning as the name takes on a life of its own, divorced from its etymological meaning and ethnic associations. So you need not be of Anglo-Saxon ancestry to be named *Edward*, or of Celtic background to be called *Brian*. And you don't have to love horses to carry the name *Philip* or to be religious to be called *Faith*; in fact, there is nothing to prevent a *Faith* from being an atheist.

Just as names can be borrowed from other languages, so too can they be borrowed internally, as it were, through extension from one lexical domain into another. Thus, originally male names such as *Billie* or *Jo* have long been used for females, and family names have been extended into use as first names, as with *Washington* or *Jefferson*. In recent years, as more women have entered originally male-dominated professions, many women have been observed to request that they be addressed by more "male-sounding" variants or clippings of their given names, such as *Sam* for *Samantha* or *Chris* for

Christine. The motivation presumably lies in the belief that male names make it easier for women to function in a male-dominated environment.

Male names such as *Sam* and *Chris* are of course themselves innovations, resulting from clipping and/or alterations in early child language. *Sam* and *Chris* are clipped versions of *Samuel* and *Christopher*, as is *Rob* for *Robert*. But beside *Rob* we also find *Bob*, with an assimilation of the initial consonant to the final that is characteristic of young children's speech. In addition some people use *Bubba* for *Robert*, although the word may also mean 'brother'. Here again we find features of early child language: A quasi-reduplicated form of *Bob* and/or assimilation and simplification of the consonants in *brother*.

HYPOCORISTICS of this sort often are quite old and reflect pronunciations or morphophonemic alternations that are no longer current. For instance, *Dotty* and *Betty* for *Dorothy* and *Elisabeth* reflect an early pronunciation with [t], before [θ] was introduced in the Renaissance on the Greek model (see Chapter 1, § 4). *Ned* most likely reflects reanalysis of an original sequence *mine Ed* 'my Ed', at a time when the possessive pronoun *my* showed a similar alternation between *mine* and *my* as Mod. Engl. *a : an*. (A clear trace of this is found in the famous *Mine eyes have seen the glory of the coming of the Lord* . . . A more opaque trace is found in Shakespeare's *nuncle* from *mine uncle*.)

Some names result from blends or coinages, and have almost a "do-it-yourself" quality to them. Popular names among African Americans such as *Latisha*, or *Latrisha* seem to derive from a blending of *La-* (from a source like *LaVerne*) and *t(r)isha* (from a source like *Tricia*). The element *La* is found in many other names, such as *LaShawn* and *Latina*.

Finally, names may carry significant social connotations. We have already observed that certain names have a strong ethnic flavor. Social factors also play a role in the popularity of certain names, with trends in naming often seeming to catch on and spread like fads or slang expressions. The abundance of *Jennifers* and *Jasons* among children born in middle-class America in the 1980s presumably reflects such a trend. Often, common cultural elements can play a role. TV soap operas, for instance, have been a source for the spread of many female names, such as *Crystal*, with all its variant spellings (*Kristal, Krystal, Cristal*, etc.).

Family names also show varied origins and are moreover of relatively recent origin. In fact, some cultures do not use them even today. They originally were labels that further identified a person who was otherwise known just by given name; they thus made it possible to specify which *John* or *Jane* was being referred to.

Many are names of professions, such as *Clark* (a variant of *clerk*), *Carpenter, Goldsmith, Miller, Fletcher, Sawyer*, and especially *Smith* – a popular source for names in many other languages, such as Germ. *Schmidt/Schmid/Schmitt*, Fr. *Ferrier*, Ital. *Ferraro* (and the derived form *Ferrari*), Sp. *Herrero*, Ru. *Kuznetsov* literally 'Smith-son', and Hung. *Kovács*. A very common alternative source consists of place names, originally the place a person came from, such as Germ. *Zumwalt/Zumwald* 'at the forest', *(von) Hinüber* 'on the other side', Engl *Milhouse* 'mill house', *Underhill, London, Hamburger, Frankfurter, Fleming, Welch/Walsh, Scott*, and hundreds of others.

Many family names are patronymic in origin, meaning 'son of X' or simply 'of X', where 'X' is the father or grandfather. Compare English names with a final *-s* (*Adams, Richards, Roberts*, etc.) representing the possessive suffix, or with a final *-son* (*Richardson, Robertson, Josephson, Adamson, Johnson, Davidson*, etc.). In some names, the *-son* is hidden by the spelling, such as *Nixon* or *Dixon* (originally 'Nick's, Dick's son'). English names in *-son* are usually of Scandinavian origin. Patronymics of Celtic origin either have *M(a)c-* 'son' or *O'*, from OIr. *ao < avi* 'grandson', so that *O'Henry* literally would be 'whose grandfather is Henry'. In addition note the rarer *Fitz*, as in *Fitzgerald*, preserving the Old French ancestor of Mod. Fr. *fils* 'son'.

Similar patterns are found in many other parts of the world, as in Hebrew names with *ben* or *bar* (e.g. *Ben Gurion, Bar Hillel*) or Georgian names in *-dze* and *-shvili* (such as *Shevardnadze* and *Shalikashvili*). The Modern Greek situation is particularly interesting, for the form of patronymics differs dialectally: *-pulos* for families originally from the Peloponnesos, *-iðis* for those from Asia Minor, *-akis* for those from Crete, and so on.

Metronymics are much rarer, but note the traditional Spanish pattern in names such as *Ramón Menéndez Pidal* = *Ramón* whose father's last name is *Menéndez*, and whose mother's last name is *Pidal*. (Traditionally, this causes difficulties for illegitimate children, who would only have one last name, thus giving away their origin.) In some areas of the world, metronymics are the norm. For instance, in Gur languages of Burkina-Faso, Ghana, and Côte d'Ivoire we find names such as *Moses Kambou* = Moses, son of Mrs. Kambou. (A father's name is acquired at initiation rites into adulthood, but that name remains secret.)

Finally, as with first names, some family names are originally epithets or nicknames, originally reflecting some noteworthy, often physical, defining characteristic, e.g. Germ. *Schwarzkopf* (literally, 'whose head is black'); Engl. *Whitehead, Armstrong, Russell* (from Fr. *Rousell* 'red-haired'); It. *Macchiavelli* 'son of the one with dirty hair'; Lat. *Cato* 'the sharp/clever one',

Caesar 'the one with the mane', *Cicero* 'the one who resembles a chickpea', *Naso* (the family name of the poet Ovid, literally 'big-nose').

While much more could be said about the origins of names, and examples from languages all over the world lined up, this survey gives a fair sampling of the range of sources for what some linguists – and many more non-linguists – have felt is the most basic function of language, that of giving a name to an object or individual.

4. Coinage in argots, jargons, and slang

As noted in Chapter 7, § 5.2, taboo may lead to a considerable turnover in the lexicon, requiring the coining of many new words. Extensive and constant vocabulary renewal is perhaps even more common in certain special forms of language use which, like taboo, are socially motivated, namely in ARGOTS, JARGONS, and SLANG. Let us conclude the chapter by taking a closer look at coinage in these forms of speech.

Although difficult to differentiate with absolute precision, these forms of language use can be distinguished roughly as follows. Argots are secret languages, intended for in-group communication that is to remain unintelligible to outsiders. Argots commonly are employed by criminals; but they may also be used by other groups, especially the suppressed or disadvantaged. The major purpose of jargon is to serve in-group communication and social cohesion. Much of its special vocabulary consists of technical terms, but there are also expressions, often humorous, that serve as markers of solidarity. Slang, finally, is to ordinary language what up-to-date, youthful, and somewhat outrageous fashion is to ordinary dress wear. Because of their nature, argots and slang are especially in need of constant lexical renewal. In the case of argots, the purpose is to maintain secrecy. If outsiders hear argot words often enough, they can catch on to their meanings, and the words are in danger of losing their secret nature. As for slang, the motivation for constant lexical renewal is similar to the motivation for the constant change in dress fashion. There is nothing more stale than outdated slang – or yesterday's fashion. Since the need for lexical renewal is strongest in slang and argots, most of the examples given below come from these two forms of speech.

Note that the interrelation of slang, jargons, and argots with each other, as well as with ordinary language, is a very complex one. In many cases the precise source for a given word or the mechanism by which it acquired its meaning is shrouded in mystery. Moreover, words often are borrowed from one sphere of language use to the other. This is especially true as far as slang is concerned. Time and again we find that in order to maintain its novelty, slang adopts words from argots and jargon. Finally, although speakers tend to resist the intrusion of slang into ordinary language use, they are far from successful in doing so; and slang (or jargon) words frequently become part of ordinary vocabulary. Such instances in a sense represent a type of borrowing from one variety of the language into another.

Consider for instance the case of *fake* which entered English through argot in the meaning of any illegal or criminal action, but especially that of stealing or robbing. Lat. *facere* 'do, make' and Germ. *fegen* 'wipe, swipe' have been mentioned as possible sources for the word, in which case the semantic development would be comparable to that in '*make* off with something' or 'swipe' = 'steal something'. But as in many other cases of argot and slang, the exact origin remains a mystery. Further developments led to meanings like 'deceive'. In these meanings the word began to enter slang, as well as jazz musicians' jargon, where it could be used for improvising without prior preparation, as in *If you don't know it, just fake it*. From these contexts, the word has come to be increasingly accepted in ordinary English, so that dictionaries like Webster's *New World Dictionary* no longer consider it necessary to label the word as slang or jargon.

Other words of similar ancestry, but now in fairly common use, are *kid* (originally 'young goat'), *keister* (originally from German or Yiddish *kiste* 'box'?), *ogle* (from Dutch *oogelijn* 'little eye'), and *pal* (from Romani *ph(r)al* 'brother'). Even phrases can be liberated into common use, as in the widespread use of *bottom line* to mean 'the essential point', originally a technical term in business jargon referring to the final line in a financial statement.

Just as examples like *daisy* or, to a lesser degree, *clear* (in expressions like *this is not clear to me*) have been referred to as faded metaphors, words like *fake*, then, can be referred to as faded slang (or faded argot/jargon).

4.1. Coinage through semantic change

Semantic change is one of the major vehicles for creating the vocabulary that distinguishes argots and slang from ordinary language use or for maintaining the distance between these forms of speech and ordinary language.

Consider for instance recent argot words for 'police' in English, such as *the heat, the fuzz*, and *smokies*. The expression *the heat* no doubt reflects the fact that the police *put the heat on criminals*. And the expressions *the fuzz* (as in the expression *Like I was rappin' to the fuzz* at the beginning of

Chapter 1) and *smokies* seem to derive from the similarity between U.S. state troopers' hats and the hat of Smokey (the) Bear (who, of course, is fuzzy). Similar developments have given rise to a veritable plethora of other argot words for 'police': *bull, danger, signal, terror, elephant ears, flatfoot,* etc.

The act of informing the police about criminal activities has similarly been expressed by many different words: *bark, belch, bleat, chirp, sing, squawk, squeak, squeal,* etc.

In the soldiers' slang or jargon of late Roman antiquity and the early Middle Ages, 'battle' was with a soupçon of gallows humor referred to at the 'smashing of pots (= heads) into shards or smithereens'. Hence heads could be referred to as 'pots' or even as 'shards'. As these words began to penetrate ordinary language, they became the ordinary words for 'head' in a number of European languages; e.g. Germ. *Kopf* (related to Engl. *cup*), and Ital. *testa*, Fr. *tête* (from Lat. *testa* 'shard'). Gallows humor can also be seen at work in argot words for the *electric chair* such as *hot seat, cinder seat,* or *barbecue stool.*

As we saw earlier, jazz musician's jargon contributed to the semantic development of *fake*. In the U.S., this jargon has been a continuing source for slang expressions. Two widely known products of jazz jargon are *cool*, originally referring to a mode of jazz performance that differed from earlier *hot* jazz by being more smooth and intellectual, and *groovy*, first attested in the 1930s and commonly used in 1940s through 1960s jargon and slang, derived from earlier *in the groove* = 'going smoothly in the groove of a record'. The word *groovy* now is clearly dated, though perhaps enjoying a bit of a retro-revival at present; *cool*, on the other hand, has shown amazing staying power, reappearing in ever-new slang forms and in ever-new combinations. An oldish, somewhat dated, slang use of *cool* is found in the combination *cool dude*, while a fairly recent slang use is *That's cool*, meaning 'that's OK; nothing wrong about it'. But given the volatile nature of slang, this use may already be beyond its prime. Note also the relatively recent pronunciation of *cool* with a protracted vowel and a rising-falling intonation, as popularized by television's Bart Simpson, or the clipped pronunciation [kūʔ] popularized by the TV characters Beavis and Butthead.

4.2. Coinage through borrowing

In addition to semantic change, argots, jargons, and slang commonly draw on borrowing as a major source for vocabulary renewal. The donors for borrowing commonly are languages of groups that are marginalized in society and thus often forced into illegal or criminal activities. In English, these are especially Yiddish and Romani (traditionally referred to as Gypsy; see

§ 3 above), as well as Shelta, a jargon spoken by tinkers and vagrants in England and Ireland and deriving much of its vocabulary from Irish and Scots Gaelic. But many other languages have contributed, including the speech of Dutch and German criminals who played a significant role in the criminal underworld of sixteenth-century England. The multicultural, multiethnic, and multilingual nature of the sources of English argot can be gauged from the selected examples in (7).

(7) | | | |
|---|---|---|
| *cuffer* | 'man' | Yid. *kuffer* 'stupid fellow' (?) |
| *keister* | 'behind; rear' | Yid. or Germ. *kiste* 'box' |
| *pal* | 'companion' | Romani *ph(r)al* 'brother' |
| *stir* | 'prison' | Romani *staripan* 'prison', *stardo* 'imprisoned' (?) |
| *cove* | 'man, rogue' | Romani *kovo* 'that man' |
| *tober* | 'road' | Shelta *tober* (from Ir. *bothar*) |
| *ogle* | 'look at covetously' | Dutch *oogelijn* 'eye (diminutive)' |
| *mongee* | 'food' | Fr. *manger* 'eat; food' |
| *feele* | 'young woman' | Fr. *fille* or Ital. *figlia* 'daughter' |
| *kinchin* | 'young' | Germ. *Kindchen* 'child (diminutive)' |
| *ken* | 'house' | Romani or Hindi *khan(a)* 'house' or Arab. *xan* 'inn' (?) |
| *hoosegow* | 'prison' | Span. *juzgado* 'court of justice' |
| *vamoose* | 'run away, get lost' | Span. *vamos* 'let's go' |

African American Vernacular English has provided a similar source for much of American English slang. Compare such expressions as *rap* 'talk, chat, converse' (which occurs in the introductory citation of Chapter 1) and *bad* in the sense of 'good'. (The latter can serve as another illustration of the extent to which semantic change can alter the meanings of words – given the right circumstances.) See also § 4.4 below.

4.3. Other devices for coinage

Beside metaphorical extensions and borrowings, argots and slang resort to a large variety of other means to coin new terms. These include abbreviatory developments, as in (8), processes similar to taboo-induced distortion (9), as well as a number of language games, such as "Pig Latin" (with transposition of initial consonants to final position and addition of [ey] (10), "rhyming slang" (11), and "back slang" (i.e. reverse pronunciation, based on spelling) (12). While rhyming slang has at least some kind of counterpart in ordinary linguistic change, in terms of the phenomenon of rhyming formation (see

Chapter 5, § 3.1), the other two phenomena normally are limited to argots and, to a lesser degree, slang. (But note the physicists' term *mho* which refers to the basic unit of conductance and is derived by back slang from its reciprocal *ohm*, the unit of resistance.) The fact that such processes are employed in these forms of speech must be attributed to the unusually great need for vocabulary renewal that is characteristic of these modes of communication.

(8)   a. Slang:

def	*definitive* (= 'excellent')
rad	*radical* (= 'excellent')
triff	*terrific*
abfab	*absolutely fabulous*

      b. Argot:

cutor	*prosecutor*
davy	*affidavit*
dan	*dynamite*

(9)   a. Slang:

grody	*grotty* (?) (an older slang term)

      b. Argot:

grift	*graft*
glee	*see*

(10)   Slang and argot:

af-g-a(y)	*f-ag*
am-scr-a(y)	*scr-am*
ix-n-a(y)	*n-ix*

(11)   Slang and especially argot:

April fools	**tools**
trouble and strife	**wife**
bat and wicket	**ticket**

(12)   Argot:

enob	*bone*
efink	*knife*

4.4. Concluding notes

While argots usually are secret languages of the underworld, they can arise under any other circumstances that call for secret communication, such as prisoner-of-war camps or slavery. Thus, it has been claimed that the African American English Vernacular words on the left side of (13) below are relics of an argot of early slavery, used to keep "the man" from understanding important communications between the slaves. It has further been suggested that these words can be traced to West African Wolof sources; see the forms on the right side of (13). For the semantic development of *honkey* compare the fact that *redneck* is a common derogatory term for lower-class whites in the South of the United States, presumably because they turn red in the sun.

(13)   *dig*   'understand'   *dega*   'understand'
        (hep/hip) cat '(smart) man'   *hep kat*   'man in the know'
        honkey   'white (derogatory)' *hong/honk*   'red'

How well argots are capable of serving as secret languages can be gauged from exchanges like the following which come from a sixteenth-century book entitled *A caveat or warning, for commen cursetors*. Can you figure them out? (For a translation see (14′).)

(14)   Argot:
        a. Question: *Why where is the **kene** that hath the **bene bouse**?*
        b. Answer: *A **bene mort** here by at the signe of the **prauncer***

(14′)   Translation:
        a.   'Now, where is the house that has the good drink?'
        b.   'A good wife close by at the sign of the horse.'

Language and dialect

Chapter 10
Language, dialect, and standard

> I speak a language, you speak a dialect, (s)he speaks like a barbarian
>
> (*Anonymous*)

> And the Gileadites took the passage of Jordan before the Ephraimites: and it was so, that when those Ephraimites which were escaped said, Let me over; that the men of Gilead said unto him, Art thou an Ephraimite? If he said, Nay;
> Then they said unto him, Say now Shibboleth: and he said Sibboleth, for he could not frame to pronounce it right. Then they took him, and slew him at the passages of Jordan; and there fell at that time of the Ephraimites forty and two thousand.
>
> (*Judges 12: 5–6; translation from the Authorized Version*)

1. Introduction

The preceding chapter has shown the effect that argots, jargon, and slang can have on lexical change. And as illustrated by examples like *pal*, a Romani word (*ph(r)al*) which entered English via a criminal argot, some of the effects may go beyond these special varieties of speech and swim into the mainstream of the ordinary language. In this chapter we take a closer and more general look at the questions raised by such terms as varieties of speech and ordinary language, including their relation to each other.

Relationships of this type are often said to involve a difference between dialect and language or substandard and standard. (Linguists commonly employ the term non-standard, instead of substandard; but at this point we are concerned with the way non-linguists think about these matters.) And, of course, the terms dialect and substandard cover much wider territory than argot, jargon, and slang. What further complicates matters is that linguists would like to use the terms language and dialect in a technical sense very different from their use by non-linguists. But, as in many other situations, the maxim holds true, "Most speakers are not linguists." Because the opinions of non-linguists often do play a considerable role in linguistic development, linguists cannot ignore them, no matter how much they may disagree. As we will see, this is especially true for the relationship between language and dialect.

2. Language and dialect

In ordinary, non-technical usage, the terms language and dialect tend to be associated with strong value judgments. "Language" is prestigious, correct, standardized, and follows the rules of grammar. "Dialects" lack prestige, are incorrect, substandard, and fail to obey the rules of grammar. They are a "depravation of what a language ought to be." Contrast the English expressions in (1)–(3) below, where those on the left are said to follow the rules of language, while the ones on the right are considered dialect.

(1)   *ask*   *aks*
(2)   *I've taken*   *I've took*
(3)   *He doesn't say anything to any-*   *He don't say nothin' to nobody*
        body at all   *nohow*

It is generally believed that the rules of grammar are sacrosanct, having been established for all eternity. Dialectal deviations, under this view, are the result of corruption brought about by carelessness and slovenly speech habits.

Linguists have difficulties with these views. They are keenly aware that even standard languages undergo changes, and that yesterday's "slovenly speech habit" may become today's standard – and conversely, the standard of yesterday may be non-standard today. For instance, in the Old English of *Beowulf*, the Anglo-Saxon Chronicle, and many other fine texts, we find counterparts to both of the forms in (1), not only with the sequence *sk* (spelled *sc*), now accepted as correct, but also with *ks* (spelled *cs*), now considered dialectal; see (1'). Constructions with the participial form *took*, considered ungrammatical or dialectal today, were perfectly normal in the language of Shakespeare, by all counts one of the best English writers ever; see (2'). And structures with multiple negation comparable to the right-side construction in (3) were perfectly acceptable in Chaucer; see (3'a). Traces persist in the language of Shakespeare (3'b) and even in the eighteenth century

(3'c), though under more restricted conditions. (See also Chapter 6, § 5.) It is only in fairly modern standard English that structures of this type became unacceptable.

(1') *eascian* : *eacsian* 'to ask'
(2') *Betwixt mine eye and heart a league is **took*** (*Sonnets* 47)
(3') a. *Ther **nas** no man **nowher** so vertuous* (*Canterbury Tales* A.251)
          'There was no man anywhere so virtuous.'
      Lit. 'There wasn't no man nowhere so virtuous.'
      b. *... and live **no** more to shame **nor** me **nor** you* (*Sonnets* 72)
      c. *No skill could obviate, **nor no** remedy dispel the terrible infection*
          (Oliver Goldsmith, *History of Greece* 1: 224)

Even today we find that different forms of Standard English disagree with each other, not only in terms of such fairly well-known vocabulary differences as the ones in (4) and the equally well-known pronunciation differences in (5), but also on other points of pronunciation (6), and even of grammar (7). The difference in (4c) is said to have caused genuine misunderstanding and, as a result, even anger in the Allied High Command during the Second World War. Speakers of (standard) British English tend to consider their *r*-less pronunciation in (5) to be superior, in spite of the fact that the *r*-ful speech of (most) Americans preserves an older stage of the language and thus is historically more correct. As for the word *herb*, both British and American English speakers can find cause for finding fault with one another; British speakers because of "that awful American *r*", Americans because of the Britishers' incorrect sounding out of the initial *h* ("next thing they'll pronounce *hour* as [hawə] and *hono(u)r* as [hɔnə] !"). The situation is even more complex in (7): Americans might take pride in being consistent in saying both *gotten* and *forgotten*, while the British might feel superior for having the same form, *got*, both in (7a) and in (7b). Historically, both *got* and *gotten* have long-standing antecedents.

(4) British English American English
     a. *flat* 'apartment' *flat* (tire)
     b. *knock up* 'call on' *knock up* (slang) 'make pregnant'
     c. *table* 'put on the table for *table* 'put on the table = the
        immediate consideration' "back burner"' '
(5) *car* [kā] [kār]
     bird [bəd] [bərd]
(6) *herb* [həb] [ərb]

(7)   a. *I haven't got your letter yet   I haven't gotten your letter yet*
       = 'I haven't received your letter yet.'
       b. *I haven't got enough money   I haven't got enough money*
       = 'I don't have enough money.'

In the technical usage of linguistics, the terms language and dialect are used in a very different manner. All the citations in (1)–(3) and (4)–(7) above are forms and structures of the English LANGUAGE (as distinct from, say, the French language); but they belong to different DIALECTS. The left-hand citations in (1)–(3) belong to the standard dialect, while the ones on the right belong to non-standard or vernacular dialects. And the differences in (4)–(7) characterize different standard dialects of the English language.

This is not to say that the non-technical understanding of the terms language and dialect is irrelevant. Further below we will see that the ideas associated with this distinction can play a considerable role in language change. But the technical usage of the terms covers important aspects of linguistic reality as well.

The technical differentiation between language and dialect can, put very simply, be characterized as follows. Varieties of speech that are relatively similar to each other, whose divergences are relatively minor, are called different dialects of the same language. A language, then, is the collection of such dialects – whether they are standard or vernacular, urban or rural, regional or supraregional. Varieties which differ from each other more noticeably, whose divergences are major, are called different languages.

Ideally, the distinction between language and dialect is based on the notion of MUTUAL INTELLIGIBILITY. Dialects of the same language should be mutually intelligible, while different languages should not be. This mutual intelligibility, in turn, would be a reflection of the linguistic similarities between the different varieties of speech.

Unfortunately, the mutual-intelligibility test does not always lead to clear results. A person from rural Maine, speaking only the local dialect, will find it extremely difficult, if not impossible, to understand someone from rural Louisiana who likewise can only speak the local dialect. Still, a person going on a slow, leisurely trip from Maine to Louisiana would find no language boundary along the way, comparable to, say, the one between German and French. Rather, any two neighboring local dialects along the way would be perfectly intelligible to each other. The dialects of Maine and Louisiana, thus, form a dialect CONTINUUM, linked to each other through a CHAIN of mutual intelligibility, and it is for this reason that they can be considered dialects of the same, English, language – in perfect agreement with ordinary, non-technical perception and usage.

The situation is more complex in cases like Scots English and American English. For instance, confronted with a Scots English expression of the type (8a), ordinary speakers of American English would have a hard time realizing that it is English, and even greater difficulties in understanding the passage as being simply a different pronunciation for the expression in (8b); in fact, Americans might well believe that (8a) is not English, but Scots Gaelic. How, then, can we justify considering Scots English a form of English?

(8) a. [its a brādlext mōnlext next tonext]
     b. *It's a broad-light moon-light night tonight*

To justify the usual belief that Scots English is in fact a variety of English, just as much as American English, we might point to the existence of a British dialect chain that links Scots English with Standard British English, and to the general mutual intelligibility of standard British and American English; American and Scots English thus are ultimately linked with each other. But knowing that there is such an indirect link does not really make it any easier for the Scots and American speakers to successfully communicate with each other in their own native varieties of English.

An alternative justification for considering Scots and American English to be different varieties of the same language might be that, given enough time (and good will), speakers of the two varieties of English can achieve mutual intelligibility. But this argument doesn't get us very far, for with an even greater amount of time (and of good will), a greater effort, and the right choice of words, French and English might likewise become mutually intelligible.

In fact, there are numerous difficulties with the concept of mutual intelligibility. For instance, Norwegian and Swedish are mutually quite intelligible, and yet, most people – including linguists – would consider them to be different languages. The reason for classifying them as different languages is that Norwegian and Swedish have different standard dialects and literary traditions and, even more important, are considered different from each other by their respective speakers. Here, then, cultural, social, and political considerations overrule the mutual-intelligibility test. A language in this sense is, as one linguist put it jokingly, "a dialect with an army and a navy". One might add, "And with schools."

But having different armies, navies, and schools does not necessarily mean a difference in "language". Consider the case of British vs. American English.

Britain and the United States certainly have different armies and navies; and as we just saw, they have different standard dialects (although their differences are smaller than those between Norwegian and Swedish). At least in the modern period, they also have distinct literary traditions. But the overwhelming majority of their speakers, on both sides of the Atlantic, continue to look upon their language as one. Here as elsewhere, the attitudes of speakers matter greatly.

Consider further the case of Norwegian and Swedish vs. Danish. Norwegian and Swedish are said to be quite readily intelligible to speakers of Danish. But the intelligibility is not mutual, since speakers of Swedish and Norwegian find Danish quite unintelligible.

A possible linguistic reason is the following. Danish had very extensive weakening (see Chapter 4, § 5.1.2) of intervocalic consonants, while Norwegian and Swedish preserved these consonants much more faithfully. Compare for instance Dan. *flue* : Swed. *fluga* 'fly' or Dan. *fjeder/fjer* (both pronounced [fyeə]) : Swed. *fjäder* 'feather'. Danes would have learned to get by without the consonants; their presence in Norwegian and Swedish would, for them, therefore be rather redundant. But Norwegian and Swedish speakers, used to the presence of intervocalic consonants in their own speech, would depend on their presence for proper understanding and, not hearing them in Danish, would fail to understand the Danes. So it seems, at least.

Linguistic factors of this type may in fact play a role in the lack of mutual intelligibility among the Scandinavian languages. However, some – more honest – speakers of Norwegian and Swedish admit that the lack of intelligibility is a consequence more of attitude than of linguistic differences. They admit that Norwegian and Swedish speakers consider the sound of Danish horrible – very guttural or throaty, in part because of the use of a uvular [ʀ] for the postdental [r] of Norwegian and Swedish. Moreover, Danish makes extensive use of glottal stops, where Norwegian and Swedish do not. Interestingly, this evaluation of Danish as guttural and unpleasant is shared by many Danes. A great Danish linguist, for instance, is said to have stated, "Danish is not a language, it is a throat disease." Here, then, even the notion of mutual intelligibility depends on speakers' attitudes, not on purely linguistic facts.

Finally consider cases like German and Dutch. A person traveling from the southernmost areas of German speech (as far south as Northern Italy), via Austria and Germany, to the Netherlands would find no boundary of mutual non-intelligibility separating one local dialect from the other. The whole territory is a single dialect continuum, although dialects that are fairly removed from each other may be mutually quite unintelligible. Yet the standard Dutch and German languages clearly lack mutual intelligibility and thus qualify for being called different languages. Moreover, they meet the sociolinguistic criteria for being considered distinct languages, since like Norwegian and Swedish, they have different linguistic standards and literary traditions and are considered different from each other by their respective speakers.

The situation is similar in the vast territory of the non-Balkan Romance languages, except that we have at least five distinct standard languages: Italian, Romantsch (one of the officially recognized languages of Switzerland), French, Spanish, and Portuguese. To these must now be added Catalan and Galician which have recently been accorded official status (see also § 5 below).

What these varying results and failures of the mutual-intelligibility test show is that there is no clear line of demarcation between "different dialect" and "different language". Linguistic similarity or difference is a matter not of yes or no, but of more or less. Moreover, mutual intelligibility depends not only on linguistic factors, but also on social ones.

Even so, the terms dialect and language are useful because they define the extreme points of a continuum. If, then, in subsequent chapters certain developments are portrayed as characteristic of dialect contact on one hand, or language contact on the other, we have to bear in mind that there may be intermediate kinds of relationship which may well show characteristics intermediate between those of the two more extreme types of relationship.

3. Social dialects

In traditional historical linguistics, the notion of dialect is almost exclusively reserved for geographically defined local and regional speech varieties; this is why Chapter 11, on dialectology, is devoted mainly to regional dialects. However, dialect differences may also be correlated with SOCIAL differences. Thus, the Chicago Chain Shift, discussed in Chapter 4, § 5.4, is limited to certain white working-class male – and macho – groups. Other speakers in Chicago do not participate in the change. In fact, where the male-macho speakers pronounce the name of their city as [šikægo], those who don't want to be caught dead being identified with these speakers affect a polarized pronunciation [šikɔgo]. The pronunciation [šikago] is rather rare in Chicago. (See also Chapter 11, § 1.)

Social dialect differentiation of this type is very common and is by no means confined to large urban areas like Chicago. We encountered the same phenomenon in the case of fairly rural Martha's Vineyard, with its socially polarized dialects of [a]-centralization vs. non-centralization. (See Chapter 4, § 6.3.)

Similarly, in Central Illinois, a chain shift polarizes two social groups in two small rural communities (Farmer City and Mansfield). The shift, involving the fronting of all back vowels, is characteristic of one group, the so-called burnouts. At the other extreme are the so-called rednecks, who refuse to participate in the change, clinging instead to the standard language. The terms *burnouts* and *rednecks* are used by local high school students as part of their school slang or argot, and their meanings are rather different from those in ordinary American English. *Burnout* no doubt is an extension of the more common term *burn out*, and probably is influenced by "drug-scene" talk. The *burnouts* are students who use drugs or alcohol and are not interested in going on to college. The use of *redneck* involves somewhat more complicated developments. In origin, the word is a derogatory term for Southern U.S. rural whites, comparable to the Wolof-derived term *honkey* (see Chapter 9, § 4). Because in the post-Civil Rights era, Southern poor whites tended to make common cause with conservative politicians, the word *redneck* appears to have locally acquired the extended meaning 'conservative'. And by an ironic twist, in this meaning the term could be used for upwardly mobile students who were not at all poor, but conservative, in the sense that they did not "do drugs" but instead went in for sports, as well as for a college education after high school.

4. Discontinuous dialects: Professional jargons and related forms of speech

In addition to continuous – social or regional – dialects, most languages have at least some discontinuous, SUPRAREGIONAL dialects, defined only in terms of social factors, which extend across the boundaries of continuous dialects. Some social dialects are by their very nature discontinuous and supraregional, because they are defined in terms of social groups living in many, geographically discontinuous locations.

Consider for instance the English dialect of lawyers, with its heavy use of borrowings from French and Latin, as in (9), as well as with certain peculiarities in grammar, such as the past tense *ple(a)d* [plɛd] of *plead* [plīd], and especially the extremely long and complex syntactic strings conjoined by *whereas, whereas, therefore.*

(9)   *feme couverte, feme sole*
        grand jury, petit jury
        oyez, oyez, oyez (at the beginning of a court session)
        habeus corpus
        nolo contendere, nolle prosequi
        venire (facias)

Social dialects of this type are commonly referred to as JARGONS or REGISTERS. Of these two terms, register can be used in a more comprehensive manner, as in academic register or professional register, while jargon tends to be employed more specifically, as in linguistic jargon or lawyers' jargon. Moreover, the two terms differ in connotations. Register focuses more on questions of rhetoric and style, while jargon emphasizes the exclusiveness of dialects of this type, which often makes it difficult for outsiders to understand them. In this regard, jargons share features with argots and slang. (See Chapter 9, § 4.)

While professional jargons and registers may share with argots and slangs the fact that they are often difficult to understand for outsiders, their basic motivation is not secrecy (or novelty, for that matter). Specialized fields of inquiry by their very nature require specialized terminology, so as to express what is intended as unambiguously and succinctly as possible. For instance, as we have seen before, in historical linguistics the term sound change is used, not to refer to just any change in sound structure, but to sound changes not conditioned by non-phonetic linguistic factors. If each time we wanted to talk about sound change we had to use the lengthy circumlocution "sound changes not conditioned by non-phonetic linguistic factors" we would never be able to get to the point. Similarly, the use of certain grammatical constructions, such as the passive, is highly appropriate in many areas of the sciences. The passive makes it possible to delete agents (as in *The experiment was conducted under the following conditions*), and this in turn makes it possible to state generally valid facts or claims, or observations that are believed to hold true no matter who observes them.

Professional jargons or registers are not necessarily limited to lawyers, scientists, and other professionals. Traditionally, they are also found in the trades and crafts.

One of the most widespread professional jargons of this type is the one of sailors and seafarers. But in some ways, this jargon is perhaps unusual. At least in the North Atlantic, the vocabulary of the jargon is highly international, with liberal borrowings back and forth among the languages of all the seafaring nations. And there is reason to believe that medieval Mediterranean nautical jargons had similar characteristics. Moreover, the vocabulary frequently comes not from the standard languages but from coastal dialects. This is especially true for the German element, which comes from the Low German (LG) dialects that differ considerably from southern-based Standard German and are much closer to Dutch and Flemish. A consequence of these special circumstances is that words may be borrowed back and forth several times over, making it impossible in many cases to determine with certainty which language was the ultimate source for a given term. Compare for instance the English, German, and French examples and their putative sources in (10). (Some of the terms in (10) may be also used in non-nautical meanings. In some cases, this is the result of secondary extension, as in Engl. *caboose, freight.*)

(10)	English	German	French	Putative source
	brig	*Brigg*	*brig/brick*	Engl., from *brigantine* ($\Leftarrow$?)
	boat	*Boot*	*bateau*	(ME from) ON
	buoy	*Boje*	*bouée*	OFr., via Dutch (?)
	cabin	*Kabine*	*cabine*	(OFr. *cabane* $\Rightarrow$ E *cabin*)
	caboose	*Kombüse*	*cambuse*	Dutch ($\Leftarrow$?)
	fleet	*Flotte*	*flotte*	early Gmc. $\Rightarrow$ Fr. *flotte* $\Rightarrow$ Germ.
	flotilla	*Flotille*	*flotille*	Fr. $\Rightarrow$ Span. $\Rightarrow$ Fr. etc.
	freight	*Fracht*	*fret*	Frisian, via Du./LG
	gaff	*Gaffel*		OFr., fr. Span. or Port.
	(larboard)	*Backbord*	*bâbord*	LG/Du./OE?
		Matrose 'sailor'	*matelot*	Du./LG or Scand. $\Rightarrow$ Fr. $\Rightarrow$ Du./LG
	lee	*Lee*		Engl.(?), or ON (?)
	luff	*Luv*	*lof*	fr. ON (?)
	packboat	*Packboot*	*paquebot*	Engl.
	pilot	*Pilot*	*pilote*	It., $\Leftarrow$ Gk.
	road	*Reede*	*rade*	ON
	schooner	*Schoner*	*schooner*	Scots Engl. (?)
	starboard	*Steuerbord*	*tribord*	early Gmc. $\Rightarrow$ Fr. (via ?)

5. Standard languages

The most important discontinuous, supraregional dialects are STANDARD DI-
ALECTS, more commonly referred to as STANDARD LANGUAGES. Historically,
these can be of very different origins. They can be regional or local dialects
which for some reason acquired sufficient prestige to be accepted as standard
on a supraregional basis; compare for instance Standard French and English
which developed out of the educated speech of Paris and London, respectively. They may develop out of "koinés" (a type of contact language to be
discussed in Chapter 12), such as the Greek Koiné of Alexandrian times or
the Swahili of present-day Tanzania. They may result from deliberate language planning or language engineering, as in the case of Nynorsk, one of
the standard languages of Norway.

To illustrate the role and effects of language planning in Norway, let us
take a closer look at the recent history of Norwegian. Centuries of Danish
domination had made Danish the language of the educated Norwegian elite,
who were concentrated mainly in the large urban areas in the south of the
country. Over time, developments similar to the ones that lead to regional
accents in monolingual societies (see further below in this section) brought
about a strongly Norwegianized form of Danish. The difference between this
form of language and the Danish of Denmark was further increased by a
variety of sound changes, especially pervasive weakening, that differentiated
Danish from the rest of the Scandinavian languages. As a consequence, the
language of Norway came to differ so much from Danish that Danes would
consider it a different language altogether, namely Norwegian. (Compare for
instance Norw. *kjøbe* [čöpə] or [čöbə] 'buy' vs. Dan. *købe* [köβə].)

In the wake of the nationalism that swept nineteenth-century Europe, the
Danish ancestry of Norwegian became suspect in the eyes of nationalistically
inclined Norwegians. One of these was the school teacher Ivar Aasen. Inspired by the puristic tendencies of Iceland (see Chapter 8, § 5.2), he set out
to construct a "truly Norwegian" rival language, drawing on the most conservative linguistic elements of conservative rural dialects. The grammar for
this Landsmaal or Nynorsk (i.e. 'Country language' or 'New Norwegian')
language was completed in 1864, and a companion dictionary nine years
later, in 1873.

Aasen's heroic attempt at single-handedly creating a new, truly Norwegian
language was greeted with enthusiasm by many nationalists. But an even
larger number of Norwegians were not impressed. They did not feel any
need to give up their variety of Norwegian, which was widely spoken by the

educated population of southern Norway and even more widely understood, in favor of what to them appeared to be a country-bumpkin language which could not claim any native speakers or regional basis. (Recall that Nynorsk was a composite language, consisting of elements from a variety of rural dialects.)

The result has been a long-standing, often uneasy, coexistence of two Norwegian standard languages, the earlier Riksmaal or Bokmaal (i.e. 'State language' or 'Book language') and Aasen's Nynorsk or Landsmaal. Both are recognized as official languages, and both are used as media of instruction in the schools, with individual localities opting for one or the other. Bokmaal still has the largest number of speakers (about 80%); but Nynorsk has acquired its own, quite loyal users. In recent years, the coexistence – and competition – of the two varieties has led to the development of an intermediate variety which combines features from both Nynorsk and Bokmaal. Perhaps this variety will some day resolve the competition by replacing both of the currently recognized official languages. (See § 6 below for a similar situation in Modern Greek.)

Standard languages may also result from a combination of any or all of these different sources. Thus, although Standard French and Standard English originated in the educated speech of the respective capital cities, Paris and London, they did experience a certain amount of language planning, too. As noted in Chapter 2, the Renaissance brought with it an increasing cultivation of the vernacular, regional languages (at the expense of Latin). That cultivation consisted not only of an expansion of vocabulary, commonly by borrowings from Latin, but also in attempts to regulate grammar, usually on the model of Latin. In France this was largely accomplished by the Académie Française. In England, which lacked such an academy, it was the work of individual scholars and writers who often disagreed with each other, especially in the area of vocabulary development. (See Chapter 8, § 5.2; for syntax, see also Chapter 6, § 5.)

For an extended example of the complex ways in which standard languages may originate, consider the case of Modern Standard German.

The ultimate source of the language was a regional written koiné of the chanceries (or administrative headquarters) of various East Central German principalities. (See Chapter 12, § 5 for the term koiné.)

The reason that this regional variety acquired wider currency must be sought in Lutheranism. Believing in the universal priesthood of all Christians, which includes the ability to read the Bible for oneself, Luther felt it necessary to translate the Bible into a language that could be understood by all Germans. And because he was familiar with the East Central German chancery koiné,

Luther naturally used this variety as a starting point. But just as naturally, he had to expand the vocabulary and diction of that bureaucratic language to make it suitable for translating the Bible. To that end, he claimed, he "watched the people's mouths" to find words in common use that were widely understood, even by those who did not use the words themselves.

The new Bible translation and its language, together with a catechism and a large stock of church hymns employing the same language, quickly spread to Luther's Protestant followers who were mainly located in the north of Germany. And both in church services and in the schools that prepared pupils for reading the Bible, the new variety of German increasingly came to be used as a spoken language. The religious divisions of Germany, however, which led to a prolonged series of wars, made not only Lutheranism, but also its language, suspect in the mainly southern and western parts of Germany, which remained with Roman Catholicism. (Calvinist Switzerland did adopt the written language of Luther's Bible translation, but retained its independence by not using it as a spoken language. This is the basis for the fact that Standard German is in a "diglossic" situation vis-à-vis Swiss German in modern Switzerland; see § 6 below.)

As time progressed, the language also came to be used for fine literature. At the same time, it underwent a certain degree of deliberate archaizing at the hands of people who were involved with attempts to purge the German language of foreign influence and who wanted to maintain a connection with earlier, Middle High German literature. In this latter respect, recall that the attempts to purify Icelandic were in part inspired by a similar desire to maintain a literary connection with Old Icelandic. However, in contrast to Iceland, the German attempts at purification were only partly successful. The result is the very mixed effect of linguistic nationalism in Modern German that we noted in Chapter 8, § 5.2.

What turned this language from a regionally based and sectarian form of German into a truly national medium was its use by the Romantic and Classical literary writers, especially by Goethe and Schiller. The sheer quality of their work was such that even those who for reasons of religious and regional loyalty had so far resisted the German of Luther's Bible translation could no longer hold back. Moreover, the topics of writers like Goethe and Schiller by and large were no longer tied to any particular form of Christianity. And perhaps, too, the political and philosophical climate had changed enough to make the old sectarian and regional differences appear less significant.

The written use by these writers and by contemporary scientists and philosophers, then, increasingly became the model for correct usage, just as the written (and oral) use of educated Paris and London speech had become the model for correct French and English. At roughly the same time, the language also became the vehicle for anti-Napoleonic and anti-French sentiments, serving as the symbol of an emerging nationalism. And slowly it came to be used as a spoken language, especially in the northern areas of Germany and in the cities.

With increasing spoken use, it finally could become a native language, for at least some speakers. Even today, however, it has remained a second language (or dialect) for many German speakers. This is especially the case in Switzerland, but even in southern Germany and Austria local and regional dialects still are the first language for most speakers.

Whatever its origins, a standard language soon becomes an entity in its own right, with a supraregional sociolinguistic basis. As a consequence, for instance, Modern Standard English no longer is tied to (educated) London speech, not even to Standard British usage. Rather, it is the language of educated speakers, no matter where they may be located. And some of its linguistic innovations, such as the "haw-haw" variety of the King's (or Queen's) English, with its [ew] for the [ow] of other dialects (as in [ew, ay dewnt bilīv sew] 'Oh, I don't believe so'), seem to have no regional basis whatsoever but are limited to socially defined sub-varieties of Standard British English.

As is shown by the case of English, which is used in Great Britain, Ireland, the U.S., Canada, Australia, New Zealand, and many other countries (see Chapter 2, § 3.3), standard languages are not necessarily restricted to a single country. Similarly, German is the standard language of Germany, as well as Austria, and part of Switzerland; and French is standard not only in France but also in parts of Belgium and Switzerland, as well as in the Canadian province of Quebec; in fact, French is recognized as an official language in all of Canada, beside English.

Like Canada, other countries, too, have more than one standard or official language: Nynorsk and Riksmaal/Bokmaal in Norway; Flemish, French, and German in Belgium; and French, German, Italian, and Romantsch in Switzerland. Within France, Provençal is clamoring for recognition as a literary standard language, in addition to Breton and Basque. And in Spain, three languages – Catalan, Galician, and Basque – coexist with the Castilian Spanish standard language.

Examples like these show that standard language and national or officially recognized language are not necessarily identical and that their relationship is open to historical variation. Those who advocate special "language" rather than vernacular status for, say, Provençal point to the fact that Provençal has a rich literature of its own and thus is distinct from French. Those opposed to special recognition argue that the "dialect" is not officially recognized as a national language, may not be taught in the schools – because it is not officially recognized, and so on.

During the reign of the Franco regime in Spain, the latter argument prevailed, and it is said that Cataluña abounded with signs that read "Don't bark, speak Spanish" (meaning "don't talk Catalan, speak Castilian Spanish"). With the demise of the regime and the introduction of democratic rule, the situation has changed drastically, and Catalan, along with Galician and Basque, has been recognized as a co-official language. All three of these languages now are used freely in schools, in publications, and in radio and television.

Finally, beside languages like German, French, English, or even Provençal and Catalan, all of which are current in fairly large areas, there may be regionally more restricted standard languages. And these may coexist with the supraregional standard languages, as well as the local dialects, with different roles assigned to each of these varieties of speech. For instance, in much of German-speaking Switzerland, Standard German is used only for written communication. A regional standard is said to be used for oral communication between speakers from different areas, while elsewhere the local dialect is employed.

Standard languages often are WRITTEN languages. In fact, in some societies they exist only in written form (which of course may be read out or recited). This was the case for early Standard German, and still is true for Standard German in much of Switzerland. In such cases, standard language and local dialect or vernacular coexist in a situation of "diglossia" (see below). However, in preliterate societies and occasionally also elsewhere, standard languages exist only in spoken form, as is the case with the regional standard German of Switzerland.

An extreme case is that of Vedic Sanskrit, the language of the oldest sacred texts of Hinduism. Until very recently this form of Sanskrit was not put into written form but handed down only through oral tradition – in spite of the fact that the art of writing has been available in India since at least the third century B.C. (See Chapter 2, § 3.10.2, and Chapter 3, § 2.1.)

At the same time, the fact that many standard languages exist first and foremost in written form may have important repercussions for linguistic change. One of the most common effects is that of SPELLING PRONUNCIATION, the replacement of the historically justified pronunciation of a given word by one which is suggested by the spelling.

It is this phenomenon which accounts for the fact that Engl. *often* frequently is pronounced as [ɔftən], rather than as inherited [ɔf(ə)n]. Similarly, the initial [h] of Engl. *humble* results from spelling pronunciation, the older pronunciation surviving only in rural dialects, such as Southern Am. Engl. *Be 'umble to the Lord.* The same explanation holds for the initial [h] of Brit. Engl. [həb] *herb* vs. North. Am. Engl. [ərb]. (Once accepted by a speech community, of course, the result of spelling pronunciations may become the norm; and the use of the older pronunciation may be considered incorrect or rustic, as in the case of *'umble.*)

Standard languages, whether written or not, also can have a retarding effect on linguistic change. After all, what characterizes standard languages is standardization. Standardization, then, becomes a measurement of correct speech, to which people purporting to speak the standard language must adhere. Standard languages therefore tend to become fettered languages, which tend to retain older patterns more tenaciously than vernaculars, especially when such patterns become SHIBBOLETHS. (For the origin of this expression see the second epigraph of this chapter. The word *shibboleth* literally means 'stream, river' – a clever word choice for testing the dialectal and ethnic identity of people at a river crossing.)

The preservation of archaic patterns can be observed in Standard German, which still retains the option of the inflected genitive, as in (11a), or of the dative singular ending *-e* [-ə], while most of the vernaculars have lost the [-ə] of the dative and have replaced the inflected genitive construction with periphrastic structures of the type (11b) and (11c). While structures like (11b) have come to be accepted in the standard language, too, the type (11c) has acquired the status of a shibboleth. Its use is not acceptable in written Standard German, and even in the spoken language it is considered either substandard or, at the least, highly colloquial.

(11)   a. *Das Haus des Vaters*   'the father's house'
      b. *Das Haus vom Vater*   'the house of the father'
      c. *Dem Vater sein Haus*   (lit. 'to the father his house')

For possible further consequences of the conservative nature of standard languages, see § 6 below.

In addition to being conservative or "defensive", standard languages may go on the offensive, as it were. In many contemporary societies the standard languages are in the process of severely threatening the existence of the local, vernacular dialects, or even of replacing them. This is often attributed to the influence of general education and of the increased effectiveness of the mass media in penetrating all layers of society. While these may be contributing factors, there are enough examples of similar developments in earlier times (when mass media played a minor role, if any) to suggest that we are dealing with a tendency that holds true for all languages, at all stages of their development.

The most celebrated and well-known instance of such a development, at a time when there was nothing comparable to the modern mass media, is the spread of the Greek Koiné during the Hellenistic period (roughly 300 B.C. to 300 A.D.), leading to the eventual replacement of virtually all of the older local dialects. (For the nature and origin of the Greek Koiné, see Chapter 12, § 5.) Only one present-day regional dialect can be clearly traced back to an ancient Greek local dialect, namely Tsakonian, a modern descendant of ancient Laconian (the dialect of Sparta). And even Tsakonian has a very heavy admixture of Koiné elements. All the other Modern Greek regional dialects are descended from the Koiné, although they may preserve a few traces of older local, or at least, regional dialects.

Standard languages, thus, can in effect completely eliminate the effects of centuries of continuous interaction between neighboring dialects. (On these effects see Chapter 11.)

However, in many cases the local, vernacular dialects do not disappear without any trace. As regional non-standard speakers adopt the standard language, they commonly retain some of the features of their original dialect and wind up speaking the standard with a REGIONAL ACCENT. For instance, speakers from the U.S. South adopting northern standard speech (which is generally considered more prestigious) may quite successfully drop their "drawl" or their "nasal twang" and, after some initial mistakes, learn where to put in a postvocalic [r], and where not. Even so, they may retain certain echoes of their original speech, especially a pronunciation of words with northern [ay], such as *mine* and *ice*, which to northern speakers sounds more like [æ] and therefore can lead to misunderstandings, hilarity, or even embarrassment.

The spread of standard languages thus may not necessarily lead to completely homogeneous and dialect-free results. In fact, the resulting regional accents of the standard may acquire a life of their own and serve to newly define regional loyalties – in opposition to the threat of homogenization, and to the political and social powers behind that threat. Thus, in many European countries, local dialects have been disappearing at a rapid rate. Their place, however, has commonly been taken by regionalized forms of the standard. And partly because of the increasing social significance of these varieties, partly also because of a greater tolerance for diversity, regional accents are increasingly heard even among newscasters on national radio. Thus, where in the past, BBC news was invariably delivered in "RP" ("received (standard) pronunciation" – received from whom, one wonders), in more recent years it has become easy to identify announcers by their regional accent as coming from England, Scotland, Wales, or Ireland – even though all of them use otherwise impeccably standard British English. Similarly, even U.S. presidents like Jimmy Carter, who hail from the South, have been speaking Standard American English, though with a Southern regional accent.

Yet a further – and paradoxical – complication is that the spread of a standard language by no means leads to everybody speaking the standard variety and nobody speaking a vernacular. This seems to be due to two factors. First, standard languages commonly have colloquial variants that are used in less formal circumstances. Although these are variants of the standard, they are not considered identical to it. It seems that these are the varieties that spread much more successfully than the formal standard, which tends to remain limited to those who need to use very formal language, or believe they ought to. Secondly, regional dialects, too, come in relatively formal, more colloquial, and downright vernacular varieties. Among these, the vernacular varieties seem to be most successful in preserving some of their linguistic features.

Regional accents thus can display a great degree of diversity. On one side of the spectrum are the standard varieties, such as the different versions of Standard British English nowadays heard on BBC. As mentioned, these differ mainly in features of pronunciation. On the other extreme we find different vernaculars which, though far removed from the original regional dialects, are perhaps equally far removed from the standard. Not only is their pronunciation vastly different, they also differ in lexicon, syntax, and style.

An interesting side effect of the development of regional accents is that not all accents are necessarily considered equally acceptable. Frequently, accents that are most different from the non-regionalized standard are considered more interesting or pleasing than varieties that are closer to the standard. In part this may involve the reverse stereotype of the noble savage, but in part it may also result from the feeling that speakers of varieties relatively close to the standard should "know better" and that their different accent, therefore, is simply due to indolence or worse.

6. Diglossia

The conservative character of standard languages, if left unchecked, will over the centuries bring about an increasing differentiation between standard and vernacular, such that the standard language ceases to be intelligible to vernacular speakers without special schooling. This is the case in many of the European languages, where the vernaculars of the local dialects differ profoundly from the standard language; see the Scots English in example (8). Even in the United States, where the differences between standard and vernacular are smaller, some speech varieties find themselves in this situation vis-à-vis the standard language, especially African American Vernacular English and the speech of Appalachian rural whites.

In some societies, this situation has progressed to the point that the standard is in effect a foreign or second language for all speakers, learned only in school, but still considered to be the same language as that of the vernacular. Take for instance the modern Arabic world and modern Greece, where in each case an ancient, ancestral prestige language (or a derivative form of it) continued to be in active use among the educated for centuries, side by side with its less prestigious and increasingly different descendants. This special coexistence between ancient prestige language and modern vernacular is now commonly referred to as DIGLOSSIA.

In some cases, such as in modern Greece and especially in the Arabic world, the ancient prestige language tends to be employed mainly in written form or in highly formal recitation, while the vernacular is used elsewhere, and not always in writing. The situation is very similar in the German-language area of modern Switzerland. In fact, it has been claimed that nowadays some Swiss Germans are so unfamiliar with the spoken use of Standard German that they prefer using English or French with native or fluent speakers of Standard German.

In other traditions, the prestige language can – or could – also be employed in freely spoken form. This was the case for instance with Latin in medieval western Europe, which was used as the common written and spoken language of the educated. In India, Sanskrit has similarly continued in spoken form down to the present time – more than three millennia after it first appeared on the scene. And in Greece, a variety of Greek known as *katharévousa* (lit. 'purifying [language]') which was based in its grammatical form on Ancient Greek and thus differed markedly from the *dimotikí* (the 'people's [language]'), gained favor in the early nineteenth century as a sign of Greek national identity and of independence from the Ottoman Turks, who had ruled over Greece for several centuries.

From the modern perspective, situations of this type may be hard to believe. Why would people not use their own native language, instead of Latin, Sanskrit, or some other non-native language? The situation becomes easier to understand if we consider that medieval western Europe, just like modern Europe, was home to a large variety of different languages, many of which clearly were not mutually intelligible. Latin made it possible for students and scholars to go anywhere in Europe and be understood by their peers, without the need of learning French in France, Italian in Italy, German in Germany, English in England, Hungarian in Hungary, etc. The case is very similar for Sanskrit in India. In both areas, incidentally, the ancient prestige language was used not only to talk about scholarly issues. It could be used for any other communication, such as asking about each other's background, gossiping, or even telling dirty jokes. Note incidentally that English now serves a very similar function in many parts of the world.

In principle, prestige languages in such diglossic situations are very conservative, resisting the normal linguistic changes which affect the vernacular. However, if they are freely used in spoken form, they often undergo what may be called VERNACULARIZATION, an intrusion of vernacular linguistic features. Thus, spoken Sanskrit has in many areas of India acquired the vernacular pronunciation [j] and [b] for initial *y-* and *v-*. Similarly, the increasing vernacularization of medieval Latin led to the compilation of dictionaries which prescribed the correct, more classical pronunciation and proscribed the incorrect, popular pronunciation. And while highly conservative in its morphological structure, Katharevousa Greek is thoroughly modern in its pronunciation.

At the same time, recall that under more ordinary circumstances the interaction between dialect and standard may give rise to regional accents of the standard language which hold a position somewhere between the pure standard and the pure dialect. In a very similar manner, the interaction of vernaculars and the prestige language in a diglossic relationship may lead to new varieties intermediate between the pure vernacular and the pure prestige language.

Developments of this sort are found both in Greece and in many parts of the Arab world (e.g., in Egypt). In the Arab world, the prestige of the language of the Qur'an is so great that intermediate varieties of this type have little chance to get recognition. In Greece, the status of the prestige language has fluctuated considerably, depending on political developments. For instance, after a period of decline it was reinstated by the conservative military junta that ruled Greece from 1968 to 1974, but lost its official status with the downfall of the junta and the ascendancy of a democratic and more progressive government. Recent political developments, moreover, have encouraged the use of an emerging intermediate language, which mixes Katharevousa with Dimotiki elements, thus not only bridging the gap between the two forms of language, but also between the generally more conservative supporters of Katharevousa and the more liberal proponents of

Dimotiki. (Note the near-parallel of Nynorsk and Bokmaal in present-day Norway.)

In addition to vernacularization, the prestige language may undergo RE-GIONALIZATION, under the influence of the local languages or dialects. For instance, in medieval times, different forms of Church Latin developed in this manner. Some of these differed only in minor details, such as the pronunciation of *c* before *i* and *e*. Italian Church Latin had [č], that of France [s], and that of Spain [ts] (later ⇒ [θ] or [s]). The most deviant of these varieties was that of England, especially after the Great English Vowel Shift had changed the English vowel system beyond recognition (from the European perspective). For instance *exempli gratia*, pronounced as something like [eksempli gratsia] in Italian Church Latin and similarly elsewhere on the continent, came out as [egzemplay grēšə]. This highly idiosyncratic character of English Church Latin is probably one of the reasons why speakers of English nowadays affect the Italian pronunciation of Latin when singing compositions based on Latin texts, such as Bach's *B-Minor Mass* or Mozart's *Requiem*, and when citing Latin expressions such as *requiescat in pace* 'may (s)he rest in peace'.

Diglossic situations may have an enormous impact on people's lives. In order to become literate it is necessary in effect to learn a foreign language. But to make things even worse, the foreignness of that language is not even acknowledged. Students are expected to learn it without great difficulty, since it is "their language". And if they do not succeed very well they will be considered dunces for "not knowing their own language".

Of course, such difficulties are not necessarily limited to diglossic situations. In languages like English, too, we find that many students speaking vernacular forms of the language have great difficulties learning the standard. Here, too, they are often considered dunces for "not knowing their own language".

The difference between diglossic situations and languages like English with their more normal distinction between standard and vernacular is one of degree, not an absolute one. The very notion of standard, with its insistence on immutable correctness, bears the seeds of diglossia. At the same time, the idea that there should be a standard seems to permeate all human languages, presumably because it is useful to have a form of speech that makes it possible to communicate across different linguistic and social groups and even across time. And no matter what the society, standard languages enjoy the highest prestige.

What is perhaps most interesting, and even puzzling at first sight, is the paradox that, in spite of the well recognized prestige of the standard, vernacular forms of language have remarkable staying power. If standard languages are so prestigious, why don't vernacular speakers fall all over themselves and switch to the standard?

Some speakers do in fact do so. But an amazingly large number of vernacular speakers refuse. They may say things like *I don't talk so good*. But if asked, *Why don't you switch?*, they will answer something like *What, and sound like a sissy?!*

It is no doubt this attitude that is responsible for the amazing stability of vernaculars. And one suspects that, ultimately, diglossia results not only from the conservatism of standard dialects, but also from the tendency of vernaculars to remain distinct and even to increase their distinctness by linguistic changes differentiating them from the standard. As in the Labovian view of sound change, group identification and group membership is a powerful factor in linguistic behavior and linguistic change.

7. Dialect borrowing

As observed in § 1 above, special speech varieties such as argots, jargons, and slang may interact by borrowing from each other, as in the case of *pal*. (As mentioned earlier, this word entered ordinary English through borrowing from an argot, probably via slang.)

Examples like this show that the picture of borrowing painted in Chapter 8 is incomplete. Borrowing can take place, not only between different, distinct languages, but also between dialects of the same language. Let us conclude this chapter by examining in greater detail the special consequences and difficulties of dialect borrowing, including borrowing in diglossic situations.

Because the linguistic differences between dialects are smaller than those between different languages, dialect borrowing does not require the same amount of adjustment in phonological and other structures and thus is much easier to accomplish. But precisely because of the greater similarities between donor and borrowing language, dialect borrowings are much more difficult to detect for the linguist. In many cases, they differ from native words in just one or two sounds. Fortunately, in many cases we have enough evidence to establish that given words are in fact borrowings, and not native words with somewhat unusual phonological developments. But in some cases it is exceedingly difficult to establish a case for borrowing.

Let us illustrate the problem with the example in (12). Normally, Old English initial *f* and *s* remain unchanged in modern English; see (12a). But in a few words we find a Modern *v* corresponding to OE *f*, and in one case, *z* corresponds to *s*; see (12b). In addition, there are a few other words which entered English with initial *f* after the Old English period, and which also have *v* in Modern English; see (12c).

(12)   Old English   Modern English

    a. *for*   *for*
       fox   *fox*
       feccian   *fetch*
       full   *full*
       fyllan   *fill*
    b. *fana*   *vane*
       fæt   *vat*
       fyxin 'female fox' *vixen*
       seax 'sword'   *zax* 'roofer's knifc-like tool'
    c. pre-Mod. Engl.   Modern English
       fente   *vent* 'slit in pack or side of coat'
          (⇐ Fr. *fendre* 'to split')
       fiole   *vial*
          (⇐ Lat. *phiala* 'drinking vessel' ⇐ Gk. *phiálē*)
       fanneer-   *veneer*
          (⇐ Germ. *fournier-*)

On the face of it, the examples in (12b) and (12c) look like examples of irregular sound change. And since no analogy or other special dialect-internal process can be invoked to account for their initial voiced fricatives, they may be considered strong counterevidence to the neogrammarian hypothesis that sound change is regular. Even in the words of (12c) which were borrowed from other languages, the initial voiced fricative cannot be explained as resulting from borrowing. The pre-Modern English forms clearly show that the words were borrowed into English with initial *f*.

A solution to our problem is possible once we consider the dialectal situation in England. While most modern dialects preserve initial voiceless *f* and *s* intact, a group of southwestern dialects, including the dialect of Somerset [zəmərzɛt], regularly change all initial voiceless fricatives into voiced ones before vowel. That is, in these dialects we get not only *vat, vane, vixen*, but also *vor, vox*, and *vill*. (For instance, in Henry Fielding's novel *Tom Jones*, situated in southwest England, Squire Western regularly talks about going hunting for *voxes*.)

What we need to assume, then, is that the words in (12b/c) were borrowed from "Somerset dialects" into the speech of London, the basis for the Modern English standard language. In fact, closer examination of the words in (12b/c) makes it possible even to venture a guess as to how and why the words may have entered London speech. Except for *vixen*, all of the words – and these are all the words with initial fricative voicing now in use in Standard English – have technical meanings in pre-modern society: *vats* and *veneer* are terms associated with woodworking, *vanes* and *zaxes* with roofers' work, *vents* with tailoring, and *vials* and *vats* with making containers for liquids or with filling containers with liquids. This raises the distinct possibility that the words entered London speech through craftsmen's jargons (compare the nautical jargon in § 3 above), and that perhaps even *vixen* found its way to London through the same vehicle.

Problems can arise, too, in diglossic situations where the standard language is in effect the linguistic ancestor of the vernacular, and where at the same time it remains in use for centuries, side by side with its vernacular descendants. Such situations are found especially in the case of Latin and (early) Romance, and of Sanskrit and its later, Middle or Modern Indo-Aryan descendants.

The continued coexistence of prestige language and vernacular may lead to the same word being borrowed repeatedly, at different chronological stages of the vernacular and the prestige language, and with very different results. Early borrowings would be more similar to dialect borrowings (as in (12)), since prestige language and vernacular would have had little time to diverge up to that point. Ironically, however, the borrowed words would later come to diverge most, because from the point of borrowing they have the longest time and therefore the greatest number of opportunities for undergoing linguistic changes that differentiate them from their sources. By contrast, very late borrowings may be more like foreign language borrowings, easy to detect, but requiring a fair amount of nativization. At the same time, they would usually be more similar to their sources than early borrowings, because they have much less time to become different through linguistic change. The words borrowed most recently thus would be the most similar to the source, while the words borrowed earliest would be the most different. As if the situation were not complex enough, a further complication arises from the fact that there may be borrowings somewhere in the middle, made at stages when the relationship between prestige language and vernacular is intermediate between dialect and foreign language.

By way of illustration, let us look at a few concrete examples from Spanish. In (13), it is possible to argue that only (13a) has a chance of being inherited from Latin. It differs most strikingly from the Latin original, with a palatal nasal *ñ*, different from both the *m* and the *n* of Latin. The form in (13b) is more likely to be an early borrowing, since it retains the vowel of the initial syllable unchanged, as well as the *m* of the Latin original. (The following *b* can be explained as epenthetic between nasal *m* and oral *r*, see Chapter 3, § 5.2.) The form differs from its Latin source by not showing a trace of the medial *-i-*, and by exhibiting an *r* where Latin had *n*. Finally, the form in (13c) is virtually identical to the Latin original. This suggests that it is a very recent borrowing and consequently had little or no chance of undergoing changes indigenous to Spanish. (In Spanish linguistics, forms of the type (13c) and (13b) are commonly distinguished as *cultismos* and *semicultismos*, where the *semi-* of the latter term indicates that such words are only half-foreign or half-learnèd, by being more firmly integrated into the fabric of the language than fully foreign or learnèd words.)

(13)   Latin   Spanish
    a. *dominum* *dueño*   'lord'
    b. *nominem* *nombre*   'name'
    c. *nomināre* *nominar* 'to name, nominate'

In (14), by contrast, the situation is much less certain. As in (13b/c) we find phonetically different reflexes of (virtually) the same Latin words. But the criteria that made it possible to distinguish inherited from borrowed reflexes in (13) do not help us in (14). The form in the middle column is phonetically closer to Latin, but the form on the right is semantically closer. How, then, can we be certain which of these forms – if any – is inherited, and which is borrowed?

(14)   Latin   Spanish
    iunctum [y-]   *yunto*   *junto*
    'joined'   'close'   'joint, united'

Fortunately, examples of the type (14) are rare. However, they show most strikingly the difficulties faced by linguists trying to establish historical developments in situations of extended diglossia, such as that between Latin and its Romance descendants.

Chapter 11
Dialect geography and dialectology

"I knowed you wasn't Oklahomy folks. You talk queer kinda –
That ain't no blame, you understan'."
"Everybody says words different," said Ivy. "Arkansas folks says
'em different, and Oklahomy folks says 'em different. And we
seen a lady from Massachusetts, an' she said 'em differentest of
all. Couldn' hardly make out what she was sayin'."
(John Steinbeck, *The Grapes of Wrath*.)

1. Introduction

The case of *fox* vs. *vixen* and other such examples in the preceding chapter
shows that different geographical dialects can interact with each other through
lexical borrowing. However, contact between speakers of neighboring dialects
tends to be pervasive, permeating all aspects of their daily lives. The effects of
contact, therefore, commonly extend beyond lexical borrowing and involve
aspects of general linguistic structure as well, including the extension of
linguistic changes from one dialect to another.

To illustrate this point let us return to a familiar phenomenon, the Chicago
sound shift discussed in Chapter 4, § 5.4, and exemplified in (1) below. Within
Chicago, the change is considered low in prestige and is confined mainly to
certain white, generally male and even macho, working-class circles. (See
also Chapter 10, § 3.)

(1)   a. *have* [hæv]   > [hæəv], [hɛəv]

               Jan [ǰæn]   > [ǰæən], [ǰɛən]

               taxi [tæksi]   > [tæəksi], [tɛəksi]

    b. *Chicago* [šikago] > [šikægo]

               John [ǰan]   > [ǰæn]

Interestingly, the change has not remained limited to the city in which it
originated. Especially its first phase, the change in (1a), has spread outside
Chicago, first in the "bedroom communities" of the "collar counties" around

Chicago, and later to other areas further downstate. If we examine the social evaluation of the change in these areas, we can see why the change has come to be adopted. Outside Chicago the change has been reinterpreted as a relatively prestigious sign of urbanization. It is therefore being affected by speakers who consider urbanization a good thing, especially younger, upwardly mobile people, residing in more urbanized localities. What is even more interesting is the response of women. In Chicago, where the change has relatively low prestige, women are reluctant to adopt the change. Outside Chicago, where the change is considered prestigious, women seem to be in the vanguard of those who adopt it.

Given its relatively low prestige in Chicago, one might wonder how the change came to be accepted by any group at all. The reason is that prestige is a relative term. What may be prestigious in society at large may be considered unacceptable in certain subgroups. In the case of Chicago, the sound shift in (1) seems to go along with a certain macho, tough-guy image cultivated by a subsection of the male white working class. And what counts as prestigious speech in other strata of society would in this group be considered sissified. (See also Chapter 10, § 5.) This social stereotyping of the change within Chicago accounts very well for the fact that in the city, women are reluctant to accept it. Outside Chicago, on the other hand, the change has a flavor of being fashionable. Women, being encouraged to be more conscious of trends in fashion than men, therefore are more likely to adopt it.

While in the present case prestige seems to be bringing about a steady and fairly extensive spread of the change into downstate Illinois, it is worth remembering that prestige can have very different effects. As may be recalled from Chapter 5, § 6, prestige differences between dialects frequently give rise to hypercorrections. A case in point is illustrated in (2) below. In a group of dialects intermediate between northern and southern U.S. speech, stretching from Maryland in the east to Kansas in the west, final [-ə] at one time had changed to [-i] or [- ɨ]. Forms like *sody* and *opry* (as in *Grand Ole Opry*) therefore were the regular counterparts of northern and southern *soda* and *op(e)ra*. Note also the *Oklahomy* (for *Oklahoma*) in the epigraph of this chapter. However, when the pronunciation with final [-ə] came to be considered more prestigious, it began to spread, not only in words with original [-ə], but also in words with original [-i], such as *Missouri*.

(2)   *sody*   : *soda*
        opry   : *opera*
        Missouri : X

The difference between the steady and extensive spread of the Chicago sound shift and the much more sporadic phenomenon of hypercorrection may be explained as follows. The prestige of the Chicago shift in downstate Illinois has come about more or less spontaneously, without outside interference. Its acceptance generally is not a matter of conscious decision but takes place below the level of conscious awareness. On the other hand, the replacement of dialectal [-i] by [-ə] was in large measure a response to a very conscious process of school instruction. It is therefore imposed from the outside and not spontaneous. Moreover, one suspects that school instruction tended to remain confined to correcting the pronunciation of individual words, without providing a reliable, general rule that would make it possible for pupils to know which words should be pronounced with [-ə] and which with [-i].

In some form or another, then, prestige can be seen to play an important role in the manner and degree to which features spread from one dialect to another.

Now, when looking at lexical borrowing, we saw that prestige finds a counterforce in linguistic nationalism. In dialect contact, prestige similarly may be countered by sociolinguistic polarization, as illustrated by the following two cases.

(i) The fact that the changes in (1) are highly stigmatized as working-class in Chicago has led to an interesting response in much of Chicago speech. First, and not surprisingly, there is no diphthongization and raising of [æ]. Second, and more surprisingly perhaps, the vowel [a] undergoes a development diametrically opposed to the working-class fronting, becoming backed and (slightly) rounded, at least in the word *Chicago*. Thus in much of Chicago, the name of the city is pronounced as something like [šikɔgo], rather than working-class [šikægo] – or general Midwestern [šikago], for that matter. (See also § 2.1 below.)

(ii) On Martha's Vineyard, centralization of [a] in the diphthongs [ay] and [aw] toward the position of [ə] served to reassert linguistically the separate identity of the islanders over against the mainlanders. In fact, as noted in Chapter 4, § 6.3, as the change was being implemented, both the degree of centralization and the number of words undergoing the process were highest for those who strongly identified themselves as islanders, and lowest for those who had a positive attitude toward the mainland.

2. Patterns of dialect interaction

2.1. The Chicago sound shift revisited

Consider again the SPREAD of the Chicago sound shift from working-class Chicago to downstate Illinois. A closer look shows that the spread first of all is correlated with relative distance from Chicago: The change applies more pervasively in the counties immediately surrounding Chicago, the area in which it originated; its effects come to be more and more attenuated with increasing distance from Chicago. In this sense, then, the change radiates out from its source area and slowly peters out on the periphery.

Secondly, because the change is associated with urbanization or a positive attitude to urbanization, it is implemented more thoroughly in urbanized than in rural areas. As a consequence, its effects may be stronger in urban locations that are quite distant from Chicago than in intervening rural areas. In this regard, then, there is a certain DISCONTINUITY to the pattern in which the change is spreading.

These patterns of spread are by no means an isolated – or recent – phenomenon. In the following sections let us take a closer look at two celebrated cases from the past which are a little more challenging because of their complexity, but at the same time, also more instructive.

2.2. The fate of long *$\bar{u}$ in the Low Countries

During the Middle Ages, old Germanic [ū] began to shift to [ü] in the Flemish/Dutch dialect area of Belgium and the Netherlands (the "Low Countries"). It is likely that the change originated in the Flemish coastal area whose port cities held special prestige at that time. Evidently it spread from that area to the south, north, and east. To the south, its spread eventually was blocked by French, and to the north, by the sea. On the eastern boundary, the situation was more complex. The prestige of the Flemish area here was encroaching on another prestige area, dominated by the Low German union of commercial cities known as the Hanseatic League; in this area [ū] was retained unshifted.

In between these two areas we find something like a no-man's land, relatively unaffected by the prestige of either area, but somewhat more open to the Low Countries. In this area the change began to peter out, leaving in its wake speech islands in which the shift of [ū] to [ü] took place incompletely, affecting some words and leaving others unchanged. Especially interesting are the differences in connotations between shifted and unshifted lexical items. Shifted forms usually have more prestigious connotations. This is for instance the case for [hūs] 'house', something that one might brag about in talking to one's neighbors (as in *Come over and look at my new* [hǖs]). Unshifted forms occur in more "homey" vocabulary, such as [mūs] 'mouse', referring to objects that one would be less likely to bring to one's neighbors attention. Here the prestige of the innovating dialects evidently is reflected in the choice of words permitted to adopt the innovating pronunciation.

Moreover, as in the case of the Chicago working-class vowel shift, this intermediate area exhibits instances of discontinuous spread. The change may leapfrog over territory that is only incompletely affected by the change, or not affected at all. Compare the eastern periphery of Map 1 below, with its pockets of solid [ǖ] territory within the larger [ū/ǖ] area, as well as the [ū/ǖ] enclave in the northeast, in otherwise solidly [ū] territory.

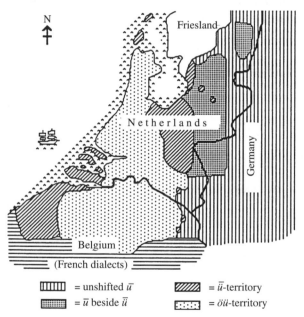

Map 1. Outcomes of **ū* in the Low Countries

What complicates matters is that in the sixteenth and seventeenth centuries, a new development affected a smaller, relatively central part of the area: The [ǖ] which had arisen from earlier [ū] now diphthongized to [öü] in the coastal cities of the Netherlands; and the prestige of these cities led to the spread of this innovation to most of the territory that had participated in the earlier change. Again, however, the change lost momentum at the periphery. As a consequence, parts of the area – in some cases only very small speech islands – have retained the older monophthongal pronunciation.

2.3. The Old High German consonant shift

A similar but even more complex pattern is presented by the shift of the Germanic voiceless stops in a dialect area which is called "High" German because it is located in the southern, "up-country", or mountainous area of Germany. In idealized form, the changes which together implement the shift can be formulated as in (3), disregarding certain minor complications. For the usual orthographic representation of the outcomes, see (4). Examples are given in (5).

(3) a. voiceless stops become affricates (e.g. *t* > *ts*) initially and after consonant (except after *s*, where the stops remain unshifted). In the case of original dental stop, the outcome is dental (here marked as *ts̩*)

   b. they become "strong" (i.e. double) fricatives elsewhere (except, again, after *s*). In the case of original dental stop the outcome is dental *s̩s̩*.

(4)

Symbol	Phonetic value	Context
pf	[pf]	(3a)
ff	[ff]	(3b)
z	[ts̩] (dental)	(3a)
zz	[s̩s̩] (dental, vs. alveolar *s(s)*)	(3b)
ch	[kx] or simplified to [x]	(3a)
hh	[xx]	(3b)

(5)

	Proto-Germanic	Old High German	
labial	**paid-*	*pfeit*	'tunic'
	*helpan-	*helpfan*	'help'
	*stump-	*stumpf*	'stump'
vs.	**hlaupan-*	*hlouffan*	'leap, run'
dental	**tō*	*zuo*	'to'
	*hert-	*herz*	'heart'
	*unt-	*unz(i)*	'unto'
vs.	**lētan-*	*lāzzan*	'let'
	*fat-	*fazz*	'vat, barrel'
	*þat	*thazz (> dazz)*	'that'
velar	**kald-*	*chalt*	'cold'
	*melk-	*milch*	'milk'
	*ank-	*ancho*	'butter'
vs.	**makō(ya)n-*	*mahhōn*	'make'
	*ik/ek	*ihh*	'I'

Before we address the more realistic picture of the Old High German shift that results from dialect spread, we may stop for a moment to take a closer look at the shift itself. In its treatment of older voiceless stops, the shift bears a great amount of similarity to Grimm's Law, especially if we assume that the Grimm's Law shift of voiceless stops to voiceless fricatives proceeded via an intermediate stage with voiceless affricates (see Chapter 4, § 5.4). Moreover, it changed earlier voiced *d* into *t*, just as did Grimm's Law.

In fact, Grimm, who was keenly aware of these similarities, believed that the parallelism of the change went even further. The Old High German shift of *þ* to *d* (as in **þat > thazz > dazz* 'that') was, to his mind, a perfect parallel to the part of Grimm's Law that turned the PIE voiced aspirates into voiced stops. This view of Grimm's was based on an identification of aspirates, affricates, and fricatives as a single class of consonants, which he called "Aspiratae" and which he contrasted with voiced stops ("Mediae"), and voiceless ones ("Tenues"). Once this identification was made, it was possible to diagram the changes from PIE to Proto-Germanic and thence to Old High German as in Figure 1 or, even, more strikingly, as a somewhat mysterious circle which kept recycling the sound system, as in Figure 2. (In both of these figures, A = Grimm's Aspiratae, M = Mediae, and T = Tenues.)

Figure 1. Grimm's conceptualization of Grimm's Law and the Old High German sound shift

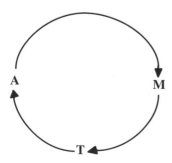

Figure 2. Grimm's "cyclical law"

While some aspects of the Old High German sound shift are indeed strikingly similar to Grimm's Law, Grimm's conceptualization of the relationship between the two shifts can no longer be accepted. First, since Grimm's time our understanding of phonetics has improved considerably, and we must now reject his identification of voiced aspirates, voiceless affricates, and voiceless fricatives as a single category, Aspiratae. Secondly and more specifically, while dental *d* and *þ* do in fact change to *t* and *d*, respectively, the development of their labial and velar counterparts was not exactly parallel. That is, unlike Grimm's Law, the Old High German sound shift was systematic only for the voiceless stops.

More important for our present discussion is the fact that, even in the voiceless stops, the Old High German shift was completely regular only in Alemannic, spoken in the southwest, along the upper Rhine valley. Outside Alemannic, the results of the High German consonant shift decrease in generality and regularity as the distance from Alemannic increases; see Map 2.

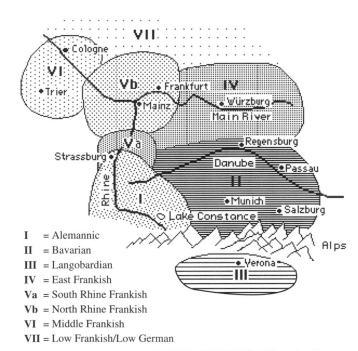

I   = Alemannic
II = Bavarian
III = Langobardian
IV = East Frankish
Va = South Rhine Frankish
Vb = North Rhine Frankish
VI = Middle Frankish
VII = Low Frankish/Low German

Map 2. Spread of Old High German sound shift

Interestingly, in some of the dialects the change becomes more general and regular with the progress of time. Thus, early Langobardian (dialect area

	Initially	After *r*	After *l*	After nasal	between vowels	word-finally
I	*z, pf, ch*	*z, pf, ch*	*z, pf, ch*	*z, pf, ch*	*zz, ff, hh*	*zz, ff, hh*
II	*z, pf, ch*	*z, pf, ch*	*z, pf, ch* *p* in relics	*z, pf, ch*	*zz, ff, hh*	*zz, ff, hh*
III	*z, p, k* > *pf, ch*	*z, p, k* > *(p)f,ch*	*z, p, k* > *(p)f,ch*	*z, p, k* > *pf*	*zz, ff, hh*	*zz, p, hh* > *ff*
IV	*z, pf, k*	*z, pf, k*	*z, pf, k* *p* in relics	*z, pf, k*	*zz, ff, hh*	*zz, ff, hh*
Va	*z, p, k* > *pf*	*z, (p)f, k* *p* in relics	*z, pf, k* *p* in relics	*z, pf, k* *p* in relics	*zz, ff, hh*	*zz, ff, hh* early: *that* vs. *fazz* later also *thazz*
Vb	*z, p, k*	*z, p, k* > *pf*	*z, p, k* > *pf*	*z, p, k*	*zz, ff, hh*	*zz, ff, hh* early: *that* vs. *fazz* later also *thazz*
VI	*z, p, k*	*z, p, k* > *pf*	*z, p, k* > *pf*	*z, p, k*	*zz, ff, hh*	*zz, ff, hh* but: *that* vs. *fazz*
VII	*t, p, k*	*t, p, k*	*t, p, k*	*t, p, k*	*t, p, k*	*t, p, k*

Chart 1. Outcomes of PGmc. *$*t, p, k$* in the older continental Germanic dialects, grouped in terms of phonetic environments

III, in northern Italy, present-day Lombardy) retains *p* and *k* unshifted after *r* and *l*; later Langobardian extends the shift to this context. Similarly, South and North Rhine Frankish (areas Va and Vb) retain unshifted *that* 'that' at an early period, but later change it to *thazz*. This increase in the number of lexical items which exhibit the shift shows that the change was still spreading at the time of our earliest documents. But as shown by relics with unshifted *p* in Bavarian, East Frankish, and Rhine Frankish (dialect areas II, IV, and Va/b), in many cases the spread remains incomplete. A more complete summary of developments and relic forms is presented in Chart 1.

In contrast to the Low Countries, lexical or overt prestige considerations have only a minor effect on the spread of the change in Old High German. The only thing coming close to the Low Country prestige differentiation between [hūs] and [mūs] is the different treatment in areas Va,b, and VI of the pronominal form *that* 'that' with unshifted *t*, vs. nominal forms like *fazz* 'vat, barrel' with shift of *t* to *zz*. In these areas, then, the spread of the Old High German sound shift affected "content" words but failed to affect pronouns, which are function words and more deeply embedded in the grammar. (As noted in the preceding paragraph, in areas Va,b, unshifted *that* soon gave way to shifted *thazz*. In these areas, then, the failure to affect pronouns was only a temporary phenomenon.)

3. Focal, transition, and relic areas

Disregarding differences in detail, all the cases of dialectal spread that we have examined so far share a general pattern.

There is a FOCAL AREA within which the change originates and in which the process is regular. This area contains the home dialect of the change, but may also include neighboring territory into which the change spread early and thoroughly.

On the other end of the spectrum is a RELIC AREA, or several such areas, which has (or have) not been affected by the spread.

Between these, there may be a TRANSITION AREA in which the spread loses in generality or peters out. The extent of this degeneralization may be determined by lexical factors, as in Dutch [hūs] vs. [mūs], Rhine Frankish *that* vs. *fazz*. Or it may be conditioned by considerations of linguistic structure. This is most strikingly the case for the spread of the Old High German sound shift, which (disregarding minor lexical relic forms such as *that*) peters out in terms of phonological parameters. In general, *p* and *k* lag behind. In East and Rhine Frankish (areas IV and Va,b) *k* remains unshifted in initial position and after liquid. And in Middle Frankish (area VI), both *p* and *k* remain unshifted in the same positions, as well as after nasal. The prestige factors responsible for the incomplete spread remain transparent in some cases; see especially Dutch [hūs] vs. [mūs]. In many other cases, such as in the majority of dialects accepting the Old High German shift, the effect of prestige may no longer be discernible. What is discernible, however, is the decreased regularity of the change.

Focal areas tend to be geographically or socially central areas, whereas relic areas tend to be geographically or socially outlying or otherwise remote areas. Thus in the case of the Low Countries, the focal area consisted of the socially central, coastal regions. Relic areas are typically found on the periphery, relatively far removed from the focal areas. However, it has been observed that other factors may play a role. For instance, location in a relatively inaccessible mountain area may turn a dialect into a relic area, even if it is geographically quite close to the focal area. On the other hand, rivers ordinarily do not present obstacles to spread. In fact, they often are conduits for accelerated spread because they tend to serve as commercial links between the communities living on either side.

4. Dialectology as a diagnostic tool

As we have just seen, an examination of historically verifiable situations shows that incomplete spread of a change may lead to irregularities in the outcome of the change in transition areas (such as Dutch *hūs : mūs*). This insight can be drawn on to account for similar prehistoric situations, even if we may not have any direct evidence for the historical sequence of events. This is especially important as regards sound change, for the notion of transition area can be used to eliminate apparent counterexamples to the neogrammarian hypothesis that sound change is completely regular. To illustrate the point let us look at a specific case in early Indo-European.

As noted in Chapter 2, § 3.6, during the last century Indo-Europeanists were excited by the discovery that at a very early time, a group of Indo-European languages changed the Proto-Indo-European (PIE) palatal stops into sibilants. Compare PIE *$\acute{k}mtom$ '100' > Avestan *satəm*. Other languages preserved the stop articulation, as in the Latin outcome *centum* [k-] '100'. The two groups of languages are distinguished as "satem" vs. "centum" languages (using the Avestan and Latin outcomes of the word for '100'). In its most regular and general form, the change can be formulated as in (6). Let us refer to the change as satem-assibilation.

(6)   PIE *$\acute{k}$ etc. > *tš* > *š, s* (etc.)

The reason for the excitement was that the satem-assibilation appeared to be a very early development which boldly divided the Indo-European languages into an eastern satem-branch, which among others included Indo-Iranian, Slavic, and Baltic, and a western centum-branch, embracing Greek, Italic, Celtic, and Germanic. The discovery that Hittite (to the south) and Tocharian (on the far eastern periphery) do not exhibit satem-assibilation and thus are centum languages has diminished the excitement somewhat, since this distribution calls into question the earlier assumption of a clear east-west distinction. Nevertheless, there can be no doubt that satem-assibilation is a very early change, one which possibly took place within a Proto-Indo-European dialect continuum.

PIE	Sanskrit	Avestan	Lithuanian	Old Ch.Slavic	Latin
*ḱlew/ḱlu- 'hear, listen'	śru-	sru-	klau-s-ī-ti vs. šlōvē 'fame'	slyšati slava 'fame'	in-clutus 'famous'
*sweḱuros 'father-in-law'	śvaśura-	xvasura-	šešuras	svekŭrŭ	socer
*ḱm̥tom '100'	śatam	satəm	šimtas	sŭto	centum

Chart 2. Satem- vs. centum forms

What is more important in the present context is that the generality and regularity of satem-assibilation is not evenly distributed. Indo-Iranian shows the change in its most complete and regular form. Slavic and Baltic, by contrast, exhibit the effect of the changes in some words, while others show unshifted segments. Even doublets can be found, in which the same original root shows reflexes with and without shifted segments. Compare the data in Chart 2. (Latin here represents all of the centum languages; Lat. *c* = [k]. Note that the Slavic word for '100' is irregular in the outcome of PIE *m̥; but this does not affect the present discussion.)

Keeping in mind the geographical distribution of the dialects (see Map 3), we are justified in explaining the distribution of satem-assibilation outcomes as follows. The change originated in a relatively centrally located focal area which included Indo-Iranian. The centum languages on the periphery are relic areas in which the change did not take place at all. Balto-Slavic, with its irregular outcomes, is a transition area between the focal area and the western relic areas; and as usual, within that transition area the change spread incompletely.

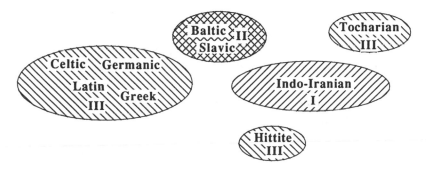

I = Focal area, II = Transition area, III = Relic areas

Map 3. Satem-assibilation in early Indo-European

5. Isoglosses and the problem of defining regional dialects

We have seen in § 2 that the patterns resulting from the spread of linguistic innovations can be quite complex. The complexities would become even more evident if, in the case of the Old High German sound shift, we had marked the boundaries, or ISOGLOSSES, of the territory in which any given word or class of words was or was not affected by the spread of the change. Compare for instance Map 4, which gives the northern boundaries for the different outcomes of the shift.

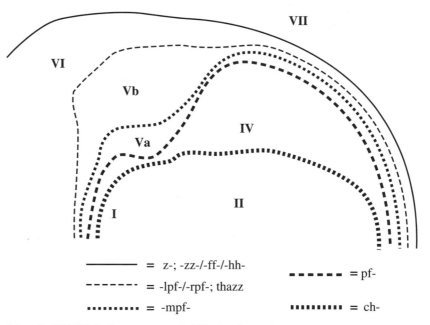

Map 4. Old High German sound shift: Isoglosses

Map 4 actually is highly simplified. It does not include the Langobardian dialect area in northern Italy, and it ignores minor relics or readjustments in the early stages of the dialects. (For instance, areas Va and Vb are included in the territory with shifted *t* in the pronoun *thazz*, even though at an early stage they show unshifted *that*.)

More significant, however, Map 4 is quite incomplete. A more complete representation would look something like Map 5 (p. 360), whose added isoglosses reflect the developments and phenomena summarized in Chart 3. But though that may be hard to believe, even this map is simplified and

(a) East Frankish inserts *w* in verbs like *sāen* 'sow' (> *sāwen*). Other dialects insert *h* or *i*, as in *sāhen/sāien*, but without any discernible dialectal differentiation.

(b) Middle and Low Frankish overlordship introduces legal terminology, such as *irteilen* 'to judge', in most of Old High German. East Frankish and Southeast Bavarian preserve the relic *tuomen* 'to judge'.

(c) Alemannic *chw* > *ch*, as in *chwedan* > *chedan* 'speak'; elsewhere *chw/kw* remains.

(d) Proto-Germanic *ō > *ua* in early Alemannic and parts of neighboring South Rhine Frankish, while elsewhere it appears as *uo*. (Hence *ruam* vs. *ruom* 'fame'.)

(e) The Low Frankish change *f* > *x* in words like *luft* > *lucht* 'air' spreads to part of neighboring Middle Frankish. Elsewhere, *f* remains.

(f) *xs > *ss*, as in *oxso* > *osso* 'ox'. The change at one point reached Alemannic and Bavarian, but later retreated toward the north.

(g) Corresponding to the southern pronominal forms *er* 'he', *in* 'him', *mir* 'to me', *dir* 'to you (sg.)', the northern dialects offer *her, hin, mī, dī*, side by side with the southern forms. (This is a transition area phenomenon: Low German, to the north, has *he, hin, mī, dī*.)

(h) The ending *-iu* of the nominative/accusative plural neuter of the adjectives, as in *blintiu* 'blind things', is replaced by *-u* in most of Frankish, except the Southern portion of East Frankish. (Hence *blintu* 'blind things'.)

(i) Earlier *scol* 'shall' appears as *sol* in most dialects of late Old High German, while Bavarian retains the original form.

Chart 3. Developments defining additional Old High German isoglosses

offers only a glimpse of the real complexity. (The developments and phenomena outlined in Chart 3 are quite complex and involve detailed aspects of Old High German phonology, morphology, and lexicon. To follow the present discussion it is sufficient to be aware of these complexities; it is not necessary to understand every single detail.)

The complex isogloss patterns of Map 5 are by no means unusual. In fact, as time progresses, the dialect map of the High German dialects becomes even more convoluted. If we include all the various lexical borrowings in such a map and allow for enough time of continuous, uninterrupted contact, then the result may well be that EVERY WORD HAS ITS OWN HISTORY – the battle cry of early dialectologists who opposed the neogrammarian regularity doctrine.

While it probably is true that in the long run every word has its own history, this does not justify the conclusion that the neogrammarian view of linguistic change is wrong. In spite of the amorphous nature of much of linguistic change, there is also a great systematicity and regularity to language,

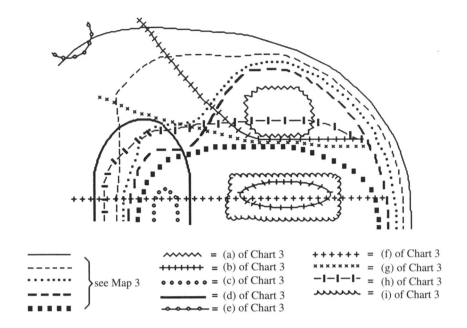

———————		∧∧∧∧∧ = (a) of Chart 3	++++++ = (f) of Chart 3
– – – – –		++++++ = (b) of Chart 3	✗✗✗✗✗✗✗ = (g) of Chart 3
· · · · · · · ·	see Map 3	○ ○ ○ ○ ○ ○ = (c) of Chart 3	–I–I–I– = (h) of Chart 3
– – – –		———— = (d) of Chart 3	∿∿∿∿∿ = (i) of Chart 3
▪ ▪ ▪ ▪ ▪		–○–○–○– = (e) of Chart 3	

Map 5. More complete isogloss map of Old High German

without which it would be difficult, if not impossible, to acquire – and understand – language effectively. And that systematicity manifests itself most
clearly in the regularity of sound change – within its home territory. To ignore this regularity and systematicity would severely limit our understanding
of linguistic change.

At the same time, it is quite clear that extensive and prolonged contact, as
it is frequently found in areas long settled by speakers of the same language,
leads to isoglosses cutting across the territory in more or less crazy-quilt fashion. While some of these isoglosses coincide with the major traditional dialectal divisions, such as Alemannic, Bavarian, or various varieties of Frankish
(see Map 2), many others do not, but cut boldly – sometimes timidly – across
these traditional dialect divisions.

This raises interesting questions for historical linguists. For instance, what
is the basis for German speakers continuing to think in terms of such dialectal divisions as Alemannic vs. Bavarian, even to the present day, if there are
isoglosses that link Alemannic more closely with Rhine Frankish, or Bavarian
with East Frankish? What makes it possible for ordinary, linguistically un-
trained speakers to classify the dialect of village X as Alemannic with strong
influence of Bavarian, but the dialect of Y, the next village to the east, as

Bavarian with strong influence from Alemannic? Are some isoglosses more salient, or more equal, than the others? That is, do some isoglosses constitute some kind of shibboleth? (See Chapter 10, § 4.) And if so, which isoglosses are they and how did they come to be shibboleths?

6. Migration and dialect leveling

The dialect interactions examined so far basically involve stationary dialects, whose speakers are fairly well settled. However, throughout the course of history we find entire linguistic groups settling new territories through colonization or conquest. In the process they may encounter speakers of very different languages, as for instance in the case of the European settlements in the Americas. But if they do not migrate very far, they may enter territory held by speakers of other dialects of the same language. And as in the case of contact with distinct, foreign languages, the result may be a complete, near-complete, or partial replacement of the native dialects.

The patterns resulting from such dialect expansion by conquest sometimes look very similar to what we find in the case of the more peaceful spread of dialectal innovations that we have examined so far. Here, too, we can often distinguish something like focal and relic areas. (There may even be transition areas, if the influence of the invaders begins to peter out on the periphery.)

A good illustration of this situation can be seen in Map 6 (p. 362), a simplified account of the ancient Greek dialects. Disregarding the mainland of Asia Minor (now modern Turkey) and its off-shore islands, whose earlier settlement history is less certain, we can observe a strong wedge of "West Greek" dialects (= Northwest Greek and Doric) cutting through the territories of Arcado-Cypriot and Aeolic. The members of the latter two dialect groups that were still extant in ancient times are located in typical relic areas. One of the Aeolic dialects, Thessalian, is located in the north, at the very periphery of ancient Greek; the other, Boeotian, is wedged into the mountainous and fairly inaccessible area between Northwest Greek, Doric, and Attic-Ionic. In the other dialect group, Arcadian is tucked away into the mountainous, forbidding interior of the Peloponnesus (the large land mass of southern Greece), and Cypriot survives on the island of Cyprus, on the southeastern periphery of the Greek dialect area.

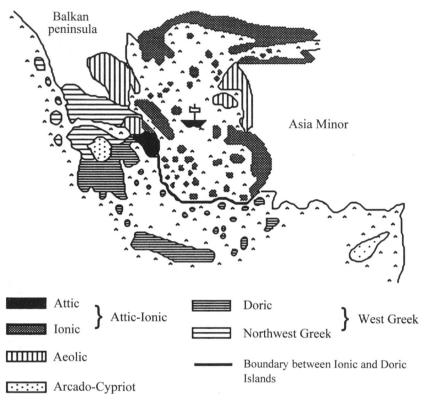

Map 6. Ancient Greek dialects

From various historical traditions of the Greeks we can discern the reason for this distribution. First, despite the large geographic separation of Arcadian and Cypriot, their linguistic connection makes sense historically, for ancient historians (e.g. Herodotus) held that Paphos, a major city of ancient Cyprus, was founded by an Arcadian colonist, Agapenor. Second, it is known that the West Greek tribes entered Greece as conquerors, considerably later than the other Greeks. And with their conquest, the West Greek invaders imposed their speech where they settled, ousting the older, indigenous Greek dialects whose distribution prior to the arrival of the West Greeks must have been more as indicated in Map 7 (p. 363).

In some cases, the ouster was not complete, and features of the local dialects were incorporated into Doric and Northwest Greek. Evidence for such a development is especially strong in Elean, in the northwest of the Peloponnesus. However, by and large, the division between West Greek and the

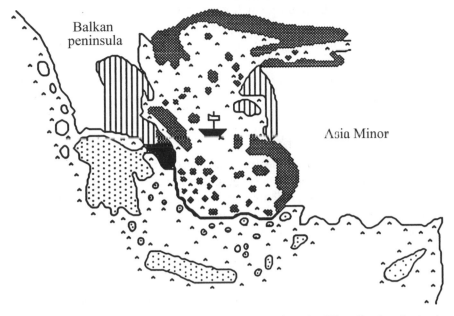

Balkan
peninsula

Asia Minor

Map 7. Approximate map of the Greek dialects before the West Greek colonization

other dialects turned out to be bold and clear-cut, with only a few isoglosses crossing the dialect boundaries between these two groups. Such relatively bold and clear-cut isoglosses seem to be a regular outcome of large-scale migration and bring about a situation quite different from the criss-crossing of isoglosses found in long-settled areas.

In addition to its effects on surrounding dialects and their relationship among each other, migration can have considerable influence on the speech of the people engaged in the migration. It has often been observed that colonial speech, i.e., the speech of groups that have left their homeland and settled in a new territory, has a much smaller degree of linguistic diversity than the dialects that have remained stationary. Thus, dialectal differences in general are much smaller in America than in Great Britain. Moreover, relatively homogeneous dialects occupy relatively large areas in the United States, while every English village of Britain tends to have a dialect markedly different from its neighbors. Finally, dialect differences in the western states, the last-settled area of the United States, are even smaller than on the East Coast or in the Middle West. (However, more recent developments, such as the Chicago Sound Shift, may introduce new divergences at the local level.)

The situation is similar in the Spanish-speaking world. Within Spain, the Castilian core area has the greatest linguistic diversity. A smaller degree of diversity is found in the South, which was settled by northern speakers after the destruction of its Islamic (or Moorish) states, the expulsion of most of its Muslim or Jewish population, and the forceful conversion of the rest to Christianity. In the same year that the last of the Moorish kingdoms fell to the forces of Catholic Spain, Columbus set sail and discovered the "New World", much of which was settled by Spanish speakers. And the dialectal diversity in the Spanish-speaking countries of the Americas is even smaller than that of Southern Spain (though, again, more recent developments have begun to introduce local differences).

The major factor responsible for this type of situation is DIALECT LEV-ELING. It is a common occurrence in migration that speakers who in the homeland lived far apart suddenly come into intensive, daily contact. Prior to migration, local loyalties and patterns of communication prevailed, and communication with the speakers of other dialects may have been minimal. As the result of migration, however, the importance of original local loyalties becomes diminished, and the job of communicating with the other settlers becomes paramount. Under these circumstances, changes which eliminate excessive differences between different speakers are highly favored, since they make communication and interaction easier. The result is a dialectally more homogeneous language.

The effects of migration, thus, may in some ways be similar to the elimination of dialect differences through the expansion of a supraregional, standard language at the expense of the local dialects (see Chapter 10).

Migration, in addition, can lead to a decrease in contact between the speech of the colonizers and that of the homeland. This often results in a relic area status for colonial speech as compared to the homeland, since innovations which sweep the homeland after the migration may reach colonial territory only incompletely, or not at all. Thus the British English loss of *r* in syllable-final position affected only the New England and Southern areas of what was to become the United States, areas which during their early history stayed in closer contact with the homeland. Other parts of the future United States remained unaffected. And as it turns out, it was the speech of these other, *r*-ful areas that eventually became more prestigious and now threatens the originally *r*-less dialects. (See Chapter 5, § 6.) Similarly the continued *h*-less pronunciation of *herb* in the United States is an archaism compared to the British spelling pronunciation with *h*.

However, here as elsewhere, being a relic area does not offer immunity from all linguistic change. Thus the strongly retroflex pronunciation of American *r*, and changes like the Chicago shift of [æ] to [æə] etc. are testimony to the fact that American English has undergone its own innovatory changes.

Finally, where migration leads to a complete severance of communication between colonial and homeland speech, different dialects become different languages. Without continued communication, the separated speech communities are free to change in completely different directions by developments which over time first reduce, and ultimately eliminate, any chance for mutual intelligibility – except through bilingualism (see the following chapters). This is no doubt how Proto-Indo-European, once a single language with dialectal diversification, turned into the different daughter languages briefly characterized in Chapter 2.

Languages in contact

Chapter 12
Language spread, link languages, and bilingualism

> So keep mei Words in Mind bei Tag und Nacht:
> A gute Noodlesupp' tut Wunders workeh.
> 'So keep my words in mind by day and night:
> A good noodle soup works wonders.'
> (Refrain of *Mama's Advice* by Kurt M. Stein)

1. Introduction: Link languages and their sources

Just as in dialect continua there are supraregional forms of speech which facilitate communication across regional differences, so in the case of distinct languages there may arise supraregional means of communication. Whatever their origin, supraregional languages may serve many different functions, ranging from that of national language to auxiliary means of communication. A term that covers all of this range is LINK LANGUAGE.

Link languages and related phenomena are of interest to students of language change because they often require the adoption of another language, generally a second, but perhaps even a third. Adoption of another language, in turn, generally leads to changes in the adopted link language, or even in the native language of the speaker, and thus can have profound effects on linguistic change.

The reasons for the supraregional use of languages are quite varied. They may range from dominance by sheer power or conquest, over a combination of political and cultural or technological/commercial predominance, to purely cultural preeminence. Examples of "conquering languages" are Latin in the Roman Empire, and English, French, and Spanish in more recent colonial empires. A combination of political and cultural, technological, or commercial predominance is seen in the case of French preeminence in eighteenth-century continental Europe, or that of English in the present, largely post-colonial world. Cultural dominance was responsible for the great prestige accorded to Greek as a link language in the Roman Empire – in spite of the fact that the Romans had conquered Greece. Cultural and religious reasons also were in part responsible for the fact that Sanskrit became the predominant interregional language of medieval and much of early modern India.

But Sanskrit may have been helped by an almost diametrically opposed factor, which can likewise lead to the selection of a particular language as a supraregional language, namely its lack of association with any particular linguistic group whose dominance might be perceived as a threat to the identity of other groups. In the case of Sanskrit, it has been argued that just prior to its expansion it was a language not tied to any particular region of India and that, moreover, in its classical form, it was the most neutral language in a society where various forms of Prakrit were the vehicles for Buddhism and Jainism, and where the sacred language of Hinduism was pre-classical, Vedic Sanskrit. For further examples see the later discussion of English in modern India, or Koiné Greek in the empire of Alexander the Great (covering Greece and most of the Middle East in the Hellenistic period from about 300 B.C. to 300 A.D.).

And just as elsewhere, LINGUISTIC NATIONALISM can act as a counterforce to cultural or political dominance.

The relationship and interaction between these opposing forces can be seen in many of the former European colonies, where debates rage over which language should become the national language or the language of wider communication in the newly independent country.

On one side are those who argue for the retention of the former colonial language as a supraregional means of communication, whether as the national language or as an officially recognized auxiliary language. Proponents of this view may in part be motivated by a desire to maintain the status which they derive from the knowledge of the colonialist language, a language not accessible to the uneducated and less privileged. Another important factor is that adoption of the foreign language makes it possible to avoid the often violent consequences of choosing one native linguistic variety over the others. And one should never underestimate the advantages that the use of English offers for interaction with the world at large.

On the other side are those who consider the former colonial language an insult to their national identity. Moreover, they argue, only through the use of indigenous languages will it be possible to compensate for the appalling lack of general education that has been the legacy of colonial rule; for it is unrealistic to expect people to become literate in an alien tongue when they do not even read or write in their own language.

In actual fact, the arguments for both views are far from cogent. It is in many cases possible to adopt an indigenous language which is just as "neutral" as the former colonialists' language and thus makes it possible to avoid the violent reactions that result when a regionally, communally, or otherwise marked language is selected. On the other hand, even if an indigenous language is chosen, that language frequently is unfamiliar to the speakers of other indigenous languages. These speakers, then, will still have to acquire literacy through a non-native language. And even for native speakers of the chosen language, the trouble may not be over, since almost invariably the variety of language chosen for administration and schooling is quite removed from the vernacular speech of the ordinary people in vocabulary, syntax, and style. In fact, the relationship between the official language and the vernacular in many cases comes very close to being diglossic (see Chapter 10, § 6).

The case of modern India is especially illuminating. When the British ruled India, Hindi, in its politically neutral, "Hindustani" variety (see Chapter 2, § 3.10.2), increasingly came to be the symbol of national unity against English, the language of the foreign oppressor. And Hindustani was learned widely throughout India, even in Bengal in the east and in the Dravidian south, areas whose speakers took great pride in their own linguistic and cultural heritage. But after independence there arose a great deal of opposition to attempts to make Hindi the national language, resulting in fierce political debate and even riots. Those opposed to Hindi argued for the retention of English as national language.

There are several reasons for this reaction. Perhaps the most important one was the fear of political hegemony: Since Hindi was the mother tongue of the largest single group of Indians, speakers of other languages considered the imposition of Hindi as a national language to be a threat to their own linguistic communities. This fear was especially great in Bengal in the east and in the Dravidian south, where the regional languages were considered to have a far greater literary tradition and prestige than Hindi. (See Chapter 8, § 4.2 on anti-Indo-Aryan linguistic nationalism in the Dravidian language Tamil.)

Whatever the motivation, the opponents of Hindi came to see English as an ideal alternative. After the departure of the British, it ceased to be a threat within India. Moreover, unlike Hindi, it was spoken as a native language by only very small and politically insignificant groups. Unlike Hindi, therefore, it did not bestow unfair advantages to large masses of native speakers. Rather, virtually all Indians were at the same advantage – or disadvantage – of having to learn English as a second or additional language.

As it turns out, the forces in favor of Hindi and those opposed to it have settled into something like a permanent stalemate. The issue of whether

Hindi or English should serve as the national link language of India remains unresolved to the present day, and both Hindi and English continue to be used.

In the modern period, there have been several attempts to avoid the difficulties connected with having to select an existing language as national or international link language through the creation of ARTIFICIAL LANGUAGES such as Volapük (invented in 1879 by the German linguist Johann Schleyer) or Esperanto (created in 1887 by the Polish physician L. L. Zamenhof). Like Nynorsk (Chapter 10, § 4), these are "constructed" languages, requiring a fair amount of linguistic engineering. But their purpose is almost diametrically different from that of Nynorsk. Where Nynorsk was constructed in the service of linguistic nationalism, languages like Volapük and Esperanto are created in the hope of bridging the narrow boundaries of nationalism by being languages that are truly international in scope.

The creators of these languages therefore have tried to develop languages that are relatively free of the idiosyncrasies of regionally based languages. However, in this regard, their success has been limited. For instance, *Volapük*, intended as the *pük* 'speech' of the whole *vola* 'world', professes to derive the components of its name from a specific language, English (*vola = world* and *pük = speak* – hard to believe but true); and in the element *pük* it uses a speech sound [ü] that is absent even from many European languages and therefore potentially difficult to acquire for their speakers. Esperanto insists on using a femininizing suffix *-ino* for words referring to females, even where not necessary (as in *fraulino* 'Miss', evidently from Germ. *Fräulein*, which does not have a male-reference counterpart) and in spite of the fact that many languages (such as Chinese) get by very well without using such suffixes. (An added problem which could not be foreseen when Esperanto was created is the late twentieth-century emergence of an increasing tendency toward using gender-neutral terminology, making specific gender marking, as in *fraulino*, quite undesirable.)

Esperanto has acquired a small, but very dedicated, number of adherents around the world who speak the language regularly and are said to use it effectively for communication across linguistic boundaries. There are even said to be some native speakers. But the attempt to make it a world language, superseding the traditional languages with all their nationalist baggage, clearly has failed.

Probably the greatest problem faced by artificial languages like Esperanto is that they are artificial. There seems to be a wide-spread prejudice against artificial languages, and that prejudice tends to be buttressed by arguments such as the following: "Esperanto is not a native language and therefore cannot adequately be used in many of the contexts that natural languages are able to serve, such as children's play, joking, or making love," or "Esperanto lacks an indigenous literature and therefore is in no position to compete with languages like English which can boast of a long and rich literary history." From an objective perspective, arguments such as these are not very strong. As the case of Nynorsk demonstrates, it is possible for a constructed language to become a native language, used in all social contexts and even boasting its own literature. But recall that the success of Nynorsk, too, has been less than spectacular. Only one sixth of the Norwegian population has embraced it. Subjective – and clearly negative – value judgments (as well as inertia) are responsible for the fact that the majority of the population continues to use Bokmaal.

The language which in today's world comes closest to functioning as a truly international means of communication, English, owes its status to a combination of different factors. Its initial spread around the world was clearly driven by a nationalist, colonialist expansion by Britain which, by the middle of the twentieth century, had spread it to every continent. But by that time already English had lost some of its cohesion, through the development of a second standard variety, American English, in the aftermath of the American Revolution. This variety itself had begun its own colonial expansion, especially in the Philippines. And even though colonial empires were crumbling, first slowly and then in a virtual avalanche, the political and technological power of the United States became ascendant, giving a further boost to the spread of English.

In the meantime, the form and function of colonial English were profoundly influenced by the bilingual context in which it took root. Post-colonial English reflects the impact of the indigenous languages of those who came to use it for their own purposes. Through the incorporation of structural and lexical features from the indigenous languages, new varieties of English have arisen which have been called INDIGENIZED, such as Indian or West African English. (See § 2 for the mechanisms that brought about indigenization.) Such indigenization has increased the development toward a PLURICENTRAL English language, with regional – standard and non-standard – varieties not only in England and the United States, and not only in the other countries with large populations of native English speakers, but also in large parts of the world where English is not used as a native language. (See Chapter 2, § 3.3.)

In many cases, the use of English in non-native contexts was motivated by social considerations, such as prestige or regional neutrality, as well as by the need for a link language in a multilingual, multicultural society (as in present-day India). The development no doubt was helped by the indigenization of

English, which made it a more adequate means of communication in its new contexts. But conversely, the increasing use of English as a link language must have reinforced the process of indigenization.

And just as success breeds success in many other spheres, so the increasingly larger domain of English use, both in native contexts and as an indigenized link language in non-native contexts, has further increased the status of English as a truly international means of communication. Even in areas of the world such as continental Europe, Latin America, or East Asia, where it traditionally competed with other languages – or was not even considered a serious candidate as an international link language – English now has become the most widely learned second language, to be used not only in order to communicate with native speakers of English, or with speakers of indigenized varieties of English (such as Indian or West African English), but with speakers of all the world's languages.

Before concluding this section, it may be worth mentioning that link languages may come to coexist with regional languages in something very similar to a DIGLOSSIC relationship. In the case of Sanskrit and the Middle Indo-Aryan Prakrits or Latin and the medieval Romance languages, we have of course classical examples of diglossia as defined in Chapter 10. But as noted in the same chapter, Sanskrit and Latin held a very similar position vis-à-vis the Dravidian languages and the non-Romance languages of western Europe, respectively. Thus, for a long time, the major language for written communication in western Europe was Latin, while the regional languages, whether Romance or non-Romance, were employed mainly as vernaculars. As noted in Chapter 9, § 3.1, this relationship is reflected in the name of the Germans for themselves, namely *deutsch*, a word that was used to differentiate the vernacular language of the ordinary people from the high-prestige language of the clerics who were able to write properly in Latin (hence the English word *clerk < cleric*).

Similarly, the prestige of Sanskrit in India, combined with the fact that most of the Dravidian languages engaged in heavy borrowing from Sanskrit, has led not only Indo-Aryans, but also Dravidian speakers to believe that the Dravidian languages are descended from Sanskrit.

This raises the possibility that English may assume a similar role vis-à-vis the languages with which it has come to coexist. However, in contradistinction to earlier times, our modern period may have a sense of historicity too consciously developed to permit us to lose sight of the historical antecedents and relationships between languages. It is therefore unlikely that speakers of languages like Hindi or Yoruba will come to think of their language as descended from English.

2. Interference and interlanguage

As time progresses, link languages – no matter what their origin – may be modified, often to a considerable degree. This phenomenon, similar to the effect of dialects on standard languages examined in Chapter 10, § 5, or of the vernacular on the prestige language in diglossic situations (see Chapter 10, § 6), is responsible for the indigenization of English mentioned in the preceding section.

Let us take a closer look at the phenomenon by examining some aspects of Indian English, a language which for most speakers differs considerably from the British model.

The linguistic component most subject to indigenous influence is the vocabulary, including fixed collocations. The reasons for adding to the lexicon often are quite straightforward, such as the need to refer to objects, concepts, customs for which there are no ready-made terms in the language chosen as a link language. Lexical borrowing, with its various routines of nativization, may serve to bridge this gap as in the Indian English examples of (1a). Some of these borrowings even spread to the English used outside of India; see (1b). However, not all lexical innovations are motivated by need. For instance, the Indian English forms in the left column of (1c) replace native English expressions like the ones on the right.

(1)   a. *saree* (a garment worn by South Asian women)
          tahsil (an administrative unit)
          lathi (a long bamboo stick used by Indian police for crowd control)
          twice-born (calque of Skt. *dvi-ja-* 'twice-born; member of the three upper castes')
    b. *khaki*
        yoga
    c. *key bunch* : *bunch of keys*
        God-love : *love of God/God's love*

Lexical innovations of this type should not be surprising. All languages have to adjust to the needs of those who use them, whether they are native languages or link languages largely used by non-native speakers. (Compare recent English innovations such as *supercomputer, prioritize,* or *dweeb.*) What is more important is that grammar may be affected, too. This is most strikingly the case in the phonology of Indian English, which is characterized by large-scale substitutions, similar to those which are used in the nativization of English vocabulary. As a consequence, expressions like *I am going to the station* may be pronounced as in (2), with post-dental retroflex sounds for the English "dentals" *t, d* (which actually are themselves post-dental, too, though alveolar), with dental *d* for the dental fricative *ð* of English, and with various other changes. (As noted in the Appendix to Chapter 1, retroflex consonants are marked by subscript dots, as in *ṭ*.)

(2)   [aī ēm gōiŋ ṭū da (i)sṭēṣan]

Morphology and syntax may likewise be affected. Thus the expression in (2) is more likely to come out without the article, as in (2′). A further deviation from the native varieties of English can be observed in (2″), found in many vernacular varieties of Indian English.

(2′)   [aī ēm gōiŋ ṭū (i)sṭēṣan]
(2″)   [aī ēm **jasṭ naū** gōiŋ ṭū (i)sṭēṣan]

The variant (2″) reflects a general tendency of Indian English to exhibit systematic differences in verb formation, compared with British English, the original, colonial source of Indian English. See the correspondences in (3). (Differences in pronunciation are ignored in this example.) Though the use of *just now* in examples like (2″) and (3c) at this point is not obligatory, we find here the makings of a complete and systematic shift in the formation of the present-tense system.

(3)   Indian English   British English
      a. *I am knowing this*   *I know this*
      b. *I am going to school*   *I go to school*
      c. *I am just now going home* I am going home

While examples like those in (1a/b) can be motivated by the need for vocabulary adequate to the new context in which the language is used, it is difficult to motivate developments like those in (1c), (2), or (3) by need. What is at work here is a principle that can be observed in all second-language acquisition.

This principle has often been called INTERFERENCE or TRANSFER, the influence of one's native language on the structure of the acquired, second language. Thus the Indian English example *God-love* in (1c) above may be considered to have been formed on the native model of *dēva-bhakti-*, a compound of *dēva-* 'God' and *bhakti-* 'devotion'. And the phonological substitutions in (2) impose on English the phonological structure of Hindi and other South Asian languages, in which post-dental retroflex consonants contrast with pure dentals, and where the post-dental alveolar stops of English therefore are perceived as retroflex. Similarly, the slightly aspirated voiceless stops of English words like *to* are replaced by unaspirated stops (as in [ṭū]), rather than the much more heavily aspirated voiceless aspirates found in the indigenous languages.

However, the concept of interference or transfer is not sufficient to account for *keybunch* in (1c) or for the correspondences in (3). In contrast to *God-love*, *keybunch* cannot be motivated in terms of an existing indigenous compound. Rather, the word must result from an overextension of the English process of compounding or, possibly, of its indigenous counterpart. In either case, the resulting structure is the product of a creative process, not simple (or simple-minded) transfer or interference.

Let us return now to the changes reflected in example (3). The substitution in (3b) can be explained by transfer or interference, as a morphological and syntactic calque of the Hindi expression in (4a) or of similar structures in other South Asian languages. Here the Hindi participle ending *-tā* is translated by the English participle (pple.) ending *-ing*, and the auxiliary (AUX) *hū̃* (lit. '(I) am') is matched by its English counterpart *am*. The elements then are combined according to the syntactic rules of English. The explanation is similar for (3a). However, there is no pattern which would directly motivate the type (3c), whose Hindi counterpart is given in (4b). (A literal translation of the auxiliary *rahā* of this construction would be 'remained' or 'remaining'.)

(4)   a. *maĩ (i)skūl jā- tā   hū̃*
       I   school go pple. AUX
       'I go to school'

    b. *maĩ ghar jā rahā hū̃*
       I   home go AUX AUX
       'I am going home'

Rather, the type (3c) seems to reflect an attempt to retain the English distinction between (3b) and (3c) and – even more important – the corresponding South Asian distinction between (4a) and (4b), within a novel, "transfer" grammar which encodes (4a) as *I am going to school*. The *just now* which may optionally be used even in the British English version of (3c), then, seems to have been recruited in order to achieve that goal.

Modifications of the "target" language in second-language acquisition thus are not always explainable as resulting exclusively from interference or transfer. They can be more satisfactorily accounted for as arising from the fact that language learners must formulate for themselves a grammatical rule system which will account for the target language. The formulation of that rule system is influenced not only by the speakers' native language but also by their – correct or incorrect – assumptions about the nature of the target language. And in the process, novel structures may arise which are unprecedented in both the native and the target language.

To account for this different conceptualization of the second-language learning process and to differentiate it from the older conceptualization as interference or transfer, the term INTERLANGUAGE has been introduced. This term will be used in the remainder of this chapter, as well as in subsequent chapters.

Interlanguage is not limited to "exotic" areas of the "Third World". It plays a role in all second-language acquisition, being responsible for the "accent" (phonetic or otherwise) with which foreigners (or in many cases, their descendants) speak our language. For instance, when Pennsylvania Dutch speakers use the English expression *Outen the light* in the meaning 'turn off/extinguish the light', the verb *outen* has come into existence as the result of interlanguage. In their native Pennsylvania Dutch, a variety of German, the speakers would express the idea of extinguishing or turning off a light by using the verb *aus-machen*, lit. 'to make or do out'). Many verbs of similar structure, such as *rot machen* 'make red', have English equivalents of the type *redden*. The verb *outen*, then, results from extending the pattern of *red : redden* to *out : X*, because of the German parallelism of *rot machen* and *aus-machen*.

A more complex example of the effect of interlanguage is found in the passage in (5a), uttered by a German graduate student when one of his American friends treated everybody to drinks. (The example has been slightly altered to simplify the discussion.) Some of the peculiarities of this utterance, which was enormously difficult to process for virtually all who were present, can be explained as transfer, such as the final devoicing in [hes] = [hæz] *has*, [dait] = *died* and [of] = [əv] *of*, or the [v-] for [w-] in [wən] *one*. And the pronunciation [aunts] for [ants] or [ænts] *aunts* was clearly influenced by the spelling. But these were not the major obstacles to comprehension. More problematic was the initial [hes dait] = *has died*, which clearly did not sound very much like English. Interestingly, it is not motivated by German grammar either. German instead would say something like (5b). Slowly it became clear that the student had meant to say something like (5c). But what had gone wrong to produce (5a)? Evidently the student had learned that English has a similar strategy for forming questions as German, namely to front the finite verb. He also had learned that English is different from German, by normally requiring the finite auxiliary to be placed next to the non-finite "main verb", as in (5d) vs. (5e). (See also Chapter 6, § 5.) Where he went wrong was in overextending the English pattern in (5d) to produce the question in (5a). As in the earlier example of Indian English, interlanguage has produced a structure that is unprecedented in either the native language or the target language.

(5)   a. *Hes dait van of yur aunts?*
       b. IST   *eine*   *deiner*   *Tanten*   GESTORBEN?
          is/has one   of your   aunts   died
       c. HAS one of your aunts died?
       d. *One of your aunts*   HAS   DIED   recently
       e. *Eine deiner Tanten*   IST   kürzlich GESTORBEN

Ordinarily the effects of interlanguage are relatively short-lived or limited to individual learners. Moreover, different learners have different interlanguages, even if their native language is the same.

However, in cases where the second language serves as a link language and is used in that capacity over an extended period, there is a greater chance that interlanguage phenomena may become a permanent feature. This is especially true if the target language is used as in South Asia – as a means of communication primarily between speakers of mutually unintelligible indigenous languages, and not with native speakers of the language. In situations of this sort, interlanguage phenomena are less likely to be eliminated under the corrective influence of the native form of the language. As a consequence they can become cumulative and the results tend to become INSTITUTIONALIZED as the linguistic norm of an entire speech community.

The extent to which the effects of interlanguage have become institutionalized in Indian English can be gauged from the fact that speakers employing varieties closer to native-speaker English may be subjected to correction or even ridicule, much as someone who speaks English with a foreign accent. This is what often happens when speakers of Indian English return to India from an extended stay in a country whose native language is English. During their stay in, say, the United States, they may have gotten used to aspirating their voiceless stops, simply in order to make it easier for native speakers of English to understand them correctly. But if they aspirate these stops after their return to India, they meet with responses such as "What's this [ṭhū ṭhū]? Do you think you've become an American? Why don't you say [ṭū] like an Indian?"

Language pedagogues tend to use the term interlanguage in a negative sense, as something that should be overcome by additional and better language instruction. And given their perspective, this evaluation is understandable. However, as examples such as Indian English show, given the right circumstances, interlanguages do not simply remain a somewhat annoying intermediate stage on the way to complete language acquisition. Rather, they can become institutionalized, and interlanguage may lead to the indigenization of the language, which makes it adequate not only on a need basis but on an emotional basis, as the unique property of its new speakers, in a manner not substantially different from the emotional functions of, say, English for monolingual native speakers in the United States or Britain.

In this way, then, new varieties of English are born, which come to coexist with the older native varieties (such as British and American English) and thereby increase the pluricentrism of the English language.

3. Code switching and code mixing

Language contact may lead to several other responses. But most of these seem to have a lesser effect on linguistic change than interlanguage.

One common response, found among many fluent bilinguals, consists of switching back and forth between the coexisting languages, such that portions of a given sentence or utterance are in one language, other parts in another language. This process is commonly referred to as CODE SWITCHING. The examples in (6) illustrate how code switching works. Example (6a) gives the pure Hindi version, while (6b–f) present different code-switched variants, with the English portions in small caps and cited in ordinary orthography for easier recognition.

(6)   a. *kahtē   haĩ   ki   ājkal   bahut lōgõ   kō   yah*
         saying   are   that   nowadays   many people to   this
         nahĩ   pasand   hai   ki   rāǰ nārāin   pāgal
         not   pleasing   is   that   Raj Narain   fool
         kē samān aikṭ kar   rahā   hai
         like   act   AUX   is
         'They say that nowadays many people don't like it that Raj Narain is acting like a fool.'

b. *kahtē haĩ ki ājkal bahut lōgõ kō yah nahĩ pasand hai ki* RAJ NARAIN ACTS LIKE A FOOL

c. *kahtē haĩ ki* NOWADAYS MANY PEOPLE DON'T LIKE IT *ki rāj nārāin pāgal kē samān aikṭ kar rahā hai*

d. *kahtē haĩ ki ājkal* MANY PEOPLE DON'T LIKE IT THAT/*ki* RAJ NARAIN ACTS LIKE A FOOL

e. *kahtē haĩ ki ājkal bahut lōgõ kō yah nahĩ pasand hai ki* RAJ NARAIN ACTS *pāgal kē samān*

f. *kahtē haĩ ki ājkal bahut* PEOPLE DON'T LIKE IT ...

Switching occurs most easily at major syntactic boundaries (between clauses), as in (b) and (c). On the other hand, the type (f), with a break in the middle of a constituent (between the modifying adjective *bahut* and its head noun *people*), borders on being ungrammatical. In addition, observe that switching tends to be limited to syntax and morphology, without a comparable switch in phonology. The phonology which is employed throughout such code-switched utterances usually is the property of the speaker's native or most dominant language. (The English portions of (6) thus are pronounced with unaspirated retroflex stops, etc., much like the passages in (2) above.)

Many linguists recognize a parallel phenomenon of CODE MIXING. While code switching takes place on the syntactic level, code mixing is a lexical phenomenon. Consider for instance the *aikṭ kar rahā hai* of (6a), where *aikṭ* is Engl. *act*, while *kar rahā hai* 'is doing/making' is Hindi and serves to make the verb *aikṭ* usable in a Hindi sentence. (On the tendency to avoid the direct borrowing of verbs, see Chapter 8, § 2.) A more extended example, actually a caricature of code mixing, is found in the motto of this chapter. Examples like this show that code mixing consists of the insertion of content words from one language into the grammatical structure of another.

It is difficult to distinguish this process from lexical borrowing. But the term code mixing may perhaps be useful to refer to varieties of language use in which the admixture of foreign elements is much heavier than in normal borrowing situations – so heavy in fact that in extreme cases virtually all content words are of foreign manufacture, while the native language furnishes only the phonology, morphology, and basic vocabulary. Such varieties of language use are currently quite common in South Asia and many other parts of the world, including varieties of Spanish spoken in the United States. In most cases, they are limited to individuals and do not appear to have lasting consequences.

However, in areas of South America, a heavily code-mixed language use appears to have become institutionalized as the norm of a particular linguistic community. In the border area between certain Spanish and Quechua speaking territories, a new, MIXED LANGUAGE, called "Media Lengua" ('Middle' or 'Halfway Language'), is said to have arisen, whose vocabulary by and large is Spanish, while grammar and basic vocabulary are Quechua. A similar form of speech, Michif, arose in the Dakotas and adjoining areas of Canada in bilingual contact between early French discoverers and speakers of Algonquian languages (especially Cree). Its nouns almost exclusively come from French, while its pronouns, verbs, and basic structure are Algonquian. Languages like these are difficult to classify in terms of their genetic affiliation. Should we base our classification on the vast majority of the vocabulary? In that case, Media Lengua is a variety of Spanish. Or should we place more trust in basic grammar and vocabulary? In that case, it is a variety of Quechua. Most historical linguists would opt for the latter classification. But the issue is controversial; and some linguists would consider such languages to be genetically unclassifiable.

The situation is at first sight very similar in written languages like "High Urdu", "High Hindi", Classical Modern Persian, or Osmanli Turkish. Here, too, we find a pervasive admixture of foreign words (Arabic and Persian in Urdu, Sanskrit in Hindi, Arabic in Persian, and Arabic and Persian in Turkish). And in certain texts, these can reach proportions similar to Media Lengua, with virtually everything but the morphology, the pronouns, and the function words in foreign garb. But in these cases we are only dealing with certain written varieties of the language, while the ordinary spoken language keeps the number of foreign words in normal limits. Similarly, it has been observed that in the South Indian language Kannada, the jargon of professional wrestlers is heavily code-mixed with English so that, again, all content words are in English and only the grammatical structure, pronouns, and function words are in Kannada. What distinguishes varieties like Media Lengua and Michif is that they constitute ordinary, every-day spoken language. Language mixture, therefore, has affected the totality of the language.

4. Substratum

As discussed above, in contrast to code mixing and especially to code switching, the effects of interlanguage are institutionalized quite frequently, leading to distinctively new language varieties. Examples in recent, observable history include Indian English and West African English, both used as link languages in their respective areas and both showing phonological, syntactic, and lexical characteristics which markedly differentiate them from native varieties of English. A less radical effect of interlanguage (involving Yiddish and English) can be seen in the special variety of English that arose in New York among Jewish immigrants.

One of the features of this variety is a much higher incidence of syntactic structures with fronting of constituents other than subject to sentence-initial position, such as *This movie I really could do without.* Note that such fronting is widespread in Yiddish and other continental European languages. In this case, it could be argued that the effect of interlanguage is relatively minor. While topic fronting is increasingly falling out of favor in many varieties of English, it still is marginally possible in the language as a whole. Yiddish speakers, thus, have simply exploited a marginal construction of native-speakers' English and used it to encode a mode of discourse organization favored in their own native speech. Other features of "Yiddish English" differ more markedly, such as expressions like *You want I should give you a ride?* These, too, reflect syntactic patterns of Yiddish (and many other continental European languages), while traditional native-speakers' English prefers structures like *Do you want me to give you a ride?* (The institutionalization of Yiddish English seems to result from the fact that for several generations, communication with speakers outside the Jewish ghetto was fairly limited. Many interlanguage phenomena therefore remained unchecked.)

Interestingly, Yiddish English, once institutionalized, took on a life of its own. Many of its current users may know little if any Yiddish and certainly cannot be identified as native speakers of the language. Similarly, South Asian and West African English have become established varieties of English, learned as such by new generations of speakers, rather than being created anew.

Extrapolating from such known cases, many linguists have postulated similar developments in earlier, often prehistoric, contact situations. The scenario most commonly envisioned is LANGUAGE SHIFT, a situation in which contact results from invasion and where one language (usually that of the invaders) eventually replaces one or more indigenous languages. In such situations, it has been claimed, the SUBSTRATUM of the indigenous languages can have as systematic and far-reaching an effect on the language of the conquerors as, say, the South Asian languages had on Indian English. (Note that this use of the term substratum is different from the one in Chapter 8, § 4.1, where a sociolinguistic distinction between substratum, superstratum, and adstratum is made. Both uses of the term are too well established in linguistics to permit replacing one of them with a less confusing term.)

It has for instance been claimed that the far-reaching Western Romance weakening, as in (7) below, is to be attributed to a Celtic substratum. For, it is said, the area in which lenition is found is coterminous with the territory settled by the Celts before the Roman expansion. Moreover, similar weakenings are found in attested Celtic languages, such as Old Irish and Middle Welsh; see (8).

(7)   Latin   Spanish   French
       amicus *amigo* [-γ-]   *amiØ*   'friend'
       vidēre *veØer > ver*   *veØoir > voir* 'see'
(8)   PIE   Old Irish   Middle Welsh
       tewtā   *tūath*[θ]   *tud*   'people'

Similarly the change of Lat. *ū* to Fr. [ü] has been attributed to a Celtic substratum. For, again, the Celts held Gaul before the Roman invasion, and a fronting change of **u* is found in Welsh, a Celtic language; see (9). Other linguists, especially native speakers of German, have attributed the fronting of *ū* to *ü* to the influence of the Germanic Franks, who gave France its first dynasty of rulers, as well as its name. This alternative account illustrates how even an objective field like linguistics is not always immune to political belief or bias.

(9)   PIE   Middle Welsh
       *uksen- *ych* [ɨx]   'ox'
       *tū   *ti* [ti]   'you (sg.)'

The Castilian Spanish and Southern French change of *f* to *h* (> Ø) in examples like (10) has been explained in terms of a Basque substratum. For, it is said, Basque had no *f* when this change occurred.

(10)   Latin   Spanish
       filius   *hijo*   'son'
       farina   *harina*   'flour'

These examples are typical of traditional "substratist" explanations. However, they also suffer from the typical weaknesses of most of these explanations.

For instance, it is not at all clear that the weakening of the relatively late-attested Insular Celtic languages Old Irish and Middle Welsh was also a feature of the Continental Celtic dialects of Gaul and Iberia (which died out very early). Moreover, the process is found in many Italian dialects that are spoken in areas not originally settled by the Celts.

As for the French change $\bar{u} > \ddot{u}$, the Celtic fronting of *u*-vowels was restricted to Welsh. There is no evidence that it occurred elsewhere in Celtic. In fact, languages like Old Irish provide positive evidence against the assumption that *u*-fronting was a general Celtic phenomenon. And here again the change in question has parallels in other Romance dialects where Celtic influence is less certain. Mutatis mutandis, the same arguments apply to the claim that French fronting reflects Frankish influence.

The substratist case is best for the change of *f* to *h·* The change is not limited to Spanish dialects that are close neighbors of Basque; it is also found in southern French dialects (Gascon) that border on Basque; see (10′a). What lends further credence to the substratum explanation is that Gascon and the Spanish *f* > *h* dialects (which include Castilian Spanish) are not direct neighbors of each other; rather, they are separated by Basque territory. Still, even within Romance the change is not limited to Gascon and Spanish. It is also found in southern Italian dialects, such as Calabrian, which are far removed from Basque; see (10′b).

(10′)   a. Latin   Gascon
          faber   *hàure*   'smith'
          festus   *hèsto*   'festive; festival'
        b. Latin   Calabrian
          farina   *harina*   'flour'
          filum   *hilu*   'string'

Perhaps even more significant is the fact that the above changes are by no means unusual and do not require an unusual or special substratum explanation. Intervocalic weakening is so widespread that it would be more noteworthy to find a language that did not undergo it at some point of its history than to find a language that did. The fronting of *u*-vowels likewise is common and recurs in a large variety of other languages and dialects, such as the Attic-Ionic of Ancient Greek, Slavic, Dutch, and most varieties of the modern Scandinavian languages. The fact that these languages were able to front their *u*'s without the aid of the Celts suggests that the same may be true for French. Finally, special weakening developments in labials, though not as common as medial weakening, are found in a number of other languages, such as early Celtic, Japanese, Armenian, and the Dravidian language Kannada. The specific change of *f* to *h* has a parallel in the history of Japanese, as well as in Hawaiian where *ʃ* > *h* goes back to earlier Malayo-Polynesian **p* (as in **pa-* 'four' > Samoan, Tongan *fa*, Haw. *ha*) and according to some scholars even in ancient dialectal Latin.

Perhaps the most striking example of the way in which substratist accounts fail to provide a meaningful explanation is that of "retroflexion", a phenomenon most consistently attributed to substratal influence, wherever it is found. This approach has been carried to an extreme in the case of the Sicilian dialectal development of *tr* to *ʈ(r)* and similar developments elsewhere in Romance: Aftcr finding that no known language could be held responsible for this change, one linguist claimed that it must be attributed to an unknown "substratum X"!

Even Grimm's Law has been attributed to some unknown substratum. Presumably the change was motivated by the fact that the substratum language had a different phonological system which required substitutions along the lines of the top part of Figure 1. But one has to ask oneself why the substitutions were not made in a more straightforward manner, along the lines of the lower part of Figure 1.

PIE   Substratum X/PGmc.

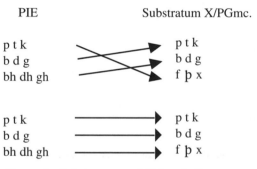

Figure 1. Substratum and Grimm's Law

A more plausible substratist explanation of Grimm's Law would assume that the initial stage of the change postulated in Chapter 4, § 5.4, the aspiration of original voiceless stops, was introduced by substratum speakers who pronounced voiceless stops with aspiration. But similar changes are found elsewhere, as in Xhosa and other Southern Bantu languages, as well as in Old High German (see Chapter 11, § 2.3). Even ardent substratists would shrink from claiming that the same substratum speakers are responsible both for Grimm's Law and for the Southern Bantu shift. The only way that a substratist explanation could be motivated for all such cases is if it could be shown that every single observable case of such a change is unambiguously the result of substratum influence. Otherwise, the fact that we have no direct evidence for the alleged substrata – not to mention the nature of their phonological systems – turns substratist explanations into nothing better than speculations.

Substratist explanations are not limited to phonological phenomena, but have also been proposed for syntax and other grammatical components. An example of a substratist account in syntax is found in the case of the Greek infinitive. Ancient Greek had a highly developed system of infinitives, used in functions similar to their English counterparts (such as Engl. *to err* in *to err is human* or *to go* in *I want to go home*). In Modern Greek, however, the infinitives have been eliminated (see Chapter 13, § 3). It has been suggested that a substratum language without infinitives was responsible for the Greek loss of the infinitive, and Thracian and Illyrian have sometimes been mentioned as likely "suspects". However, the substratum account runs afoul of the problem of circularity, for very little is known about either Thracian or Illyrian (see Chapter 2, §§ 3.6 and 3.12), and the claim that they lacked an infinitive is based entirely on the effect they supposedly had on Greek! There are also problems with the chronology, for we would have to believe that Thracian or Illyrian had an effect on Greek syntax about a thousand years after they were last attested!

The conclusion we draw must be that although examples like Indian English demonstrate that interlanguage may result in far-reaching structural changes, many of the commonly alleged prehistoric instances of substratal changes are dubious. Not that the proposed solutions are completely impossible. In fact, in the case of Gascon and Spanish *f* > *h*, a substratist explanation looks very attractive. But in most cases, substratist accounts simply are either unnecessary and unenlightening, or difficult to establish beyond a reasonable doubt, or both.

It is in the more specific areas of koiné formation, "convergence", and the development of pidgins and similar varieties of language that interlanguage plays a more clearly relevant role. One of these, koiné formation, is discussed in the next section of this chapter. Convergence and pidginization are sufficiently different in their characteristics to be treated in separate chapters.

5. Koinés

A special type of link language, commonly referred to as KOINÉ, tends to arise under very special linguistic conditions, characterized by the following features.

- The varieties of speech that are in contact with each other are closely related languages or even mutually intelligible dialects.
- For cultural or political reasons, these linguistic varieties are considered by their speakers to be of about equal prestige, each being the proper linguistic vehicle for a group with its own cherished identity. Speakers therefore are not willing to give up their speech in favor of one of the other speech varieties.
- No outside language suggests itself as a link language.

Put simply, koinés may be defined as deregionalized languages or dialects which because of their DEREGIONALIZATION become potential vehicles as link languages in areas meeting the above description. The mechanism for deregionalization, in turn, no doubt lies in interlanguage.

The classical example of koiné, which gave its name to the type of link language we are concerned with, is the Hellenistic Koiné, the *koiné glôssa* 'common language' of the Greece of Alexander the Great and subsequent times. This language transcended the local languages (or rather, dialects) of the various Greek city states and confederations of cities, with their jealously guarded separate political, cultural, and linguistic identities. In fact, as noted in Chapter 10, § 5, the Koiné eventually replaced virtually all of the dialects of ancient Greece.

The Koiné was essentially a (partially) de-Atticized variant of the Attic Greek dialect. It was based on the Attic dialect of Athens, a city which had become one of the most important, perhaps the most important state in Greece, both culturally (in terms of its arts, literature, and learning) and politically (in terms of heading the Attic League, the main line of defense against the Persians). Even so, without de-Atticization, its dialect might not have been acceptable as a link language, since accepting it would have given the undesirable impression of accepting the political hegemony of Athens. Fortunately for posterity, however, a de-Atticized version arose.

This form of speech probably first came about in the harbor of Athens, where Attic came into daily contact with virtually all the other Greek dialects, especially with Ionic. Under these circumstances an interlanguage variety of Attic could readily develop. The language received further impetus from the contact between different seafaring Greek city states in the Attic League. Whatever its early origins, however, this non-standard de-Atticized Attic was ideally suited as a link language, since it could be looked at as unaffiliated with any of the competing standard local dialects.

Some examples may illustrate the way in which de-Atticization was accomplished.

The majority of Greek dialects have *-ss-* as the outcome of earlier **-ky-*, **-khy-*, and other consonant clusters, while Attic has *-tt-*, a development shared by only a few other dialects. The Koiné instead generally offers the *-ss-* of the majority of dialects, as in (11a). Similarly, older *-rs-* was assimilated to *-rr-* in Attic and a few other dialects. Elsewhere, the unchanged *-rs-* prevailed. Again, the Koiné went with the majority pattern, against the idiosyncratic Attic usage; see (11b). Attic, together with parts of Ionic, had changed earlier **-ayw-* into *-ā-* before vowel, whereas the majority of dialects had *-ai-*. And yet again, the Koiné sided with the majority; see (11c).

(11)   Attic   Koiné
   a. *glôtta*   *glôssa*   'tongue, language'
      phuláttō   *phulássō*   'guard, watch'
      téttares   *téssares*   'four'
   b. *árrēn*   *ársēn*   'male'
   c. *eláā*   *elaíā*   'olive'

The developments that brought about the Koiné did not, of course, arise from speakers going into a huddle or having a council meeting and deciding to subvert Attic. Rather they must have resulted from a slow process of – semiconscious or even subconscious – selection of the non-Attic features which had fortuitously arisen through the Attic interlanguage in Athens harbor and which differentiated this form of speech sufficiently from standard Attic to make it acceptable as a general link language.

We can see similar developments in various African koinés, especially in the Bantu area. What is interesting is that in many cases the deregionalization is brought about by SELECTIVE SIMPLIFICATION, the reduction or elimination of just those grammatical features which differ most widely in the various languages and dialects involved.

For instance, there is good reason to believe that the Bantu languages originally had either an accent which was not bound to any particular syllable, or something more like the tonal system of languages like Chinese. However, as the result of linguistic change, the accent or tone systems differ considerably from one Bantu language to the other. Languages like Swahili, which appear to have originated as koinés, instead show an accent that is fixed on the next-to-last syllable of all words. The reason for this simplificatory development may have been that by dropping a feature which is idiosyncratically different from language to language, and by substituting in its stead a completely predictable feature, Swahili achieved a degree of deregionalization which made it more suitable as a koiné.

In the case of Swahili we must depend on speculation, since the developments in question took place prehistorically. However, similar examples of selective simplification are found in observable history. These include deregionalized varieties of Bantu languages which have become koinés more recently.

These koinés exhibit a considerable simplification in the system of "concord" prefixes, the area of Bantu morphology which exhibits the greatest degree of idiosyncratic differentiation, both within given languages and across linguistic boundaries. The Bantu languages are characterized by a complex system of prefixes which distinguish different nominal classes. Pronouns, adjectives, and verbs must show agreement with these noun class prefixes. Agreement markers, however, in many cases are not identical but may differ considerably, as in the Lingala examples of (12) and (13). (Singular formations are given under a., plurals under b. CL = (noun) class prefix, AG = agreement marker, TA = tense/aspect marker.)

(12)   a. ***mw****-ana*   ***o****-yo*   ***mo****-lamu*   ***a*** *- ko-kweya*
          CL   AG   AG   AG TA
          child   this   beautiful   fall
          'This beautiful child will fall.'

      b. ***ba****-na*   ***ba****-ye* ***ba****-lamu*   ***ba****-ko-kweya*
          CL   AG   AG   AG TA
          'These beautiful children will fall.'

(13)   a. ***Ø****-ndako*   ***e****-ye*   ***e****-lamu*   ***e****-ko-kweya*
          CL house   AG   AG   AG TA
          'This beautiful house will fall.'

      b. ***Ø****-ndako*   ***i****-ye*   ***n****-damu*   ***e****-ko-kweya*
          CL   AG   AG   AG TA
          'These beautiful houses will fall.'

      (The alternation between *l* and *d* in (13a/b) *-lamu : -damu* is regular.)

Moreover, agreement markers differ considerably across different languages. Contrast the Lingala examples in (12) and (13) with their Swahili counterparts in (12′) and (13′).

(12′)   a. ***m****-toto*   ***hu****-yu* ***m****-zuri*   ***a****-ta-nguka*
          CL   AG   AG   AG TA
          'This beautiful child will fall.'

      b. ***wa****-toto*   ***ha****-wa* ***wa****-zuri* ***wa****-ta-nguka*
          CL   AG   AG   AG TA
          'These beautiful children will fall.'

(13′)   a. ***Ø**-nyumba **hi**-i   **n**-zuri   **i**-ta-nguka*
            CL   AG   AG   AG TA
            'This beautiful house will fall.'
        b. ***Ø**-nyumba **hi**-zi   **n**-zuri   **zi**-ta-nguka*
            CL   AG   AG   AG TA
            'These beautiful houses will fall.'

Given these disagreements, it is not surprising that in the course of dere-gionalization, Bantu koinés often radically simplify the system. Compare the examples from Kinshasa Lingala, a Koiné based on Standard Lingala, in (12″) and (13″) with the Standard Lingala and Swahili versions of (12/13) and (12′/13′).

(12″)   a. ***mw**-ana o-yo ma-lamu **a**-ko-kweya*
            CL   AG
            'This beautiful child will fall.'
        b. ***ba**-na   o-yo ma-lamu **ba**-ko-kweya*
            CL   AG
            'These beautiful children will fall.'
(13″)   a. ***Ø**-ndako o-yo ma-lamu **e**-ko-kweya*
            CL   AG
            'This beautiful house will fall.'
        b. ***Ø**-ndako o-yo ma-lamu **e**-ko-kweya*
            CL   AG
            'These beautiful houses will fall.'

As these examples show, agreement in Kinshasa Lingala now is marked only on the verb. The demonstrative pronoun and the adjective no longer show agreement but offer an invariable prefix. And in many cases, the lack of variability in that prefix leads to its being reanalyzed as part of the following root. In some of the Bantu koinés, such as Kituba, the process has gone even farther and has led to the virtual elimination of the noun class system.

What is interesting – and shows that simplification is a selective process – is that there has been no similar reduction in other areas of the morphology. Thus the Bantu tense/aspect system remains considerably more intact than the class prefixes; see the Kinshasa Lingala examples in (12″/13″). And derivational suffixes seem to be the most resistant to change.

6. Outlook

The development of koinés brings us back to the two themes established in the first two sections of this chapter, the development of link languages and the role of interlanguage in linguistic contact. But note that ordinary link languages can have many sources other than koinés; and the phenomenon of interlanguage is not restricted to link languages but operates in all situations of second-language learning. Moreover, in other link languages, interlanguage in effect is a response phenomenon, conditioned by the fact that a language has come to be used as a means of inter-language communication. In koiné-formation, by contrast, interlanguage is the very foundation for the development of the link language; without interlanguage there would be no koiné.

In the next chapter we will look at another area of language contact in which interlanguage plays a fundamental role. But whereas the effects of interlanguage that we examined in this chapter are essentially unidirectional, from substrate languages to link languages, the phenomena to be examined in the next chapter involve bidirectional effects of interlanguage, with results that are perhaps even more profound than the ones that we encountered in this chapter.

Chapter 13
Convergence: Dialectology beyond language boundaries

> He spoke more than ten different languages fluently – all in Russian.
>
> (*A common claim about the famous Russian-born linguist Roman Jakobson, co-founder of the modern approach to convergence studies*)
>
> The division between them, in their leading character, blends away.
>
> (Charles Darwin, *Fertilisation of Orchids*, V: 159.)

1. Introduction: Convergence defined

Until recently, the ideal of modern western societies has been that of the nation-state with a single national language. There are a few European countries like Switzerland and Belgium with a clear and long-established policy of bi- or multilingualism; and in North America, Canada has tried its hand at English-French bilingualism. However, the linguistically inspired strife or even violence which keeps flaring up in Belgium and the threat of Canada's splitting in two along linguistic lines demonstrates how precarious the notion of bilingualism tends to be in modern western society. In fact, until very recently, the norm in western European countries has been one of discouraging, even suppressing the use of minority languages. As a consequence, many languages have died out, such as Cornish, the Celtic language indigenous to Cornwall (the southeastern tip of England), and Dalmatian, a variety of Romance once spoken in Dalmatia (along the east coast of the Adriatic Sea). Cornish was replaced by English, and Dalmatian, as we have seen in Chapter 2, § 3.4, by Italian and varieties of Slavic. Other languages have undergone severe attrition in use, in the number of speakers, even in linguistic structure, such as Upper and Lower Sorbian in Germany (see Chapter 2, § 3.4), or Welsh, Irish, and Scots Gaelic in the British Isles. (See also Chapter 15.)

And as observed in Chapter 11, § 4, the repression of Catalan, Galician, and Basque in the Spain of Franco's fascist regime has only very recently given way to official toleration, recognition, and even cultivation.

In many ways, however, this aversion to bi- or multilingualism is anomalous. Large areas of the world are habitually bilingual or even multilingual. (Henceforth the term BILINGUAL and its derivatives will be used to cover both bi- and multilingual situations.) These include not only the Balkans, South Asia, much of Africa and the Americas, but even premodern, medieval western Europe. In addition, of course, bilingualism is widespread at national/linguistic boundaries, such as between France and Germany.

Such habitual bilingualism may be most likely to occur if the languages in contact are more or less equal in strength, or if they are more or less equal in prestige. However, there may be other social reasons for maintaining a pattern of bilingualism.

In South Asia, for instance, one's position within society, especially within the complex caste system, has traditionally been intimately tied up with language. Bengalis, for instance, would marry Bengalis (from the appropriate caste); and to establish yourself as a Bengali you had better speak the Bengali language – even if you live in Hindi-speaking territory. Religious affiliation, too, is often linked to language, especially among Muslims, most of whom speak Urdu, no matter where they live. In either case, in traditional Indian society you can't simply decide not to be Bengali, Muslim, or whatever your affiliation may be, and to give up the language that is appropriate for your affiliation – unless you want to become an outcast from society, unable to marry and have a family. At the same time, over the centuries there has been a fair amount of group mobility across political and linguistic lines, generally for cultural and economic reasons. So, even if you have to speak Bengali or Urdu at home (to establish your credentials as a Bengali or a Muslim and therefore your place in society), you may need to know one or more other languages to interact with the people on the outside.

Although the details differ, the situation is remarkably similar in the Balkan peninsula of southeastern Europe. Repeated conquests and reconquests and other migrations have in many areas introduced settlement patterns where speakers of different languages are thrown together in the same locality or where their villages are intermingled in a crazy-quilt fashion, situations which guarantee daily bilingual contact. At the same time, as recent developments in former Yugoslavia remind us, the old ethnic identities – and differences – remain a potent force, precluding linguistic amalgamation or the victory of any of the rival languages.

In short, it is not necessary to love your neighbors in order to engage in daily bilingual contact with them.

Whatever the social motivations, in societies with long-standing bilingualism, the use of different languages is in many ways comparable to the use of different social or regional dialects in monolingual societies. Different varieties of speech are appropriate under different social conditions. One language might be used at home, another on the job, a third in religious contexts. But to a large extent their spheres of usage are mutually exclusive; each has its own appropriate niche in society.

Conditions of this sort commonly give rise to a phenomenon that is referred to as CONVERGENCE, the increasing agreement of languages not only in terms of vocabulary (which may in fact remain quite distinct), but especially in aspects of their overall structure.

If bilingual contact is prolonged, often extending over more than a millennium, the interlanguage or interlanguages that naturally arise in the process of speaking a second language can have a much more profound effect on the structure of languages than the fairly short-lived substratum situations examined in the preceding chapter.

This is not simply because interlanguage has a longer time span within which it can operate. Rather, with the passage of time, a syndrome of the following sort will arise. Let the interaction begin with two languages, A and B, producing the interlanguages A^B, based on native knowledge of language A and acquired knowledge of B, and its counterpart B^A, based on native language knowledge of B and acquired knowledge of A. These interlanguages, in turn, will interact with each other, as well as with relatively unchanged A and B. The result will be a build-up of increasingly complex and mixed interlanguages, with increasingly longer – and more complex – series of "superscripts". Compare the illustration in (1) which ignores the continued coexistence of earlier, less mixed varieties. In the long run it may become impossible to determine which of the features shared by given languages originated where.

(1)

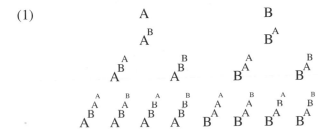

In contrast to the phenomena discussed in the preceding chapter, then, convergence saliently involves not just a unidirectional effect of interlanguage, but a bi- or multidirectional one. In fact, some evidence suggests that interlanguage itself may have a BIDIRECTIONAL side to it. True, under ordinary circumstances we tend to notice the effects of interlanguage mainly in the "accent" with which a foreigner speaks our language. But when that foreigner returns home after many years abroad, those who remained behind will likewise notice a certain "accent" in his or her speech. (Compare for instance the case of aspirated [thū] in Chapter 12, § 2.) This is often considered an affectation, and to some extent it may be. But to a certain degree this "foreign accent" in one's native language is as natural and normal as the "foreign accent" in one's second, non-native language.

While the precise reason for this "backflow" of interlanguage into one's native language is not well understood, recent research does establish that the internalized grammars of native bilinguals are different from the grammars of persons who only speak one of the two languages, no matter which of these two it may be. If interlanguage thus is indeed to some extent bidirectional, its bidirectionality may play an important role in convergence, in addition to the complex interaction of interlanguages modeled in (1) above.

In addition, one suspects, a certain degree of quasi-Darwinian SELECTION plays a role, too, accelerating convergent developments and eliminating more divergent ones. As we saw in Chapter 8, when borrowing foreign words we need to nativize them, especially phonetically, but in many cases also in terms of other aspects of linguistic structure. If we fail to do so, we need to "reconfigure" our articulation in mid-sentence, a feat that even linguists find difficult to accomplish, at least in ordinary speech. This is no doubt the reason, too, for the fact noted in the preceding chapter (§ 3) that in code switching between different languages the phonology tends to be solidly from one of these languages (usually one's native language). Naturally, then, somebody who has to function as a bilingual on a daily basis likewise has to deal with the problem of reconfiguring from one of the languages to the other. Under the circumstances, those varieties of interlanguage will be favored which are most conducive to making the job of switching back and forth easier. In fact, the ideal outcome would be varieties of language which are virtually identical in linguistic structure, so that speakers only have to plug in different words or morphological elements in order to satisfy the requirement of bilingualism.

There may even be a further factor, allied to the last one, namely ACCOMMODATION: In addition to selecting variants which make it easier to function as a bilingual speaker, it is possible that there also is a selective use of variants that make it easier for the listener to understand.

Note finally that for convergence to take place it is not necessary for all speakers of the involved languages to be bilingual (or even equally proficient as bilinguals), or for all dialectal areas of these languages to be bilingual. It is perfectly possible for convergence to start in a relatively small area of intense bilingualism, such as the border between two different linguistic groups. From this area, then, the results of convergence can spread to new speakers and to new dialect areas by the usual processes of dialectal spread (see Chapter 11). The loss of past tense distinctions in modern French, Romantsch, northern Italian dialects, and Southern German discussed in § 4 below may well be an example of such a development.

2. Convergence illustrated: Kupwar

In the most famous and large-scale convergence areas, the Balkans and South Asia, the exact manner in which convergence arose is partly shrouded in the mystery of the unobservable past and, therefore, also partly controversial.

Fortunately, however, there are cases where convergence has happened quite recently and where, therefore, we have a good idea of how it came about. Perhaps the most celebrated of these is the case of Kupwar, a small locality of about 3,000 inhabitants at the border of the modern Indian states of Maharashtra and Karnataka. Its population includes three major groups, speaking the following languages which outside Kupwar are clearly distinct and whose history is well understood:

Urdu (Indo-Aryan): used by Muslim landholders, a socially prestigious or powerful group.

Kannada (Dravidian): spoken by Jain landholders and Hindu craftspeople who likewise hold a fairly high prestige.

Marathi (Indo-Aryan): used by Hindu "untouchables" and landless laborers, i.e., persons on the lower end of the prestige spectrum. In addition, however, it is the state language and the primary means of education.

In spite of the obvious prestige differences, the languages coexist without any appreciable threat of one replacing another. Within its own communal setting, each of the groups or communities sticks to its own language as a mark of its separate identity. In intergroup relations, however, there is a great amount of bilingualism and multilingualism, especially among the men and largely, though not exclusively, in favor of Marathi. Most speakers are at least passively competent in all the languages of the locality.

This complex and intensive bilingualism is known to have extended over more than 300 years. And during that period it has brought about such a remarkable degree of convergence that the phonology and syntax of the individual languages have been claimed to be virtually identical. Only the vocabularies and grammatical elements have remained clearly distinct, with borrowing limited to a few lexical items.

Presumably it is this lexical distinction which makes it possible for people to have nearly identical structures and still feel that they are speaking different, communally appropriate languages. This should actually not be surprising, given that non-linguists, when trying to characterize differences between dialects or languages, find it much easier to talk about different lexical choices than structural differences.

The structural parallelism of the examples in (2) below may provide an initial glimpse of the extent of this convergence. While there are some differences in detail, such as the fact that the "absolutive marker" is an independent (but clitic) word in Urdu and Marathi, but a suffix in Kannada, there is an exact, word-by-word, suffix-by-suffix parallelism in the linear arrangement of the sentences and in the meanings and functions of the morphological elements and words that are used. Put differently, the sentences are exact calques of each other. (The non-italicized words represent one of the rare examples of recent lexical borrowing; the source language is Urdu. – Abs. = marker of the so-called absolutive, a non-finite verbal form which functions as something like a verbal adverb and whose literal translation is 'having Xed'; TA = tense/agreement marker.)

(2) Ur. *pālā* *jarā* *kāṭ* *kē* *lē* *kē ā-* *yā*
     Ma. *pālā* *jarā* *kāp* *un* *ghē* *un ā-* *lō*
     Ka. *tāplā* *jarā* *khōd - i* *tagōnd - i* *ba-* *yn*
          greens some cut Abs. take Abs. come TA
          'Having cut some greens, having taken (them), I came.'
          = 'I cut some greens and brought them.'

What complicates matters is that some of the structural agreement is shared by (virtually) all the South Asian languages, as the result of historically earlier and geographically more widespread convergence. But the Kupwar varieties of Urdu, Marathi, and Kannada have converged far beyond the ordinary convergence of the South Asian languages, specifically of the ordinary varieties of Urdu, Marathi, and Kannada that are spoken outside Kupwar.

Thus, Urdu and Marathi both have arbitrary or grammatical gender, just like German (see Chapter 8, § 3): Nouns not referring to human beings are arbitrarily assigned masculine (see Urdu *pālā* in (2)), or feminine gender (see Urdu *kitāb* 'book'). And Marathi has yet a third, neuter gender. Like Marathi, Kannada has a three-gender system, but with a clear semantic basis for gender assignment, like English: Nouns referring to male humans are masculine; to female humans, feminine; and all others are neuter. The similarities and differences of these three systems are summarized in (3).

(3)

	masculine	feminine	neuter
Ur.	± human	± human	————
Ma.	± human	± human	± human
Ka.	+ human	+ human	− human

Just as in German, nominal gender assignment has important grammatical consequences, for it controls agreement on adjectives and verbs, as in (4). The differences between the Urdu, Marathi, and Kannada systems therefore were not resolved simply by giving up gender marking altogether. Rather, the semantically more transparent system of Kannada was extended to Kupwar Marathi and Kupwar Urdu. As a consequence, Kupwar Marathi has neuter agreement for non-human nouns that are masculine or feminine in Standard Marathi. And Kupwar Urdu, lacking a separate neuter gender, employs the "unmarked" masculine gender for the same purpose. Compare the examples in (5). (Here and elsewhere below, St. = Standard, Ku. = Kupwar variety; m. = masculine, f. = feminine, n. = neuter; Adj. = adjective, N = noun, V = verb.)

(4) Ur.

aččhī	*kitāb*	*paṛhī*
Adj. f.	N f.	V f.
good	book	read

'(I) read a good book.'

(5)

St.Ur.	*vahã̄*	*nadī*	*ā-ī*
		f.	f.
St.Ma.	*tith*	*nadī*	*ā-lī*
		f.	f.
Ku.Ur.	*hvā*	*nadī*	*ā-yā*
			m.
Ku.Ma.	*tith*	*nadī*	*ā-lō*
			n.
Ka.	*yalli*	*hwaḷi*	*ba-ttu*
			n.
	there	flood	came

'A flood came there.'

In other areas of structural disagreement, the pattern of Urdu and/or Marathi has won out. Thus, Standard Kannada does not have a verb 'to be' after predicate adjectives. On the model of Urdu and Marathi, Kupwar Kannada has come to employ a form of 'be' in this context; see (6).

(6)	St.Ka.	*ii*	*mane*	*nim-da*	Ø	*i-du*	*nim*	*mana*	Ø
	Ku.Ka.	*id*	*mani*	*nimd*	*eti*	*id*	*nimd*	*mani*	*eti*
	Ku.Ma.	*hē*	*ghar*	*tumčā*	*hāi*	*hē*	*tumčā*	*ghar*	*hāi*
	Ku.Ur.	*yē*	*ghar*	*tumhārā*	*hai*	*yē*	*tumhārā*	*ghar*	*hai*
		this	house	your	is	this	your	house	is
		\multicolumn{4}{}{'This house is yours.'}			'This is your house.'			

Example (6) further illustrates that as in the development of koinés, convergence may bring about SELECTIVE SIMPLIFICATION. In Standard Kannada, adjectives and demonstratives appear in two morphologically distinct forms. One occurs when the form is used as a predicate or as a noun (as in *nim-da, i-du*), the other is used elsewhere (as in *ii, nim*). Kupwar Kannada has given up the distinction in favor of the predicate/nominal forms (as in *id* and *nimd*).

Significantly, then, convergence in Kupwar has not been unidirectional, with one language doing all the giving and the others doing all the taking. Rather, the common features of the Kupwar varieties of Kannada, Marathi, and Urdu reflect influence from all of the three languages.

3. The Balkans

One of the classical examples of convergence is the area of the Balkans, home to languages which belong to four distinct subgroups of Indo-European: (i) Bulgarian, Macedonian, part of Serbo-Croatian (all Slavic); (ii) Romanian (Romance); (iii) Albanian; and (iv) Modern Greek. (In addition, there are a number of less well-represented languages. Their behavior does not substantially differ from the other Balkan languages.) Moreover, as we have seen earlier, the area is characterized by a high degree of long-standing bilingualism and multilingualism.

It should therefore not be surprising that the languages of the area have over the centuries come to share remarkable similarities in structure. Many of the shared features are clearly common innovations, since they were absent from Proto-Indo-European or from earlier forms of the Balkan languages (such as Ancient Greek). What makes the languages of the Balkan so interesting, then, is not just their mutual convergence, but also their individual and collective divergence from their historical antecedents, as well as from their non-Balkan relatives. The innovated features which Bulgarian, Macedonian, and part of Serbo-Croatian share with the other Balkan languages are absent in the rest of Slavic; and the case is similar for Romanian and the rest of Romance. In fact, it was the study of this area that gave rise to one of the terms used to refer to such areas, SPRACHBUND, lit. 'language league', a term which has been adopted in many English-language publications on convergence. Other terms used in English are CONVERGENCE AREA and LINGUISTIC AREA. Of these, the term convergence area is probably the most transparent in English and will therefore be used in the remainder of this chapter. (It has already been used informally in the preceding section.)

The features shared by all or most Balkan languages range over phonology, morphology, and syntax. Unlike the Kupwar situation, there are also many shared loan words, many of them having spread from one Balkan language or another, but even some that have diffused from Turkish, which was very influential despite being a relative late-comer to the Balkans. Compare examples like Mod. Gk. *drómos*, Alb. *dhrom*, Bulg., SCr., Rom. *drum* 'way, road' (from Greek) or Mod. Gk. [boyá] (spelled μπογιά = mpogiá !), Bulg., SCr. *boja*, Rom. *boia*, Alb. *bojë* 'paint, color' (from Turk. *boya*).

The important structural features shared by many or most of the Balkan languages include the following:

- The absence of nasalized or long vowels. Thus, even though early Slavic had nasalized vowels and Polish still does, Bulgarian, Macedonian, and Serbo-Croatian lack distinctive vowel nasalization. Similarly, none of the Balkan languages show distinctive long vowels, even though earlier stages of the languages had a contrast between long and short vowels.
- A postposed definite article, as in (7). This feature is found in Albanian, Romanian, Bulgarian, Macedonian, and the southeastern dialects of Serbo-Croatian (which are geographically closest to Bulgarian and Macedonian). The rest of Serbo-Croatian does not use a definite article; and Greek has a preposed article, as in *o fílos* 'the friend'. The articles of the Slavic and Romance Balkan languages have outside relations, such as the demonstrative pronoun *(*)tŭ* 'that' in Slavic or the article of It. *il duomo* 'the house', Fr. *le chat* 'the cat', Sp. *el lobo* 'the wolf'. However, outside the Balkan area, the articles and demonstratives are preposed; see Sp. *el lobo* vs. postposed Rom. *lupu-l*. Note further that though the Balkan languages (other than Greek) agree on the placement of the article, they do not agree on its form. Each language employs an indigenous form.

(7)   plain noun   noun + article

Mac. ⎫
Bulg. ⎬   *voda*   *voda-ta*   'water'/'the water'
SEScr. ⎭
Rom.   *lup*   *lupu-l*   'wolf'/'the wolf'
Alb.   *shok*   *shok-u*   'comrade'/'the comrade'

- Infinitival structures tend to be replaced by dependent (or coordinate) clauses; see for example (8a). The development has been carried through most consistently in Greek, Macedonian, and Bulgarian. It peters out in Serbo-Croatian, with Serbian generally using the dependent-clause structure and Croatian preferring the old infinitive construction; see (8b). The related non-Balkan languages and earlier stages of the Balkan languages have structures with infinitives, as in Fr. *je veux écrire* or Ancient Greek *thélō gráphein* 'I want to write'.

(8)   a. Mod. Greek *θélo*   *na*   *γráfo*
            Rom.   *voi*   *să*   *scriu*
            Alb.   *dua*   *të*   *shkruaj*
                        I want   that   I write
                        'I want to write.'
        b. Serbian   *hoću*   *da*   *pisam*
                        I want   that   I write
            Croatian   *hoću*   *pisati*
                        I want   to write
                        'I want to write.'

- The marker used to form the future tense is based on the verb 'want, wish' used as an auxiliary, except in certain, mostly northern, Albanian dialects which use the verb *kam* 'have'. Compare the examples in (9). This future marker generally is an invariant, uninflected particle and is followed by the dependent clause construction illustrated in (8); the only exception is Serbo-Croatian which, outside the southeastern dialects, uses an auxiliary that is inflected for person and number and can combine with an infinitive or a dependent clause structure. Historically, the invariant future markers derive from full verbs, generally third person singular forms, which usually have undergone clitic reduction. For instance, Gk. *θa* derives from *θéli na* (lit. 'it wants that', see (8a)) and SCr. *ću* from the *hoću* of (8b). Again the outside languages and earlier stages of the Balkan languages have very different constructions; see (10).

(9)   Gk.   θα γράφο   'I will write' (*'it wants that I write')
      Rom.   *o să scriu*
      Alb.   *do të shkruaj*
      SCr.   *pisa-ću*   (*'I want to write')
(10) Span.   *escribir-é* < *escribir hé* 'I will write' (= infinitive of
            'write + 'have')
      Anc.Gk.   *gráp-s-ō* 'I will write' (= 'write' + future suffix + first
            singular ending)

While it is easy to state that the languages of the Balkans have come to converge in terms of the above features, as well as others not listed, there has been considerable disagreement about the exact sources for these features. Moreover, as in the case of Kupwar, it is not possible to point to a single language that might have been the source for all of the Balkanisms.

The elimination of long and nasalized vowels, for instance, seems to have been a communal effort, so to speak. It could well be the result of selective simplification, stripping away more complex features, a move toward a lowest common denominator.

As for the "loss" of the infinitive, i.e., its replacement by dependent clause structures, recall first of all the (failed) substratum explanation discussed in Chapter 12, § 4, in which an unknown single language (perhaps Thracian or Illyrian) was claimed to be the source. A more viable hypothesis is the claim that the loss of the infinitive is of Greek provenience, since the development is found attested earliest in that language. This view finds support in the fact that the replacement has taken place most completely in Greek and in the Slavic languages neighboring Greek – Macedonian and Bulgarian. Both Romanian and Albanian show what can be interpreted as traces of the old infinitive.

The problem with this hypothesis is that the first attestations of Albanian and Romanian come from the sixteenth century, considerably later than those of Greek. We therefore have no way of knowing the earlier history of the infinitive in these languages. Moreover, some evidence suggests that a number of Balkanisms may have been a shared feature of Greek and Latin in a convergence area of the late Roman Empire. One of the features of that area was a competition between infinitive and subordinate constructions. This competition, in turn, has been claimed by some linguists to be a Latin contribution, raising the possibility of the following, rather complex scenario.

Let us accept as the starting point the just-noted competition between infinitive and dependent clause constructions in the late Roman Imperial convergence area – a feature of Latin provenience. After the collapse of the Western Roman Empire, the convergence area, including its competition between infinitive and dependent clause structures, survives mainly in the Eastern Empire. Under the influence of that empire it then spreads through-out the Balkans. At a later stage the competition is resolved in favor of the dependent clause construction – an innovation that may have started in Greece. This innovation, finally, likewise spreads to the rest of the peninsula, petering out at the northwestern and western periphery. If this scenario is on the right track, then the Balkan "loss" of the infinitive is not the result of a single cataclysmic event, but the consequence of a series of developments, some of which were not limited to the Balkans.

Note however that this scenario is merely a possibility, entertained by some scholars; it has by no means come to be accepted by the majority of Balkanists.

Some further support for the scenario might be found in the choice of future auxiliary. Again we find that there was a competition in the Late Roman Empire, involving not only 'want, wish' and 'have', but in part of the area also 'begin'. The modern situation, with 'want, wish' in the majority of Balkan languages, but 'have' in non-Balkan Romance (as in Span. *escribir-é* < *escribir he* 'I have to = will write'), may be attributed to different resolutions of this competition. And just as some Balkan languages did not fully participate in the generalization of the subordinate construction, so in this case we have an exception to the generalization of 'want, wish' in one of the dialects of Albanian. (In fact, Old Church Slavic, the earliest attestation of South Slavic, offers the triple choice 'want, wish', 'have', and 'begin' of the Late Roman Empire convergence area.) What complicates matters is that the Greek 'have' future is attested much earlier than the 'want' future, which appears only in the tenth to twelfth centuries; and the chronology of the 'want' future in the other Balkan languages is still not fully understood.

Some considerations might even suggest that we should not look for a special convergence explanation of the Balkan auxiliary 'want, wish': Constructions meaning 'want, wish' are a very common source for future tense formations. We find parallels in Sanskrit and many other early Indo-European languages, as well as in Engl. *will*, originally 'want, wish'. In fact, 'have' in the sense of 'have to' is likewise a plausible choice as future auxiliary and is paralleled for instance in Engl. *shall*, originally 'be obliged to'.

The fact that English and other Germanic languages, including all the old Germanic dialects, offer both *will* and *shall* as future auxiliaries raises further questions about the uniqueness not only of Balkan 'want, wish', but also of the Late Imperial competition between 'want, wish' and 'have (to)'. These questions are reexamined in § 5 below.

While the replacement of the infinitive by subordinate structures and the use of 'want, wish' as future auxiliary thus may possibly go back to a Late Imperial convergence area dominated by Greek and Latin, features like the postposed article would be difficult to attribute to the same source. After all, neither Greek nor the modern non-Balkan Romance languages have postposed articles. The postposed article of Romanian thus is likely to be due to regional convergence. And since the postposed articles of Bulgarian and Macedonian likewise seem to be innovations, the logical choice for the feature might appear to be Albanian. However, as noted earlier, we know nothing about the earlier history of Albanian and thus would be in no position to substantiate the claim that postposed articles originated in that language. Moreover, some linguists have speculated that certain complexities in the use of articles in Greek structures with nouns plus adjectives may be indirectly connected with the postposed article of the other Balkan languages. But if there was a connection, then it is remarkable that Greek did not participate in the development of the postposed article.

4. South Asia

Another famous convergence area is that of South Asia: Beside Burushaski in the Northwest, for which we have no known outside relations, there are at least four major linguistic families which over the course of millennia have come to show an increasing agreement in a large number of overall structural features. These are:

- Indo-Aryan and some of the neighboring Nuristani and Eastern Iranian languages (such as Pashto), belonging to the Indo-European language family
- the Dravidian languages, which may perhaps be distantly related to the Uralic or Finno-Ugric family
- the Munda languages, related to Southeast Asian ("Austro-Asiatic") languages such as Mon and Khmer
- Tibeto-Burman languages on the northern periphery of South Asia, which share many features of the convergence area

For the approximate location of these language groups in modern South Asia, see Map 1.

All of these languages tend to share certain features. Exceptions do occur, such as some Munda languages which lack absolutives, or Kashmiri which

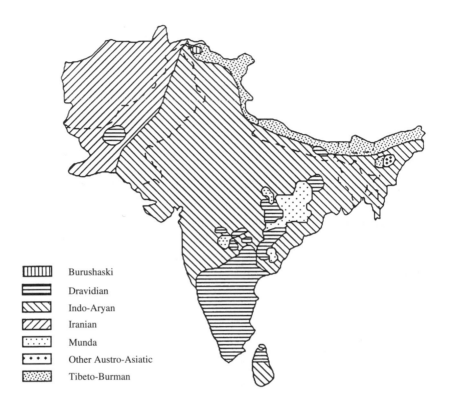

Burushaski

Dravidian

Indo-Aryan

Iranian

Munda

Other Austro-Asiatic

Tibeto-Burman

Map 1. Approximate distribution of modern South Asian languages

has innovated in the area of word order; but such exceptions are rare. The common features are as follows:

– A contrast between dental and retroflex consonants, as in (11)
– An unmarked SOV order, as in (12)
– The tendency to use "absolutives", something like verbal adverbs, where European languages would employ dependent or coordinate clauses; see (13)

(11)   Skt.   *pāta-*   'flight'   :   *pāṭa-*   'portion'

(12)   Hindi   *maĩ   kitāb   paṛh rahā   hũ*
                I (**S**)   book (**O**)   read AUX AUX (**V**)
                'I am reading a book.'

(13)   Hindi a.   *kitāb*   ***paṛh kē***   *baiṭh lō*
                     book   read Abs.   sit   take
                     'Having read the book/after you have read the book, sit
                     down.'
           or: 'Read the book and sit down.'
           b.   ***baiṭh kē***   *kitāb*   *paṛh lō*
                     sit   Abs.   book   read take
                     'Having sat down/after you have sat down, read the
                     book.'
           or: 'Sit down and read the book.'

Controversy continues as to when the convergence of South Asian languages began and which language group is responsible for the features listed above. Some scholars argue that the source is Dravidian, since all three features can be reconstructed for Proto-Dravidian. And, these scholars maintain, the ancestors of the other languages lacked some, or even all of these features. Moreover, since all of the features are found in the earliest attested stage of Indo-Aryan, it is claimed that convergence between Indo-Aryan and Dravidian must have begun in the second millennium B.C. Under this view, then, the similarities between Dravidian and the other South Asian languages are due, not to bidirectional convergence, but to unidirectional substratum influence.

Other linguists have pointed to evidence which supports the view that all the syntactic features also are indigenous in Indo-Aryan and that the basic principles of syntactic organization underlying these structures are inherited from Proto-Indo-European. SOV plus absolutive structures also appear to be inherited in Tibeto-Burman, as well as in many languages to the north and west of South Asia, including Altaic, Uralic, and a number of ancient Near Eastern languages, such as Elamite, Akkadian, and Sumerian. If these features are not inherited in the respective languages or language families, they may, therefore, have arisen in an earlier, much larger Eurasian convergence area which extended far beyond South Asia.

Interestingly, both Indo-Aryan and Dravidian, throughout their history, offer an alternative to subordination by means of absolutives (or other non-finite formations), namely a special type of relative construction in which the relative clause is not embedded into the main clause, but is juxtaposed before (or after) that clause. In this type of construction the main clause commonly contains a "correlative" pronoun (CP) which answers to the relative pronoun (RP) of the relative clause. The pairing of relative and correlative pronouns, then, accomplishes the same purpose as the English placement of relative clauses after the constituents that they modify. Compare the examples in (13′).

(13′) a. Skt.

yaḥ	*puruṣaḥ*	*paṭhati*	*saḥ*		(*puruṣaḥ*)
RP	human	studies	**CP**		human
vidvān	*bhavati*				
wise	becomes				

       lit. 'Which human (being) studies, that human (being) becomes wise.'

             'A human being who studies becomes wise.'

   b. Tamil

evan	*nanṟāka*	*uṟaikkiṟāṉ*	*-ō*		*avan*
RP	hard	works	Clitic	Particle	**CP**
vāṟkkaiyil	*munnāruvān*				
in life	will succeed				

       lit. 'Which (being) works hard, that (being) will succeed in life.'

             'He/She who works hard, will succeed in life.'

Unaware of their wide distribution in Dravidian and their appearance even in the earliest Dravidian texts, some linguists have attributed these structures to Indo-Aryan influence. Ironically, one linguist has made the converse claim, that the difference between the relative-correlative construction of Sanskrit and the embedded relative clause structures of English indirectly results from Dravidian influence. Recent research suggests that these structures, too, are inherited in both language families.

If the arguments that the overall syntactic agreements reflect common inheritance are correct, then the substratum hypothesis loses much of its cogency. It should be noted, however, that many adherents of the substratum hypothesis remain unconvinced of these alternative arguments.

There is controversy even over whether Dravidians and Indo-Aryans were in contact early enough for the allegedly substratum-induced features to be present in the earliest Indo-Aryan. One piece of evidence which seems to favor early contact is the appearance of one modern Dravidian language, Brahui, in today's Pakistan, i.e., in the extreme northwest which is commonly assumed to have been the place of earliest Indo-Aryan settlement in South Asia. But the present-day location of Brahui could be the result of migration from further south. True, the general direction of migrations has been from the northwest toward the south and east of South Asia. But other Dravidian-speaking groups have moved northward. And one Indo-Aryan group, that of the Romani (formerly called Gypsies), has moved even beyond northwestern South Asia, into Central Asia, and thence into Europe.

Similar uncertainties exist over another issue which might support the hypothesis that Indo-Aryan and Dravidian were in contact early enough for Dravidian to influence the structure of Indo-Aryan. This is the question of early Indo-Aryan borrowings from Dravidian. The reasoning here goes as follows: If there is evidence for such borrowings then it may be safely assumed that there must have been contact.

Some linguists find massive evidence for borrowings. But even substratists now consider many of these uncertain. Linguists on the other side of the argument have claimed that none of the proposed early borrowings from Dravidian stands up under scrutiny. But even if they are right, an absence of lexical borrowing does not preclude the possibility of contact. As noted earlier, the languages of Kupwar have undergone extensive structural convergence, while lexical borrowing has been minimal.

This leaves the retroflex/dental contrast, as in (11) above. Opponents of the substratist hypothesis have pointed out that such a contrast has arisen in other parts of the world (see Chapter 12, § 4) and that it is therefore unnecessary to assume Dravidian influence on Indo-Aryan. They also have observed that the sound systems of early Dravidian and Indo-Aryan are much more divergent than should be the case if Indo-Aryan retroflexion resulted from Dravidian influence: As Figure 1 shows, early Dravidian actually has a triple contrast between dental (unmarked), alveolar (post-dental; marked by underlining), and retroflex. In Sanskrit, the earliest attested form of Indo-Aryan, only [r] is phonetically alveolar; for the rest the contrast is one between dental and retroflex. Dravidian has a retroflex sound, r, very similar to Modern American English [r], which is absent in Indo-Aryan. On the other hand, Sanskrit has a retroflex sibilant $ṣ$ absent in Dravidian. And so on.

	Sanskrit			Dravidian		
	DENT.	ALV.	RETR.	DENT.	ALV.	RETR.
STOP	*t*		*ṭ*	*t*	*t̲*	*ṭ*
	th		*ṭh*			
	d		*ḍ*			
	dh		*ḍh*			
SIB.	*s*		*ṣ*			
NAS.	*n*		*ṇ*	*n*	*n̲*	*ṇ*
LIQU.	*l*	*r̲*			*l̲*	*ḷ*
					r̲	*ṛ*

Figure 1. Early Indo-Aryan and Dravidian systems

Contrast this situation with the modern one, especially as it obtains in the central area of South Asia, where Dravidian and Indo-Aryan languages are in closest contact. Except in the extreme south and northwest, the idio-syncratically Dravidian *ṟ* and the equally idiosyncratic retroflex sibilant *ṣ* of Sanskrit have been eliminated; and so has the alveolar series of early Dravidian. Moreover, secondary developments have given rise to a retroflex flapped *ṛ*, and in some of the languages to a retroflex liquid *ḷ*. And in both groups of languages, dental nasals are conditioned variants of more basic alveolar nasals. Compare Figure 2. Here, then, we have genuine convergence by way of mutual accommodation, while the early situation in Figure 1 looks more like divergence.

	INDO-ARYAN			DRAVIDIAN		
	DENT.	ALV.	RETR.	DENT.	ALV.	RETR.
STOP	*t*		*ṭ*	*t*		*ṭ*
	th		*ṭh*			
	d		*ḍ*			
	dh		*ḍh*			
SIB.	*s*					
NAS.	*n*	*ṉ*	*ṇ*	*n*	*ṉ*	*ṇ*
LIQU.		*ḻ*	*ḷ*		*ḻ*	*ḷ*
		ṟ	*ṛ*		*ṟ*	*ṛ*

Figure 2. Modern Indo-Aryan and Dravidian systems

Finally, there even is evidence that the Dravidian contrast between dental, alveolar, and retroflex stops may be secondary, the result of assimilation of dentals to preceding alveolar and retroflex nasals and liquids, as in **cen-t-ēṉ* > Tamil *ceṉṟēṉ* 'I went', **āḷ-t-ēṉ* > *āṇṭēṉ* 'I ruled'. The claim that retroflexion is inherited in Dravidian therefore is open to question.

Nevertheless, the fact that both early Dravidian and early Indo-Aryan have a retroflex : dental contrast is difficult to attribute to pure chance, even if it looks like an innovation in both groups. The very fact that it looks like an innovation in both groups of languages, at roughly the same time and in roughly the same area, makes the assumption of chance similarity even more difficult to accept. The fact that both groups seem to have innovated, however, makes unilateral substratum influence from Dravidian on Indo-Aryan (or vice versa, for that matter) just as unlikely. Perhaps, then, we should entertain the idea that the contrast arose from sound changes which were convergent even though they yielded different outcomes because they operated on different inputs – a retroflex : dental contrast in Sanskrit, and a retroflex : alveolar : dental contrast in Dravidian. These differences subsequently would have been eliminated by convergent accommodating developments.

While this alternative view of retroflexion is quite speculative, it has the virtue of overcoming some of the objections to the substratist view. Perhaps even more important, it replaces that view with a convergence analysis which is much more in keeping with later South Asian historical developments that in most cases are convergent, rather than reflecting unilateral substratum influence.

Only for the Munda languages do we need to assume extensive unidirectional influence. SOV order and the retroflex : dental contrast must be the result of contact; for the Austro-Asiatic languages of Indo-China have basic SVO and lack the retroflex : dental contrast. Note however that there is independent evidence that the speakers of Munda languages have a very different social status from that of (most) Dravidians and Indo-Aryans. Munda speakers only live in so-called tribal societies, in relatively isolated and economically disadvantaged areas. Their languages and customs, and they themselves are the subjects of widespread discrimination. Further, many areas now inhabited by Indo-Aryans and Dravidians bear place names suggesting that they originally were settled by Mundas who must have been displaced by Indo-Aryans and Dravidians. Given these circumstances, it should not be surprising if the Munda speakers were also linguistically on the receiving end.

5. Pre-Modern Europe

Convergence has not always been limited to "exotic" areas. There is good reason for believing that prior to the development of the notion of the monolingual nation-state, much of medieval and early modern Europe was a convergence area. In this section we examine several common innovations which resulted from this earlier convergence and which, to varying degrees, diffused through the languages of Europe.

One development which swept virtually the whole area is the movement of auxiliaries (AUX) into clause-second position; see Chapter 6, § 6. The only exceptions are: (i) the Insular Celtic languages, including Breton (originally spoken on the British Isles), which have VSO; (ii) Basque, with SOV; and at an early period, (iii) the Uralic languages (Finnish, Estonian, Hungarian, etc.) which likewise had SOV.

The precise source of the change is unknown. However, the earliest attestations of Lithuanian (in the sixteenth century) exhibit a very early stage of the development, which suggests that the change did not originate in or near Lithuanian, but farther south and west, in Germanic and/or Romance, where the effects of the change can be observed in the Middle Ages.

A further extension of this development, the shift of all finite verbs to second position, covered the same area, except that German, Dutch, and Frisian generalized verb-final AUX in dependent clauses. The same languages also resisted the last phase of the word order change, the movement of originally stranded non-finite main verbs into the position after clause-second AUX. See again Chapter 6, § 6.

Through this change the unmarked word order of most of the Indo-European languages of Europe became SVO. This order also spread to the Uralic languages which had settled in Europe (Finnish, Estonian, Hungarian). In Hungarian, however, the spread was incomplete, and older SOV patterns continue to exist beside the innovated SVO.

Other innovations extended over more limited territory. For instance, Greek, Romance, and Germanic developed a system with contrasting definite and indefinite articles, as in Fr. *l'homme* 'the man' : *un homme* 'a man' or their English counterparts. But Icelandic and early Celtic, on the northwestern periphery, acquired only a definite article. Since Greek was the first of the attested Indo-European languages to develop a definite article, it is likely that the feature originated in that language. A more southern and eastern origin would also explain why the languages on the western and northern periphery did not participate in this innovation.

Greek, Romance (including Romanian), Albanian, and the Balkan Slavic languages Macedonian and Bulgarian share the development of a system of pronominal clitics in which the position of clitic pronouns depends on the function of the verb. Position after the verb ("enclisis") is the norm after imperatives; see (14a). Position in front of the verb ("proclisis") is found elsewhere; see (14b). (There are some complications next to non-finite verbs, and such complications are found even next to finite verbs in older stages of Romance. These are unimportant for the present discussion and are therefore ignored.) The geographical source of this innovation is not clear.

(14)	a.	Span.	*mostrad **me***	'show me'
		Fr.	*dis-**le***	'tell it'
		It.	*mostrate **mi***	'show me'
vs.	b.	Sp.	*(yo)* ***te*** *quiero*	'I love you'
		Fr.	*je t'aime*	'I love you'
		It.	*(io)* ***ti*** *amo*	'I love you'

Yet another innovation is the development of a redundant marker of negation and the subsequent ellipsis of the original negative marker, as in (15). This change is also found in Old Norse, German, French, and a number of other, neighboring languages. (For further details on the individual developments see Chapter 5, § 3.2 and Chapter 6, § 1.)

(15)	OE	*ic ne wāt*	: *ic ne wāt (nā)wiht*
		'I don't know'	'I don't know at all'
	Chaucer	*ic ne woot*	: *ic ne woot naught*
		'I don't know'	'I don't know'
			: *ic woot naught*
			: 'I don't know'
	Shakespeare	*I wot(e) not*	
		'I don't know'	

The change appears to have started in the north. In Old Norse, it was virtually complete by about 1000 A.D. German carried it through by the fourteenth century. The English implementation of the process appears to have been a little slower; Chaucer still has a fair amount of variation in the fourteenth century. In French, on the other hand, redundant negation becomes obligatory only in the fifteenth century; and ellipsis still has not been carried through consistently in the modern conservative standard language. It is approaching greater consistency in colloquial French and especially in vernacular variants.

Finally, a more recent and geographically more limited development can be observed in the replacement of the simple past by the present perfect in colloquial French, Romantsch, northern Italian dialects, southern German, and Dutch/Flemish; see example (16). The phenomenon is most widespread in French, whereas in Italian and German it is limited to dialects that are geographically close to French. This suggests that the change originated in French and spread from there into the neighboring languages. Within Germany it is now spreading into more northern dialects, presumably through ordinary dialect diffusion. Given the lateness of the spread into non-French territory, it is possible that it took place, not within the larger convergence area of earlier Europe, but through border-area bilingualism.

(16)	a. Traditional German	Innovative southern German	
	ich bin gegangen	*ich bin gegangen*	'I have gone'
	ich ging	*ich bin gegangen*	'I went'

    b. Traditional French Innovative French
je suis allé	*je suis allé*	'I have gone'
j'allais	*je suis allé*	'I went, used to go'
j'allai	*je suis allé*	'I went'

6. The dialectology of convergence areas

Interestingly, the various innovations of the European convergence area that we have examined in the preceding section have spread across language boundaries in just about the same way as innovations cross dialect boundaries in a dialect continuum. And just as in the case of dialect continua, it is possible to capture the effects of spread by means of isogloss maps. Compare for instance Map 2 (p. 415), which accounts for the effects of some of the above developments by about the sixteenth century. (For ease of orientation, several geographical areas are identified by name. The map has been simplified to some extent. For instance, Finnish, Estonian, and other neighboring Uralic languages are listed as still having SOV, and Hungarian has been ignored altogether; similarly, Lithuanian is listed as SVO, even though at this point it has only begun to move finite verbs into second position. The abbreviation S Fin. OV / SOV is used to refer to the peculiar word order type of German, Dutch, and Frisian.)

As it turns out, a closer look at the Balkan convergence area reveals a similar picture of criss-crossing isoglosses. Several features commonly considered to be characteristic of the area do not necessarily extend over the whole territory. Other features extend far beyond the Balkans. In our earlier discussion in § 3 above we tacitly ignored these facts, since they appeared to be minor complications. Now that we have seen that isoglosses of this type are not unusual in convergence areas, we can recognize that these facts are not just minor complications, but that they are a meaningful feature of convergence areas. Let us therefore take another, closer look at the Balkan convergence area.

As we saw in § 3, the postposed definite article occurs in most of the Balkan languages, but not in Greek. The replacement of the infinitive by dependent clause constructions has been less complete in Romanian and Albanian than in Greek, Bulgarian, and Macedonian. The characteristic Balkan feature of 'want, wish' as future auxiliary is not found in part of Albanian.

On the other hand, the feature is found in much of Germanic (coexisting with 'be obliged to', as in Engl. *will* and *shall*) and was even more widespread in early Germanic. And there is evidence that 'want, wish' and 'have (to), be obliged to' once competed in a Late Imperial Roman convergence area. In addition, recall that some of the members of the Late Imperial convergence area employed an additional future auxiliary, 'begin to, set out to'.

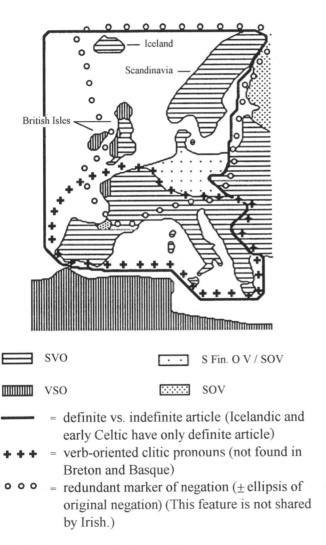

▤	SVO	⊡	S Fin. O V / SOV
▥	VSO	▦	SOV

— = definite vs. indefinite article (Icelandic and early Celtic have only definite article)

+ + + = verb-oriented clitic pronouns (not found in Breton and Basque)

o o o = redundant marker of negation (± ellipsis of original negation) (This feature is not shared by Irish.)

Map 2. Some major isoglosses of pre-modern Europe

Given that Germanic peoples were an important ingredient in the multilingual melting pot of the Late Roman Empire, one suspects that the Germanic competition between 'want, wish' and 'be obliged to' in early Germanic is not just an accident, but is a legacy of the Late Imperial convergence area. In the modern period, then, the link between the Balkans and the Germanic languages has been disrupted by several divergent linguistic developments which suggest a disintegration of the bilingualism responsible for earlier convergence. Most of the Balkan languages have generalized 'want, wish' at the expense of 'be obliged to'; the non-Balkan Romance languages instead have generalized 'have to, be obliged to'; and Modern German has innovated by employing a completely different future auxiliary, *werden* 'become'.

Further investigation reveals that German exhibits an encroachment of dependent clause constructions on the infinitive similar to what we find in the Balkans, but under more restricted conditions. Ordinarily, German is like English in only permitting infinitive constructions and disfavoring subordinate clauses with the verb 'want'; see (17a). However, in structures of the type (17b), where the logically subordinate proposition contains modal verbs such as *dürfen* 'be permitted to', both infinitive and subordinate constructions are possible. Given our new "dialectological" perspective on convergence, German (and other languages like it) can be considered something like a transition area between the Balkan core area and the rest of Europe.

(17)   INFINITIVE   SUBORDINATE CONSTRUCTION

 a. *Ich will   gehen*   *Ich will, dass ich gehe**
    I   want to go   I   want that I   go
                  'I want to go.'

 b. *Ich will   gehen dürfen*   *Ich will, dass ich gehen*
    I   want to go   be permitted   I   want that I   to go
                                        darf
                                        am permitted
              'I want to be permitted to go.'

As in the case of the European convergence area, the geographical distribution of these "Balkan features" can be plotted on a dialect map; see Map 3 (next page).

And again we find a picture of intersecting and criss-crossing isoglosses very similar to the traditional dialect maps of monolingual societies. We also observe that the features commonly considered characteristic of the Balkan convergence area do not define the area as boldly as one might expect. This is reminiscent of the fact discussed in Chapter 11, § 5, that the isoglosses of ordinary dialect maps often fail to set off traditionally defined major dialect divisions as boldly as one might expect.

This similarity between convergence area and dialect continuum should perhaps not be surprising, for as noted at the beginning of this chapter, the use of different languages in bilingual societies is in many ways comparable to the use of different dialects in monolingual societies. The isogloss evidence now permits us to state this insight even more boldly: Languages spoken in bi- or multilingual societies are the functional equivalent of dialects in monolingual societies, not only in their social function, but also in their interaction, including the spread of linguistic features and innovations.

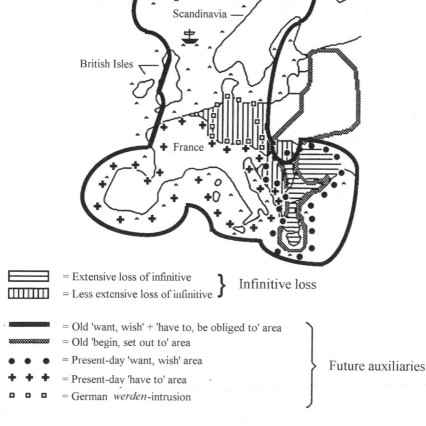

= Extensive loss of infinitive
= Less extensive loss of infinitive   } Infinitive loss

= Old 'want, wish' + 'have to, be obliged to' area
= Old 'begin, set out to' area
= Present-day 'want, wish' area
= Present-day 'have to' area   } Future auxiliaries
= German *werden*-intrusion

Map 3. Isogloss map of "Balkan features"

Chapter 14
Pidgins, creoles, and related forms of language

1. Introduction: Foreigner Talk, "Tarzanian", and other simplified forms of speech

In the last two chapters we examined various effects of ordinary bilingual contact between speakers of different languages. Let us now turn our attention to more extreme results of contact which include the development of pidgins. To set the stage for our discussion, let us begin with a look at a rather ordinary form of language contact which, however, in spite of its ordinariness bears the seeds for the more extraordinary developments that will occupy us in the rest of this chapter.

In response to the enormous and ever-growing international demand for instruction in English, the profession of teaching English as a Second Language (ESL) has become a highly attractive and lucrative business. The ranks of ESL teachers have been filled by many people who are highly trained and qualified professionals. But there are also individuals whose only qualification is that they speak English. Teachers of the latter type generally do not know the native languages of their students and the grammars of those languages. They may be quite unfamiliar with the formal grammar of their own language, English. And they may even lack the most rudimentary acquaintance with language pedagogy.

Now, imagine what happens when such teachers are confronted with students who have no previous knowledge of English – not an unlikely event, since the students have come to them to become familiar with English. Clearly, such situations can be highly frustrating for both teacher and students. What interests us in the present context is the manner in which such teachers often respond to the situation. This response can be best illustrated by the following anecdote.

An ESL teacher, let us call him or her Jan Johnson, was confronted with a group of foreign students who had no prior knowledge of English but were clearly eager to learn. At the same time, the teacher had no knowledge of the students' native language. After spending most of the first class session explaining at length the purposes of the course, the requirements, and so on, and feeling reassured by the students' polite smiles that they understood, Jan concluded the session, saying

> *For the next class, read chapter one.*

The blank gazes in the students' faces made Jan realize that the students did not understand the instruction. At best, they had come to realize that the initial pleasantries were over, and that their teacher now was telling them to do something. But what that something was clearly eluded them.

Jan's first response was to repeat the same message, only at a much SLOWER pace and somewhat more LOUDLY. The results were no better than after the first try. One or more additional tries, at an even slower pace and even greater volume, met with the same results.

At this point, feeling highly frustrated, Jan held up the book and said the following – at an even slower pace, even greater volume, and in a HEAVY, CHUNKY RHYTHM, with each word intoned as if it were a complete sentence:

(1)   *Here – book. See – book? Open – page – one.*

And to make sure that the students would understand their assignment, Jan pointed to the chapter title on the first page and added in the same voice:

(2)   *Chapter – one. Read. Next – time.*

The story does not tell us how successful this last effort was. But one suspects that the students figured out that they were supposed to read Chapter One (or Page One?), even if they could not actually do so – since they did not know English as yet. At any rate, their eagerness to acquire English would sooner, rather than later, enable them to learn enough of the language to complete the course and to employ it in the contexts of their choice – with, of course, varying degrees of success.

Jan's case is not an isolated one, and utterances such as the ones he or she resorted to in sheer desperation are not limited to certain ESL contexts. They are extremely common when any two or more people not knowing each other's language try to communicate. In fact, they are such a common phenomenon that linguists have introduced a special term to refer to this type of communication, namely FOREIGNER TALK.

Most of us have encountered Foreigner Talk more than once in our lives; and while our examples are drawn from English, virtually all languages – or rather, their speakers – have a form of Foreigner Talk. Modern tourism is a prime context for utterances such as (3), uttered to a taxi driver by a tourist afraid she might miss her plane.

(3)   *No – speak – Spanish. Go – airport … … airplanes – zoom-zoom-zoom. Quick. You – get – me – airport – me – pay – big bucks. Kapeesh?*

Another common context is warfare. Thus, in one of the episodes of the American television series **M*A*S*H**, Colonel Potter finds himself saying something like (4) to one of the Koreans he is trying to communicate with, only to stop himself by uttering (5).

(4)   *Me – no – want – watch*
(5)   *My God, I'm beginning to talk pidgin!*

In fact, not only have most of us come across Foreigner Talk; many of us have used it ourselves, under similar circumstances. There is indeed only one common alternative, a practice which anthropologists refer to as SILENT BARTER. In many parts of the world, people not knowing each other's language engage in trade without any serious attempt at using language, simply by displaying their wares, selecting, rejecting, and finally trading objects. The whole procedure is conducted in silence. If the trade is not mutually satisfactory, the whole cycle begins again. While evidently quite effective for simple trading purposes, silent barter is very limited in its application. It could conceivably have been used in the situation that gave rise to utterance (4), but not in the situations addressed by the utterances in (1)–(3).

Even those of us who might have a personal prejudice against the use of Foreigner Talk are quite familiar with it and its linguistic peculiarities, and we are able to judge whether a particular utterance is a proper example of Foreigner Talk or not.

We know that in addition to increase in volume, decrease in speed, and a chunky, word-by-word delivery, Foreigner Talk exhibits a number of peculiarities in its lexicon, syntax, and morphology, most of them consisting in ATTRITION and SIMPLIFICATION.

In the lexicon we find most noticeably an attrition in terms of the omission of function words such as *a, the, to, and*. There is also a tendency to use onomatopoetic expressions such as *(airplanes –) zoom-zoom-zoom*, colloquial expressions such as *big bucks*, and words that sound vaguely international such as *kapeesh*.

In the morphology we find a tendency to simplify by omitting inflections. As a consequence, where ordinary English distinguishes *I* vs. *me*, Foreigner Talk tends to use only *me*.

Syntactic simplification consists of the absence of complex syntax (such as the use of relative and other dependent clauses). The latter feature, combined with a number of lexical and morphological ones, can best be illustrated by comparing (3) above with (3′) below. Even a cursory glance will convince us, whether we use Foreigner Talk or not, that (3) is a much more appropriate example of Foreigner Talk than (3′).

(3′)   *I – do – not – speak – Spanish. Go – to – the – airport. Quickly. If – you – get – me – to – the – airport – I – will – pay – more – money. Understand?*

Part of our familiarity with the structural peculiarities of Foreigner Talk and our ability to judge its quality may stem from our familiarity with another widespread form of speech that is structurally very similar, namely BABY TALK. This is a form of speech commonly employed by adults, or even older children, with babies.

The term Baby Talk reflects the common assumption that "this is the way babies talk". But linguists who study the early stages of children's language acquisition know that this view is not founded in fact. Rather, Baby Talk is a response by adults to a situation remarkably similar to the contexts in which Foreigner Talk tends to arise – the desire or need to communicate with somebody whose language we don't understand and who apparently

422   *Pidgins, creoles, and related forms of language*

does not understand our language either. Scholars working on early child language acquisition therefore prefer to use terms such as NURSERY TALK or CARE-GIVER TALK to refer to this form of speech. But the term Baby Talk has a certain usefulness, in that it more accurately reflects what ordinary, linguistically naive adults believe; and as noted on several earlier occasions, such a belief often is more important for linguistic change than the more objective accounts of trained linguists.

Given the communicative similarities between the contexts in which Baby Talk and Foreigner Talk arise, it is not surprising that, like Foreigner Talk, Baby Talk is characterized by extensive lexical attrition and morphological and syntactic simplification, as in (6). At the same time, the differences between the two types of situation also have consequences in linguistic structure and in "delivery". Baby Talk tends to exhibit a great degree of phonological simplification, as in *seep* for *sleep*; and while Foreigner Talk tends to be characterized by a chunky and rather loud delivery, Baby Talk features a more "lilting" or "sweet" delivery.

(6)   *Baby wan(t) seep ?*
        'Does the baby/do you want to sleep?'

Many people extend Baby Talk when talking with their lovers or even their pets, i.e., in other situations in which a lilting, sweet delivery seems appropriate. Dogs, however, may also be subjected to a form of simplified speech that is anything but lilting and sweet. This is the special form of language used in dog obedience training, especially in expressions like *No sniff* 'do not sniff around' or *No scratch* 'don't scratch yourself' – or even *no lick paw*, to discourage a dog from licking her paws till they get sore.

In addition to these forms of simplified speech we can draw on yet another, similar form of speech as a model for producing Foreigner Talk. This is the literary caricature of something like Foreigner Talk that we find exemplified in the famous *Me Tarzan – You Jane* in the cartoon at the beginning of this chapter. This form of language is found in numerous other literary contexts, many of them much earlier than the Tarzan stories. See for instance the passage in (7). Even so, linguists have begun to use the term TARZANIAN to refer to this form of language use.

(7)   *"Kill-e," cried Queequeg, twisting his tattoed face into an unearthly expression of disdain, "ah! him bevy small-e fish-e; Queequeg no kill-e so small-e fish-e: Queequeg kill-e big whale!"* (Herman Melville, *Moby Dick*)

Interestingly, then, by at least partly drawing on the model of Tarzanian, Foreigner Talk may be drawing on a caricature of itself – in a kind of circular development. But while Tarzanian no doubt draws partly on Foreigner Talk and our quasi-intuitive understanding of its peculiarities, it also tends to caricature another form of speech which, in spite of great structural similarities, differs considerably in its use and social setting from Foreigner Talk. This form of speech is called PIDGIN. (Notice in this regard Colonel Potter's use of the term pidgin in example (5) above.)

The pidgin influence is especially clear in the passage cited in (7). Both the general setting of Melville's novel and the specific use of expressions like *tattoed face* places the utterance in the prototypical context for pidgins to arise – the interaction between Europeans and non-Europeans in the period of European colonial expansion. At the same time, there is clear empirical evidence that, in spite of their similarities, pidgin and Foreigner Talk are very distinct forms of speech. These matters are discussed more fully in the next two sections.

2. Pidgins defined

In the wake of the European colonialization of much of today's "Third World", there arose all over the globe a series of speech varieties that are commonly referred to as PIDGINS. These languages in many ways differ radically from any of the other types of language resulting from linguistic contact. True, here too, we find evidence of interlanguage influence from the various indigenous languages. And one of the major characteristics of pidgins, structural simplification, may be found in other types of language contact, such as koiné formation or convergence. But in other situations, structural simplification is selective and merely serves to eliminate (excessive) linguistic differences. In pidgins, by contrast, there is a RADICAL SIMPLIFICATION of linguistic STRUCTURE, plus a radical REDUCTION or attrition of VOCABULARY. Thus, all inflection, all morphophonemic alternation, major syntactic phenomena such as the passive, and all syntactic embedding tend to be eliminated. And the lexicon tends to be limited to 1,000 or 2,000 words. Most significant, by all appearances, simplification and reduction take place rapidly, within one or two generations.

Before trying to determine the precise linguistic developments and the special social conditions that give rise to pidgins, let us take a brief look at an often-cited example from an English-based pidgin spoken in New Guinea and Melanesia. This is a structure used to express the notion 'piano':

(8)

	Big	*pela*	*bokas*	*yu*	*pait-im*	*i*	*krai*
Literally:	big	fellow	box	you	fight-him	he	cry (= cries)
Actually:	big	*	box	you	fight *	*	cry
	large		(suit)case	one	hit		shout
	great		wooden		touch		make sounds
	...		container		...		...

...

= 'A big type of wooden structure which, if you touch it (or its keys), emits (musical) sounds'

Even a cursory glance will show that this is a rather lengthy expression for the notion 'piano'. The length of the expression is a consequence of the extremely limited lexicon of pidgins. If you have only 1,000 to 2,000 words, it does not pay to have special terms for such notions as 'piano', or 'philosophy' for that matter. Especially terms for things and ideas like 'piano' and 'philosophy' that are far removed from the social context in which pidgins must function are likely to be expressed by circumlocution, as in (8).

But even some very basic notions may be expressed by circumlocution. For instance, the New Guinean/Melanesian pidgin expression for hair is *gras (bi)loŋ hed*, lit. 'grass belong head' ≈ 'grass-like growth on the head'.

Moreover, the words actually used in circumlocutions of this type exhibit characteristics attributable to the extremely limited size of the lexicon. As the "Actually" glosses in (8) for *big, bokas, pait,* and *krai* illustrate, to cover enough semantic territory each word has to have a wide range of POLYSEMY, that is, multiple meanings for a given word (see Chapter 7, § 2). Thus, *big* covers 'big', 'large', 'great', and a large number of other related meanings.

At the same time, all of the vocabulary used in (8) is of European origin. This is the normal pattern in the classical pidgins that arose in the context of European colonialization. Non-European words are quite rare, except for names of places, flora, and fauna which tend to come from the indigenous languages. A few other non-European words may likewise derive from the indigenous languages, such as *kanæka* 'native' in Melanesian/New Guinean pidgin. But they may also stem from other languages, such as Melanesian/New Guinean pidgin *kau-kau* 'food', which has been traced to Hawaiian sources.

Further, note the evidence for extensive structural simplification which manifests itself in the absence of inflectional morphology in *krai*, rather than *crie-s*; in the absence of a relative pronoun (or other type of relative marker); and in the absence of the conditional marker 'if'. (In our examples, both markers of subordination must be supplied in the interpretation.) Again, these characteristics are a general feature of classical pidgins.

Other features include the use of just one universal preposition. New Guinean/Melanesian pidgin, for instance, employs the all-purpose preposition *(bi)lɔŋ* to express the notions covered by ordinary English *of, to, for, at, in, with*, and all the other prepositions. Compare for instance the expression *gras (bi)lɔŋ hed* 'hair', discussed earlier.

Similarly, our pidgin uses *mi* and *ɛm* not only for the object *me* and *him*, but also for the subject *I* and *he*. In the third person, *ɛm* indicates not only the singular masculine 'he', but also feminine 'she' and neuter 'it'. And so on.

The last statement seems to be contradicted by the use of *im* and *i* in example (8), whose literal translation is 'him' vs. 'he'. However, here as elsewhere, the "Literally" gloss at best gives us an indication of the English source, not of the actual meaning or function of a given word. In the case of *im* and *i*, the "Actually" gloss supplies an asterisk, just as it does for *pela*, lit. 'fellow'. This is because in both cases, English words have been recruited, as it were, to express grammatical features of the indigenous languages: *im* serves to indicate that the preceding verb is transitive and *i* is used to signal aspects of discourse continuity. Both of these elements, thus, serve as something like function words or affixes, calquing grammatical peculiarities of the indigenous languages. (A parallel to *im* as a transitive marker seems to have existed in a North American pidgin used in communication between speakers of English and certain Indigenous American languages. This is reflected in caricature expressions such as *You want-**um** wampum?*)

The use of *pela* generally is motivated by the fact that the indigenous languages employ "classifiers". Classifiers are marginally present in English, too, where they are used to "individualize" mass nouns, as in *rice : one **grain** of rice/two **grains** of rice, bread : a **loaf** of bread, a **slice** of bread*. In the indigenous languages of New Guinea/Melanesia (and in many other languages around the world) classifiers are obligatory with all nouns that are preceded by modifiers. The use of *pela*, then, is a calque of this important grammatical pattern. At the same time, like all other structural and lexical pidgin features, it exhibits extreme attrition, being expressed by a single, all-purpose form. (A second use of *pela*, not illustrated in (8), is to turn the pronouns *mi* and *yu* into plurals, yielding *mi-pela* 'we (all)' (including

persons other than 'you' and 'I') and *yu-pela* 'you all', beside *yu-mi* 'we' =
'you and I only'. Here again, the use of *pela*, in *mi-pela* vs. *yu-mi*, serves to
encode an important grammatical distinction of the indigenous languages.)

Finally, yet another consequence of the extreme lexical and grammatical reduction has occasionally been commented on, namely the need to use
gestures, facial expressions, and changes in voice quality to make up, as it
were, for the limited linguistic means that speakers can use to convey their
ideas. This phenomenon has perhaps been most strikingly described in the
following late-nineteenth-century account of a pidgin-like form of language,
Chinook Jargon, spoken in the northwestern United States, British Columbia,
and Alaska. The account betrays its date by its use of expressions such as "a
party of the natives". (See § 4 below for more on Chinook Jargon.)

> The Indians in general are very sparing of their gesticulations. No languages,
> probably, require less assistance from this source than theirs ... We frequently
> had occasion to observe the sudden change produced when a party of the na-
> tives, who had been conversing in their own tongue, were joined by a foreigner,
> with whom it was necessary to speak in the Jargon. The countenances, which
> had before been grave, stolid, and inexpressive, were instantly lighted up with
> animation; the low, monotonous tone became lively and modulated; every fea-
> ture was active; the head, the arms, and the whole body were in motion, and
> every look and gesture became instinct with meaning. (Hale 1890)

3. Pidgin origins

The question of how pidgins originated, and why so many of them arose
in the wake of European colonialist expansion, has elicited many different
responses.

3.1. "Imperfect learning"
One explanation, coming in different variants, boils down to the assertion that
pidgins resulted from the inability of the non-Europeans to learn European
languages correctly, i.e., pidgins result from "imperfect learning".

However, one must ask why pidgins arose only among non-Europeans.
And why should the non-Europeans have exhibited this peculiar inability
only in learning European languages, while having no difficulties with learning other non-European languages? Note in this regard that the indigenous

populations of most non-European areas of the world have a long tradition of bilingualism (and multilingualism). That bilingualism, however, did not typically result in pidgins or pidgin-like languages, but in convergence, koiné-formation, and similar developments. (See Chapters 12 and 13.) Moreover, in more recent times large numbers of non-Europeans have learned European languages very well – evidently because they were both permitted and encouraged to do so.

There is, in fact, a further difficulty with the assumption that pidgins arose from imperfect learning of the European languages. This difficulty is connected with the very process of structural simplification. If we only had English-based pidgins, it would be easy to attribute the lack of inflection in forms such as the *krai* of (8) above to the fact that the non-European learners, not understanding the function of inflectional endings such as *-s, -ing, -ed*, ignored them altogether. The result is the simple root *krai*, whose choice would be further supported by the fact that most forms of the present, as well as the imperative and infinitive, consist of the simple root, without inflectional ending. But in Romance-based pidgins the case is much more complex. Consider for instance the following (incomplete) Portuguese paradigm of the verb 'to speak'.

(9) Present   singular   plural
                    1 *falo*   *falamos*
                    2 *falas*   *falais*[1]
                    3 *fala*   *falam*
    Imperative   2 *fala*   *falai*[1]
    Infinitive   *falar*
    Gerund   *falando*
    Past Participle   *falado*

([1]The second plural form has become obsolescent in present-day Portuguese.)

How should this complex set of forms be simplified, reduced to a single, invariant form? Should we use the simplest form, without any inflectional ending, i.e., the second person singular imperative *fala*? But this form is just one of many. And in fact, it is not the form that was used as the invariant, uninflected form of the verb. Perhaps the third person singular should have been used, since this is the form that most frequently occurs in speech? Or the first person singular, since we like to talk about ourselves? Again, these forms were not used. Or should we just randomly choose the first verbal form we come across? That would mean that the invariant pidgin verb forms should randomly reflect any verbal form of Portuguese. And again, that is not what we find.

Instead, the normal invariant pidgin form of the verb is that of the infinitive, *falar* in our case.

Since the late nineteenth century, many linguists have argued that this consistent choice is unexplainable under the assumption that pidgins arose from imperfect learning. To be able to consistently choose one grammatical structure, the infinitive, as the invariant shape of the verb requires a degree of grammatical knowledge of the European language which is far from imperfect. Moreover, one must ask, if the non-European learners had such a high degree of grammatical knowledge of the European language that they could recognize the infinitive, why did they not use the full range of grammatical forms of that language – or at least a much larger range than the mere infinitive?

3.2. The "racial-inferiority" argument

The claim that pidgins result from the imperfect learning of European languages by non-Europeans has often – especially in colonialist times – been supported by the racist allegation that the non-European "natives" are genetically inferior to the European colonizers and that this is the reason they are unable to learn the European languages. This view has often been supported by asserting that the highly reduced structure and vocabulary of pidgins are prima facie evidence for the intellectual inferiority of the "natives". The similarity between pidgins and Baby Talk "confirms" that the "natives" only have the mental capacity of infants.

The strongest linguistic arguments against this racist view can be based on the following facts. Many of the native languages of these "natives" can rival any European language in structural complexity. Moreover, as just noted, the "natives" had no difficulties with being bilingual in non-European languages. (If anything, many of them were much better at bilingualism than most modern Europeans.) And, when given the opportunity and encouragement to do so, they were perfectly able to learn the European languages. Beyond this linguistic evidence, it is sufficient to note that there is simply no credible evidence to support the view that non-Europeans are mentally inferior to Europeans.

Nevertheless, several elements in the traditional racist arguments are significant, since they provide us with important information on the social attitudes of the European colonizers and since, as we will see a little further down, the belief that the "natives" are mentally inferior may have indirectly contributed to the institutionalization of pidgins.

3.3. The Portuguese Proto-Pidgin hypothesis

It has also been alleged that all – or at least most – pidgins are descended from a single source, a "Proto-Pidgin". This claim, if correct, would be highly attractive, since it would automatically explain the similarities in structural and lexical attrition found in all of the pidgins.

Some scholars claim that the Proto-Pidgin consisted in the original Lingua Franca or SABIR, a Romance-based contact language employed in the Mediterranean area from the time of the Crusades into the last century, and sharing with the pidgins of the colonialist period a high degree of lexical and structural reduction. According to these scholars, Sabir was taken as a contact language from the Mediterranean to the world at large by the Portuguese, who were the first to engage in the explorations that ultimately led to the domination and exploitation of most of the non-white world by a tiny minority of European, white nations. Other scholars, instead, believe that the Portuguese developed their own Proto-Pidgin contact language, without influence from Sabir.

As other European nations, with different languages, entered the colonialist scene, it is claimed, they took over the ready-made pidgin of the Portuguese – together with their nautical and other relevant non-linguistic expertise. But instead of taking it over intact, these nations adjusted the Portuguese pidgin to their languages by substituting words from their own lexica for the Portuguese lexical items. This process, which has been called RELEXIFICATION, would a priori seem to be relatively easy, given that we are talking about a very limited vocabulary of at most 2,000 words.

The relexification hypothesis receives apparent empirical support from the fact that many, if not most, of the non-Portuguese European-based pidgins have certain lexical items which are most likely to be of Portuguese origin. Most notable among these are the words in (10) below. Significantly, the earlier English form *sabby*, clearly Romance in origin, agrees best with Port. *saber* [-b-] 'know', whereas Fr. *savoir* and Sp. *saber* have [v] and [β] respectively. Similarly, *pickaninny* and its relatives are most easily derived from Port. *pequeno,* diminutive *pequenino* 'small', while Spanish has *pequeño* with palatal nasal. More than that, a few pidgins, such as Saramaccan (spoken in Surinam), seem to have stopped relexifying in midstream. About 27 percent of Saramaccan vocabulary is traceable to Portuguese; the rest is mainly of English origin.

(10)   Engl. pidgin   *savvy*
        Earlier Engl. pidgin   *sabby*
        Fr. pidgin   *sabé*

Engl. pidgin *pickaninny*
Du. pidgin *pikien*
Span. pidgin *piquinini*

This theory likewise is open to several doubts and reservations. First, even if it were established beyond a reasonable doubt that all pidgins are descended from a single Proto-Pidgin, we must still explain how that Proto-Pidgin came about. Relexification does not solve the problem; it merely pushes it back farther in history.

Secondly, some pidgins or pidgin-like languages (see § 4 below) clearly arose independently, in areas and social situations without any possible access to Sabir, the hypothetical Portuguese Proto-Pidgin, or any of the pidgins supposedly descended from it. Even some of the alleged descendants of the Portuguese Proto-Pidgin exhibit features suggesting that they arose independently. Thus, early reports show that in the French-based pidgins of the West Indies the issue as to which structure should be used as the uninflected, general verb form was not yet fully resolved. Both the infinitive (as in *savoir* 'know') and, less commonly, a regularized form of the participle (*savé* 'known') still were in competition. Had there been simple relexification of an already established Proto-Pidgin, we would not expect such fluctuations. It is only later, as the pidgins come to be more established, that the infinitive form is used across the board, just as it is in any other pidgins based on languages with relevant verb morphology. (English-based pidgins, of course, are not helpful in this regard, since their invariable verb form is identical not just to the English infinitive, but to the verbal root.)

More than that, the heterogeneous vocabulary of Saramaccan and a few other similar cases can be explained by a different scenario, which has the added advantage that it is much less hypothetical than the relexification hypothesis: Let us assume that Saramaccan started as a Portuguese-based pidgin, a likely assumption since we know that the Portuguese had a significant South American presence (which still survives in Brazil) and since, moreover, the Portuguese were heavily involved in the slave trade to South America. Under the circumstances, we would expect a Portuguese-based pidgin to have arisen. Now, while in many colonial situations the speakers of the source language for the pidgin remained in power, Surinam, formerly known as Dutch Guyana, experienced a rather checkered colonial history. At an early period the colony came under British control, which continued in British Guyana but gave way to Dutch control in Surinam by the late seventeenth century. It is the early change from Portuguese to British influence which can be held responsible for the lexically mixed character of Saramaccan. As we will see in § 5, pidgins – if they survive for an extended period – tend to undergo a process of creolization or depidginization which most prominently manifests itself in vocabulary expansion. For the majority of pidgins, the source for the original pidgin lexicon and the source for the expanded creole lexicon were the same European language. But in Saramaccan, the situation must have been different. While Portuguese furnished the source for the pidgin lexicon, lexical expansion must have taken place largely during the period of British control and therefore drew on English vocabulary. (There is, in fact, a fair amount of additional, Dutch vocabulary which reflects the later Dutch control of the colony.)

In the majority of pidgins the words of Portuguese origin are much more limited. The most widespread are the ones in (10) above. The wide diffusion of this limited lexical set, however, can be explained without the assumption of a Portuguese Proto-Pidgin. The fact is undeniable that there was a great amount of contact between Portuguese navigators, sailors, and (slave) traders and their counterparts from other European nations as they entered the colonialist and slave-trading "enterprise". In the process, a fair amount of vocabulary connected with the enterprise must have been passed on from the Portuguese to the other Europeans, as part of a special conquistador/slave trader jargon. (A possible parallel is the North Atlantic nautical jargon of Chapter 10, § 4.)

Probable traces of this jargon, which are not limited to pidgins (and creoles, discussed in § 5 below), can be found in a fair amount of the terminology of the slave trade, including Engl. *Negro, mulatto, quadroon*, and their counterparts in other European languages, as well as the term *creole*, whose original meaning is said to have been 'child of a non-European mother and a European father, born in the house of the father'. (Many of these terms are generally claimed to be of Spanish origin; but from the formal perspective, Portuguese origin is equally possible; and from the social perspective of early colonialism and slave trade, it is much more likely.) There is nothing to prevent us from assuming that *savvy* and *pickaninny* were likewise diffused from Portuguese through the medium of the conquistador/slave trader jargon, rather than through relexification from a Portuguese Proto-Pidgin.

That words of this sort, together with their social connotations, can be picked up by people who do not speak a pidgin – or are in the process of relexifying a pidgin – is shown by the fact that *savvy* and *pickaninny*, as well as *Negro, mulatto, quadroon*, and *creole* have entered the general vocabulary of English and are used by people who have no firsthand acquaintance with pidgins. Similarly, the word *kapeesh* of example (3) above was no doubt first picked up by American soldiers in World War II who fought in Italy and learned a smattering of Italian, including *capisci* 'do you understand?', regionally pronounced more like [kapiš]. Having done so, they transferred the word to similar contexts, i.e., when talking with speakers of other foreign languages that they did not understand. Subsequently, many Americans who have never been to Italy have adopted the word and use it in similar situations, without of course knowing its origin. Note similarly the word *kau-kau* 'food' in Melanesian/New Guinea pidgin, a word which has been traced to Hawaiian origin and which, significantly, is believed to have come to the area through South Sea sailors' jargon.

3.4. Foreigner Talk and the origin of pidgins

So far, the most plausible hypothesis is that (beside interlanguage), the most potent force in the development of pidgins is FOREIGNER TALK, the form of speech discussed in detail in § 1 above.

As we have seen, there are great formal similarities between Foreigner Talk and pidgins. Both exhibit a great amount of structural and lexical reduction. Moreover, there is good reason to believe that pidgins originated in contexts very similar to those that give rise to Foreigner Talk: Speakers find themselves in a situation – in this case the context of colonial expansion and the slave trade – where they are forced to communicate with others whose language they do not understand and who do not understand their language.

Given these great similarities between Foreigner Talk and pidgins, it is tempting to view pidgins simply as institutionalized forms of Foreigner Talk. However, the link cannot be quite so direct. We know that Foreigner Talk is a very common tendency in the context of first linguistic contact. We must therefore ask ourselves why it is not institutionalized more commonly.

A plausible answer to this question can be given if we consider sociolinguistic factors. Under normal circumstances, the expectation is that a foreign language (or even several languages in contact) will be learned to the point of complete or at least adequate mastery. Foreigner Talk therefore generally is only a transitory, first-generation or first-contact, phase.

The expansion of European colonialism brought with it a very different expectation on the part of (most of) the Europeans: The "natives" were held to be inferior and thus proper objects of colonialist and racist exploitation, even of slavery. As we have seen in § 3.2 above, they were also commonly believed to be incapable of correctly learning the European languages. If, then, they began to imitate the Foreigner Talk of the Europeans, the similarity of their production to Baby Talk only strengthened the colonialists' and slave-traders' mistaken belief that these "natives" had the mentality of infants and that Foreigner Talk therefore was the only proper way of speaking to them.

Under the circumstances, the use of Foreigner Talk did not just remain a transitory phenomenon, but became institutionalized as the proper vehicle for communication with the "natives".

The extent to which attitudes of this type permeated society can be gauged from the fact that even in the early part of the twentieth century, the *Encyclopedia Britannica* characterized Pidgin English as an "unruly bastard jargon, filled with nursery imbecilities, vulgarities, and corruptions." Except for the function words, virtually every lexical item in this passage expresses prejudice. Note further the use of the word *nursery*, a clear echo of the belief that Pidgin = Baby Talk.

Another important factor may have been that by providing Foreigner Talk as the only model which the "natives" could imitate, the Europeans were able to keep them "in their place". Foreigner Talk, then, became a marker of the social distance between European masters – who spoke the "real, proper" form of European language – and their non-European subjects or slaves – who were confined to an "inferior, bastardized" form of the language. Being relegated to Foreigner Talk excluded the subject peoples from the European language of power, while the reduced structure of the European-based Foreigner-Talk made it both easy to learn and perfectly adequate for the limited communication – mainly giving orders – that the Europeans wanted to engage in.

(There were of course dissenting voices who looked at Foreigner-Talk or pidgin as at least ideally a transitory phenomenon. Thus, in *Moby Dick* [Chapter 99], Melville eventually has Queequeg begin to learn "proper English" by memorizing such paradigms as *I look, you look, he looks; we look, ye look, they look* from Murray's *Grammar*, thus "improving his mind".)

Recent research suggests that Portuguese pidgins arose from a deliberate decision by the Portuguese to use Foreigner Talk, rather than their normal language. In the early phase of Portuguese expansion down the western coast of Africa, attempts were made to communicate with the local population through interpreters familiar with Portuguese and with Arabic, which at that time served as the major link language in all of northern Africa. As the Portuguese moved farther south, this approach no longer was feasible. At first, the Portuguese tried to teach their language to members of the local community who would then serve as interpreters. After a while, realizing that this was a very time-consuming process, they switched to teaching a simplified, Foreigner Talk variety of Portuguese. It is this variety which seems to have been the basis for the Portuguese pidgins.

In addition to having sociolinguistic plausibility on its side, as well as the general similarities between Foreigner Talk and pidgins, the Foreigner Talk hypothesis has the advantage of explaining an important linguistic feature of pidgins which other theories find very difficult to explain. This is the fact, noted in § 3.1, that the invariable verb form of Romance-based pidgins generally is the infinitive of the European source language, rather than another specific form – or, randomly, any form – of the verbal paradigm. As it turns out, the infinitive also is the normal invariable verb form in the Foreigner Talk varieties of the Romance languages.

The Foreigner Talk hypothesis further explains why many pidgins have picked up highly colloquial, even vulgar, expressions from the European languages, such as Melanesian Pidgin Engl. *bagerap* 'destroy, ruin ...' from vulgar Engl. *bugger up*. As observed in § 1 above, such expressions are quite common in Foreigner Talk.

While the Foreigner Talk hypothesis thus is the most fruitful account of pidgin origins, there is clear evidence that pidgins, once established, differ markedly from Foreigner Talk. After the First World War, the former German colony of New Guinea was placed under Australian trusteeship. Australian officials who took over the administration believed that they could talk to the "natives" simply by using their own version of Foreigner Talk, with a few elements (*im, i,* and *pela*) thrown in randomly to capture the most striking features of New Guinea Pidgin. But it is reported that the "natives" were not impressed. At least when amongst each other, they laughed derisively at what to them was an incompetent imitation of their pidgin.

4. Trade Jargons and other pidgin-like languages

The importance of sociolinguistic factors can also be seen in a more recent and therefore more observable development. In Germany (and similarly in a number of other European countries), the industrial boom of the 1960s led to a heavy influx of foreign laborers or "guest workers" who were brought in from economically less advantaged countries to do work which Germans considered undesirable. Most guest workers had no prior knowledge of German, and their languages were equally unfamiliar to most of their German supervisors. Out of the Foreigner Talk employed by the socially more powerful Germans there developed a special variety of language called Gastarbeiterdeutsch ('guest worker German', abbreviated GAD). GAD has undergone a certain degree of institutionalization and may for instance be used by guest workers of different linguistic backgrounds when talking to each other. Moreover, although in the early stages, native Germans apparently used Foreigner

Talk quite freely with guest workers, recent studies suggest that Foreigner Talk now is used rather sparingly. That is, foreign laborers no longer seem to need the input of native speakers' Foreigner Talk for acquiring GAD.

At the same time, sociolinguistic conditions are not conducive for the development of a fully institutionalized pidgin. In spite of considerable difficulties with a bureaucracy that tries to prevent their acquiring citizenship and in spite of widespread social segregation and recurring episodes of xenophobic excesses, most foreign laborers and their families try to stay in Germany and therefore make considerable efforts to learn German more fully. Most native speakers of German, on their part, tend to switch to normal, non-simplified German as soon as they feel that a particular foreign laborer has begun to acquire more than cursory control of the language. It is only among those guest workers who develop a very negative attitude to Germany and to German society (because of cultural disillusionment or because they have been victims of xenophobia) that GAD becomes relatively "fixed". But workers with this attitude tend to return to their home countries. Their version of GAD therefore has no chance of becoming institutionalized.

The relatively unsettled sociolinguistic nature of GAD is mirrored by relatively unsettled linguistic characteristics. For instance, instead of generalizing a single morphological form as the all-purpose, uninflected form of the verb, GAD has at least three different formations: an uninflected form of the verb, formally similar or identical to the imperative, a form identical to the infinitive, and the past participle; see (11). Interestingly, each of these can be used in ordinary German to give orders; see (11′). It has been observed that the generalization of formations which can be used as imperatives is a common feature of pidgins. Thus the infinitive, commonly used in Romance-based pidgins, can also be used as an imperative in the Romance languages. Presumably, this choice reflects the social context in which the more privileged or powerful give orders to the less privileged. (In German, the use of infinitives and past participles is especially common in more impersonal commands, as for instance in the military. These forms are therefore especially appropriate for giving orders to people with whom one does not want to be in close, personal contact. The choice of the imperative may, however, also be motivated by the fact that it is virtually identical to the root and thus morphologically the simplest verb form.)

(11)   GAD   Ordinary German
    a. *mach* arbeit   ich *mache/tue* die Arbeit   'I do the work'
                        wir *machen* /... die Arbeit   'we do the work'
                        ich *habe* die Arbeit *getan*   'I did the work'

b. *nix nach haus*   *ich **gehe** nicht nach*   'I don't go home'
   gehn   *hause*

c. *tag **geschlafen***   *ich **schlafe** am Tag /...*   'I sleep during the
                                     day'
   (said by a guest worker who was working night shifts)

(11′)   a. ***iss** deine Suppe!* (sing. 2 imperative)   'eat your soup'
       b. *Essen **fassen!*** (infinitive (distancing))   'get (your) chow'
       c. ***stillgestanden!*** (past pple. (military))   'stand still; (stand at) at-
                                         tention'

While pidgins and pidgin-like languages such as GAD arise in an environment of rather extreme inequality, similar types of language can come about under conditions of equality. Interestingly, the different social conditions are reflected in the fact that such TRADE JARGONS also differ from pidgins in their linguistic characteristics.

One such language may be the so-called Chinook Jargon referred to in § 2 above, which used to be employed by trappers and traders in the northwest of the United States, British Columbia, and Alaska. Extant descriptions show that when the Europeans arrived, the jargon was used for relatively short-term trading relations in a social setting of equality. Here, too, we find a great degree of structural and vocabulary simplification, exceeding what one encounters in normal language contact. However, there is an important difference: The vocabulary and the linguistic structures employed, as well as their simplification, are much more variable than those of the classical pidgins. Thus, the vocabulary did not predominantly come from a single source; but a variety of languages contributed to it. Moreover, the extent to which different groups contributed to the vocabulary was subject to considerable fluctuation. (Some linguists believe that Chinook Jargon began as a pidgin, because there are some indications that it was used with slaves; but for all we know, slavery in the Native American context of the northwest was very different in nature from the chattel slavery of European colonialism and its successors in countries like the United States.)

A similar language, called Russenorsk, arose in the north of Norway, as a means of communication between Russian traders and Norwegian fishermen during the relatively short fishing season. Just like Chinook Jargon, the language was employed for relatively short-term trading relations between social equals. Here, too, we find considerable reduction in structure and vocabulary. And again, the vocabulary is heterogeneous, with Russian and Norwegian elements mixed in roughly equal proportions, in addition to a few lexical items which seem to have come from the nautical jargon of the northern Atlantic. Moreover, some areas of grammatical structure exhibit the effect of something like SELECTIVE SIMPLIFICATION. For instance, the all-purpose preposition *po* is phonetically more or less identical to the Norwegian preposition *på* and the Russian *po* (although the meanings of these two prepositions are not identical).

Trade jargons like Russenorsk and Chinook Jargon give the impression of being semi-institutionalized forms of Foreigner Talk, without the homogeneity of fully institutionalized classical pidgins. However, in spite of their linguistic and social differences, they share one feature with pidgins: In both types of contact, there is no expectation of full acquisition of the other's language. What differs is the specific reason for not expecting full acquisition. In the case of pidgins, that reason is the colonialists' notion of extreme social inequality. In the case of trade jargons, by contrast, the reason is that two or more groups engage in contact which (by design or necessity) is restricted to just a few activities. What is interesting in this regard is that when the Russian merchants decided to engage in less limited trading relations with Norway, they sent their sons to Oslo (or, as it was called then, Christiania) to learn "proper" Norwegian; and conversely, Norwegians went to the city of Archangel to learn Russian.

5. Creoles

Many pidgin-like forms of language may have developed in the extended history of human language, only to disappear later – usually without any distinct trace. But under certain conditions they came to be employed in a manner that ensured them a more lasting place in history, as link languages or even as native languages.

Given their severe limitations in grammar and especially in vocabulary, pidgins and similar varieties of language may be very useful, even appropriate for the very restricted social conditions in which they arose. However, the limitations are considerable obstacles when languages of this type are to be used in a broader range of social and linguistic contexts. At a minimum, an expansion of context requires a vastly expanded vocabulary which more unambiguously accommodates the large range of meanings ordinarily expressed through language. A certain expansion of grammar is no doubt required as well.

This process of expansion, called CREOLIZATION (or DEPIDGINIZATION), is commonly believed to take place only when a pidgin "acquires native speakers". According to this view, the starting point is a linguistically highly diversified community in which parents begin using pidgin with each other as their only common means of communication. The pidgin therefore becomes the sole basis for a new generation of speakers to acquire as a native language. And, it is argued, while the pidgin may have been sufficient as an auxiliary language for the parents, it is clearly inadequate as a native language and therefore must undergo expansion and elaboration. Linguists subscribing to this view will reserve the term CREOLE for languages which arose in this manner.

The American linguist Derek Bickerton, in fact, has based an elaborate – but highly controversial – theory of creolization on this view. According to him, the need to create a native language makes it necessary for children to draw on a "bioprogram", part of the innate endowment of human beings, which determines the structure of the creole and, at the same time, explains idiosyncratic features that, Bickerton claims, are shared by all creoles and cannot be attributed to the influence either of the European or of the non-European languages. Among these is the phenomenon of "double negation" and "negative spread" as in (12). Double negation involves the use of more than one negative marker to express simple negation, as in (12b.i). Negative spread involves the use of double or even multiple negative words, without the negatives canceling each other out, as in (12a) and (12b.ii).

(12)   a. English-based creoles:
            Cameroon Pidg. *i nɛva giv **no nɔting** fɔ papa*
                        'He never gave anything to the old man.'
        b. Portuguese-based creoles:
            i. São Tomé: *i'nẽ   **na**   ka 'tlaba na'i   **fa***
                                    negative   negative
                            'They do not work here.'
                Angolares: *ɛ'nɛ   **na**   ka 'taba   ngɛ   **wa***
                                    negative   negative
                            'They do not work here.'
            ii. Papiamentu: *Mi   **no**   tin   **nada***
                                    no(t)   nothing
                            'I have nothing.'

There are several reasons why Bickerton's theory is highly controversial. Most important is the fact that the allegedly idiosyncratic features of creoles are not as unusual as Bickerton claims and that many, perhaps all, can be explained as reflecting influence from relevant European – and non-European – languages. For instance, while the negative spread in (12a) may look strange from the perspective of Standard English, it ceases to do so if we consider non-standard or vernacular English, as in (12′a). And note that the majority of early slave traders and colonialists were not highly educated and were therefore more likely to speak the vernacular than the standard. In the Romance languages, negative spread is found even in the standard languages, see (12′b.ii). And one study of early Portuguese Foreigner Talk provides examples of double negation in that form of speech; see (12′b.i). Moreover, many of the languages of West Africa, where most slaves came from, have similar features; see (12″).

(12′) a. Vernacular English: *He **never** gave **nothin'** to the old man*

    b. Portuguese:

    i. Foreigner Talk:

nunca	*a*	*mi*	*cadella*	***nam***
never	be(?)	me	dog	not

'Never am I a dog.'

    ii. Standard:

não dou		***nada***		***nunca***
not		nothing		never

*a **ninguém***
nobody

'I do not ever give anything to anybody.'

(12″) Hausa:

Halima	*ba-ta yi*	***ba***
	negative	negative

'Halima didn't do it.'

While Bickerton's theory therefore is considered dubious by most linguists specializing in pidgin and creole research, the general belief that creoles arise when pidgins acquire native speakers has remained remarkably unshaken.

Perhaps developments of this sort did take place in the slave-holding societies of the New World, where slave owners, fearful of African slave revolts (especially after the successful revolution in Haiti), may have attempted to prohibit the use of African languages and to force slaves to resort to pidgin. However, if such attempts were made, they were not very successful. For instance, reports that early North American fugitive slave patrols frequently had Wolof interpreters suggest that instead of pidgin, Wolof and perhaps other African languages were used as link languages among the slaves. (See Chapter 9, § 4.4 for direct traces of Wolof in African American English.)

More important, it must be seriously doubted whether a language as re-stricted as a pidgin would have been picked up as a native language by large groups of children, or whether it would have been used as the only means of communication in the parental generation. In order for anything of that sort to happen, the pidgin must have undergone considerable prior expansion and elaboration. Note further that studies of plantation populations have shown that there were not always large numbers of children who would have been in a position to acquire and expand the pidgin.

In fact, creolization or depidginization can take place without a pid-gin's acquiring native speakers. This suggests that creolization ordinarily is a slow, continuous process of depidginization, rather than an overnight, "catastrophic" phenomenon.

Especially illustrative is the case of the varieties of Pidgin English used in Papua New Guinea and the Solomon Islands. (These are now commonly referred to as Tok Pisin or Neo-Melanesian, and Neo-Solomonic, respec-tively.) These languages came to be employed as **administrative** auxiliary languages by the European colonial administrations in communicating with a linguistically highly diversified indigenous population, as increasingly pop-ular **link languages** between the various local communities, and as vehicles for **missionary** activities. Each of these expanded uses brought with it an elaboration in vocabulary and structure so as to enable the language to be employed in its new social contexts. Tok Pisin has now become a language of parliamentary debates and of the news media, requiring yet further expansion and elaboration.

Acquisition of native speakers, on the other hand, has proceeded at a much slower pace. Even now, only about five percent of all Tok Pisin users are native speakers. Moreover, while native speakers are reported to use a more "advanced" form of language in their early years, during their teens they are said to adjust to the norm of the majority population of non-native (but fluent) speakers.

Although the exact earlier history of other creoles is to a large extent shrouded in mystery, a fair amount of circumstantial evidence suggests that similar developments took place here, too. Thus, our early information about Caribbean pidgins comes from missionaries' reports or, even more signifi-cant, from grammars and translations of the Bible and the catechism, which they produced for the purpose of converting slaves to Christianity. Clearly, such activities required considerable expansion of the pidgin, especially of the lexicon – a vocabulary of 1,000 to 2,000 words would hardly have sufficed to translate the Bible. The form of language that we can discern from these sources, therefore, is no longer the simple, highly reduced pidgin, although it may not be the full creole either.

More than that, though the colonialist establishment strongly disapproved of the practice, we have numerous reports of Europeans having "gone native", living with, or even marrying, non-European women, begetting children with them, accepting the children as their own legal offspring, or even altogether adopting non-European ways. From all we can tell, these practices were much more widespread than the extant – generally highly disapproving – reports let on. In fact, it is in this context that the word *creole* is believed to have arisen, to refer to the children of European/non-European matches. (The source word, Port. *crioulo*, is said to be derived from *criar* 'to create, beget'.)

This "domestic" context, too, can be expected to have encouraged an expansion in vocabulary and structure, to make the language usable for the more expanded communicative demands within the family or household. As in Tok Pisin, it is possible that some children acquired the resulting form of speech as their native language; but there is nothing to guarantee that their form of speech immediately became dominant. In fact, in many areas, the majority of pidgin speakers did not become part of a "crioulo" household, but remained "field slaves". Under the circumstances, the influence of native pidgin speakers on the general pidgin-speaking population must at first have been quite limited, just as in Tok Pisin.

The clear evidence of Tok Pisin and the more circumstantial evidence of other pidgins/creoles, then, suggest that the distinction between pidgins and creoles is gradient, rather than absolute. The distinction pidgin vs. creole may be useful for linguistic classification, but just like distinctions such as Old English vs. Middle English, it would seem to be an idealization. And just as in reality, speakers of Old English did not one fine morning wake up finding themselves speaking Middle English, so pidgin-speaking societies probably did not switch to creole in a short, cataclysmic upheaval.

What is more important is that, once the process of depidginization has run its full course and the language thereby has acquired the lexicon and grammar necessary for full communication, the resulting creoles will be indistinguishable from any other form of "full" language. It is only their history which makes them different.

In the majority of cases, the resulting language is a vernacular which is used only for ordinary everyday communication, while another language (usually a European standard language) serves as a means of more intellectual and written communication. This result, then, is something very similar to diglossia (see Chapter 10, § 6). In fact, the Haitian relationship between the speech of the educated elite (modeled on Parisian French) and the French-based creole of the majority population has been cited as a paradigm case of diglossia.

However, creoles are not "condemned" to forever remain vernaculars. The case of Tok Pisin shows that creoles are just as much usable as intellectual and written languages as any other form of speech, if there is the need.

6. Decreolization and African American Vernacular English

Where creoles are used as a vernacular, their relationship to the coexisting European prestige language may be of two types. On one side is the diglossic relationship between Haitian Creole and French. On the other side, where society is less rigidly stratified, as in the post-slavery English-speaking Caribbean, the result may be quite different. In this environment, an ever-increasing section of the population has found it possible, convenient, or necessary to become actively bilingual in the creole and the European standard language. Through interlanguage, then, varieties of language have arisen which are intermediate between the European standard and the creole. Note the similar development of intermediate varieties in the modern Greek diglossic relationship between Katharevousa and Dimotiki (Chapter 10, § 6) and the Norwegian competition between Nynorsk and Bokmaal (Chapter 10, § 5).

In the Caribbean, the process probably was helped by the fact that both creole and (more or less) Standard English speakers consider the creole a dialect, i.e., a vernacular variety of English. Creole speakers trying to approximate the standard therefore do not see this as learning a different language; and standard speakers expect such approximation, with the justification that "They really should know their own language!"

Interestingly, here again, speakers behave in accordance with their own social attitudes and prejudices and not according to the linguists' view. Linguists would argue that the creole is really a separate language, not just a dialect of English, because of its special historical origins and its formidable structural differences compared to the standard. But such distinctions evidently are of no great significance to most ordinary speakers.

In fact, the common assumption among professional linguists that the linguistic approximation necessarily involves a full-fledged creole and a European standard language is open to some question. Nothing prevents speakers from beginning to approximate the European standard language even at the pidgin stage, if the need should arise – or to approximate the European vernacular, for that matter! As a matter of fact, the very process of creolization or depidginization can be considered as simply a first step in this process of linguistic approximation. Here as elsewhere linguists need to constantly reexamine their views, so as not to fall victims to their own idealizations.

Whatever the truth may be in a particular situation, the ultimate result of the creole's (or pidgin's) approximation to the European prestige language is noteworthy enough to have received a special name, namely CREOLE CONTINUUM. The continuum is characterized by a range of speech varieties which extend from the more or less pure European language to the more or less pure creole (or pidgin), with all kinds of intermediate varieties which, depending on education, motivation, or attitude, exhibit a varying admixture of standard and creole elements. The different layers within this creole continuum then function much like the social dialects of monolingual societies, such that different speakers will be proficient in a number of different varieties (but not necessarily in all). That is, for all practical purposes, the two languages have merged into a single entity.

The ultimate outcome is complete DECREOLIZATION. The grammar of the original creole becomes more or less fully integrated into the grammar of the European language, the pure creole disappears, and its vestiges acquire characteristics which even linguists would term social dialects of the European language.

A probable example is found in African American Vernacular English (AAVE) or, as it became known in important research of the 1970s and 1980s, Black Vernacular English. In its more conservative or archaic variants, AAVE still preserves traces of the original pidgin or creole grammar, such as the "completive" marker *done* in (13a) or the lack of gender distinction in (13b). But these are definitely on the wane.

(13) a. *He **done** tole me*
      b. ***He** a nice girl*

Other creole features have proved much more vigorous, such as the absence of the past tense marker *-(e)d* in *tole* of (13a) or the absence of the verb 'to be' in (13b). However, they have done so in a curious fashion.

In the case of the past tense, there is evidence that AAVE now generally has acquired the ending *-(e)d*: Forms like *lied, teed (off)* have practically invariant final [-d]. Where the addition of *-(e)d* results in a final consonant group, the ending is variably absent or present, as in *clean(ed), walk(ed)*. Its absence is especially common in forms like *tole*, where the vowel change in the verb root is sufficient to mark the form as the past tense of *tell*, even without any affix. What seems to have happened here is that the original absence of the past-tense marker has been "salvaged", by having been reinterpreted as resulting from word-final simplification of consonant groups, a phenomenon also widely present in the fast speech of white English speakers.

Similarly, the absence of the "copula" verb 'to be' in structures like (13b) has been integrated into the system of non-creole English grammar: Unlike prototypical creoles, AAVE does in fact have a copula. But that copula may be "deleted", and deletion takes place under the same conditions under which standard English "contracts"; see (14a). Where standard English cannot contract, AAVE does not delete (14b). Put differently, AAVE only differs from standard English by having deletion where the latter has contraction.

(14)   Standard English   Black Vernacular English
    a. *She's a nice girl*   *She a nice girl*
    b. *She ís*[1]   *She ís*[1]
       She isn't nice, is she?   *She ain't nice, is she?*
       The girl I saw yesterday is *The girl I saw yesterday is*
       nice   *nice*
       ([1]response to the claim that she is not)

Through the integration of its creole features into the grammar of "ordinary" English, AAVE has become a decreolized dialect of English. But note that much of the decreolization took place in the American South, based on Vernacular (Southern) White English, and not on the standard language. This factor probably accounts for the fact that AAVE has been rather slow to adopt the third-person singular present ending *-s*. The absence of this ending (or its generalization throughout the present, as in *we goes*) appears to be an old feature of non-standard white Southern speech, carried over from regional dialects on the British Isles, especially the so-called Midland dialects. In this case, then, the structure of the European-based speech which was available as a model for decreolization reinforced the pidgin/creole feature of not having inflectional endings.

The fact that some of the features of AAVE thus can be traced to European sources has given rise to theories that AAVE can be exhaustively explained as a regional dialect, just like any other dialect of American English. However, features like the variable presence of the copula, peculiarities of the past tense formation, and relics like the ones in (13) persuasively argue that it did start out as a creole. Further evidence comes from African American speech in the so-called Tidewater Area, islands off the southern East Coast of the United States. This variety of English is considerably more creole-like than AAVE. Its conservatism is explained by the fact that when the northern troops retreated after the liberation of the slaves during the Civil War, the former white landholders of this area did not return: unlike the rest of the South, the islands no longer provided an economically viable opportunity for plantation farming. Until the islands were "opened up" again to the outside world during the 1930s, the population had relatively little contact with white speech and thus maintained a form of language much closer to the original creole.

While decreolization thus is a possible final development in what sometimes is called the "life cycle" of pidgins, it is not a necessary event. The major developmental step lies in the process of creolization (or depidginization), which turns a radically simplified and socially highly restricted form of communication into a full-blown language, with the complexity and social versatility of ordinary languages. From this perspective, decreolization is simply a step "sideways", from one form of fully developed language to another.

Chapter 15
Language death

Gaelic's no use to you through the world.
(Said by a Gaelic speaker justifying why she is teaching her children English, not Gaelic. Reported by Nancy Dorian in *The loss of language skills*, ed. by R.D. Lambert & B.F. Freed, 1982.)

But today, by reason of the immense augmentation of the American population ..., the Indian races are more seriously threatened with a speedy extermination than ever before in the history of the country.
(Donehogawa, first Indigenous American to be Commissioner of Indian Affairs, Report of the U. S. Department of the Interior, 1870.)

To continue in the "life-cycle" metaphor introduced at the end of the preceding chapter, we turn our attention now to developments at the end of the life cycle of languages when, in essence, a language loses its native speakers and thus undergoes LANGUAGE DEATH. Like the birth of languages through pidginization and creolization, language death results from language contact.

Throughout history, speakers have given up their native language in favor of another, more prestigious – or powerful – form of speech, whether the latter be the language of a foreign conqueror, a link language, a koiné, a creole, or perhaps even a pidgin. While this much has been known for a long time, the manner in which linguistic communities switch language loyalties and the effects of this switch on linguistic structure were only poorly understood. An even less well examined issue is the related one of dialect death; for dialects, too, can lose their speakers and thus die out. In fact, dialect death is an even more widespread phenomenon than language death. Although we will continue in this chapter to speak of the death of languages, the observations that we make also apply to dialects.

Traditional linguistic literature may mention the date at which "the last speaker" of a given language died (or more rarely, when a dialect ceased to be spoken). But it does not examine questions such as "Whom did that last speaker speak to?" or "What was his or her language like?"

It is only fairly recently that systematic research has begun on the issue of language death. Findings therefore still are limited in number and spotty in terms of the languages and the aspects of grammar that have been studied. Nevertheless, certain very general patterns are beginning to emerge.

First of all, given the metaphor of language death, it is useful to distinguish different manners in which languages may be said to die: "language suicide", "language murder", and other language death. Second, we must distinguish between individual loss of language skills and the disappearance of entire speech communities. While both are interesting, only the latter development has permanent effects on language history.

Language suicide generally is a matter of individual decision. As such, of course, it is very common among immigrants to areas with a linguistically relatively homogeneous population and without any significant tradition of bi- or multilingualism. Thus, many immigrant families in the United States decide soon after entering the country that their children should be fluent in English so as to be able to compete with native speakers of English. To this end the parents decide not to use their native language any more, but only English. Sometimes the decision to abandon one's native language is motivated by special social or political considerations. For instance, many of those fleeing Nazi Germany, both Jews and non-Jews, were so strongly opposed to what was happening in Germany and in the name of Germany that they decided never to speak German again. Similarly, immigrants to Israel generally decided to switch from their native languages to Modern Israeli Hebrew, the language of the country which they felt would give them a clear identity and freedom from persecution.

Although quite widespread as an individual phenomenon, language suicide does not seem to be a common occurrence for whole speech communities. At the same time, its effects should not be underestimated. Yiddish, the language of most Eastern European Jews, has undergone severe attrition as the result of language suicide – either in Israel (in favor of Modern Hebrew) or in the United States (in favor of English). (In addition, of course, the number of Yiddish speakers has been severely diminished by the mass murder of Jews under the Nazi regime.)

Language murder can be said to take place if individuals or whole speech communities are forced to abandon their native language in favor of a language favored by a politically more powerful group. Again, this is not an uncommon phenomenon, at least on an individual basis. For instance, starting from the First World War, U. S. schools, with support from powerful national teachers' organizations and various forms of government, strongly discouraged or even prohibited the use of any language other than English by the children of immigrants from non-English speaking countries. And in the early part of the twentieth century the United States collected Indigenous American children into government schools and forced them to abandon their native languages and cultures in favor of the language and customs of the English-speaking population. Most teachers' organizations and governments have since then taken a very different position, and the repression of languages other than English has to a large extent given way to greater tolerance. Bilingual programs have been set up, generally conceived as transitions to full acquisition of English. Many educators have argued in favor of bilingualism as a goal in itself. On the other hand, new organizations, and an entire new movement ("English Only"), have been formed with the express goal of making English the official, national language and of doing away with more permissive bilingual programs – and with bilingualism in general. (Closer examination reveals that much of the English Only movement is motivated not just by a rejection of bilingualism and multilingualism but by xenophobia.)

Similarly, until very recently non-private schools in Wales and Brittany have, as a matter of policy, prohibited the use of Welsh and Breton by school children, even during recess, requiring them to use English and French (respectively) at all times. Other minority languages have generally received the same treatment throughout early modern Europe and into the present century.

Although by their very nature such repressive policies are directed at entire speech communities, they do not necessarily meet their goals. In many cases, enough individuals have braved social ostracism or even severe punishment to maintain their language, or at least to prevent the immediate death of the language. At the same time, there is no denying that many languages have disappeared and are still dying around the globe. One recent estimate is that more than half of the world's approximately 6,000 distinct languages are facing extinction. Significantly, although being distinct languages, almost all of them lack the "army and navy" which one linguist jokingly claimed are needed to define a form of speech as a language, not a dialect; see Chapter 10, § 2.

On the level of the speech community, language death commonly does not take place suddenly, within just one generation. Rather, it is a slow process which may extend over more than three generations. Death, moreover, is not necessarily caused by overt repression. It often arises in situations where a non-native language is considered more prestigious or useful (compare the first quotation at the beginning of the chapter). Or use of the non-native language may be required in certain contexts (such as school or dealing with governmental authorities), but not necessarily in others. As a consequence, the non-native language may begin to be used with increasing frequency and in increasingly larger social contexts, while the native language is employed less frequently and in fewer contexts.

Even for individuals, language attrition tends to be a fairly slow process. Speakers who have been abroad for only a short period and have regularly used a foreign language during that time, may return with a noticeable "accent". They also may have missed out on some of the most recent innovations in their home country, especially in vocabulary and colloquialisms or slang. However, they generally have no difficulty expressing themselves. Extended stays abroad can have more serious results. Thus, when the lead author of this book returned to his native Germany after thirteen years in the United States, he experienced an excruciatingly frustrating first week. Having used English not just for speaking but for teaching, publishing, even thinking, he found even the most simple sentences difficult to produce without at least some errors in grammar and usage. (Eventually, fluency returned, and he was complimented on how good his German was after so many years of absence.)

Interestingly, losing much of one's native language skills does not imply for all practical purposes becoming a native speaker of the "other" language. Depending on motivation and opportunity, the outcome may be a lack of native competence in both the native and the second language.

Language attrition of this sort becomes most relevant if for some reason it becomes a feature of whole speech communities. In that case, reduction in use and competence limits the "input" on which new speakers of the language can draw in order to learn their language. In many cases, this may not affect the most common constructions in the language. The effect, however, may be considerable on less frequently used structures. These structures may come to be heard so rarely that the next generation of learners finds it difficult, if not impossible, to determine how to use them correctly.

The new generation of speakers may therefore avoid using such constructions, thus further reducing the input for the next generation of speakers, and so on. In this manner the rule system of the language undergoes a slow process of atrophy. Studies on language death in very different locations, focusing on very different grammatical phenomena, agree on the fact that grammatical attrition is not across the board or random, but that it takes place in terms of the fading out of general rules of the language and that in this process, certain rules which are from some perspective more difficult are lost first.

What is interesting is that grammatical atrophy is not matched by a similar decrease in vocabulary or in the younger generations' ability to understand older speakers. Passive and active command of the language thus may differ considerably.

At a certain point, the atrophy in the grammatical system progresses to the extent that a new generation of speakers no longer is able to learn the grammatical rule system of the language. The members of this generation, often referred to as semi-speakers, fluently understand even their grandparents' speech, but will generally admit that they are unable to speak the language themselves. At this point, the transmission of the language has come to an end, and the language has effectively died. One suspects that many of the last speakers mentioned in traditional accounts were in fact the last remaining members of such a generation of semi-speakers.

Even when language death has happened, the language is not necessarily dead forever. As long as there are sufficient records of the language as it once had been used, it is possible to resurrect a language, as it were. Similarly, it is possible for a speech community that has been experiencing language death to reverse the process and to revive the language to its earlier status, by turning to the more fully intact speech of the older generation.

The most celebrated example of the resurrection of a language that had died out as a normal spoken medium is that of Modern Israeli Hebrew. While Hebrew continued to be used as a language of scripture, ritual, and – to a lesser degree – scholarship, it had died out as a spoken language among most Jews. The first steps toward its revival were undertaken by the nineteenth and twentieth century Zionist movement in its attempt to assert the Semitic identity of the Jewish people. But its call to use Hebrew as an overt sign of this identity was challenged by other groups who advocated Yiddish as the language of Jewish identity. As a consequence, the revival of Hebrew as a spoken language was limited to relatively small groups. The Nazi holocaust and the foundation of the state of Israel as a country where Jews would be able to live without fear of further persecution radically changed the situation, and within a very short time there was an almost complete switch from Yiddish and many other European languages to Modern Hebrew.

Many other peoples have attempted to revive their language, but generally with more mixed success. For instance, there have been recent attempts in the British Isles to revive Manx and Cornish, ancient, (near-)extinct Celtic languages spoken on the Isle of Man and in Cornwall, respectively. The European continent is witnessing attempts to revive Latin as a spoken language. Some even hope to make Latin the common language of the European Union, thus avoiding the problems with having to decide which link language to use. (While English is the most widely used language, many Europeans – especially the French, but increasingly the Germans as well – have severe reservations about accepting English as the only link language.) Similarly, there are groups in India that are attempting to revive Sanskrit, which since the 1970s has been dying rapidly in its use as a spoken language among traditionally educated scholars. Here, too, it can be argued that the use of Sanskrit as a common link language avoids the problems with having to decide between Hindi and English (see Chapter 12, § 1). It combines within itself the advantages of both Hindi and English: Like Hindi it is an indigenous language, and like English it is not a native language for any sizable community within India and therefore does not bestow special privileges on one community while discriminating against the others.

In the United States, too, there have been repeated attempts by Indigenous Americans to revive or resurrect their languages. In part, these attempts are motivated by the fact that the United States accords special legal status to peoples who can demonstrate cultural, including linguistic, continuity with their indigenous roots. To succeed in these attempts, many indigenous communities have asked linguists and anthropologists to make available to them recordings of indigenous languages made in the nineteenth century and the beginning of the twentieth century, when the languages were still spoken, or were spoken in fuller, less diminished form.

Language death presents interesting challenges to linguists. The most important one is the question whether we, as linguists, have a special responsibility to ensure that languages do not die out. Some linguists take a "Darwinian" position on this issue, arguing that languages always have died and always will die, when they no longer are useful to their speakers, and that linguists have no business to interfere with this natural development. Other linguists feel that, even if we wanted to, we would not be able to prevent languages from dying: We cannot force speakers to maintain their languages if they do not want to. A third group of linguists takes a more interventionist position, arguing that any loss of language diminishes the world, just as the death of any animal or plant species threatens our ecosystem. These linguists, therefore, actively support groups that are trying to preserve or revive their language, or even encourage them to do so.

The truth probably is on the side of those who argue that one cannot force speakers to maintain their language. In fact, it is probably just as imperialist to try to tell speakers that they must do so as it is to try to suppress other people's languages.

At the same time, linguists need not remain on the sidelines. They can help groups trying to revive or preserve their language by providing relevant information on grammar, vocabulary, and usage, or even by preparing teaching materials which enable the members of these groups to provide formal instruction in their language. Through such efforts these groups can counter or overcome the common prejudice that a form of speech is a language only if it is taught in school and has a formal grammar, while all other forms of speech are dialects and therefore do not merit preservation. Linguists can also help in developing the technical vocabulary necessary to permit the language to branch out from its traditional setting and to become competitive and meaningful in the modern world. (In fact, such language planning activities have been undertaken rather successfully for many languages in the former European colonial empires, and several programs of this type are under way in the United States, too.)

Linguists can serve the cause of language preservation in another, more indirect way, by collecting the greatest possible amount of grammatical and lexical information, as well as entire texts of languages that are in danger of becoming extinct. These materials can then be made available to speakers who may decide at some future point to reverse the course of language death or even to revive the language. Without such materials, even the most successful attempt at language resurrection, that of Modern Hebrew, would have come to naught.

Ultimately, of course, we must accept the fact that no linguist can stem the course of language death. Only the speakers of the language can do so – if they have the motivation, the opportunity, and the wherewithal.

Language relationship

Chapter 16
Comparative method: Establishing language relationship

The Sanscrit language, whatever be its antiquity, is of a wonderful structure; more perfect than the Greek, more copious than
the Latin, and more exquisitely refined than either, yet bearing
to both of them a stronger affinity, both in the roots of verbs and
in the forms of grammar, than could possibly have been produced
by accident; so strong indeed, that no philologer could examine
them all three, without believing them to have sprung from some
common source, which, perhaps, no longer exists: there is a similar reason, though not quite so forcible, for supposing that both
the Gothick and the Celtick, though blended with a very different idiom, had the same origin with the Sanscrit; and the old
Persian might be added to the same family, if this were the place
for discussing any question concerning the antiquities of Persia.
*(Sir William Jones, Third Anniversary Discourse, on the Hindus,
Royal Asiatic Society, 1786.)*

1. Introduction

The epigraph above, which readers will remember from Chapter 2, has had
a double significance for the history of linguistics. On one hand, it provided
one of the most important stimuli for research in comparative Indo-European
linguistics, a field which soon became the most thoroughly investigated area
of historical and comparative linguistics and which to the present day has remained the most important source for our understanding of linguistic change.
This is the issue which we pursued in Chapter 2.

On the other hand, Jones's statement is important because, perhaps for
the first time, it offered a very succinct and explicit summary of what have
turned out to be the basic assumptions and motivations of comparative linguistics: accounting for similarities which cannot be attributed to chance, by
the assumption that they are the result of descent from a common ancestor. It

is the purpose of comparative linguistics to establish that certain similarities are indeed not due to chance and that, moreover, they can only be accounted for as genetically related, by descent from a common ancestor.

Work of this sort most naturally starts out by looking for languages which seem to share enough similarities to suggest genetic relationship. In many cases, this is not all too difficult, once we accept the notion that languages may be genetically related to each other. To illustrate the point, consider Table 1 below on the relationship of major European languages.

As the table shows, even seven lexical items – if selected with care – can furnish strong evidence that the Indo-European languages (Breton – Latvian) are related to each other. The case is similar for the Uralic languages (Finnish, Estonian, and Hungarian), although the case for Hungarian may be less obvious. Moreover, the table permits us to distinguish subgroups within, say, Indo-European: Celtic (Breton, Welsh, Irish), Germanic (Icelandic – German), Romance (French – Romanian), Slavic (Bulgarian – Russian), and Baltic (Lithuanian and Latvian); Greek and Albanian constitute subgroups of one each.

Given the evidence of just the seven words in Table 1, there might appear to be a somewhat weaker case for a Turkish-Basque relationship. Compare the similarities in the words for 'one', 'head', and possibly also 'three'. As far as we can tell, however, the similarities are misleading. Once the basis for comparison is enlarged to, say, a hundred lexical items, it turns out that the Turkish-Basque similarities are most likely the result of chance. In fact, up to this point it has not been possible to successfully establish a genetic relationship between Basque and any other language or language group. The fact that there can be such accidental similarities raises important questions about our ability to establish genetic relationship by sheer inspection of vocabulary. (This matter is pursued further in § 2 below and Chapter 17.)

The situation gets much more complex once we introduce selected Asian languages, as in Table 2 (p. 458), a continuation of Table 1.

On one hand, the sets Hindi *dō* : Marathi *dōn* : Persian *do* : Osset. *dɨwwə* 'two', Hindi and Marathi *tīn* : Kashmiri *triʔ* : Tocharian *trai/tarya* 'three', and Kashmiri *nas* 'nose' (perhaps also Hindi *nākh* 'nose') may suggest relationship to the Indo-European languages of Europe because of the phonetic similarities between the words. Note also Hindi *mūh* 'mouth' and especially Marathi *muṇḍ* 'head' on one hand, and the Germanic words for 'mouth' on the other.

On the other hand, Hindi/Marathi *ēk*, Kashm. *akh*, Pers. *yek* 'one' look more similar to Finn. *üksi*, Est. *üks*, Hung. *ej̆*, and so do Hindi *kān*, Kashm. *kan* 'eye' to Finn. *korva*, Est. *kõrv* – as well as to Kannada *kivi*. In fact, Hindi

Table 1. Vocabulary correspondences in the major European languages

	'one'	'two'	'three'	'head'	'ear'	'mouth'	'nose'
Breton	*ünan*	*dau*	*tri*	*penn*	*skuarn*	*genu*	*fri*
Welsh	*in*	*dai*	*tri*	*pen*	*klist*	*keg*	*truin*
Irish	*ōn*	*dɔ*	*tri*	*kyan*	*kluəs*	*byal*	*srōn*
Icelandic	*eidn*	*tveir*	*þrīr*	*hȫfüð*	*eira*	*münnür*	*nēf*
Danish	*en*	*tō?*	*trē?*	*hōðə*	*ōrə*	*mon?*	*næsə*
Norwegian	*ēn*	*tō*	*trē*	*hōvəd*	*ȫrə*	*mund*	*næsɔ*
Swedish	*ēn*	*tvō*	*trē*	*hȫvud*	*öra*	*mun*	*næsa*
Dutch	*ēn*	*tvē*	*drī*	*hōft*	*ōr*	*mont*	*nȫs*
English	*wən*	*tuw*	*θrɪy*	*hɛd*	*ɪyr*	*mawθ*	*nowz*
German	*ʔains*	*tsvai*	*drai*	*kɔpf*	*ʔōr*	*munt*	*nāzə*
French	*æ̃/ün*	*dö*	*trwa*	*tēt*	*orēy*	*buš*	*ne*
Spanish	*uno*	*dos*	*tres*	*kaβeθa*	*orexa*	*boka*	*nariθ*
Portuguese	*ũ*	*doš*	*treš*	*kəbesə*	*oreλa*	*bokə*	*nariz*
Italian	*un(o)*	*due*	*tre*	*testa*	*orɛkkyo*	*bokka*	*naso*
Romanian	*un*	*doy*	*trey*	*kap*	*ureke*	*gurə*	*nas*
Albanian	*ñə*	*dü*	*tre*	*kokə*	*veš*	*goyə*	*hundə*
Greek	*énas*	*ðyó*	*trís*	*kefáli*	*aftí*	*stóma*	*míti*
Bulgarian	*yedan*	*dva*	*tri*	*glava*	*uxo*	*usta*	*nos*
Serbo-Croatian	*yedan*	*dva*	*tri*	*glava*	*uho*	*usta*	*nos*
Czech	*yeden*	*dva*	*tři*	*hlava*	*uxo*	*usta*	*nos*
Polish	*yeden*	*dva*	*tši*	*gwova*	*uxo*	*usta*	*nos*
Russian	*adʸin*	*dva*	*trʸi*	*galavá*	*úxo*	*rot*	*nos*
Lithuanian	*vʸíenas*	*du*	*trʸīs*	*galvá*	*ausʸís*	*burná*	*nōsʸis*
Latvian	*viens*	*divi*	*trīs*	*galva*	*auss*	*mute*	*deguns*
Finnish	*üksi*	*kaksi*	*kolme*	*pǟ*	*korva*	*sū*	*nenä*
Estonian	*üks*	*kaks*	*kolm*	*pea*	*kõrv*	*sū*	*nina*
Hungarian	*ej̆*	*kēt*	*hārom*	*fȫ/fey*	*fül*	*sāy*	*orr*
Turkish	*bir*	*iki*	*üč*	*baš*	*kulak*	*āɪz*	*burun*
Basque	*bat*	*bi*	*hirür*	*bürü*	*belari*	*aho*	*südür*

(Note: Except for French 'one', the numerals are cited without gender variation. Finnish and Estonian *ä* = [æ].)

nākh 'nose', perhaps also Kashm. *nas*, could just as well be considered related to Finn. *nenä*, Est. *nina* as to the words for 'nose' in the European members of the Indo-European language family. And while Hindi *mūh* and Marathi *muṇḍ* bear strong resemblances to the Germanic words for 'mouth', they are similar, too, to Kannada *mūti*.

But there are more problems. For instance, the evidence accumulated by more than a century of comparative linguistics suggests an especially close

Table 2. Further data from selected Asian languages

	'one'	'two'	'three'	'head'	'ear'	'mouth'	'nose'
Hindi	ēk	dō	tīn	sir/sar	kān	mūh	nāk
Marathi	ēk	dōn	tīn	ḍōī, muṇḍ	kān	tõī	nāk
Kashmiri	akh	z̄iʔ	triʔ	kalʲ	kan	is	nas
Persian	yek	do	se	sær	guš	dæhɔn	bini
Ossetic	iw	diwwə	ərtə	sər	qus	dzix	find
Armenian	mi	erku	erekh	glux	unkn	beran	r̄əngunkh
Tocharian B	ṣe, sana	wi	trai, tarya	āśce	klautso	koyṁ	meli
Tamil	ondrɨ	iraṇḍɨ	mūndrɨ	talɛi	kāḍɨ, sevi	vāy	mūkkɨ
Kannada	ondu	eraṛu	mūru	tale	kivi	bāy, mūti	mūgu

(Note: Unlike the other forms, the Classical Armenian and Tocharian B forms are not given in phonetic transcription but in a transliteration of their original spelling. The Tocharian words for 'one' and 'three' distinguish between masculine and feminine forms.)

relationship between Indo-Aryan Hindi, Marathi, and Kashmiri on one hand and Iranian Persian and Ossetic (Iron dialect) on the other. This relationship, however, does not come out very well in Table 2, except perhaps for the word for 'head'.

Further, the evidence for considering Tocharian an Indo-European language appears to be limited to one word, the numeral 'three', and there seems to be no evidence for considering Armenian an Indo-European language. Again, this conflicts with what we know as the result of extensive work in comparative Indo-European linguistics.

Finally, the evidence does correctly indicate that the Dravidian languages Tamil and Kannada (in the south of India) are not particularly closely related to any of the other language families. However, it fails to indicate that there are recurrent similarities between Dravidian and Uralic which suggest a possible relationship (see Chapter 17).

As it turns out, a number of the similarities that we just noted are accidental, just like those between Turkish *bir* and Basque *bat* 'one', and therefore do not reflect genetic relationship.

This is the case for instance for the Hindi/Marathi and Germanic words for 'mouth'. Hindi *mūh* derives from Sanskrit *mukha-* which, if inherited, would reflect an earlier **mukho-*; Marathi *muṇḍ* goes back to Skt. *mūrdhan-*, a reflex of PIE **melədh-*; while the Germanic words reflect PGmc. **munþa-* which must go back to PIE **mn̥to-*. Note further that Kannada *mūti* is related to Tam. *mūñči* 'face', which appears to be older both in its phonetic shape and in its semantics. That is, as we trace these similar forms back in history we find that they become less similar. The modern similarities, thus, must be due to chance.

The similarities between the Hindi/Kashmiri/Persian and Finnish/Estonian/Hungarian words for 'one' likewise are accidental. For instance, the Indo-Aryan words go back to Skt. *ēka-*, derived from PIE **oy-ko-*'one, single', which in turn represents an extension by a suffix *-ko-* of the same root which, extended by the suffix *-no-*, underlies the numeral 'one' that is found in the majority of the Indo-European languages of Europe.

The similarities between Hindi and Persian/Ossetic in the word for 'head' reflect the fact that the Hindi word has been borrowed from Persian. Here, too, then, the similarities do not reflect inheritance from a common ancestor.

On the other hand, a number of genuine cognates are very difficult to detect without extensive comparative research. For instance, the Tocharian and Armenian words for 'one' are ultimately related to the one found in Greek; all three of these derive – believe it or not – from PIE **sem-* 'same, similar, identical'. The Armenian and Ossetic words for 'three' are perfect cognates of the words found in the rest of the Indo-European languages. Again, given the evidence in Tables 1 and 2, this may be hard to believe; but more than a century of research has shown that the Armenian and Ossetic words are in fact related. The Armenian form results from a change of **tr-* > *þr-*, loss of the *þ*, and prefixation of a vowel before the resulting initial *r*; the Ossetic form involves metathesis of initial **tr-* to **-rt*, an areal phenomenon in the Caucasus, plus prefixation of a vowel before initial **rt-* and other changes. The Armenian word for 'two' can likewise be related to its counterparts elsewhere in Indo-European, through a sequence of even more complex developments.

The upshot is that not all similarities – or dissimilarities – between languages in their vocabulary are indicative of genetic relationship, and that in order to establish genetic relationship we have to go significantly beyond comparing just seven vocabulary items.

2. Chance similarities, onomatopoeia, and "nursery words"

Probably any given pair of languages will offer at least some formally and semantically similar linguistic items whose similarities are simply due to chance. We have seen a few examples of this type in the preceding section, such as the Hindi, Marathi, Kannada, and Germanic words for 'mouth' (or 'head'). Even among the Indo-European languages of Table 1, some resemblances are accidental. This is certainly true for the similarity between the words for 'one' found in most of the languages and Modern Greek *énas* 'one'. The Modern Greek form reflects Ancient Greek *heîs, mía, hén* 'one (m., f., n.)'. As suggested in the preceding section, this form, in turn, derives from earlier **sem-s, *sm-ia, *sem*, with a root **sem-* related to Engl. *same*. The remainder of the words for 'one' derive from a different ancestor, **oy-no-*.

Modern Greek has a word *máti* 'eye' whose phonetic and semantic resemblance to Malay *mata* is remarkable. But again, from what we know about the earlier history of these languages, the similarity between the words is due to chance. Mod. Gk. *máti* goes back to earlier Gk. *ommátion*, a diminutive form of *ómma* 'eye', which in turn derives from an earlier **ok^w-m(e)n-*, in which **-m(e)n-* was a derivational suffix, and only the first element **ok^w-* originally meant 'eye'. Ironically, this element, found also in *óps* 'eye, face', as well as in *Kúklōps* 'Cyclops, lit. having a (single) circular eye' and related to Engl. *eye*, has disappeared from Mod. Gk. *máti*. What is left consists only of suffixal material, historically speaking. (Except for those familiar with the history of the word, Modern Greek speakers are not aware of this fact; to them, *máti* is a perfectly good lexical item, rather than just an agglomeration of suffixes.)

There are similar problems for Mal. *mata*. While most Malayo-Polynesian languages have cognates of *mata* 'eye', many also offer evidence for an obviously related form *kita* 'see' (e.g. Tagalog *kita*), and others testify to a form *buta* 'be blind' (e.g. Fiji *buto*). These variant forms suggest that *mata* is morphologically composite in origin, consisting of a root *-ta* meaning something like 'sight' and a prefix *ma-* which fixes the meaning of *-ta* to 'eye', while *ki-* and *bu-* alter the meaning to 'see' and 'be blind' respectively.

Similarly, Modern English and Modern Persian have phonetically and semantically virtually identical forms for 'bad': *bad* [bæd] and *bad* [bæ˘d] (with a vowel slightly more retracted than that of the English word). The origin of the English word is somewhat controversial. Two derivations have been proposed, one from OE *bæddel* 'hermaphrodite, effeminate man', the other from OE *(ge)bæded* 'captured'. (Both of these involve extensive semantic shifts, generally involving pejoration.) The Persian word, on the other hand, derives from earlier Pahlavi *wad*, whose initial *w-* cannot possibly be related to the *b-* of the English form, either of its putative Old English ancestors, or any other imaginable ancestral form.

We can avoid being misled by chance similarities if we insist that our comparison be based on a very LARGE data base. For if we find striking similarities in pronunciation and meaning in, say, a thousand words, the possibility that these similarities are due to chance becomes rather remote. Note that the data base must be very large, for as (1) below shows, it is not at all difficult to find a fairly large number of chance similarities between any given pair of languages. (Sanskrit and English are of course related to each other. However, we know their linguistic histories sufficiently well to be certain that the similarities in (1) do not reflect genetic relationship. On this matter see also Chapter 17.)

(1)   Sanskrit Mod. Engl.

kōṇa-	*corner*	
jhampa-	*jump*	
taru-	*tree*	(correct cognate: Skt. *dāru-*)
tōraṇa-	*door*	(correct cognate: Skt. *dvāra-*)
krōśati	*cries*	
gati-	*gait*	
lōkati	*looks*	
marīčikā	*mirage*	
rāga-	*rag*	(musical terms)
vāmā	*woman*	

(and others, the total being at least 26 items)

In addition, certain types of vocabulary are notoriously unreliable for establishing genetic relationship. One of these is ONOMATOPOEIA. Although details may differ, onomatopoetic expressions may come out remarkably similar in different languages. See for instance the rooster calls in examples (17) and (17′) of Chapter 7. In spite of their differences, Engl. *cockadoodledoo*, Germ. *kickericki*, Fr. *cocorico* share a repetition of velar stops, an inserted liquid (generally an *r*-sound), as well as, generally, accent on the last syllable.

Another area in which caution is advisable consists in vocabulary such as Engl. *dad(dy)*, *mom(my)*, *baby*, It. *papà*, *mamma*, *bambino*, Hindi *bāp*, *mã̄*, *baččā*. The structure, sounds, and often also the connotations of these words suggest that they are NURSERY WORDS, i.e., words and meanings which adults assign to the early babbling of infants. Like other items that occur in this kind of language, the words tend to have reduplicated consonant-vowel syllables (as in *pa-pa*). And the predominance of the vowel *a* and of the consonants *p/b*, *t/d*, *m*, and *n* in these words is a common feature of early babbling. (See Chapter 9, § 2.)

3. Similarities due to linguistic contact

Even if we eliminate chance similarities, onomatopoeia, and nursery words, we are not necessarily home free. We may be confronted with situations of the type (2). Here it appears as if English is simultaneously and equidistantly related to two quite distinct languages, French and German, with no evidence for genetic relationship between these two languages if we limit ourselves to the evidence in (2). (Of course, we know that French and German are related to each other; but at least in part that knowledge derives from the fact that previous generations of linguists have established that relationship. At this point, we are concerned with how genetic relationship can be established if we start from scratch.) In biology, such a dual relationship might not be entirely unexpected, since there is such a thing as cross-breeding. But in genetic/comparative linguistics, this type of relationship is always considered suspect. The suspicion always arises that such a relationship is attributable to borrowing. And in fact, in the present case we know from the history of English that the correspondences between English and French result from the secondary contact between the two languages after the Norman conquest of England.

(2)   English French German
       calf   *Kalb*
       veal   *veau*
       cow   *Kuh*
       beef   *bœuf*
       swine   *Schwein*
       pork   *porc*

Even if we did not have this direct historical knowledge, we would be able to make a good case for a borrowing relation between English and French by looking at other vocabulary items, such as the ones in (3).

(3)   English French German
       to   *à*   *zu*
       too   *trop*   *zu*
       two   *deux*   *zwei*
       twenty *vingt* *zwanzig*
       eat   *manger* *essen*

English	French	German
bite	*mordre*	*beissen*
father	*père*	*Vater* [f-]
mother	*mère*	*Mutter*
three	*trois*	*drei*
thou	*tu*	*du*

In these correspondences (which could be multiplied many times over), it is easy to see that there is a very close relationship between English and German, while French generally offers very different forms. True, closer examination now reveals some recurrent similarities which also involve French (see the last four words in (3)); but it is also clear that French does not exhibit any closer affinities with English than it does with German (or vice versa). In fact, in the words for 'father' and 'mother', and in many others like them, the similarities between English and German are much more striking than those of either of the two languages to French. The special affiliation of English with French that was suggested by the correspondences in (2) thus turns out to be contradicted by the evidence of additional data.

What is even more significant, a comparison of the data in (2) with those in (3) shows that the English/French similarities are restricted to certain, limited, spheres of the vocabulary. On the other hand, the German/English similarities pervade the whole lexicon, including BASIC VOCABULARY. As noted in Chapter 8, borrowing tends to be limited to certain spheres of the lexicon. In addition, it is often restricted to technical vocabulary. And it has the least effect in the area of basic vocabulary.

Cases like the English/French/German relationship are important because they provide insights that make it possible to detect borrowings in other cases, where we do not have direct historical evidence: If the similarities between two given languages are limited to certain spheres of the lexicon and if they cover little, if any, basic vocabulary, then there is a strong reason to suspect that they result from borrowing, not from genetic relationship.

Contact-induced similarities can also be found in overall structure, as the result of convergence. Recall for instance the case of the Balkans, of South Asia, or – even more strikingly – of Kupwar (Chapter 13, § 2). On the other hand, divergence in overall structure does not necessarily argue against genetic relationship. For instance, the modern Indo-European languages, though clearly related, exhibit the following basic word orders: Indo-Aryan, Iranian, and Armenian have SOV; Celtic offers VSO; German, Dutch, and Frisian have a mixture of SOV and SVO characteristics; and most of the others exhibit SVO. Similarities and differences in overall structure, thus, are not a reliable guide to establishing relationship. (But see § 5 below on similarities in specific aspects of structure.)

Comparative linguists therefore usually concentrate on VOCABULARY and on correspondences that emerge from an examination of vocabulary. Moreover, since basic vocabulary is less likely to be borrowed, the evidence of such vocabulary receives the highest priority.

4. Systematic, recurrent correspondences

We can strengthen our argument for genetic relationship between given languages by showing that the similarities between them are not just helter-skelter or sporadic, but that they are SYSTEMATIC and RECUR in large sets of words. In fact, given that sound change is overwhelmingly regular, we must expect a great degree of systematicity and recurrence in the phonetic similarities between putatively related languages.

Consider again the case of English and German. If we add the data in (4) to those in (2) and (3), we note some important phonetic differences between English words with *t* and their German counterparts. However, within these differences, we can establish a great systematicity; see the summary in (5). Moreover, even though there may be differences, the German counterparts of English *t* are phonetically similar, in that like *t*, they are dental. And if we expand our horizon to include words with English *p* and *k*, we find (mutatis mutandis) a very similar situation; see (6). Given these facts, the conclusion becomes almost inescapable that these words, and many others like them, go back to a common ancestor and have become different through the operation of regular sound change. The ability to find such regular and systematic correspondences between languages is the cornerstone of establishing genetic relationship.

(4)	English	German
	frost	*Frost*
	chest	*Kiste*
(5)	English	German
	t	*z* [ts] (initially and after consonant)
	t	*ss* [s] (intervocalically)
	t	*t* (after *s*)

(6)	English	German				
	pound	*Pfund*	}	p-	:	pf-
	penny	*Pfennig*				
	ape	*Affe*	}	-p-	:	-f-
	hope	*hoffen*				
	aspen	*Espe*	}	-sp-	:	-sp-
	wasp	*Wespe*				
	cool	*kühl*	}	k-	:	k-
	card	*Karte*				
	make	*machen*	}	-k-	:	-x-
	cook	*Koch*				

5. Shared aberrancies

We can yet further improve our case if we can find shared "aberrancies", or idiosyncrasies, in morphology.

Consider the English and German comparatives of Engl. *good* and its German counterpart *gut*, which are formed from what looks like a completely different lexical item – *better, best* and *besser, best-*; see (7a) (next page). Morphological relationships of this type are commonly referred to as SUPPLETION. Contrast the suppletion in (7a) with the normal pattern in Engl. *warm : warmer : warmest*, Germ. *warm : wärmer : wärmst-*. Now, (7a) demonstrates that French likewise has suppletion; but significantly, the English and German data exhibit systematic and recurrent similarities with each other, while the French forms are radically different. If we had to choose which of these patterns of suppletion must result from genetic relationship, we would surely have to opt for the patterns found in English and German. To select English and French would border on the perverse.

Similarly, the early Indo-European languages and even some modern ones exhibit striking similarities in the third person singular and plural forms of the verb 'to be', including a remarkable morphophonemic alternation between *Vs-* in the singular and *s-* in the plural. Compare (7b).

Highly idiosyncratic morphophonemic alternations such as those in (7b) do not normally get borrowed, nor do suppletive patterns like the ones in (7a). The morphological aberrancies exhibited by these patterns, therefore, combined with the fact that they involve systematic phonological correspondences, would be difficult to explain except as reflecting common heritage. In fact, evidence of patterns like (7b) no doubt contributed greatly to William Jones's proposal that "Sanscrit", Greek, Latin, and perhaps "Gothick" and "Celtick", too, are descended from a common ancestor.

(7)   a. English German French
          good   *gut*   *bon*
          better *besser* *meilleur*
          best   *best-*   *le meilleur*

(For the correspondences *-t- : -s-, -st- : -st-*, see (4) above. The other correspondences are similarly supported by "outside" evidence; compare the *g-:g-* in Engl. *great, give* : Germ. *gross, geben*.)

    b. Sanskrit   Latin   Mod. Germ.   Old Church Slavic
       as-ti 'is'   *es-t* 'is'   *is-t* 'is'   *es-tŭ* 'is'
       s-anti 'are' *s-unt* 'are' *s-ind* 'are' *s-ǫtŭ* 'are'

6. Reconstruction

Most historical linguists believe that the ultimate proof of genetic relationship lies in reconstruction, i.e., in reversing linguistic history, as it were, by postulating linguistic forms in an ancestral or PROTO-language from which the attested forms can be derived by plausible linguistic changes. Note that "proof" here is to be understood more or less as in a court of justice, as establishing a case beyond a reasonable doubt. Moreover, to be probative, the reconstruction must be based on a large amount of lexical items and at the same time conform to a set of evaluative principles that are detailed below.

For an illustration, consider the data in (8) (next page) as they bear on the reconstruction of Proto-Indo-European vowels.

In reconstructing, we must keep in mind the following principles which determine the acceptability and plausibility of our reconstruction:

– Reconstructed items and systems, and postulated linguistic changes should be NATURAL. A corollary of this principle is that postulated sound changes must be REGULAR, in conformity with the regularity principle of Chapter 4.

(8)

		Sanskrit	Greek	Latin	Germanic			Reconstruction
	a.	*idam*		*id(em)*	Go. *ita*	'it, that'		**i*
		rikta-	*é-lip-on*	*(re-)lic-tus*		'left'		
	b.	*yugam*	*zugón*	*iugum*	Go. *juk,*	'yoke'		**u*
					OE *geoc*			
		budh-	*puth-*		OE *budon,*	'(a)bide,		
					geboden	awake'		
	c.	*asti*	*estì*	*est*	Go. *ist,* OE *is*	'is'		**e*
		atti	*édomai*	*edō*	Go. *itan,*			
					OE *etan, itiþ*	'eat'		
	d.	*aṣṭau*	*oktṓ*	*octō*	Go. *ahtau*	'eight'		**o*
	e.	*ajati*	*ágō*	*agō*	ON *aka*	'drive'		**a*
	f.	*pitar-*	*patḗr*	*pater*	Go. *fadar*	'father'		**ə*

(Note: The data above are representative of larger sets. Given the overall available evidence, it is not possible to assume that (some of) the above sets can be "collapsed" in the process of reconstruction and that the observed differences might be attributed to special developments in the individual languages. That is, each set must be reconstructed separately for the proto-language.)

A further corollary of this principle is that there must be a phonetic value attached to a reconstructed sound. For instance, it would be unacceptable to reconstruct set (8f) as *. What would be the phonetic value of such a symbol? We must assume that a reconstructed (proto-)language is essentially like any language observable today – since known languages do not have sounds like , presumably neither did Proto-Indo-European. A natural reconstruction would instead be *[ə]; for as (9) shows, [ə] can naturally change to either [a] or [i].

(9)   *i*   *u*

       ↖

   e   *ə*   *o*

        ↓

       a

Moreover, it would be dubious to reconstruct *[a] for both sets (8e) and (8f) – or for sets (8d) and (8e), for that matter. To do so would require the assumption that contrary to normal expectations, sound change operates in a sporadic, irregular fashion, such that *[a] can change either to *i* or to *a* in Indo-Iranian, without any discernible motivation for the different developments.

– The reconstruction must not violate OCCAM'S RAZOR. According to this maxim, attributed to the medieval English philosopher William of Occam, *Entia (*or *essentia) non sunt multiplicanda praeter necessitatem* 'Entities [in an argument] should not be multiplied beyond necessity.' (This maxim, incidentally, is fundamental to all scientific inquiry.)

In comparative reconstruction, such "entities" are (i) reconstructed items, and (ii) changes required to convert these items into the forms attested in the descendant languages.

For instance, it would be a perverse violation of Occam's Razor if we reconstructed *[æ] for set (8a). This reconstruction would require the entirely unnecessary assumption either that all the languages innovated by changing *[æ] to [i] or that there was such a change in the ancestor language.

On the other hand, while the reconstruction *[ə] for set (8f) introduces an additional reconstructed sound, beyond the ones that we find attested in the daughter languages, it does so by necessity. To do otherwise would result in a violation of our first principle, since it would entail the unnecessary assumption of irregular sound change.

Finally, Occam's Razor argues that set (8d) should be reconstructed as *[o]. This reconstruction makes it possible to distinguish the behavior of this set from set (8e), in accordance with the expectation that sound change is regular. In addition, the reconstruction *[o] makes it possible to account for the attested forms with a minimum of changes. All we need to assume is that outside of Greek and Latin, the distinction between *[o] and *[a] was lost in favor of [a]. The Greek and Latin forms, then, represent unchanged outcomes. If however we reconstructed, say, *[ɔ], then we would have to unnecessarily assume that the original sound was changed in all the languages, including Greek and Latin.

– Wherever we can, we use the OLDEST available stages of languages. This makes reconstruction simpler, since less time has passed, and thus there has been less chance for linguistic changes to obscure the relationship between the languages.

Consider for instance the data in (10): Most striking are the examples in (10a), where the similarities – and correspondences – between Sanskrit and Old English are quite clear, while their modern counterparts have come to differ greatly as the result of linguistic change (mainly through lexical replacements). As examples such as (10b) illustrate, in some cases the relationship remains quite transparent, even in the modern languages. But compared to the older stages, such modern correspondences are much rarer. In fact, (10c) shows that in some cases even the oldest stages of the languages have undergone enough changes that the relationship of words which we know to be inherited from the Indo-European ancestor has become greatly obscured. Their relationship can be established only after extensive research in comparative reconstruction.

(10)

	Sanskrit	Old English		Hindi	Modern English	
a.	*asti*	*is*		*hai*	*is*	
	sa	*sē*		*vō*	*he*	
	vayam	*wē*		*ham*	*we*	
	śvasar	*sweostor*		*bahan*	*sister*	
	śvaśrū	*sweogor*		*sās*	*mother-in-law*	
	vēda	*wāt*		*jā́ntā hai*	*(he) knows*	
b.	*dvā(u)*	*twā*		*dō*	*two*	
	trayas	*þrī*		*tīn*	*three*	
	pād-	*fōt*		*pã̄v-*	*foot*	
c.	*čakra-*	*hweogol*		*čakkā*	*wheel*	*(< *kʷekʷlo-)*
	śr̥ṅga-	*horn*		*sī̃g*	*horn*	*(< *ḱer/kr̥-)*
	bhavati	*bēon*		*hōnā*	*be*	*(< *bhū-)*
	ṣaṭ	*seox*		*čhah*	*six*	*(< *s(w)eḱs)*
	pluśi-	*flēah*		*pissū*	*flea*	*(< *pl(o)uḱ-)*

We are able to assert that the words in (10c) are in fact related to each other partly because of the evidence of cognates in the early stages of other related languages, such as Gk. *kéras* 'horn'. In other cases, such as Skt. *čakra-*, OE *hweogol*, the relationship can be demonstrated only because we have reconstructed the Proto-Indo-European ancestral language, established the sound changes from PIE to languages such as Sanskrit and Old English, and are therefore able to show that both forms are derivable from a PIE form **kʷekʷlo-*, which is also reflected in Gk. *kúklos* 'wheel, circle'. Moreover, because we have reconstructed not just the sound system and the lexicon of Proto-Indo-European, but also its morphology, we are able to explain **kʷekʷlo-* as a morphological derivative of the independently reconstructed PIE root **kʷel-* 'move, turn' with an original meaning along the lines of 'the thing that keeps turning around'. (The morphological processes are quite complex, involving among other things a productive morphophonemic alternation between *el* and *l* [hence **kʷel-* beside **-kʷl-*] and a process of reduplication, which copies the initial consonant and vowel of the root [hence the initial **kʷe-* of **kʷe-kʷlo-*].)

Evidence of the type (10a), combined with that of (10c), suggests that there may be an optimal closeness of related languages that is necessary to successfully establish genetic relationship. If too many centuries of different linguistic changes have increased divergence beyond that optimal stage, the evidence may become too limited, and establishing genetic relationship may become extremely difficult or even impossible. (See also Chapter 17.)

7. What can we reconstruct and how confident are we of our reconstructions?

As we have seen earlier, comparative linguistics places the greatest amount of confidence in sound correspondences found in lexical comparisons, especially in basic vocabulary. Nevertheless, we can reconstruct other aspects of the ancestral language, in addition to the lexicon. Based on the methods and assumptions illustrated in the preceding section, we can reconstruct a fair amount of the phonology of the proto-language; and using somewhat different and more sophisticated methods, we can gain a pretty good picture of the morphology of the proto-language and of aspects of its syntax.

Ironically, although we base our reconstructions on lexical evidence, lexical reconstruction in many cases is done with much less confidence than the reconstruction of phonology, morphology, and syntax. Consider for instance the case of Algonquian 'fire-water' in example (11). There is no doubt that the words for 'fire' and 'water' are inherited. Given the evidence in (11), we might feel similarly confident about reconstructing a word 'fire-water'. But appearances are deceiving. We know that the product 'fire-water', i.e., alcohol, was introduced with the arrival of Europeans, long after Proto-Algonquian was spoken. We must therefore conclude that the words for 'fire-water' were assembled secondarily, from indigenous roots and according to inherited processes of compounding. Moreover, we can assume that the words were not created independently, but that they were diffused through the Algonquian languages by calquing (for which see Chapter 8.)

(11)   Fox   Cree   Menomini   Ojibwa
          'fire'   aškotēwi   iskotēw   eskōtēw   iškotē
          'water, liquid' -āpō-   -āpō-   -āpō-
          'fire-water'   iskotēw-āp-oy eskōtēw-āp-oh iškotēw-āp-ō

Examples like this one very strikingly show that in many cases we are more successful in reconstructing basic morphological elements, such as the roots for 'fire' and 'water', and the morphological patterns according to which they can combine, than we are able to reconstruct complete, complex words.

The best we can do in this regard is to establish that Proto-Algonquian had the morphological elements and the morphological machinery to assemble a word like 'fire-water' – if the occasion had arisen. The problem, of course, is that the occasion arose only much later.

Such problems are not limited to lexical reconstruction. In syntax, too, we are much more successful at reconstructing syntactic patterns. Reconstructing specific sentences runs into even greater difficulties than reconstructing complex words. True, we may be quite certain that a speaker of Proto Indo-European must have been able to utter a simple sentence like *$p\partial t\bar{e}r$ (e)$g^w emt$* 'the father came/arrived/went'. But even for a simple sentence like this there are problems, such as the fact that Indo-Europeanists are not in full agreement as to whether we should reconstruct *$g^w emt$* or *$eg^w emt$* for the form meaning 'came/arrived/went'. Moreover, there is the problem that the same idea may be expressed in more than one way. For complex sentences, the problems are obviously even greater.

The problem runs even deeper, for as the example of *$g^w emt$* vs. *$eg^w emt$* illustrates, comparative linguists often disagree with each other. Their disagreement may concern matters of relatively minor detail, such as whether past-tense forms of the type *$g^w emt$* should be reconstructed with the "augment" *e-* for all of Proto-Indo-European or for only some dialects of the proto-language, or whether the prefix was introduced in the early stages of some of the descendant languages.

The reason for this disagreement, briefly, is this: Among the ancient Indo-European languages, the augment is limited to Indo-Iranian, Armenian, Greek, and a few other, less well attested languages. These languages were close geographical neighbors. On the other hand, Hittite, Latin, and the other early Indo-European languages show no clear traces of the augment. What is especially embarrassing is that Hittite lacks it, since Hittite is attested earlier than either Sanskrit or Greek (or Latin). Some linguists therefore consider the augment a regional innovation, either in dialectal Proto-Indo-European (comparable to the centum : satem phenomena discussed in Chapter 11, § 4) or even later (presumably as the result of convergent developments; see Chapter 13). Other linguists argue that Hittite, Latin, and other early languages that lack the augment exhibit other innovations in verbal morphology and that, therefore, the absence of the augment in these languages can be considered a similar morphological innovation.

Even the reconstruction of the Indo-European sound system has been a matter of controversy and/or change of opinion. For instance, in the nineteenth century the stop system was reconstructed as in (12a), with a neat four-way contrast between voiceless, voiceless aspirated, voiced, and voiced aspirated, just as is found in Sanskrit. (See also Chapter 2.) More recently, scholars have argued that the voiceless aspirated series of Sanskrit (indirectly attested also in Iranian) can be explained as the result of secondary developments. Occam's Razor, therefore, should prevent us from postulating it as a feature of the proto-language. As a consequence, the system in (12b) was postulated.

Even more recently it has been claimed that the system in (12b) is unnatural. The most important argument in favor of this view is the claim that no known languages have voiced aspirates without also having voiceless aspirates. Scholars adhering to this view therefore reconstruct the system in (12c), with voiceless stops (± aspiration), "glottalized" stops (accompanied by a glottal-stop element), and voiced stops (± aspiration) corresponding, respectively, to the voiceless, voiced, and voiced aspirated stops of (12b).

(12)   a. Nineteenth-century reconstruction

	Labial	Dental	Palatal	Velar	Labiovelar
voiceless	p	t	$\acute{k}$	k	k^w
voiceless aspirated	ph	th	$\acute{k}h$	kh	k^wh
voiced	b	d	$\acute{g}$	g	g^w
voiced aspirated	bh	dh	$\acute{g}h$	gh	g^wh

   b. Standard twentieth-century reconstruction

	Labial	Dental	Palatal	Velar	Labiovelar
voiceless	p	t	$\acute{k}$	k	k^w
voiced	b	d	$\acute{g}$	g	g^w
voiced aspirated	bh	dh	$\acute{g}h$	gh	g^wh

   c. "Glottalic" reconstruction

	Labial	Dental	Palatal	Velar	Labiovelar
voiceless (± asp.)	$p(h)$	$t(h)$	$\acute{k}(h)$	$k(h)$	$k^w(h)$
glottalized	p'	t'	$\acute{k}'$	k'	$k^{w'}$
voiced (± asp.)	$b(h)$	$d(h)$	$\acute{g}(h)$	$g(h)$	$g^w(h)$

The so-called glottalic system in (12c) differs markedly from the ones in (12a) and (12b) and, if correct, would have enormous consequences for comparative Indo-European linguistics. The system is virtually identical to the one found in certain modern Armenian dialects and postulated for early Armenian by the advocates of the "glottalic theory". This has the virtue that the system is precedented and therefore can be considered natural. But another consequence is that the sound shift traditionally postulated for Armenian (see Chapter 4) can no longer be maintained. Instead, we must assume that Armenian essentially retained the stop system of Proto-Indo-European. An extension of this argument is that Grimm's Law, which, as noted in Chapter 4, is remarkably similar to the traditionally postulated Armenian sound shift, must likewise be rejected. The Germanic sound system, then, is claimed to be nearly as archaic as that of Armenian.

Note, however, that this approach has further consequences. The striking differences between Armenian and Germanic on one hand and the rest of Indo-European on the other must now be attributed, not to innovations on the part of Armenian and Germanic, but to sound shifts in the other Indo-European languages. These shifts must be of similar proportions to the ones traditionally postulated for Armenian and Germanic. Moreover, it may be necessary to assume that these shifts were independent of each other. If this assumption is correct, we would have to postulate some ten or twelve major sound shifts, instead of the two traditionally assumed for Armenian and Germanic. Such a proliferation of shifts, in turn, could be considered an argument against the reconstruction in (12c), since it would violate Occam's Razor.

Moreover, as noted in Chapter 2, the glottalic system found in some of the modern Armenian dialects may well be attributed to convergence with the neighboring Caucasic languages. In this regard, note that Ossetic, an Iranian language which likewise is spoken in this region, has a similar glottalic system. But in this case, the evidence of the other Iranian languages makes it clear that the glottalic system is an innovation, no doubt the result of convergence with the other languages of the Caucasus. These facts weaken the arguments for considering the glottalic system of Armenian to be an archaism. At the same time, they do not necessarily prove that the system must be an innovation, either.

Finally, it has been observed that there are in fact some languages that have voiced aspirates (or at least, stops more similar to voiced aspirates than to voiceless ones) without contrasting voiceless aspirates. One area in which such languages are found is part of the Indonesian archipelago, where Javanese (in Java), Madurese (Madura and parts of Java), Kelabit (Sarawak), and Lun Daye (Sabah) exhibit systems with contrasts between voiceless stops and voiced aspirates (Javanese) or voiceless stops, voiced stops, and voiced aspirates (Madurese, Kelabit, and Lun Daye). Members of the West African group of Kwa languages likewise offer such supposedly impossible sound systems. The evidence of these languages shows that one of the most important foundations of the glottalic theory cannot be maintained, namely the claim that languages with voiced aspirates but no contrasting voiceless aspirates are unnatural.

There are thus a number of arguments that weaken the cogency of the glottalic theory. But does this mean that they invalidate it? Proponents of the glottalic theory could still argue that the rarity of languages with voiced aspirates that do not have voiceless aspirate counterparts favors their theory

and that, at any rate, it does not particularly strengthen the standard reconstruction. Whatever the correct answer might be, at this point, the issue of
whether we should prefer the reconstruction in (12b) or the one in (12c) must
be considered unresolved. Both reconstructions have their strong partisans,
and the adherents of both views continue to marshal new arguments in favor
of their theory, or against the other theory.

Such disagreements must appear disconcerting to the non-linguist, and
even to linguists working in other areas of specialization, who are unfamiliar with the often arcane arguments of comparative linguists. In principle,
however, the disagreement should come as no surprise. All reconstructions
basically are HYPOTHESES about the nature of the proto-language. By their
very nature, however, hypotheses are – well, hypothetical. True, we try to
exclude questionable hypotheses by appealing to such principles as Occam's
Razor and naturalness. But these are only very general guidelines. They do
not really help us in dealing with many specific issues, such as the reconstruction in (12b) vs. the reconstruction in (12c). Moreover, they are not
simple algorithms which, if properly applied, will automatically yield correct
solutions. They require judgments on the part of comparative linguists. And
that is where most disagreements arise.

At the same time, we don't really have any choice; we have to develop
hypotheses, even if they are "hypothetical" and often controversial. If we
really knew what the proto-language was like, we wouldn't have to do reconstruction.

8. Language families other than Indo-European

The present chapter, just like much of the rest of this book, so far has concentrated on Indo-European. This is because since their "discovery" in the late
eighteenth century, the Indo-European languages have received the attention
of more comparative and historical linguists than any other language family.
In part this reflects the fact that until relatively recently, most linguists were
speakers of Indo-European languages.

But this is not a sufficient explanation. Much of the work on the Semitic
languages and the larger Afro-Asiatic family of which Semitic is a member
has also been done by native speakers of Indo-European languages, and similarly, pioneering fundamental research on language families such as Bantu,

Malayo-Polynesian, or the languages of the Americas has been conducted by speakers of Indo-European languages.

What may be more important is that most Indo-Europeanists begin with a good foundation in the classical languages of Greek and Latin. Since these are clearly Indo-European, it is natural for such scholars to expand their horizon (if they choose to do so) to other, related, Indo-European languages.

It may, however, also be true that the early Indo-European languages present something close to the optimal stage for comparison mentioned in § 6 above. This makes the initial task of establishing genetic relationship, as well as the job of reconstruction, relatively easy. True, even the Indo-European family includes members whose earliest attestations come from less optimal times (such as Albanian and Tocharian), or whose written attestations present other difficulties (such as Hittite). But just as in the case of examples like Skt. *čakra-*, OE *hweogol* 'wheel' in (10c) above, it is possible to at least begin to unravel the mysteries presented by such languages, because – in spite of the difficulties outlined in § 7 – we do have a fairly firm understanding of reconstructed Proto-Indo-European and therefore are able to draw on that understanding to make hypotheses as to how recalcitrant forms like *čakra-* and *hweogol* or recalcitrant languages like Albanian, Tocharian, and Hittite may be derived from Proto-Indo-European.

The following presents a brief look at the often more mixed successes of comparative linguistics as regards other language families. For selected languages the relationships are illustrated with examples of lexical correspondences. In some cases, the phonetic similarities in the correspondences are strong enough to strike even the non-specialist. In others, the similarities are more remote, but extensive comparative work makes it certain that the forms are cognate. In a few cases (especially Altaic), sets of highly dissimilar correspondences are included specifically to illustrate the problems that lead linguists to disagree on whether the languages in question should be considered genetically related.

The highly controversial issue of whether it is possible to establish longer-range genetic relationships (such as between Indo-European and Semitic or Afro-Asiatic) or even a genetic relationship between all of the world's languages is taken up in the next chapter.

As we saw in the introduction to this chapter, beside Indo-European there are members of at least two other language families in Europe. One of these families is the FINNO-UGRIC group which includes Finnish, Estonian, and Hungarian, as well as a number of other less well-known languages such as Lapp (now often called Saami, in the northern parts of Norway, Sweden, and Finland), Ostyak (also called Hanty, in western Siberia). Finno-Ugric, in turn, is part of a larger group, called URALIC, which includes Samoyed (in the northern part of the Russian Republic, east of the Ural mountains). The relationship between these languages can be illustrated by the sample correspondences below, given here in traditional transcription. Some of the forms are obviously similar, such as the words for 'winter' in all three languages, or the words for 'fish' in Finnish and Hungarian. In others, the relationship is less obvious, such as the words for 'one' and 'two'; but a closer look yields better results. For instance, the words for 'one' all begin in vowel, and the Finnish -*k*- of this word can be related to the -*gy* = [ɟ] in Hungarian; and so forth. In fact, more than a century of comparative work on Finno-Ugric/Uralic makes it possible for us to be certain that all the correspondences involve genuine cognates, descended from a common ancestor.

	Finnish	Hungarian	Ostyak
'one'	*yksi*	*egy*	*it, ij*
'two'	*kaksi*	*kettő/két*	*katən, kăt*
'three'	*kolme*	*három*	*xutəm*
'fish'	*kala*	*hal*	*xut*
'heart'	*sydän*	*szív*	*sam*
'winter'	*talvi*	*tél*	*tatə, tał*

The other family represented in Table 1 above is ALTAIC, of which only one language with a literary tradition is found in Europe, namely Turkish. Turkish is part of a closely-related subgroup of Altaic, called Turkic, members of which are found as far east as Central Asia and Siberia. Other members of the Altaic group include Mongol, Manchu, and Tunguz. Recent research suggests that Korean, and perhaps also Japanese, may be related to the Altaic languages, But both claims, especially the claim that Japanese is related, are controversial.

Even the Altaic group as more traditionally defined is controversial. Some scholars deny the validity of the "Altaic hypothesis" altogether and claim that Manchu and Tunguz are related to Korean and possibly to Japanese, but that there is no relationship between this group and the rest of what traditionally has been called Altaic. A comparison of the data below with those for Uralic readily illustrates how much more remote the Altaic languages are from each other. (Some of the Tunguz forms are missing, due to insufficient information.) Similarities are limited to Mong. *jirin* : Tung. *jū(r)* 'two', and Tu. *yürek* : Mong. *dzürx* 'heart'. However, semantically less exact correspondences such as Turk. *balık* 'fish' : Mong. *balgu* 'carp', and Turk. *kıš* 'winter' : Mong. *kul-de*, Tung. *kēl-di* 'cold' can easily be added.

	Turkish	Mongol	Tunguz
'one'	*bir*	*negen*	*umun*
'two'	*iki*	*qoyor/jirin*	*jū(r)*
'three'	*üč*	*gurban*	*ilan*
'fish'	*balık*	*dzagas*	
'heart'	*yürek*	*dzürx*	*mēwan*
'winter'	*kıš*	*öböl*	

Some scholars have argued for genetic relationship not just between the Altaic languages, but even between Uralic and Altaic, pointing to lexical similarities such as those given below. (The glosses on the left in many cases are only approximate. For instance, the range of meanings for Alt. **al-* includes 'underside, side', 'frontside', 'lower part, backside, rump', and so on). Some of the correspondences are indeed quite striking; others, such as **ñele-* : **dalag-* 'lick' are less impressive. Whatever the merits of such similarities, the Ural-Altaic hypothesis is considered even less well established than the Altaic one, and therefore even more controversial.

	Uralic/Finno-Ugric	Altaic
'under, below'	**al-*	**al*
'tongue, language'	**kelä*	**kele*
'we'	**me-*	**min-*
'what'	**mə*	**mu*
'lick'	**ñele-*	**dalag-*
'three'	**kolme*	Mong. *gurban*

As noted in the introduction to this chapter, in addition to Indo-European, Uralic, and Altaic, Europe also is host to BASQUE, which does not seem to belong to any of the other well-established language families. It may well be that Basque had relatives in prehistoric times that died with the coming of the Indo-Europeans to Europe in the second millennium B.C., but there are no records of such languages. Many other LANGUAGE ISOLATES like Basque are found around the world, such as Sumerian in ancient Mesopotamia and Burushaski in the extreme north of South Asia. Languages like these present even greater challenges to comparative linguistics than controversial groupings like Altaic.

Language families spoken in the Asian part of Eurasia are discussed below. Illustrative correspondences are given only for selected language families. In most cases, these are the words for the numerals 'one', 'two', and 'three', but for some groups other words have to be cited.

The Caucasus area is home to a number of Indo-European and Altaic (Turkic) languages, including Armenian and Ossetic (an Iranian language), as well as Azeri (Azerbaijani, a Turkic language). In addition, there are three groups of CAUCASIC languages which are commonly considered unrelated (i.e., unrelatable) to any outside languages or language families: the Northwest Caucasic languages (e.g. Abkhaz); the Northeast Caucasic languages (e.g. Chechen-Ingush and Dagestani); and Kartvelian. The best known Kartvelian language, and the one with the longest literary attestation (since the fifth century A.D.) is Georgian.

The Caucasic languages are notorious for very rich consonant systems. One feature, shared by the Indo-European languages Armenian and Ossetic, is the existence of a series of glottalized stops. (See § 7 above.) Some of the languages, especially those of Northwest Caucasic, have consonant systems said to be unexcelled in any other attested human language. Ubykh, for instance, is said to have close to 80 consonants. And some of the same languages have been claimed to have the lowest vowel inventories. Abkhaz, for example, probably only has two vowels, a low vowel *a* and a central vowel *ə*.

In the eastern area we find SINO-TIBETAN, a family that includes the Chinese language family, as well as TIBETO-BURMAN, of which Tibetan and Burmese are the major members. Chinese has been attested since probably the seventeenth century B.C., Tibetan since the eighth century A.D., and Burmese from the twelfth century A. D. Although the Sino-Tibetan family is generally considered well established, reconstructive work has not progressed very far as yet, and many aspects of the internal subgrouping of Sino-Tibetan are still uncertain. There have been proposals in the past that Thai belongs to Sino-Tibetan, but recent research suggests that it may rather be distantly related to Austronesian. The following correspondences may illustrate the relationship between Chinese, Tibetan, and Burmese. As in many other cases, some word sets exhibit much more transparent similarities than others; compare the words for 'three' and 'I' vs. the words for 'two'; but all forms can be considered cognates. (Chinese forms are from the Middle Chinese period; the Tibetan and Burmese forms come from the written forms of these languages.)

	Chinese	Tibetan	Burmese
'two'	*ñžyi-*	*gnyis*	*hnac*
'three'	*sam*	*gsum*	*sûm*
'I'	*nguo*	*nga*	*ŋa*
'name'	*myäng*	*ming*	*ə-mañ*
'tree, wood'	*syen*	*shing*	*sac*

South Asia is home to DRAVIDIAN, a family of languages spoken mainly in the south of India and parts of Sri Lanka. But one member, Brahui, is spoken much farther north, in present-day Pakistan. The major literary languages are Tamil, Malayalam, Kannada, and Telugu. The following correspondences, in traditional transcription, may illustrate the degree to which the Dravidian languages are related to each other.

	Tamil	Malayalam	Kannada	Telugu	Brahui
'one'	*oṉṟu*	*onnu*	*ondu*	*okaṭi*	*asi(ṭ)*
'two'	*iraṇḍu*	*raṇḍu*	*eraṛu*	*reṇḍu*	*ira(ṭ)*
'three'	*mūṉṟu*	*mūnnu*	*mūru*	*muṛu*	*musi(ṭ)*

The AUSTRO-ASIATIC language family includes Mon and Khmer in present-day Kampuchea, as well as the Munda languages in Central and East-Central India.

The MALAYO-POLYNESIAN or AUSTRONESIAN languages form a far-flung, but linguistically fairly close-knit family. They include Malay, Indonesian, Javanese, Tagalog (in the Philippines), Maori, Hawaiian, Samoan, as well as Malagasy, the language of Madagascar just east of Africa. Compare for instance the following correspondences.

	Indonesian	Javanese	Tagalog	Samoan	Malagasy
'one'	*satu*	*siji*	*isa*	*tasi*	*isa*
'two'	*dua*	*loro*	*dalawa*	*lua*	*rua*
'three'	*tiga*	*telung*	*tatlo*	*tolu*	*telu*

AFRO-ASIATIC, as the name suggests, extends from Asia into Africa. The group includes the SEMITIC languages (Hebrew, Arabic, as well as Assyrian and Babylonian, spoken in ancient Mesopotamia), Ancient EGYPTIAN (and its descendant, Coptic), as well as BERBER (in North Africa), CUSHITIC (including Somali), and CHADIC (including Hausa). Compare the following correspondences. (Only putatively related words are given. This accounts for some of the blanks. The hieroglyphic script of ancient Egyptian indicates only the consonants, not the vowels; this accounts for the absence of vowels in the transcriptions below.)

	Hebrew	Arabic	Egyptian	Berber	Cushitic	Chadic
'to beat'	*dɔqaq*	*daqqaqa*	*dkw*	*dəgdəg*	*daku*	*dōka*
'bone'	*qaṣṣ*	*qs*		*ixs, iɣs*		*k'ašī*
'ear, hear'	*šmaʕ*	*samiʕa*	*sĭm*	*asim*	*māsuw*	*sim*
'heart'	*lēv*	*lubb*	*yb*	*ul*	*lēb, nibbo*	*nəfu*
'mouth'	*pɛ*	*fam*		*emi*	*(y)af*	*po*
'nose, smell'			*snsn*		*san*	*sunsunā*

In Africa, the following families are recognized, in addition of course to Afro-Asiatic.

The most widespread language family is BANTU, ranging from Swahili in Kenya and Tanzania to Setswana and Zulu in southern Africa. The Bantu languages are generally considered part of a larger family, NIGER-CONGO, which includes West African and sub-Saharan languages like Wolof, Fula, and Yoruba. An even larger putative language family is NIGER-CORDOFANIAN, which in addition to Niger-Congo embraces most of the remaining West African languages. Of these different genetic classifications, Bantu is by far the best established; Niger-Congo is a little more uncertain; and Niger-Cordofanian is rather controversial. The correspondences below are from selected members of the Niger-Congo family.

	Bantu			Other	
	Swahili	Lingala	Setswana	Ahlõ	Efik
'one'	*moja*	*m-ɔkɔ*	*ŋŋwe*	*ili*	*kiet*
'two'	*mbili/wili*	*mi-bale*	*pedi*	*iwa*	*iba*
'three'	*tatu*	*mi-sato*	*tharo*	*ita*	*ita*

In the extreme south of Africa are located the KHOISAN languages, famous for their click sounds, which are indicated by such arcane symbols as ≠*k*, ≠*g*, and *!k(x)*. (Formerly these languages were called Bushman and Hottentot; but the names have been given up because of their negative connotations.) Two languages of Tanzania, Sandawe and Hatsa, have been claimed to be distant relatives of the Khoisan languages. The following correspondences may illustrate the relationship.

	Sandawe	Khoisan	
		Naron	Khoi
'ear, hear'	*keke*	≠*kē*	≠*gai*
'four'	*haka*	*haga*	*haka*
'valley'	*Goʔa*	*!xubi*	*!kxowi*

It has been argued that the majority of the remaining African languages (including Nubian, Sudanic, and Songhai) form a single language family, called NILO-SAHARAN. But like many others, this genetic classification is relatively controversial.

The Americas are home to a large variety of indigenous languages. According to some scholars, most of these are related to each other, and there are only three "super-families" in the Americas. But this view remains highly controversial. A more conservative approach would recognize, among others, the following groups, but would consider the genetic affiliation of many languages to be still unsettled.

ESKIMO-ALEUT is a group of languages extending from Alaska and Northern Canada to Greenland, of which Eskimo, now often referred to as Inuit, is the best-known member. (As noted in Chapter 9, the term Eskimo originally is a derogatory word, apparently derived from Micmac *eskameege* 'raw fish eaters'. The term, however, is still used in technical writing and by Indigenous Americans in Alaska.)

The ATHABASKAN family is named after Athabaskan, spoken in Alaska and Northwest Canada, but includes many other languages, known for their rich consonant systems, a large number of glottalized consonants, and highly complex consonant groups. Navajo, with the largest number of speakers of any Indigenous American language in the United States (some 150,000), and Apache, are also members of the Athabaskan family, though spoken much father south (in present-day Arizona and adjacent areas). The Athabaskan family is considered related to two other groups, the nearly extinct Eyak (Alaska), and the Tlingit group (Alaska and Northwest Canada). Some linguists argue for a larger family, "NA-DENE", which also includes Haida (Alaska and British Columbia); but that affiliation is highly controversial.

ALGONQUIAN is a widespread family of relatively closely related languages, extending from the Great Lakes area to northeastern North America, and originally along the eastern seaboard as far south as Virginia. Well-known members include Blackfoot, Cheyenne, Cree, Chippewa or Ojibwa, Fox, Menomini, Ottawa, the Illinois Confederation, and Shawnee. The correspondences below, which include the (in)famous word for 'fire-water', may illustrate the relative closeness of the members of this family. Reconstruction of the linguistic ancestor, Proto-Algonquian, has made considerable process during the twentieth century.

	Fox	Cree	Menomini	Ojibwa
'one'	*nekoti*	*nikot-*	*nekot*	*ninkot-*
'two'	*nīšwi*	*nīso*	*nīs*	*nīš*
'three'	*neswi*	*nisto*	*neʔniw*	*nisswi*
'fire'	*aškotēwi*	*iskotēw*	*eskōtēw*	*iškotē*
'water'	*nepi*	*nipiy*	*nepēw*	*nimpi*
'water, liquid'	*-āpō-*		*-āpō-*	*-āpō-*
"fire-water"		*iskotēwāpoy*	*eskōtēwāpoh*	*iškotēwāpō*

Two languages spoken in California, Wiyot and Yurok, have been shown to be related to Algonquian, but at a much greater distance. The fact that Algonquian thus has relatives in California raises interesting questions about the earlier distribution of the larger language family, or about prehistoric migrations in North America.

IROQUOIAN is a family of languages in the eastern United States and Canada with members that bear some particularly familiar names from American history, for it comprises the members of the "Five Nations" confederacy (also known as the "Iroquois League"): Cayuga, Mohawk, Oneida, Onondaga, and Seneca, along with Tuscaroara, which as a later addition, turned the confederacy into the "Six Nations". Other Iroquoian languages are Cherokee (see Chapter 3, § 5.3 for its writing system), Erie, Huron, and Wyandot. Iroquoian is sometimes classified as related to Siouan.

SIOUAN is a very far-flung family, embracing the languages of the Sioux or Dakotas, as well as Crow, Iowa, Omaha, Osage, Winnebago and many others. The family at one time extended as far north as the Dakotas and Central Canada, as far east as Virginia and the Carolinas, and as far south as the Gulf coast. There have been attempts to relate Siouan to HOKAN, languages spoken in the Southwest of the United States, which include Mohave, Chumash, and Yuman. But that classification is generally doubted; and there are even doubts as to whether all the Hokan languages are really related to each other or whether similarities are mainly attributable to centuries or even millennia of mutual borrowing.

UTO-AZTECAN is a large family in the western United States, Mexico, and Central America, including Nahuatl (the language of the ancient Aztec empire), Hopi (in Arizona), and Ute (in Utah and Colorado). The following correspondences may illustrate the relationship.

	Comanche	Tübatulabal	Luiseño	Hopi	Papago	Nahuatl
'one'	*səmə?*	*čïč*	*supúl*	*sə́ka*	*həmako*	*seem-*
'two'	*waha(h)-*	*wō*	*wéx, wé?*	*lóyö-m*	*gōk*	*oomi*
'three'	*pahi-*	*pāi-*	*pắhi*	*pắyo-m*	*vaik*	*eeyi*

MAYAN, in Mexico and Central America, is a group of fairly closely related languages, named after their most well-known member, the language of the ancient Maya civilization. As observed in Chapter 3, the Mayan civilization developed a writing system of its own, long before the arrival of the Europeans. The decipherment of the writing system has been increasingly successful in recent years.

ARAWAKAN now is found mainly in northeastern South America, but once extended into the Caribbean as well.

QUECHUA, a far-flung family with members in Peru, Ecuador, Bolivia, as well as in border areas of Argentina, Chile, and Colombia, was the language of the ancient Inca empire. The modern varieties of Quechua are very closely related to each other, as can be seen from the following correspondences. Some scholars have grouped Quechua and Aymara into a larger, "Andean" or "Quechumara" family. But like most other attempts at establishing larger genetic families in the Americas, this proposal has remained controversial.

	Ancash	Junín	Cajamarca	Amazonas	Ecuador	Ayacucho	Cuzco
'two'	*iškē*	*iškay*	*iškay*	*iškē*	*iškay*	*iskay*	*iskay*
'three'	*kimsa*	*kimsa*	*kimsa*	*kimsa*	*kimsa*	*kimsa*	*kinsa*
'six'	*hoxta*	*suʔta*	*soxta*	*suχta*	*suχta*	*soxta*	*soxta*
'language'	*qaλu*	*aλu*	*qažu*	*kadžu*	*kažu*	*kaλu*	*qaλu*

AUSTRALIA, too, is home of a large number of languages. By some estimates, at least 200 languages were spoken in Australia at the time of the European arrival. The languages have suffered an enormous degree of language death. About fifty percent of the original number of languages are now extinct. Many others are dying. Some scholars claim that all the indigenous languages of Australia are related. Others class the large majority into a PAMA-NYUNGAN family, distributed over most of Australia, and assume a relatively large number of smaller genetic groups for the remaining languages, many of which are found in the northwest. But many details of these and other proposed genetic classifications still need to be worked out. In the meantime, Australian languages continue to die out at a rapid rate; and with the languages the evidence dies out that they might contribute to a more complete understanding of Australian genetic relationships.

In addition, we can mention various SIGN(ED) LANGUAGES and the question of their genetic affiliation. The number of such manually-based languages is generally assumed to be very large – at least in the hundreds, but possibly in the thousands. In their natural state (i.e., leaving aside codes such as finger-spelled versions of spoken languages), true signed languages are unrelated to their "co-territorial" oral languages. For instance, American Sign Language (ASL) has nothing to do with American English, either historically or structurally or lexically. The same holds true for the relationship between British Sign Language (BSL) and British English, French Sign Language (FSL) and French, and so on. Interestingly, however, ASL and FSL are related to each other historically, and neither is related to BSL. FSL originated around 1760 through the efforts of a French teacher to the deaf, Abbé de l'Épée, and later spread to America (where it became the basis for ASL), to Russia, to Ireland (from where it spread to Australia), and to several other European countries, whose sign languages thus are related and form a language family. Through similar developments, Japanese and Korean Sign Language are related to each other. BSL and Chinese Sign Language, by contrast, constitute something like signed counterparts to oral language isolates such as Basque.

Our knowledge of relatedness among signed languages is partly based on what is known about the their historical spread, but also on applying the standard methods of comparative linguistics – by comparing systematic similarities and differences in hand shapes, hand orientation, and hand movements for particular signs, in the meanings associated with these signs, and in the morphology and syntax of signed languages. Thus, just as examples in the earlier chapters have shown that sign languages are affected by the same kinds of linguistic change that are observable in oral languages, so also is it true that the principles of comparative linguistics apply equally well to signed languages as to oral languages.

Chapter 17
Proto-World? The question of long-distance genetic relationships

> And the Lord said, Behold, the people is one, and they have all
> one language; and this they begin to do: and now nothing will
> be restrained from them, which they have imagined to do. Go
> to, let us go down, and there confound their language, that they
> may not understand one another's speech. So the Lord scattered
> them abroad from thence upon the face of all the earth: and they
> left off to build the city.
>
> *(Genesis 11: 6–8)*

1. Introduction

The question whether all of the world's languages are related, i.c., whether we
can establish a "Proto-World" from which all human languages are descended,
has intrigued humankind for centuries, even millennia. Perhaps the earliest,
and certainly the most famous testimony to this interest in the western world
is the story about the tower of Babel (cited above, from the "Authorized
Version" of the English Bible translation). Similar stories are told in other
parts of the world, including in many indigenous languages of the western
United States. Consider the following two examples.

> Mouse was sitting on top of the assembly house, playing his flute and
> dropping pieces of coal through the smokehole, when Coyote inter-
> rupted him. Those who sat closest to the smokehole received fire and
> therefore cook their food and speak correctly. Those farther removed
> did not receive fire and remained in the cold; that is why their teeth
> chatter when they talk. If Coyote had not interrupted Mouse, all people
> would have received the fire and would have spoken in one language.
> (Adapted from a tale by the Maidu of California.)

> When the people emerged from the lower world to the upper world
> through the sipapuni, Mocking Bird stood beside Old Spider Woman

and assigned them to different groups. "You will be Hopi and speak Hopi," he said to one group. "You will be Navajo and speak Navajo," he said to another group. In this way he assigned everyone to a tribe and language – the Hopis, the Navajos, the Apache, the Paiutes, the Zunis, and so on, down to the whites. (Adapted from a myth of the Hopi of Arizona.)

Traditional historical linguists consider it impossible at the present state of our knowledge to establish that all the world's languages are genetically related. More than that, many doubt whether it is possible to establish relationships more distant than, say, Indo-European, Uralic, Bantu, or Algonquian. In fact, as we have seen in the preceding chapter, even relatively well-established, smaller, language families such as Altaic are a matter of continuing controversy.

At the same time, since nearly the beginning of comparative linguistics, there have been repeated attempts to establish longer-distance relationships. And time and again, traditional historical linguists have claimed that these attempts are premature or poorly established. For instance, the Ural-Altaic hypothesis (see Chapter 16, § 8) has been doubted, since it was proposed mainly on the basis of general structural similarities, features which could easily be attributed to convergence. Vocabulary correspondences, on the other hand, are quite limited, too limited to convince scholars that they cannot possibly be borrowings, onomatopoeia, nursery words, or even due to accident. Adopting an expression used in second-language teaching, let us refer to such non-cognate similarities as FALSE FRIENDS.

The situation is similar for the nineteenth-century proposal of an INDO-SEMITIC family, consisting of Indo-European and Semitic. An additional problem in this case is that Semitic belongs to a larger family, now referred to as Afro-Asiatic (see Chapter 16, § 8). The comparison, therefore should be of Indo-European with Afro-Asiatic, not just with Semitic. More recent work meets this objection by comparing Indo-European with Afro-Asiatic and proposing a larger family which one scholar refers to as LISLAKH (lit., 'language of the people', from *lisan*, the Arabic word for 'tongue, language', and **laHHuwa-* 'people', a form reconstructed by one scholar for the ancestor of Hittite and the other Indo-European languages).

Probably the largest language family proposed by scholars attempting to establish relationship by traditional methods is NOSTRATIC, a family consisting of Indo-European plus a range of other languages which differs from researcher to researcher and tends to include such languages as Semitic or Afro-Asiatic, Uralic, Altaic, Caucasic languages, and/or languages like ancient Sumerian or Basque which most traditional scholars consider to be without known relatives. The term Nostratic is somewhat ethnocentric, meaning 'belonging to us/to our part of the world', i.e., to Eurasia plus Northern Africa. Depending on one's views on this matter, this may be considered exciting or deplorable. What is more significant is that even more than such shorter-distance groupings as Ural-Altaic or Lislakh, the Nostratic hypothesis has failed to convince most traditional comparative linguists because of concerns that the similarities in vocabulary and structure may be of the false-friend type.

Most recently, the American linguist Joseph Greenberg and some associates of his have claimed that long-distance relationships can be established more effectively – and more easily – by employing an approach totally different from the traditional methods. This is an approach of lexical "mass comparison" or "multilateral comparison" which establishes relationship through comparison of a large number of languages, on a fairly limited lexical basis (including function words and affixes), simply by means of scoring cognates based on similarities in sound and meaning.

Greenberg has used this method to establish a genetic classification of the languages of Africa and, more recently, of the indigenous languages of the Americas. He argues that most of the latter languages can be grouped together into a single family which he calls AMERIND.

Greenberg further claims that his approach makes it possible to establish a relationship between Amerind on one hand and, on the other hand, Eskimo-Aleut, and four linguistic families of the "Old World": Afro-Asiatic, Indo-European, Uralic, and Dravidian. In principle, he claims, his method will make it possible to show that all of the world's languages are related. Some of the "Nostraticists" have made similar claims recently.

Not unexpectedly, Greenberg's claims and the similar claims of certain Nostraticists have created a lot of excitement among non-linguists, since they promise, at least in principle, to provide a positive answer to the question raised at the beginning of this section: "Are all the world's languages related?" At the same time, traditional comparative linguists have subjected Greenberg's methodology and claims to close scrutiny – and severe criticism.

The debate that ensued between Greenberg and his critics has at times been highly acrimonious. Greenberg has been accused of having predetermined the outcome of his work on Amerind before actually applying his methodology. A close associate of Greenberg has suggested that opposition to Greenberg's methodology is based either on indolence or, worse, on a Eurocentric refusal to even entertain the idea that the languages of Europe might be related to non-European languages. Moreover, despairing of finding acceptance among traditional historical linguists, many advocates of such long-distance genetic comparisons have taken to the semi-popular press, especially *Scientific American*. Even popular journals, such as *US World and News Report* and *Der Spiegel* have carried features on their work.

In the following let us take a closer look at the kinds of arguments and evidence that are relevant in discussions of this type.

Our focus will be on oral languages, since they are the topic of the controversy between Greenberg (and his followers), the Nostraticists, and what may be called the Traditionalists. But as noted at the end of Chapter 16, there are numerous signed languages throughout the world, some related to each other but, crucially, none connected to or derived from any oral language. Whatever may emerge from the "Proto-World" controversy, therefore, affects the genetic relationship of oral languages – sign languages seem to require the assumption of different origins. (See also § 5 below.)

2. Longer-distance comparison

For language families like Indo-European and Uralic, the evidence that the members of each respective family are indeed related amongst each other is so strong and overwhelming that to doubt the relationship would be bordering on the perverse. Perhaps most important, in both of these families it has been possible to successfully reconstruct the phonology, much of the morphology, and the basic outlines of the syntax. Controversies (as in the case of the Indo-European "glottalic theory") are concerned with details of the reconstruction or with the precise nature of the reconstruction (phonetic or otherwise), not with the overall results of comparative reconstruction or the question of whether it is possible to reconstruct at all.

For many other putative language groups, the evidence is not sufficient to engage in comparative reconstruction and thus to establish genetic relationship. In fact, in many cases the available evidence is so limited that most linguists would consider hypotheses of genetic relationship extremely dubious.

In some cases, the evidence is at least strong enough to establish a shared aberrancy, or the number of recurrent lexical similarities is massive enough to make genetic relationship very likely, even if it cannot be established beyond a reasonable doubt. A handy term for a group of this sort is PHYLUM. The term was originally introduced in comparative work on Indigenous American languages to refer to "super-families" consisting of putatively related

languages. But it is useful for designating any group of languages for which
there is tantalizing – but insufficient – evidence of relationship.

A case in point is the question of the possible relationship between Uralic
and Dravidian. Earlier comparisons of the modern members of these language
families suggested relationship to some scholars, while many others remained
skeptical. The completion of etymological dictionaries and the working out
of (approximate) reconstructions for each of the two families have pushed
back our knowledge of each family by several thousand years by essentially
undoing some of the effects of linguistic change. Comparison of the resulting reconstructed forms of Uralic and Dravidian has made it considerably
easier to establish similarities; and many systematically recurring correspondences in non-technical, basic vocabulary have been uncovered. Compare the
selected examples in (1).

(1)   Proto-Uralic Proto-Dravidian
       *taγ-   *ta(-r)-   'give'
       *täm-   *tev-   'fill'
       *tuγ-   *tur̤-   'river'
       *käte-   *kay-   'hand'
       *kele-   *kēl̤-   'speech'
       *sükese-   *čuk(k)-   'autumn'
       *pekse-   *pak-   'arrow'

In addition we find systematically recurrent phonetic correspondences in
the shared syntactic aberrancy of expressing negation by a finite verb; see (2).
For an illustration of how such negative verbs operate, compare the Finnish
example in (3), in which it is the negation which is inflected for person and
number, while the accompanying main verb appears in an uninflected form.

(2)   Ural. *äl- : Drav. *al(l)-
(3)   sg. 1 *juo-n*   'drink' | e-n juo   'do not drink'
          2   *juo-t* | e-t juo
          3   *juo* | ei juo
       pl. 1 *juo-mme* | e-mme juo
          2   *juo-tte* | e-tte juo
          3   *juo-vat* | ei-vät juo

Now, we do find "negative verbs" elsewhere, such as in a number of Australian languages; and the modern Tsakonian dialect of Greek developed one
through regular sound changes affecting combinations of a negative marker
and an obligatory auxiliary verb. Marathi, an Indo-Aryan neighbor of Dravidian, has developed something like a negative verb, too, presumably by

convergence with Dravidian. However, as usual in convergence situations, the actual form of this negative verb consists of inherited, Indo-Aryan elements (compare the present stem *nāhī* ≈ Hindi *nahī̃* 'not'). It is thus quite different and exhibits no systematic recurrent correspondences with either Dravidian or Uralic. The correspondence in (2), by contrast, does.

The only reservation which one must have concerning the value of the shared aberrancy in (2) is that the morphemes involved are very short. This raises the possibility that we might be dealing with a case of chance similarity. The longer, more complex, and more idiosyncratic putative cognates are, the less the likelihood that their similarities are due to chance; but in short elements, consisting of just one or two sounds, the chance of accidental similarity is much greater.

Moreover, while the shared aberrancy might persuade some linguists that Uralic and Dravidian are related, others would not consider the relationship established beyond a reasonable doubt, since up to this point it has not been possible to propose a satisfactory reconstruction even of the phonological structure of the common ancestor.

In the case of many other languages, the evidence is even more limited, such that the encountered similarities could very well be the result of borrowing or convergence, or might even be attributable to chance.

For instance, there are a number of intriguing correspondences between Uralic and Proto-Indo-European, including pronominal forms, as well as verb and noun endings. These similarities include some twenty lexical items such as the words for 'name' and 'water' (4a), demonstrative and personal pronouns (4b), and even inflectional endings (4c).

(4)　　　Uralic　　　Proto-Indo-European
　　a. *nime-　　*nomen-　　'name'
　　　*wete　　*wodor/weden/uden-　'water'
　　b. *tä-　⎫
　　　*to-　⎬ *te/o-　　'this, that'
　　　*se-　　*se/o-　　'this, that'
　　　*ke-, ku-　*kʷe/o-　'who, what'
　　c. *-m　　*-m　　(Accusative singular)
　　　*-n　　*-om　　(Genitive plural)

However, the number of correspondences, proposed by one of the most ardent proponents of the Indo-Uralic hypothesis, is highly limited. Some of them are controversial. For instance, one Uralicist has doubted the reconstruction of the accusative singular and genitive plural endings in (4c). No shared aberrancies involving systematically recurring correspondences seem to be found. And given the extremely limited number of correspondences, the possibility cannot be excluded that the similarities are false friends.

As we saw in example (1) of Chapter 16, chance similarities are by no means rare. And example (10) of the same chapter, repeated as (5) below, shows that given enough time of separation and independent development, clearly related languages can come to be different enough that many of their genuine cognates are difficult or even impossible to recognize.

(5)

		Sanskrit	Old English	Hindi	Modern English
	a.	*asti*	*is*	*hai*	*is*
		sa	*sē*	*vō*	*he*
		vayam	*wē*	*ham*	*we*
		svasar	*sweostor*	*bahan*	*sister*
		śvaśrū	*sweogor*	*sās*	*mother-in-law*
		vēda	*wāt*	*j̆āntā hai*	*(he) knows*
	b.	*dvā(u)*	*twā*	*dō*	*two*
		trayas	*þrī*	*tīn*	*three*
		pād-	*fōt*	*pā̃v-*	*foot*
	c.	*čakra-*	*hweogol*	*čakkā*	*wheel*
		śṛnga-	*horn*	*sīg*	*horn*
		bhavati	*bēon*	*hōnā*	*be*
		ṣaṭ	*seox*	*chah*	*six*
		pluśi-	*flēah*	*pissū*	*flea*

Let us pursue this issue a little further by taking a closer look at the relationship between Modern Hindi and English – pretending that we do not yet know that they are related, and trying to establish their relationship by vocabulary comparison. This is actually more difficult than it appears. It is all too easy to be influenced by one's knowledge of the historical relationship between the two languages and therefore to notice the genuine cognates, or even to underestimate the effects of linguistic change on the recognizability of genuine cognates.

An open-ended search of Modern Hindi and English dictionaries yields some 55 genuine cognates which still are close enough phonetically and semantically to look like they are related; see the selected examples in (6a). There are some 30 further genuine cognates which probably would be unrecognizable without one's knowing their historical antecedents; see (6b) for examples. In fact, without that knowledge, one might well feel that if forms like these can be related, then anything can. In addition, there are at least 45 Hindi borrowings from Sanskrit which have English cognates but which –

since they are borrowings – are not strictly speaking genuine cognates between Hindi and English. See (6c) for a few examples. Some of these, such as the first four items under (6c) are difficult to recognize, just like the words in (6b). Words of the type (6c) probably should be disregarded since on one hand they are borrowed from Sanskrit but, on the other hand, their Sanskrit sources are cognates of their English counterparts. These words, thus, are simultaneously cognate and non-cognate. Some 5 correspondences involve borrowings from Persian into Hindi (6d), and another 10 or more other borrowings not directly involving Hindi and English; see (6e) for selected examples. Finally, and most significantly, there are some 60 correspondences which, given our knowledge of the history of these languages, clearly are accidental similarities; see the selected examples in (6f).

(6)

	Hindi	English	Hindi	English
a.	*bãdh-nā*	*bind*	*bhāī*	*brother*
	bhaũ	*brow*	*āṭh*	*eight*
	pãč	*five*	*pãv, pãy*	*foot*
	čār	*four*	*māī*	*mother*
	dãt	*tooth*	*dō*	*two*
	kaun	*who*		
b.	*hō-nā*	*be*	*ǰān-nā*	*can, know*
	gayā 'went'	*come*	*harā*	*green*
	sĩg	*horn*	*sun-nā*	*listen*
	ǰī-nā 'live'	*quick*	*sūkhā* 'dry'	*sear*
	thā 'was'	*stand*	*ǰuā*	*yoke*
c.	*hanu*	*chin*	*švān* 'dog'	*hound*
	hiraṇya	*gold*	*vāñčhā*	*wish*
	pitā	*father*	*ant*	*end*
	mānav	*man*	*nābhī*	*navel*
	tanu	*thin*	*vidhavā*	*widow*
d.	*band* 'string'	*bond*	*sar(a)d*	*cold*
	dar(vāzā)	*door*	*nāf*	*navel*
	gar(a)m	*warm*		

	Hindi	English
e.	*kēndra* (from Greek via Sanskrit)	*center* (from Greek via Latin)
	mistrī 'craftsman' (from Portuguese)	*master* (from Latin)
	path	*path* (from Iranian)
	vāk (from Sanskrit)	*voice* (from French)

f. | Hindi | English | Hindi | English |
|---|---|---|---|
| *gannā* | *cane* | *gā̄r̄ī* | *car, cart* |
| *čakhnā* 'taste' | *to check* | *čabānā* | *chew* |
| *kōylā* | *coal* | *kōnā* | *corner* |
| *gin-nā* | *to count* | *kāṭ-nā* | *cut* |
| *dūn* 'valley' | *downs* | *gati* | *gait* |
| *ghās* | *grass* | *kēš* | *hair* |
| *xudā/khudā* | *God* | *kuttā* 'dog' | *hound* |
| *lōčan* 'eye' | *look* | *tōṛ-nā* 'break' | *tear* |

Disregarding Sanskrit borrowings of the type (6c) which, as noted, are simultaneously cognate and non-cognate, we find that the ratio of cognates that are both genuine and recognizable (6a) to false friends (6d-f) is about 55 to 75. Even if we add the difficult type (6b) to the genuine cognates we wind up with a ratio of about 85 to 75. That is, no matter what we do, there is only about a 50 : 50 chance that correspondences are genuine cognates.

The situation is very much the same when we look at similarities in pronouns, function words, and grammatical suffixes. Compare the data in (7). Here again we find that in languages that are clearly related, the ratio of genuine cognates to false friends is not much better than 50 : 50.

(7) | Hindi | English | |
|---|---|---|
| *hū-ṁ* | *a-m* | (directly or indirectly from PIE *-mi*) |
| **maiṁ** | **me** | (directly or indirectly from PIE *me*) |
| **kaun/kyā** | **who/what** | (related, from PIE *k^we/o/i*-, but hard to recognize as cognates) |
| **aur** [ɔ̄r] 'and' | **or** | (false friends; Hindi *aur* < Skt. *aparam* 'other; moreover'; Engl. *or* < OE *oþðe*.) |
| *jā-nā* (infinitive) | *go-ing* (gerund) | (false friends; the cognate of the Hindi suffix has been replaced by *-ing* in English) |

Given these fairly dismal results on the basis of languages which we know to be related, the small number of correspondences between Indo-European and Uralic must be considered too limited to be persuasive. Much more massive evidence would be required for traditional comparativists even to entertain the possibility of genetic relationship.

The question, then, must be "How massive is 'massive'?" Clearly, one correspondence is not enough; nor are twenty. And just as clearly, a thousand correspondences with systematic recurrences of phonetic similarities and differences would be fairly persuasive. Are 500 enough, then? And if not, are 501 sufficient? Nobody can give a satisfactory answer to these questions.

And this is no doubt the reason that linguists may disagree over whether a particular proposed genetic relationship is sufficiently supported or not.

Traditional historical linguists would believe that ultimately, the question is irrelevant, since genetic relationship is safely established only through reconstruction, not just through simple vocabulary comparison. After all, they would argue, only reconstruction gives us the ability to state with confidence that the similarities in (6c–e) are false friends.

Moreover, traditional comparativists feel that in order to be successful, reconstruction has to be based on a certain minimal amount of lexical evidence. Without such evidence it becomes difficult, if not impossible, to decide on a particular reconstruction, rather than another, a priori equally possible one. For example, there was a recent attempt to show that Dravidian is related to Elamite, the language of the rulers who preceded the Old Persian king-emperors (6th–4th c. B.C.).

The corpus of Elamite texts is very small, providing an extremely limited basis for comparison. Nevertheless, the Elamo-Dravidian hypothesis at first looked very promising, since it went beyond vocabulary comparison and proposed a reconstruction. Many traditional comparativists, however, felt that the evidence of Elamite is too limited to permit reconstructing a sufficiently large number of lexical items (or enough aspects of linguistic structure) to establish the case beyond a reasonable doubt. Under the circumstances, it would be very difficult to be certain that the reconstructions – and the postulated changes relating the reconstructed forms to their attested descendants – might not be ad hoc. They might work just for the limited number of lexical items on which the reconstruction is based; but there is no guarantee that they would work at all if new data were to be added. Only a very large amount of data would make it possible to test the basic validity of the reconstruction. (This argument is vulnerable to some degree; for even in Indo-European, for which we have a very large amount of data, the addition of new data from Hittite and other Anatolian languages changed our reconstruction. But the changes involved only parts, not the entire system of reconstructed PIE. Moreover, in some cases the Anatolian evidence merely helped to confirm analyses proposed earlier, based on the evidence of the non-Anatolian languages.)

Critics soon felt that their skepticism was confirmed, because the author of the Elamo-Dravidian hypothesis proposed another, radically different reconstruction, on the basis of the same limited data and without being able to convince other linguists that this reconstruction was any better than the first one. Clearly, it was felt, if two radically different reconstructions can be proposed without any persuasive arguments for choosing one over the other, then the data base must be too limited and, thus, there must be something wrong with the entire approach.

Traditional historical linguists, therefore, are equally skeptical about recent attempts at establishing a Nostratic family, even though these attempts, too, go beyond lexical comparison and propose reconstructions. Again, they feel that the vocabulary evidence is too limited to be certain that the reconstructions are on the right track.

The traditionalists' skepticism is confirmed by the fact that Nostraticists disagree amongst each other over whether particular words should be considered genetically related, or rather ancient borrowings.

This is the case, for instance, for relationships such as Altaic **poku-* (or the like) 'ox, bovine animal', inferable from Monguor *fuɣuor*, Mong. *hüker*, Turk. *öküz*, and possibly related to Ainu *peko*, Jap. *beko* vs. PIE **peḱu-* 'cattle, property'. Some Nostraticists believe that the words are related, descended from Proto-Nostratic, others consider the words of the Altaic and other non-Indo-European languages to be borrowings from Indo-European. Yet others claim that the Indo-European word is borrowed from Semitic. (Note incidentally that Turk. *öküz* : Engl. *ox* are a perfect example of chance similarity.)

Skeptics find further grounds for doubt in reconstructions such as **kuyon* or **küyna* 'dog, wolf', **mad/med-* 'honey, mead', or **ʔam(m)/ʔem(m)* 'mother'.

Cases like **ʔam(m)/ʔem(m)* 'mother' may be nursery words, comparable to *mama, amma* 'mother' in many modern languages. (See Chapter 16, § 2.)

The type **mad/med-* 'honey, mead' can be suspected to belong to the category of words for cultural artifacts or techniques which are notoriously easily diffused through borrowing. Compare Chapter 16, § 7 on Algonquian 'fire-water', and Chapter 18, § 4.2 on the word for 'hemp'. See also Chapter 8, § 1, for the wide diffusion of words for 'sugar' and 'candy' which originated in Sanskrit.

Some linguists have also suspected the value of the reconstruction **kuyon* or **küyna* 'dog, wolf' since, they would argue, dogs are not descended from wolves but are related to jackals. (Actually, specialists on dogs do not seem to be so certain on this matter; one hears again and again that important aspects of canine behavior reflect lupine (i.e., wolf) origin.) Proponents of the Nostratic hypothesis can counter by pointing to Southern Arabic dialects which use the same word for 'dog' and 'wolf'.

What seems to have escaped both sides of this issue is that the phonetic similarities in words such as PIE **ḱuwon-* which form the basis for the reconstruction, can be attributed to onomatopoeia. As noted in Chapter 7,

§ 5.3, in a number of Indo-European languages, the original word for 'dog' was replaced by words with initial *ku-*, such as Sanskrit *kurkura-*, literally no doubt 'the one that snarls, growls, or barks, i.e., makes the sound [kurkur]', Mod. Hindi *kuttā*, Modern English *cur*, and its semantic Modern German equivalent *Köter*. Similar developments are found outside Indo-European, as in Tamil *kurai* 'to bark' : *kūraṇ* 'dog'.

Strictly speaking this does not prove that the reconstruction **kuyon* or **küyna* is impossible. However, the fact that *ku*-initial words for 'dog' evidently can arise independently, presumably as a result of onomatopoeia, casts doubt on the cogency of the reconstruction.

It is possible that as linguists keep adding to the evidence in favor of longer-range groupings such as Indo-Uralic or Nostratic, they will eventually reach the point where the majority of comparativists will accept the relationship between these languages (if they come to the issue with an open mind). At this point, however, the evidence still appears to be too limited. If the languages in question are related, their relationship may be too remote, too far removed from that optimal stage for comparison mentioned in Chapter 16, § 6, to be establishable beyond a reasonable doubt.

3. Are there any unrelated languages?

In the case of many other languages, traditional comparative linguists feel that there is no probative evidence whatsoever for outside genetic relationships. Such languages include Basque along the western part of the French/Spanish border, Sumerian in ancient Mesopotamia, and Burushaski in Northwest India. Languages of this sort are often called ISOLATES. Even more commonly they are referred to as "unrelated" to any other languages.

Strictly speaking, the term unrelated is not accurate – the word "unrelatable" would give a much better description. Except perhaps in the case of trying to relate a signed language with an oral language, we can never prove that two given languages are not related. It is always conceivable that they are related, but that the relationship is of such an ancient date that millennia of divergent linguistic changes have completely obscured the original relationship.

Ultimately, this issue is tied up with the question of whether there was a single or a multiple origin of Language, writ large (see § 5 below). And according to traditional comparativists, this question can be answered only in terms of unverifiable speculations, given the fact that even with the added time depth provided by reconstruction, our knowledge of the history of human languages does not extend much beyond ca. 5000 B.C., a small "slice" indeed out of the long prehistory of language. And as we have seen in (5) above, even shorter time-spans can obscure the evidence for genetic relationship.

4. Lexical mass comparison: Can it establish "Proto-World"?

As noted in § 1 above, the American linguist Greenberg claims that the difficulties that beset traditional comparative linguistics in trying to establish longer-range genetic relationships can be overcome by the method of lexical "mass comparison". Under this approach, genetic relationship can be established through comparison of a large number of languages, on a fairly limited lexical basis (about 200 to 250 lexical notions), simply by means of scoring cognates based on similarities in sound and meaning. While up to this point his work has been concerned with establishing long-distance genetic groupings such as a proposed Amerind family, Greenberg claims that his method in principle makes it possible to show that all (or most) of the world's languages are related.

Critics have argued that the ease with which chance-similarity sets of the type (6f) can be established casts doubt on Greenberg's method of determining cognation merely on the basis of phonetic and semantic similarities. They argue that false friends can only be eliminated by traditional comparative methodology which, as noted earlier, makes it possible to distinguish between true cognates and false friends.

Greenberg has replied to such criticism by claiming that his method yields correct insights in spite of these difficulties because it operates as MASS or MULTILATERAL comparison, comparing a large number of languages at the same time: "The method of multilateral comparison is so powerful that it will give reliable results even with the poorest of materials. Incorrect material should have merely a randomizing effect." Put differently, under mass comparison, errors will cancel each other out.

Greenberg's claim has recently been subjected to a rigorous statistical test on the basis of randomly generated lists of artificial vocabulary items. The test suggests that rather than reducing the possibility of chance similarities, an increase in the number of compared languages actually increases the chance of accidental resemblances in lists of lexical items comparable in size to those used by Greenberg.

Similar conclusions have been reached in empirical tests of Greenberg's methodology, using a limited word list, vis-à-vis Hindi, English, and Finnish, languages whose earlier history is known to us. As in the open-ended comparison of Hindi and English presented in § 2 above, the method produced not only genuine cognates, but also false friends. In fact, the ratio between genuine cognates and false friends is nearly 1 : 2 (no better than the results of the open-ended Hindi/English comparison reported in § 2 above). That is, even for clearly related languages, the method has less than a 50 : 50 chance of yielding correct results. Moreover, application of the method also suggests relationship between Hindi and English on one hand, and Finnish on the other. Interestingly, however, except for one correspondence, all of these similarities are false friends. Finally, expanding the basis by including data from German and Marathi fails to reduce the ratio of false friends.

Given this evidence, Greenberg's methodology of mass comparison must be considered to be of dubious reliability.

However, Greenberg and his associates, especially Merritt Ruhlen, find further support for his approach in the fact that it is possible to establish individual etymologies which they believe show that many, perhaps most, languages of the world are related. One of these etymologies is *tik* 'finger', with alleged reflexes in fifteen linguistic families. However, numerous empirical and methodological difficulties have been pointed out for this etymology, suggesting again that the similarities are simply due to chance. Given that the root consists of only three sounds, the possibility of chance similarity should not be surprising. Traditional historical linguists always have argued that chance similarities are more likely to occur in short words than in longer ones.

Most of Greenberg and Ruhlen's other long-range etymologies suffer from the same difficulty, of being overly short. There is, however, one exception. This is the etymology *maliq'a* 'throat, swallow' which Greenberg finds attested in his postulated Amerind family, in Eskimo-Aleut, and in four linguistic families of the "Old World" – Afro-Asiatic, Indo-European, Uralic, and Dravidian. See Table 1. (The organization of Table 1 closely follows that of Greenberg and Ruhlen; the major difference consists of the addition of identifying letters in the left margin for easier cross-reference.)

Unlike etymologies such as *tik* 'finger', this is a "robust" etymology, consisting of three syllables, and including three consonants and three vowels. Intuitively, this robustness seems to support Greenberg and Ruhlen's assertion that the "probability for a random similarity among [the] six fam-

Table 1. Greenberg & Ruhlen's **MALIQ'A* 'swallow, throat'

	Language family	Language	Form	Meaning
a.	Afro-Asiatic	PAfr.-As.	**mlg*	'to suck, breast, udder'
b.		Arabic	*mlǰ*	'to suck the breast'
c.		Old Egyptian	*mndᵞ*	'woman's breast, udder'
d.	Indo-European	PIE	**melg-*	'to milk'
e.		English	*milk*	'to milk, milk'
f.		Latin	*mulg-ēre*	'to milk'
g.	Uralic	P-Finno-Ugric	**mälke*	'breast'
h.		Saami	*mielga*	'breast'
i.		Hungarian	*mell*	'breast'
j.	Dravidian	Tamil	*melku*	'to chew'
k.		Malayalam	*melluka*	'to chew'
l.		Kurux	*melkhā*	'throat'
m.	Eskimo-Aleut	Central Yupik	*melug-*	'to suck'
n.	Amerind	Proto-Amerind	**maliq'a*	'to swallow, throat'
o.	Almosan	Halkomelem	*məlqw*	'throat'
p.		Kwakwala	*m'lXw-'id*	'chew food for the baby'
q.		Kutenai	*u'mqolh*	'to swallow'
r.	Penutian	Chinook	*mlqw-tan*	'cheek'
s.		Takelma	*mülk'*	'to swallow'
t.		Tfaltik	*milq*	'to swallow'
u.		Mixe	*amu'ul*	'to suck'
v.	Hokan	Mohave	*malᵞaqé*	'throat'
w.		Walapai	*malqi'*	'throat, neck'
x.		Akwa'ala	*milqi*	'neck'
y.	Chibchan	Cuna	*murki-*	'to swallow'
z.	Andean	Quechua	*malq'a*	'throat'
α.		Aymara	*malᵞq'a*	'to swallow, throat'
β.	Macro-Tucan.	Iranshe	*moke'i*	'neck'
γ.	Equatorial	Guamo	*mirko*	'to drink'
δ.	Macro-Carib	Surinam	*e'mōk*	'to swallow'
ε.		Faai	*mekeli*	'nape of the neck'
ζ.		Kaliana	*imukulali*	'throat'

ilies [examined]" is "about one chance in 10 billion", as well as the added remark, "So much for accidental resemblances."

As it turns out, however, the etymology is not at all as robust as it appears on first sight. First, Greenberg permits a fair amount of latitude in the phonetic correspondences, including metathesis (in items u., q., ε., and ζ. of Table 1) and loss of one or another root consonant (e.g. β., δ.). Moreover, vowel correspondences are ignored altogether. (In this context note the epigraph at the beginning of Chapter 4.) Similarly there are considerable variations in the semantics, including 'swallow, throat', 'suck', 'chew', 'milk', 'breast', and 'neck'.

Now, most of the developments that might be responsible for these variations are quite natural, or at least not unusual. In fact, given enough time, such variations in form and meaning are not only possible; they arc to be expected. Compare example (5c) above for the phonetic divergences between Modern Hindi and English as compared to the earlier, Sanskrit and Old English stages.

The real problem lies first of all in the fact that some of Greenberg's data are suspect. For instance, the Dravidian (Tamil) *melku* most likely consists of a root *mel-*, actually attested in the same meaning, plus a suffix *-ku-*. The etymology of the Indo-European words for 'milk' is highly controversial; but most Indo-Europeanists prefer derivation from a root **melĝ-* 'stroke, wipe', attested in this meaning in Sanskrit *mr̥j-*, with a semantic development comparable to that found in Latv. *slaukt* 'to milk' vs. Lith. *šliaukti* 'sweep'. (There are numerous parallels both in Indo-European and in Dravidian for the notion 'to milk' being expressed by verbs referring to the action of manipulating an udder to produce milk.) The Finno-Ugric words for 'breast' ordinarily refer to the chest or forepart of animals, not to women's breasts.

Even more important, given enough phonetic and semantic leeway – which we should expect, given the great time-depth at which the languages must be related (if they are indeed related) – it is amazingly easy to find alternative candidates as descendants of **maliq'a* 'throat, swallow'. See for instance the examples in (8), with in each case an indication (i) of the phonetic developments and (ii) the semantic changes that would putatively relate a given word to **maliq'a* 'throat, swallow'.

(8)   a. Afro-Asiatic

        Egypt. *ʕm* 'swallow', Cushitic *am* 'eat, devour', Somali *ʕon/ʕun* 'eat'

            (i) *l* > Ø; metathesis of stop and nasal; *q'* > ʕ

            (ii) No significant changes

        Arab. *qmm* 'devour', Cushitic *qam* (etc.)

            (i) *l* > Ø; metathesis of stop and nasal; Arabic doubling of *m* (?)

            (ii) No significant changes

        Sem. *lqq* 'lick', Egypt. Demotic *lkh* 'lick', etc., Cushitic *lanqi* (etc.) 'tongue'

                             (i) $m > \emptyset$, in a form like *$mliq$'a*; stop doubling
                             (ii) 'swallow' → 'suck' → 'lick' → 'tongue'

b. Indo-European:

leigh- 'lick'
    (i) $m > \emptyset$, in a form like *$mliq$'a*
    (ii) 'swallow' → 'suck' → 'lick'

melH- 'grind'
    (i) q' > "laryngeal" H
    (ii) 'swallow' → 'chew' → 'grind'

gel- 'throat, swallow'
    (i) $m > \emptyset$, in a form like *$mliq$'a*; metathesis of l and stop
    (ii) No change

g^wer- 'throat, swallow'
    (i) Similar to preceding; but velar > labiovelar (as in items o. and r. of Table 1; and $l >$ r as in item y. of Table 1)
    (ii) No change

c. Uralic:

ñele 'swallow'
    (i) Palatalization of m; loss of stop
    (ii) No change

ñole 'lick'
    (i) Palatalization of m; loss of stop
    (ii) 'swallow' → 'suck' → 'lick'

ñɤkkɜ 'neck'
    (i) Palatalization of m; assimilation of l
    (ii) see item β. in Table 1.

kelä 'tongue, language'
    (i) $m > \emptyset$; metathesis of stop and l
    (ii) 'swallow' → 'suck' → 'lick' → 'tongue' etc.

d. Dravidian

miṟuŋku 'swallow'
    (i) $l > ṟ$, "prenasalization" of k, common in Dravid.
    (ii) No change

mār 'breast'
    (i) $l > r$, q' $> \emptyset$
    (ii) See items a.–c., g.–i. of Table 1

mulai 'breast'
    (i) $k > \emptyset$
    (ii) See items a.–c., g.–i. of Table 1

mukku 'gobble'
    (i) Assimilation of l to k
    (ii) 'swallow' → 'gobble (up)'

Alternatives like these are by no means limited to the languages in example (8). Similar alternatives can be found in numerous Indigenous American languages, as well as in such families as Altaic, Bantu, and Austronesian.

The fact that it is so easy to find alternatives of this type raises important questions about Greenberg's long-range etymology: What are the criteria for choosing among different alternatives without arbitrariness? Which are the genuine cognates, if any? And which are the false friends? Important here is the fact that barring special circumstances, at most one form per language or language family can be a true cognate; the others must be false friends.

Greenberg does not address this issue. Implicitly he seems to be operating with the idea that the forms should be maximally similar both phonetically and semantically. But this is hardly a realistic approach. As examples like (6b) above illustrate, given enough time, genuine cognates often become differentiated beyond recognition.

There may in fact be no answer to this question, short of comparative reconstruction. But to do reconstruction requires much richer evidence and a methodology markedly different from Greenberg's mass comparison.

Further, the very ease with which alternatives of the type (8) can be found calls into question Greenberg's claim that the similarities in his data cannot be due to chance. Whatever may be the mathematical foundation of his calculation that the chance of finding the similarities in Table 1 is one in ten billion, the empirical evidence suggests that the conclusion is incorrect.

Far from corroborating Greenberg's mass comparison, the long-range etymology *maliq'a* 'throat, swallow' actually casts further doubt on any approach that involves setting up "cognates" merely on the basis of similarities in sound and meaning. What it suggests instead is that only the traditional approach, however cumbersome and time-consuming it may be, makes it possible to distinguish true cognates from false friends.

At this point, then, there is no credible alternative to the cumbrous and time-consuming traditional method of comparative linguistics. And, as noted earlier, this method is at this point incapable of successfully establishing even longer-range relationships, not to mention settling the question of whether all the world's (spoken) languages are related.

This may be considered regrettable, for it would indeed be marvelous if we could establish longer-distance relationships or even prove that all the world's languages are descended from a common ancestor. But perhaps it is better to acknowledge our ignorance, our inability to come up with definite conclusions, rather than to believe that we have found the answers.

This way the challenge remains to look farther and deeper. And even if we may never reach the goal of establishing relationship for all the world's languages, we are bound to gather new insights in our quest for that goal and over time we may even succeed in more firmly establishing longer-range relationships such as those of Ural-Altaic, Indo-Uralic, Lislakh, or even Nostratic.

5. The origin of Language

The controversy over Proto-World is really about the origin of all known (oral) languages; and indeed, under ideal, but most likely unattainable, conditions, we might perhaps catch a glimpse of the nature of the mother tongue from which all spoken languages are derived – either through application of the traditional method of comparative linguistics (if sufficient new evidence is found) or through Greenberg's mass comparison (if strict controls make it possible to eliminate the difficulties with this method). Still, catching a glimpse of the mother tongue is a far cry from receiving an answer to what might be thought of as the ultimate question in historical linguistic research: How did the mother tongue itself originate? That is, How did Language (writ large) come about?

Over the centuries, some peoples have sought the solution by looking to the heavens or to supernatural forces, as in the myths of various Indigenous American peoples (see § 1 above), and as also supposed by the ancient Egyptians, and early Christian writers such as Origen (3rd c. A.D.). Others saw language as a human invention and worried about what the inspiration was for the form of the invented words – did they arise as imitations of sounds in nature (the so-called bow-wow theory), or as derivatives from human interjections (the so-called pooh-pooh or yo-he-ho theory), or in yet other ways? In 1866, the Linguistic Society of Paris declared that any theories on the origin of language were by their very nature so speculative that they should no longer be discussed in its meetings. But the issue of language origin is too important to human beings for its discussion to be forever banished from popular or scholarly consideration.

Since at this point, comparative linguistics (whether Greenbergian, Nostraticist, or Traditionalist) evidently cannot provide answers to the question of language origin, scholars interested in this issue have drawn on a wide range of other resources. The evidence that researchers have looked at includes the following:

– observable examples of language genesis, including normal language development in children; language development in hearing or deaf children

with no exposure to language input of any sort; the origination of pidgin languages; and the development of creoles
- physiological evidence that might reveal aspects of the evolutionary development of the human capacity for language, such as comparative anatomy and fossil records
- the language abilities of creatures evolutionarily related to humans, as these abilities manifest themselves both under natural conditions and under training by human instructors or intimate exposure to human linguistic behavior

We briefly examine below some of the insights that might emerge from these sources.

The study of language development in children seems quite promising at first sight. The stages of normal development have been studied and are fairly well understood. It is tempting to extrapolate from these stages and to hypothesize that they recapitulate the evolutionary stages of human language development, in accordance with the Biogenetic Law, "Ontogeny recapitulates phylogeny", first formulated by Ernst Haeckel in 1866. However, one finding of child language development research is that, to be successful, the acquisition of language depends on the stimulus of other language users (generally the adult care-givers at first, but later the child's peer group). This finding is reinforced by the differences between normal child language acquisition and abnormal – and fortunately, quite rare – cases, in which children have to develop a language without human stimulus. (In fact, well-documented cases of abnormal language development always involve some kind of human stimulus, even though the stimulus may come very late, or in spoken form when signed language input is needed.) The study of child language development, therefore, cannot provide definite answers to the question of how human language may first have arisen – when by definition there was no prior human input.

The case is very similar as far as the development of pidgins and creoles is concerned; for these, too, depend on human language input, in the form of already-existing languages. Bickerton's "bioprogram" hypothesis (Chapter 14, § 5) might prove more useful, in that it postulates an innate form of grammar that manifests itself exclusively in creolization and therefore differs substantially from the grammar of ordinary languages. It might be hypothesized that this innate grammar is closer to the grammar of the early stages of human linguistic evolution. But as noted in Chapter 14, Bickerton's hypothesis is controversial; it therefore does not provide a solid foundation for theories on the origin of language.

Some researchers have looked for clues to the origin of language in evidence from physical anthropology, including the study of human fossils, comparative anatomy, or structures in non-humans – or even non-primates – that are analogous to the human organs of speech (such as the vocal tracts of apes or even the air passages of frogs and lungfish). Some important findings have emerged, such as the observation that the speech organs did not evolve for the purpose of speech, but rather, that speech is an "overlay" function, superimposed on a vocal tract originally developed for other purposes. Measurements of the vocal tracts of apes show them to be quite different from those of adult humans, and actually somewhat similar to those of human newborns. The study of fossil skulls of Neanderthals, evolutionary cousins to modern humans, has suggested that Neanderthals may not have been able to articulate the full range of speech sounds found in known human languages, and thus may also have lacked the perceptual apparatus to process the full range of human speech sounds. These observations, taken together, suggest that human language as we know it today may be a fairly recent evolutionary innovation, perhaps on the order of 50,000 to 100,000 years old, although less complex and less highly structured forms of communication in pre-human ancestors could be much older. These claims, however, remain controversial. For instance, the claim that Neanderthals were incapable of producing and understanding language as we know it is based on examination of a single skull that may have been damaged by arthritis and physical trauma. Moreover, the evolutionary situation is very complex: As many as 100 developmental factors have been identified by some scholars as contributing, directly or indirectly, to the ultimate emergence of human language; and the evolutionary history of many of these factors is still poorly understood. Nevertheless, the comparative physiological approach has improved our understanding of the physical developments associated with the emergence of language.

Other researchers have turned to the linguistic abilities and behavior of primates, such as chimpanzees and gorillas, as they can be inferred from both their natural call systems in the wild and their latent abilities, drawn out through instruction in a sign language (often a modified form of an existing signed language) or in the use of representational symbols such as plastic tokens. The idea here is that the study of primate abilities and behavior can help us understand the linguistic abilities and behavior of human beings just before the development of language as we know it. The natural communication systems of apes consist of a closed set of calls, about twenty in number, and certainly show nothing resembling the complexity of human language. However, some observers have seen in these systems the potential for developing the open-endedness and complexity of human language. The attempts to tap the latent linguistic abilities of apes have resulted in some dramatic claims of language learning by these apes; but many linguists consider these claims quite controversial. More important, it is not at all obvious that the linguistic training of apes by human instructors can tell us anything about how humans may have first acquired language at a time when there were no other living beings that could have instructed them.

What may be more significant is that the successes in training apes in some kind of language (however far removed that language may have been from human speech) were accomplished by employing non-oral means of communication – modified forms of signed language or systems based on plastic tokens. Moreover, as we have seen in Chapter 16, § 8, numerous signed language systems have developed spontaneously around the world. One theory of language origin, therefore, becomes quite attractive, namely the so-called gestural theory, according to which human language first originated in a gestural "channel", and the shift to the speech channel was a secondary development. This switch in channel, it is suggested, may have started with movements in the vocal organs, especially the tongue, that mimicked manual gestures. An alternative hypothesis, not necessarily in conflict with this view, is that vocal sounds at first were emphasizing accompaniments to meaningful manual gestures, just as facial expressions and gesticulations now can accompany speech as a form of non-verbal "paralanguage". Some researchers further claim that the complete switch to the speech channel was motivated by the fact that it enabled human beings to use their hands for purposes other than communication and still to effectively communicate through the speech channel. Nevertheless, many researchers remain skeptical.

While all these different theories, lines of investigations, and threads of evidence are fascinating and provocative, we must admit that there is no definitive answer as yet to this most interesting and far-reaching question of how human language originated. The controversy over this issue will therefore go on, perhaps forever. But if language really is one of the defining characteristics of human beings – a view dear to most of us, even if open to debate – it may well be a good thing that the answer to what started us on the road to humanity lies beyond our grasp, for this will encourage us to continue to examine ourselves, our place in the world, and the role language plays for us as human beings.

Chapter 18
Historical linguistics, history, and prehistory: Linguistic paleontology and other applications of our methods

> We have found a strange footprint on the shores of the unknown. We have devised profound theories, one after another, to account for its origin. At last we have succeeded in reconstructing the creature that made the footprint. And lo! it is our own.
> (Arthur Stanley Eddington, *Space, Time, and Gravitation*, Chapter 12.)

> The past is a foreign country; they do things differently there.
> (Lesley Poles Hartley, *The Go-Between*, prologue.)

1. Introduction

One of the most exciting aspects of doing historical work of any kind is the thrill of getting a glimpse of events that may have happened eons before our time. While the results of doing historical work are sometimes speculative, they are always interesting. In this chapter we examine a number of ways in which historical linguistics, and especially comparative linguistics, can contribute to historical and prehistorical debates, thus allowing us, in a sense, to reveal the "history" in historical linguistics.

2. Linguistic comparison as a detective's tool: The Tasaday of the Philippines

In 1971 an incredible discovery was reported in the Philippines by Manuel Elizalde, Jr., a government official responsible for national minorities.

Elizalde announced that a heretofore isolated community of some twenty-five people had been found living in caves in the rain forest of Cotabato, a region on Mindanao, the southernmost island of the Philippines – seemingly following a way of life that was described as "Stone Age". They came to be called the Tasaday, after the name of their mountain ridge home. Since virtually every part of the world has been explored and opened to contact with modern civilization, a discovery of this sort naturally stirred up considerable interest among anthropologists, archaeologists, historians, and the general public, not just in the Philippines but around the world.

What makes this case fascinating is that not long after their discovery, suspicions about the authenticity of the Tasaday began to emerge. Some charged that Elizalde had staged a hoax, partly perhaps for purposes of political gain or for the celebrity that followed the "discovery".

After 1974, the Tasaday were no longer in the news, and martial law in the Philippines imposed by then-President Ferdinand Marcos made entry into the Tasaday area and contact with them illegal, thus effectively closing off further access by Philippine scholars or anyone from the outside world. In 1986, after the fall of Marcos's government, access to the Tasaday again became possible, and visitors reported evidence that the whole "discovery" had indeed been a hoax. These claims too, however, have not gone unchallenged, and the controversy remains, though with the added twist that there have now been several, heretofore unsuccessful, lawsuits filed by Elizalde countering those who accuse him of perpetrating a fraud. The potential for uncovering a scandal in the Marcos government gave the story an extra dimension that enhanced its already considerable intrinsic interest.

On the scientific side, the researchers interested in the Tasaday controversy naturally included linguists, since the uncovering of a new speech community immediately raised questions about the nature and affinities of the language spoken by the community. Even more significant, it was realized that linguistic evidence could play a role in deciding the issue of authenticity. Questions to be investigated included whether the language of the Tasaday can be shown to be a member of an existing language group, whether it shows noticeable divergences from its linguistic relatives, and whether their relative degree of isolation thus can be substantiated by linguistic evidence. All of these, of course, are questions for historical and comparative linguists, offering them an opportunity to apply their methods to a real world issue – getting at the truth about the Tasaday.

It was clear from the start, based on a comparison of vocabulary and on general structural characteristics, that the Tasaday language is a Malayo-Polynesian language and is probably closely related to the language known as Cotabato Manobo. It was further claimed that the Tasaday language has no loan words from neighboring languages, in keeping with its presumed isolation. One linguist found added support for the Tasaday community's isolation by applying a method called glottochronology, in which one compares word-lists of related languages and measures the degree of divergence against a formula for the supposed rate of lexical replacement through time (see § 5 below). The results were at first intriguing: Evaluation of a limited word list of the Tasaday language suggested a divergence from sibling languages of at least 125 years and possibly as much as 750 years, consistent with the claim that the isolation of Tasaday is authentic. However, beyond the problematic nature of glottochronology (see § 5 below), this study suffered from the fact that it was not carried out by a specialist in the group of languages to which Tasaday supposedly belongs. More careful study of the language by experts on Cotabato Manobo has revealed that the Tasaday speak nothing more than a different variety of that language, and one not really too divergent at all.

Thus it would appear in the end that the linguistic evidence supports the hoax theory. The interesting thing from our perspective is that even though the glottochronological evidence turned out not to be conclusive, a different application of historical and comparative linguistics was helpful in deciding this fascinating scientific and human problem, with all its political ramifications.

As is often the case in any attempt at proof, a positive result on a single test is not necessarily sufficient, since the test itself may have to be tested and evaluated. That is in the nature of scientific inquiry. Still, in the case of the Tasaday, it was through an investigation of the historical and comparative linguistic evidence that we could come to a better understanding. The methods and results of historical and comparative linguistics thus can indeed contribute to public debates and public issues, and therefore deserve a fair hearing where appropriate.

3. Comparative linguistics and comparative law

Linguistic comparison played an important role in the Tasaday case, although the comparative method itself (as we have come to know it in Chapter 16) played only a minor role. In many other cases, however, comparative linguistics can be a remarkably powerful tool, serving as a time machine, as it were, offering a window into the past, often into distant prehistory. The utility of the comparative method extends well beyond the reconstruction of sounds and sound patterns. The reconstructed sounds "spell out" words of the ancestral language. It is in this way that we are able to say that the word for 'father' sounded something close to [pətēr] in the mouths of the speakers of Proto-Indo-European (or perhaps [p(h)ət(h)ēr, if the glottalic theory is correct; see Chapter 16, § 7).

Along with the words, moreover, we are able to reconstruct different inflected forms, the endings that define these forms, and much of the remaining morphology. Thus we can reconstruct for the word 'father' not just a nominative singular form *pətēr, but also an accusative singular *pətérm̥ (based on, for instance, Greek *patéra* = Sanskrit *pitáram*), a dative singular *pətr-(e)i (based on, for instance, Greek *patrí*, Sanskrit *pitré*, Latin *patri*), and forms for all the other cases enumerated in Chapter 2, § 2.

We are also able to isolate a stem *pətér-, and a set of vowel alternations keyed to particular grammatical categories (here, specifically, case forms): lengthening of the suffix vowel in the nominative *pətēr, suppression of that vowel in the dative *pətr-(e)i = *pətØr-(e)i, and so on. This morphological process of vowel change, referred to as ablaut, is found throughout the Indo-European languages, and is responsible, for instance, for English alternations such as *sing / sang / sung* (from PIE *seng^wh- / *song^wh- / *sn̥g^wh-, respectively).

We can even reconstruct aspects of the syntax of the ancestral language, even though we would be hard put to reconstruct real texts.

But the comparative method is not limited to linguistic structure and the lexicon. It can be extended to other domains and can be put to work to reconstruct aspects of culture.

To take an example from Indo-European law: In the ancient Roman, Greek, and Hittite legal traditions, one finds a parallel treatment of offenses committed by someone who is not considered a legal person – a slave, a child, a cow, or the like. In principle, several outcomes are possible; for example, declaring the offense to be a nonoffense (as is done with some juvenile offenses in the United States); providing restitution; turning the offender over to the person who suffered from the offense; and so on. What is interesting is that all three ancient traditions offer the same resolution – a choice is allowed between restitution and turning the offender over to the plaintiff. Thus, the structures of the legal codes are completely parallel, with not just one outcome being prescribed but a choice between two outcomes and, moreover, the same choices (out of several conceivable ones) being specified in all three traditions. Further, cognate vocabulary is used: Latin uses the verb *sarcire* 'to make amends for' and Hittite the related verb *sark-* 'make restitution for'.

For the alternative action, of 'giving over', Greek uses the verb *para-dídōmi* (root: *dō-* 'to give') and Latin the verb *dedere* (also from the root *dō-*).

The structural parallels combined with the linguistic parallels thus permit us to infer a common origin for the legal practices being compared and even provide us with an idea of the technical legal language covering such situations in Proto-Indo-European.

In fact, even through the reconstruction of more mundane individual lexical items, the comparative method can provide information about the society, culture, and ecology of the ancestral speech community.

These and other applications and implications of the comparative method are examined in the following sections.

4. Comparative reconstruction as a window on prehistory: Linguistic paleontology

The fact that we can reconstruct vocabulary of the proto-language raises interesting questions beyond the sheer pleasures of linguistic discovery – questions that are of intense concern to prehistorians.

For instance, if we can reconstruct PIE words for 'horse' (**eḱwos*), 'cow, bovine animal' (**gʷōws*), and 'dog' (**ḱuwōn*), this tells us a great deal about the degree to which the speakers of PIE had succeeded in domesticating animals; for clearly, it makes no sense to have the words without also having the animals, objects, ideas, and concepts that the words refer to.

Drawing on linguistic evidence of this type to make inferences about the culture, society, and ecology of prehistoric peoples is commonly known as LINGUISTIC PALEONTOLOGY.

Although linguistic paleontology can in principle be applied to the ancestor of any established language family, the following examples are drawn from Indo-European, since research both on reconstruction and on linguistic paleontology has been conducted most successfully for this family. Even so, many issues of Indo-European linguistic paleontology are controversial – especially the ones that would be of greatest interest to the student of general prehistory.

4.1. Material culture and economy

As just noted, we can reconstruct names for domestic animals such as 'horse' and 'cow, bovine animal' for Proto-Indo-European. Other names for domesti-

cated animals that we can reconstruct are 'pig' and 'sheep', and perhaps also
'goat'. We are therefore entitled to believe that the Indo-Europeans (short for
"the speakers of Proto-Indo-European") had a fairly well developed cattle-
raising economy.

The importance of domestic animals in Proto-Indo-European economy can
be gauged from the fact that the word *pek̂us* could be used to refer both
to 'cattle' (compare Skt. *paśu-* 'cattle, esp. bovine cattle', Lat. *pecus* '(herd
of) cattle', Germ. *Vieh* 'cattle, beast') and to 'property, wealth' in general
(Lat. *pecunia* 'property, wealth; money', Engl. *fee*). Opinions are divided on
whether we should reconstruct 'cattle' or 'property, wealth' as the original
meaning. But one thing we can be certain of – cattle and cattle raising formed
a significant basis, perhaps the major one, for measuring wealth in Indo-
European society.

The strong evidence in favor of cattle raising contrasts with the much
weaker – and controversial – evidence with regard to farming. We find cognate words for 'field', 'plough', and 'sow, seed' in many Indo-European languages. But cognates for these words, in these meanings, are systematically
absent in Indo-Iranian.

As it turns out, the widespread words for 'field' and 'sow, seed', which
could be reconstructed as *aĝros* and *sē-* respectively, can be derived from
roots with more general, less specifically agricultural meanings: *aĝ-* 'drive
(especially of cattle)' and *sē-* 'throw, cast'. In the case of the word for
'field', therefore, one suspects that its original meaning was 'area where the
cattle are driven' = 'pasture'. As for 'sow' it is interesting to note that words
for 'throw, cast' or 'put, place' are used to refer to sowing in several Indo-
European languages, such as Gk. *speírō*, Mod. Ir. *cuirim*, and Skt. *vap-*. The
specialization of *sē-* to refer to 'sow', therefore, could well be an innovation,
perhaps in late Proto-Indo-European or, less likely, in the individual daughter
languages. Moreover, even if *sē-* was used to refer to sowing in PIE, it is
conceivable that the sowing was not done into ploughed, permanent fields,
but into holes dug into the soil of cleared areas in temporarily occupied
territory. According to this view, then, the Indo-Europeans may have been
pastoralists who were just at the threshold of agriculture.

However, a different view is possible, too. The absence of cognate words
for 'field', 'plough', and 'sow, seed' in Indo-Iranian could result from the
fact that the Indo-Iranians migrated away from a mixed pastoral/agricultural
society. And because they migrated over vast distances and for many generations, they gave up agricultural life and the words that went along with it
and concentrated on pastoralism, which was easier to maintain during their
long treks.

There is even a third hypothesis: The fact that cognate words for agricultural terminology are lacking in Indo-Iranian reflects a division within Proto-Indo-European society. The more western tribes or clan groups had begun to develop at least some rudimentary forms of agriculture, presumably because they lived in areas with soil and climate conditions that were more conducive to farming. The more eastern tribes, by contrast, lived in an area with less fertile soil and harsher climate and therefore stuck to pastoralism.

In this regard a word for 'bull', shared by the more western languages, might be significant. The word is attested in Gk. *taûros*, Lat. *taurus* and cognates in other old Italic languages, Gaulish *tarvos* and other Celtic languages, Old Icel. *þjórr* and other Germanic languages, Old Prussian *tauris*, possibly in Engl. *steer*, Germ. *Stier* 'bull', and perhaps also in Lith. *tauras*, OCS *turŭ* 'wild ox'. An Indo-European derivation from something like *təw-* 'be strong' is possible. But we find similar words in Semitic, such as Arab. *θawr-*. Some scholars attribute this similarity to common inheritance from Nostratic or Lislakh (see Chapter 17, § 1). But given its restricted distribution in Indo-European and its absence in Indo-Iranian – even though it is a pastoral, not an agricultural word – it is more likely that it is an early borrowing from Semitic or Afro-Asiatic.

A number of other words connected with agriculture and cattle raising seem to be similarly connected to Semitic or Afro-Asiatic. For instance, the Germanic words for 'goat' (including Engl. *goat*) and their Latin cognate *haedus* 'kid' bear strong resemblance to Semitic words like Hebr. *gəðî* 'kid'; and the Greek, Latin, Armenian, and Hittite words for 'wine' (*oînos* < **woyno-*; *vinum, gini* < **weyno-*; *wiyana-*) are commonly acknowledged to be of Near Eastern, probably Semitic or Afro-Asiatic origin (compare Arab. *wayn-* 'black grapes', Akkadian *īnu-* 'wine'). (The Germanic words, such as Engl. *wine*, are borrowings from Latin.) See also § 4.2 below on the word for 'hemp'.

Given the evidence of 'bull' and other pastoral/agricultural words in western Indo-European languages that are likely to be borrowed from Semitic or Afro-Asiatic, one may begin to wonder whether the western Indo-European agricultural words for 'field', 'plough', and 'sow, seed' may likewise owe their origin to Semitic or Afro-Asiatic influence. Archeologists find much evidence indicating that many important aspects of European agriculture, perhaps even all of agriculture, spread from the ancient Near East. While words such as 'bull' may be taken to testify to this spread directly – as words adopted from Semitic or Afro-Asiatic – words such as 'field' may reflect the spread indirectly – as calques or loan shifts, using indigenous Indo-European elements to recreate the designations coming from the Near East (see Chapter 8, § 3).

At the same time, we do have evidence for at least one Proto-Indo-European word for a cereal grain, **yewo-*, attested in Skt. *yava-* 'corn, grain', later 'barley', Avest. *yava-* 'grain', Lith. *javai* 'grain', and with semantic specialization comparable to later Skt. 'barley', Gk. *zeaí* 'spelt'. But as noted earlier, grain may have been sown in holes dug in temporary plots, rather than in established, ploughed fields. Note further that the Indo-European word for 'grain' was borrowed into Finno-Ugric, compare Finn. *jyvä* 'corn, grain', Votyak *ju* 'threshed corn'. The fact that the word could later diffuse into Finno-Ugric suggests that it could have done the same thing in earlier Indo-European – as a "Wanderwort" comparable to many other agricultural items that are borrowed from language to language, often through a long chain of intermediate languages. (See Chapter 8, § 1 on the words for 'sugar' and 'candy'.)

Possible further complications arise in connection with the word for 'horse'. It has been claimed that Hittite and the other Anatolian languages lack inherited reflexes of this word, or for any other word connected with horses, such as especially the light, two-wheeled battle chariot used by most other early Indo-Europeans in their conquests. True, the Hittites, too, came to use horse-drawn battle chariots and thus became famous – or infamous – as a powerful force in the area (note the Biblical references to the Hittites). But there is strong evidence that they learned the art of horse training from the Mitanni, speakers of an Indo-Iranian language (see Chapter 2, § 3.10.3). This has led some linguists to conclude that the Hittites and other Anatolians acquired not only the art of horse training, but also the use of the two-wheeled battle chariot, and even the general use of horses from the Mitanni. This conclusion, however, is not inevitable. It is not at all clear that the art of horse training conveyed by the Mitanni to the Hittites concerned battle chariots; it is at least equally possible that it merely concerned the training of race horses. Even if the Hittites learned the use of the two-wheeled battle chariot from the Mitanni, this does not mean that they did not know horses. They may have used them for more mundane purposes or for riding. Finally, as noted in Chapter 3, § 2.3, the Hittite texts are written in a composite system, employing symbols – and words – not only in their Hittite value, but also in the values of Akkadian (an earlier form of Assyrian) and Sumerian. Many words – including the numeral 1 – therefore happen to be attested only in "Akkadograms" or "Sumerograms". In fact, the word for 'horse' is expressed by the Sumerogram ANSU.KUR.RA, which may explain the absence of an Indo-European word for 'horse' in the Hittite texts.

There are Anatolian languages with more helpful writing systems. And in some of these we do find words for 'horse'; compare Hieroglyphic Luwian *asu(wa)-* and Lycian *esbe* < **eswe-*. Some scholars consider these words inherited from Proto-Indo-European **ekwos*, pointing to the recurrence of the sound change **ḱ* > *s* in inherited words for 'dog' and 'horn'. Other linguists dismiss this view and claim that all of the words are cultural borrowings from Indo-Iranian. (The claim that even a word like 'horn' can be borrowed should not be dismissed lightly: Finno-Ugric did in fact borrow the word from Indo-Iranian.) Those who advocate a borrowing hypothesis point to the fact that Hittite does not shift **ḱ* to *s* in words that happen to have survived – or are attested – in the language. But this overlooks the fact that Hittite and Luwian/Lycian belong to different subgroups of Anatolian, differentiated by a number of other developments. The different outcomes of **ḱ* in Hittite and Luwian/Lycian may be ascribed to similar differences in historical development. The arguments against the inheritance hypothesis therefore do not carry conviction. (See also the next section.)

As the controversy over "Anatolian horses" shows, disputes regarding linguistic paleontology often are fought out on the basis of very limited evidence and of arguments that – at least from the perspective of the non-linguist – are highly arcane.

While it is fairly certain, then, that the Indo-Europeans were pastoralists, other aspects of the use of domesticated animals and of agriculture are much less clear. This may come as a disappointment to prehistorians. Pastoralism is a widespread phenomenon at the relevant period in prehistory. If the comparative evidence permitted us to be certain that the Indo-Europeans used the plough or employed horse-drawn two-wheeled battle chariots, this would provide much more specific information for identifying the Indo-Europeans with physical artifacts that have been unearthed by archaeologists, and with the particular cultural sphere in which those artifacts were used.

Nevertheless, prehistorians may derive some comfort from the fact that, except perhaps for 'reindeer', words for domesticated animals apparently cannot be reconstructed for Proto-Uralic, a putative eastern neighbor of early Indo-European. This negative evidence could possibly be drawn on to establish the eastern boundary of Proto-Indo-European – if we could be certain that Uralic was in fact the closest neighbor to the east.

Let us round out this incomplete sketch of Indo-European material culture and economy by briefly examining the question of whether the Indo-Europeans are to be assigned to the Stone Age or to the (early) Metal Age. The available evidence suggests a weak "yes" on both counts. We can only reconstruct one word for metal that is usable for tools. This is **ayos/ayes*, the ancestor of Engl. *ore*, Goth. *aiz* 'copper', Lat. *aes* 'copper (ore), bronze', Skt. *ayas-* 'metal, iron'. The original meaning most likely included both 'copper' and its principal alloy, 'bronze'. The evidence of this word, then, would place the Indo-Europeans in the Bronze Age.

But there is much more evidence pointing in the direction of the Stone Age, presumably the Neolithic. Many of the tools bear names suggesting that they were originally made of stone or rock. Thus Germanic *sahs*, a short sword that proved very handy in battle against the Romans and provided the base for the name *Saxon*, is related to Lat. *saxum* 'rock, stone'. A modern reflex of the word is Engl. *zax*, the name of a cutting tool used by roofers (with "Somerset" voicing of *s* > *z*; see Chapter 10, § 7). The word also survives, in much more hidden form, in Mod. Germ. *Messer* which, believe it or not, is derived from an earlier **mati-sahs* 'food-sword' via *mezzira(h)s* (with **s* > **z* by Verner's Law, and then **z* > *r*; the *zz* of *mezzira(h)s* spells a "strong" or double [s̠s̠]; see Chapter 11, § 2.3). The English word *saw* and its cognates in other Germanic languages have been considered derived from the same root.

Similarly, *hammer* is a cognate of Slav. *kamy* 'rock'; and Greek *ákmōn* 'anvil' and Lithuanian *ašmens* 'cutting edge' are related to Sanskrit *aśman-* 'rock, stone'.

Further support for the view that the Indo-Europeans had a strong neolithic background comes from the fact that wooden and stone instruments, rather than metal ones, are used in many early Indo-European rituals. Rituals tend to be the most conservative aspects of religion and therefore to preserve both linguistic and material archaisms.

We may conclude, then, that the Indo-Europeans essentially had a neolithic background but had recently, in the late stages of Proto-Indo-European, entered the Bronze Age.

4.2. Ecology and the question of the "original home"

The fact that we can reconstruct words for three seasons (winter, spring, and summer) and for snow suggests that the Indo-Europeans lived in a relatively northern climate in which a cold season (with snow) alternated with a warm, summery season, with spring forming a kind of bridge between the two.

This impression is reinforced by the fact that while we can reconstruct words for 'wolf' and 'bear', we cannot do so with confidence for 'lion' and 'tiger', animals that are found farther south, in the warmer climates of the Mediterranean, Asia Minor, Iran, and South Asia. Some scholars, to be sure, have claimed that a word for 'lion' must be reconstructed for Proto-Indo-European, on the basis of correspondences such as Gk. *léōn*, Lat. *leō*, OHG *leo, lio, lewo*, Lith. *levas*, Pol. *lew*. But in languages such as Old High German, Lithuanian, and Polish, the words can hardly be inherited, since the animal they designate is not found in the areas in which the languages are spoken – and have been spoken throughout their attested history. When they appear in the early literature of these languages they refer to lions found in other parts of the world – or to lions in the metaphorical sense, as symbols of power and heroism, a use which of course likewise can have originated only in countries with lions. Moreover, South Asia, where Sanskrit was (and still is) spoken, includes areas where lions roam; but Sanskrit uses an entirely different word, *siṁha-* of somewhat uncertain origin. (This word, too, is used to indicate valor and power and underlies the common Indian name *Singh*, as well the name of the city-state *Singapore*, lit. 'the lion city'.) On balance, then, similar-sounding words for 'lion' are limited to Greek and Latin and to languages (Germanic, Baltic, and Slavic) in which they are likely to have been borrowed from Greek or Latin. Indo-Europeanists tend to be leery of words that are geographically limited in this way since such words may well be regional innovations (see the "beech tree" argument below). The evidence for reconstructing an Indo-European word for 'lion' therefore must be considered quite weak.

Attempts have also been made to use reconstructed names for fauna and flora to identify the ORIGINAL HOME of the Indo-Europeans (some linguists refer to the home area by the German term "Urheimat" ≈ 'proto-home'). The basic assumption is highly plausible: If we can reconstruct a word which refers to a particular plant or animal, then the speakers of Indo-European must have found that plant or animal in their environment. Through pollen samples in the appropriate layers of moors and through skeletal remains, it should then be possible to establish the area in which that plant or animal flourished some 5000 to 6000 years ago, at the time when it is commonly assumed Proto-Indo-European must have been spoken. And if we limit our investigation to those plants and animals whose habitat was geographically highly limited or even unique, we should be able to pinpoint the exact area in which the Indo-Europeans lived.

Using this approach, some scholars have claimed that the original home of the Indo-Europeans must have been in an area of central and western Europe, to the west of a line which runs roughly from today's Polish/Ukrainian border to the Crimea (a peninsula in the north of the Black Sea). That area is defined by the coexistence of BEECH trees and BIRCH trees. And it has been claimed that words for both of these trees can be reconstructed. Other scholars, using different approaches, have come to similar – or widely divergent – conclusions. In recent years, the disputes between different scholars have increased, and their battles are often fought out, not only in scholarly journals, but also in semi-popular publications, especially *Scientific American*.

Let us begin with a closer look at the "beech tree" argument.

Of the two defining terms, 'beech tree' and 'birch tree', the former is the more significant one: Birch trees thrive under relatively cold conditions and are not hardy in warmer climates. They are therefore found in a large northern area of Eurasia, as well as in mountainous areas further south. Beech trees, on the other hand, require a fairly moderate climate. Areas where both beech and birch trees are found, then, must naturally constitute a small subpart of the large birch tree territory. So far, so good.

The problem is that the evidence for reconstructing the word for 'beech' is limited to three language groups: Greek, Latin (Italic), and Germanic; see (1). Only these languages offer words which can be derived by straightforward changes from a common PIE source, *bhāgos*. To the extent that other European languages have a term for 'beech', it is most probably borrowed from one or the other of these three language groups. This is the case for instance for MIr. *fagh-vile* and Russian Church Slavic *buky*. (According to one view, a number of Slavic words meaning 'elder' should be considered reflexes of our word for 'beech'. But their phonetic shape precludes deriving them from the same ancestral form as the words in (1).)

(1)   Gk.   *phēgós*   (a kind of oak tree with edible acorns)
       Lat.   *fāgus*   'beech tree'
       Gmc.   *bōk-*   'beech tree' (compare OHG *buohha* > NHG *Buche*,
                     OE *bēc* > Mod. E *beech*)

More than that, the claim that the words in (1) are descended from a common PIE source requires the subsidiary assumption that only Latin and Germanic preserved the original form and meaning, and that other languages either retained the word and changed its meaning (Greek) or lost the word altogether (all the other languages). Presumably, the semantic change or loss was brought about by migration into areas where beech trees did not grow. The fact that the Greek term refers to an oak with edible acorns may be considered significant, since the nuts (or acorns) of beech trees also are edible. That is, proponents of this view can argue that the Greeks transferred the term *bhāgos* to a tree which shared a salient characteristic with the original beech tree, i.e., edible acorns.

While this beech-tree scenario is possible, it is not probable beyond a reasonable doubt. Several equally possible alternative explanations can be advanced. And the availability of such alternative explanations raises serious doubts about the cogency of the beech-tree hypothesis.

First, Latin (or Italic) and Germanic were neighbors, located in areas with beech trees. It is therefore entirely possible that the meaning 'beech tree' is a common innovation on their part, reflecting the fact that they moved into beech-tree territory. The Greek meaning, in that case, might represent an archaism. Or alternatively, both the Latin/Germanic and Greek meanings might be innovations, replacing an original reference to some other large deciduous tree with edible acorns or nuts. Consider the different uses of the term *Korn* 'corn, grain' in different areas of Germany. The word may refer to wheat, rye, barley, or oats, depending on which was the traditional major crop grain of the area. Similarly, different British English varieties use *corn* to refer to wheat or oats, and in American English the term refers to maize. (Note also the semantic specializations of **yewo-* 'grain' mentioned in § 4.1 above.)

Even more important, the fact that our word is limited to just a few geographically neighboring languages raises the possibility that it is a regional innovation, perhaps a borrowing from another, non-Indo-European language originally spoken in the region. The fact that the word later was borrowed into other, neighboring Indo-European languages lends credence to this assumption. The word behaves just like other terms for agricultural (and general technical) products and processes, which keep diffusing from language to language to language.

The fact that our beech tree word looks as if it is inherited from a common Proto-Indo-European source is no obstacle to this view. All that needs to be assumed is that the word was borrowed early enough, before the sound changes took place which differentiated Greek, Latin, and Germanic from each other.

It is precisely through developments of this sort that Greek and Germanic are generally considered to have come to share the word for 'hemp'; see (2). Note that this borrowing, too, took place early enough for the word to undergo Grimm's Law, the development which most strikingly differentiated Germanic from the rest of Indo-European. (If the glottalic theory is accepted, we would have to claim that the borrowing was made before the changes which differentiated Greek from Germanic.) Moreover, while the view that the word for beech tree was borrowed is based on conjecture, we have something close to a "smoking gun" for the word for 'hemp': The Sumerian word for the same plant, *kunibu*, is close both in meaning and in form; and it is attested at a considerably earlier period. (Keep in mind that Sumerian died as a spoken language by the eighteenth century B.C., well before our Greek and Germanic words are attested.) And by now we know that the putative direction of this borrowing, from the ancient Near East of Sumer to Europe, follows the general pattern of borrowings for agricultural products and processes.

(2)   Gk.   *kánnabis*
       PGmc.   **hanipiz*, OE *hænep* > Mod. Engl. *hemp*, OHG *hanaf* >
       NHG *Hanf*

As a matter of fact, the beech-tree scenario probably involves circular reasoning. It assumes that the meaning found in Latin and Germanic is the original one and that the word is inherited. Having done so, it reconstructs an ancestral form **bhāgos* with the meaning 'beech tree'. The reconstruction then is "confirmed" by the Latin and Germanic forms together with their meanings, while the different meaning in Greek and the absence of the word in other languages are attributed to special developments.

There is good evidence that the way of caution lies in avoiding reconstructions of this type, which are merely possible, but not probable beyond reasonable doubt, or – at a minimum – that we should not put excessive faith in such merely possible reconstructions. In this regard, recall the case of Algonquian 'fire-water' discussed in Chapter 16 § 7. In spite of considerable differences in detail, it constitutes an important warning about the dangers involved in over-reconstructing.

The collapse of the 'beech tree' argument, of course, is cold comfort to the prehistorian who would like to have the Indo-Europeanist provide information that is specific enough to form a basis for correlating language with archeological artifacts. But given what we know about possibilities and limits of reconstruction, there is not much that can be done about that. Here as elsewhere, it is probably better to admit that we don't know, rather than to claim that we know what we have no way of knowing.

Other approaches to the problem that are based on specific linguistic data have not fared much better. For instance, in recent years several linguists have tried to locate the original home of the Indo-Europeans in an area near the Caucasus, or in Anatolia. The arguments are partly based on claims of early borrowings from or into Caucasic languages, Semitic or Afro-Asiatic, and other, less well known ancient languages once spoken in the area. Some linguists have additionally used the "glottalic" reconstruction of the Proto-Indo-European stop system as evidence: In its overall structure, the system is remarkably similar to the system reconstructed for the ancestor of modern Caucasic languages. This similarity, it is claimed, must be due to convergence under close bilingual contact. Finally, linguists have drawn on the alleged absence of the word for 'horse' in Anatolian as supporting evidence for the view that the Anatolians remained in the original homeland and that the rest of the Indo-European acquired knowledge and use of domesticated horses only after moving farther north (to the steppes of Ukraine).

The evidence adduced for early borrowings essentially consists of words that are probable borrowings from Semitic or other Near Eastern languages to Indo-European, such as the word for 'hemp' just discussed and many of the items covered in § 4.1. But these words generally are limited to the more western Indo-European languages. This suggests that the borrowing was made, not into Proto-Indo-European, but into its daughter languages or, at best, into a dialectal subgroup of late Proto-Indo-European.

Moreover, as noted in Chapter 16, § 7, the glottalic theory still is quite controversial and thus offers at best weak support for the "Caucasic hypothesis". Even if it were stronger, it would not require the assumption of direct bilingual contact between Proto-Indo-European and the Caucasic proto-language. As we saw in Chapter 13, § 5, innovations can spread from a convergence area to neighboring territory by ordinary dialect diffusion. There is nothing to prevent the same thing from happening in a chain of bilingual groups, through intermediate bilingual areas.

Finally, as we have seen in the preceding section, the claim that the Anatolians did not have the Indo-European word for 'horse' is controversial at best. But even if it were true, the following alternative scenario could just as easily account for an absence of the word 'horse' in early Anatolian: The original homeland was farther north, say, in Ukraine. The Anatolians were the first to move away from the homeland, at a time when the horse had not yet been domesticated. After their departure, the rest of the Indo-Europeans acquired the use of horses.

Additional facts of a non-linguistic nature cast doubts on the "Anatolian hypothesis". We have good reasons for believing that the Indo-European Anatolians were relatively recent arrivals in the area. When they first appear on the horizon in the eighteenth or seventeenth century B.C., the Hittites replace earlier, non-Indo-European dynasties and rule over their peoples or absorb them. No references to Hittites or other Indo-European Anatolians are found at a significantly earlier time. These facts suggest that they were immigrants to Anatolia. And there is no evidence to suggest that they migrated from more southern points. Given the nature of the geography, the conclusion must be that they migrated from the north.

In fact, to the extent that it is inferable from the traditions of the early Indo-European peoples or their neighbors, the general picture of early Indo-European migrations is one of movement to the south (into India, Iran, Anatolia, Greece, Italy) and west (Germany, Gaul, the British isles). Only within

Europe do we find evidence for a relatively early northern migration, of Germanic tribes into southern Scandinavia.

Given the evidence for the general directions of early migrations, one approach to solving the riddle of the original home might lie in determining the putative starting point of these movements, by projecting back from the southern and western direction of the migrations. The "core" area thus defined ranges from somewhere in Russia to somewhere in East Central Europe.

Some prehistorians have tried to use this relatively uncontroversial insight as a starting point for attempts to define an original home on the basis of archeological evidence. The assumption is as follows. Take the core area and see what kind of material culture prevails in it at the time Proto-Indo-European is assumed to have been spoken. Then determine whether at the putative time(s) of migration, the traits of this culture are diffused into the areas of new settlement. If the match is reasonable, then the assumption is reasonable, too, that the core area is the original home of the Indo-Europeans. This is the type of reasoning that underlies one of the currently most popular hypotheses, which places the home of the Indo-Europeans in the so-called Kurgan culture of Southern Russia. (Kurgans are special forms of burial mounds.)

Unfortunately, we are not able to fix the date of Proto-Indo-European with certainty (see § 5 below). Different educated guesses therefore may lead to different results.

Moreover, the method is fraught with other difficulties. Underlying the method is the – tacit – assumption that culture and language are coterminous. But that assumption is dubious. Take for instance South Asia. The Indian subcontinent is home to at least three different language families – Indo-Aryan, Dravidian, and Munda. As noted in Chapter 13, § 4, centuries of linguistic convergence have made these languages increasingly similar in their overall structure. Similar developments in the cultural sphere have yielded a similar convergence in culture. As a consequence, the three different language families are spoken in a single cultural area. But the picture of a single cultural area still is incomplete, for within the area we find a major division between two different cultural sub-areas. Traditional South Asia makes a fundamental distinction between "tribal" and "civilized" society, with significant cultural and even political implications. And again, we do find that language and culture to a large degree are not coterminous. True, all Munda speakers belong to "tribal" societies; but so do many Dravidian and Indo-Aryan groups. Other Dravidians and Indo-Aryans belong to "civilized" society.

Linguistic – and cultural – convergence, as we find it in such areas as modern South Asia, is by no means limited to recent history. If anything, the bilingualism that is the "engine" behind convergence has been declining in recent history. There is thus no reason to assume that Proto-Indo-European was spoken in a completely monolingual setting. Under the circumstances, the possibility cannot be ruled out that all – or part – of Indo-European was part of a larger linguistic and cultural convergence area (or several such areas), a fact which renders suspect any argument that is based on the tacit assumption of an identity between Indo-European language and culture.

There is finally an additional piece of linguistic evidence. This is the fact that in the early historical period the linguistic diversity among Indo-European languages appears to be greatest in the area of the Balkans and closely adjacent territory. On the other hand, the Indo-Iranian languages or dialects occupy a vast territory, with amazingly little differentiation at an early time. Now, as we saw in Chapter 11, § 6, where the history is known, linguistic diversity usually is greatest in the homeland, and smallest in colonial territory. By extrapolation, then, we might consider the area of the Balkans the original home of the Indo-Europeans and the Indo-Iranian area a late colonial extension.

Even this argument is not infallible. It could well be argued that the Balkans were a favorite passage way for migration from more northern or eastern areas to the south and the southwest. The linguistic diversity, then, might result from the fact that some of the many, linguistically highly diverse groups passing through the area simply "got stuck". This view, too, can be buttressed by evidence from known history. The Balkans have witnessed an enormous amount of migration – of the Huns and their linguistically highly diversified allies, the Goths, the Vandals, and other Germanic (and non-Germanic) tribes; of the Bulgars (a Turkic tribe that gave Bulgaria its name); of the Magyars (Hungarians); of the Slavs; of the Turks. And the present highly diverse linguistic map of the Balkans and closely adjacent areas is in large measure the result of different groups "getting stuck".

As a kind of compromise between these two "diversity-based" views, one scholar has proposed that the Balkans were an intermediate homeland for the western Indo-Europeans after the disintegration of Proto-Indo-European unity.

All things considered, the area from East Central Europe to Eastern Russia does appear to be the most likely candidate for being the original home of the Indo-Europeans. But that area is vast. The question of where within that vast expanse we should pinpoint the home territory of Proto-Indo-European cannot be considered settled. And given the nature of the evidence, it is not at all certain that it can ever be settled to the satisfaction of most (reasonable) scholars.

4.3. Religion, mythology, and poetic tradition

Indo-European religion is often portrayed as a strongly male-oriented one, whose deities are associated with the sky. Support for this view comes in the fact that *dyēw-s*, lit. 'sky', is the only divine name that we can reconstruct with confidence for Proto-Indo-European. The name refers to a male God who plays a prominent role in Greek and Latin, as *Zeús* or *Juppiter*, chief of the Gods. (Note also the Germanic deity hidden in Engl. *Tuesday*; see Chapter 4, §3.3.) Moreover, words for 'God' that are in widespread use in early Indo-European languages, such as Skt. *dēva-*, Lat. *deus*, OIr. *dia*, and Lith. *dievas*, are derivable from an adjective *deyw-os*, whose literal meaning is 'of the sky'.

Note further that Lat. *Juppiter* reflects a collocation *dyew pəter* which literally means 'O **father** sky'. The collocation evidently is old, since it has counterparts in Greek *Zeús Patḗr* and Vedic Sanskrit *dyaús (...) pitā́*.

Significantly, we have no evidence for reconstructing the name of a female deity, comparable to the image of the Mother Goddess found throughout much of prehistoric Eurasia. When Mother Goddesses do occur in early Indo-European texts, their presence is said to reflect the substratum of conquered, pre-Indo-European indigenous populations who worshiped the Goddess.

So, at least, the story goes.

But there are difficulties with this traditional view of early Indo-European religion. And these difficulties concern not only our picture of the Indo-Europeans, but also of the pre-Indo-European indigenous peoples. Perhaps the major problem is that for the Indo-Europeans we have to rely on traditions conveyed through language; for the pre-Indo-European populations of Europe and Asia we depend on artifacts. Now, there can be no doubt that the textual traditions of the Indo-Europeans – just as those of the ancient Near East, of Egypt, or of Meso-America – were handed down by males and that this male dominance may well have skewed the information that was preserved for posterity. Artifacts, in this regard, may be more "gender-neutral". But here, too, the evidence may have been skewed, even if unintentionally. Archeologists have been impressed with the widespread presence of Mother Goddess images in early prehistoric sites and have inferred from this presence a female-dominated religion. But recent, more fine-grained research in Malta suggests that in at least one society of this type, the female-dominated religious sphere coexisted with a male-dominated one. The former was found in subterranean burial complexes, the latter, in above-ground sanctuaries. The heavy presence of female images in earlier archeological digs, then, might reflect the fact that such digs often unearth burial sites which, being placed underground, had a better chance of being preserved than above-ground sanctuaries.

The new archeological evidence invites reexamination of early Indo-European tradition. True, we find strong evidence for male deities associated with the sky; but we also find recurrent myths and other references to female deities associated with the earth and the fertility that lies in the earth – and even to the impregnation of 'earth' by 'sky' as the act through which the world was created. (Impregnation, of course, may still be interpreted as an act of male domination; but if we take this interpretation to its strict conclusion, then all human societies are male-dominated, and the distinction between male-dominated and female-dominated societies becomes meaningless.)

The primordial embrace of father sky – above – and mother earth – below – is no doubt the ideology underlying the following Vedic Sanskrit passage, which actually juxtaposes 'father sky' and 'mother earth'. Note further that the Mother Goddesses of the Greek "Mysteries" generally were associated with the earth or with underground caves.

> ***dyaúr*** *me **pitā** janitā́ nā́bhir átra*
> *bándhur me **mātā́ pṛthivī́** mahīyám*
> 'Father sky is my creator, the navel here;
> Mother earth is my kin, this great one.'

As the discussion of 'father sky' and 'mother earth' shows, the comparative method permits us to reconstruct a fair amount of Indo-European non-material culture, especially if it draws not only on individual words, but also on collocations of words, as well as on the literary traditions of the early Indo-European peoples.

Especially in the area of poetic language we find numerous fixed collocations that have been handed down as a part of Indo-European poetic heritage. Compare for instance Gk. *áphthiton kléos* : Skt. *ákṣiti śravas*, both meaning 'imperishable fame' and, in spite of their phonetic differences, derivable from a common source, PIE $* \acute{\eta}\text{-}g^w hdhi\text{-}tom$ or $*\acute{\eta}\text{-}g^w hdhi\text{-}ti\ \acute{k}l\acute{e}wos$. Scholars have also begun to reconstruct elements of Indo-European myths, especially of one in which a great hero or God slays a large snake or dragon. In fact, in a paper titled "How to kill a dragon in Indo-European", the American linguist Calvert Watkins has proposed to reconstruct a sentence which must have formed part of the traditional telling of the myth and which states quite simply and appropriately that "He [the hero] killed the dragon". (Compare the reconstructed legal language in § 3 above.)

4.4. Society

From similar evidence it can be gathered that the structure of Indo-European society was strongly patriarchal, with the woman moving into the husband's father's extended family; that it was organized around the clan as its smallest unit beyond the extended family; and that clans could form tribes, the basic units of early Indo-European ethnicity.

The early traditions of the Indo-Europeans tell us that they were warlike people whose leaders were heroes: They could even slay dragons and, under more mundane conditions, could lead their people to victory over others. In historical times we find one Indo-European group after the other invading other peoples' territory. Note, for instance, the ransacking of Rome and Delphi by the Celts, the imperialist expansions of the Romans, the raids on the Roman Empire by Germanic and other tribes, or the Slavic incursions into the Byzantine empire and much of present-day Russia.

This evidence is generally taken to indicate that the Indo-Europeans spread over most of their later territory by military expansion. Recently, an eminent English prehistorian, Colin Renfrew, has painted a very different picture: The Indo-European languages spread peaceably, along with agricultural innovations, from a much more southern heartland in Anatolia (see also § 4.2 above).

The facts, as they are preserved in early Indo-European tradition and in the historical records, favor the traditional interpretation. However, it is quite possible that the military exploits of the early Indo-European peoples are only part of the total story and that there was another, more peaceful dimension in which agricultural and other cultural innovations spread from village to village. In fact, we know that in many cases the invaders did not replace the local populations, but merely constituted a thin – but powerful – overlay. This makes it at least possible that preexisting networks of communication between different local populations remained relatively undisturbed by the comings – and goings – of conquerors. It may have been by this route that the agricultural words of §§ 4.1 and 4.2 spread into much of Western Indo-European. Put differently, the conflict between Renfrew's archeologically founded scenario and the traditional view of linguists and philologists can be resolved if we envisage the world of early Indo-European expansion as consisting of at least two levels: one being the "heroic" one of military conquest, the other being a more peaceful one of agricultural and general cultural diffusion. In this regard note the similar division between father sky and mother earth discussed in the preceding section.

The image of the division of labor between father sky and mother earth can be extended in an even more appropriate manner. A recent book by the archeologist-linguist E. J. W. Barber shows that far from being relegated to being the helpmates of their heroic husbands, fathers, or sons, Indo-European women dominated an important and much more peaceful sphere of their own, the production of textiles; and in that sphere they either developed important new technological innovations, or passed them on from one prehistoric society to the other. (This, of course, does not mean that Indo-European women were treated as true equals. But none of the societies for which we have early records accorded equal status to women. In this regard, too, the Indo-Europeans may have differed little from other contemporary cultures – whether we approve or not.)

In fact, it is highly unlikely that all (male) Indo-Europeans were militaristic conquerors who, in the manner of traditional warfare, raped, pillaged, and plundered peaceful non-Indo-European populations and their territories. True, early historical records emphasize the military exploits; but we also get scenes of love, tenderness, and compassion, as well as great thinkers like Socrates and compassionate visionaries like the Buddha. We probably make a mistake in imagining the early Indo-Europeans as exclusively great heroes – or great brutes, depending on our perspective. In the area of human nature it is most likely that the "strange footsteps" that we discover "on the shores of the unknown" are "our own".

Although social structure probably was not as rigid in early times as in later Greek, Roman, medieval European, and especially Indo-Aryan society, there was no doubt some differentiation. As noted before, the early traditions tell of heroic leaders, who could even fight dragons. There must also have been priests who took care of the people's spiritual needs and watched over the rituals to father sky and perhaps also mother earth. In addition, there must have been people who tended the cattle, cultivated the crops, and otherwise saw to it that everybody could eat. Such a threefold division of society into warriors, priests, and common people is, in a way, so mundane as to be unremarkable. But under the French scholar Georges Dumézil, the division was turned into an "ideology", which supposedly governed all of Indo-European culture.

Dumézil's views have given rise to an extended debate, which is still continuing. Similar to the homeland issue, arguments have been met by counterarguments, and so on. What has largely been ignored in the context is the fact that early Indo-European society had at least one additional, fourth, component – the slaves. As in all ancient societies, prisoners of war – if they were permitted to live at all – were enslaved (see Chapters 2, § 3.4, and 9, § 3.1 on *Slav : slave*), and even members of the dominant group could become slaves if, for instance, they committed certain crimes. True, unlike the chattel slavery of the Caribbean and the Americas, traditional slavery was not hereditary, and "manumission" often offered a release from serfdom. But the life of slaves was a difficult one; and many societies depended on the work of slaves to maintain them. (This is most strikingly true for Athenian democracy, which was built on the backs of slaves who, of course, were barred from participating in the democracy that made Athens famous.)

In addition to slaves, another group may have formed a special layer of early Indo-European society, beyond the warriors, priests, and commoners, namely the traders and artisans who provided tools and luxuries of foreign origin or introduced the production of such items. A recent article argues that the presence of traders and artisans accounts for striking similarities between prehistoric artifacts from northern India to the Balkans and even Scandinavia; and it points to parallels in historical times of artisans and other specialists who migrate from society to society, including the so-called Gypsies (Romani speakers). Like the slaves, such migrant specialists would have been an important component of society and yet, would not have been given full legal standing within society. In this sense, then, they were outside society or, at best, on its margins.

It is interesting to note that one early Avestan text divides society into four, not just three, strata: Warriors, priests, cattle-herders [i.e., commoners], and finally artisans. Even more interesting, a similar explicit division of society, underlying the later caste system is found in early Sanskrit texts. But here the fourth stratum consists both of artisans and of slaves. Here, then, the fourth estate included all persons who were outside society, even though they formed an important – and indispensable – component of that society.

4.5. The question of "race"

What is far more difficult – and controversial – to determine than any of the issues so far examined is the question of what the Indo-Europeans looked like.

There have been many attempts to establish the "race" of the speakers of Indo-European. The Nazi-inspired efforts to identify their race as "Aryan", i.e. blond, blue-eyed, and "Nordic" are especially notorious.

However, these and other less racist attempts vastly overestimate the value of the available evidence. True, by some of their own accounts, the early Indo-Europeans were lighter-skinned than the peoples they subjugated. However, this evidence does not prove that the Indo-Europeans as a whole were "white", blond (or light-haired), blue-eyed, or that all Indo-European invaders were lighter-skinned than all non-Indo-Europeans.

The situation may well have been like that of present-day Europe, where different areas present different ratios of blond/blue-eyed vs. dark-haired/brown-eyed, but where no area has an exclusively blond/blue-eyed or dark-haired/brown-eyed population. Nevertheless, because of the greater preponderance of the latter type in Italy, brown-haired/gray-eyed Germans may refer to themselves as "white" in contrast to the "black Italians" – ignoring the existence of Italians blonder and lighter-skinned than they are.

Clearly, speaking the same language does not, and should not, imply that the speakers are racially homogenous. Look for example at the United States, where members of every "race" under the sun have come to speak the same language. Although the racial diversity of the United States may be unusual, we know that even prehistoric societies exhibited some degree of diversity. For instance, skeletal evidence from the Indus Valley Civilization suggests a fair amount of "racial mixture" as early as the third and second millennia B.C. There is no reason to believe that the early Indo-Europeans were any more homogeneous in their "racial" characteristics (whatever they may have been).

More than that, not only is there evidence for "racial mixture" in the ancient Indus Valley Civilization, it has also been observed that the mix of different skeletal types in the third and second millennia B.C. is virtually identical to what we find in the same area in modern times. Now, the Indus Valley has time and again been a key geographic area for foreign invaders, who in historical times included both the Mediterranean Greeks and the Central Asiatic Huns. Evidently, however, the effect of these different "races" on the skeletal mix of the Indus Valley has been negligible; for as just noted there is no appreciable difference between the third and second millennia B.C. and the present. The probable reason is that as noted earlier, conquerors commonly constitute only a thin overlay over the local population.

5. Dating the Indo-Europeans

In trying to deal with controversies like the original home of the Indo-Europeans, one issue comes up again and again – the question of when Proto-Indo-European was spoken. Scholars have tried to answer this question by using several different approaches, but so far, none of these has been completely satisfactory.

One approach tries to estimate how much time must have passed between Proto-Indo-European and the earliest attested languages to account for the differences between them. Unfortunately, there is no simple algorithm that tells us that X number of changes can be expected in X number of centuries. In fact, study of change in historically observable times suggests that different languages can change at very different rates. For instance, within the Germanic languages, noun inflection has been virtually lost in Modern English and the continental Scandinavian languages, while Modern Icelandic and Modern Standard German have preserved an inflection for four cases.

In early Indo-European we run into what may be a comparable situation: As we have seen in Chapter 2, § 3.8, the Anatolian languages exhibit a number of features that are markedly different from those found in the other early Indo-European languages. Some of these are very modern in appearance, such as the use of a verb 'to have'. Other features are quite archaic. And yet others are still the topic of hot debate.

Some scholars ascribe all or most of the divergent Anatolian features to archaism. They argue that Anatolian constitutes a separate branch of Indo-European that broke away very early, before the rest of the Indo-European languages underwent common innovations that differentiated them from Anatolian. Adherents of this view like to use the term Indo-Hittite to signal the special status of Anatolian vs. the rest of Indo-European.

Other scholars acknowledge that Hittite preserves many archaic features, but believe that some features are innovations specific to Hittite. Moreover, they would argue, other early Indo-European languages likewise preserve archaisms – although in different components of grammar and lexicon. Under this view, then, the Anatolian languages do not have a special status, and the traditional term Indo-European is perfectly adequate.

These different interpretations of the evidence have clear implications for attempts to estimate the date of the proto-language. First, they affect the number of changes that we want to attribute to the different languages and the amount of time required for these changes. Secondly, the Indo-Hittite approach has to fix two dates, one for "Proto-Indo-Hittite", the other for "Proto-(Rest-of-)Indo-European", of which the former clearly must precede the latter by a period long enough to permit the non-Anatolian languages to undergo the changes that differentiate them from Anatolian.

As we can see from this discussion, even if there were – roughly – a constant rate of change, our estimates of time depth still would to a large degree depend on interpretation, not just on simple facts.

For several decades, during the 1950s through the 1970s, there was a lot of excitement about a different method of estimating time depth by linguistic means, a method which promised to be easier than the traditional approach. Fundamental to this GLOTTOCHRONOLOGICAL approach (sometimes also referred to as lexicostatistical) is the notion of a constant rate of replacement in basic vocabulary. Given this assumption, it was possible to collect basic vocabulary data from related languages, determine the number of lexical items that look similar or different, and then to determine the amount of time required for the different-looking items to be replaced. The method was frankly modeled on the radiocarbon method, which also operates with a constant rate of change (the notion of half-life) and which has yielded spectacular results in prehistoric research. What was additionally attractive about glottochronology was that all it required was a collection of basic vocabulary items – no need to worry about problems such as whether the Hittite verb 'have' is an archaism or an innovation!

The enthusiasm for glottochronology soon came to an end, however. Problems arose that were similar to the false-friend syndrome discussed in the preceding chapter: How can we tell by simple inspection whether given words are similar due to chance, to borrowing, or to inheritance? And what if we do not determine genuine cognates because their shape has been changed beyond recognition?

Questions arose, too, about the appropriateness of the radiocarbon model, since radioactive carbon decays only once, while words may change over and over again. As a consequence, if corresponding items in two languages A and B are different, we cannot tell whether the difference is the result of one replacement in A, one replacement each in A and B, or several replacements in A and/or B. Since the method is concerned with the number of vocabulary replacements, not just the number of differences in vocabulary, these subtle distinctions can make a great difference.

Most significant, however, was the fact that the method was disconfirmed by empirical evidence. Especially persuasive was a study that showed that glottochronology failed when confronted with languages like English on one hand, whose rate of vocabulary replacement significantly exceeded expectations (presumably because of its proclivity to borrow), and Icelandic on the other, with a significantly lower rate of replacement (perhaps because of the conservative influence of linguistic nationalism).

A third approach to determining the date of Indo-European adopts the spirit of linguistic paleontology: If we can reconstruct a particular word for Proto-Indo-European and if this word refers to a cultural innovation, then we can infer that the language must have been spoken after the innovation took place. Currently, the domestication of horses is a popular topic in this regard. Recent research shows that horses were domesticated for riding purposes as early as the fourth millennium B.C. If, then, we can reconstruct a word for domesticated 'horse' in Proto-Indo-European, this would mean that the language was spoken in the fourth millennium or soon thereafter. But this is where controversy sets in. While many Indo-Europeanists do believe that a reconstruction *eḱwos* 'horse' is justified, we have seen in §§ 4.1 and 4.2 above that some linguists do not. At least, they do not believe that the reconstruction is justified for "Indo-Hittite", but only for the proto-language of the rest of the Indo-European languages. This belief would require setting the date of the Indo-Hittite proto-language before the domestication of horses in the fourth millennium, and the date of the "Rest-of-Indo-European" proto-language, after.

This, of course, brings us back to the quandary that we faced in the first part of this section. Determining the date of the proto-language depends, not on objective, verifiable facts, but on theories and hypotheses that interpret these facts. As long as scholars disagree, and do so not just frivolously but with reasonable arguments, the chances of determining the date of Proto-Indo-European with any degree of certainty are very poor.

6. Realism in reconstruction

Attentive readers may begin to wonder at this time, if they haven't done so before: If there is so much disagreement among the experts, how can we be sure that anything they reconstruct has any right to be taken seriously?

Some historical linguists, too, have expressed doubts about whether our reconstructions can make any claim to being realistic.

These skeptics argue that we can never hope to fully reconstruct the ancestral language, since lexical items and grammatical forms tend to become obsolete. The impact is so pervasive that many forms may be lost from many of the related languages, leaving no evidence that might be used for reconstruction. (Consider the rapid and extensive loss of horse-and-buggy terminology in recent times, after the introduction of the internal combustion engine.)

Even in phonological reconstruction, the greatest success story of the comparative method, we can never be certain about the precise pronunciation of what we reconstruct as, say, voiced, or aspirated, or palatal. In fact, the controversy over the glottalic theory shows how little we can be certain about the phonetic details of Proto-Indo-European sounds.

Finally, the skeptics argue, the comparative method by its very design has to reduce all the variation found in the daughter languages to invariance. Real, natural languages always have some variation: This may range from morphophonemic alternations like Engl. *sing : sang : sung* to dialectal variation such as [šikægo] : [šikɔgo] : [šikago] for *Chicago*. Languages without variation, especially without different dialects, are unnatural. If the comparative method forces us to reconstruct such languages, then our reconstructions by necessity are unrealistic.

The skeptics conclude that the best we can say for reconstructions is that they serve as convenient cover formulae, summarizing our understanding of the linguistic relationship between given languages.

Now, it is perfectly true that our reconstructions are hypotheses and thus necessarily somewhat hypothetical. It is also true that there is disagreement over issues such as the glottalic theory. And as we have seen in the preceding sections, there are also controversies over the reconstruction of particular lexical items and even over whether the language we reconstruct should be called Indo-European or Indo-Hittite. But these disagreements and controversies concern matters of detail. Lexical items whose reconstruction is controversial constitute a minute fraction of the hundreds, even thousands of lexical items, roots, and morphemes that we can reconstruct without difficulties – items such as the words for 'father', 'mother', 'brother', 'sister'; or 'eat', 'drink', 'sleep'; or even personal pronouns and the function word 'and'. It is just that these well-assured items are not particularly interesting for linguistic paleontology: What language does not have words for basic concepts like these?

Even disagreements over issues such as the glottalic theory are not as serious as they might appear. True, we may be arguing over whether particular sounds were voiced unaspirated or whether they were glottalized. But we do agree on the need to reconstruct three series (either voiced : voiceless : aspirated, or glottalized : voiceless (aspirated) : voiced (aspirated)), rather than just one or two. Further, where most of the languages present a labial stop or a plausible outcome of such a stop, none of us would reconstruct a glottal stop instead. There are many more aspects of phonological reconstruction that we agree on – even the skeptics – than those that we do battle over.

The claim that the comparative method by necessity eliminates all vestiges of variation likewise is exaggerated. It is only through the comparative method that we can postulate for Proto-Indo-European morphophonemic alternations of the type **seng^wh- / *song^wh- / *sng^wh-* which, as noted in § 3 above, are the source for Engl. *sing : sang : sung*. Moreover, the comparative method even furnishes evidence of dialectal variation in Proto-Indo-

European, such as the centum : satem division mentioned in Chapter 2, § 3.6 and Chapter 11, § 3.

Here again, specialists may differ on matters of detail. And it is certainly possible, even likely, that some aspects of Proto-Indo-European variation escape us – because the evidence for the variation has been irretrievably lost. But this does not detract from the fact that we are able to reconstruct aspects of the morphophonemic and dialectal variation characteristic of natural languages.

More than that, the American linguist Robert A. Hall, Jr. has put the comparative method to the test by doing reconstruction in Romance and comparing the results with Latin. Making allowances for the fact that the Classical Latin of Caesar and Cicero is not identical with the vernacular Latin from which the Romance languages descended, the results are impressive. Most striking is the fact that Hall was able to reconstruct something approximating the Latin length distinction in vowels – even though all Latin long vowels had become short in Romance! True, the evidence of the Romance languages does not permit us to define the feature distinguishing the two vowel sets as length; it could conceivably be characterized by other terms such as "tense". In this sense, then, we are in a situation similar to the glottalic controversy. But the fact remains that the reconstructed contrast, however defined, closely corresponds to the length contrast of Latin and thus is a realistic one, not just a figment of one scholar's imagination.

On balance, a proper assessment of the value of our reconstructions would be that they approximate some prehistoric reality, even if some aspects of that reality may escape us. Where different scholars disagree with each other in respect to such issues as the glottalic theory and linguistic paleontology, their disagreement is not so much over the goal of approximating reality, but over which road leads more effectively to that goal. In fact, if they were resigned to considering reconstructions mere "convenient cover formulae", there would be very little reason for disagreement: Any cover formula is as good as the next, as long as it manages to sum up "the facts".

7. Conclusions and outlook

In this chapter we have examined a variety of ways in which the methods and results of historical and comparative linguistics can be applied to issues outside linguistics proper. By looking at Proto-Indo-European, we have seen that the comparative method permits us to go beyond the mere reconstruction of sounds, morphology, syntax, and words, and to reconstruct aspects of prehistoric culture and civilization. As a consequence we have realized that the "footprints on the unknown shore" are, to some extent, ours: Human beings tend to be the same no matter where or when they live. Some aspects of Indo-European culture, such as the limited use of agriculture (if any) or of metals, will remain to us "a foreign country". But even if the Indo-Europeans "did many things differently", we may have become a little more familiar with them – through the fruits of the comparative method.

At the same time, we have come to know that there are serious limitations to the comparative method. And unfortunately, these limitations most seriously affect precisely those areas which are of the keenest interest to the prehistorian – the time and place at which Indo-European was spoken. But perhaps there is some benefit in having traveled the road to this realization. Examining the different proposals and hypotheses in some detail has given us a better understanding of the arcane world of the Indo-European specialists and should prepare us for a better appreciation of new claims that we might come across in the future, whether they involve Indo-European and the Indo-Europeans or other proto-languages and their speakers.

Chapter notes and suggested readings

We have deliberately written this book with no footnotes in the text and without a large number of references worked into the presentation, for we feel that they might be distracting as you read through the text. However, such notes and references can serve a very useful purpose, by pointing you in the direction of further readings if you want to explore certain issues more fully; by giving you information on the standard sources of the ideas we present and the findings we discuss; by generally acknowledging contributions that others have made to our understanding of the processes of language change over the years; or by making additional comments of interest that are not quite appropriate in the main text. In these chapter notes, we give relevant additional information, mainly keyed to publications listed in the References, with reference to specific chapter sections where possible or appropriate.

Many of these publications are at an advanced level, representing the findings of professional linguists investigating language change. Our expectation is that seeing them listed here will give you a feel for the full range of scholarship on language change that has provided the basis for what we have distilled in this book.

At the same time, many topics we have covered lend themselves particularly well to popular and thus highly accessible treatments (e.g., writing, etymology, the origin of language, linguistic paleontology). Indeed, some of the works cited below come from sources such as *Scientific American* or the publications of the British Museum, and are designed for the interested, intelligent, and intellectually curious non-specialist reader. We specifically note those works which are appropriate for beginners in the field.

As you can see, historical linguistics is a vast field and there is a great amount of information available; these notes will give you an idea of where to start looking to go beyond what we have presented.

Chapter 1.
Introduction

Since we survey briefly in this chapter what is in store in the rest of the book, we start these notes with references to some general works on historical linguistics. Among these are classic works that are basically manifestos on the nature of language and so treat language change as an essential part of understanding language in general. Others are textbooks more in the familiar modern sense, though often aimed at student populations with backgrounds in linguistics quite different from that assumed in this textbook.

Among the classic works are L. Bloomfield 1933 ([1965]), Jespersen 1921, Paul 1920, Sapir 1921, de Saussure 1916.

Textbooks at the beginning level include Aitchison 1991, Arlotto 1972, Crowley 1987/1992, and Trask 1994.

More advanced introductions, presupposing greater familiarity with linguistics, include Fox 1995 (focus on reconstruction), Goyvaerts 1975, Jeffers & Lehiste 1979, Lehmann 1962, 1973, 1992, and Sturtevant 1917, 1947.

Advanced introductions and handbooks are Anttila 1972 and 1988, Bynon 1977, Hock 1986a/1991, Hoenigswald 1965, Labov 1994, and McMahon 1994. Somewhat advanced historical linguistics texts in German include Boretzky 1977, Sternemann & Gutschmidt 1989, and Szemerényi 1970/1989a.

Additionally, though they are aimed at quite advanced students and professional practitioners of historical linguistics, we mention two anthologies that survey the field: Polomé 1990a and Chs. Jones 1993. All of the works listed in this note offer many more examples of the types of changes given in this book.

Throughout the book, we draw on many examples from English. We note here just a few of the extremely large number of useful sources on English and its history: Chs. Barber 1976, M. Bloomfield & Newmark 1963, Crystal 1988, Crystal 1995 (organized in a highly readable and innovative way), and Pyles & Algeo 1982 (somewhat traditional in style but solid).

Similarly, since our references to change in sign languages and to their history are spread here and there across the chapters, we note several relevant, and generally highly accessible works: Battison 1978, Frishberg 1975, Frishberg 1976, Lane 1980, Perlmutter 1986, Stokoe 1974.

As for phonetics, presented in the Appendix to this chapter, virtually any introductory textbook in linguistics – and there are dozens – gives essentially the same information and symbols. A standard text on phonetics itself, which goes into far greater detail than is presented here, is Ladefoged 1993.

Finally, an excellent resource, aimed at a generalist audience, in which a brief overview of linguistic concepts and terms given throughout this book can be found, is Bright 1992.

Chapter 2.
The discovery of Indo-European

§1. Pedersen 1959 gives an intriguing and readable history of the development of historical linguistic research, and especially of early Indo-European studies, including pictures of eighteenth and nineteenth century scholars known otherwise just by name.

The term "vernacular" is an important one that occurs frequently in this book (e.g. in Chapters 1, §2; 10, §2; 12, §1). It refers to a form of speech that is spoken by "ordinary people" and thus has lower status than another "prestige" (or more properly, "high prestige") variety with which it coexists. Depending on the circumstances, a vernacular may be a different language from the prestige variety (such as early forms of French, Spanish, English, or German in medieval Europe, which were vernaculars compared to the prestige language, Latin); or it may be something more like a non-standard dialect (such as non-standard forms of English compared to Standard English).

§2. The field of Indo-European studies is covered in such a vast literature that we cannot do it justice here. The following all provide some general information on the individual languages and the proto-language: Baldi 1983, Krahe 1970, Lehmann 1993, Meillet 1937, Lockwood 1969 and Lockwood 1972 (both of these designed for interested nonlinguists), and Beekes 1995.

Classic treatments of Proto-Indo-European grammar, in whole or in part, include Brugmann 1897-1916 and 1904, more recently Watkins 1969 (on the verb) and Mayrhofer 1986 (on phonology); see also Sihler 1995 (focus on Greek and Latin). The 1879 publication by de Saussure, written when the author was just nineteen years old, eventually revolutionized our understanding of the Proto-Indo-European vowel system (this is translated in part in Lehmann 1967). Gamkrelidze & Ivanov 1984/1994 gives a still controversial reassessment of much of the classical view of Proto-Indo-European grammar (see Chapter 16, §7 on their view of Proto-Indo-European phonology).

Buck 1949 is an interesting source on the Proto-Indo-European lexicon, and Gvozdanović 1992 a quite advanced compendium on one sector of the Proto-Indo-European lexicon, the numerals (see also Winter 1992 and Justus 1988). Cardona, Hoenigswald, & Senn 1970 and Polomé 1982 offer important collections of high-level papers on various aspects of Indo-European.

§3. Useful reference works on each of the branches of Indo-European, often with surveys of the important languages and/or bibliography, include the following.

Celtic: MacAuley 1992, Ball & Fife 1993, and Gregor 1980

Latin (Italic) and Romance: Palmer 1954 (Latin); Posner 1966 and Hall 1976 (Romance)

Germanic: König & van der Auwera 1994 and Robinson 1992; see also Haugen 1982 for the Scandinavian languages and Antonsen 1975 for early runic

Slavic: Comrie & Corbett 1993

Lithuanian (Baltic): Fraenkel 1950, Senn 1942 (for Lithuanian)

Baltic-Slavic or Balto-Slavic: Szemerényi 1957

Albanian: Hamp 1972 (a primarily bibliographic essay)

Greek: Palmer 1980

Iranian: Schmitt 1989a

Indo-Aryan: Burrow 1973 (Sanskrit, with information on Indo-Iranian in general), Masica 1991 (modern Indo-Aryan)

Anatolian (Hittite): Ceram 1973 and Gurney 1954; unfortunately, no generally accessible survey of the Anatolian languages exists; Melchert 1994 covers Anatolian historical morphology

For Armenian and Tocharian there are no generally accessible surveys. On the dialectally highly diverse foundations of Classical Armenian see Winter 1966. On Etruscan, see Wellard 1973, intended for a general audience.

Chapter 3.
Writing: Its history and its decipherment

General references: Diringer 1962, J. Friedrich 1957, Gelb 1963, and Naka- nishi 1992, all designed for a general audience; Carter & Schoville 1984, Daniels 1990, Daniels & Bright 1995, Günther & Ludwig 1994-1995, Jensen 1958, 1970, Trager 1974.

§2.1. On orality in early India see Falk 1990 and 1993 (the latter is an advanced scholarly survey of the issue). *Roots* was published in 1976 by Doubleday & Co. It is a powerful testimony to the vitality and accuracy of oral traditions, since Haley reports that when he finally visited the West African village that his ancestors came from, he heard a *griot* recite the family history. He describes the moment thus: "This man [the *griot*] whose lifetime had been in this back-country African village ... had just echoed what I had heard all through my boyhood years on my grandma's front porch in Henning, Tennessee".

§2.2. Denise Schmandt-Besserat has initiated the important research into the role of tokens in the prehistory of writing, as described, for instance, in her 1992 book.

§§2.3–6. General histories of writing abound; particularly well-worth consulting are Diringer 1962, Gelb 1963, and J. Friedrich 1957, all designed for a general audience; note also Carter & Schoville 1984, Jensen 1958, 1970. These works all treat the ancient Near Eastern developments in considerable detail and discuss the development of the alphabet.

On cuneiform writing, see Walker 1987; Chiera 1938 describes what has been learned from the cuneiform tablets about life in this part of the world in ancient times. On the Egyptian hieroglyphs, see W. Davies 1987. The writing system of the Mayans, as well as its decipherment, is described well in Coe 1992, Houston 1989, and Stuart & Houston 1989. All of these publications are aimed at a general audience.

On the development of the Persian syllabary, see Schmitt 1989b. Daniels 1990 deals with Semitic "abjads". Senner 1989 offers an interesting collection of papers, dealing in part with the spread of writing and the alphabet. Jeffery 1961 offers an excellent account of the development of the Greek writing system out of Semitic originals. A very accessible discussion of the Germanic runes is found in Page 1987. The issue of the Germanic "feather runes" and their possible relation to the Old Irish Ogham script is discussed in Pedersen 1959.

§3. Cleator 1962, J. Friedrich 1957, Gelb 1963, Gordon 1982, and Pedersen 1959 give interesting details on the decipherments of cuneiform and the Egyptian hieroglyphs, and of other decipherments. See also Walker 1987 on cuneiform, Chadwick 1958, 1987 on the decipherment of Linear B, and Andrews 1981 on Egyptian hieroglyphs, all quite accessible works.

§4. On the interpretation of written records (philology) in general, see the many articles in Fisiak 1990, some of which also address the specific question of phonetic interpretation. See Sturtevant 1940/1967 for a survey of evidence that helps us in determining the pronunciation of ancient languages known only through writing. The problem of the Old English "digraphs" is discussed in Antonsen 1967, S. Kuhn 1961, Stockwell & Barritt 1961.

§5. Sampson 1985 is an excellent source on East Asian writing systems, and writing typology in general. Many of the works mentioned above, but especially Diringer 1962 and Gelb 1963, as well as Daniels 1990, Daniels &

Bright 1995, and Trager 1974, give typologies of writing systems. Nakanishi 1992, a popular treatment, gives samples of the various writing systems of the world. Fuller discussion of the different types is found in Trager 1974, Daniels & Bright 1995, and Günther & Ludwig 1994–1995.

Chapter 4.
Sound change

§§2–3. Lehmann 1967 provides, in English translation with annotations, many of the nineteenth century works that reported the important breakthroughs in Indo-European linguistics mentioned here, including Grimm 1819–1834, Lottner 1862, Rask 1818, and Verner 1877 (Sir William Jones 1786, the source of the quotation in Chapter 2, is also included). Bopp 1816 and Pott 1833–1836 were among the early explorations of Indo-European grammar. Vennemann 1984 gives a novel interpretation of the Germanic sound shifts (partly in accordance with the "glottalic theory" of Proto-Indo-European consonants; see Chapter 16, § 7). On the Southern Bantu sound shift, see Doke 1954. For other parallels to Grimm's Law see Sapir 1931 and Labov 1981.

§4. On taboo deformations, see Havers 1946. For a fairly advanced discussion of the neogrammarian hypothesis, see Jankowsky 1990, and Labov 1981, 1994. Osthoff & Brugmann 1878, the source of the epigram for this chapter, is the classic statement of the regularity hypothesis. Schuchardt 1885 is the most outspoken representative of those who were opposed to the neogrammarian regularity hypothesis.

§5. Additional examples of the various types of sound change can be found in virtually any of the textbooks mentioned in the notes to Chapter 1 (though in some instances the terminology may be slightly different). An especially comprehensive treatment is found in Hock 1986a/1991, Chapters 3–8. For the phenomenon of loss with compensatory lengthening see Hock 1986b with examples from many languages and references to earlier discussions. Martinet 1964 is the standard source concerning chain shifts, and Labov's highly influential work draws on some of these insights and elaborates on them (see especially Labov 1994).

The Great Vowel Shift of English, along with Grimm's Law, is one of the most celebrated sound changes that have been studied, and the literature on this subject is enormous; see M. Bloomfield & Newmark 1963, Pyles

& Algeo 1982, or any other work on the history of English for additional discussion of this change.

Hoenigswald 1964 discusses the issue of sporadic changes. The connection of sporadic changes with speech errors goes back to Paul 1920. The aspiration dissimilation now known as Grassmann's Law was discovered by Hermann Grassmann, a noted mathematician whose work is still important in modern mathematics; Grassmann 1863 is translated in Lehmann 1967.

§6.1–2. Jespersen 1941 and Whitney 1877 discuss the notion of change as improvement rather than decay, while Zipf 1929 and Mańczak 1987 try to establish a link between word frequency and sound change. The various neogrammarian attempts to deal with the motivation of sound change are discussed in Paul 1920. Arguments against the claim that linguistic change originates in early child language learning are found in Bybee & Slobin 1982 and in Vihman 1980.

§6.3. Forerunners of Labov's work are Gauchat 1905, Hermann 1929 (a follow-up study on Gauchat), and Sturtevant 1917. Labov 1963 is the ground-breaking study that led to the general recognition that sound change is observable and is directed by social factors. See also Labov 1965, Weinreich, Labov, & Herzog 1968 (an important early position paper), and especially Labov 1994 for a full discussion, at a very advanced level, of the nature of sound change.

Chapter 5.
Analogy and change in word structure

Analogy has a directly psychological basis, inasmuch as it involves a relationship being drawn between two (or more) linguistic entities, whether separate but semantically related words, forms linked together in a grammatical paradigm, sound-alike words, or whatever. Anttila & Brewer 1977 has references to hundreds of works on analogy, both linguistic and psychological. B. Joseph 1997 provides a compendium of types of morphological change, with extensive examples, but the discussion is at a somewhat advanced level.

§2.1. See Lipton 1991 for an entertaining look at collective terms of the type *a pride of lions*. See Winter 1989 for discussion of some parallels in Welsh, Armenian, and Russian to the English zero-plurals.

§3.1. See for instance Winter 1969. D. Baron 1989 (especially Part III) is a highly readable work with several examples of blends and related formations, especially in advertising. The Yiddish rhyming pattern with *shm-* has parallels in Tamil, Marathi, and other South Asian languages, Turkish, Bulgarian, and Greek, and many other languages from India across central Asia and the middle East into Europe. The Yiddish pattern may well be the result of a long-range geographical diffusion (see Chapter 8, §1 for examples of the long-distance spread of words).

§3.2. Probably any parents you ask can give you examples of their children's reinterpretations and folk etymologies, though these processes clearly are not restricted just to children. Parker 1883 is a huge collection of forms created by these sporadic processes (though some may now be dated).

Chapter 6.
Syntactic change

Much of this chapter deals with aspects of usage that are commented on routinely by prescriptivists, who are interested more in what they feel speakers ought to be saying than in what speakers actually do say. As indicated, there is a long history of prescriptivism in English; see Crystal 1995 for a brief overview, as well as any source on the history of English (see the notes to Chapter 1 above). Pinker 1994, Chapter 12 has a highly readable discussion of prescriptivism in contemporary America. Many examples of syntactic change due to language contact are given in Chapter 13 below.

§3. See Pullum & Zwicky 1983 for arguments that *n't* is an affix in modern English.

§6. Hock 1982 is the source for the discussion of the role of auxiliary clitics in the change from SOV to SVO word order. Winter 1961 (especially pp. 197–200) presents the results of an extensive text frequency count in German which showed that only 2.9% of all sentences in the sample had initial objects, while 66.7% had initial subjects.

Chapter 7.
Semantic change

General references: See for instance Algeo 1990a, Ogden & Richards 1923, Stern 1931, Ullman 1957, 1962, Trier 1931, 1973.

§4. The notion of the arbitrary relation between linguistic form and linguistic meaning was first emphasized by Ferdinand de Saussure (see de Saussure 1915).

§5.1. Crystal 1995 and D. Baron 1989 (Chapter 11) discuss "doublespeak" (euphemism in officialese and in daily use). D. Baron 1989 (Chapter 18) has numerous examples of punning in business names (you should be able to find examples in your own area). See also Lutz 1989 and Cutts & Maher 1984, similarly aimed at the general reader.

§5.2. Pisani 1937 and Winter 1982 discuss 'tongue' in Indo-European; see Havers 1946 on the effects of taboo in general.

§5.4. Gilliéron 1915 and 1918 are the classical sources on "intolerable homonymy".

§6.2.1. Buck 1949 organizes the Indo-European lexicon by meanings, and thus provides numerous opportunities to view semantic changes, including the extended Indo-European example given here. The non-Indo-European data are based on research by H. H. Hock; sources include Cohen 1947 and information provided by Iwona Kraska-Szlenk.

§6.2.2. For the English changes in the second person pronoun forms, see any book on the history of English, including the ones cited in the notes to Chapter 1.

Chapter 8.
Lexical borrowing

For general references, see Algeo 1990b and Haugen 1950, as well as Hock 1986a/1991, Chapter 14.

§3. See Hock 1986a/1991, § 14.3. Arndt 1973 deals with the issue of gender assignment in German loanwords.

§4. See Janda, Joseph, & Jacobs 1994 for more examples of hyperforeignisms and discussion of the significance of this phenomenon.

§5.2. For general discussion, see Hock 1986a/1991, § 14.5.3. The information on Icelandic is based on research by H. H. Hock (conducted in 1962–1963); see also Haugen 1982: 204–205. See Sampson 1985: 166–167 for some discussion of the nativization of foreign words in Chinese, where he notes that the nature of the writing system makes adaptation a difficult strategy. He also notes that as speakers of the language of high culture in East Asia, the Chinese have felt little motivation throughout history to borrow from neighboring languages.

Chapter 9.
Lexical change and etymology: The study of words

General reference: A recent survey is found in Zgusta 1990.

§1. For numerous examples of phonesthematic attraction in English, see Samuels 1972. Popular books on English etymology and the origins of phrases, all of which make for fascinating reading, include Black 1988, D. Feldman 1989, Flexner 1982, Funk 1985, Funk 1986, Hendrickson 1983, Partridge 1961. Works on English word origins that are on a more scholarly level include: *The American Heritage Dictionary* (especially the 1992 edition), Onions 1966, and especially the *Oxford English Dictionary* (first or second edition), which traces the history of English words from their earliest attestation to the present, providing extensive examples of usage and changes in usage. P. Davies 1981 is a popularized collection of Indo-European roots, whereas Watkins 1985 is a highly readable but more scholarly collection of all the Indo-European roots that have a reflex in English, whether by inheritance or by borrowing, together with a listing of all the English words that are derived from these roots. Buck 1949, organized in terms of semantic classes, makes it possible to trace lexical change in the Indo-European languages. Works dealing more with the practice of etymology include Malkiel 1993 and Schmitt 1977.

§2. On words that derive from names (eponyms), see Partridge 1950a and Hendrickson 1988. Feldman & Feldman 1994 provides a popularized account of new acronyms in English. The loss of the middle part of three-element compounds (such as *cheese hamburger* → *cheese burger*) was already noted

by the indigenous Sanskrit grammarians and is discussed briefly in Wackernagel & Debrunner 1942 (especially pp. 164–165).

§3. For the etymological sources of names, there are literally dozens of popular books that provide information, vignettes, derivations, and the like. A
few of the more useful ones for English given names and surnames, both in
the United States and in England, are: Dunkling 1977, Ewen 1931, Hanks &
Hodges 1988, Hanks & Hodges 1990, Harrison 1918, Hook 1982, E. Lambert
& Pei 1961, McKinley 1990, G. Stewart 1979, and Withycombe 1977. It is
possible to find similar books on names in other languages and for various
ethnic traditions, such as Woods 1984 on Hispanic names, Kolatch 1989 on
Hebrew names, Puckett 1974 on African American names, or Guggenheimer
& Guggenheimer 1992 and Kaganoff 1977 on Jewish names (ask your refer-
ence librarian for help regarding other languages and/or ethnic backgrounds).

§4. On slang, see Beale 1989, Dillard 1976, Grose 1796, Partridge 1950b,
1967. An interesting exercise is to compare your local college slang tempo-
rally (e.g. with what your parents or professors recall of their college slang)
or geographically (e.g. with what your friends at other schools report), for
some insights into variation and lexical replacement in slang. On argot, see
Kluge 1901 and Partridge 1967. On African elements in African American
Vernacular English, see Turner 1949 and Dalby 1972 (the latter deals with
the Wolof elements discussed in this section).

Chapter 10.
Language, dialect, and standard

General references: Chambers & Trudgill 1983; Francis 1983; and Trudgill
1983, 1986, 1990a, 1990b, 1994.

§2. The exact source of this (half-)joking statement about the difference
between dialects and languages is disputed; but whatever its source, it is
particularly apt.

§3. For the Central Illinois chain shift see Habick 1980.

§4. The nautical jargon example comes from Hock 1986a/1991, Chapter 15.
For mediterranean nautical jargon see Kahane, Kahane, and Tietze 1958.

§5. A good discussion of the development of Nynorsk and its relation to Bokmaal is found in Haugen 1982. On the Hellenistic Greek Koiné, see Thumb 1901; for a briefer and highly readable discussion, see Browning 1982. J. Joseph 1987 has extensive discussion of the standardization process in various European countries. On regional accents, see Trudgill 1983.

§6. The landmark study of diglossia, in which the phenomenon was first brought to light, is Ferguson 1959. The emotional side of the "language question" in Greece has been so strong at times that there have literally been riots over the use of katharevousa versus dimotiki.

Chapter 11.
Dialect geography and dialectology

General references: Chambers & Trudgill 1983, Francis 1983, Hock 1986a/ 1991 (Chapter 15), Jaberg 1908, Mattheier 1983, and Trudgill 1983, 1986, 1990a, 1990b, 1994.

§2.1. On the geographical spread of the Chicago Sound Shift, see Callary 1975.

§2.2. See Kloeke 1927.

§2.3. See Grimm 1893 for the Old High German sound shift, and Hock 1986a/1991, § 15.2.3 for general discussion with references.

Chapter 12.
Language spread, link languages, and bilingualism

General reference: Hock 1986a/1991, § 16.1, Lehiste 1988, Thomason & Kaufman 1988.

§1. Esperanto and Volapük are two of the better-known artificial languages but there have been others; see Large 1985 for more information.

§2. On Indian English (and more generally, world-wide varieties of English), see Kachru 1965, 1983/1992, 1986; for the notion of interlanguage, see Selinker 1972 and the recent reappraisal in Sclinker 1992; for a different view on interlanguage and a discussion of indigenization see Sridhar & Sridhar 1986.

§3. Muysken 1981 discusses Media Lengua. See also Thomason & Kaufman 1988. Information on Michif is in part based on current dissertation research at the University of Illinois by James Kapper.

§4. See Millardet 1933 for "substratum X". The Balkan loss of the infinitive is discussed in B. Joseph 1983; see also Hock 1988. See the notes on Chapter 10, § 5 concerning the Koiné. Data on Swahili, Lingala, and Kinshasa Lingala courtesy of Eyamba Bokamba.

Chapter 13.
Convergence: Dialectology beyond language boundaries

General references: Hock 1986a/1991 (§16.3), Lehiste 1988, Southworth 1990, Thomason & Kaufman 1988, Ureland 1990, and Weinreich 1968 (a true classic in the field).

§1. On the internalized grammar of native bilinguals see Mack 1986, 1989, as well as Caramazza, Yeni-Komshian, Zurif, & Carbone 1973.

§2. The Kupwar convergence is described in Gumperz & Wilson 1971.

§3. The classic work on the Balkans is Sandfeld 1930; see also Schaller 1975 and Solta 1980. There are no comparable books in English (see B. Joseph 1986, 1992 for brief and readable presentations). The shared loan words include calques (loan translations) not just of words and expressions but also proverbial sayings, indicating long-standing intimate and intense contact.

§4. The standard descriptive source on the South Asian convergence area is Masica 1976. On the historical development of convergence, see Emeneau 1956 and the collection of papers in Emeneau 1980; a different view is advocated in Hock 1975 and 1984.

§6. See Hock 1988 on the dialectology of convergence areas.

Chapter 14.
Pidgins, creoles, and related forms of language

General references: Hall 1966, Hancock 1990, Holm 1989, Schuchardt 1883–1888, 1978, 1980, Singler 1988, Thomason & Kaufman 1988; see also N. Baron 1977 and Hock 1986a/1991 (§ 16.4).

§1. As far as H. H. Hock can recall, the anecdotal characterization of the unprepared ESL teacher is adapted from Hatch 1978. Ferguson 1971 is the standard reference on foreigner talk and baby talk and their relation to other types of simplification. See also the collection of articles in Clyne 1981.

§2. On Melanesian Pidgin English/Tok Pisin, see Hall 1943, Mühlhäusler 1970, 1982, 1983. The passage on Chinook Jargon at the end of this section comes from H. Hale 1890.

§3. The idea that foreigner talk is the most important source for the development of pidgins goes back to Schuchardt (1883–1888). Schuchardt, too, appears to be the first one to have discussed the significance of the choice of the infinitive as the all-purpose, uninflected form of the verb. On the deliberate use of foreigner talk by the Portuguese, see Naro 1978. On the attempts of Australian officials to "fake" Tok Pisin, see Mühlhäusler 1981.

§4. GAD is discussed in Clyne 1968; Rost-Roth 1995 has some observations about the extent of guest worker integration into German society. Regarding specific trade jargons, see Broch 1927 on Russenorsk, and Thomason 1983 on Chinook Jargon.

§5. See Bickerton 1981 concerning the "bioprogram" hypothesis. Muysken & Smith 1986 provides a good sampling of views critical of Bickerton's claims.

§6. On the AAVE copula, see Labov 1969. Dillard 1972 is a survey of African American Vernacular English; Schneider 1989 offers information on early stages of AAVE.

Chapter 15.
Language death

Ground-breaking studies on language death are Dressler 1972, Dressler & Wodak 1977, and Dorian 1981. Dorian 1989 is an important anthology, with case-studies of a number of different language-death situations. See also A. Schmidt 1985. The studies in Hock 1983 and 1992 deal with language attrition in an ancient prestige language, Sanskrit, which is now dying out in its spoken use. R. Lambert & Freed 1982 treats language loss in individuals. On the "English Only" or "Official English" movement, see for instance D. Baron 1990 and Adams & Brink 1990. Fishman 1991 discusses language maintenance and language revival.

A fascinating debate on the role of the linguist in dealing with endangered languages is provided by the exchange involving K. Hale et al. 1992, Ladefoged 1992, and Dorian 1993.

Chapter 16.
Comparative method: Establishing language relationship

General references: See Anttila 1972/1988, Hock 1986a/1991, Fox 1995, Winter 1990.

§§1–6. For a good summary see Winter 1970. The most cogent statement of the principles of the Comparative Method is Meillet 1925 (available in an English translation), but see also L. Campbell 1988. Baldi 1990 contains a number of important articles on the results and methods of comparative linguistics applied to a variety of language families (e.g. L. Campbell & Goddard 1990). Anttila 1972 and 1988 illustrates comparative reconstruction with Uralic data; Hock 1986a/1991, with data from Germanic.

§7. For an application of the comparative method to syntax, see Hall 1968 and Hock 1985. The issue of Proto-Indo-European syntactic reconstruction is discussed at length in Hock 1986a/1991, Chapter 19 and the references cited there.

On the "Glottalic Theory", developed more or less at the same time by Gamkrelidze working with Ivanov, and by Hopper, see Gamkrelidze & Ivanov 1973, 1984, 1994, Hopper 1973, Gamkrelidze 1988, all rather advanced works. Relevant are also Vennemann 1989, Haider 1985, Hock 1986a/1991 (§ 19.5.2), J. Stewart 1989 (on voiced aspirates in West African Kwa languages), Stevens 1992; see also Vogt 1958 (on Armenian glottalized stops). Salmons 1993 provides a good overview of the theory, pro and con, while Szemerényi 1989b gives a critical appraisal (see also his 1967 pre-glottalic appraisal of Proto-Indo-European phonology).

The validity of the Comparative Method has been tested against controls provided by the Romance languages by Hall 1950 and 1976.

§8. Sources on some of the language families mentioned include the following.

> Uralic: Collinder 1965a, 1965b, Décsy 1990, Rédei 1986–88; Sajnovics 1770
> Altaic: Poppe 1960, Ramstedt 1957–66; R. A. Miller 1971, 1991 (Japanese included), Unger 1990 (doubts about Altaic)

Basque: Tovar 1957
Caucasic languages: Hewitt 1989
Chinese and Sino-Tibetan: Haudricourt 1954, Karlgren 1949, Norman 1988
Austro-Asiatic and Munda: Pinnow 1959, Parkin 1991
Dravidian: Andronov 1970, Caldwell 1974
Malayo-Polynesian/Austronesian: Blust 1990, Dempwolff 1938, Kahlo 1941
Afro-Asiatic: Cohen 1947, S. Lieberman 1990 (the Cushitic and Chadic sub-groups comprise a variety of related languages; the forms that we cite come from different languages within each group)
Bantu: Doke 1954, Meinhof 1899 (see also Greenberg 1966 on the relatives of Bantu within Africa)
Khoisan: Data from Greenberg 1966
Indigenous languages of America: L. Campbell and Mithun 1979
Algonquian: L. Campbell & Goddard 1990, Goddard 1990
Uto-Aztecan: W. Miller 1967
Siouan: Chafe 1976
Hokan-Siouan: Langdon 1974
Mayan: L. Campbell 1990a, 1990b
Quechua: Cerrón-Palomino 1987
Australian languages: Dixon 1990

We are grateful to Marianne Mithun for valuable feedback on the genetic classification of the indigenous languages of North America.

For a sympathetic and intriguing account of the diversity of the indigenous languages in California, written for a general audience, see Hinton 1994. Surveys of languages of the world, intended for a general audience, are found in G. Campbell 1991, 1995, Katzner 1995, Wendt 1961; these books typically provide a thumbnail sketch (at best) of a number of languages, including quite obscure ones. A collection of more scholarly accounts is found in Comrie 1987. On sign languages, see Lane 1980, Perlmutter 1986, and Stokoe 1974.

Chapter 17.
Proto-World? The question of long-distance genetic relationships

General reference: See the papers in Lamb & Mitchell 1991.

§1. The quoted passages from Indigenous American languages are based on Hinton 1994 and Courlander 1971. On Nostratic, which comes in different "varieties" depending on the researchers involved, see Bomhard 1984, 1990, Bomhard & Kerns 1994, Collinder 1965b, 1974, Illič-Svityč 1964, 1971, 1976.

§2. On Uralic and Dravidian, see Tyler 1968. For attempts to link Indo-European and Uralic, see Collinder 1965b, 1966, 1974, and Ringe 1995; Décsy 1990 expresses doubts about reconstructing the Uralic case endings. On the proposed connection between Dravidian and Elamite, see McAlpin 1974, 1975, 1981. Other connections involving Indo-European have been proposed over the years, most notably, Indo-European and Hamito-Semitic or Afro-Asiatic; see e.g. Cuny 1946, Hodge 1990, Møller 1907, 1917. On the question of the meaning 'wolf' for Nostratic *kuyon* or *küyna*, see Manaster-Ramer 1992.

§4. Greenberg's controversial claims about lexical mass comparison, leading to his classification of Indigenous American languages, are presented in Greenberg 1987, and condensed for a general audience in Greenberg & Ruhlen 1992; Ruhlen 1994 presents evidence for Proto-World. (Earlier statements and applications of Greenberg's views are found in Greenberg 1957 and 1966.) See also Ross 1991 and Shevoroshkin 1990, both aimed at the general reader.

Greenberg's method of mass comparison is critically examined by Peter 1991 (an empirical test of the methodology) and Ringe 1992 (an evaluation of the statistical foundation of the methodology). Hock 1994 is the source of the critical discussion of the putative reconstruction *maliq'a*, while Salmons 1992 critically examines the *tik* reconstruction; Hamp 1992 is generally skeptical of Greenberg's methods.

An interesting scholarly debate on methodology and results in this area is represented in a series of publications by L. Campbell 1988, Greenberg 1989, and Matisoff 1990.

§5. Valuable resources on the origin of language include Jespersen 1921 and Ph. Lieberman 1975, 1984, and the anthologies of de Grolier, Lock, Peters, & Wind 1983; Lock 1978; von Raffler-Engel, Wind, & Jonker 1991; Wind, Chiarelli, Bichakjian, Nocentini, & Jonker 1992; Wind, Jonker, Allott, & Rolfe 1994; and Wind, Pulleyblank, de Grolier, & Bichakjian 1989. Armstrong, Stokoe, & Wilcox 1995 presents a case for the role of sign language in language origin. See also Pinker 1994, Chapter 11, for a highly readable account of the origin of language.

Chapter 18.
Historical linguistics, history, and prehistory: Linguistic paleontology and other applications of our methods

General references on linguistic paleontology: Winter & Polomé 1992 (an important anthology), Polomé 1990b. Early work on Indo-European cultural reconstruction includes Schrader 1886, 1890, 1906–1907. General works on linguistic paleontology as applied to various aspects of Indo-European prehistory include Scherer 1956, K. H. Schmidt 1992, Skomal & Polomé 1987, and Polomé 1990b.

§2. For a full and highly readable discussion of the Tasaday controversy, with numerous suggestions for further reading, see Berreman 1991.

§3. For an analysis of Proto-Indo-European institutions, based on lexical items and their use in the individual languages, including some observations on Indo-European law, see Benveniste 1973. The example of Indo-European comparative jurisprudence is adapted from Calvert Watkins's class lectures (Harvard University, 1973).

§4.1. Benveniste 1973 is an excellent source on Proto-Indo-European material culture and economy. Gamkrelidze & Ivanov 1984/1990, 1985, 1990 discuss prehistoric contacts among Indo-European, Semitic, and Caucasian languages, as do Dolgopolsky 1989 and the papers in Markey & Greppin 1990. Anthony, Telegin, & Brown 1991 presents relevant points on equestrian history.

§4.2. On the question of the Proto-Indo-European homeland, see Diebold 1985, Djakonov 1985, Gimbutas 1970, 1985, Shevoroshkin 1987, Thieme 1954. On Indo-European trees, see also P. Friedrich 1970.

§4.3. On Indo-European poetics and mythology, see Watkins 1982, 1987, 1989, and 1995. Lehmann & Zgusta 1979 presents an attempt at reconstructing a Proto-Indo-European connected text. See Malone et al. 1993 on recent archeological finds in Malta that bear on the issue of male vs. female deities.

§4.4. The spread of the Indo-Europeans is discussed in A. Jones 1992, A. Kuhn 1845, Mallory 1989, Renfrew 1987, 1989. On the tripartite division in Proto-Indo-European society, see Dumézil 1958, who in other works has extended this notion to an analysis of Indo-European religion. The role of traders in early societies has been dealt with in Taylor 1992. On Indo-European women and textiles, see E. Barber 1991.

§5. On the method of Glottochronology, pro and con, see Bergsland & Vogt 1962 (empirical disconfirmation), Hymes 1960, Lees 1953 (comparison with carbon dating), Hock 1976 (questioning the carbon-dating analogy), Rea 1990, and Swadesh 1967 (statement by the founder of the method).

§6. The question of the reality or realism of reconstructions is debated by Pulgram 1959 and Hall 1960.

Copyright acknowledgments

References

Adams, Karen, and Daniel T. Brink (eds.)
  1990   *Perspectives on official English: The campaign for English as the official language of the USA.* Berlin: Mouton de Gruyter.
Aitchison, Jean
  1991   *Language change: Progress or decay?* 2nd ed. Cambridge: University Press.
Algeo, John
  1990a   Semantic change. In: Polomé 1990a: 399–408.
  1990b   Borrowing. In: Polomé 1990a: 409–413.
American Heritage Dictionary of the English Language
  1992   3rd ed. Boston: Houghton Mifflin Co.
Andrews, Carol
  1981   *The British Museum book of the Rosetta Stone.* New York: Dorsett.
Andronov, Mikhail Sergeevich
  1970   *Dravidian languages* [translated from the Russian by D.M. Segal]. Moscow: Nauka.
Anthony, David, Dimitri Y. Telegin, and Dorcas Brown
  1991   The origin of horseback riding. *Scientific American*, December 1991: 94–100.
Antonsen, Elmer H.
  1967   On the origin of the Old English digraph spellings. *Studies in Linguistics* 19: 5–17.
  1975   *A concise grammar of the older runic inscriptions.* Tübingen: Niemeyer.
Anttila, Raimo
  1972   *An introduction to historical and comparative linguistics.* New York: Macmillan.
  1988   *Historical and comparative linguistics.* [Revised edition of the preceding.] Amsterdam: Benjamins.
Anttila, Raimo, and Warren A. Brewer
  1977   *Analogy: A basic bibliography.* Amsterdam: Benjamins.
Arlotto, Anthony
  1972   *Introduction to historical linguistics.* Boston: Houghton-Mifflin. (Repr. 1981, Washington, DC: University Press of America.)
Armstrong, David F., William F. Stokoe, and Sherman E. Wilcox
  1995   *Gesture and the nature of language.* Cambridge: University Press.

Arndt, Walter W.
  1973   Nonrandom assignment of loan words: German noun gender. *Word* 26: 244–253 (1970–1972).
Baldi, Philip
  1983   *An introduction to the Indo-European languages.* Carbondale and Edwardsville: Southern Illinois University Press.
  1990   (ed.) *Linguistic change and reconstruction methodology.* Berlin: Mouton de Gruyter.
Ball, Martin J., and James Fife (eds.)
  1993   *The Celtic languages.* London and New York: Routledge.
Barber, Charles
  1976   *Early Modern English.* London: Andre Deutsch.
Barber, Elizabeth J. W.
  1991   *Prehistoric textiles.* Princeton: University Press.
Baron, Dennis
  1989   *Declining grammar and other essays on the English vocabulary.* Urbana, IL: National Council of Teachers of English.
  1990   *The English-only question: An official language for Americans?* New Haven: Yale University Press.
Baron, Naomi S.
  1977   Trade jargons and pidgins: A functionalist approach. *Journal of Creole Studies* 1977: 5–28.
Battison, Robin
  1978   *Lexical borrowing in American Sign Language.* Silver Spring, MD: Linstok Press.
Beale, Paul (ed.)
  1989   *Partridge's concise dictionary of slang and unconventional English.* New York: Macmillan.
Beekes, Robert S. P.
  1995   *Comparative Indo-European linguistics: An introduction.* Amsterdam and Philadelphia: Benjamins.
Benveniste, Emile
  1973   *Indo-European language and society.* Translated from the French (Le vocabulaire des institutions indo-européennes. Paris: Les Éditions de Minuit [1969: 2 volumes]) by E. Palmer. Coral Gables, FL: University of Miami Press.
Bergsland, Knut, and Hans Vogt
  1962   On the validity of glottochronology. *Current Anthropology* 3: 115–153.
Berreman, Gerald D.
  1991   The incredible "Tasaday": Deconstructing the myth of a "Stone-Age" people. *Cultural Survival Quarterly* 15: 1: 2–45.
Bickerton, Derek
  1981   *Roots of language.* Ann Arbor, MI: Karoma.

Black, Donald C.
1988   *Spoonerisms, sycophants, and sops.* New York: Harper & Row.
Bloomfield, Leonard
1933   *Language.* New York: Holt, Rinehart & Winston. (Repr. 1984, Chicago University Press; chapters on historical linguistics issued separately as "Language history", New York: Holt, Rinehart & Winston, 1965.)
Bloomfield, Morton W., and Leonard Newmark
1963   *A linguistic introduction to the history of English.* New York: Alfred A. Knopf.
Blust, Robert
1990   Summary report: Linguistic change and reconstruction methodology in the Austronesian language family. In: Baldi 1990: 133–153.
Bomhard, Allan R.
1984   *Toward Proto-Nostratic: A new beginning in the reconstruction of Proto-Indo-European and Proto-Afro-Asiatic.* Amsterdam: Benjamins.
1990   A survey of the comparative phonology of the so-called "Nostratic" languages. In: Baldi 1990: 331–358.
Bomhard, Allan R., and John C. Kerns
1994   *The Nostratic macrofamily: A study in distant linguistic relationship.* Berlin and New York: Mouton de Gruyter.
Bopp, Franz
1816   *Ueber das Conjugationssystem der Sanscritsprache in Vergleichung mit jenem der griechischen, lateinischen, persischen und germanischen Sprache.* Frankfurt: Andreä.
Boretzky, Norbert
1977   *Einführung in die historische Linguistik.* Reinbek: Rowohlt.
Bright, William
1992   *Oxford International Encyclopedia of Linguistics.* London and New York: Oxford University Press.
Broch, Olaf
1927   Russenorsk. *Archiv für slavische Philologie* 41: 209–262.
Brugmann, Karl
1897–1916 *Vergleichende Laut-, Stammbildungs- und Flexionslehre der indogermanischen Sprachen.* 2 volumes in 5. Straßburg: Trübner. [Revised edition of K. Brugmann and B. Delbrück 1886–1900, Grundriß der vergleichenden Grammatik der indogermanischen Sprachen. 5 vols. Straßburg: Trübner.]
1904   *Kurze vergleichende Grammatik der indogermanischen Sprachen.* Straßburg: Trübner.
Buck, Carl Darling
1949   *A dictionary of selected synonyms in the principal Indo-European languages.* Chicago: University Press.
Burrow, Thomas
1973   *The Sanskrit language.* New and revised edition. London: Faber.

Bybee, Joan L., and Dan I. Slobin
    1982   Why small children cannot change language on their own: Suggestions from
            the English past tense. In: *Papers from the 5th International Conference on
            Historical Linguistics,* ed. by A. Ahlqvist, 29–37. Amsterdam: Benjamins.
Bynon, Theodora
    1977   *Historical linguistics.* Cambridge: University Press.
Caldwell, Robert.
    1974   *A comparative grammar of the Dravidian or South-Indian family of lan-
            guages.* Revised and edited by J. L. Wyatt and T. Ramakrishna Pillai. New
            Delhi: Oriental Books Reprint Corp. (Reprint of the 1913 edition, London:
            Kegan Paul, Trench, Trubner.)
Callary, Robert E.
    1975   Phonological change and the development of an urban dialect in Illinois.
            Language in Society 4: 155–169.
Campbell, George L.
    1991   *Compendium of the world's languages.* Two volumes. London and New
            York: Routledge.
    1995   *Concise compendium of the world's languages.* London and New York:
            Routledge.
Campbell, Lyle
    1988   Review article on Greenberg 1987. *Language* 64: 591–615.
    1990a   Mayan languages and linguistic change. In: Baldi 1990: 115–129.
    1990b   Philological studies in Mayan languages. In: Fisiak 1990: 87–105.
Campbell, Lyle, and Ives Goddard
    1990   Summary report: American Indian languages and principles of language
            change. In: Baldi 1990: 17–32.
Campbell, Lyle, and Marianne Mithun (eds.)
    1979   *The languages of native America.* Austin: University of Texas Press.
Cardona, George, Henry Hoenigswald, and Alfred Senn (eds.)
    1970   *Indo-European and Indo-Europeans.* Philadelphia: University of Pennsyl-
            vania Press.
Caramazza, Alfonso, Grace Yeni-Komshian, Edgar Zurif, and E. Carbone
    1973   The acquisition of a new phonological contrast: The case of stop consonants
            in French-English bilinguals. *Journal of the Acoustical Society of America*
            54: 421–428.
Carter, Martha L., and Keith N. Schoville (eds.)
    1984   *Sign, symbol, script*: [Guide to] *An exhibition on the origins of writing and
            alphabet.* Madison: University of Wisconsin, Department of Hebrew and
            Semitic Studies.
Ceram, C. W. (pseudonym for Karl W. Marek)
    1973   *The secret of the Hittites: The discovery of an ancient empire.* Transl. by
            R. and C. Winston from the 1955 German original. New York: Schocken
            Books.

Cerrón-Palomino, Rodolfo

1987   *Lingüística quechua.* Cuzco: Centro de los studios rurales andinos.

Chadwick, John

1958   *The decipherment of Linear B.* New York: Vintage Books.

1987   *Reading the past: Linear B and related scripts.* Berkeley and Los Angeles: University of California Press and British Museum.

Chafe, Wallace L.

1976   *The Caddoan, Iroquoian, and Siouan languages.* The Hague: Mouton.

Chambers, John K., and Peter Trudgill

1983   *Dialectology.* Cambridge: University Press.

Chiera, Edward

1938   *They wrote on clay.* (Reprinted 1966.) Chicago: University Press.

Cleator, Philip E.

1962   *Lost languages.* New York: New American Library.

Clyne, Michael

1968   Zum Pidgin-Deutsch der Gastarbeiter. *Zeitschrift für Mundartforschung* 35: 130–139.

1981   (ed.) *Foreigner talk.* (International Journal of the Sociology of Language, 28.)

Coe, Michael D.

1992   *Breaking the Maya code.* New York: Thames & Hudson.

Cohen, Marcel

1947   *Essai comparatif sur le vocabulaire et la phonétique du chamito-sémitique.* Paris: Librairie Ancienne Honoré Champion.

Collinder, Björn

1965 (a)   *An introduction to the Uralic languages.* Berkeley and Los Angeles: University of California Press.

1965 (b)   *Hat das Uralische Verwandte? Eine sprachvergleichende Untersuchung.* (Acta Universitatis Upsaliensis: Acta Societatis Linguisticae Upsaliensis, n.s., 1: 4.) Uppsala: Almqvist & Wiksell.

1966   Distant linguistic affinity. In: *Ancient Indo-European dialects*, ed. by H. Birnbaum and J. Puhvel, 199–200. Berkeley: University of California Press.

1974   Indo-Uralisch – oder gar Nostratisch? Vierzig Jahre auf rauhen Pfaden. In: *Antiquitates Indogermanicae ... Gedenkschrift für Hermann Güntert ...*, ed. by M. Mayrhofer et al., 363–375. (Innsbrucker Beiträge zur Sprachwissenschaft, 12.) Innsbruck.

Comrie, Bernard (ed.)

1987   *The world's major languages.* New York: Oxford University Press.

Comrie, Bernard, and Greville Corbett (eds.)

1993   *The Slavonic languages.* London: Routledge.

Courlander, Harold

   1971   *The fourth world of the Hopis: The epic story of the Hopi Indians as preserved in their legends and traditions.* 5th printing 1992. Albuquerque: University of New Mexico Press.

Crowley, Terry

   1987   *An introduction to historical linguistics.* Suva, Fiji: University of the South Pacific.

   1992   *An introduction to historical linguistics.* Second edition. Auckland: Oxford University Press.

Crystal, David

   1988   *The English language.* London: Penguin.

   1995   *The Cambridge encyclopedia of the English language.* Cambridge: University Press.

Cuny, Albert

   1946   *Invitation à l'étude comparative des langues indo-européennes et des langues chamito-sémitiques.* Bordeaux.

Cutts, Martin, and Chrissie Maher

   1984   *Gobbledygook.* London: George Allen & Unwin.

Dalby, David

   1972   The African element in Black American English. In: *Rappin' and stylin' out,* ed. by T. Kochman, 170–186. Urbana: University of Illinois Press.

Daniels, Peter T.

   1990   Fundamentals of grammatology. *Journal of the American Oriental Society* 110: 727–731.

Daniels, Peter T., and William Bright (eds.)

   1995   *The world's writing systems.* Oxford University Press.

Davies, Peter

   1981   *Roots: Family histories of familiar words.* New York: McGraw-Hill.

Davies, William Vivian

   1987   *Reading the past: Egyptian hieroglyphs.* London: British Museum.

Décsy, Gyula

   1990   *The Uralic protolanguage: A comprehensive reconstruction.* Bloomington, IN: Eurolingua.

Dempwolff, Otto

   1938   *Vergleichende Lautlehre des austronesischen Wortschatzes.* Vol. 3: Austronesisches Wörterverzeichnis. (Beihefte zur Zeitschrift für Eingeborenen-Sprachen, 19.) Berlin: Reimer.

Diebold, A. Richard, Jr.

   1985   *The evolution of Indo-European nomenclature for salmonid fish.* (The Journal of Indo-European Studies, Monograph 5). McLean (VA): Institute for the Study of Man.

Dillard, Joe L.

1972   *Black English: Its history and usage in the United States.* New York: Random House.

1976   *American talk: Slang and American usage.* New York: Random House.

Diringer, David

1962   *Writing.* London: Thames and Hudson.

Dixon, Robert M. W.

1990   Summary report: Linguistic change and reconstruction in the Australian language family. In: Baldi 1990: 393–401.

Djakonov, Igor M.

1985   On the original home of the speakers of Indo-European. *The Journal of Indo-European Studies* 13: 92–174.

Doke, Clement Martyn

1954   *The Southern Bantu languages.* London, New York, Capetown: Oxford University Press and International African Institute.

Dolgopolsky, Aron

1989   Cultural contacts of Proto-Indo-European and Proto-Indo-Iranian with neighbouring languages. *Folia Linguistica Historica* 8: 3–36.

Dorian, Nancy D.

1981   *Language death: The life cycle of a Scottish Gaelic dialect.* Philadelphia: University of Pennsylvania Press.

1989   (ed.) *Investigating obsolescence: Studies in language contraction and death.* Cambridge: University Press.

1993   A response to Ladefoged's other view on endangered languages. *Language* 69: 575–579.

Dressler, Wolfgang U.

1972   On the phonology of language death. *Papers from the 8th Regional Meeting of the Chicago Linguistic Society*, 448–457. Chicago.

Dressler, Wolfgang U., and Ruth Wodak (eds.)

1977   *Language death.* (International Journal of the Sociology of Language 12; published also as vol. 191 of the journal Linguistics, 1977.)

Dumézil, Georges

1958   *L'idéologie tripartite des Indo-Européens.* (Collection LATOMUS, 31.) Brussels: LATOMUS, Revue d'Études Latines.

Dunkling, Leslie

1977   *First names first.* New York: Universe Books.

Emeneau, Murray B.

1956   India as a linguistic area. *Language* 32: 3–16.

1980   *Language and linguistic area*: Essays selected by A. S. Dil. Stanford, CA: University Press.

Ewen, Cecil L.
  1931   A *history of surnames of the British Isles: A concise account of their origin,
          evolution, etymology, and legal status.* London: K. Paul, Trench, Trubner.
          (Reprinted 1968, Detroit: Gale Research Co.)
Falk, Harry
  1990   Goodies for India: Literacy, orality, and Vedic culture. In: *Erscheinungsfor-
          men kultureller Prozesse,* ed. by W. Raible, 103–120. (Script Oralia, 13.)
          Tübingen.
  1993   *Schrift im alten Indien: Ein Forschungsbericht mit Anmerkungen.* Tübingen:
          Gunter Narr.
Feldman, David
  1989   *Who put the butter in butterfly?* New York: Harper & Row.
Feldman, Gilda, and Phil Feldman
  1994   *Acronym soup: A stirring guide to our newest word form.* New York:
          William Morrow and Co.
Ferguson, Charles A.
  1959   Diglossia. *Word* 15: 325–340.
  1971   Absence of copula and the notion of simplicity: A study of normal speech,
          baby talk, foreigner talk, and pidgins. In: Hymes (ed.) 1971: 141–150.
Fishman, Joshua A.
  1991   *Reversing language shift.* Clevedon: Multilingual Matters.
Fisiak, Jacek (ed.)
  1990   *Historical linguistics and philology.* Berlin: Mouton de Gruyter.
Flexner, Stuart B.
  1982   *Listening to America: An illustrated history of words and phrases from our
          lively and splendid past.* New York: Simon and Schuster.
Fox, Anthony
  1995   *Linguistic reconstruction: An introduction to theory and method.* Oxford:
          University Press.
Fraenkel, Ernst
  1950   *Die baltischen Sprachen.* Heidelberg: Winter.
Francis, W. Nelson
  1983   *Dialectology: An introduction.* New York: Longman.
Friedrich, Johannes
  1957   *Extinct languages.* Philosophical Library.
Friedrich, Paul
  1970   *Indo-European trees.* Chicago: University Press.
Frishberg, Nancy Jo
  1975   Arbitrariness and iconicity: Historical change in American Sign Language.
          Language 51: 696–719.
  1976   *Some aspects of the historical development of signs in American Sign Lan-
          guage.* Ph. D. Dissertation, University of California, San Diego.

Funk, Charles E.

1985   *A hog on ice and other curious expressions.* New York: Harper & Row.

1986   *Heavens to Betsy! and other curious sayings.* New York: Harper & Row.

Gamkrelidze, Thomas Valerianovich

1988   The Indo-European glottalic theory in the light of recent critique. *Folia Linguistica Historica* 9: 3–12.

Gamkrelidze, Thomas Valerianovich, and Vjacheslav V. Ivanov

1973   Sprachtypologie und die Rekonstruktion der gemeinindogermanischen Verschlüsse. *Phonetica* 27: 150–156.

1984   *Indoevropejskij jazyk i indoevropejcy: Rekonstrukcija i istoriko-tipologičkij analiz prajazyka i protokul'tury* [Indo-European and the Indo-Europeans: A reconstruction and historical typological analysis of a protolanguage and a proto-culture.] Tbilisi: Publishing House of the Tbilisi State University.

1985   The ancient Near East and the Indo-European question and the migration of tribes speaking Indo-European dialects. *The Journal of Indo-European Studies* 13: 2–91.

1990   The early history of Indo-European languages. *Scientific American*, March 1990: 110–116.

1994   *Indo-European and the Indo-Europeans.* Berlin: Mouton de Gruyter.

Gauchat, Louis

1905   L'unité phonétique dans le patois d'une commune. In: *Aus romanischen Sprachen und Literaturen: Festschrift Heinrich Morf*, 175–232. Halle: Niemeyer.

Gelb, Ignace J.

1963   *A study of writing.* Rev. ed. Chicago: University Press.

Gilliéron, Jules

1915   *Pathologie et thérapeutique verbales.* Paris: Champion.

1918   *Généalogie des mots qui designent l'abeille.* Paris: Champion.

Gimbutas, Marija

1970   Proto-Indo-European culture: The Kurgan culture during the fifth, fourth, and third millennia BC. In: Cardona et al. (eds.) 1970: 155–197.

1985   Primary and secondary homeland of the Indo-Europeans. *The Journal of Indo-European Studies* 13: 185–202.

Goddard, Ives

1990   Algonquian linguistic change and reconstruction. In: Baldi 1990: 99–114.

Gordon, Cyrus H.

1982   *Forgotten scripts: Their ongoing discovery and decipherment.* Repr. 1993, New York: Barnes & Noble.

Goyvaerts, Didier L.

1975   *Present-day historical and comparative linguistics: Introductory guide to theory and method.* Ghent: E. Story-Scientia P.V.B.A.

Greenberg, Joseph H.
  1957   *Essays in linguistics.* Repr. as Phoenix Book P 119, 1963.
  1966   *The languages of Africa.* Bloomington, IN and The Hague: Indiana University and Mouton.
  1987   *Language in the Americas.* Stanford, CA: University Press.
  1989   Classification of American Indian languages: A reply to Campbell. *Language* 65: 107–114.

Greenberg, Joseph H., and Merritt Ruhlen
  1992   Linguistic origins of Native Americans. *Scientific American*, November 1992: 94–99.

Gregor, Douglass Bartlett
  1980   *Celtic: A comparative study of the six Celtic languages: Irish, Gaelic, Manx, Welsh, Cornish, Breton seen against the background of their history, literature, and destiny.* Cambridge and New York: The Oleander Press.

Grimm, Jacob
  1819–1834 *Deutsche Grammatik.* 4 vols. Göttingen: Dieterich.
  1893   *Deutsche Grammatik.* Second ed., v. 1. Gütersloh: Bertelsmann. (Engl. transl. of pp. 580–592 in Lehmann (ed.) 1967: 46–60.)

de Grolier, Eric, Andrew Lock, Charles R. Peters, and Jan Wind (eds.)
  1983   *Glossogenetics: The origin and evolution of language.* (Models of scientific thought, 1). Chur and London: Harwood Academic Publishers.

Grose, Francis
  1796   *A classical dictionary of the vulgar tongue.* Edited by E. Partridge. Repr. 1992, New York: Dorset Press.

Guggenheimer, Heinrich W., and Eva H. Guggenheimer
  1992   *Jewish family names and their origins: An etymological dictionary.* Hoboken (NJ): Ktav Publishing House.

Gumperz, John J., and Robert Wilson
  1971   Convergence and creolization: A case from the Indo-Aryan/Dravidian border. In: Hymes (ed.) 1971: 151–168.

Günther, Hartmut, and Otto Ludwig
  1994–1995 *Schrift und Schriftlichkeit/Writing and its use: Ein interdisziplinäres Handbuch internationaler Forschung/An interdisciplinary handbook of international research.* 2 vols. Berlin: de Gruyter.

Gurney, Oliver R.
  1954   *The Hittites.* 2nd ed. Baltimore: Penguin Books.

Gvozdanović, Jadranka (ed.)
  1992   *Indo-European numerals.* Berlin: Mouton de Gruyter.

Gyármathi, Samuel
  1799   *Affinitas lingvae hvngaricae cvm lingvis fennicae originis grammatice demonstrata.* Göttingen: Dieterich. (Engl. transl. 1983 by V. E. Hanzell, "Grammatical proof of the affinity of the Hungarian language with languages of Fennic origin", Amsterdam Studies in the Theory and History of Linguistic Science, Series 1, v. 15.)

Habick, Timothy
  1980   *Sound change in Farmer City: A sociolinguistic study based on acoustic data.* Urbana: University of Illinois Ph.D. dissertation in Linguistics.

Haider, Hubert
  1985   The fallacy of typology: Remarks on the PIE stop-system. *Lingua* 65: 1–27.

Hale, Horatio
  1890   *An international idiom: A manual of the Oregon Trade Language or Chinook Jargon.* London.

Hale, Kenneth, et al.
  1992   Endangered languages. *Language* 68: 1–42.

Hall, Robert A., Jr.
  1943   *Melanesian Pidgin English.* Baltimore: Linguistic Society of America.
  1950   The reconstruction of Proto-Romance. *Language* 26: 6–27.
  1960   On realism in reconstruction. *Language* 36: 203–206.
  1966   *Pidgin and creole languages.* Ithaca, NY: Cornell University Press.
  1968   Comparative reconstruction in Romance syntax. *Acta Linguistica Hafniensia* 11: 81–88.
  1976   *Proto-Romance phonology.* (Comparative Romance grammar, 2.) New York: Elsevier.

Hamp, Eric P.
  1972   Albanian. In: *Current trends in linguistics*, vol. 9: Linguistics in western Europe, ed. by T. A. Sebeok, 1626–1692. The Hague: Mouton.
  1992   On misusing similarity. In: *Explanation in historical linguistics*, ed. by G. W. Davis and G. K. Iverson, 95–103. Amsterdam: Benjamins.

Hancock, Ian
  1990   Creolization and language change. In: Polomé 1990a: 507–525.

Hanks, Patrick, and Flavia Hodges
  1988   *A dictionary of surnames.* New York: Oxford University Press.
  1990   *A dictionary of first names.* New York: Oxford University Press.

Harrison, Henry
  1918   *Surnames of the United Kingdom: A concise etymological dictionary.* London. Repr., Baltimore: Clearfield Co.

Hatch, Evelyn M.
  1978   Discourse analysis and second language acquisition. In: *Second language acquisition: A book of readings*, ed. by E. M. Hatch. Newbury House.

Haudricourt, André-Georges
  1954   Comment reconstruire le chinois archaique. *Word* 10: 351–364.

Haugen, Einar
  1950   The analysis of linguistic borrowing. *Language* 26: 210–231.
  1982   *The Scandinavian languages: A comparative historical survey.* Minneapolis: University of Minnesota Press.
Havers, Wilhelm
  1946   *Neuere Literatur zum Sprachtabu.* (Sitzungsberichte der Akademie der Wissenschaften Wien, phil.-hist. Klasse, 223: 5.)
Hendrickson, Robert
  1983   *Animal crackers: A bestial lexicon.* New York: Viking Press.
  1988   *The dictionary of eponyms: Names that became words.* New York: Dorset Press. (Reprint of Human words, 1972, Philadelphia: Chilton Book Co.)
Hermann, Eduard
  1929   Lautveränderungen in der Individualsprache einer Mundart. *Nachrichten der Gesellschaft der Wissenschaften zu Göttingen*, phil.-hist. Klasse, 9: 195–214.
Hewitt, B. George (ed.)
  1989   *The indigenous languages of the Caucasus.* Delmar, NY: Caravan Books.
Hinton, Leanne
  1994   *Flutes of fire: Essays on California Indian languages.* Berkeley, CA: Heyday Books.
Hock, Hans Henrich
  1975   Substratum influence on (Rig-Vedic) Sanskrit? *Studies in the Linguistic Sciences* 5: 2: 76–125.
  1976   Review article on Anttila 1972. *Language* 52: 202–220.
  1982   AUX-cliticization as a motivation for word order change. *Studies in the Linguistic Sciences* 12: 1: 91–101.
  1983   Language-death phenomena in Sanskrit: Grammatical evidence for attrition in contemporary spoken Sanskrit. *Studies in the Linguistic Sciences* 13: 2: 21–35.
  1984   (Pre-)Rig-Vedic convergence of Indo-Aryan with Dravidian? Another look at the evidence. *Studies in the Linguistic Sciences* 14: 1: 89–107.
  1985   Yes, Virginia, syntactic reconstruction is possible. *Studies in the Linguistic Sciences* 15: 1: 49–60.
  1986a/1991 *Principles of historical linguistics.* Berlin: Mouton de Gruyter. 2nd rev. and augm. ed., 1991, Berlin: Mouton de Gruyter. [Except for the chapter notes and references, the second edition is substantially the same as the first one.]
  1986b   Compensatory lengthening: In defense of the concept 'mora'. *Folia Linguistica* 20: 431–60
  1988   Historical implications of a dialectological approach to convergence. In: *Historical dialectology*, ed. by J. Fisiak, 283–328. Berlin: Mouton de Gruyter.

1992   Spoken Sanskrit in Uttar Pradesh: Profile of a dying prestige language. In: *Dimensions of sociolinguistics in South Asia: Papers in memory of Gerald Kelley*, ed. by E. C. Dimmock, B. B. Kachru, and Bh. Krishnamurti, 247–260. New Delhi: Oxford University Press.

1994   Swallow tales: Chance and the "world etymology" MALIQ'A 'swallow, throat'. *Papers from the 29th Regional Meeting of the Chicago Linguistic Society*, 1: 215–238. Chicago.

Hodge, Carleton T.

1990   The role of Egyptian within Afroasiatic(/Lislakh). In: Baldi 1990: 639–659.

Hoenigswald, Henry M.

1964   Graduality, sporadicity, and the minor sound change processes. *Phonetica* 11: 202–215.

1965   *Language change and linguistic reconstruction*. Chicago: University Press.

Holm, John

1989   *Pidgins and creoles*. Vols. 1–2. Cambridge: University Press.

Hook, Julius N.

1982   *Family names: How our surnames came to America*. New York: Macmillan.

Hopper, Paul J.

1973   Glottalized and murmured occlusives in Indo-European. *Glossa* 7: 141–166.

Houston, Stephen D.

1989   *Reading the past: Maya glyphs*. London: British Museum.

Hymes, Dell

1960   Lexicostatistics so far. *Current Anthropology* 1: 3–44 and 340–345.

1971   (ed.) *Pidginization and creolization of language*. Cambridge: University Press.

Illič-Svityč, Vladislav Markovič

1964   Drevnejšie indoevropejsko-semitskie jazykovye kontakty [The oldest contacts between Indo-European and Semitic languages]. In: *Problemy indoevropejskogo jazyknoznanija*, ed. by V. Toporov, 3–12. Moscow: Nauka.

1971, 1976   *Opyt sravnenija nostratičeskix jazykov* [An attempt at reconstructing Nostratic]. 2 vols. Moscow: Nauka.

Jaberg, Karl

1908   *Sprachgeographie*. Aarau: Sauerländer.

Janda, Richard D., Brian D. Joseph, and Neil G. Jacobs

1994   Systematic hyperforeignisms as maximally external evidence for linguistic rules. In: *The reality of linguistic rules*, ed. by S. D. Lima et al., 67–92. Amsterdam and Philadelphia: Benjamins.

Jankowsky, Kurt R.

1990   The Neogrammarian hypothesis. In: Polomé 1990a: 223–239.

Jeffers, Robert J., and Ilse Lehiste

1979   *Principles and methods for historical linguistics*. Cambridge, MA: MIT Press.

Jeffery, Lilian Hamilton
  1961   *The local scripts of archaic Greece.* Oxford: Clarendon Press.
Jensen, Hans
  1958   *Die Schrift in Vergangenheit und Gegenwart.* Berlin.
  1970   *Sign, symbol, and script.* Transl. of 3rd ed. of Jensen 1958. London: Allen & Unwin.
Jespersen, Otto
  1921   *Language: Its nature, development, and origin.* Repr. 1964, New York: W. W. Norton & Company.
  1941   *Efficiency in linguistic change.* (Det Kgl. Danske Videnskabernes Selskab, 27: 4.)
Jones, Alex I.
  1992   Language and archeology: Evaluating competing explanations of the origins of the Indo-European languages. *Journal of Indo-European Studies* 20: 31–44.
Jones, Charles (ed.)
  1993   *Historical linguistic: Problems and perspectives.* London and New York: Longman.
Jones, Sir William
  1786   The third anniversary discourse, on the Hindus. Published 1788. *Asiatick Researches* 1: 422. (Repr. in Lehmann 1967.)
Joseph, Brian D.
  1983   *The synchrony and diachrony of the Balkan infinitive: A study in areal, general, and historical linguistics.* Cambridge: University Press.
  1986   A fresh look at the Balkan Sprachbund: Some observations on H. W. Schaller's Die Balkansprachen. *Mediterranean Language Review* 3: 105–114.
  1992   The Balkan languages. In: *International encyclopedia of linguistics*, ed. by W. Bright, 1: 153–155. Oxford: University Press.
  1997   Diachronic morphology. In: *Handbook of morphology*, ed. by A. Zwicky and A. Spencer. Oxford: Blackwell Publishers.
Joseph, John
  1987   *Eloquence and power: The rise of language standards and standard languages.* London: Pinter.
Justus, Carol F.
  1988   Indo-European numerals and numeral systems. In: *A linguistic happening in memory of Ben Schwartz*, ed. by Y. L. Arbeitman, 521–541. Louvain: Peeters.
Kachru, Braj B.
  1965   The Indianness in Indian English. *Word* 21: 391–410.
  1983   (ed.) *The other tongue: English across cultures.* Oxford: Pergamon Press.
  1986   *The alchemy of English.* Oxford: Pergamon Press. (Repr. 1990, Urbana: University of Illinois Press.)

1992   (ed.) *The other tongue: English across cultures*. 2nd ed. Urbana: University of Illinois Press.

Kaganoff, Benzion G.
1977   *A dictionary of Jewish names and their history*. New York: Schocken Books.

Kahane, Henry, Renée Kahane, and Andreas Tietze
1958   *The Lingua Franca in the Mediterranean: Turkish nautical terms of Italian and Greek origin*. Urbana: University of Illinois Press. (Repr. 1988, Istanbul: ABC Kıtabevi.)

Kahlo, Gerhard
1941   *Kleines vergleichendes malayo-polynesisches Wörterbuch*. Leipzig: Harrassowitz.

Karlgren, Bernhard
1920   Le proto-chinois: Langue flexionelle. *Journal asiatique* 1920: 205ff.
1949   *The Chinese language: An essay on its nature and history*. New York: Ronal Press.

Katzner, Kenneth
1995   *The languages of the world*. London and New York: Routledge.

Kloeke, Gesinus Gerhardus
1927   *De Hollandsche expansie in de zestiende en zeventiende eeuw*. 's Gravenhage: Nijhoff.

Kluge, Friedrich
1901   *Rotwelsch: Quellen und Wortschatz der Gaunersprache und der verwandten Geheimsprachen*. Repr. 1987, Berlin: de Gruyter.

Kolatch, Alfred J.
1989   *The new name dictionary: Modern English and Hebrew names*. Middle Village, NY: J. David Publishers.

König, Ekkehard, and Johan van der Auwera (eds.)
1994   *The Germanic languages*. London and New York: Routledge.

Krahe, Hans
1970   *Einleitung in das vergleichende Sprachstudium*, ed. by W. Meid. (Innsbrucker Beiträge zur Sprachwissenschaft, 1.) Innsbruck.

Kuhn, Adalbert
1845   *Zur ältesten Geschichte der indogermanischen Völker*. Berlin: Nauck.

Kuhn, Sherman M.
1961   On the syllabic phonemes of Old English. *Language* 37: 522–538.

Labov, William
1963   The social motivation of a sound change. *Word* 19: 273–309.
1965   On the mechanism of linguistic change. *Georgetown University Monographs on Languages and Linguistics* 18: 91–114.
1969   Contraction, deletion, and inherent variability of the English copula. *Language* 45: 715–762.
1981   Resolving the neogrammarian controversy. *Language* 57: 267–308.

572   *References*

1994   *Principles of linguistic change: Internal factors.* Cambridge, MA and Oxford, England: Blackwell.

Ladefoged, Peter

1992   Another view of endangered languages. *Language* 68: 809–811.

1993   *A course in phonetics.* 3rd ed. Fort Worth: Harcourt Brace Jovanovich College Publishers.

Lamb, Sydney, and E. Douglas Mitchell (eds.)

1991   *Sprung from some common source: Investigations into the prehistory of languages.* Stanford: University Press.

Lambert, Eloise, and Mario Pei

1961   *Our names, where they come from and what they mean.* New York: Lothrop, Lee & Shepard Co.

Lambert, Richard D., and Barbara F. Freed (eds.)

1982   *The loss of language skills.* Rowley, MA: Newbury House.

Lane, Harlan

1980   Historical: A chronology of the oppression of sign language in France and the United States. In: *Recent perspectives on American Sign Language*, ed. by H. Lane and F. Grosjean, 119–161. Hillsdale, NJ: Lawrence Erlbaum Associates.

Langdon, Margaret

1974   *Comparative Hokan-Coahuiltecan studies.* The Hague: Mouton.

Large, Andrew

1985   *The artificial language movement.* Oxford: Basil Blackwell.

Lees, Robert B.

1953   The basis of glottochronology. *Language* 29: 113–127.

Lehiste, Ilse

1988   *Lectures on language contact.* Cambridge, MA: MIT Press.

Lehmann, Winfred P.

1962   *Historical linguistics.* New York: Holt.

1967   (ed.) *A reader in 19th century historical Indo-European linguistics.* Bloomington: Indiana University Press.

1973   *Historical linguistics.* 2nd ed. New York: Holt.

1992   *Historical linguistics: An introduction.* 3rd ed. London and New York: Routledge

1993   *Theoretical bases of Indo-European linguistics.* London: Routledge.

Lehmann, Winfred P., and Ladislav Zgusta

1979   Schleicher's tale after a century. In: *Festschrift für Oswald Szemerényi*, ed. by Bela Brogyanyi, 1: 455–466. Amsterdam: Benjamins.

Lieberman, Philip

1975   *On the origins of language: An introduction to the evolution of human speech.* New York: Macmillan.

1984   *The biology and evolution of language.* Cambridge, MA: Harvard University Press.

Lieberman, Stephen J.
   1990   Summary report: Linguistic change and reconstruction in the Afro-Asiatic languages. In: Baldi 1990: 565–575.
Lipton, James
   1991   *An exaltation of larks: "The ultimate edition."* New York: Viking Books.
Lock, Andrew (ed.)
   1978   *Action, gesture. and symbol: The emergence of language.* London and New York: Academic Press
Lockwood, William B.
   1969   *Indo-European philology: Historical and comparative.* London: Hutchinson University Library.
   1972   *A panorama of Indo-European languages.* London: Hutchinson University Library.
Lottner, Carl
   1862   Ausnahmen der ersten Lautverschiebung. *Zeitschrift für vergleichende Sprachwissenschaft* 11: 161–205. (Transl. in Lehmann 1967.)
Lutz, William (ed.)
   1989   *Beyond nineteen eighty-four: Doublespeak in a post-Orwellian age.* Urbana, IL: National Council of Teachers of English.
MacAlpin, David W.
   1974   Toward Proto-Elamo-Dravidian. *Language* 50: 89–101.
   1975   Elamite and Dravidian: Further evidence of relationship. (With discussion by M. B. Emeneau, W. H. Jacobsen, F. B. J. Kuiper, H. H. Paper, E. Reiner, R. Stopa, F. Vallat, R. W. Wescott, and a reply by D. W. MacAlpin.) *Current Anthropology* 16: 105–115.
   1981   *Proto-Elamo-Dravidian: The evidence and its implications.* (Transactions of the American Philosophical Society, 71: 3.) Philadelphia.
Macaulay, Donald (ed.)
   1992   *The Celtic languages.* (Cambridge Language Surveys.) Cambridge: University Press.
Mack, Molly
   1986   A study of the semantic and syntactic processing in monolinguals and fluent early bilinguals. *Journal of Psycholinguistic Research* 15: 6: 443–488.
   1989   Consonant and vowel perception and production: Early English-French bilinguals and English monolinguals. *Perception & Psychophysics* 46: 2: 187–200.
Malkiel, Yakov
   1993   *Etymology.* Cambridge: University Press.
Mallory, John P.
   1989   *In search of the Indo-Europeans: Language, archaeology, and myth.* London and New York: Thames and Hudson.

Malone, Caroline, et al.

1993   The death cults of prehistoric Malta. *Scientific American*, December 1993: 110–117.

Manaster-Ramer, Alexis

1992   On anecdotal universals in historical linguistics. *Diachronica* 9: 135–137.

Mańczak, Witold

1987   *Frequenzbedingter unregelmässiger Lautwandel in den germanischen Sprachen*. Wrocław: Polska Akademia Nauk.

Markey, Thomas, and John Greppin (eds.)

1990   *When worlds collide: Indo-Europeans and pre-Indo-Europeans*. Ann Arbor, MI: Karoma.

Martinet, André

1964   *Économie des changements phonétiques*. 2nd ed. Bern: Francke

Masica, Colin P.

1976   *Defining a linguistic area: South Asia*. Chicago: University Press.

1991   *The Indo-Aryan languages*. Cambridge: University Press.

Matisoff, James A.

1990   On megalocomparison. *Language* 66: 106–120.

Mattheier, Klaus J.

1983   *Aspekte der Dialekttheorie*. Tübingen: Niemeyer.

Mayrhofer, Manfred

1986   *Indogermanische Grammatik*, 1. Heidelberg: Winter.

McKinley, Richard A.

1990   *A history of British surnames*. London and New York: Longman.

McMahon, April M. S.

1994   *Understanding language change*. Cambridge: University Press.

Meillet, Antoine

1925   *La méthode comparative en linguistique historique*. Paris: Librairie Honoré Champion. ("The comparative method in historical linguistics", transl. by Gordon B. Ford, Jr., 1970).

1937   *Introduction à l'étude comparative des langues indo-européennes*. 8th ed. Paris: Hachette. (Reprinted. 1964, Alabama University Press.)

Meinhof, Carl

1899   *Grundriss einer Lautlehre der Bantusprachen*. (Abhandlungen für die Kunde des Morgenlandes, 11: 2.) Repr. 1966, Kraus Reprint Limited.

Melchert, H. Craig

1994   *Anatolian historical morphology*. Amsterdam and Atlanta: Rodopi.

Millardet, Georges

1933   Sur un ancien substrat commun à la Sicile, le Corse, et la Sardaigne. *Revue de linguistique romane* 9: 346–369.

Miller, Roy Andrew

1971   *Japanese and the other Altaic languages*. Chicago: University Press.

1991   How many Verner's Laws does an Altaicist need? In: *Studies in the historical phonology of Asian languages*, ed. by W. G. Boltz and M. C. Shapiro, 176–204. Amsterdam: Benjamins.

Miller, Wick R.

1967   *Uto-Aztecan cognate sets*. (University of California Publications in Linguistics, 48.) Berkeley and Los Angeles: University of California Press.

Møller, Hermann

1907   *Semitisch und Indogermanisch*. Vol. 1. Copenhagen.

1917   *Die semitisch-vorindogermanischen laryngalen Konsonanten*. (Mémoires de l'Académie Royale des Sciences et Lettres de Danemark, 7me série, 4: 1.) Copenhagen.

Mühlhäusler, Peter

1970   *Growth and structure of the lexicon of New Guinea Pidgin*. Canberra: Pacific Linguistics, C-52.

1981   Foreigner Talk, Tok Masta in New Guinea. In: Clyne 1981: 93–113

1982   Tok Pisin in Papua New Guinea. In: *English as a world language*, ed. by R. W. Bailey and M. Görlach, 439–466. Ann Arbor, MI: The University of Michigan Press.

1983   The development of word formation in Tok Pisin. *Folia Linguistica* 17: 463–487.

Muysken, Pieter

1981   Halfway between Quechua and Spanish: The case for relexification. In: *Historicity and variation in creole studies*, ed. by A. R. Highfield and A. Valdman, 52–78. Ann Arbor, MI: Karoma.

Muysken, Pieter, and Norval Smith (eds.)

1986   *Substrata versus universals in creole genesis*. Amsterdam: Benjamins.

Nakanishi, Akira

1992   *Writing systems of the world: Alphabets, syllabaries, pictograms*. Rutland, VT: Charles E. Tuttle Co.

Naro, Anthony Julius

1978   A study on the origins of pidginization. *Language* 54: 314–347.

Norman, Jerry

1988   *Chinese*. (Cambridge Language Surveys.) Cambridge: University Press.

Ogden, Charles Kay, and Ivor Armstrong Richards

1923   *The meaning of meaning*. New York: Harcourt.

Onions, C. T.

1966   *The Oxford dictionary of English etymology*. Oxford: Clarendon Press.

Osthoff, Hermann, and Karl Brugmann

1878   (Preface to) *Morphologische Untersuchungen auf dem Gebiete der indogermanischen Sprachen*, 1. (Engl. transl. in Lehmann 1967.)

Oxford English Dictionary
 1884–1928 Oxford University Press. (Repr. 1933 with supplements.)
 1989   2nd ed. Oxford University Press.
Page, Raymond Ian
 1987   *Reading the past: Runes.* London: British Museum.
Palmer, Leonard R.
 1954   *The Latin language.* London: Faber & Faber.
 1980   *The Greek language.* Atlantic Highlands, NJ: Humanities Press, Inc.
Parker, A. Smythe
 1883   *Folk-etymology: A dictionary of verbal corruptions or words perverted in form or meaning, by false derivation or mistaken analogy.* Repr. 1969, New York: Greenwood Publishers.
Partridge, Eric
 1950a   *Name into word: Proper names that have become common property: A discursive dictionary.* 2nd ed. London: Secker & Warburg.
 1950b   *A dictionary of the underworld.* London: Routledge & Kegan Paul.
 1961   *Adventuring among words.* Oxford: University Press.
 1967   *Dictionary of slang and unconventional English.* 6th ed. New York: Macmillan.
Paul, Hermann
 1920   *Prinzipien der Sprachgeschichte.* 5th ed. Halle: Niemeyer. (Engl. translation of 2nd ed.: Principles of language history, 1889, New York: Macmillan.)
Pedersen, Holger
 1959   *The discovery of language.* (Transl. by J. W. Spargo from the 1931 Danish original.) Repr. 1959, Bloomington: Indiana University Press.
Perlmutter, David M.
 1986   No nearer to the soul. *Natural Language and Linguistic Theory* 4: 515–523.
Peter, Steven Joseph
 1991   *Barking up the wrong family tree? Greenberg's method of mass comparison and the genetic classification of languages.* Urbana: University of Illinois B.A. honors thesis.
Pinker, Steven
 1994   *The language instinct: How the mind creates language.* New York: William Morrow and Co.
Pinnow, Heinz-Jürgen
 1959   *Versuch einer historischen Lautlehre der Kharia-Sprache.* Wiesbaden: Harrassowitz.
Pisani, Vittore
 1937   Toch. A *käntu* und das idg. Wort für 'Zunge'. *Zeitschrift für vergleichende Sprachwissenschaft* 64: 100–103.

Polomé, Edgar C.
  1982   (ed.) *The Indo-Europeans in the fourth and third millennia.* Ann Arbor,
          MI: Karoma.
  1990a   (ed.) *Research guide on language change.* Berlin: Mouton de Gruyter.
  1990b   Linguistic paleontology: Migration theory, prehistory, and archeology cor-
          related with linguistic data. In: Polomé 1990a: 137–159.
  1990c   Etymology. In: Polomé 1990a: 415–440.
Poppe, Nikolaus
  1960   *Vergleichende Grammatik der altaischen Sprachen.* Wiesbaden: Harras-
          sowitz.
Posner, Rebecca
  1966   *The Romance languages: A linguistic introduction.* Anchor Books. Repr.
          1970, Gloucester, MA: Peter Smith.
Pott, August F.
  1833–1836 *Etymologische Forschungen auf dem Gebiete der indogermanischen
          Sprachen.* Lemgo: Meyer.
Puckett, Newbell N.
  1974   *Black names in America: Origins and usage.* Boston: G. K. Hall.
Pulgram, Ernst
  1959   Proto-Indo-European reality and reconstruction. *Language* 35: 421–426.
Pyles, Thomas, and John Algeo
  1982   *The origins and development of the English language.* 3rd ed. New York:
          Harcourt Brace Jovanovich.
Ramstedt, Gustaf John
  1957–1966 *Einführung in die altaische Sprachwissenschaft.* 3 vols. (Suomalais-
          Ugrilaisen Seuran Toimituksia, 104: 1–3) Helsinki: Suomalais-Ugrilainen
          Seura.
Rask, Rasmus
  1818   *Undersögelse om det gamle Norske eller Islandske Sprogs Oprindelse.*
          København: Gyldendal.
Rea, John A.
  1990   Lexicostatistics. In: Polomé 1990a: 217–222.
Rédei, Károly (ed.)
  1986–1988 *Uralisches etymologisches Wörterbuch.* Wiesbaden: Harrassowitz.
Renfrew, Colin
  1987   *Archaeology and language: The puzzle of Indo-European origins.* Cam-
          bridge: University Press.
  1989   The origins of the Indo-European languages. *Scientific American*, October
          1989: 106–114.
Ringe, Donald R.
  1992   *On calculating the factor of chance in language comparison.* (Transactions
          of the American Philosophical Society, 82: 1.)
  1995   "Nostratic" and the factor of chance. *Diachronica* 12: 1: 55–74.

Robinson, Orrin W.
    1992   *Old English and its closest relatives: A survey of the earliest Germanic languages*. Stanford: University Press.

Ross, Philip E.
    1991   Hard words: How deeply can language be traced? Radical linguists look back to the Stone Age, traditionalists disagree. *Scientific American*, April 1991: 138–147.

Rost-Roth, Martina
    1995   Language in intercultural communication. In: *The German language and the real world: Sociolinguistic, cultural, and pragmatic perspectives on contemporary German*, ed. by Patrick Stevenson. Oxford: University Press.

Ruhlen, Merritt
    1994   *On the origin of languages: Studies in linguistic typology*. Stanford: University Press.

Sajnovics, Joannis
    1770   *Demonstratio idioma ungarorum et lapponum idem esse*. Tyrnavia. (Repr. 1968, Indiana University Publications, Uralic and Altaic Series, 91.)

Salmons, Joe
    1992   A look at the data for a global etymology: **tik* 'finger'. In: *Explanation in historical linguistics*, ed. by G. W. Davis and G. K. Iverson, 207–228. Amsterdam: Benjamins.
    1993   *The glottalic theory: Survey and synthesis*. (The Journal of Indo-European Studies, Monograph 10.) McLean, VA: Institute for the Study of Man.

Sampson, Geoffrey
    1985   *Writing systems: A linguistic introduction*. London: Hutchinson & Co.

Samuels, Michael Louis
    1972   *Linguistic evolution, with special reference to English*. Cambridge: University Press.

Sandfeld, Kristian
    1930   *Linguistique balkanique: Problèmes et résultats*. Paris: Librairie Ancienne Honoré Champion.

Sapir, Edward
    1921   *Language*. New York: Harcourt.
    1931   The concept of phonetic law as tested in primitive languages by Leonard Bloomfield. In: *Methods in social science: A case book,* ed. by S. A. Rice, 197–306. Chicago: University Press.

de Saussure, Ferdinand
    1879   *Mémoire sur le système primitif des voyelles dans les langues indo-européennes*. Repr. 1968, Hildesheim: Olms. (Excerpts in Engl. transl. in Lehmann 1967.)
    1915   *Cours de linguistique générale*, ed. by Charles Bally, Albert Sechehaye, and Albert Reidlinger. Paris: Payot.

Schaller, Helmut W.
  1975   *Die Balkansprachen: Eine Einführung in die Balkanphilologie.* Heidelberg: Winter.
Scherer, Anton
  1956   Hauptprobleme der idg. Altertumskunde. *Kratylos* 1: 3–21.
Schmandt-Besserat, Denise
  1992   *Before writing. Vol. 1: From counting to cuneiform.* Austin: University of Texas Press.
Schmidt, Annette
  1985   *Young people's Dyirbal: An example of language death from Australia.* Cambridge: University Press.
Schmidt, Karl Horst
  1992   Celtic movements in the first millennium B.C. *Journal of Indo-European Studies* 20: 145–178.
Schmitt, Rüdiger
  1977   (ed.) *Etymologie.* Darmstadt: Wissenschaftliche Buchgesellschaft.
  1989a (ed.) *Compendium linguarum iranicarum.* Wiesbaden: Reichert.
  1989b Altpersisch. In: Schmitt 1989a.
Schneider, Edgar W.
  1989   *American Earlier Black English: Morphological and syntactic variables.* Tuscaloosa and London: The University of Alabama Press.
Schrader, Otto
  1886   *Linguistisch-historische Forschungen zur Handelsgeschichte und Warenkunde,* 1. Jena.
  1890   *Prehistoric antiquities of the Aryan peoples: A manual of comparative philology and the earliest cultures.* (Transl. of first ed. of Schrader 1906–1907.) London: Griffin.
  1906–1907 *Sprachvergleichung und Urgeschichte: Linguistisch-historische Beiträge zur Erforschung des indogermanischen Altertums.* 3rd ed., 2 vols. Jena.
Schuchardt, Hugo
  1883–1888 *Kreolische Studien.* 8 vols. Wien: Gerold.
  1885   *Über die Lautgesetze: Gegen die Junggrammatiker.* Berlin: Oppenheim.
  1978   *The ethnography of variation: Selected writings on pidgins and creoles.* Transl. and selected by T. L. Markey. Ann Arbor, MI: Karoma.
  1980   *Pidgin and creole languages*: Selected and transl. by G. G. Gilbert. Cambridge: University Press.
Selinker, Larry
  1972   Interlanguage. *International Review of Applied Linguistics* 10: 209–231.
  1992   *Rediscovering interlanguage.* London: Longman.
Senn, Alfred
  1942   *The Lithuanian language: A characterization.* Chicago: Lithuanian Cultural Institute.

Senner, Wayne M. (ed.)
  1989   *The origins of writing*. Lincoln: University of Nebraska Press.
Shevoroshkin, Vitaly
  1987   Indo-European homeland and migrations. *Folia Linguistica Historica* 7:
          227–250.
  1990   The mother tongue: How linguists have reconstructed the ancestor of all
          living languages. *The Sciences*, May/June 1990: 20–27.
Shevoroshkin, Vitaly, and Thomas L. Markey (eds.)
  1986   *Typology, relationship, and time*. Ann Arbor, MI: Karoma.
Sihler, Andrew L.
  1995   *New comparative grammar of Greek and Latin*. New York and Oxford:
          Oxford University Press.
Singler, John Victor
  1988   The homogeneity of the substrate as a factor in pidgin/creole genesis. *Lan-
          guage* 64: 27–51.
Skomal, Susan N., and Edgar C. Polomé
  1987   *Proto-Indo-European: The archeology of a linguistic problem*. Washington,
          DC: Institute for the Study of Man.
Solta, Georg Renatus
  1980   *Einführung in die Balkanlinguistik mit besonderer Berücksichtigung des
          Substrats und des Balkanlateinischen*. Darmstadt: Wissenschaftliche Buch-
          gesellschaft.
Southworth, Franklin C., III
  1990   Contact and interference. In: Polomé 1990a: 281–294.
Sridhar, Kamal, and S. N. Sridhar
  1986   Bridging the gap: Second language acquisition and indigenized varieties of
          English. *World Englishes* 5: 1: 3–14.
Stern, Gustaf
  1931   *Meaning and change of meaning*. Bloomington: Indiana University Press.
Sternemann, Reinhard, and Karl Gutschmidt
  1989   *Einführung in die vergleichende Sprachwissenschaft*. Berlin: Akademie-
          Verlag.
Stevens, Christopher M.
  1992   The use and abuse of typology in comparative linguistics: An update of
          the controversy. *Journal of Indo-European Studies* 20: 45–58.
Stewart, George R.
  1979   *American given names: Their origin and history in the context of the En-
          glish language*. New York: Oxford University Press.
Stewart, John M.
  1989   Kwa. In: *The Niger-Congo languages*, ed. by J. Bendor-Samuel, 217–245.
          Lanham, New York, and London: University Press of America.
Stockwell, Robert P., and C. Westbrook Barritt
  1961   Scribal practice: Some assumptions. *Language* 37: 75–82.

Stokoe, William C., Jr.
　1974　Classification and description of sign languages. In: *Current trends in linguistics, vol. 12: Linguistics and adjacent arts and sciences*, ed. by T. A. Sebeok, 345–371. The Hague: Mouton.
Stuart, David, and Stephen D. Houston
　1989　*Maya writing*. Scientific American, August 1989: 82–89.
Sturtevant, Edgar H.
　1917　*Linguistic change*. Chicago: University Press.
　1940　*The pronunciation of Greek and Latin*. Baltimore: Linguistic Society of America. (2nd ed., 1967.)
　1947　*An introduction to linguistic science*. New Haven: Yale University Press.
Swadesh, Morris
　1967　Lexicostatistic classification. In: *Handbook of Middle American Indians*, ed. by N. McQuown, 5: 79–115. Austin: University of Texas Press.
Szemerényi, Oswald
　1957　The problem of Balto-Slav unity: A critical survey. *Kratylos* 2: 97–123.
　1967　The new look of Indo-European: Reconstruction and typology. *Phonetica* 17: 65–99.
　1970　*Einführung in die vergleichende Sprachwissenschaft*. Darmstadt: Wissenschaftliche Buchgesellschaft.
　1989 (a)　*Einführung in die vergleichende Sprachwissenschaft*. 3rd ed. Darmstadt: Wissenschaftliche Buchgesellschaft.
　1989 (b)　The new sound of Indo-European. *Diachronica* 6: 237–269.
Taylor, Timothy
　1992　The Gundestrup cauldron. *Scientific American*, March 1992: 84–89.
Thieme, Paul
　1954　*Die Heimat der indogermanischen Gemeinsprache*. (Akademie der Wissenschaften und der Literatur, Mainz.) Wiesbaden: Steiner.
Thomason, Sarah Grey
　1983　Chinook Jargon in areal and historical context. *Language* 59: 820–870.
Thomason, Sarah Grey, and Terrence Kaufman
　1988　*Language contact, creolization, and genetic linguistics*. Berkeley and Los Angeles: University of California Press.
Thumb, Albert
　1901　*Die griechische Sprache im Zeitalter des Hellenismus: Beiträge zur Geschichte und Beurteilung der Koinē*. Straßburg: Trübner.
Tovar, Antonio
　1957　*The Basque language*. Transl. by Herbert Pierrepont Houghton. Philadelphia: University of Pennsylvania Press.
Trager, George L.
　1974　Writing and writing systems. In: *Current trends in linguistics, vol. 12. Linguistics and adjacent arts and sciences*, ed. by Thomas A. Sebeok, 373–496. The Hague: Mouton.

Trask, Robert Lawrence
1994   *Language change*. London and New York: Routledge.
Trier, Jost
1931   *Der deutsche Wortschatz im Sinnbezirk des Verstandes: Die Geschichte eines sprachlichen Feldes, 1: Von den Anfängen bis zum Beginn des 13. Jahrhunderts*. Heidelberg: Winter.
1973   *Aufsätze und Vorträge zur Wortfeldtheorie*, ed. by A. van der Lee and O. Reichmann. The Hague: Mouton.
Trudgill, Peter
1983   *On dialect: Social and geographical perspectives*. New York: University Press.
1986   *Dialects in contact*. Oxford: Blackwell.
1990a   *The dialects of England*. Cambridge, MA and Oxford, England: Blackwell.
1990b   Dialect geography. In: Polomé 1990a: 257–271.
1994   *Dialects*. London and New York: Routledge.
Turner, Lorenzo Dow
1949   *Africanisms in the Gullah dialect*. Chicago: University Press.
Tyler, Stephen A.
1968   Dravidian and Uralic: The lexical evidence. *Language* 44: 798–812.
Ullmann, Stephen
1957   *The principles of semantics*. 2nd ed. Glasgow: University Publications.
1962   *Semantics: An introduction to the science of meaning*. Oxford: Blackwell.
Unger, J. Marshall
1990   Japanese and what other Altaic languages? In: Baldi 1990: 547–561.
Ureland, P. Sture
1990   Contact linguistics: Research on linguistic areas, strata, and interference in Europe. In: Polomé 1990a: 471–506.
Vennemann, Theo
1984   Hochgermanisch und Niedergermanisch: Die Verzweigungstheorie der germanisch-deutschen Lautverschiebungen. *Beiträge zur Geschichte der deutschen Sprache und Literatur* 106: 1–45.
1989   (ed.) *The new sound of Indo-European: Essays in phonological reconstruction*. Berlin: Mouton de Gruyter.
Verner, Karl
1877   Eine Ausnahme der ersten Lautverschiebung. *Zeitschrift für vergleichende Sprachforschung* 23: 97–130. (Engl. transl. in Lehmann 1967.)
Vihman, Marilyn May
1980   Sound change and child language. In: *Papers from the 4th International Conference on Historical Linguistics*, ed. by E. C. Traugott et al., 303–320. Amsterdam: Benjamins.
Vogt, Hans
1958   Les occlusives de l'arménien. *Norsk Tidskrift for Sprogvidenskap* 18: 143–161.

von Raffler-Engel, Walburga, Jan Wind, and Abraham Jonker (eds.)
  1991   *Studies in language origins.* Volume 2. Amsterdam/Philadelphia: Benjamins.
Wackernagel, Jacob, and Albert Debrunner
  1942   Indo-Iranica. *Zeitschrift für vergleichende Sprachforschung* 67: 154–182.
Walker, C. B. F.
  1987   *Reading the past: Cuneiform.* London: British Museum.
Watkins, Calvert
  1969   *Indogermanische Grammatik, 3: 1: Formenlehre: Geschichte der indogermanischen Verbalflexion.* Heidelberg: Winter.
  1982   Aspects of Indo-European poetics. In: Polomé 1982: 104–120.
  1985   (ed.) *The American heritage dictionary of Indo-European roots.* Boston: Houghton Mifflin Co.
  1987   How to kill a dragon in Indo-European. In: *Studies in Memory of Warren Cowgill (1929–1985): Papers of the Fourth East Coast Indo-European Conference*, ed. by C. Watkins, 270–299. Berlin: de Gruyter.
  1989   New parameters in historical linguistics, philology, and culture history. *Language* 65: 783–799.
  1995   *How to kill a dragon: Aspects of Indo-European poetics.* New York and Oxford: Oxford University Press.
Weinreich, Uriel
  1968   *Languages in contact: Findings and problems.* The Hague: Mouton.
Weinreich, Uriel, William Labov, and Marvin I. Herzog
  1968   Empirical foundations for a theory of language change. In: *Directions for historical linguistics*, ed. by W. P. Lehmann and Y. Malkiel, 95–195. Austin: University of Texas Press.
Wellard, James
  1973   *The search for the Etruscans.* New York: Saturday Review Press.
Wendt, Heinz F.
  1961   *Sprachen.* Frankfurt: Fischer Bücherei.
Whitney, William D.
  1877   The principle of economy as a phonetic force. *Transactions of the American Philological Association* 8: 121–134.
Wind, Jan, Brunetto Chiarelli, Bernard Bichakjian, Alberto Nocentini, and Abraham Jonker (eds.)
  1992   *Language origins: A multidisciplinary approach.* (NATO ASI Series D: Behavioural and Social Sciences, 61.) Dordrecht: Kluwer Academic Publishers.
Wind, Jan, Abraham Jonker, Robin Allott, and Leonard Rolfe (eds.).
  1994   *Studies in language origins.* Volume 3. Amsterdam and Philadelphia: Benjamins.

Wind, Jan, Edward G. Pulleyblank, Eric de Grolier, and Bernard H. Bichakjian (eds.).
  1989   *Studies in language origins*. Volume 1. Amsterdam and Philadelphia: Benjamins.
Winter, Werner
  1961   Relative Häufigkeit syntaktischer Erscheinungen als Mittel zur Abgrenzung von Stilarten. *Phonetica* 7: 193–216.
  1966   Traces of early dialectal diversity in Old Armenian. In: *Ancient Indo-European dialects*, ed. by H. Birnbaum and J. Puhvel, 201–211. Berkeley and Los Angeles: University of California Press.
  1969   Analogischer Sprachwandel und semantische Struktur. *Folia Linguistica* 3: 29–45.
  1970   Basic principles of the comparative method. In: *Method and theory in linguistics*, ed. by P. J. Garvin, 147–156. The Hague: Mouton.
  1982   IE for 'tongue' and 'fish'. *Journal of Indo-European Studies* 10: 167–186.
  1989   Thoughts about markedness and normalcy/naturalness. In: *Markedness in synchrony and diachrony*, ed. by O. M. Tomić, 103–109. Berlin: Mouton de Gruyter.
  1990   Linguistic reconstruction: The scope of historical and comparative linguistics. In: Polomé 1990a: 11–21.
  1992   Some thoughts about Indo-European numerals. In: Gvozdanović 1992: 11–28.
Winter, Werner, and Edgar C. Polomé (eds.)
  1992   *Reconstructing languages and cultures*. Berlin: Mouton de Gruyter.
Withycombe, Elizabeth G.
  1977   *The Oxford dictionary of English Christian names*. 3rd ed. New York: Clarendon Press.
Woods, Richard D.
  1984   H*ispanic first names: A comprehensive dictionary of 250 years of Mexican-American usage*. Westport, CT: Greenwood Press.
Zgusta, Ladislav
  1990   Onomasiological change: *Sachen*-change reflected by *Wörter*. In: Polomé 1990a: 389–398.
Zipf, George Kingsley
  1929   Relative frequency as a determinant of phonetic change. *Harvard Studies in Classical Philology* 40: 1–95.
Zwicky, Arnold M., and Geoffrey K. Pullum
  1983   Cliticization vs. inflection: English *n't*. *Language* 50: 502–51.

Language index

(NB: Names of language families or major subgroups are in SMALL CAPITALS)

CELTIC 42, 43-5, 242, 272, 309, 311, 356, 383, 385, 393, 411, 412, 415, 450, 456, 463, 466, 513
CHADIC 479
Chechen-Ingush 478
Cheremis 303
Cherokee 108-9
Cheyenne 481
CHIBCHAN 499
Chinese 14, 18, 71, 72, 106, 178-179, 181, 182, 183, 253, 275, 278, 282, 283, 372, 389, 478
Chinese, Mandarin 178
Chinese, Proto- 178-9
Chinese Sign Language 483
Chinook 499
Chinook Jargon 426, 436-7
Chipewyan 117
Chippewa – *see* Ojibwa
Chumash 482
Comanche 482
Coptic 97, 98, 479
Cornish 44, 393, 450
Cotabato Manobo 509
Cree 109, 226, 382, 470, 481
Crow 482
Cuna 499
CUSHITIC 479, 500
Czech 52, 457

Dagestani 478
Dakota 482
Dalmatian 45, 393
Danish 16, 50, 258, 277, 281, 326, 331, 457
DRAVIDIAN 33, 37, 60, 61, 135, 283, 371, 374, 385, 397, 405-410, 458, 478-9, 487, 489-90, 494, 498, 500, 501, 522
Dutch 13, 16, 50, 134, 209, 243, 277, 313, 315, 326-7, 330, 349, 355, 356, 385, 412, 413, 414, 430, 431, 457, 463

Efik 480
Egyptian 84, 97, 247, 248, 479, 499, 500
Elamite 98, 407, 494
English 4, 5, 6, 7, 9, 12, 14, 15, 16, 18, 19, 20, 23, 24, 26, 27, 28, 29, 41, 45, 48, 49, 50, 53, 68, 76, 79, 96, 101, 103, 104, 113, 120, 124, 125, 127, 128, 129, 130, 136, 137, 140, 141, 142, 143, 144, 145, 146, 151, 153, 154, 155, 156, 157, 159, 160, 162, 166, 167, 168, 172, 173, 174, 176, 177, 179, 180, 181, 182, 183, 184, 189, 190, 192-4, 195, 197-202, 203-210, 216-8, 224, 225, 226, 227, 229, 234, 235, 240, 241, 243, 244, 245, 248, 249, 250, 251, 253, 254, 255, 256, 258, 259, 260, 262, 263, 264, 265, 266, 268, 269, 270, 271, 276, 280, 281, 283, 284, 285, 286, 287, 288, 289, 290, 291, 292-3, 294, 295, 296, 297, 298, 299, 301, 302, 304, 305, 306, 309, 321, 313, 314, 321, 322, 323, 325, 328, 330, 331, 332, 334, 335, 339, 343, 344, 369, 371-2, 373-4, 375, 378, 382, 393, 404, 407-8, 415, 416, 420, 425, 429, 430, 321, 439, 442, 443-5, 447, 448, 451, 457, 460, 461, 462-3, 464-6, 491-3, 496, 498, 499, 500, 512-4, 516, 530, 531
English, African American Vernacular 315-7, 339, 442-5
English, American 5, 6, 15-16, 19, 28, 124, 129, 162, 163, 187, 210, 224, 230, 245, 269, 279, 294, 309, 323, 336, 364, 373, 378, 409, 444, 483, 519
English, Black Vernacular – *see* English, African American Vernacular
English, British 6, 15-6, 18, 19, 31, 117, 129, 136, 166, 184, 185,

Subject and name index

[NOTE: See the detailed Table of Contents also for topic coverage; information in the Table of Contents is generally not repeated here. Names given are of important scholars in historical linguistics or of people who figured in some important linguistic development mentioned in text.]